Britain's Greatest Prime Minister

Britain's Greatest Prime Minister

Lord Liverpool

Martin Hutchinson

The Lutterworth Press

The Lutterworth Press

P.O. Box 60
Cambridge
CB1 2NT
United Kingdom

www.lutterworth.com
publishing@lutterworth.com

Hardback ISBN: 978 0 7188 9563 1
Paperback ISBN: 978 0 7188 9564 8
PDF ISBN: 978 0 7188 4821 7
ePub ISBN: 978 0 7188 4822 4

British Library Cataloguing in Publication Data
A record is available from the British Library

First published by The Lutterworth Press, 2020

For more information, please visit
www.lordliverpool.com
Additional information on the following subjects, *inter alia*:
The life and career of Charles Jenkinson
Biographical notes on Liverpool and his colleagues
Discussion of Britain's other 54 prime ministers, and their claims to greatness.

Table of Contents

List of Illustrations

Note on Nomenclature

One difficulty for historians of this period is that the names of many statesmen changed several times during their lives as they were granted or inherited peerages.

Liverpool's father, Charles Jenkinson, is a case in point; he became Lord Hawkesbury in 1786 and then in 1796 first Earl of Liverpool. (He was also Sir Charles Jenkinson, seventh Baronet, from 1790.) Liverpool himself was plain Robert Jenkinson until 1786, the Hon. Robert Jenkinson from 1786 until 1796, Lord Hawkesbury from 1796 until 1808 (he held this name as a courtesy title between 1796 and 1803 and then in his own right after he was called to the Lords in 1803) and then the second Earl of Liverpool (and 8th Baronet) on his father's death in 1808.

The problem exists for other statesmen also. Henry Addington was known as 'Addington' during his prime ministership, 1801-04, but 'Sidmouth' (Viscount Sidmouth) as Liverpool's Home Secretary, 1812-21. Robert Stewart was 'Stewart' until 1796, his courtesy title was 'Castlereagh' (Viscount) from 1796 to 1821, and 'Londonderry' after he inherited his father's Irish marquessate in 1821. Henry Dundas was 'Dundas' until 1802, first Viscount Melville thereafter; his son Robert was 'Dundas' until 1811, then second Viscount Melville on the death of his father.

The normal convention is to be pedantic, referring to each statesman according to his title in the year you are discussing, so the familiar 'Castlereagh' becomes an unfamiliar 'Londonderry' in the last year of his life and (another example) the familiar 'Vansittart' becomes 'Bexley' after 1823. (Addington and Sidmouth are both familiar; I suspect most readers think they are different people!)

I have followed this, except in the case of Liverpool and his father, who sat in the same Cabinet together between 1801 and 1804, at which point the whirligig of names becomes just plain confusing (and has confused many well-regarded historians of the period, if you read their accounts carefully).

Therefore, in this book Charles Jenkinson remains 'Jenkinson' even in old age after he has rightly, through his own unaided efforts, earned an earldom, while Robert Banks Jenkinson is referred to throughout as 'Liverpool' even when he is a toddler and the earldom is non-existent, a quarter of a century in the future. I hope this will help readers to distinguish them.

Finally, for millennials and Americans, before 1998 the English peerage had five grades of hereditary title entitled to sit in the House of Lords: in descending order, dukes, marquesses, earls, viscounts and barons ('lords'). Archbishops, some bishops and, after 1958, life peers were also entitled to sit in the Lords but were not hereditary. There were also Irish and Scottish peers, only some of whom by election could sit in the Lords (so Castlereagh, from 1821 an Irish marquess, continued to sit in the Commons). Below the peers were knights and baronets ('sirs'), the latter hereditary, who were not entitled to sit in the House of Lords.

Note on Money

It is now nearly half a century since Britain went decimal, so I include a note on the currency system and coinage of Liverpool's time. Moreover, the regrettable abandonment of the gold standard has made modern money worth the equivalent of early nineteenth-century confetti. I therefore give some hint to readers of the modern equivalent of the various wage, price and budgetary sums mentioned in the text.

In Liverpool's time, the British currency consisted of pounds, shillings and pennies, with twelve pence (pennies) to the shilling and 20 shillings to the pound (see table below). Until 1817, no gold pound coins (sovereigns) were minted; the common gold coin was the guinea, worth 21 shillings. Coins such as shillings, sixpences, crowns and half-crowns were minted in silver; twopenny pieces, pennies and fractions thereof in copper (notably by Charles Jenkinson's 1797 coinage). The pound was, from 1819, fixed in value against gold, at £3/17/10½ per troy ounce of 22 carat gold, or £4.25 (in decimals) per ounce of pure gold.

Roderick Floud, in 'The Changing Value of Money',[1] sets out three different ways in which we can compare money items of the distant past to those today. We can multiply an 1820 price by the change of a price index from 1820 to today, by the change of a wage index or by the change in gross domestic product (GDP). Using Floud's example, the £10,000 annual income of Jane Austen's Mr Darcy from the period of Liverpool's ascent (*Pride and Prejudice* was published in 1813) becomes £620,000 p.a. today (March 2019, when the article appeared) inflating by prices, £7,305,000 today inflating by wages and about £40 million inflating by GDP (which Floud uses not for earnings but for public construction, state budgets etc.).

There was considerable deflation between 1813 and 1826, Liverpool's last full year in office; prices fell by 42 per cent, while factory wages fell by 37 per cent. Thus, if Mr Darcy had been lucky enough to earn £10,000 a year in

1. Roderick Floud, 'The Changing Value of Money', *History Today*, Vol. 69, Issue 3 (March 2019).

1826 (he might not have as agricultural incomes declined substantially after the war ended), he would have earned £1,069,000 in 2019 inflating by prices or £11,600,000 inflating by wages.

Floud prefers the wage index to the price index – we buy different things today, for example, relatively less food. I disagree; we are all richer than 200 years ago and inflating by wages overinflates an 1813-26 income as if today's technology had been available then. GDP indexing overinflates even more. Mr Darcy was rich, but not the richest man in England. Liverpool's income was £15,000 a year and the Marquess of Stafford's about £100,000. Mr Darcy is thus not quite equivalent to a modern CEO, as Floud suggests. Pemberley is a much nicer home than the CEO's, but Mr Darcy's plumbing, transportation and medical care were pathetic by modern standards.

There is an easier way: to use the gold standard. Gold was worth £4.25 per troy ounce between 1819 and 1827; it is worth about \$1,500 or £1,200 per ounce today. By this measure, Mr Darcy's £10,000 a year in 1813 paper money is worth about £8,000 gold standard pounds (gold traded around 25 per cent above par in 1813) or £2,259,000 today. That's between Floud's price and wage calculations; it shows what a good long-term store of value gold is. I suggest therefore that to get a modern (2020) equivalent you should multiply 1812-14 prices and wages by 226 and 1819-26 prices and wages by 282. The 282x conversion multiple also works for Charles Jenkinson's world before 1793, which from 1717 was on a bimetallic standard (in practice, tied to gold) with the same gold parity. As for foreign money, where a sterling equivalent was needed, I have used representative exchange rates for the period of \$5 = £1 for US dollars and FF 25 = \$1 for French francs.

Finally, here is a table to equip you for your journey into this world of proper money:

Coin	Symbol	Material	Made of d	Made of 1/-	Made of £
Farthing	$\frac{1}{4}$d	Copper	$\frac{1}{4}$	$\frac{1}{48}$	$\frac{1}{960}$
Halfpenny	$\frac{1}{2}$d	Copper	$\frac{1}{2}$	$\frac{1}{24}$	$\frac{1}{480}$
Penny	d	Copper	1	$\frac{1}{12}$	$\frac{1}{240}$
Twopence	2d	Copper	2	$\frac{1}{6}$	$\frac{1}{120}$
Sixpence	6d	Silver	6	$\frac{1}{2}$	$\frac{1}{40}$
Shilling	1/-	Silver	12	1	$\frac{1}{20}$
Half crown	2/6d	Silver	30	$2\frac{1}{2}$	$\frac{1}{8}$
Crown	5/-	Silver	60	5	$\frac{1}{4}$
Pound	£	Gold	240	20	1
Guinea	1£/1s	Gold	252	21	$1\frac{1}{20}$

1.
Introduction

If you look at him – especially the unflattering Hayter[1] portrait of 1823, rather than the kinder Lawrence[2] portraits of 1796, 1808, 1820, 1821 and 1826 – with his double chin and his watery eyes Robert Banks Jenkinson, second Earl of Liverpool does not look like the greatest anything. Benjamin Disraeli[3] famously termed him 'the Arch-Mediocrity'. He had only one full-scale biography, written in 1868. Yet look at his achievements in economics, foreign policy and financial management, his record in some of Britain's most dangerous, difficult years and at the calibre of his colleagues, and the picture looks different. Ruling at the apogee of British power, winning a major global war, managing a historically unprecedented economic transformation, in office longer than any of his successors, he stands revealed as Britain's Greatest Prime Minister. Liverpool was prime minister for fifteen years, with an unequalled record:

i. he organised victory in the Napoleonic Wars;
ii. he managed (with Castlereagh)[4] the peace settlement that followed;

---

1. George Hayter (1792-1871), knighted 1841. Portrait of Lord Liverpool, 1823. Hayter was a second-rate artist and an ardent Whig but this unflattering portrait, a sketch prepared for a group picture of the Queen Caroline trial, is the Liverpool image generally used by Whig historians.
2. Thomas Lawrence (1769-1830), knighted 1815. FRS 1822. President of the Royal Academy, 1820-30. Portraits of Lord Liverpool, 1796, 1808, 1820, 1821, 1826. A solid Tory as well as a top-notch artist, albeit one who tended to flatter his sitters; his 1826 portrait of Liverpool a year before his retirement is magnificent and suggests Liverpool's real stature much better than the Hayter one.
3. Benjamin Disraeli (1804-81). 1st Earl of Beaconsfield from 1876. Small-time swindler and unsuccessful novelist, who went on after Liverpool's death to become MP for Maidstone, Shrewsbury and Buckinghamshire, 1837-76. Conservative Leader in the Commons, 1849-76. Chancellor of the Exchequer, 1852, 1858-59, 1866-68. Prime Minister, 1868, 1874-80.
4. Robert Stewart, Viscount Castlereagh, 2nd Marquess of Londonderry (1769-1822).

iii. he directed Britain's economy through the most difficult years of the industrial revolution;
iv. he managed (with Sidmouth) [5] the social unrest of the difficult years 1816-20 without a major uprising;
v. he brought down (with Vansittart) [6] without default or inflation the highest debt level ever incurred by the British government;
vi. he designed two versions of the Corn Laws that determined British trade policy for the next generation;
vii. he took Britain back onto the gold standard against strong opposition and reformed the coinage;
viii. he ended his term in office with a vigorous period of social reform and trade liberalisation (with Peel,[7] Robinson[8] and Huskisson[9]);
ix. he reformed the English banking system, making it sound, stable and flexible; and
x. he led an outstandingly able government containing six past and future prime ministers.

I elaborate on these achievements in the Conclusion, where Liverpool is compared briefly with other prime ministers.

Chief Secretary for Ireland, 1798-1801. President of the Board of Control, 1802-6. Secretary for War and the Colonies, 1805-06, 1807-09. Foreign Secretary, 1812-22.

5. Henry Addington (1757-1844). MP for Devizes, 1784-1805. 1st Viscount Sidmouth from 1805. Speaker, 1789-1801. Prime Minister, 1801-04. Lord President of the Council, 1805, 1806-7, 1812. Lord Privy Seal, 1806. Home Secretary, 1812-22.

6. Nicholas Vansittart (1767-1851). 1st Baron Bexley from 1823. MP for Hastings, Old Sarum, East Grinstead and Harwich, 1796-1823. Chancellor of the Exchequer, 1812-23. Chancellor of the Duchy of Lancaster, 1823-28.

7. Robert Peel (1788-1850). 2nd Baronet from 1830. MP for Cashel, Chippenham, Oxford University, Westbury and Tamworth, 1809-50. Chief Secretary for Ireland, 1812-18. Home Secretary, 1822-27, 1828-30. Prime Minister, 1834-35, 1841-46.

8. Frederick John Robinson (1782-1859). 1st Viscount Goderich from 1827. 1st Earl of Ripon from 1833. MP for Carlow and Ripon, 1806-27. Vice-President of the Board of Trade, 1812-18. Joint Paymaster of the Forces, 1813-17. President of the Board of Trade, 1818-23. Treasurer of the Navy, 1818-23. Chancellor of the Exchequer, 1823-27. Secretary of State for War and the Colonies, 1827. Prime Minister, 1827-28. Secretary of State for War and the Colonies, 1830-33. Lord Privy Seal, 1833-34. President of the Board of Trade, 1841-43. President of the Board of Control, 1843-46.

9. William Huskisson (1770-1830). Son of a Staffordshire country gentleman. Tory MP for Morpeth, Liskeard, Harwich, Chichester and Liverpool, 1796-1802, 1804-30. Privy Councillor, 1814. Senior Secretary to the Treasury, 1804-06, 1807-09. First Commissioner of Woods and Forests, 1814-23. President of the Board of Trade, 1823-27. Secretary of State for War and the Colonies, 1827-28. Killed by Stephenson's 'Rocket' at the opening of the Liverpool and Manchester Railway, 15 September 1830.

Despite his long tenure and many achievements, Liverpool has an odd lack of prominence in the memoirs, cartoons, mob house trashings and Radical jeremiads of the period. A self-effacing man, Liverpool preferred it that way – for one thing, his wife Louisa was of a nervous disposition and in delicate health – she died in 1821, just as the government became more popular. Liverpool had no need to seek popular acclaim on the hustings, which he left to his able Commons lieutenants.

House of Commons debates were better reported than those in the Lords. However, Liverpool, himself an excellent speaker, faced Grenville, Grey[10] and Lansdowne[11] in the Lords and so had much tougher opposition than the feeble Ponsonby[12] and Tierney,[13] Whig Commons leaders from 1808-21, or the Whig Commons leadership in 1821-27, when no leader was selected.

Thus, with his speeches under-reported and the government's limited publicity machine concentrated on his Commons colleagues, Liverpool was much less in the public eye than others who have led the government for comparable periods. Nevertheless, Liverpool's dominance of an outstandingly able group of ministers was unquestioned. Partly this was due to his excellent grasp of economic matters, a subject on which both Canning and Castlereagh were uncertain and his followers were self-effacing men like Vansittart, distrusted by the bulk of the government's followers, like Huskisson, or younger, feebler and more junior like Robinson. Furthermore, even on foreign policy, military strategy and home affairs, he was deferred to by prominent colleagues like Castlereagh, Wellington, Sidmouth and Peel. (Canning after 1822 is an exception, although he deferred to Liverpool on policy outside foreign affairs.)

Finally, on one measure Liverpool's stature is unchallengeable. One of the most important tasks of a Prime Minister is to win general elections and Liverpool, with four outright victories (1812, 1818, 1820 and 1826) and

---

10. Charles Grey (1764-1845). 2nd Earl Grey from 1807. Whig MP for Northumberland 1786-1807. First Lord of the Admiralty, 1806. Foreign Secretary and Leader of the House of Commons, 1806-07. Reform Bill Prime Minister, 1830-34. Inspired a teabag!
11. Henry Petty-Fitzmaurice (1780-1863). 3rd Marquess of Lansdowne from 1809. Whig MP for Calne, Cambridge University and Camelford, 1802-09. Chancellor of the Exchequer, 1806-07. Home Secretary, 1827-28. Lord President of the Council, 1830-34, 1835-41, 1846-52. Leader of the House of Lords, 1846-52. Minister without Portfolio, 1852-58.
12. George Ponsonby (1755-1817). Whig MP (Ireland) for Wicklow Borough, Inistioge and Galway, 1778-1801. MP for Wicklow, Tavistock and Peterborough, 1801-17. Lord Chancellor of Ireland, 1806-07. Leader of the Opposition, 1808-17.
13. George Tierney (1761-1830). Whig MP for Colchester, Southwark, Athlone, Banden, Appleby, Knaresborough, 1796-1830. Treasurer of the Navy, 1803-04. President of the Board of Control, 1806-07. Master of the Mint, 1827-28. Leader of the Whigs in the House of Commons, 1818-21.

no general elections lost, leads all contenders in this area. His three closest competitors were Sir Robert Walpole,[14] William Gladstone[15] and Harold Wilson[16] but none of their records quite matches Liverpool's.

It may be objected that in the eighteenth century elections were won largely by patronage rather than through popular opinion. Nevertheless, by Liverpool's time that had already changed, with the power of patronage sharply restricted by various Acts of Parliament from 1780 onwards up to Curwen's[17] Act of 1809. The first truly popularly decided election was the landslide victory of the Duke of Portland[18] in 1807 on the issue of Catholic Emancipation (which the Duke and his followers opposed, in line with majority public opinion). Thus, in terms of winning elections, politically a Prime Minister's most important objective, Liverpool was unparalleled.

Liverpool's historical stature appears undistinguished – he was after all ranked only nineteenth among 50 prime ministers by *The Times* in 2010,[19] and other rankings have been similarly mediocre. Yet this book will show he was much better than that, and I believe Liverpool should rank ahead of the field.

The philosophy by which Liverpool governed was in the January 1830 *Quarterly Review*[20] first defined as 'Conservatism' (a 'Conservative' being defined as a follower of that philosophy, by then mostly embodied in Wellington's administration) and thus should be honoured as the original definition of that much-used term.

---

14. Sir Robert Walpole (1676-1745). 1st Earl of Orford from 1742. MP for Castle Rising and King's Lynn, 1701-12, 1713-42. Secretary at War, 1708-10. Treasurer of the Navy, 1710-11. Paymaster of the Forces, 1714-15 and 1720-21. First Lord of the Treasury and Chancellor of the Exchequer, 1715-17, 1721-42. Prime Minister, 1721-42.
15. William Ewart Gladstone (1809-98). MP for Newark, Oxford University, South Lancashire, Greenwich and Midlothian, 1832-95. President of the Board of Trade, 1843-45. Secretary of State for War and the Colonies, 1845-46. Chancellor of the Exchequer, 1852-55, 1859-66, 1873-74, 1880-82. Prime Minister, 1868-74, 1880-85, 1886, 1892-94.
16. Harold Wilson (1916-95). Lord Wilson of Rievaulx (life peer) from 1976. MP for Ormskirk and Huyton, 1945-83. President of the Board of Trade, 1947-51. Prime Minister, 1964-66, 1974-76.
17. John Curwen (1756-1828). MP for Carlisle, 1786-1812. MP for Carlisle and Cumberland, 1816-28.
18. William Henry Cavendish-Bentinck (1738-1809). 3rd Duke of Portland from 1762. MP for Weobley, 1761-62. Lord Chamberlain, 1765-66. Lord Lieutenant of Ireland, 1782. Prime Minister, 1783, 1807-09. Home Secretary, 1794-1801. Lord President of the Council, 1801-05. Minister without Portfolio, 1805-06.
19. *The Times*' Top 50 Prime Ministers, 5 May 2010. Of the 55 prime ministers since Sir Robert Walpole, *The Times* rating pre-dated David Cameron, Theresa May and Boris Johnson and left out Wilmington and Goderich.
20. 'Article IX – Internal Policy', *The Quarterly Review*, Vol. XLII, no. LXXXIII (January 1830) p. 276. At first attributed to John Wilson Croker, now thought to be by John Miller of Lincoln's Inn (?-1841).

Despite his philosophical importance, his long period in power and his manifold successes, Liverpool's low biographical profile is strange. There have been only five biographies in 192 years, only one of them a full-length study. Compare that to the numerous studies of Wellington,[21] Castlereagh and Canning,[22] all of whom were Liverpool's subordinates, and the omission is extraordinary. Even Sidmouth, another unfashionable figure, has enjoyed several rehabilitating biographies in the last half-century. The omission extends to Liverpool's papers; those of Wellington, Castlereagh and Canning were published in multiple-volume editions in the nineteenth century while Liverpool's papers remain in handwritten obscurity in the British Library's archives.

The first biography of Liverpool had some advantages over its successors. Written anonymously, *Memoirs of the Public Life and Administration of the Rt Hon. The Earl of Liverpool* was published in 1827, after Liverpool's retirement but while he was still alive. It had access to no correspondence and so was based on Liverpool's public speeches only but, being written before Catholic Emancipation and the Reform Act, was usefully respectful of Liverpool's position on those issues and his political views in general. Overall, like Aurelian Cook's 1685 biography of Charles II,[23] it has special value in being written before scepticism took hold, thus showing the way to a more balanced and generous appraisal than biographies that followed the change of regime.

Before the second full biography of Liverpool, Disraeli had his say. Disraeli started life as a Radical and by 1844, despite his wealthy older wife, was still paying off the debts he had incurred in the 1825 South American bonds bubble. Disgruntled at the Conservative Party establishment (Peel denied him a job in 1841), he tried to build his political position on the back of a 'Young England' Tory/Radical ginger group. The theory of history Disraeli came up with in his novel *Coningsby* thus relied on denigrating Liverpool's administration as a

21. Arthur Wellesley (1769-1852). 1st Viscount Wellington from 1809. 1st Earl of Wellington from 1810. 1st Marquess of Wellington from 1812. 1st Duke of Wellington from 1813. MP (Ireland) for Trim, 1790-97. MP for Rye, Tralee, Mitchell, and Newport, 1806-09. Chief Secretary for Ireland, 1807-09, Master-General of the Ordnance, 1818-27. Prime Minister, 1828-30, 1834 (briefly). Foreign Secretary, 1834-35. Ensign, British army, 1787. Lieutenant-Colonel, 1793. Served in Flanders, 1793-95, then served in India 1798-1805 becoming Major General in 1802 and winning Battle of Assaye in 1803. Served in Copenhagen expedition 1807. Lieutenant-General, 1808. General, 1812. Field Marshal, 1813. Portugal and Spain, 1808, 1809-14. Battle of Waterloo, 1815.

22. George Canning, 1770-1827. MP for Newtown, Wendover, Tralee, Petersfield, Liverpool, Harwich and Seaford, 1793-1827. Paymaster of the Forces, 1800-01. Foreign Secretary, 1807-09, 1822-27. Prime Minister, 1827.

23. Aurelian Cook, *Titus Britannicus: an essay of history royal, in the life & reign of His late Sacred Majesty, Charles II, of ever blessed and immortal memory* (James Partridge, 1685).

period of 'mediocrity' and Liverpool as 'the Arch-Mediocrity' – being a Tory MP he did not dare do this to Pitt. [24] This would not have mattered much to Liverpool's reputation – *Coningsby* is not a very good novel – except that Disraeli improbably became leader of the Conservative Party and a much-admired prime minister.

Disraeli's success combined with Peel's attempt to re-brand the 'Conservatives' in the 1830s and his flashy 1846 repeal of Liverpool's Corn Laws to make Liverpool deeply unfashionable. Not only were most historians Whigs, but even the Tory ones, such as fifth Earl Stanhope (biographer of Pitt), sought to meld with the prevailing zeitgeist and not attempt the resurrection of other pre-Peel Tories. Wellington never went out of fashion, Castlereagh's reputation was rehabilitated by the future Lord Salisbury in 1862 and Canning, in any case a quasi-Whig, was helped by the prominence of his son (Governor General of India, 1856-62). Liverpool had no such assistance.

The first major biography, and so far the only full-length one, is the three-volume *Life and Administration of Robert Banks Jenkinson, Second Earl of Liverpool* published in 1868 by Charles Duke Yonge, a second-tier academic historian (then Professor of History at Queens College, Belfast) and prolific writer. Yonge's biography was workmanlike but viewed Liverpool from a Canningite perspective, perhaps inevitable by the time it was written. Canning's abilities are overrated, his character even more so (Mrs Arbuthnot's diaries being then unavailable). This warps Yonge's view of Liverpool's activities. Inevitably, the Canningite period after 1822 is treated with more sympathy than the period of greatest achievement in Liverpool's earlier years. An equally serious problem is that Yonge devotes little space or analysis to economic, monetary and fiscal policy.

Yonge's is a perfectly competent biography but damns Liverpool with faint praise and, with its dull prose, makes him seem uninteresting. With Yonge as a 'standard biography' and Disraeli having suggested there was nothing much there, it is unsurprising that no further biography appeared for 80 years.

After a 70-year gap, W.R. Brock's *Lord Liverpool and Liberal Toryism, 1820-27*, published in 1941 and not a full biography of Liverpool, took the Canningite error to new lengths by claiming that the post-1822 Liverpool ministry was in essence a new government, with new policies of 'Liberal Toryism'. While the Liverpool government's policies indeed changed after 1820, the primary drivers of that change were the economic upturn, the reduction in unrest to which it led and the easing of fiscal and budgetary constraints. Even after he became Foreign Secretary, Canning had little influence on policy outside foreign affairs; he remained passive, for example, at the crucial December 1825 Cabinet meeting which discussed the financial crisis and possible reactions to it.

24. William Pitt the Younger (1759-1806). MP for Appleby and Cambridge University, 1781-1806. Chancellor of the Exchequer, 1782-83, 1783-1801, 1804-06. Prime Minister, 1783-1801, 1804-06.

Sir Charles Petrie's *Lord Liverpool*, published in 1954 and the first biography since Yonge, is short but generally favourable. However, its influence was lessened by Petrie's own eccentricities; he was a keen Jacobite supporter, writing an alternative history in which the 1745 rebellion succeeded, and had connections with the British far-right. Like previous biographers of Liverpool, Petrie lacked a grasp of economic and financial matters.

The biographers' inattention to economic policy was finally reversed in the 1970s with two books, J.E. Cookson's *Lord Liverpool's Administration, 1815-22*, published in 1975 and Boyd Hilton's *Corn, Cash, Commerce: The Economic Policies of the Tory Governments, 1815-1830* in 1977. Both books dealt primarily with economic policy, Hilton's entirely, and recognised the importance of the early post-war years to the fiscal, monetary and economic stabilisation that laid the foundation for the century's later prosperity. Even Hilton, however, missed the importance and quality of Liverpool's 1826 banking reform. In the same decade (1974) Asa Briggs, in his survey of prime ministers, recognised Liverpool's 'sheer professionalism',[25] a quality that was to cause an upward reappraisal in Liverpool's standing in decades to come.

Norman Gash, whose *Lord Liverpool* appeared in 1984, was the most distinguished historian of Liverpool's biographers, and brought additional know-how from his life's work on Peel. Alas, he too did not focus on economic questions. However, for the first time he provided some details of Liverpool's private life, humanising him. He also took an appropriately sceptical view of Canning's activities and relationship with Liverpool. Gash's final verdict was significantly more positive than the prevailing consensus among historians: 'In any analysis of his premiership three features are outstanding: his competence in every important branch of public business, his successful handling of an extraordinary variety of problems, and his gift for getting the best out of his colleagues.'[26]

Most recently, William Anthony Hay's *Lord Liverpool: A Political Life*, published in 2018, is a high-quality addition to Liverpool's biographies, with particularly helpful information on his early life, drawn from his still-unpublished correspondence. Hay focusses on Charles Jenkinson as well as Liverpool, tracing the career of Liverpool's formidable and formative father. Like other biographers, he underemphasises the economic area, though his title indicates this will be the case. Hay, like Gash shares the generally higher opinion of Liverpool that has prevailed in recent decades.

This book takes further the last forty years' rehabilitation of Liverpool's reputation and suggests that, by a modest margin, he was the greatest of all Britain's prime ministers.

25. Asa Briggs, *Sir Robert Peel* in Herbert van Thal (ed.), *The Prime Ministers, Volume 1: Sir Robert Walpole to Sir Robert Peel* (London: Allen & Unwin, 1974) pp. 287-96.
26. Norman Gash, *Lord Liverpool* (London: Weidenfeld & Nicolson, 1984) p. 254

II.

Early Years until the Death of Pitt, 1770-1806

Robert Banks Jenkinson, second Lord Liverpool, was an intriguing mixture. On his father's side, he came from Oxfordshire squires, descended from one of Elizabethan England's foremost merchant/explorers. On his mother's side, he came from the commerce and mixed marriages that made up the first century of Britain's relationship with India.

The founder of the family fortunes was Anthony Jenkinson (1529-1611), who was born at Market Harborough, Leicestershire, into a mercantile family. He travelled extensively throughout Europe and in the Eastern Mediterranean from 1546-56, obtaining a safe conduct for travel in the Ottoman Empire from Suleiman II ('the Magnificent') in 1553. In 1557 he was appointed captain-general of the quite new Muscovy Company (the first major chartered joint stock company) after its founder Richard Chancellor was killed in a shipwreck.

Anthony Jenkinson made four voyages to Russia between 1557 and 1572, penetrating to Bokhara and opening English contacts with Persia. He also negotiated with Ivan the Terrible, being given secret instructions, 'That he should seriously solicit the Queen for a mutual League of Defence and Offence against all men'. As William Camden said in his biography of Elizabeth, 'Thus did a Tyrant, from whom no man can keep anything safe, seem to himself be without Safety.'[1] Jenkinson wrote about his travels to Russia and Persia, which were incorporated in Richard Hakluyt's *Principal Navigations* in 1589. As Camden said: 'No man had a more perfect knowledge of the North part of the World than he.'

Anthony Jenkinson's substantial fortune was invested by his descendants in country estates. His grandson, Sir Robert Jenkinson of Walcot, Oxfordshire, was knighted by James I in 1618 and around 1620[2] acquired the manor of Hawkesbury, Gloucestershire, dying in 1645. The manor house at Hawkesbury, built around 1500, was by the late eighteenth century in ruin,

1. William Camden, *The History of the Most Renowned and Victorious Princess Elizabeth, Late Queen of England* (London: E. Flesher, 1675) p. 103.
2. *The Gentleman's Magazine*, March 1829, p. 201.

and was abandoned some time before 1770. Even though Liverpool's father took the title 'Lord Hawkesbury' in 1786, neither he nor Liverpool lived there, although both are buried in the parish church and Liverpool owned 3,000 acres of land centred on Hawkesbury.[3]

Sir Robert's son, Sir Robert Jenkinson, Bt (c. 1620-77) entered the First Protectorate Parliament of 1654 as MP for Oxfordshire. He was re-elected to the Second Protectorate Parliament of 1656 and the Third Protectorate Parliament of 1659 but played no role in the Convention Parliament of 1660 or the Cavalier Parliament of 1661-79. Nevertheless, he received a baronetcy in 1661 from the restored Charles II. At some point he married Mary Bankes, younger daughter of a doughty Royalist landowner, Mary Bankes, *née* Hawtry (1603-61), who held Corfe Castle in Dorset for an intermittent three-year siege against the Parliamentarians in 1643-46.[4] By his baronetcy, the family's position was established for future generations; its motto was "*Pareo, non servio*" (I obey, but not as a slave).

Based primarily at Walcot, the Jenkinsons became a leading Oxfordshire political family, with strong Tory views. The first baronet's son, the second Jenkinson baronet, Sir Robert (1655-1710) was a Tory/'Country' MP for Abingdon and then Oxfordshire from 1689 and a good friend of Henry Hyde, second Earl of Clarendon. The second baronet's eldest son, Robert (third baronet), elected for Oxfordshire in 1710, was described as 'a gentleman of great virtues and of singular integrity and probity, of a courteous, affable temper, a lover of his country and an enemy to rebellion'.[5] After his death in 1717 he was succeeded in the seat by his brother Robert Bankes, fourth baronet, who retired from Parliament in 1727, aged only 40, probably because of his pronounced Jacobite sympathies, and died in 1738. Robert Bankes Jenkinson's sons Robert (fifth baronet, died 1766) and Banks (sixth baronet, died 1790) did not sit in Parliament, possibly because the family's financial position was declining (they sold Walcot in 1758).

3. According to the Hawkesbury Local History Society website, the manor was the scene of a tragic occurrence, in which the pro-Hanoverian Sir Robert Jenkinson's daughter Catherine fell in love with the son of a local Catholic and Jacobite squire and, after her father's rejection of his suit, fell from the window of the decrepit building when part of the masonry collapsed as she was leaning out to speak to her lover. It's a nice story, though the details are questionable. The legend inspired a fine early-Victorian poem printed in an 1845 book *Chavenage: A Tale on the Cotswolds* by R.W. Huntley, which begins evocatively:

   'O Hawkesbury Manor, Hawkesbury Manor
   Why so empty stand thy halls?
   Why in dampness droops thy banner,
   Rust the weapons on thy walls?'

4. See *History Today*, February 2015, for a discussion of her role.
5. *The Remains of Thomas Hearne, M.A. of Edmund Hall*, by Philip Bliss, p. 183, 24 February 1709/10.

The second Jenkinson baronet's third son was Lieutenant-Colonel Charles Jenkinson (1693-1750), who married Amarantha Cornewall (1702-85), daughter of Wolfran Cornewall (1658-1719), a Royal Navy captain, and then lived at a modest house, Burford Lawn Lodge, in Shipton-under-Wychwood, Oxfordshire, four miles from the Jenkinson baronets' Walcot seat. Lieutenant-Colonel Jenkinson was a major in the Blues (the Royal Horse Guards) at the 1745 Battle of Fontenoy[6] and a graduate of Christ Church College, Oxford. As well as Liverpool's father Charles Jenkinson, his eldest son, who inherited the family baronetcy in 1790, Lieutenant-Colonel Jenkinson's children included a younger son, John Jenkinson (1734-1805) himself MP for Corfe Castle, 1768-80, a third son, Robert, who died of fever in 1761 while undertaking military service in Hesse and a daughter, Elizabeth (c. 1736-1809), who in 1764 married her cousin, Charles Wolfran Cornwall, who was Speaker of the House of Commons from 1780 until 1789 and a close colleague of Charles Jenkinson.[7]

Before discussing Charles Jenkinson, I will deal with the family of Liverpool's mother. His mother Amelia Watts (1750-70), who married Charles Jenkinson in 1769 but died after Liverpool's birth in 1770, was the daughter of William Watts of the East India Company. Amelia was 'a girl of great beauty and accomplishments'[8] but alas we don't know much about her character, what she looked like or where she was educated. The portrait traditionally held to be of her, by Joshua Reynolds, in the guise of the Roman goddess Flora, is dated by art historians to 1745-46, before she was born.[9]

Amelia had an adventurous early childhood before returning to England at the age of eight. In 1756, her parents, brother and sister were captured at Kasimbazar by Siraj-ud-Daulah, the Nawab of Bengal. Fortunately, the Nawab's grandmother befriended the women and took them into the *zenana*, where they remained for over a month before sending them under escort to the French factory (or trading post). There they remained until the Battle of Plassey liberated them the following year.[10]

---

6. The admirable *Lord Liverpool: A Political Life* by William Anthony Hay (Martlesham, Suffolk: Boydell & Brewer, 2018) says Col. Jenkinson commanded the Blues at the 1745 Battle of Dettingen (actually fought in 1743). The sources I can find say that he was a Major in the Blues at the 1745 Battle of Fontenoy, where he was mentioned in the Duke of Cumberland's Dispatches. Hay's source is an 1820 letter by Liverpool to Croker, which I suspect inflated his grandfather's rank and substituted a more glorious (in British eyes) battle – the British lost Fontenoy, while Dettingen is famous as the last time a British monarch led his troops to victory.
7. Charles Wolfran Cornwall (1735-89). MP for Grampound, Winchelsea and Rye, 1768-89. Speaker of the House of Commons, 1780-89.
8. 'An Echo from old Bengal', *Blackwood's Magazine*, Vol. 182 (1907) p. 420.
9. The portrait is available on poster and claimed to be of Amelia Watts, whose dates are given as 1750-70, yet the picture is dated to 1745. Art historians can be clueless!
10. 'An Echo from Old Bengal', p. 420.

Amelia's father William Watts (1722-64) was probably the son of William Watts of London, an academy master (teacher) and possibly the nephew of Thomas Watts (1689-1742), the 'presiding genius' of the Sun insurance office and an anti-Walpole MP in 1734-42. Watts went to India with the East India Company in his teens, where he met Robert Clive.[11] While lacking Clive's early military exploits, Watts rose quickly in the East India Company's service, became fluent in Bengali, Hindustani and Persian and was appointed chief of the company's Kasimbazar factory, a subsidiary of the Kolkata presidency.

His second in command here was the young Warren Hastings,[12] born about four miles from Charles Jenkinson into impoverished gentry. He would later become the first Governor-General of the East India Company's Indian possessions and face impeachment under Pitt and a seven-year House of Lords trial before his acquittal on all charges in 1795. Hastings would be rehabilitated under Liverpool, with a triumphant House of Commons appearance in 1813 and a Privy Councillorship in 1814.

In April 1756 the old Nawab of Bengal, who had maintained a tolerant attitude to European interlopers in return for massive subsidies, died and was succeeded by his 23-year-old grandson, Siraj-ud-Daulah. Both the British and the French factories began to improve their fortifications. When the British refused Siraj's orders to cease their fortifications, he attacked their factory at Kasimbazar with a force of 3,000 men. Kazimbazar was captured on 4 June and Watts, Hastings and other British officials were taken prisoner, then released a month later.

With an army of 50,000 men, Siraj then marched on Kolkata it after a short siege. The prisoners were confined in the common dungeon of Fort William known as the Black Hole. He then proceeded to sack the French and Dutch factories in the area, extracting large sums from them 'to demonstrate his general distaste to Europeans'.[13]

When news of the capture of Kolkata reached British headquarters in Madras, it was decided to send an expeditionary force under Clive, to establish the Company's privileges in Bengal on a more permanent basis. The force, with a squadron commanded by Vice-Admiral Charles Watson,[14] arrived off Kolkata in December 1756, where Watts joined them. Kolkata was retaken on 2 January 1757.

11. Robert Clive (1725-74). 1st Baron Clive (Ireland) from 1762. MP for Mitchell and Shrewsbury, 1754-55, 1761-74. Commander-in-Chief, India, 1756-60, 1765-67.

12. Warren Hastings (1732-1818). Governor (from 1773 Governor-General) of the Presidency of Fort William, 1772-82. Governor-General of the Presidency of Fort Sala, 1782-85. FRS, 1801. PC, 1814. The first Governor-General of India and married to Jane Austen's cousin.

13. William Watts, *Memoirs of the Revolution in Bengal, Anno. Dom. 1757* (London: A. Millar, 1760) p. 15.

14. Watson was a cousin of the Marquess of Rockingham and got his early promotion as nephew of the Walpolean First Lord of the Admiralty, Sir Charles Wager (1666-1743).

Siraj responded by marching on Kolkata, where he arrived on 3 February. The following day, Clive launched a surprise attack on Siraj's 50,000-strong army with a force of 600 sailors, 650 Europeans and 800 sepoys, which produced a tactical victory with some 600 killed of Siraj's force compared to 57 Europeans. The attack was accompanied by a letter from Admiral Watson, indicating this was 'a specimen only of what British Arms, when provoked, could perform'.[15] The partially cowed Siraj signed the Treaty of Alinagar, restoring the Company's properties, and Watts accompanied Siraj back to his capital as advisor and administrator of the treaty's provisions.

The day after the treaty was signed, news arrived of the outbreak of Britain's war with France. Siraj accordingly opened negotiations with the French, who convinced him falsely that they had large forces nearby. As Watts put it: 'his Project was too great for his Capacity; he did what he could to execute it, but it was beyond his force, and his very manner of managing it defeated his Design'.[16] Thus, after Watts had, through judicious bribery, convinced Siraj to remain neutral, Clive attacked the French trading post at Chandannagar (formerly, Chandernagore), their most important post in Bengal, which he captured on 24 March, assisted by information from Watts on Siraj's movements.

From this point, Siraj was firmly in league with the French and Watts' situation at his court became perilous and unpleasant – Siraj several times threatened to have him executed. However, Siraj's court was seething with discontent and Watts was approached by Mir Jafar, the paymaster of Siraj's army, offering to support the British. On advice from Watts, Clive and the council drew up a treaty offering to make Mir Jafar Nawab of Bengal if British arms were successful.

The treaty with Mir Jafar was signed on 5 June and Watts escaped from Siraj on 11 June. After Watts arrived at their encampment, the British forces, totalling around 3,000 men, of which 800 were Europeans, began an advance towards Siraj's capital. On 23 June, the force arrived at Plassey, to be faced by about 60,000 enemy troops, of which the left wing was commanded by Mir Jafar. A French detachment to reinforce Siraj was expected, but only 50 French troops were present. The battle lasted all day, with the crucial engagement taking place after a tropical downpour, during which the British kept their powder dry while Siraj's forces did not.

At the end of the day, Siraj fled, to be murdered on the order of Mir Jafar's son. Mir Jafar became Nawab of Bengal and a large indemnity was paid to cover British costs. Of that indemnity, Watts was given £114,000 for his services surrounding Plassey. He also starred in a heroic painting by Benjamin Wilson (1721-88): 'Mir Jafar and his son Miran delivering the Treaty of 1757 to William Watts'.[17]

15. Watts, ibid., p. 21.
16. Watts, ibid., p. 34.
17. The British Library has an 1890 platinotype reproduction of this picture; the

Mir Jafar and his son delivering the 1757 Treaty to William Watts, Liverpool's maternal grandfather.

Watts returned to England in 1758 and wrote *Memoirs of the Revolution in Bengal*, published in 1760. He bought a Buckinghamshire family seat Hanslope Park, in June 1764 but died there in August.

Watts' wife, Liverpool's grandmother, Frances Croke (1728-1812), was the second daughter of Edward Croke (1690-1769), the Governor of Fort St David. She was married four times, Watts being the third (both her first two husbands died young). After a few years at Hanslope, Frances returned to India following Amelia's wedding. There she married the chaplain William Johnson in 1774 and stayed on in Kolkata after his return to England in 1789, dying in February 1812, well-known and well-liked throughout Kolkata society as 'the Begum Johnson' (from her frequent references to the Nawab's grandmother's kindness). By the time she died, she was the oldest British resident in Bengal and a leader in Kolkata society, flourishing for a decade after her grandson became Foreign Secretary in 1801. Charles Jenkinson helped her with her affairs, including her divorce from Johnson, and she corresponded with Liverpool until her death. She was granted a public funeral, attended by the Governor-General Lord Minto[18] and Wellington later talked of having known her while in India.[19]

---

original, oil on canvas measuring 52¾ x 107½ inches was sold at a London auction in 1979 for £12,000.

18. Gilbert Elliott (1751-1814). 4th Baronet from 1777. 1st Baron Minto from1797. 1st Earl of Minto from 1813. Whig MP for Morpeth, Roxburghshire, Berwick and Helston, 1777-95. PC, 1793. Viceroy of the Corsican Kingdom, 1794-96. British Minister to Austria, 1799-1801. President of the Board of Control, 1806. Governor-General of India, 1807-13.

19. C.E. Buckland, *Dictionary of Indian Biography* (London: Swan Sonnenschein & Co., 1906) p. 224.

Edward Croke's wife, Isabella Beizor (c. 1710-80), was a Portuguese Indian creole, thus giving Liverpool a trace (probably about one sixteenth, but maybe less) of Indian blood.

On both sides therefore, Liverpool's ancestry was not aristocratic – there is a remarkable absence of the peerage from his direct ancestry. There was not a huge amount of money around, other than that earned by Charles Jenkinson from political offices and sinecures. (Only a modest part of Watts' £114,000 and other Indian earnings went to Amelia.)

Before dealing with Charles Jenkinson and then Liverpool himself, it is worth examining Liverpool's contemporary relatives, who mostly played limited roles in his life, although he provided many of them with assistance and occasionally money.

Edward Watts (1752-1828), Liverpool's maternal uncle, led a long and apparently blameless life at the family seat, Hanslope Park, marrying in 1778 Florentia Wynch, daughter of Alexander Wynch (1721-81), former Governor of Madras. He otherwise touched modern records only peripherally, notably when he employed the landscape architect, Humphry Repton (1752-1818), to produce designs for remodelling Hanslope's grounds in 1791-92. His descendants lived at Hanslope until 1933.

Sophia Watts (1753-1830), Liverpool's maternal aunt, helped with Liverpool's early childhood, then in December 1772 married George Poyntz Ricketts (1749-1800), a sugar planter in the West Indies who in 1794 – helped by intervention from Charles Jenkinson – became Governor of Barbados.

Ricketts' second son, Charles Milner Ricketts (1776-1867), served in India and benefited from Liverpool's patronage, becoming Lord Moira's[20] secretary in 1813 and member of the Indian Council in 1817 before returning to England to become MP for Dartmouth (1820-22). Alas, in 1822 Ricketts and his wife separated acrimoniously and he was compelled to abandon hope of high office in England. Instead, he learned Spanish quickly and was sent as Consul to Peru in 1825, after which his life descended into obscurity. Liverpool wrote:

> I procured him an easy seat in Parliament . . . and gave him thereby the opportunity of making himself known, and of forming English connections. Whether anything further would have resulted from this it is impossible for me to say . . . but the road was certainly open to him and it is no fault of mine he has not been able to take advantage of it.[21]

20. Francis Rawdon-Hastings, (1754-1826). Baron Rawdon, 1783. 2nd Earl of Moira from 1793. 1st Marquess of Hastings from 1816. Financially troubled Whig grandee. Friend of the Prince of Wales. Colonel, Adjutant-General and amateur actor in the American War of Independence, 1774-81. Commander-in-Chief, Scotland with rank of full General, 1803-6. Master-General of the Ordnance, 1806-7. Governor-General and Commander-in-Chief of India, 1812-23. Governor of Malta, 1824-26.
21. D.R. Fisher (ed.), *The History of Parliament: The House of Commons 1820-32*

On his father's side, Liverpool's uncle, John Jenkinson's eldest son, Sir Charles Jenkinson (1779-1855), served in the army, rising to Captain. Then, following Liverpool's appointment as Lord Warden of the Cinque Ports, he was elected MP for Dover at the 1806 election. He was a safe government vote throughout his parliamentary service, although he opposed his cousin in voting for Catholic relief in 1813. However, Charles left unpaid debts in Dover in 1812, resigned from Parliament at the 1818 election and in 1825 wrote a begging letter to his cousin from Paris, which resulted in a pension of £50 a year each to his two eldest daughters and £100 towards liquidation of his debts. Late in life he was to become the tenth Jenkinson baronet on the death of Liverpool's half-brother, Charles Cecil Cope Jenkinson, in 1851. Nonetheless, he died in Paris four years later.[22]

John's second son, John Banks Jenkinson (1781-1840), was the star of the family, other than Liverpool himself. He was appointed Bishop of St Davids, Pembrokeshire by Liverpool in 1825 and Dean of Durham by Canning two years later; he also produced the eleventh Baronet, and another Conservative MP, Sir George Samuel Jenkinson (1817-92).[23] As Bishop of St Davids he was the official petitioner to the Crown for the charter of the University of Wales, Lampeter (in 1828); as Dean of Durham he performed the same function for Durham University (in 1837).

John's third son, George Jenkinson (1783-1823), served in the Peninsular War in the Royal Artillery, was wounded at Talavera in 1809 and rose to Lieutenant-Colonel in 1814 at Wellington's recommendation. He was trusted by Liverpool as special envoy to the French royal family when Napoleon escaped from Elba, and their relationship appears to have been both close and friendly. George IV sent Liverpool condolences when George Jenkinson died.

John's fourth and youngest son, Robert Henry Jenkinson (1786-1857), was appointed Lieutenant-Governor of Dover Castle in 1806, at the age of only 20, by his cousin the Lord Warden. He was to hold the appointment until Liverpool's retirement in 1827 and then reciprocated Liverpool's help by buying a modest estate, Norbiton Hall in Kingston, jointly with Liverpool's widow, Mary,[24] in which she lived until her death in 1846.

Finally, John also had a daughter, Fanny Jenkinson (1787?-1838), who in 1805 married William Boothby (1782-1846), the son of a Derbyshire baronet and from 1824 the Baronet himself. Liverpool paid the fees for their son at a boarding school in 1815-16, after which the entire Boothby family came to live with him at Coombe Wood and Fife House before he got William

---

(Cambridge: Cambridge University Press, 2009).

22. R. Thorne (ed.), *The History of Parliament: The House of Commons 1790-1820* (Cambridge: Cambridge University Press, 1986).

23. The fourteenth Baronet, Sir John Banks Jenkinson (1945-), descended from the eleventh Baronet, lived in the village of Hawkesbury in 2013.

24. Mary Chester (1777-1846). Married Liverpool 24 September 1822.

Boothby a £300-per-annum post in HM Customs. Liverpool left two of the Boothby children, Cecil and Fanny, £10,000 each in his will, together with £2,000 each to their four brothers and sisters,[25] so the Boothbys clearly played a useful emotional role in Liverpool's life.

Liverpool's brother-in-law, James Grimston (his half-sister Charlotte's husband), was Tory MP for St Albans from 1802 until 1808, before succeeding as fourth Viscount Grimston in 1808, and was rewarded by Liverpool, becoming first Earl of Verulam in 1815. He was a solid Tory vote in both Commons and Lords, but his primary interest was the turf, though he served as Lord Lieutenant of Hertfordshire from 1823 until his 1845 death.

Finally, Liverpool's half-brother, Charles Cecil Cope Jenkinson, who succeeded Liverpool to the earldom, was considerably younger than Liverpool and made his career in Liverpool's shadow. He was educated privately, rather than at Charterhouse, then at Christ Church, Oxford, where he matriculated in 1801, after a short spell in the navy, but did not take a degree. He acted as his brother's private secretary and undersecretary in 1804-10, then, finding official business tiresome, retired to a lengthy career on the Commons backbenches, as MP for Sandwich, Bridgenorth and East Grinstead before moving to the Lords on Liverpool's death. His later career included a spell as Lord Steward of the Household to Queen Victoria during Peel's government of 1841-6.

In 1810 Charles married Julia Shuckburgh-Evelyn, daughter of Sir George Shuckburgh-Evelyn, sixth Baronet.[26] An independent country gentleman of 'inadequate' fortune, Sir George remarked to Pitt in 1787: 'I have the honour of the county of Warwick in my hands and I will surrender it to no individual on earth.'[27] Alas, Julia died in 1814, leaving Charles with no sons and three daughters, and he never remarried, thus extinguishing the Hawkesbury and Liverpool titles on his death in 1851. However, his second daughter Selina (1812-83) married twice, the second time in 1845 to George Savile Foljambe (1800-69) whose only son, Cecil George Savile Foljambe (1846-1907), was Liberal MP for North Nottinghamshire and Mansfield from 1880-92. He was raised to the peerage as Baron Hawkesbury in 1893 and then, on his appointment as Lord Steward of the Household, he was made Earl of Liverpool in 1905. The title has descended to the present day in Edward Foljambe, fifth Earl of the 1905 creation (1944-).

Turning now to the main protagonists, Liverpool's father, Charles Jenkinson (1729-1808), was a major political figure from 1763 and a key member of both North's and Pitt's governments, granted both a barony and an earldom. He was educated at Charterhouse, and University College, Oxford, matriculating in 1746. He remained at Oxford until 1752, intending to enter the Church

25. Gash, *Lord Liverpool*, p. 213, gives some details on the Boothbys and their legacies.
26. Sir George Shuckburgh-Evelyn, 6th Baronet (1751-1804). MP for Warwickshire, 1780-1804, voting with Fox until the Fox-North coalition, then for Pitt until 1791, after which he opposed Pitt but supported Addington from 1801.
27. Quoted in Thorne, *The History of Parliament*. "Shuckburgh-Evelyn, Sir George"

Charles Jenkinson, Liverpool's father, in 1788, by George Romney. A satisfied man; his ambitions are being achieved.

through a family connection, but then became involved as pamphleteer on the Whig side in the Oxfordshire election of 1754, the most expensive election of the eighteenth century.[28] (By 1754, Toryism appeared a dead-end for a young

28. R.J. Robson's *The Oxfordshire Election of 1754* (Oxford: Oxford University Press, 1949) describes the election in detail and throws some light on Jenkinson's role.

politician seeking paid office.) Using his Oxfordshire connections and those from this campaign, notably, Simon, Earl Harcourt[29] and George Grenville,[30] he became unpaid secretary in 1756 to the fourth Earl of Holderness,[31] Secretary of State for the Northern Department.

With his Tory family history and beliefs, Charles Jenkinson's future was boosted when the Tory-friendly George III became king in 1760. He became an MP in 1761 and secretary to the third Earl of Bute,[32] who from 1762 was the first Tory Prime Minister since 1714. Then, when Bute was succeeded by George Grenville the following year, Charles Jenkinson became Senior Secretary to the Treasury. Here he played a major role in drafting the 1765 Stamp Act, a sensible piece of legislation that was stymied by the fall of the Grenville government and its replacement by Whigs under the second Marquess of Rockingham,[33] who allowed Colonial opposition to the Act to force its repeal. Jenkinson resigned on Grenville's fall, but had formed a friendship with George III that he never lost.

In minor but increasingly well-paid offices, Jenkinson's influence gradually grew after 1770, because he was close to both the King and Lord North.[34] He was active in Indian policy, proposing the Tea Act of 1773 that led to the Boston Tea Party, and in the gold recoinage of 1774, becoming Britain's leading coinage expert. He became Secretary at War in 1778, still outside the Cabinet but responsible for the American War's logistics. From 1778, North became increasingly dilatory, so Jenkinson and the Treasury secretary John Robinson[35] managed affairs at the direction of the King – 1778-82 was the last period of effective Royal rule in British history.

---

29. Simon Harcourt (1714-77). 2nd Viscount Harcourt from 1729. 1st Earl Harcourt from 1749. Governor to the Prince of Wales, 1751-60. Special Ambassador to Mecklenburg-Strelitz, 1761. Ambassador to Paris, 1768-72. Lord Lieutenant of Ireland, 1772-77. Drowned in a well while rescuing his dog.
30. George Grenville (1712-70). MP for Buckingham, 1741-70. Treasurer of the Navy, 1756-62. Secretary of State for the Northern Department, 1762. First Lord of the Admiralty, 1762-63. Prime Minister and Chancellor of the Exchequer, 1763-65. Brother of William Grenville, 2nd Earl Temple (1711-79). Father of William Wyndham Grenville.
31. Robert Darcy (1718-78). 4th Earl of Holderness from 1722. Minister at Venice, 1744-46, and at the Hague, 1749-51. Secretary of State for the Southern Department, 1751-54, 1757. Secretary of State for the Northern Department, 1754-61.
32. John Stuart (1713-92). 3rd Earl of Bute from 1723. Tutor to George, Prince of Wales, 1755-60. Secretary of State for the Northern Department, 1761-62. Prime Minister, 1762-63.
33. Charles Watson-Wentworth (1730-82). 2nd Marquess of Rockingham from 1750. Prime Minister, 1765-66, 1782.
34. Frederick North (1732-92). Lord North from 1752. 2nd Earl of Guilford from 1790. MP for Banbury, 1754-90. Paymaster of the Forces, 1766-67. Chancellor of the Exchequer, 1767-82. Prime Minister and First Lord of the Treasury, 1770-82. Home Secretary, 1783.
35. John Robinson (1727-1802). MP for Westmorland and Harwich, 1764-1803. Secretary of the Treasury, 1770-82.

In 1782 with North, Jenkinson lost office. He then helped to engineer the Royal coup that brought William Pitt the Younger to power in December 1783. Pitt initially believed himself a Whig and distrusted Jenkinson but Jenkinson remained involved in economic matters, his area of greatest expertise. He was rewarded in 1786 by being made President of the Board of Trade with a barony, albeit still outside the Cabinet. Nudged by Jenkinson, the Regency Crisis and the French Revolution, Pitt shifted gradually towards Toryism, forming a fully Tory government by the 1790s. Cabinet membership for Jenkinson followed in 1791 and an earldom in 1796; he continued playing an active role in Cabinet (with Liverpool from 1801) until his retirement in 1804. Together with Pitt (and not always in agreement with him) he was the principal economic specialist in government from 1786, designing the Navigation Act of 1786, several trade treaties, the famine relief measures of the 1790s and the 'Cartwheel' copper recoinage of 1797.

Charles Jenkinson married twice: Liverpool's mother, Amelia, in 1769 and a second wife, Catherine Bishopp Cope (1744-1827), in 1782. This second marriage produced two children, a daughter, Charlotte, in 1783 and a son, Charles Cecil Cope Jenkinson (1784-1851), who succeeded Liverpool as third Earl.

Charles Jenkinson's political position and philosophy were crucial to Liverpool's own early career and central to the development of the Tory party, Conservatism and much of Liverpool's economic policy. The £150,000 he left in 1808, the proceeds of a lifetime of lucrative political activity, were also useful.[36]

Liverpool was born on 7 June 1770, probably at Charles Jenkinson's London house, and baptised on 26 June at St Margaret's, Westminster, ten days before his mother died on 7 July, apparently while travelling from London to Hawkesbury, where the air was thought to be healthier. His godfather was his father's bachelor cousin, Sir Banks Jenkinson, sixth baronet.

The son of a single father with an active parliamentary career, Liverpool spent much of his early childhood with his widowed grandmother, Amarantha, and his aunt Elizabeth either at her home in Winchester or at Speaker Charles Wolfran Cornwall's home nearby. His maternal aunt Sophia was a paying guest and helped with his upbringing until her marriage to Ricketts. There were also visits to his scholarly godfather Banks' house in Oxford.

Liverpool briefly attended school in Winchester then, a few weeks before his eighth birthday, transferred to his father's house at North End, where he had a French tutor. A year later in September 1779 he entered Albion House, a preparatory school at Parsons Green.

Liverpool's childhood was generally healthy, except for an alarming attack of worms in 1781. He was a docile and intelligent child, although stories suggest shyness, an inability to pick up non-verbal clues and a certain gullibility which

36. More on Charles Jenkinson at the website www.lordliverpool.com/chronology

Sir Banks Jenkinson, 6th Bt Liverpool's godfather. Impoverished gentry, given sinecure by Charles Jenkinson while Bute's 'right hand' in 1762.

he was to retain into early adulthood.[37] Although without a mother, he was surrounded by capable and kindly family members, male and female, whose attentions left him with a sweetness of disposition which remained with him even as Prime Minister.

In 1783, Liverpool followed in his father's footsteps to the Charterhouse School in London. Since his father was both wealthy and eminent, the choice of Charterhouse, surrounded by Smithfield Market and urban grime, can be held as deliberate. The school had two advantages: its curriculum was broader

37. Hay, *Lord Liverpool*, is helpful on Liverpool's childhood, with details about which relatives played a role in his upbringing and a few tales of his childhood character.

than most, offering considerable mathematics and encouraging general reading, as well as the usual Latin and Greek, while the school also paid more attention to the boys' welfare than the lackadaisical Eton.

Liverpool's upbringing in this respect was more akin to Castlereagh's at The Royal School, Armagh, or even Eldon's[38] at Newcastle Grammar School, than to Canning's at Eton – in the period 1790-1820 Charterhouse produced 35 of the 1,240 MPs whose education is known, compared to Eton's 400.[39] This became significant in later life; Whig historians, admirers of Canning, have deliberately misinterpreted the relationship between Canning and Liverpool, which in that class-ridden society was somewhat typical of that between an Old Etonian and one who, in his view, had a socially inferior education.

History is surprisingly lacking in anecdotes of Liverpool's schooldays, partly because in the Whig-dominated nineteenth century, when such anecdotes would have surfaced, Liverpool was very undervalued by historians and the general public. The 1894 *Charterhouse, Old and New*,[40] for example, has a chapter on notable Old Carthusians, drooling about Thackeray, but does not mention either Charles Jenkinson or Liverpool – the latter surely the school's most notable alumnus. However, Liverpool himself left us one anecdote, in an 1826 House of Lords speech: 'I was once, when a schoolboy, attacked by a highwayman. I was very young at the time, but I remember losing all the money I had about me.'[41]

With the encouragement of his father, Liverpool was a diligent scholar, with interests far beyond the traditional classics. In a letter to his 14-year-old son in his second year at Charterhouse, Jenkinson praised his progress in Latin and Greek but warned him not to read any novels, since they would only waste time which he would not find 'more than sufficient for the pursuit of more useful and important studies'.[42] Liverpool also paid attention to his appearance and presentation – something his father never quite mastered – and would continue in this respect over the years

By the time he left Charterhouse, Liverpool was adept not only in classics, but also in mathematics, French, history, European politics and political economy – the latter study through a reading programme recommended by his father, now President of the Board of Trade. As Liverpool's first biographer noted, 'As the eldest

---

38. John Scott (1751-1838). 1st Earl of Eldon from 1799. Solicitor General, 1788-93. Attorney General, 1793-99. Lord Chief Justice, 1799-1801. Lord Chancellor, 1801-06, 1807-27.
39. R. Thorne (ed.), *The History of Parliament: The House of Commons 1790-1820* (Cambridge: Cambridge University Press, 1986). Survey III – The Members
40. E.P.E. Wilmot and E.C. Streatfield, *Charterhouse, Old and New* (London: John C. Nimmo, 1894).
41. *Hansard's Parliamentary Debates: The Official Report* (HL) Vol. 14, col. 1355 (14 March 1826) (London: Hansard). Hay, *Lord Liverpool*, says this happened when Liverpool was 14.
42. Quoted in Gash, *Lord Liverpool*, p. 12.

son of a peer with the greatest personal influence with the crown, his destination to the highest offices of state was never equivocal; but no man ever felt and exemplified more than that peer, the importance of early and solid acquirements.'[43]

Like his grandfather, but unlike his father, Liverpool went in 1787 to Christ Church, Oxford, now restored to its traditional Toryism, as was the see of Oxford under John Butler, a strong supporter of Lord North, appointed in 1777. More important for Liverpool's development, the Dean, Cyril Jackson,[44] was also a Tory and one of the greatest of Christ Church's deans, with substantial political influence and connections as well as a sterling academic reputation and a commitment to sound discipline.

Christ Church was the greatest producer of MPs of any Oxford or Cambridge college. Between 1790 and 1820, 285 of Oxford's 531 graduates who became MPs were Christ Church graduates, compared to the runner-up, Trinity College, Cambridge, with 151 of Cambridge's 414 (but note that Eton still beats it).[45] Thus, with Christ Church restored to its traditional Toryism and his ambitious father's friendship with Dr George Jubb, the professor of Hebrew,[46] it was a natural destination for Liverpool.

Liverpool was awarded his MA on 19 May 1790. His college career included a nine-month gap in 1789-90, which he used for travel, and the social contacts he made were also important to his later career. These included Lord Henry Spencer,[47] Charles Arbuthnot,[48] the rather younger Granville Leveson-Gower[49] and, above all, George Canning. Nicholas Vansittart was a near contemporary, graduating in 1787, who also played a major role in Liverpool's future career.

As an old Etonian with the fashionable leftism of youth – a strong Foxite Whig at this stage – Canning's political contacts at Christ Church included the Whig leaders, Henry Vassall-Fox, Lord Holland[50] and George Howard,

43. Anon., *Memoirs of the Public Life and Administration of the Rt Hon. The Earl of Liverpool*, p. 15.
44. Cyril Jackson (1746-1819). Dean of Christ Church, Oxford, 1783-1809.
45. Thorne, *The History of Parliament*, Survey III – The Members
46. Gash, *Lord Liverpool*, p. 12. George Jubb (1718-87).
47. Lord Henry Spencer (1770-95). Second son of the 4th Duke of Marlborough. Pittite MP for Woodstock, 1790-95. Envoy to Stockholm and Berlin, 1793-95.
48. Charles Arbuthnot (1767-1850). MP for East Looe, Eye, Orford, St Germans, St Ives and Ashburton, 1795-96, 1809-31. Joint (Senior) Secretary to the Treasury, 1809-23. First Commissioner of Woods and Forests, 1823-27, 1828. Chancellor of the Duchy of Lancaster, 1828-30. Second marriage 1814 to Harriet Arbuthnot, the diarist (1793-1834).
49. Granville Leveson-Gower (1773-1846). Viscount Granville, 1815. Earl Granville, 1833. Second son of the 1st Marquess of Stafford, brother of the 1st Duke of Sutherland. Ambassador to Russia 1804-05, 1807-12. Ambassador to France 1824-28,1830-41. Secretary at War, 1809. Follower of Pitt, then vacillated between Canning and the Whigs, becoming a firm Whig after Canning's death.
50. Henry Vassall-Fox (1773-1840). 3rd Baron Holland from 1774. Lord Privy Seal, 1806-07. Chancellor of the Duchy of Lancaster, 1830-34, 1835-40.

heir to the earldom of Carlisle.[51] Another good friend of both Canning and Liverpool, John Frank Newton, in 1828, wrote a reminiscence of their Oxford days, entitled *Early Days of the Right Honorable George Canning*.

Newton describes how Canning and Liverpool formed a political discussion club (the Oxford Union was still 30 years in the future) which met every Thursday, with its own brown uniform jacket adorned with buttons representing Demosthenes, Cicero, Pitt and Fox.[52] In a letter to Newton in 1788 announcing the winding-up of the club, Canning explained that a motive for setting it up had been to debate against Liverpool, who had arrived at Christ Church seven months earlier:

> Connected with men of avowed enmity in the political world, professing opposite principles, and looking forward to some distant period when we might be ranged against each other on some larger field, we were perhaps neither of us without the vanity of wishing to obtain an early ascendency over the other.[53]

However, within a year of its formation, Canning had left the club, having been advised by Dean Jackson that too ardent an espousal of Foxite Whiggery would damage his earning capacity at the Bar.

Newton describes Liverpool at Christ Church as:

> not only a first rate scholar, but he had confessedly acquired a greater share of general knowledge than perhaps any other undergraduate of that day. He was an excellent historian, and his attention had been directed so early by his father to the contending interests of the European nations, that intricate political questions were already familiar to his mind.[54]

His good nature and 'conciliatory temper' were also remarkable, as they were to remain until around 1820.

Canning's friendship with Liverpool did far more for Canning than for Liverpool, who rescued Canning's career on several occasions, without many signs of reciprocation. Even at Oxford, Canning patronised 'Jenky' and 'once, it is believed, Canning put him under the college pump'.[55] Liverpool introduced

---

51. George Howard (1773-1848). 6th Earl of Carlisle from 1825. Lord Privy Seal, 1827-28, 1834. Minister without Portfolio, 1830-34.
52. Charles James Fox (1749-1806). MP for Midhurst, Malmesbury and Westminster, 1768-1806. Foreign Secretary and Leader of the House of Commons, 1782, 1783 and 1806. Second son of Henry Fox, 1st Lord Holland.
53. John Frank Newton, *Early Days of the Right Honorable George Canning: First Lord of the Treasury and Chancellor of the Exchequer* (London: T. Cadell, 1828) pp. 20-21.
54. Ibid., p. 15.
55. C.R.L. Fletcher, *Historical Portraits, 1700-1850* (Oxford: Clarendon Press, 1919) Vol. 2, p. 173.

Canning to Pitt (they are believed to have met first at a dinner at Charles Jenkinson's seat of Addiscombe), thereby gaining him the patron who brought him into the House of Commons in 1793 as member for the rotten borough of Newtown, Isle of Wight. After Canning entered the House, Pitt's patronage of him came rather at the expense of Liverpool. Then, over 1801-04, Canning sneered at Liverpool's membership of Addington's government, from 1804 to 1812, the two clashed several times as rival members of the same Cabinet and, in 1812, Canning attempted without success to oust Liverpool. After 1812 Liverpool bailed out Canning's career despite the opposition of several of his colleagues, bringing him back first into the Cabinet and then, in 1822, making him Foreign Secretary in the face of determined Royal and Cabinet opposition.

It is unclear what Liverpool got in return for all this, and Canning's attitude to Liverpool throughout remained mostly friendly but almost always deprecating and patronising. Gash says: 'Canning's feelings towards [Liverpool] still had an element of contempt of a kind not uncommon in a clever, witty man towards a duller, loyal companion.'[56] We are not told in what respect Liverpool was 'duller' – his academic record at Christ Church was excellent and his early House of Commons speeches were praised very highly. One is drawn to the suspicion that much of Canning's attitude derived from the eternal contempt of Old Etonians for those not blessed with that magic accolade, exacerbated by the *lacunae* in Canning's own social position. As Canning was media savvy, his version of history has dominated.

Liverpool was a diligent and sober undergraduate, studying classical authors and Euclidean mathematics and, in his first year, failing to spend his whole allowance of £200.[57] Despite the occasional pump incident, Liverpool reported later, 'I had the good fortune [while at Oxford] of living in a very quiet and orderly set.'[58]

One excursion from Oxford was to give him valuable practical experience. In February 1789, Liverpool and some friends, helped John Pitt, a Gloucester attorney (no relation to the Prime Minister), in an expensive by-election at Gloucester, where he was opposed by the Whig Duke of Norfolk's cousin. The by-election had national significance because it occurred in the middle of the Regency Crisis – polling day was 5 February, the day Pitt's Regency Bill was introduced to the Commons. After heavy canvassing by Liverpool and his friends of individual electors (something Liverpool was not to do much in later years despite his political success), John Pitt won by one vote (837 to 836) and was to remain in Parliament as a reliable government supporter until 1805. The total cost of John Pitt's election exceeded £10,000, far beyond his means, so his Oxford supporters doubtless helped there, too. (The Duke of Norfolk spent £20,000 on behalf of his cousin.)[59]

56. Gash, *Lord Liverpool*, p. 26.
57. Ibid., p. 14.
58. Quoted in ibid., p. 15.
59. I am indebted to Hay, *Lord Liverpool*, p. 32, for this anecdote. John Pitt (1725-

After 26 months at Oxford, Liverpool set off on a prolonged visit to France, arriving in Paris on 7 July 1789.[60] He was just in time for the storming of the Bastille, which took place a week after on 14 July. In 1819 Liverpool was to claim in Parliament that he had been an eyewitness 'and had seen even women busy in the work of destruction and slaughter'.[61] Definitive proof of this is available in a National Archives Education Service handout,[62] which contains a letter from the young Liverpool dated 15 July, probably to his father, saying, 'The Consternation that has prevailed in Paris for the last two days, is beyond all description . . . the whole sight has been such, that nothing would have tempted me to miss it.' A modern observer, even of student age, might have had a better sense of self-preservation in a revolutionary situation; those were innocent days!

Liverpool was also in Paris on 22 July when the mob murdered Joseph Foulon de Doue, Necker's successor as interim Finance Minister, and his son-in-law, Louis Benigne François Berthier de Sauvigny. Five years later, Liverpool in a House of Commons debate was to suggest that, according to the Paris gossip of the time, Lafayette,[63] then Commander-in-Chief of the National Guard of France, had not done all he might to prevent the murders, which somewhat justified his 1793-97 imprisonment by Prussia and Austria.

One contemporary who decided Paris was getting too dangerous was the British Ambassador, the Duke of Dorset,[64] who by late July was advising British nationals to leave Paris. Dorset himself left the city on 8 August, leaving his Paris residence to be sacked by the mob, and met at Dover the nucleus of a cricket side he had invited to tour France with him – abortively, the world's first international cricket tour, an experiment not to be repeated until 1859.[65] Dorset in the following year married Liverpool's stepsister Arabella Cope.

1805). MP for Gloucester, 1789-1805. Attorney; steward of Hardwicke's Gloucester properties. The timing of this by-election explains its expense, and probably Liverpool's involvement.

60. The exact timing of this trip is uncertain; Yonge contradicts himself and suggests he went to Italy first.

61. Quoted in Yonge, *The Life and Administration of Robert Banks Jenkinson*, Vol. II, p. 442.

62. The National Archives, *French Revolution: How did the British react to July 1789*, Source 4 comprises a letter from 'a Mr. Jenkinson', dated 15 July, which appears from the facsimile to be in Liverpool's handwriting, available at: https://www.nationalarchives.gov.uk/education/resources/french-revolution/. Accessed 29 June 2020.

63. Gilbert du Motier, Marquis de Lafayette (1757-1834). Served with US Continental Army, 1777-81, ending as Major-General. Leader of moderates in the French Revolution and Commander of the National Guard, ousted in 1791. Member of the Chamber of Deputies, 1815-23, where he opposed the restored Bourbon monarchy.

64. John Sackville (1745-99). 3rd Duke of Dorset from 1769. MP for Kent, 1768-69. Ambassador to France, 1783-89.

65. John Goulstone and Michael Swanton, 'Carry on Cricket – the Duke of Dorset's 1789 Tour', *History Today*, Vol. 39, Issue 8 (August 1989).

The events of the next few tumultuous months made a lasting impression upon the young Liverpool. He appears to have observed events as they unfolded both accurately and shrewdly, and to have been uncontaminated by Radical enthusiasm for the early months of the French Revolution. 'How this matter will end it seems more and more difficult every day to determine,'[66] wrote Liverpool to his father in October, after a detailed dissection, 'all who understand the plan condemn it', of Necker's[67] latest financial plan, which involved an income tax of 25 per cent and a loan of 30 million francs. He also shrewdly noted to his father, 'the nobility and men of property would readily consent to pay part of their fortune for the positive security of the rest'[68] – an impossible bargain, alas, in any revolutionary situation.

Liverpool returned to London in November 1789 to study law under the barrister, John Reeves, later a well-known High Tory polemicist and founder in 1792 of the highly successful Association for Preserving Liberty and Property against Republicans and Levellers.[69] Then, in the spring of 1790, he returned to Christ Church, after which he received the degree of Master of Arts in May 1790 without taking an examination.

Although more than a year short of his 21st birthday, Liverpool began his political career by standing for two constituencies at the June 1790 election, being elected for both. The precipitancy of his application to Parliament was justified by the infrequency of parliamentary elections; by the following election of 1796 he would be 26 years old. For a young man with Liverpool's connections and money, parliamentary seats were easy to find, but by-elections were infrequent.

In the event, Charles Jenkinson exerted his influence in two directions in favour of his son. Liverpool was elected both for Appleby, the notorious Lowther[70] pocket borough for which his father had briefly sat, and for Rye, which was under the control of the Treasury. Since Liverpool had no wish to have his policy stances dictated by the incorrigibly autocratic Lowther, he accepted the Rye nomination.

Being under age, Liverpool did not begin his Commons career immediately; instead, he embarked on a second and longer Grand Tour, taking in Holland, Germany and Italy.[71] From Italy he wrote back to his father letters full of

66. Yonge, *The Life and Administration of Robert Banks Jenkinson*, Vol. I, p. 14.
67. Ibid., p. 13. Jacques Necker (1732-1804). Chief Minister to the French Monarch, 1788-89, 1789-90.
68. Letter to Charles Jenkinson, 23 September 1789, quoted in Hay, *Lord Liverpool*, p. 36.
69. John Reeves (1752-1829). Chief Justice of Newfoundland, 1791-93. November 1792 founded the Association for Preserving Liberty and Property against Republicans and Levellers, which by the following year had over 2,000 Crown and Anchor Club branches around the country. Reeves' 1795 *Thoughts on the English Government* was prosecuted by Fox for 'libel on the British Constitution' because of its anti-Whig views.
70. James Lowther (1736-1802). 1st Earl of Lonsdale from 1784. MP for Cumberland, Westmorland, Cockermouth and Haslemere, 1757-84.
71. Yonge has him in both Holland and Italy before returning to France in 1789 but,

classical allusions, although he found modern Italy a beautiful country full of rather unattractive people: 'Nothing is more common than assassinations in Naples: the week does not pass in which you do not hear of four or five, and in cases of murder little redress is to be found.'[72] He returned to England just before the end of the parliamentary session in June 1791, but did not take the oath until the following year.

His Christ Church contemporary, Granville Leveson-Gower saw him again at this time and remarked, 'I do not think his abilities are of the highest class, but a wonderful fluency of words and no share of *mauvaise honte* may cause his making some figure in the House of Commons.'[73] That view seems largely governed by aristocratic hauteur; Liverpool was not an exceptionally pushy personality and could hardly be described as 'shameless'.

Liverpool gave his maiden speech in the House of Commons in February 1792 after Pitt chose him to answer the opposition's censure motion moved by Samuel Whitbread[74] on the armaments programme undertaken to combat Russian expansion With France apparently weakened by post-Revolutionary disturbances, Russia began to reassert its policy of expansionism into the territories of the ailing Ottoman Empire. Pitt, early to recognise the new strategic situation, had issued an ultimatum to Russia demanding its surrender of Oczakov, a Black Sea Turkish fortress seized in 1788.

The opposition spotted ministerial weakness and attacked both the ultimatum and the armaments programme instituted to back it, forcing Pitt to abandon the ultimatum. In the event, it did the ministry a favour; a war with Russia would have led to horrible complications when his assumption that Revolutionary France posed no threat proved a year later to be nonsense.

Liverpool, in his speech, maintained that France was our eternal rival, that Britain needed to support Holland against France and that Prussia was Britain's natural ally because of its interests in Holland. Austria, recently allied to France and Prussia's natural rival, would be weakened by strengthening Turkey, which would give Prussia freedom to support Britain against France, whose enfeebled state he did not expect to last for long. He made the argument that Russia would back down if it saw that Parliament supported the British ultimatum,

---

if you look at the dates (and bear in mind the speed of travel in the eighteenth century), this was physically impossible. Hence, I conclude (along with Gash) that his observations on Italy, quoted by Yonge, date from 1790-91.

72. Quoted in Yonge, *The Life and Administration of Robert Banks Jenkinson*, Vol. I, p. 13.

73. Quoted in Gash, *Lord Liverpool*, p. 19. '*Mauvaise honte*' translates literally as 'bad shame' or bashfulness.

74. Not the Samuel Whitbread (1720-96), who founded the eponymous brewery in 1742, who was MP for Bedford, 1768-90, for Steyning, 1792-96, who according to *The Gentleman's Magazine*, was worth over £1 million at his death and was a sound Pittite, but his Radical son of the same name (1764-1815), who was MP for Bedford, 1790-1815.

and suggested that free navigation of the River Dniester, another demand in Britain's ultimatum, would enable Turkey to aid Poland, which was likely to become a power of considerable consequence. Finally, he ended the speech with a panegyric on the balance of power.[75]

Liverpool's prescience was greater than Pitt's in recognising that France could recover quickly, though his optimism on Poland proved misguided – that country was partitioned by Russia, Austria and Prussia over the next three years, with no more than feeble protests from Britain.[76] However, his overall reasoning was reminiscent of the manoeuvring between the Great Powers before the Seven Years War; the Oczakov crisis was an odd hybrid, containing elements of the diplomacy of 40 years earlier and that of 60 years later.

Liverpool's maiden speech was a great success, praised by Pitt in his daily report to the King ('it went through the whole subject in a manner so masterly both in point of matter and stile as to excite general admiration'[77]) and by various potentates in congratulatory letters to his father. It was additionally useful to Liverpool's career in dealing with a great foreign policy question, indicating to Pitt that he had acquired a valuable new Commons debating talent.

The year 1792 was an eventful parliamentary session; it included Pitt's great economic speech of 17 February, quoted by Canning 35 years later. After a three-year period from 1789 in which British exports had increased by 50 per cent, Pitt postulated that Britain could achieve, given peace and good government, a permanent economic growth derived from the effect of compound interest on the nation's capital stock. While Pitt's optimism about the lack of danger from France ('There never was a time in the history of this country when, from the situation of Europe, we might reasonably expect fifteen years of peace'[78]) proved excessive, his speech marked the beginning of transition in political thought to the idea of living in a world of continuous economic growth and increasing prosperity.

Previous statesmen had seen the world as unchanging, falling short of the glories of ancient Rome so that economic ups and downs were cyclical or random movements, due to a run of peace or good harvests, in an economy that was essentially static. Six years later Thomas Malthus[79] was to propound

75. Liverpool's speech is given almost verbatim in Anon., *Memoirs of the Public Life and Administration of the Rt Hon. The Earl of Liverpool*, pp. 18-28.

76. An indication of the folly of the 1939 Polish guarantee. Britain had been unable to protect Poland even at the height of its powers in 1792-95 and so should not have attempted or rather, pretended, to do so without a guarantee of American support in its relatively enfeebled state of 1939.

77. A. Aspinall (ed.), *The Later Correspondence of George III* (Cambridge: Cambridge University Press, 1962) Vol. 1, p. 584.

78. W.S. Hathaway (ed.), *The Speeches of William Pitt in the House of Commons*, 3 vols (London: Longman, Hurst, Rees, Orme and Brown, 1817) p. 350.

79. Thomas R. Malthus (1766-1834). Cleric and political economist. Author of *An*

the opposite thesis, that mankind was destined for inevitable starvation as population outran growth. Pitt's optimism proved correct and liberating, although he alluded only peripherally ('the improvement which has been made in the mode of carrying on almost every branch of manufacture'[80]) to technological change. That was already happening at a considerable rate, but its effects entered political thinking only gradually, with Liverpool himself becoming one of its major proponents.

Liverpool absorbed his great chief's new message of optimism and in his own premiership 20 years later was to show a firm faith in the country's ability to achieve long-term, even perpetual, growth – not so much through the operation of compound interest on the nation's capital stock as through technological change and productivity growth therefrom, which by then had fully entered the political lexicon.

The 1792 session also saw the second great debate on the abolition of the slave trade. (A bill had been passed in 1788 restricting the trade and an abolitionist motion had been introduced in the previous year, losing by 163 to 88.) Here Liverpool followed his father, a leading anti-abolitionist in the Lords; as his first biographer, writing in 1827 before the abolition of slavery itself, said 'the advocates of abolition were not, at this time, distinguished either by their mercantile knowledge, their individual discretion, or their respect for established opinions'.[81]

Within the British Empire the moral case against slavery was becoming generally agreed and opposition to abolition was primarily economic – there were few equivalents of John C. Calhoun[82] proclaiming slavery a 'positive good'. Lord Mansfield's 1772 decision in the Somersett Case had effectively forbidden it in England and Wales, while Upper Canada (today's Ontario), where the only significant pro-slavery economic interests were a few former Loyalist Americans from the southern states, was in 1793 to pass an 'Act Against Slavery' providing for immediate abolition of the trade and gradual abolition of slavery itself.

Liverpool's own speech admitted that the slave trade was indefensible but pointed out that British trade would lose £6 million annually by its abolition. He then introduced an economic argument of doubtful validity, suggesting that regulation improving the lot of existing slaves would increase their fertility,

---

Essay on the Principle of Population (1798), a work which remains influential and appears increasingly prescient more than 200 years later.

80. Hathaway, *The Speeches of William Pitt*, p. 357.
81. Anon., *Memoirs of the Public Life and Administration of the Rt Hon. The Earl of Liverpool*, p. 33.
82. John C. Calhoun (1782-1850). Representative from South Carolina, 1811-17. US Secretary of War, 1817-25. Vice-President, 1825-32. Senator from South Carolina, 1832-43, 1845-50. US Secretary of State, 1844-45. Claimed that slavery was a 'positive good', not simply a necessary evil, in a US Senate speech on 6 February 1837.

thus rendering the import of new slaves unnecessary and causing the trade to die a natural death. This may have looked plausible in relation to Britain's possessions in the West Indies and the coastal US slave states, but it ignored the slaveholding potential of the future US Deep South states, which would open to extended slave cultivation after the United States' Louisiana Purchase of 1803.

Liverpool's motion to bring forth a plan for this purpose was defeated by 234 votes to 87, after which Dundas'[83] motion, inserting the word 'gradually' before the provision for abolition (he later proposed a date of 1 January 1800), was carried by a majority of 193 to 125. The amended motion was carried by 230 to 85 but died in the face of Lords' opposition, after which the war told against further abolition attempts.

Although Liverpool would continue to oppose the abolition of the slave trade until the Act was passed in January 1807, as Prime Minister he would devote considerable naval and diplomatic resources to stamping out the slave trade and in the 1820s he was mildly helpful in early attempts to abolish slavery.

After the session ended, Liverpool made his third European trip, through Holland to Coblenz, the headquarters of the Austrian and German forces now at war with Revolutionary France. In this trip, Liverpool probably had a watching brief from Pitt (though any formal brief from Pitt was denied in a letter to *The Times*).[84]

He travelled with Leveson-Gower and, while on the journey composed a project of government for France, which divided the country into provinces, each with a provincial parliament of two houses imposing taxes locally. Leveson-Gower thought the project good but that the nobility might object to spending so much time in the provinces, away from Paris. Essentially, Liverpool was here attempting to replace France's overcentralised constitution with a version of Britain's mixed eighteenth-century government. It might well have worked better but ran directly contrary to France's constitutional tradition, still apparent today both in France and in the institutions of the European Union, of centralisation and authoritarianism.[85]

Liverpool's letters to his father were full of detailed information on the Allied forces' diplomatic and military positions. He was not optimistic: 'It is not easy to conceive the sovereign contempt with which the Prussians of every description, soldiers as well as officers, treat the French. . . . In the French *émigré* army there are about 16,000 men. In this number there are about 500 soldiers; all the rest are officers.'[86]

---

83. Henry Dundas (1741-1811). 1st Viscount Melville from 1802. Lord Advocate of Scotland, 1775-83. Home Secretary, 1791-94. Secretary for War and the Colonies, 1794-1801. First Lord of the Admiralty 1804-05.
84. Hay, *Lord Liverpool*, p. 44.
85. Ibid., pp. 44-45, presumably quoting from correspondence during the trip.
86. Quoted in Yonge, *The Life and Administration of Robert Banks Jenkinson*, Vol. I, p. 21.

Three days later he commended as 'moderate' the manifesto of the Duke of Brunswick, commander of the joint Prussian and Austrian forces, by which he threatened to burn to the ground any French village which opposed his troops and to destroy Paris if the royal family was harmed. This threat further radicalised the French regime, produced massive additional opposition to the royal family and spurred a rising on 10 August that stormed the Tuileries Palace, massacred the Swiss Guard and deposed Louis XVI.

Liverpool's commendation of Brunswick was an unexpected youthful misjudgement; he should have learned from his reading of Clarendon's *History of the Rebellion and Civil Wars in England*[87] that the opposite policy, to be as lenient as possible, was greatly preferable in what was potentially a civil war. Fortunately, by the time he had the command of military matters in 1809-15, he would have mastered this lesson.

Liverpool was more sure-footed in his analysis of economic and strategic questions, writing in a subsequent letter that Prussia was so small that, if anything interrupted its military success, it would, except under a very able prince, decline to a second-class power, whereas Austria, far less effective and impressive though its army was, would always maintain its strength because of its population and resources.

Liverpool spent over a month with the Allied armies, witnessing their first incursion into France and commenting favourably on the King of Prussia's recompensing French villagers for war damage. However, the French armies succeeded in stopping the Allied advance on 20 September at the Battle of Valmy and thereafter Britain was drawn inexorably into the war, the final step being the execution of Louis XVI in January 1793.

Having spent a month with the Allied armies, Liverpool was more aware than most that war with France was inevitable. Accordingly, in the winter of 1792-3 he obtained a commission in the militia, although Canning, supportive as always, remarked that with his knowledge of music he was best suited to be a trumpeter.[88]

In the new session which opened in December, Liverpool took a prominent part in opposing Fox's motion calling for 'every species of honourable negotiation' to avoid war with France. He took a financial viewpoint, claiming that France's dire financial position made it a uniquely favourable moment to declare war on her and suggesting it was pointless to negotiate with the 'band of sanguinary ruffians' who now ruled France. He also suggested that war with France would make it far easier to quell British sedition, which the French had

87. Edward Hyde, Earl of Clarendon, *The History of the Rebellion and Civil Wars in England* (Oxford: Oxford University Press, 1703). The issue came up repeatedly during the Civil War during which Clarendon was a strong voice for a lenient policy in opposition to the punitive proposals of others.

88. Gash, *Lord Liverpool*, p. 26. Liverpool was generally musical but I cannot find any evidence for activity that would have caused Canning's quip.

been busily supporting from their national treasury, to the tune of 25 million livres (£1million) in dodgy *assignats*.[89] His speech received warm accolades from Edmund Burke, whose earlier career before the French Revolution had been spent in Whiggish opposition to Charles Jenkinson.[90]

Liverpool's contribution to the February debate accompanying the declaration of war against France was described by Pitt to the King as 'a speech of uncommon ability and effect',[91] from which point he became a frontbench spokesman for the government. With most senior ministers in the Lords, governments were perennially short of debating talent in the Commons, so promotion was quick for a good speaker of reliable politics.

Liverpool's participation was also notable in favour of what was to become the Aliens Act of 1793. This legislation, prompted by the massive surge in immigration by French fleeing the Jacobins, introduced compulsory registration with the local justice of the peace by aliens entering the country and provided that those violating the act could be held without bail and, if necessary, deported. Even as a supporter in general of free trade, Liverpool was aware that immigration and trade were different issues, on which enlightened policy should differ.

In May he took a leading role in opposing Charles Grey's motion for Parliamentary Reform, which was believed to embarrass the administration, since Pitt had supported Reform in 1782 and 1785, and it was now backed by agitators in the various Corresponding Societies. Showing the reaction against the Terror in even the mind of young and fairly radical Whigs, Grey's speech claimed: 'it is impossible that any set of men, who had not actually lost their sense, should ever propose the French revolution as a model for imitation'.[92] He then went on to denounce electoral corruption, claiming that a wider franchise would alleviate it, and to suggest that parliaments elected under the existing narrow franchise had involved the country in repeated expensive wars, running up debt.

In response, Liverpool began by pointing out that Grey's resolutions proposed no reform plan. He defended the existing constitution on the grounds that its variety of representation, including the landed interests, the mercantile community and the professions, was indispensable to securing a proper advocacy for all the nation's interests. However, the House of

89. Anon., *Memoirs of the Public Life and Administration of the Rt Hon. The Earl of Liverpool*, p. 47.
90. Edmund Burke (1729-97). MP for Wendover, Malton and Bristol, 1765-94. Paymaster of the Forces, 1782, 1783-84. Author of *Reflections on the Revolution in France* (1790).
91. Aspinall, *The Later Correspondence of George III*, Vol. 2, p. 8.
92. Quoted in Anon., *Memoirs of the Public Life and Administration of the Rt Hon. The Earl of Liverpool*, p. 66. Having been written in 1827, before the 1832 Reform Act, Anon. is particularly useful on the Reform question; subsequent Liverpool biographers are mealy-mouthed on the issue.

Commons was a deliberative assembly and should therefore not be directed by every breeze of popular opinion but should be expected to pursue unpopular policies from time to time. As for wars, Liverpool pointed out that the War of Jenkins' Ear had been got up by popular demand, against the wishes of Walpole's government, while the American war, once it became unpopular, had resulted in the ejection of North's ministry within eighteen months of an election at which it had triumphed:

> Form a House of Commons as you please, assemble the people in Salisbury Plain; you cannot prevent their having improper attachments and improper aversions. You cannot prevent their placing too much confidence in one minister, because they approve of him, or too little in another, because they disapprove of him. The defect is not in the representation; it is human nature, and our eyes had better be turned to an improvement of that.

Finally, he concluded, 'That there are theoretic defects in the composition of the House of Commons cannot be denied; but it is incumbent on those who propose a reform, to prove, if they can, that those defects affect the practice of the constitution.'[93]

Grey's motion lost by a vote of 181 to 109. It was the closest Parliament ever came to broad-based parliamentary reform during Liverpool's career. Only after his retirement did it again approach success.

In June 1793, Pitt offered Liverpool his first official appointment, a seat on the reconstituted Board of Control for India, which he would hold until 1796, under its new President, Henry Dundas, already Home Secretary. Given Charles Jenkinson's knowledge of India since the 1760s, friendship with Dundas, and continued presidency of the Board of Trade, there was a natural synergy between the activities of father and son.

We have an image of Liverpool at this period from Karl Anton Hickel's picture, *The House of Commons, 1793-94.*[94] He is on the front bench, probably after his appointment to the India Board, sitting fifth to the right of Pitt, who is addressing the House. Liverpool's fawn-yellow trousers, tight boots, cream waistcoat and elaborately ruffled shirt give him a dandified appearance alongside his more soberly-dressed colleagues, all of whom were older. But

93. Anon., *Memoirs of the Public Life and Administration of the Rt Hon. The Earl of Liverpool*, pp. 63-73, summarises Grey's speech and quotes much of Liverpool's verbatim.

94. National Portrait Gallery: https://www.npg.org.uk/collections/search/portrait/mw00119/The-House-of-Commons-1793-94. Accessed 30 June 2020. Karl Anton Hickel (1745-98) was court painter to the emperors of Austria; the picture was unveiled at 28 Haymarket in 1795 and presented to the gallery by Emperor Franz Josef I in 1885.

The House of Commons in 1793-94, Karl Anton Hickel. Liverpool is sitting back, five to the right of Pitt, who is speaking.

then this was the era of Sir Percy Blakeney![95] (It is also possible that the yellow trousers of both Liverpool and the fictional Sir Percy were inspired by Goethe's 1774 novel, *The Sorrows of Young Werther*, which inspired a fashion for yellow trousers, high boots and a blue jacket, all of which Liverpool is wearing in the Hickel picture.) Nevertheless, this and the Lawrence portrait of 1796 on the jacket of this book show the young Liverpool as a considerably 'cooler' cat than the sober statesman of later years.[96]

Liverpool spent a considerable time in the next few years on militia duties. In April 1794, he was appointed Colonel of Pitt's new Cinque Ports Regiment of Fencible Cavalry, raised by the Prime Minister as Lord Warden of the Cinque Ports. (Canning was to put his recruiting handbill into doggerel verse and read the verses at a dinner party at which Liverpool was present – another nasty Old Etonian putdown.) This was a less grand appointment than it sounds – by October 1795, after having been presented with its colours by Dundas at a parade near Windsor Castle, the regiment numbered 80 effectives.

95. Hero of the historical romances of Baroness Orczy (1865-1947) and played by Leslie Howard in the classic 1934 film, *The Scarlet Pimpernel.*

96. Sir Thomas Lawrence, *Robert Banks Jenkinson*, c. 1796, National Portrait Gallery: https://www.npg.org.uk/collections/search/portrait/mw09420/Robert-Banks-Jenkinson-2nd-Earl-of-Liverpool. Accessed 30 June 2020.

Still, Liverpool was quickly in the front line of maintaining public order – his regiment was ordered to Brighton in May 1795, where the execution of two soldiers had caused a disturbance.[97]

Liverpool's performance in the next Parliamentary session was less successful. It included one much mocked speech when he got carried away and announced that 'marching to Paris is attainable and practicable, and I, for one would recommend such an expedition'.[98] This exhortation appeared over optimistic at the time and was to appear absurd as defeat followed defeat. It was to remain part of his legend, being brought up from time to time by the opposition in both Houses and mocked by the Prince Regent eighteen years later.[99] In the first months of the war, Liverpool's aggressive strategy might have succeeded better than the hesitant posture adopted by the Duke of York[100] in command of the British forces, but the time for that was already past.

In a later debate on the same subject, Liverpool demolished both the arguments for an early peace and the uselessness of moderation in revolutionary circumstances:

> What was it overthrew the administration of Necker? Moderation. What destroyed the Constitutionalists, the Girondins, the Brissotines and the various parties that have risen and sunk in that agitated hemisphere? Moderation! Or what has confirmed the power lodged in the hands of the present possessors? The total want of it! Should they ever depart from their usual system of violence, by thinking of so humane and moderate an idea as treating for peace, their downfall would be inevitable.[101]

97. Hay, *Lord Liverpool*, p. 51, and Roger Knight, *Britain Against Napoleon: The Organization of Victory, 1793-1815* (London: Penguin Books, 2014) p. 79.
98. Quoted in Anon., *Memoirs of the Public Life and Administration of the Rt Hon. The Earl of Liverpool*, p. 80.
99. Sir Augustus Foster (1780-1848; Minister Plenipotentiary to the United States, 1811-12), 'Foster's Notes on the United States', *The Quarterly Review*, Vol. 68 (1841), p. 56. 'The Prince Regent then desired us to sit down, and began questioning me about the American government, saying, jokingly, that he had heard not only the Minister for War but the Minister for Foreign Affairs had become soldiers, and commanded corps; and when I told him it was very true, he laughed, and turning round, exclaimed, "By God, Liverpool, you should copy their example and then, by God, you know, you might execute your favourite plan of a march on Paris."' In the event, a 'march on Paris' was executed successfully twice in the next three years.
100. Prince Frederick Augustus (1763-1827). Duke of York and Albany from 1784. Second son of George III. Bishop of Osnabruck, 1764-1803. General, 1793. Commander, British forces in Flanders, 1793-95. Field Marshal, 1795. Commander, British forces in Holland, 1799. Commander-in-Chief of the Forces, 1795-1809, 1811-27.
101. Quoted in Anon., *Memoirs of the Public Life and Administration of the Rt Hon. The Earl of Liverpool*, pp. 86-7.

Louisa, Lady Liverpool in 1793,
around the time she met Liverpool, by George Romney.

In response, Sheridan[102] mocked Liverpool's confidence: 'No other supposition indeed could warrant the manner in which that honourable

102. Richard Brinsley Sheridan (1751-1816), the playwright. Foxite Whig MP for Stafford, Westminster and Ilchester, 1780-1812. Treasurer of the Navy, 1806-07.

gentleman delivers his opinions, unless we are to suppose that he has an *hereditary* [author's italics] knowledge of politics, and that a deep insight into the secrets of cabinets runs in his blood.'[103]

Liverpool's principal activity for the next year was to get married, which he did on 25 March 1795 at Wimbledon, with the Dean of Canterbury, his third cousin, Folliott Cornewall, officiating.[104] His wife, Lady Louisa Hervey, was the third and youngest daughter of Frederick Augustus Hervey, fourth Earl of Bristol and Bishop of Derry (1730-1803).[105] The Earl was a radical, supporting the Irish Volunteer rebel movement in 1782-83 and favouring both political and religious equality (for example, he objected to tithes, at that time the financial bulwark of the Church of England). In addition, Louisa's elder sister, Elizabeth, was the live-in mistress (and later wife) of the Whig fifth Duke of Devonshire.

Charles Jenkinson was thus strongly opposed to the match on political, religious and eugenic grounds (there was considerable madness in the Hervey family, beyond the eccentricities of the Earl-Bishop himself). He also believed Liverpool at 24 was too young and early in his career to marry – comparing his own first marriage at the age of 40. (It didn't help that the proposed bride was three years older than Liverpool himself.) Louisa, however, was very different from her rakish father and sister; she was a diffident soul and an Evangelical, with a seriousness which appealed to Liverpool.

Liverpool appears to have met Louisa some time in 1793 and to have kept the relationship secret from his father in the early stages. By November 1794 Liverpool's wooing had been successful. The pair then made the mistake of asking the Earl-Bishop's consent first (he was, as usual travelling on the Continent). This was returned with great benevolence. However, being left to last did nothing for Jenkinson's equanimity – he had refused to believe a romance was in train when informed of it by a third party.

When Jenkinson was finally told officially, initially in a letter from Liverpool, he refused to accept the match, whereupon Liverpool, after consulting with Pitt and Dundas, informed his father that, if thwarted in love, he would be compelled to give up his Parliamentary career. As Pitt and Dundas agreed (according to the possibly malicious, Canning), 'the pride which he feels in his son's consequence is a passion much more powerful, and to which it is much more prudent to appeal, than his affection'.[106] Eventually, even the King

103. Quoted in Anon., *Memoirs of the Public Life and Administration of the Rt Hon. The Earl of Liverpool*, p. 91.

104. Sir Lewis Namier and J. Brooke (eds), *The History of Parliament: The House of Commons 1754-1790*, (Martlesham, Suffolk: Boydell & Brewer,1964). Folliott Cornewall (1754-1831). Dean of Canterbury, 1792. Bishop of Bristol, 1797. Bishop of Hereford, 1803. Bishop of Worcester, 1808.

105. Frederick Augustus Hervey, 4th Earl of Bristol (1730-1803). Bishop of Derry, 1768-1803. See Gash, *Lord Liverpool*, pp. 31-32.

106. Quoted in Gash, *Lord Liverpool*, p. 32.

got involved, not surprisingly, given his long friendship with Jenkinson, to persuade Jenkinson that, despite the highly unsatisfactory character of the bride's father, true love should be allowed to prevail.

Liverpool's judgement proved admirable. Louisa was an excellent wife until her relatively early death in 1821, although the Liverpool household was notable for the dullness of its entertainments and the fashionable Whig hostess Lady Holland accused her of 'extreme prudery'.[107] Louisa was also a good judge of people; in particular, she disliked and distrusted Canning, a useful corrective to Liverpool's enthusiasm for him.

Their married life was only later to include a settled home. Charles Jenkinson's Addiscombe was rented and left the family on his death in 1808, while a possible inheritance of Pitchford Hall, a beautiful Tudor country house in Shropshire, went in 1807 to his half-brother Charles, as he had fewer means of his own.

Liverpool was to lease a magnificent Whitehall residence, Fife House, only in 1809 after his father's death and the death of the second Earl of Fife (1729-1809). Given this large and convenient base, Liverpool never used 10 Downing Street, assigning it to his Chancellors of the Exchequer, Nicholas Vansittart and Frederick Robinson, although he had used the Foreign Office's house at 16 Downing Street as Foreign Secretary in 1801-4, albeit primarily as an office.

In the country, Hawkesbury Manor, which Liverpool owned from 1808, was in a state of disrepair and he appears never to have lived there. There are, however, two houses in Gloucestershire which claim a Liverpool connection. One is Eastwood Park, about ten miles west of Hawkesbury, where Liverpool is said to have started but never completed a house. The second is the Manor House at Petty France, about four miles from Hawkesbury, which Liverpool is said to have had built with completion in 1812. It is likely that Liverpool attempted to build at Eastwood, then realised that Petty France was much closer to his ancestral lands and the family church. Petty France is also only sixteen miles from Bath, where he convalesced frequently in his later years as the strains of high office began to tell. Overall, as Prime Minister he spent little time in Gloucestershire, even though he owned 3,000 acres in the county.

Much nearer to London and hence more convenient for his work in those days of achingly slow travel, in 1801 or 1802 Liverpool bought a modest country home, Coombe Wood, near Kingston, which he had enlarged under the direction of the fashionable architect, Sir John Soane.[108] (In its enlarged

107. Ibid., p. 32. Elizabeth Fox, *née* Vassall (1771-1845), married 3rd Baron Holland in 1797, having been divorced two days earlier from her previous husband on grounds of her adultery. She had five children with her first husband, seven with Holland and introduced the dahlia to England. A bossy woman, she admired Napoleon and was admired by the Whig diarist, Charles Greville, but NOT by Mrs Arbuthnot.

108. Sir John Soane (1753-1837). Knighted, 1831. Neo-classical architect, *protégé* of 4th Earl of Bristol, Liverpool's father-in-law. Rebuilt Bank of England, 1790-1827, and made renovations to Coombe Wood and Fife House.

1995 monument to 1797 'Massacre of Tranent' by militia troops of which Liverpool was Colonel. Liverpool's peripheral involvement is useful modern agitprop. Source: Kim Traynor

state, the house was sold to the Duke of Cumberland[109] in 1837.) This was close enough to London for entertaining George III (in 1805), the Prince Regent and Czar Alexander I, as well as being large enough for house parties.

Liverpool's position on the India Board was largely a sinecure, so he was able to spend most of the next few summers drilling his volunteer regiment. He suffered a notably uncomfortable camp in Dumfries in the summer of 1796, where the hospitality was trying: 'the bottle passes more quickly than I like'.[110]

The following year, when his regiment was in the Haddington area east of Edinburgh, it was involved in a riot at the mining village of Tranent, since romanticised by some as the 'Massacre of Tranent'.[111] Following the 1797 Militia Act, which authorised the recruitment of 6,000 militia in Scotland, a recruiting

109. Ernest Augustus (1771-1851). Duke of Cumberland from 1799. King of Hanover from 1837. Fifth son of George III, a noted reactionary, especially active in the 1829 Catholic Emancipation crisis.

110. Quoted in Yonge, *The Life and Administration of Robert Banks Jenkinson*, Vol. I, p. 38.

111. The best account of this incident is in *The Lamp of Lothian or the History of Haddington* by James Miller (Edinburgh: James Allan, 1844) pp. 309-30. Modern accounts are not to be trusted, being corrupted by leftist and nationalist political agendas.

squad of about 80 soldiers under Major Wight, which included a party of the Cinque Ports light cavalry under Captain Finlay, was attacked with rocks and bottles by an organised mob of protesters against army recruiting activities.

After several attempts to quell the rioters, Major Wight ordered the dragoons to fire, killing some of the rioters but dispelling them, after which the soldiers appear to have lost discipline and killed various innocent people in the surrounding countryside, to a total of eleven dead and eight injured. Liverpool, the Cinque Ports light cavalry's commanding officer, was not present, being at the county town of Haddington about ten miles away. The facts of the case were laid before the Lord Advocate of Scotland but no action was taken.

The 'massacre', as it can correctly be called with respect to the non-rioters, apparently seven of the eleven killed, has recently been played up locally, with an ugly monument to the rioters erected in 1995. Liverpool's collateral involvement has fuelled nationalist and leftist agendas. The accusation that he should have been present at Tranent makes little sense as only a small part of his regiment was involved, and Major Wight, not of his regiment, was the senior officer present. Liverpool can, however, be criticised for the poor discipline of his men and for Captain Finlay's failure to control them.

Liverpool's military activities continued until the disbandment of the regiment sometime in early 1800, when the invasion threat was thought to have passed, although his ministerial promotion in March 1799 severely curtailed his activities. His activities as Colonel of the Cinque Ports Fencible Cavalry had been unpleasant in parts but had given him an invaluable understanding of two things. First, he had a worm's eye view of an army's needs and capabilities, useful after he became War Minister in 1809. Second, he had acquired an understanding of the difficulties of maintaining order and enforcing law in a society, much of which was from time to time on the edge of destitution.

Parliament reassembled on 29 October 1795, 'its opening being attended by a disgraceful demonstration of the influence of the new democratic doctrines on the mob'.[112] (There was a riot outside Westminster, shouts of 'No King', stones were thrown at the Royal coach, and its glass was broken by a bullet apparently fired from an airgun.) Liverpool declared in seconding the address that no peace with France was possible until she could be persuaded to give up her recent conquest of Holland, which had taken place only because of the dilatory actions of the anti-French coalition.

His next major speech was on commercial matters, in response to a Grey motion on the state of the nation. He remarked that:

> the commercial situation of Great Britain, notwithstanding the weight of so great a war, is more prosperous than at any antecedent period. . . . The advantage in the borrowing of money, at present, is 1½ per cent

112. Anon., *Memoirs of the Public Life and Administration of the Rt Hon. The Earl of Liverpool*, p. 96.

> greater than during the American war. . . . It is unfair to complain of increasing expenses. The augmentation of price in all the articles of life and social intercourse, adds, of consequence, the same proportion of increase to military expenses.[113]

Liverpool assumed the courtesy title of Lord Hawkesbury in May 1796, on his father's elevation to the earldom of Liverpool, and was easily re-elected at the general election of May-June 1796, at which the Pittite Tories maintained the large majority they had enjoyed since the Portland Whigs crossed the floor of the house two years earlier.

The same year, he produced his only published work (other than a few speeches), *Reflections on the Present State of the Resources of the Country*.[114] It was a sensible career move, since it attached his rising reputation to his father's established economic expertise. The pamphlet attempted to prove that Britain was as well able to bear its debt load in 1795 and 1796 as it had been in the peace year of 1788. To this end, Liverpool proved that British exports had increased by 50 per cent from 1788 to 1795, more than the increase in debt service payments. Despite France and Holland being cut off from British exports directly, exports to Germany had quadrupled, suggesting that increased costs imposed by war had not prevented some British exports from finding their way to French and Dutch buyers.

He then examined 'navigation bills' for canal construction, which had leapt in value since 1788, and 'enclosure bills' allowing technological improvements in agriculture, which had also increased. Finally, he proposed the modern notion that since the national debt was primarily held domestically, it did not represent a burden on the economy similar to an individual's debt. The decline in bond prices was thus not an indication of doubts about the country's credit, simply the law of supply and demand in action.

Liverpool's confidence was partly belied by the Bank of England's suspension of specie payments in February 1797. The pamphlet also took no account of inflation, already virulent in 1795. Liverpool's overall conclusion, that, given the relatively robust financing system of the City of London, the British economy should prove strong enough to deal with the stresses facing it and the costs of war, was surely, in retrospect, correct. Britain's capacity to wage global war was an issue that Liverpool would deal with repeatedly in future years. The slim published pamphlet of 1796 remains the basis of his thinking about the matter.

Liverpool spoke at length on the Bank of England's suspension of payments in the parliamentary debate on 9 March 1797, in answer to heated accusations of national bankruptcy by Fox. He began by asserting that national credit

113. Quoted in Anon., *Memoirs of the Public Life and Administration of the Rt Hon. The Earl of Liverpool*, pp. 98-99.

114. Robert Banks Jenkinson, *Reflections on the Present State of the Resources of the Country* (London: John Stockdale, 1796).

was 'the most delicate and important subject that could possibly be agitated', then pointed out that the term 'bankruptcy' could not be applied to a country whose assets greatly exceeded its liabilities and whose economy was flourishing. He showed that the value of land was greater than at any previous time and suggested that the drain of specie was due to a 'panic that has causelessly seized on the public mind'. He ended by suggesting that the paper money supply should be increased rather than diminished, as Fox was suggesting, since to do otherwise would prove impossibly destructive of trade.[115] As he was to prove triumphantly in 1819, Liverpool was a sound money man like his father. However, he knew that a paper currency issue became essential when wartime trade imbalances destabilised the gold standard; provided it remained limited, it need not lead to hyperinflation.

Liverpool spoke against a parliamentary reform motion proposed by Grey. He declared himself opposed to Reform, not only at that particularly difficult time, but at any time. The principal objection to it was that the evil addressed by Reform did not exist and its non-existence could be demonstrated by the vagueness of proposals for Reform and the lack of any commonality between them. Parliament well reflected the will of the public, both in its support of Pitt's ministry and in its initial enthusiasm for the American war. This could be demonstrated by examining the 1796 election results in the counties and populous towns, which showed an even larger majority for Pitt's ministry than did the close boroughs. The current proposal pointed in the direction of universal suffrage, a principle that almost nobody in the House supported.[116]

In the following session (1797-98) Liverpool spoke in favour of Pitt's income tax, first proposed in that year. He said the tax was nowhere near as unpopular in the country as it was in London (since it applied only to incomes above £60, far above the annual wages of a working man, this should not have been surprising). Later in the year, he twice spoke in favour of the land tax, still in 1797 the principal bastion of government finances. This year saw the rise of the ephemeral but influential *Anti-Jacobin*, sponsored by the young Canning and edited by William Gifford,[117] the future first editor of *The Quarterly Review*. Liverpool, through his friendship for Canning, was a significant contributor.

Liverpool returned twice in December 1798 to the subject of Pitt's income tax, saying that: 'Perfection is not in human nature, but this comes as near it as human wisdom could devise.' He pointed out that income tax would fall most heavily on the City merchants, whose income typically vastly exceeded their expenditure, rather than the poor whose expenditure matched or exceeded their income – yet the City merchants were welcoming the new measure. The

115. *The Parliamentary Register; or, History of the Proceedings and Debates of the House of Commons* (London: John Debrett, 1797) Vol. 1, pp. 807-8.

116. Ibid., Vol. 2, pp. 613-14.

117. William Gifford (1756-1826). Editor, *Anti-Jacobin*, 1797-98; Editor, *The Quarterly Review*, 1809-24.

income tax also had the singular merit of 'keeping all the orders of society in their relative situation'. Also, 'the objections to its inequality had been illustrated by a comparison of taking a tenth off a man's height, but this bill took nothing from the height of the dwarf' [118] – the poorest being spared by the £60 minimum income for tax to be charged.

The following month, Liverpool supported warmly Castlereagh's motion for consideration of a union with Ireland, which would only be acceptable if wholeheartedly backed by the Irish parliament as well as the English one. (Ireland's majority Catholic population was not represented in the Irish parliament, although they could vote in Irish parliamentary elections.) Liverpool had seen Pitt's plan for Irish union the previous year and had written to Wellesley that he agreed with it in every part and remarked that Pitt proposed 'to find some substitute for the tithes on potatoes, as I believe it is the greatest practical grievance in that country'.[119]

Opponents of union pointed out the prosperity of Ireland under the independent parliament it had enjoyed since 1782 but:

> whatever that prosperity may have been, the course of events which has for some years past taken place in that country has firmly riveted me in the opinion that there must be something radically wrong in the internal situation of that country. The interests of the Protestant and Catholic are so distinct and different, and form so continual a food for jealousy, that I am afraid that nothing but a grand Legislative Union will ever be able effectually to reconcile them one to the other.

Again:

> It would be my desire to extend the blessings of this Constitution to all my fellow creatures; it is my particular wish that the people of Ireland should derive every benefit from it that results to us: I am desirous to pledge my own property in Great Britain, as well as the property of Britons in general, for the security of property in Ireland.[120]

Liverpool received his reward for years of steady Commons service to the government, and for his father's labours on the currency front, when he was created Master of the Mint in February 1799 and admitted to the Privy

---

118. *The Parliamentary Register*, Vol. 7, pp. 294-95 (17 December 1798).

119. Richard Colley Wellesley, (1760-1842). Earl of Mornington, 1781-99. Marquess Wellesley from 1799. Governor-General of India, 1798-1805. Foreign Secretary, 1809-12. Lord Lieutenant of Ireland, 1821-28, 1833-34. Lewis Melville (ed.), *The Wellesley Papers: The Life and Correspondence of Richard Colley Wellesley, 1760-1842* (London: Herbert Jenkins, 1914) Vol. 1, pp. 79-81.

120. *The Parliamentary Register*, Vol. 7, pp. 670-74 (31 January 1799).

Council. As Master of the Mint, Liverpool became involved in his father's ambitions for a silver re-coinage, following on from the highly successful emergency copper coinage created by his father two years earlier. However, in the event, the financial situation was so serious that silver re-coinage had to be postponed, revived by Liverpool as Prime Minister in 1816. One reform which Liverpool introduced was to replace the perquisites to which previous masters had been accustomed with a fixed salary of £3,000 per annum – increased from £2,500 after a vigorous intervention by his father.

By the end of the 1790s, Liverpool was becoming somewhat disillusioned with Pitt. He had never hero-worshipped him in the way Canning did, since his father was on cool terms with him. In the autumn of 1798, illness, which Liverpool believed to be more serious than gout, began to make Pitt's attendance to his duties intermittent. In the following year Pitt and the Cabinet sent a major expedition to Holland, again under the Duke of York, the naval part of which successfully turned the allegiance of the Dutch fleet, but the land part failed to coordinate properly with Russian forces and the army was forced to evacuate. Liverpool had been sceptical of the expedition and in October wrote to his father: 'I agree with you that our Government is completely disgraced, for what can be more disgraceful to a Minister than to fail in an expedition, when your troops have been uniformly victorious, in consequence of the impracticability of the country which you have chosen for your scene of action.'[121]

Liverpool intervened in February 1800 against the projected peace with France, saying that in the previous seven years they had seen in France seven great revolutions and four smaller ones, while the character of the new government (Napoleon Bonaparte's[122] First Consulship) could be no better than the character of its members, which was poor. Britain's position remained strong: 'Thank God, I believe that the only part of Europe which does not speak well of the country was confined to that very small portion which constitutes the Opposition in this country; whatever remains of property, religion and social order, remains in this country.'[123] Later in the month Liverpool re-affirmed that the government was not fighting to restore the French monarchy but merely required that the French establish some government with which agreements could reliably be made.[124]

Liverpool made another economic speech later in February, supporting a bill prohibiting the sale of bread less than 24 hours old (this saved a considerable amount of corn, at that time scarce and expensive). In it he recommended free imports of foreign corn, while pointing out that wartime price rises had

121. Quoted in Yonge, *The Life and Administration of Robert Banks Jenkinson*, Vol I., p. 39.
122. Napoleon Bonaparte (1769-1821). Second Lieutenant, French army, 1785. Brigadier General, 1793. General, 1796. First Consul, 1799-1804. Emperor, 1804-14, 1815. Won battles (*inter alia*) of Rivoli, 1797, Marengo, 1800, Ulm, 1805, Austerlitz, 1805, Jena, 1806, Friedland, 1807, Wagram, 1809, and Borodino, 1812.
123. *The Parliamentary Register*, Vol. 10, pp. 409-11 (7 February 1800).
124. Ibid., pp. 745-50 (28 February).

benefited agriculture by encouraging the enclosure movement – the number of enclosure bills had doubled to 479 in 1793-99 from the 1786-92 total of 227. However, even with this increase, it was most unlikely that Britain could feed itself in most years, because of the rapid increase in population.[125]

From this point, Liverpool began to act as a junior Treasury minister under Pitt's direction, proposing bills to place bounties on imports of corn, flour and rice from America and the Mediterranean, to prevent wheat from being used in making starch, to cultivate potatoes on waste lands and to eliminate temporarily the ban on Swedish herring imports. Later, in March, he proposed a duty on exports of copper items, the scale varying according to the price of copper ore, with the objective of expanding production from high-cost domestic mines when the price was high, as it was in 1800. As he said, at that war-ravaged point the only exportable item other than copper on which there was no export tax was tin.

The following month, Liverpool came back to the proposed union with Ireland, accepting the principle of Catholic Emancipation, but only after the countries had been united for 20 years, by which time their commercial and social systems would have inexorably drawn together and the principle of Catholic Emancipation would have lost much of its danger.[126]

Liverpool also spoke against Parliamentary Reform, on a Grey motion.[127] He began by agreeing with Grey that it was a practical question and that Parliament should not 'acquiesce in the wild projects of men of speculative minds or heated imaginations'. He then enquired to which period Grey was referring at which the constitution was properly balanced, as it had been gradually broadening throughout history because, as a result of inflation, the 40-shilling freehold set down as the qualification for a vote in 1295 was equivalent to £20 by 1800. Furthermore, since the original arrangement for the Grand Council had barons sending their retainers to attend parliament, representation was then no part of the constitution, which was based entirely on property. The Crown could grant the right to representation but could not take it away and, when James I had attempted to disenfranchise some rotten boroughs, his action was shown to be unconstitutional by the great jurist Sir Edward Coke.

Grey attempted to justify radicalism, because the principles of the French Revolution had been abused, but Liverpool responded that the principles themselves were fundamentally false. The Revolution had held out equality as a goal for the lower orders but equality did not exist in nature and was not a proper object of government, which is a regulation of the natural inequalities of man. If Reform was to be justified on practical grounds, then a powerful grievance should exist which it might correct but, if you examined the record of Pitt's government, no such grievance existed and indeed the nation's liberties were better protected than ever before. The Constitution was doing its job and

125. Ibid., pp. 601-6 (18 February).

126. *The Parliamentary Register*, Vol. 11, pp. 320-21 (22 April 1800).

127. Ibid., pp. 361-71 (25 April).

no practical argument for reforming it existed. The corruption of earlier times was greatly diminished; for example, since 1782 the number of MPs holding offices of profit under the Crown had fallen from 118 to 52.

Schemes of universal or household suffrage would subvert the Constitution because they would change the basis of representation from property to population. Even the Whig Burke had celebrated the present system because it made the House of Commons a deliberative council and assembly and not an assembly of deputies bound to vote as their constituents wished. As for Irish union, it would add 100 Members to the House, but it was necessary for other reasons, and safeguards had been designed to ensure that the Irish members were not markedly different in character from existing members. The union certainly did not provide a propitious moment for Parliamentary Reform.

Liverpool's own responsibility as Master of the Mint was the subject of debate in December, when a motion demanded a committee of inquiry on coinage. Liverpool explained that the dearth of 1800 had necessitated importing large quantities of corn, the corn had to be paid for, and paying for it had driven bullion out of the country and lowered the pound's exchange rate against gold. Accordingly, since there was little bullion in the country and its price was high, it was economically disadvantageous for the Mint to attempt to coin it.[128] Liverpool was supported by the banker/economist Henry Thornton[129] and the motion was defeated by 32 votes to 16.

Liverpool's first parliamentary intervention in 1801 was to congratulate the Speaker on his reappointment. His flattery was well-timed; within a month that Speaker, Henry Addington, would be appointed prime minister and would grant Liverpool the job of Foreign Secretary.

Pitt's fall came over Catholic Emancipation, which he had privately promised to Irish leaders as an incentive for the Act of Union. He had not, however, broached the subject properly with the King (this lack of straightforwardness shows why the King preferred both the Jenkinsons to Pitt). Pitt's Cabinet was hopelessly split on the issue; Jenkinson was strongly opposed, for example, and, when the chance of a break-up came, saw the possibility of advancement for Liverpool, according to Sir John Sinclair.[130]

128. *The Parliamentary Register*, Vol. 13, pp. 414-15 (5 December 1800). The Mint Office return (ibid., p. 612) was to show that only £189,937 was coined in 1800 (before 20 November) compared to £2,000,297 in 1797 and £2,967,505 in 1798.

129. Henry Thornton (1760-1815). MP for Southwark, 1782-1815. In 1784 joined and a year later became partner in the banking firm of Down, Thornton and Free, the bank would fail in December 1825 (by which time it was Pole, Thornton, Free, Down and Scott). Leader of the Clapham Sect of evangelical reformers seeking the abolition of the slave trade, and later slavery, and sponsor of William Wilberforce. In 1802 wrote *An Enquiry into the Nature and Effects of the Paper Credit of Great Britain* (London: George Allen & Unwin), later recognised as a foundation stone of monetary economics and reissued in 1939 with an introduction by Friedrich Hayek.

130. *The Correspondence of the Right Honorable Sir John Sinclair, Bart* (London: Henry Colburn

Pitt's secrecy also meant he had not properly canvassed the legal implications of Emancipation. Two senior law officers, one the future Lord Chancellor, Eldon, gave their opinion that that Catholic Emancipation did not violate the Coronation Oath. However, Lord Chancellor Loughborough[131] convinced the King that he could not agree to Emancipation without violating his oath. Consequently, Pitt had to resign, even though his supporters still had a substantial majority in the House of Commons.

Pitt advised the King to send for Addington, thought to be a competent and safe pair of hands without much independent political influence, and Addington set about forming a ministry. Liverpool hesitated as to whether he should resign with Pitt but, with Pitt's own acquiescence and his father's encouragement, he decided to continue in Addington's new ministry. After all, his father, a strong opponent of Catholic Emancipation and no great admirer of Pitt, would undoubtedly stay, although his powers were beginning to fail.

Addington, needing colleagues with real debating skill in the Commons, was happy to promote Liverpool to the Cabinet. It is not immediately clear, however, why he felt compelled to raise him to the eminence of Foreign Secretary. With Grenville[132] and Dundas (two of the three Secretaries of State) withdrawing, there were vacancies at the top. Of the younger members around Pitt, Castlereagh was identified with Catholic Emancipation and had been a conduit for Pitt's assurances of Emancipation to Irish leaders. Canning was a Pitt loyalist and despised Addington. Perceval,[133] six years older, was as yet purely a law officer with no executive experience.

Of Pitt's outgoing Cabinet Addington accordingly decided to retain Portland, Chatham,[134] Westmorland[135] and Jenkinson, all of whom opposed Catholic Emancipation. The King, in his letter of instruction to Addington,

---

and Richard Bentley, 1831) Vol. 1, Appendix, p. 33. Sir John Sinclair, 1st Baronet (1754-1835). MP for Caithness, Lostwithiel, Petersfield, 1780-1811. Privy Counsellor, 1810. Economist/statistician, first user of the word 'statistics' in the English language.

131. Alexander Wedderburn (1733-1805). 1st Baron Loughborough from 1780. 1st Earl of Rosslyn from 1801. MP for Ayr Burghs, Richmond, Bishop's Castle, 1761-69, 1770-74, 1778-80. Solicitor General, 1771-78. Attorney General, 1778-80. Chief Justice of the Common Pleas, 1780-93. Lord Chancellor, 1793-1801.

132. William Grenville (1759-1834). 1st Baron Grenville from 1790. MP for Buckingham and Buckinghamshire, 1782-90. Speaker, 1789. Home Secretary, 1789-91. Foreign Secretary, 1791-1801. Prime Minister, 1806-07.

133. Spencer Perceval (1762-1812). Attorney General, 1802-06. Chancellor of the Exchequer, 1807-12. Prime Minister, 1809-12.

134. John Pitt (1756-1835). 2nd Earl of Chatham from 1778. Colonel in the British army, 1793, Major-General, 1795, General, 1812. Commander of the Walcheren Expedition, 1809. First Lord of the Admiralty, 1788-94. Lord Privy Seal, 1794-98. Lord President of the Council, 1796-1801. Master-General of the Ordnance, 1801-06, 1807-10.

135. John Fane, 10th Earl of Westmorland (1759-1841). Lord Lieutenant of Ireland, 1789-94. Master of the Horse, 1795-98. Lord Privy Seal, 1798-1806, 1807-27. First cousin and head of the family to Harriet Arbuthnot, the diarist.

made only one stipulation, that Eldon should replace Loughborough as Lord Chancellor. With Portland remaining at the Home Office, the third Secretary of State was Lord Hobart[136] at War and the Colonies, ten years older than Liverpool and a former Governor of Madras, but of no great distinction.

No doubt Jenkinson himself, by now a decade in Cabinet and possessing vast experience, might have been elevated to the Foreign Office if he were still fit, possibly with his son succeeding him at the more junior Board of Trade. However, by 1801 Jenkinson was old and sick. Hence, overpromoting his able if inexperienced son seemed the best solution and caused Addington no hesitation, visible from his correspondence. However eminent the position, the Foreign Office was unlikely to gain Liverpool much reputation, since it would involve negotiating a peace treaty with the rampant First Consul of France, Napoleon Bonaparte.

Liverpool's rapport with George III, largely gained through his father's 40-year friendship with the King, was such that, when the King delivered him the seals of office as Foreign Secretary, he said that he 'had often given them away, but in no instance with so much pleasure'.[137] Pitt was also impressed. He said to the House of Commons:

> I am ready to ask, without the fear of receiving any answer that would disappoint me, whether Gentlemen on the other side knew any man who was superior to the Noble Lord, who for the last ten years had experience of State affairs, and who has given proof of steady attention to public business; of a better understanding, of more information; who from all the habits of life, from hereditary habits of attention to business, of perseverance, and of all those qualities which go to qualify a man for great affairs.[138]

On the other hand, Fox had his doubts: 'If you had polled the country, not an individual could be found in it less suited for the peculiar department he occupies than the Noble Lord.'[139] Fox's doubts presumably related to Liverpool's introversion, which would cause difficulties in his relations with foreign ambassadors.

---

136. Robert Hobart (1760-1816). 4th Earl of Buckinghamshire from 1804. MP for Bramber and Lincoln, 1788-96. PC, 1793. Governor of Madras (Chennai), 1793-97. Baron Hobart (acceleration), 1798-1804. Secretary of State for War and the Colonies, 1801-04. Chancellor of the Duchy of Lancaster, 1805 and 1812. President of the Board of Control, 1812-16.
137. Told to Glenbervie by Charles Jenkinson; see Francis Bickley (ed.), *The Diaries of Sylvester Douglas, Lord Glenbervie* (London: Constable, 1928) Vol. 1, p. 179.
138. *The Parliamentary Register*, Vol. 14, p. 611 (25 March 1801). Gash, *Lord Liverpool*, p. 39, claims Pitt said he 'knew no one superior in capacity for business' but in fact he confined this comparison to the opposition, presumably excluding Grenville, Dundas and other members of his former government and, explicitly, excluding Fox.
139. *The Parliamentary Register*, Vol. 14, p. 643 (25 March 1801).

The change of government was complicated by a return of the King's illness, which threw into question the continuation of any government in the event of a regency. However, on this occasion, unlike in 1789, the Prince of Wales indicated his preparedness to continue temporarily with his existing ministers if a regency was declared. Thus, the formation of the new administration was only delayed, rather than thrown into complete confusion as it would have been in 1789. The new ministers were received in Council on 20 February but were not formally invested with the seals and powers of office until 14 March.

By agreement with the outgoing government and support from the opposition, the new ministry's first priority was to arrange a peace with France, possible terms of which had been outlined in a Cabinet minute by Pitt. Addington had nothing like Pitt's reputation as finance minister and so was keen to arrange a peace that might restore British finances to an even keel. Although France was attempting to arrange a Northern Confederacy to lock Britain out of the Baltic, she too was believed to be in financial difficulties and keen for peace – Bonaparte had put out feelers in late 1799, which had been rejected by Pitt's Cabinet led by the hard-line Grenville. Thus, four days after Liverpool took office he was directed by the Cabinet to intimate to the French government 'the disposition of His Majesty to enter into immediate negotiations', which he did in a letter to Louis-Guillaume Otto,[140] in London as Commissioner for Prisoners of War.

Bonaparte's commitment to peace notoriously not being what it might be, it was fortunate for the success of Liverpool's negotiations that three events in the spring of 1801 greatly strengthened his hand. On 21 March, General Sir Ralph Abercromby[141] defeated the French army in Egypt at the Battle of Alexandria, alas dying from a musket ball wound a week later. The British then besieged the city, which finally surrendered on 2 September. This removed a huge weight from the British official mind, since the French army in Egypt was considered a major threat to British interests in India.

The second fortuitous benefit to Britain's position was the assassination of the Russian Czar Paul I; he had been the leading proponent of his country's pro-French alignment. His successor Alexander I[142] was at this stage anti-Bonapartist and mildly pro-British; hence, the Northern Confederacy arranged by France became a dead letter.

140. Louis-Guillaume Otto (1754-1817). French diplomat. *Chargé d'affaires* in America, 1785-92. Envoy to London, 1800-3. Ambassador to Vienna 1810-14, where he negotiated Napoleon's marriage to Marie-Louise. Known as Citizen Otto while in London but became Comte de Moloy in 1810.

141. Ralph Abercromby (1734-1801). KB, 1795. MP for Clackmannanshire, 1774-80, 1796-98. Colonel, British army, 1781. Lieutenant-General, 1797. Commander-in-Chief, Ireland, 1797-98. Lord Lieutenant of Clackmannanshire, 1798-1801. Commander-in-Chief, Mediterranean, 1800-1.

142. Alexander I (1777-1825). Czar of All Russia from 1801. King of Poland, 1815-25. A complex character, with mystical tendencies and mild liberal inclinations.

The third, triumphant benefit occurred on 2 April, when a British fleet under Admiral Sir Hyde Parker, with Vice-Admiral Lord Nelson, defeated the Danish fleet in Copenhagen harbour, thus knocking Denmark effectively out of the Northern Confederacy and preventing Bonaparte from using the Danish fleet to cut Britain's lifeline to the Baltic.

Once these three events were known in France and Britain, the chance of a satisfactory peace became much higher. Equally, as would become apparent later, British public opinion was buoyed and expectations of an advantageous peace raised, so the terms eventually obtained quickly became unpopular.

Bonaparte's first response to Liverpool's letter proposed an immediate cessation of hostilities, to which Britain could not agree, given her imminent victories in Copenhagen and Egypt. However, Liverpool professed to be encouraged by peaceable signs from the First Consul and offered to enter into immediate negotiations on the basis of Britain relinquishing some of its colonial conquests since 1793, and the French evacuating Egypt – although he included the caveat that, were the French forced out of Egypt, these concessions would no longer apply. As an alternative, he later offered France a full relinquishment of all conquests, with France returning to its boundaries of 1792; he knew, however, that this would be unacceptable to Bonaparte.

Bonaparte, hearing in mid-April of Abercromby's victory, accused the British government of harbouring Royalist conspirators against him, thus producing a delay in negotiations, which he thought likely to be advantageous. Bonaparte hoped to take Portugal with a combined Spanish/French invasion during the summer, thus enabling him to trade Portugal for the British colonial gains in the West Indies.

Liverpool steered a subsidy for Portugal through the Commons on 28 May saying, 'this is not a subsidy intended to encourage offensive, but merely to enable an old and faithful ally to maintain defensive operations, till a peace can be made on terms consistent with her honour'.[143] Even this measure caused controversy; one opposition member called it 'this horrible subsidy' and conjured him by 'the bloody ghost of the brave Abercromby' not to pass it.

However, the subsidy was insufficient to prevent Portugal's defeat. An unprovoked Franco-Spanish attack in the brief 'War of the Oranges' ended by the Treaty of Badajoz, signed on 6 June, and the subsequent Treaty of Madrid, signed on 29 September. By these treaties, Portugal agreed to close its ports to British shipping and pay France an indemnity of 20 million francs (about £800,000). Fortunately, the French generals had proved eminently bribable by Portugal, so Bonaparte's hope of a truly massive indemnity and

143. Anon., *Memoirs of the Public Life and Administration of the Rt Hon. The Earl of Liverpool*, p. 145.

the addition of Portugal to his burgeoning empire was thwarted. Nevertheless, given this humiliation, much resented by Portugal's ruler John VI,[144] Portugal's enthusiasm for the anti-Napoleonic cause from 1808 is unsurprising.

Once the Treaty of Badajoz was concluded, Bonaparte no longer wanted to delay matters, since his troops in Egypt might have to surrender, removing a valuable bargaining chip. Naturally, there were further demands for Britain to give up all her West Indian conquests, and accusations of dishonourable dealing, but Liverpool resisted stoutly. Thus, with inevitable delays during the French August, negotiations proceeded smoothly and preliminaries of peace were signed in London on 1 October – it appears, when Otto, but not Liverpool, was aware of the final French evacuation of Egypt.

By the preliminary terms of peace, Britain kept some but not all her conquests in the West Indies, including Trinidad (formerly Spanish), as well as Ceylon, but ceded Malta to its original owners, the Knights of St John. France made several territorial acquisitions in Europe (for which Britain's colonial gains were thought to be compensation) but ceded Egypt back to the Ottomans (a provision rendered nugatory by her surrender there).

Liverpool's relations with his former colleagues were an important dynamic of the Addington administration. During the peace negotiations Pitt remained supportive but Grenville, while supportive at first, by the time preliminaries of peace were signed had decided that they were inadequate. Indeed, Liverpool was told by Pitt not to communicate the terms to Grenville until they were signed.

While Grenville's hostility was primarily one of policy, much more damage was done by Canning, who, despite his long friendship with Liverpool, spent the summer of 1801 denigrating him, saying of the Amiens peace that it was made by Addington, not by '[Liverpool] who merely held the pen'.[145] Another mutual friend and Canning follower, Granville Leveson-Gower said, 'we that have known [Liverpool] well at Oxford cannot certainly look on him with any admiration'.[146] Once again, Liverpool's friendship with Canning and his circle was proving one-sided.

Lord Cornwallis,[147] master of the nation's dirty jobs for the previous 20 years, was sent to Paris to carry out the supposedly routine business of negotiating the final terms of peace and Liverpool defended the preliminaries in the House

144. João (John) VI (1767-1826). Prince Regent of Portugal, *de facto* from 1792, *de jure* 1799-1816. King of Portugal and the Algarves, 1816-26. King of Brazil, 1816-22. Emperor of Brazil (*in absentia*) 1825-26.

145. Quoted in Yonge, *The Life and Administration of Robert Banks Jenkinson*, Vol. I, p. 156.

146. Quoted in Gash, *Lord Liverpool*, p. 39.

147. Charles Cornwallis, 1st Marquess Cornwallis, KG (1738-1805). MP for Eye 1760-62. Earl Cornwallis from 1762. Lieutenant-General, 1777, commanding forces in North America. Surrendered at Yorktown, 19 October 1781. Governor-General of India, 1786-93, 1805. Marquess, 1792. Master of the Ordnance, 1794-98. Lord Lieutenant of Ireland, 1798-1801. Minister Plenipotentiary to France, 1801-2.

of Commons on 3 November. Liverpool's support for the terms was heavily qualified and even in the initial euphoria of peace he was realistic about its likely durability: 'I do not attempt to pledge myself for the security which the Peace will give to this country, or to be responsible for the stability of the Treaty; but under all the circumstances in which we were situated, I maintain that it is honourable and advantageous.'[148]

Liverpool argued that France had started the war, that its initial objective for Britain was the removal of extreme French republicanism and that this objective had been attained. The First and Second Coalitions had failed to stop French aggression, the naval power of Britain and the land power of France could achieve little militarily against each other, and there seemed no possibility in 1801 of assembling a third coalition from the exhausted Continental powers. He then went through the peace provisions item by item and noted that Malta was in peace primarily valuable for the Levant trade, which had produced only exports valuing £112,000 during the war, out of total exports of £24 million. He also extolled the virtues of Ceylon (which he envisaged as a kind of proto-Singapore) and Trinidad, both gained by the treaty, and pronounced them superior to both Gibraltar and Minorca (gained by the 1713 Treaty of Utrecht) and Canada and Florida (gained by the 1763 Treaty of Paris) which he pronounced 'with all that extent of territory, I am strongly inclined to think that they were not real acquisitions'.[149]

Finally, Liverpool admitted that France was more powerful in 1801 than in 1793 but pointed out that the partition of Poland and the addition of Venice to Austrian territories had made her adversaries more powerful also. Moreover, Britain should not fear an enlarged France: France's trade had diminished, while Britain's trade had nearly doubled with areas such as the United States and had increased everywhere by more than a third (here Liverpool failed to adjust for inflation); and British naval superiority was far greater than in 1793. If war was resumed after 'seven, eight or ten years', Britain would be in a much better position to meet it.

As both Pitt and Fox supported the peace, Fox remarking that he 'could not flatter himself that we could have obtained peace on better terms',[150] Liverpool's reputation was enhanced by the peace negotiations. Regrettably, further developments between the preliminaries and the final treaty, followed by the slide back into war, tarnished this achievement.

Liverpool's first year as Foreign Secretary contained another useful accomplishment: the Anglo-Russian Convention of 1801. This followed the forcible break-up of the Second League of Armed Neutrality following Nelson's victory at Copenhagen and the accession of Alexander I. It steered a careful path between British demands to search neutral vessels and Russia's assertion of its right to freedom from search, providing a procedure and limits for vessel

148. *The Parliamentary Register*, Vol. 16, p. 83 (3 November 1801).

149. Ibid., p. 96.

150. Quoted in Yonge, *The Life and Administration of Robert Banks Jenkinson*, Vol. I, p. 63.

search, requiring it to be carried out by an accredited naval vessel and not a privateer. The convention became more important as other countries acceded to it and was the basis for maritime law in this area until superseded by the Paris Declaration of 1856.

In the debate on the Anglo-Russian Convention, Liverpool said that, 'to gain anything new was not the object of the contest, but to preserve those ancient principles which came into dispute'.[151] He then proceeded by economic argument to show that Britain's maritime system lay in carrying the great bulk of her trade in her own ships, while France in times of war used other nations' ships to carry her goods. Hence, overthrowing Britain's right of search, which had existed since Cromwell's time, and establishing the principle that 'free ships make free goods' would hugely damage British interests and benefit those of France. He then ended with a peroration of universal applicability:

> I again enter my protest against the principle that things can best be done by violence. On the contrary, both in public and private life, I shall always hold it to be the truest and most manly policy, not only to let off an enemy easy, but even to assist him in extricating himself.[152]

The period between the preliminaries of peace and the final ratification of the Treaty of Amiens saw some erosion in the provisions for Britain. For one thing, the modest cession of territory by Portugal in the Treaty of Madrid, which Liverpool believed had been reversed in the preliminary provisions, was confirmed by the Madrid treaty's final ratification in November. The negotiation between Cornwallis, Talleyrand and Joseph Bonaparte[153] began with Joseph Bonaparte proclaiming himself a simple man with no experience in such matters, which Cornwallis implicitly believed, and continued with the French adopting such tricks as changing sentences of the draft after they had been agreed. Napoleon also caused a collapse in British confidence in his *bona fides* when in January 1802 he accepted the presidency of the Italian Republic, contrary to the provisions of the Treaty of Lunéville, signed with Austria less than a year earlier.

Nevertheless, while some concessions were attributed by Cornwallis' assistant to 'his drowsiness, and his total want of practice and experience in matters of that kind',[154] the differences from the original treaty were modest

151. *The Parliamentary Register*, Vol. 16, p. 223 (13 November 1801).
152. Ibid., p. 228.
153. Joseph Bonaparte (1768-1844). Elder brother of Napoleon. Ambassador to Rome, 1797-1801, negotiating the Treaty of Mortefontaine with the United States, 1800, and the Treaty of Lunéville with Austria, 1801. King of Naples, 1806-08. King of Spain, 1808-13. Lived in United States, 1817-32. Claimant Emperor of the French, 1832-44.
154. Quoted in Yonge, *The Life and Administration of Robert Banks Jenkinson*, Vol. I, p. 66.

and became nugatory when war was resumed a year later. The main provision that was to give trouble was the status of Malta, which was to be returned after three months to the Knights of St John. Since the Knights had dissolved after the French seizure of the island in 1798, it was left unclear how they would be re-established, so Britain did not withdraw its troops, which Napoleon used as a *casus belli* the following year.

Liverpool's defence of the final treaty on 13 May 1802 went through the changes from the preliminaries point by point, correcting opposition errors:

> We so arranged it for [Portugal] that her navigation of the river Amazon is perfectly secured, and not at all exposed to that interruption from the possessions which the French had obtained by the Treaty, that Gentlemen on a former evening so strenuously maintained, upon the authority of a map not quite so accurate as they have been taught to believe.[155]

He also pointed out that the British position in India had been immeasurably strengthened by the defeat of Mysore, while France's West Indian possessions were in chaos because of the revolt in Haiti. In the event, the main opposition amendment condemning the Treaty failed by 276 votes to 20.

The conclusion of peace, and the abolition of income tax that came with it, rendered the Addington government momentarily both popular and powerful, with Foxite Whigs, such as Sheridan, becoming more supportive. Its strength was increased in July 1802 by Castlereagh joining as President of the Board of Control, responsible for the government's relations with the East India Company.

As Chief Secretary for Ireland, Castlereagh had been instrumental in pushing through the Act of Union. He had then left office in 1801, as he supported Catholic Emancipation and was thought to have encouraged the Irish to expect it. Indeed, the pecuniary and other deceptions relating to union led Castlereagh to a severe fit of depression, lasting several months, foreshadowing his suicide two decades later. Nevertheless, unlike Canning, he liked Addington and supported both the preliminaries of peace in the November 1801 debate and the final Treaty of Amiens in May 1802.[156]

Castlereagh was a Cambridge man (St John's) and something of a radical in his youth. Thus, he and Liverpool had not previously been close, although they had become friends as fellow-acolytes of Pitt after Castlereagh entered the Commons in 1794. From this point forward, however, they were firm allies. Liverpool had more in common politically with Castlereagh than he did with Canning and there were fewer emotional crises in the relationship, which was altogether more supportive and less one-sided for Liverpool.

155. *The Parliamentary Register*, Vol. 18, p. 387 (13 May 1802).

156. See *The Parliamentary Register*, Vol. 16, p. 96 (3 November 1801) and Vol. 18, pp. 404-13 (14 May 1802).

Gillray cartoon 'The nursery: with Britannia reposing in peace'. Liverpool and Addington, with Fox in background, December, 1802.

The 1802 election that followed the end of the parliamentary session was a highly successful one for the Addington government, with *The History of Parliament* reckoning, out of a total of 658 MPs, 467 administration supporters being returned, 124 Foxites, 25 members of the 'new opposition' (supporting Grenville and Windham[157] in their gradual move towards the Whiggery they adopted in 1806) and 42 independents.[158] However, the renewal of war the following year was to weaken fatally the Addington ministry's credibility, put further strain on old friendships and alliances, and eventually end Addington's ability to command a Commons majority.

For Liverpool, 1802 was the last Commons election he faced. He was easily re-elected for Rye but his election expenses were doubled to £2,596 by gratuitous padding on the part of Rye Corporation. Since there were fewer than 20 electors in Rye (though the borough's 1801 population was 2,187), this was regarded as excessive and certainly surprised Liverpool and his father.

157. William Windham (1750-1810). Chief Secretary for Ireland, 1783. Secretary at War, 1794-1801. Secretary of State for War and the Colonies, 1806-7.

158. Thorne, *The History of Parliament* 1790-1820. *"Parliaments – 1802"*. See: https://www.historyofparliamentonline.org/volume/1790-1820/parliament/1802

(He had been elected unopposed at two previous general elections and at two by-elections, following his appointments as Master of the Mint and Foreign Secretary, without any trouble.) As Liverpool's cash flow was strained from moving into Coombe Wood, this necessitated a bailout from his wealthy and liquid father.[159]

Liverpool's private life during these years underwent several upheavals. Louisa's mother, to whom she was close, died in 1800, then the reprobate Earl-Bishop, her father, was to die on an Italian roadside in 1803. (The Bristol hotels scattered about the Continent are said to be named after him, representing the kind of luxury accommodation he would use when travelling.[160]) Then in August 1802 the Liverpools moved into Coombe Wood, the house near Kingston which Liverpool had bought the previous year and had rebuilt – as well as the house itself, the land was said to comprise 670 acres, an expensive park when situated so close to London. That proximity was its main advantage; they could leave their town house after a parliamentary sitting and be at Coombe Wood within 90 minutes, dining on cold meat in their chaise on the way and returning to London after a country walk the next day in time for the parliamentary sitting.

Liverpool in these years developed an increasingly close relationship with George III, fuelled by the frequent interaction necessary as Foreign Secretary. He was several times invited to join the King at his summer retreat in Weymouth for a day's sailing. In September 1801, the King expressed severe doubts to Liverpool as to whether any treaty with France would last 'till it has a settled government' but acquiesced in Liverpool's negotiations, and was cheered a month later when Liverpool told him that Prussian troops were evacuating Hanover. Jenkinson was becoming less and less active, so the King grew increasingly to trust Liverpool as he had trusted his father, with the two men's opposition to Catholic Emancipation becoming a particular bond after Pitt returned in 1804 with an administration including supporters of it.

Normal relations with France necessitated the appointment of an ambassador, and Liverpool appointed Charles, Lord Whitworth in June 1802.[161] Whitworth's new wife was the daughter of Jenkinson's second wife by a previous marriage and this family connection may have helped him obtain what seemed a prize appointment. However, Whitworth did not arrive in Paris

159. Gash, *Lord Liverpool* p. 45.

160. The first Hotel Bristol opened in Paris in 1816, during the post-war Anglomania; there are now more than 200 Bristols worldwide, most, but not all, luxury, including a 12-hotel chain in Brazil.

161. Charles Whitworth (1752-1825). Baron Whitworth, 1800. Viscount Whitworth, 1813. Earl Whitworth, 1815. Minister to Poland, 1785-88, Russia, 1788-1800, France, 1802-3. Lord Lieutenant of Ireland, 1813-17. His second wife, Arabella Cope Sackville Whitworth, the widow of the cricketing Duke of Dorset, was Liverpool's stepsister, her mother being Charles Jenkinson's second wife.

until November, by which time relations with France were fast deteriorating. Napoleon had already in January1802 annexed the Cisalpine Republic (northern Italy) and in October 1802 he sent French troops into Switzerland, both in contravention of the Treaty of Lunéville, though not that of Amiens. Malta remained a bone of contention, though at one stage the Bonaparte family offered to allow Britain to remain there in return for a bribe.

The French government complained about libels in the British press but Liverpool responded that liberty of the press was 'secured by the constitution of this country', that laws existed under which neither the British government nor foreign governments could be libelled, so French complaints should go through the courts, rather than attempting to change British libel law. France also attempted to get the Bourbons expelled from Britain, which Liverpool refused. A prosecution was brought against a M. Peltier for libelling Napoleon and the defendant was convicted in February 1803, although the renewal of war prevented a sentence from being imposed.[162]

Britain signed two new conventions with the United States during Liverpool's period as Foreign Secretary: one in January 1802 settling the last debt claims from the American War; the other the following year settling the Maine boundary. Although the anti-British Thomas Jefferson had become President in the previous year, relations were helped by the American negotiator, Rufus King,[163] being a strongly pro-British Federalist.. Relations improved further when Britain offered the United States naval assistance in its war with the Barbary pirates of Tripoli.

By the end of 1802 Liverpool's early optimism about the Amiens peace was badly dented, partly by evidence that Napoleon had sent phony commercial agents into British ports to survey their harbours. So was the prestige and power of the Addington administration and the reputation of Liverpool himself. One straw in the wind was Pitt's distancing himself; Liverpool had been in the habit of sending papers over for his opinion but in November 1802 Pitt returned a set without commenting.

Liverpool took a major role in defending the government in the Commons and was thus forced to defend the government's actions at the beginning of the new Parliamentary session in November 1802. He disclaimed any temptation to pursue a policy of isolation from the Continent, pointing out that Britain's interests were so large that isolation was impossible. At the same time, Britain had not been able to intervene effectively in the partition of Poland in 1792 and could not intervene effectively in the landlocked Switzerland now without help from Austria, which was not available. He ended by admitting that France

162. Anon., *Memoirs of the Public Life and Administration of the Rt Hon. The Earl of Liverpool*, pp. 191-95.

163. Rufus King (1755-1827). Minister to the United Kingdom, 1796-1803, 1825-26; U.S. Senator from New York 1789-96, 1813-25; Federalist party nominee for Vice President, 1804, 1808; for President, 1816.

hated Britain but that had been the case after all three preceding peace treaties and did not prevent Britain from following a pacific policy, even while keeping up its military and, especially, naval strength.[164]

In December, Liverpool supported a government motion to increase the peacetime naval establishment from 30,000 seamen to 50,000 seamen, plus 12,000 marines. He pointed out that ministers could not give the House confidential information on the state of Europe but enough information was public to indicate that a larger establishment was necessary while 'preserving the spirit of peace . . . that should not hold out any species of irritation, which could never answer any good end but must, if pursued, inevitably lead to hostility'.[165]

In another December debate, the opposition began to demand the restoration of Pitt as Prime Minister. Liverpool spoke against this demand from Sheridan, pointing out that the opposition had supported the Addington ministry's peace policy and its increased military establishment, so there was constitutionally no occasion for dismissing the ministry while its measures were still approved.[166]

Early in 1803, it became clear that Napoleon intended to renew the war. On 9 and 11 March Liverpool announced to the House that preparations in France and Holland, suggesting contemplation of a cross-channel invasion, made it necessary to reinforce the militia. At the same time, this re-armament did not mean the government was yet committed to renewing the war; it was a precautionary measure, given the belligerent approach followed by Napoleon's government.

Napoleon had already threatened Whitworth at public meetings on 18 February, 'Unite rather than fighting us and we will settle the fate of the whole world', and did so again more directly in a tantrum on 13 March, 'Woe to those who do not respect treaties! They will be responsible to all Europe' – immortalised by Gillray[167] in a cartoon, 'Maniac ravings, or Little Boney in a Strong Fit'. Thus, when Czar Alexander offered in April 1803 to step in and take nominal control of Malta, the evacuation of which by Britain was the principal ostensible unfulfilled provision of the Amiens treaty, French preparations for war were too obvious to be ignored. Whitworth demanded his passport from Napoleon and on 18 May Britain once again declared war on France.

The spring of 1803 saw the first negotiations for Pitt's return to government. The crucial meeting took place on 10 April, at the house of Charles Long,[168] a friend of Pitt who had been a junior Treasury Secretary. At this meeting, Pitt

164. *The Parliamentary Register*, Vol. 19, pp. 80-90 (23 November 1802).
165. Ibid., pp. 190-94 (2 December 1802).
166. Ibid., pp. 301-8, 9 December, 1802.
167. James Gillray (1756-1815). Leading caricaturist, active 1780-1811. 'Maniac Ravings' published 24 May 1803.
168. Charles Long (1760-1838). MP for Rye, Midhurst, Wendover and Haslemere, 1790-1826. Junior Treasury Secretary, 1791-1801. Lord of the Treasury, 1804-5. Chief Secretary for Ireland, 1805-6. Paymaster of the Forces, 1807-26. Created Baron Farnborough, 1826.

Addington and Liverpool (Foreign Secretary) brace themselves for renewed war, May 1803. Gillray gives us a heroic Addington!

told Addington that Liverpool should be removed from the Foreign Office, while Dundas, Grenville, Spencer[169] and Windham should be admitted to the Cabinet. Addington asked Pitt not to insist on office for Grenville, Spencer and Windham, and negotiations broke down.

At the subsequent Cabinet meeting, Liverpool was strongly of the view that inclusion of the belligerent Grenville would unbalance the administration and convince neutrals that Britain was to blame for the resumption of the war. Grenville had already objected to Liverpool remaining in office in the spring of 1802; when he was told of Liverpool's attitude, he declared that Liverpool would never serve in any Cabinet of which he was a member. At least, unlike his father with Charles Jenkinson in 1766, he did not order his footman to throw Liverpool out of the house! In the event, when after 1818 Grenville drifted back towards the Tories, Liverpool was Prime Minister.

Liverpool's last year at the Foreign Office was difficult, although improved by the appointment as Under Secretary of Charles Arbuthnot, who was to serve Liverpool faithfully for most of the next quarter-century – Liverpool thought him well qualified for the post by his experience in the forms of the office, his

169. George Spencer, 2nd Earl Spencer (1758-1834). Lord Privy Seal, 1794. First Lord of the Admiralty, 1794-1801. Home Secretary, 1806-07.

good temper and his good manners.[170] The Addington ministry was clinging to power but the abortive peace had deprived it of all prestige, so it seemed only a question of time before Pitt resumed office. Liverpool's reputation had also suffered from the peace's failure, though he must have known when he took office that he had been handed a poisoned chalice.

Liverpool's experience of the Peace of Amiens convinced him for the remainder of the war that peace with Napoleon was unlikely to be lasting. He was to be sceptical of the Whigs' attempt to obtain peace in 1806 and of subsequent similar opportunities. As he was to articulate when determining Peninsular War strategy, Napoleon's empire was economically unstable and required continual new conquests to loot. The Emperor's apologists among subsequent historians have failed to address this point: while Napoleon remained in power, Europe was condemned to perpetual war.

During the spring and summer of 1803, Liverpool was subjected to vilification by the long-standing Russian ambassador, Count Woronzow,[171] who had been incensed in 1801 by Liverpool's refusal to deal with him until he had been officially reinstated by Alexander I (he had been removed by Czar Paul I in his pro-French phase the previous year) and spent the next three years complaining of Liverpool's utter incompetence for his post. Of Liverpool's opponents, Pitt concentrated his fire mainly on Addington, and Grenville was safely in the Lords, but Canning and his coterie had taken to open hostility in the Commons and through their contacts in the press, as well as pressing Pitt towards open opposition.

Liverpool defended the government's foreign policy on 3 June in response to a speech by Pitt criticising the government and moving the adjournment without fully approving the motion of censure proposed by the independent Colonel Patten,[172] who had been put up to it by Canning. Canning piled in, claiming that the government ought to have been more belligerent. In the event Pitt's adjournment was voted down by 333 to 56, after which Patten's motion was voted down by 275 votes to 34, with the Foxites leaving the House and only Canning and Grenville's family and placemen voting against the government.

In a secret session on 30 June (not reported in the parliamentary debates) Liverpool showed that a French invasion was impracticable. Five days later, he supported the re-introduction of the income tax, opposing the idea of imposing it at different rates on earned and unearned income, pointing out that those with unearned income from property generally had duties and costs attached to it, not the case for those earning their income. Later in the month

170. Namier and Brooke, *The History of Parliament. 'Charles Arbuthnot'*

171. Count (of the Holy Roman Empire) Simeon Romanovich Woronzow (1744-1832). Russian minister to Vienna, 1783-85, to London 1785-1800, 1801-6. Remained in London until his death in 1832. According to Charles Greville, the diarist, he never learned a word of English.

172. Peter Patten (later Patten Bold) (1764-1819). MP for Newton, Lancaster, Malmesbury, 1797-1818.

he returned to this subject, pointing out that multiplying exemptions made the tax complicated and necessitated a higher rate; he therefore proposed as close to a flat tax as possible.

Addington, a better administrator than Pitt, reintroduced the tax at a flat rate of five per cent, compared with Pitt's graduated rate to ten per cent, but made one change by withholding it at source (for example, by the Bank of England on Consol interest payments). Consequently, the first year's yield of Addington's tax was £4.8 million with a five per cent tax, compared with only £5.6 million netted by Pitt in 1799 with a ten per cent tax.[173] The finances of the Napoleonic Wars in 1803-14 were thereby made considerably sounder than those of the French Revolutionary Wars of 1793-1802.

The Foxite Whig, George Tierney[174] joined the government as Treasurer of the Navy in June and this temporarily prevented the return of Pitt, with whom Tierney had fought a duel in 1798. With Castlereagh and Tierney available to support him in the Commons, Addington felt he needed reinforcements to face Grenville in the Lords and therefore asked Liverpool to accept a Writ of Acceleration for his courtesy title of Lord Hawkesbury and take his seat in the upper house. Jenkinson opposed this move, believing that Pitt was on his last legs (although he was only 44) and that Liverpool would have a better chance of succeeding him if still in the Commons (of course, the 74-year-old Jenkinson would have to outlive Pitt, as indeed he did, for this ploy to become effective). However, on 15 November, Liverpool entered the Lords, as Leader of the House, an office he was to hold for the next 23 years, with only a year's respite between 1806 and 1807.

Liverpool's first substantive Lords intervention came on 5 March 1804 on the Bank of Ireland and the monetary conditions following the war's resumption, in relation to the Irish Bank Restriction Bill. Grenville argued that the Bank of Ireland ought to be forced to pay its bills in specie, but Liverpool responded that the Bank of Ireland's paper currency, and that produced by the Bank of England, had not driven specie out of the country; that had been caused by the costs of the war and by food importation in the dearth years of 1795-96 and 1800. With the paper currency inconvertible, 'speculators might suffer, but I think it is better to leave the evil to work out its own cure, than to hold out encouragement to persons of this description'. Even with a partially successful invasion, the country's credit could be maintained, as shown in 1715 and 1745.[175]

173. Hay, *Lord Liverpool*, p79, and HM Revenue and Customs, *A Tax to Beat Napoleon*, 1999, National Archives. https://webarchive.nationalarchives.gov.uk/+/http://www.hmrc.gov.uk/history/taxhis1.htm Accessed August 12, 2020.

174. George Tierney (1761-1830). MP for Colchester, Southwark, Athlone, Bandon, Appleby and Knaresborough 1788-90, 1796-1830. Treasurer of the Navy, 1803-4. President of the Board of Control, 1806-07. Master of the Mint, 1827-28. Whig leader in the House of Commons, 1818-21.

175. Hansard, *Parliamentary Debates from the Year 1803 to the Present Time*, Vol. 1, cols 705-8 (5 March 1804).

Then on 27 March he moved the second reading of the Volunteer Consolidation Bill, an anticipation of the responsibilities he would soon assume. He began by claiming a right of the King to demand service from everyone in the case of a real danger of invasion. He then continued by pointing out that the regular army in Britain of 180,000 was 40,000 stronger than in 1801, on top of which he claimed a volunteer force, to be used as auxiliaries, totalled about 330,000. The volunteers – 'an armed peasantry' – would be most useful if an invader intended long-term occupation but, if the invasion was a short-term one, aimed at the capital or the major naval installations, regular troops were needed. The Bill provided regulations for the 'good order and discipline of a force which I, for one, would be glad to see last as long as the necessity that has given rise to it'.[176]

At the end of April 1804, the Addington ministry collapsed and on 30 April Liverpool as Leader of the Lords took the first formal step in the process of replacing it. The Cabinet had decided it needed to seek outside support to continue and to shut down all controversy while the King had discussions with possible combinations of ministers. Accordingly, when the Marquess of Stafford[177] rose to propose a motion on national defence, Liverpool immediately asked Stafford to postpone his motion, for unspecified reasons – a request not normally denied, by the conventions of the House.

Stafford agreed to postpone his motion but Grenville then rose, complained about the lack of explanation and demanded that the House adjourn until Stafford's motion could be discussed. Liverpool reiterated:

> I will state again to your Lordships, and I will state it not only upon my official credit, but on my character as a man, that the circumstances I allude to are neither light nor trivial but weigh sufficiently upon my mind to induce me to make the application I did to the noble marquess.

After Grenville complained again and insisted that no business of substance be discussed in the interim, the motion was postponed until 3 May.[178]

On 3 May, Stafford's motion was again postponed until 7 May. On that day, Eldon rose and told the House that discussion of Stafford's motion was now even more inopportune and its discussion was postponed again until 11 May, when, as the formation of a new ministry with Pitt at its head was imminent,

176. Ibid., cols 1022-26 (27 March 1804).

177. George Leveson-Gower (1758-1833). 2nd Marquess of Stafford from 1803. 1st Duke of Sutherland from 1833. Pittite MP for Newcastle-under-Lyme and Staffordshire 1779-84, 1787-99. (Whig from 1804.) Ambassador to Paris, 1790-92. Elder half-brother of Granville Leveson-Gower.

178. Hansard, *Parliamentary Debates from the Year 1803 to the Present Time*, Vol 2, cols 334-44, 362-64, 392-93 and 409 (30 April, 3 May, 7 May and 11 May 1804).

Stafford withdrew his motion. On 12 May Addington resigned. The crisis had been worsened by another recurrence of the Royal malady but Pitt's return was the only realistic outcome, if only grudgingly accepted by Addington. Pitt wanted to form a broad-based coalition but Grenville refused to enter the government without Fox, to whom the King made a firm objection.

Without Grenville, Pitt's government was weak in the Commons and he was forced to buy Grenville's neutrality by making several changes among senior ministers, the most important among which was the removal of Liverpool from the Foreign Office. Liverpool initially consented to move to allow Pitt to replace him with Lord Moira, a leading Whig who would increase the administration's voting strength. Moira, however, turned Pitt's offer down, so Pitt was forced to replace him with Lord Harrowby,[179] who had no great claim to Liverpool's office. He attempted to assuage Liverpool with the especially feeble excuse that Harrowby's poor health meant that only the Foreign Office was feasible for him (he lived until 1847).

Dudley Ryder, 1st Earl of Harrowby. The news of Waterloo arrived at his house in Grosvenor Square; the Cato St conspirators fortunately didn't.

At this point Jenkinson objected strongly, believing Harrowby unqualified to replace his son, but was mollified by the King assuring him that he particularly wanted Liverpool at the Home Office, the ministry with the greatest level of Royal contact. Liverpool further assisted the King by persuading Pitt to retain Westmorland, a Royal favourite, less than halfway through his 38-year ministerial tenure.

The wound to Liverpool's *amour propre* at his removal from the Foreign Office was exacerbated in June by Canning, who had been made Treasurer of the Navy, a lucrative non-Cabinet post in the new government (and who would have preferred a greater position). Canning also objected to Thomas Wallace,[180] a friend of Liverpool, being kept on as

179. Dudley Ryder (1762-1847). MP for Tiverton, 1784-1803. 2nd Baron Harrowby, 1803. Created Earl of Harrowby, 1809. Paymaster of the Forces, 1791-1800. Treasurer of the Navy, 1800-1. Foreign Secretary, 1804-5. Chancellor of the Duchy of Lancaster, 1805-6. Minister without Portfolio, 1809-12. Lord President of the Council, 1812-27.

180. Thomas Wallace (1768-1844). 1st Baron Wallace from 1828. MP for Grampound, Penryn, Hindon, Shaftesbury, Weymouth and Cockermouth, 1790-1828.

a member of the Board of Control. In a typically spiteful speech, Canning claimed that Pitt's ministry was greatly improved on Addington's by the removal of four incompetent ministers, St Vincent, Hobart, Addington (all out of office) and Liverpool. Pitt made no attempt to deny this aspersion and Liverpool, after reflecting for 24 hours and consulting some friends, sent in his resignation.

Pitt, not wanting to lose Liverpool, let alone Castlereagh, who threatened to resign also if Liverpool went, attempted to dissuade him and then offered to fire Canning. Canning, panicking at the potential collapse of Pitt's new government, came three times to the Home Office to say he didn't mean it and to beg Liverpool to withdraw his resignation. Liverpool, a sucker as always for Canning's charm, withdrew his resignation, extracting a promise from Pitt to tell the House of Commons that his removal to the Home Office was made for Pitt's convenience in arranging his administration.

It was a great moral victory, strengthening Liverpool's position immensely. Castlereagh had proved himself Liverpool's staunchest friend and Canning a dangerous and unreliable one. Jenkinson saw through Canning's machinations, remarking, 'I think he [Liverpool] does right in setting them [Canning and his friends] at defiance. He must destroy their influence, or they must destroy him.'[181]

Canning's true attitude to Liverpool poured out in a meeting with Pitt in the autumn of 1804. According to the account by Norman Gash:

> He complained that Pitt had been ready to make 'a propitiatory sacrifice' of him to please Liverpool and had aggravated this by subsequently praising Liverpool in the House of Commons. He indulged in some hysterical abuse of his rival – 'a liar and a coward, for such he is – I know him to be so' and admitted that he believed Liverpool responsible both for the rejection of Canning's Foreign Office proposal the previous year and for systematically influencing the King against him. It was galling enough for Canning to think that he had only been retained in office by the magnanimity of a man he thought his inferior; but what mortified him most was that Liverpool should apparently rank higher in Pitt's estimation than himself. It must have been a distressing interview for Pitt which only calmed down when he dexterously turned the subject to the possibility of bringing Canning into the cabinet.[182]

Commissioner, Board of Control 1800-06, 1807-16, 1828-30. Vice-President of the Board of Trade, 1818-23. Master of the Mint, 1823-27.

181. Letter to Folliott Cornewall, Bishop of Hereford, 16 July 1804, quoted in Yonge, *The Life and Administration of Robert Banks Jenkinson*, Vol. I, p. 153.

182. Norman Gash, 'The Tortoise and the Hare: Liverpool and Canning', *History Today*, Vol. 32, Issue 3 (March 1982).

As Home Secretary and Leader of the House of Lords, Liverpool's parliamentary interventions became more frequent. Economically, the most important legislation of the session was the 1804 Corn Law, the immediate predecessor to the great 1815 Corn Law. The bill's main effect was to raise sharply from the previous 1773 Act the price below which corn imports would suffer a heavy duty from 44 shillings to 65 shillings per quarter (or eight bushels of grain). (Under the 1815 law imports were to be prohibited below 80 shillings.)

According to modern price statistics calculated for the period, the 1804 legislation raised the price at which heavy duties were imposed by just about the 47 per cent inflation between 1773 and 1804, while the 1815 Corn Law reduced the limit by about two per cent in real terms. Only with the deflation after the wars ended did the corn price at which imports were freed rise sharply in real terms, by 38 per cent by 1825. Whether or not the Corn Laws were economically sound, they were skilfully designed to maintain constant corn prices in real terms.

'The best security that the country could have against famine, laying out of consideration the accidents of seasons, against which human precaution is to no avail, is to encourage the farmer to cultivate as much of the soil as he could,'[183] said Liverpool. He knew from his father's Board of Trade experience of the dearths of the 1790s that the risks between high and low corn prices were asymmetric; in a situation of 'sticky' international markets, rapidly rising population and uncertain climate it was much better to maximise domestic production than to rely on cheap imports that might not always be available.

After the session ended, Liverpool became embroiled in Royal Family disputes, another duty of the Home Secretary that was particularly unpleasant during the turbulent years of George III's unruly brood. The Prince of Wales and his wife were now leading separate lives, and George III, exasperated over his son's ostentatious support of the opposition and his rejoicing at the recurrence of the King's illness earlier that year, wanted control over the upbringing of the young Princess Charlotte, eventual heiress presumptive to the throne. After considerable negotiation this was achieved, adding to George III's favourable view of Liverpool's capabilities, character and tact.

In the autumn of 1804, Liverpool became involved in the question of trade unions, then a novel type of organisation, stimulated by the political societies formed after the French Revolution and prohibited by Pitt's Combination Acts of 1799 and 1800. The boot- and shoemakers of London had formed a trade union in combination with boot- and shoemakers throughout the country. Their objective was largely increased wages (which had declined in real terms because of the effects of wartime inflation) but they were also attempting to impose a closed shop, with compulsory union membership.

183. Hansard, *Parliamentary Debates from the Year 1803 to the Present Time*, Vol. 2, cols 1047-49 (16 July 1804).

Some of the masters of the trade had appealed to Liverpool to institute a prosecution and he referred the matter to Spencer Perceval, the Attorney General. Perceval opined[184] that the combination was clearly illegal under the 1799/1800 Acts but the question of whether the Crown should prosecute was a difficult one. If this were an isolated case, the Crown could reasonably prosecute, but since trade unions existed in many occupations, a prosecution in this case would lead to demands from the masters in every other trade for prosecution of the union members. Both in the interests of better industrial relations and because of the difficulty of getting evidence, Perceval felt the masters rather than government should bear the burden of prosecution – it was after all their 'inertness and timidity' that had allowed the problem to grow to the extent it had.

Liverpool took Perceval's advice and did not prosecute; this largely made the 1799/1800 laws inoperable. The problem was to recur with the Luddite disturbances in 1812 and Liverpool's government would institute a broader solution with its legislation of 1824-25.

As Home Secretary, Liverpool was also responsible for handling Irish agitation, which broke out again in the autumn of 1804, when the young Daniel O'Connell[185] and some others revived agitation for Catholic Emancipation. Since Ireland was at this time vulnerable to a French invasion (one was then being planned for the Irish East Coast) even Pitt, formerly a friend of Emancipation, agreed that reviving agitation for it was ill-timed. In a letter to Lord Hardwicke,[186] the Lord Lieutenant, intended to be communicated to the Catholics, Liverpool argued that it was impolitic to a degree 'little short of insanity' for the Catholics to press their claims at that time.

Towards the end of 1804, Liverpool was instrumental in reconciling Pitt and Addington, thereby for a short time forming a stronger base in the House of Commons for Pitt's government. Liverpool first contacted Addington in October and after some delay Addington dined with Liverpool on 1 December, when Liverpool opened negotiations for a reconciliation between Addington and Pitt with Addington going to the House of Lords – Liverpool offered to give up his leadership thereof in Addington's favour.

There was some negotiation about places for Addington's followers. Then on 23 December Pitt and Addington met for dinner at Coombe Wood, after which the King wrote to Liverpool that he was, 'the happy instrument of

184. Quoted in Yonge, *The Life and Administration of Robert Banks Jenkinson*, Vol. I, pp. 166-69.

185. Daniel O'Connell (1775-1847). Radical agitator for Catholic Emancipation and repeal of the Act of Union between Great Britain and Ireland. MP for Clare, County Waterford, Kerry, Dublin City, Kilkenny City, Meath and Cork County, 1828-47. Lord Mayor of Dublin, 1841-42. Founded Catholic Association, 1823, to agitate first for Catholic Emancipation, then against tithes (sparking off the Tithe War of 1831-36) and for repeal of the Act of Union.

186. Philip Yorke (1757-1834). 3rd Earl of Hardwicke from 1790. Whig MP for Cambridgeshire, 1780-90, afterwards Pittite. Lord Lieutenant of Ireland, 1801-5.

effecting the reconciliation of two men who ought ever to have been friends, and may now easily remain so . . . that is one of the greatest eases to my mind that, in a political view, could have been effected'.[187]

Addington became Viscount Sidmouth and succeeded Portland as Lord President of the Council, though Liverpool remained Leader of the Lords. Sidmouth's follower, Hobart, now Earl of Buckinghamshire, became Chancellor of the Duchy of Lancaster and minor places were found for Sidmouth's other followers. At this time Harrowby fell downstairs at the Foreign Office and felt compelled to resign; he was succeeded by the undistinguished Lord Mulgrave,[188] a staunch Pittite. Canning was annoyed not to be offered the Foreign Office but took consolation in Liverpool being denied a return to it. In the event, Lord Mulgrave was to gain temporary acclaim as the negotiator, under Pitt's direction, of the Third Coalition against Napoleon. Nevertheless, as with Liverpool's Treaty of Amiens, the acclaim ceased when the Third Coalition was defeated at Ulm and Austerlitz.

Peace within the government did not last long. In February 1805 a naval commission of inquiry, appointed by Addington in 1802, at the instigation of his First Lord of the Admiralty, St Vincent,[189] produced its Tenth Report which suggested that Dundas (since 1802, Viscount Melville), when Treasurer of the Navy before 1800, had allowed his deputy to invest public money on his own behalf (a practice that, in relation to the army, had made the fortunes of Robert Walpole a century earlier and Henry Fox 50 years earlier, but which was now frowned upon). A motion of censure against Melville brought by Samuel Whitbread produced a tied vote 216-216 on 8 April. The Speaker gave his casting vote for the motion and Melville had to resign.

Liverpool sided with Sidmouth rather than Pitt, agreeing that Melville should go. However, when the case reached the Lords, Liverpool would be active in defending him, insisting on Melville's right for an impeachment trial by the House of Lords, rather than the Commons, citing impeachment attempts against the Duke of Buckingham in 1626 and the Earl of Arlington in 1673.[190]

---

187. Quoted in Yonge, *The Life and Administration of Robert Banks Jenkinson*, Vol. I, p. 177.
188. Henry Phipps (1755-1831). 2nd Baron Mulgrave (Ireland) 1792. 1st Baron Mulgrave (Britain) 1794. 1st Earl of Mulgrave, 1812. MP for Totness and Scarborough, 1784-94. Chancellor of the Duchy of Lancaster, 1804-5. Foreign Secretary, 1805-6. First Lord of the Admiralty, 1807-10. Master-General of the Ordnance, 1810-19.
189. John Jervis (1735-1823). 1st Earl St Vincent from 1797. Whig/Pittite MP for Launceston, Great Yarmouth and Great Wycombe, 1784-94. Captain, Royal Navy, 1760, Rear-Admiral 1787, Vice-Admiral, 1793, Admiral, 1795 Commander-in-Chief, Mediterranean Fleet, 1796-99. Battle of Cape St Vincent, 1797. Commander-in-Chief, Channel Fleet, 1800-1, 1805-7. Admiral of the Fleet, 1821. First Lord of the Admiralty, 1801-4.
190. Hansard, *Parliamentary Debates from the Year 1803 to the Present Time*, Vol. 4, cols 588-89 (3 May 1805).

At Sidmouth's suggestion, Pitt offered the Admiralty to Liverpool, who declined it on the advice of his father, who observed that no minister within his recollection had added to his reputation by going to the Admiralty. Another problem was that Liverpool would probably have had to give up the leadership of the Lords, which would have further weakened the government. In this case, however, the office might have added further lustre to Liverpool's reputation, since the new First Lord would have dispatched Nelson to Trafalgar.

Pitt then appointed Sir Charles Middleton (created Lord Barham), an experienced naval administrator, albeit 79 years old, over strong objections from Sidmouth, who backed the return to the admiralty of St Vincent, almost universally hated by his former subordinates. Liverpool attempted to persuade Sidmouth to stay in the government, though with only short-run success.

Liverpool's first House of Lords intervention in 1805 concerned the declaration of war with Spain. A modest British squadron had attacked the Spanish treasure fleet the previous November and had succeeded in capturing it. Since Spain was still at peace with Britain at the time, the attack was questionable but Liverpool argued that Spain had essentially been France's tool since the 1800 Treaty of Ildefonso, by which it had ceded Louisiana to France, and was simply awaiting the arrival of the treasure fleet before a formal declaration of war on Britain. Spain was an example of a large empire which had 'mouldered away through apathy, inertness and pusillanimity. . . . Sunk as she is under the vassalage and dictation of the person who now rules France, friendly to us she dare not be; neutral she cannot be and hostile she must be, at the mandate of her ally.'[191]

The following month, Liverpool defended the administration's management of its military forces, which he calculated totalled 810,000 men, taking regular army and volunteer forces together, more than one in four of the adult male population, a higher proportion even than in countries which employed conscription.[192]

The most important speech Liverpool made in 1805 was on Grenville's motion for Catholic Emancipation. He began by deprecating Grenville's timing, raising the question when Britain and Ireland were still under imminent danger of attack. He agreed that religious differences were less dangerous than they had seemed a century previously for:

> We have seen a Republic of atheists established, for a time, in the very heart of Europe. . . . We must be sensible that the bigotry, intolerance, persecution and cruelty of the most condemned systems of superstition and enthusiasm, are as clemency, moderation and mercy, when compared with the same qualities in the atheists of France. With such

191. Hansard, *Parliamentary Debates from the Year 1803 to the Present Time*, Vol. 3, cols 361-64 (11 February 1805).
192. Ibid., cols 806-15 (8 March 1805).

> an example before our eyes, we can no longer hesitate in believing that those who possess any religion, be it what it may, are to be preferred, both as men and subjects, to those who have none.

He then drew a distinction between civil liberty and civil rights, which 'should be denied to no man, except upon the strongest reasons' and political power 'which should always be extended with that degree of jealousy and circumspection which may enable us to guard against the abuse of it, and which may prevent its being made the instrument to destroy the very government, for whose protection and support it was alone created'. He argued that since the British constitution required a Protestant monarch, it should require the great officers of state also to be Protestants, if only because of the Catholics' allegiance to a foreign authority (who in 1805 was under the thumb of Napoleon).

Membership of the legislature was a different question but as long as Catholics would not take the Oath of Supremacy (by which the King was declared to be Head of the Established Church) in his view they could not be MPs. In Ireland, the position was worsened by the Act of 1793, which had enacted a very broad (40-shilling) suffrage, which would cause undue conflicts between the Catholic Church and the interests of property if Catholics could stand for Parliament. In any case, following liberalising legislation in the 1780s and 1790s, the Irish Catholics could occupy all but about 38 offices and stand for Parliament, so their practical disabilities were slender.

Liverpool continued that Catholic Emancipation would not be the last concession; it would lead to an irresistible demand for disestablishment of the Church of Ireland and the abolition of tithes. He objected to the principles of the penal laws against Irish Catholics that had been imposed in Queen Anne's reign but, after those laws had been imposed, there was a lengthy period of tranquillity in Ireland, whereas, since concessions had begun in 1782, unrest had been almost continuous. Above all, 'It has been till within these few years a principle uniformly recognized, that the state and the established religion of a country must be connected; and that those who possess political power in the former, owe a certain degree of obedience and homage to the latter.'

Liverpool ended with a peroration that set out his view of the current party system:

> I call upon the Whigs, who have ever gloried in the lead they took in the revolution of 1688 . . . to support the system of King William, and the laws enacted under his auspices; I call upon the Tories, the firm, steady and persevering supporters of the monarchy and the Established Church; I call upon them to maintain the laws which are the bulwarks of those establishments."[193]

---

193. Ibid., Vol. 4, cols 673-92 (10 May 1805).

Grenville's motion was rejected by 178 to 49, to the King's great rejoicing.

At some time in 1805, Liverpool oversaw and secured funding for Britain's first uniformed police force, the Bow Street Horse Patrol, set up to address the menace of highwaymen in the roads around London. An earlier horse patrol had been set up by Sir John Fielding in 1763, after his brother, Henry Fielding, instituted the Bow Street Runners, but it consisted of fewer than a dozen men, too small to be effective. Working with Sir Richard Ford,[194] Bow Street's Chief Magistrate, Liverpool obtained backing for a force of around 60 men, large enough to rid London of the highwayman menace. The Horse Patrol proved completely effective, almost eliminating the highwayman menace before either the railways or the Metropolitan Police came along; Liverpool would refer to it with pride in a Lords speech in 1826.[195]

July 1805 saw the final resignation of Sidmouth from the government; he had sought further preferment for one of his followers, Nathaniel Bond, who had attempted to turn Melville's impeachment into a criminal prosecution. Administratively, there was no problem: Harrowby, recovered from his fall, came back as Chancellor of the Duchy of Lancaster, replacing Hobart; Camden[196] became Lord President of the Council; and Castlereagh was promoted to War and the Colonies in Camden's place, keeping the Board of Control as well. Sidmouth was already negotiating with Fox, whose government he was to join the following February. Liverpool's unsuccessful attempts at mediation caused a coolness between them, which fortunately proved temporary.

However, Sidmouth's departure did further weaken the government. As the tied vote on Melville's censure had shown in April, without Sidmouth's followers even Pitt was not sure of a majority. Pitt attempted in September to form a broad-based administration with Grenville and Fox, but Liverpool declared to his father that he would never join such a combination. The King also raised a firm objection, possibly prompted by Liverpool, with whom he was now close.

Liverpool was only peripherally connected with the world-changing events of the autumn of 1805: the formation of the Third Coalition; the decision by Napoleon in August 1805 to turn his attention from England towards the powers forming against him; the Coalition's defeats at Ulm and Austerlitz; and the naval victory at Trafalgar. His main responsibility was to arrange for a Day of Thanksgiving on 5 December and for Nelson's funeral, which took

194. Richard Ford (1748-1806). Knighted, 1801. Tory MP for East Grinstead and Appleby, 1789-91. Bow Street Chief Magistrate, 1801-6. Predecessor of William IV in the affections of Dorothea Jordan (1761-1816) with whom he had three children.

195. T.C. Hansard, *Parliamentary Debates, New Series, Commencing with the Accession of George IV*, Vol. 14, cols 1353-56 (14 March 1826).

196. John Jeffreys Platt (1759-1840). 2nd Earl Camden from 1794. 1st Marquess Camden from 1812. MP for Bath, 1780-94. Lord Lieutenant of Ireland, 1795-98. Secretary of State for War and the Colonies, 1804-5. Lord President of the Council, 1805-6, 1807-12.

place on 9 January 1806. He also gave Nelson's eulogy in the House of Lords introducing a Vote of Thanks to the Navy, in which he claimed (amusingly to modern eyes who know the full story) that, 'His [Nelson's] conduct in private life was equally admirable with that which he uniformly manifested in his professional career'.[197]

By this time, Pitt was dying. Liverpool invited him on 7 January to convalesce at Coombe Wood on his return from Bath, where he was attempting to recover. Instead, Pitt returned to his 'damp and cold' house on Putney Heath. Liverpool visited him there on 13 January with Castlereagh, to tell him that the British expeditionary force in north Germany would have to be withdrawn. Parliament opened on 21 January with a deliberately uncontroversial King's Speech drafted by Liverpool. Two days later, Pitt died at 4.30 a.m.

Liverpool had been leading the Cabinet on Pitt's behalf during his last illness and, given his close relationship with the King, was his obvious successor. The problem was that even with Pitt, the government was unsure of its majority; it had not been subjected to a Parliementary vote since Sidmouth's resignation the previous July. Liverpool called a special Cabinet the evening after Pitt died, at which it was decided not to carry on in view of the close rapport between Fox and Grenville and the ongoing discussions with Sidmouth.

The following day Liverpool had a three-hour interview with the King; the King pressed him to accept the Prime Ministership but he reluctantly declined. In view of the divisions within Pitt's Cabinet, Liverpool's own relative youth and inexperience and, above all, the impossibility of keeping a Commons majority, Liverpool's refusal was well-founded. Although Liverpool would have had the faithful Castlereagh and Perceval to lead the House of Commons, Canning had been a solid supporter of Pitt but would have been unreliable and probably hostile to a Liverpool ministry. Liverpool urged the King to abandon his veto on the return of Fox and allow Fox, Grenville and Sidmouth to form what became the so-called 'Ministry of All the Talents', which took over in early February.

Liverpool was not without consolation; the King insisted on giving him the office of Lord Warden of the Cinque Ports, which had become vacant on Pitt's death. This was worth £3,000 per annum and came with the use of Walmer Castle, an attractive converted Tudor fort that Liverpool used as a country retreat and was much liked by Louisa. Given his father's successful acquisition of sinecures over his 40-year public career, this caused some adverse comment: 'The Jenkinson craving disposition will revolt the whole country' remarked the junior minister, Lord Sheffield.[198]

197. Hansard, *Parliamentary Debates from the Year 1803 to the Present Time*, Vol. 6 cols 75-78 (28 January 1806).

198. John Baker Holroyd (1735-1821). Baron Sheffield (Ireland),1781, (UK) 1802. Earl of Sheffield, 1816. MP for Coventry and Bristol, 1780-1802. President of the Board of Agriculture, 1803. Board of Trade, 1809-1821. Quoted in Gash, *Lord Liverpool* p. 67.

III.

De Facto Primus inter Pares, 1806-11

Liverpool was now in a strong political position. From here on he was arguably the most powerful single figure on the conservative side of politics, albeit without complete control or the popular stature of Fox on the left (who was within six months of death). He could not command a Commons majority, because the factions led by Grenville and Sidmouth (the latter with about 30 followers) supported the Whigs and Canning's faction, while generally Tory, was jealous of Liverpool himself. Nevertheless, within an overall Tory administration, which became possible in 1807 when Sidmouth left the Whigs, Liverpool was, along with Eldon, the first consulted by the King and the central figure in the construction of ministries.

Policy remained partly decentralised under the stronger departmental ministers, so that Canning ran foreign policy and Castlereagh ran the war in 1807-9, Perceval ran finance (with considerable input from Liverpool) in 1807-12 and Wellesley ran foreign policy in 1809-12, just as Castlereagh and Canning were successively to run foreign policy after 1812. Moreover, the King's disability from late 1810 temporarily weakened Liverpool's position, because he had no comparably close relationship with the Prince Regent. However, the architect of the great Tory governments of 1807-27 was primarily Liverpool, even though he became their nominal leader only after Perceval's assassination in May 1812.

In February 1806, while Liverpool and his colleagues could not form a majority government, they had every prospect of an early return to office. The Ministry of All the Talents, formed by Fox and Grenville, had a stellar assembly of talent, even though its Whig majority element had not held office for over 20 years. However, it was split from top to bottom on policy.

Fox and Grey, the two principal Whig leaders, were well to the left of most of their party and had lost credibility by opposing the war against France and supporting radical parliamentary reform and Catholic Emancipation. Indeed, after the collapse of the Third Coalition, Fox was determined on a compromise peace with France, taking the post of Foreign Secretary to attempt one.

Grenville, the other main pillar of the ministry, was a highly difficult colleague whose attitude to the war was more hawkish than the Pittites, even though on Catholic Emancipation he sided with the Whigs. Finally, Sidmouth, whose supporters they needed for a Commons majority was a strong Tory, differing from the outgoing ministry only on one issue, the Melville impeachment, while differing from his new colleagues on Catholic Emancipation and most other issues.

Thus, provided Liverpool could keep the opposition acting together, the former ministers had every chance of an early return to office, as soon as one or other ministerial faction split from its colleagues. Conversely, it was strongly in the interest of the Talents' leaders to try to pick off one of the Pittites to strengthen their Commons position, thereby preventing Sidmouth from holding them to ransom over some issue. The most obvious potential recruit to the Talents was Canning, who agreed with the Whigs on Catholic Emancipation, was at least partly sympathetic on other issues (though not on the war) and combined intense ambition with jealousy of his former colleagues, notably, Liverpool and Castlereagh.

Political tactics therefore dictated that the Pittites should make every effort to hold their followers together, which they did through frequent meetings and dinners, the first, to set opposition tactics, as early as 19 February. It also made sense to attempt to split the ministry, which could be achieved by agreeing ostentatiously with a factional position within it when that faction disagreed with the majority Whig view. Generally, the ex-Pittites attempted to detach Grenville from his colleagues, even though Sidmouth was closer to them in beliefs. Presumably they felt that no reunion with Sidmouth would be possible until the Melville impeachment had been settled, which would take most of the 1806 session.

The formation of the Talents' coalition caused an immediate difficulty when they attempted to include Lord Ellenborough[1] in the Cabinet while retaining him in his post of Lord Chief Justice. Ellenborough had entered the Commons as a follower of Addington (Sidmouth) who had promoted him Lord Chief Justice in 1802, where he proved to be peppery and excessively anti-defendant, even by the standards of the day. The inclusion of the Lord Chief Justice in the Cabinet had happened only once before since 1688 (Lord Mansfield[2] in 1757-65) – the principal objection was the separation of the judicial and executive function, which was thought more important than in the case of the Lord Chancellor because the Lord Chancellor did not normally preside over

1. Edward Law (1750-1818). 1st Baron Ellenborough from 1802. PC, 1801. Addingtonian MP for Newtown, 1801-2. Attorney General, 1801-2. Lord Chief Justice, 1802-18. Third Wrangler, 1771 (i.e. third in Cambridge Mathematics Tripos). Lead defence counsel in Warren Hastings impeachment, 1792-95.
2. William Murray (1705-93). 1st Baron Mansfield from 1756. 1st Earl of Mansfield from 1776. MP for Boroughbridge, 1742-56. Solicitor General, 1742-54. Attorney General, 1754-56. Lord Chief Justice, 1756-88.

criminal cases. Liverpool spoke on a motion introduced by his brother-in-law, Lord Bristol,[3] to disqualify Ellenborough from sitting in the Cabinet. He quoted both Montesquieu and Blackstone on the separation of judicial and executive powers and suggested that the problem arose most severely in cases of libel and riot against the government.[4]

Towards the end of the session, Liverpool objected to Windham's plan for a fixed seven-year service term in the army, suggesting that it ran the danger of a mass expiry of service terms just before the outbreak of a war, leaving the country unprotected. He also objected to ministers bringing in such a major innovation as an amendment to the annual Mutiny Bill, which had to be agreed within ten days. He proposed an amendment making the term of service 20 years instead of seven, to keep a core of more experienced soldiers, but this was rejected. In the event, Windham solved the practical problem by raising army pay for the second and third seven-year terms of service.

Liverpool opposed the slave importation bill, which prevented slaves being imported into islands which Britain had captured during the war and then spoke briefly against slave trade abolition when it was brought up to the Lords by resolutions in June. He agreed with the moral principle of ending slavery ('If a trade is carried on, which is contrary to humanity and justice, there is no question as to its being contrary to sound policy'). However, since it was not proposed to abolish slavery itself he saw little benefit in ending the slave trade with Africa alone, since it would merely divert the trade to less scrupulous hands.[5] The resolutions passed the Lords by 41 votes to 20 and would become a bill in January 1807.

Before the end of the session, during which opposition to the Ministry of All the Talents had been modest, Liverpool had coordinated with Castlereagh, Melville and Canning what should be done if the government fell. They agreed that a Pittite ministry should be formed led by Perceval, to give it the strongest possible support in the Commons (the Pittites were stronger in the Lords, partly because of Pitt's many peerage creations). This was fortunate, for Fox fell ill at the beginning of the summer and died in September, necessitating a reconstruction of the government.

After the Pittites refused to join a government that contained the mainstream Whigs, Grenville made considerable efforts to bring Canning into the government, but Canning felt required to discuss this matter with his former colleagues and eventually turned Grenville down. Part of the problem was that both Sidmouth and Grey, for different reasons, detested Canning, so it was difficult to include him harmoniously in the Talents' administration.

---

3. Frederick Hervey (1769-1859). 5th Earl of Bristol, from 1803. 1st Marquess from 1826. Under Secretary for Foreign Affairs, 1801-3.
4. Hansard, *Parliamentary Debates from the Year 1803 to the Present Time*, Vol. 6, cols 274-77 (3 March 1806).
5. Ibid., cols 805-6 (24 June 1806).

After Fox's death and the failed attempt to form a truly broad-based administration, Grenville decided to call an election, in the hope that the normal ministerial accretion of strength would bring him enough additional followers to have a safe majority. This was contrary to eighteenth-century precedent, although not to later nineteenth-century practice. The 1802 parliament was only four years old out of a possible seven-year life and the only previous parliament since the 1716 Septennial Act to be terminated so early was that assembled by Lord North in 1780, which had been dissolved in 1784 after Pitt and the King ousted the Fox-North coalition. Given the 1784 precedent, Grenville was lucky to be granted the dissolution; George III remarked that Grenville treated him 'in the way he should have expected from Buonaparte after the Battle of Austerlitz'.[6]

Liverpool, with the support of Eldon, wrote to the King before the dissolution urging him not to grant it. He claimed that:

> Since the change which took place in Your Majesty's councils in the beginning of February last, an alteration has been produced in the relative state of parties much more rapid and extensive than could have been expected in so short a space of time. . . . The number of county members of Great Britain favourably disposed to the present Administration are forty-nine; those favourably disposed to their opponents are forty-five; there are eight undecided, but more inclined to the latter than to the former; and seventeen altogether doubtful. . . . [A dissolution] would have the inevitable effect of throwing the whole influence of Government into the hands of the present Administration.[7]

Liverpool's attempt to prevent the King from being bounced into a dissolution was unsuccessful. Nevertheless, the resulting election proved a disappointment to the Grenville administration, which increased its majority by only 30-50,[8] with the Sidmouth supporters losing twelve seats, showing that Liverpool had been right about popular opinion. One reason for the government's unpopularity was that Lord Henry Petty's[9] budget on 28 March had raised the income tax from a sliding scale reaching up to 6½ per cent to a flat ten per cent on all income over £50. He admitted that this massive increase

6. Quoted in Yonge, *The Life and Administration of Robert Banks Jenkinson*, Vol. I, p. 220.
7. Quoted in Yonge, *The Life and Administration of Robert Banks Jenkinson*, Vol. I pp. 218-20. In his tally, Liverpool counted only 119 of the 122 non-Irish County seats; some seats may have been vacant, of course.
8. Namier and Brooke, *The History of Parliament*, say a net gain of 30 in the majority, i.e. a net fifteen seats changing hands. However, Hilton, *Corn, Cash, Commerce*, p. 180, gives a table showing the 1806 election producing a net 27 additional supporters of the government and 23 fewer supporters of the Pittite opposition.
9. Petty would succeed as 3rd Marquess of Lansdowne in 1809.

was 'alarming to the public' but preferred it to a more gradual increase because it set income taxes at their 'natural limit, [so] there will be less suspicion of their future augmentation'.[10] Frankly, the Ministry of All the Talents was lucky not to suffer a landslide defeat!

Liverpool returned to the subject of the dissolution in the new session of Parliament in the debate on the King's Speech. He claimed there was no dispute between the King and the government that could justify a dissolution (thus the precedent of 1784 was inapplicable), nor any inability by the government to carry on its prime responsibility of prosecuting the war.[11] Grenville, in response, partially justified Liverpool's criticism by claiming that the dissolution had been caused by the breakdown of abortive peace negotiations with France.

That subject came up early in the 1806-7 session, when Liverpool gave 'qualified support' to the King's Speech. With experience of the Amiens negotiation behind him, he pointed out that, while ministers claimed that peace could be achieved on the basis of actual possession of particular territories, the French had not agreed to this anywhere in writing, and their verbal agreements could not be relied upon. He questioned the value of extending British colonial possessions (by the capture of Buenos Aires in June 1806) since: 'Colonies are undoubtedly valuable to a commercial country, but they are not valuable to us beyond what we can protect and govern.' Overall, 'I cannot conceive how, in the present disposition of France, any permanent peace can be obtained.'[12]

The main legislative achievement of the session was the abolition of the slave trade, which Liverpool opposed on several occasions in the Lords debates. He began by asking whether any other governments had shown themselves ready to abolish the trade, demanding papers on any negotiations following the previous year's slave trade resolutions:

> Considering that slavery had been permitted under the Jewish dispensation, that there was no express prohibition of it in the Christian; that it was a condition of man that many great and wise men in all ages had sanctioned, I am not prepared to say, that to allow slavery is a crime. Nevertheless, combining slavery and the slave trade, I think that it is a matter of regret the latter ever existed, and that it is desirable to abolish it. . . . I deny, however, that our withdrawing from it will abolish the trade; and if it only shifts hands, the change will only be to the disadvantage of the negroes, and of the cause of humanity.[13]

10. Hansard, *Parliamentary Debates from the Year 1803 to the Present Time*, Vol. 6, cols 564-75 (28 March 1806).
11. Ibid., Vol. 8, cols 21-25 (19 December 1806).
12. Ibid., Vol. 8, cols 270-78 (2 January 1807).
13. Ibid., Vol. 8, col. 671 (5 February 1807) and cols 679-80 (6 February 1807).

The second reading of the bill was carried by 100 votes to 36, with Liverpool in the minority, after which he confined himself to an amendment in the committee stage striking out the words 'inconsistent with the principles of justice and humanity' on the grounds that those words might arose unrealistic expectations in the existing slave population; the amendment was defeated.

Slave trade abolition was a great triumph for the Ministry of All the Talents but was quickly followed by disaster. Irish Catholics had in 1793 been allowed to hold commissions in the army up to the rank of colonel for regiments serving in Ireland; the ministry decided to extend that privilege to all regiments through the annual Mutiny Bill, a measure to which George III grudgingly acquiesced. Given false encouragement by this success, they substituted for this measure a separate bill giving Catholics the right to hold all ranks in both the army and navy, which they introduced without properly informing the King (whose eyesight was now very bad).

Sidmouth warned his colleagues that neither the King nor he could agree to such a measure and on 11 March he resigned from the government. When the King found out, he not only refused to agree to this measure (which would not have passed the Lords) but demanded assurances from his ministers that no further attempts to emancipate Catholics would be made during his lifetime. Grenville, who had developed increasingly strained relationships with his colleagues, had another unsuccessful attempt to recruit Canning and then resigned on 18 March. As Sheridan said: 'I have often heard of people knocking out their brains against a wall, but never before knew of any one building a wall expressly for the purpose.'[14]

The King had been encouraged to take a hard line by Portland, who wrote to him indicating that an alternative ministry could be formed – a fact which the King already knew from Liverpool. After Liverpool got home from visiting his father that night, he was wakened after only two hours of sleep to receive a letter summoning him to accompany Eldon to meet the King at 10 a.m. the following day. At that meeting, which lasted two and a half hours, the King again offered Liverpool the premiership. However, since all the opposition ministers, including Canning, were prepared to serve under Portland (Canning and Portland's eldest son were married to sisters), Liverpool and Eldon advised the King that Portland should act as the figurehead of a government, with Liverpool leading the House of Lords and returning as Home Secretary. Liverpool was accordingly tasked by the King to make arrangements with Portland to form a government.[15]

Canning, to ensure the support of his debating talent and Commons faction, was jumped up the ladder to Foreign Secretary and was allowed to veto the

14. Quoted in Anon., *Memoirs of the Public Life and Administration of the Rt Hon. The Earl of Liverpool*, p. 302.
15. See Liverpool's letter to the King in Aspinall, *The Later Correspondence of George III*, Vol. 4, p. 530.

re-entry of Sidmouth (who would have brought useful Commons votes but remained outside the government although friendly to it). However, Perceval as Chancellor of the Exchequer was, at Liverpool's suggestion, made Leader of the House of Commons (and Chancellor of the Duchy of Lancaster to boost his income, as the Exchequer paid only about £1,300 per year).

Liverpool wrote to the King recommending Perceval, by implication slighting the claims of both Canning and Castlereagh to the House of Commons leadership and supporting Wellesley's claim ahead of Canning to be Foreign Secretary:

> [I am] thoroughly convinced that under the present circumstances he [Perceval] is the only person fully competent to conduct Your Majesty's Government in the House of Commons, that the support of many respectable individuals depends on the choice being made, and that he will have great advantages in his situation from being of an old English family.[16]

Perceval would be supported in debate by Canning, by Castlereagh back at War and the Colonies and (whenever he was available) by Sir Arthur Wellesley (the future Duke of Wellington) as Chief Secretary for Ireland.

The government's parliamentary position was perilous but Liverpool was optimistic: 'If we have good nerves, we should get through it.'[17] In the event they did, though with a majority of only 32 in a full House on 9 April on a motion relating to the outgoing government's conduct in refusing the King a Catholic Emancipation pledge. Liverpool gave a lengthy speech on that subject in the Lords on 26 March, saying, 'There are fundamental laws, which ought not to be altered, except on the utmost pressing necessity. The right of petition, the trial by jury, and the independence of the judges are fundamental principles of the constitution, and a Protestant government and establishment are equally so.'[18]

Liverpool also intervened in the debate on finance the following month. With Pitt's death and his father's retirement, he had become the principal financial and economic expert within the new government, with deeper knowledge than Perceval, the Chancellor of the Exchequer (who trained in the law). Accordingly, he intervened in the Lords debate on 25 April, to indicate that the government was prepared to follow only for the current fiscal year Petty's ambitious scheme put forth in January, by which the duty on tonnage

---

16. Ibid., p. 535. Perceval was the seventh son of the 2nd Earl of Egmont (Ireland) and Baron Lovel (UK).
17. Quoted in Yonge, *The Life and Administration of Robert Banks Jenkinson*, Vol. I, p. 228, and Gash, *Lord Liverpool* p. 69.
18. Hansard, *Parliamentary Debates from the Year 1803 to the Present Time*, Vol. 9, cols 247-52 (26 March 1807).

and the nation's export and import duties should be mortgaged for the next 20 years, to provide security for additional loans: 'The duty on tonnage, in particular, was originally and professedly imposed by the late Mr Pitt, as a mere temporary war tax, in order to pay for the expenses of convoys.'[19] He considered the hypothecation of these taxes 'rash and improvident'.

Despite the ministry's majorities in both Commons and Lords, just as for Pitt in 1784 and Grenville the previous year, it was clear that the ministers needed to dissolve Parliament, this time with less than a year of its seven-year term elapsed, to solidify their position. There was a better pretext for dissolution than for Grenville's dissolution the previous year, namely, validation by a general election of the King's insistence that no measures of Catholic Emancipation be brought before him.

In the event, with the Protestant cry supporting them and the usual Treasury management, the ministry increased its majority by about 130,[20] gaining a majority of 195 on the debate on the Address in the new House of Commons. As the 1807 *Annual Register* said: 'The most striking feature in the general election . . . was that the progress of public opinion appeared to have, in a great measure, superseded the influence of faction and party.'[21] It was the greatest popular election victory in terms of seats gained since Pitt's triumph of 1784.

If we compare the roughly 65 seats gained by the Portland ministry in 1807 (adding 130 to its majority) with the 20 net seats (subtracting 40) lost in 1806, and remember that Sidmouth was now generally friendly, we can see that Portland from 1807 enjoyed a majority roughly 90 larger than Pitt had during the 1805 session. Moreover, given Sidmouth's move with 30 supporters into opposition in July 1805, Portland's majority was about 150 more than Liverpool, had he succeeded Pitt as Prime Minister, or indeed Pitt himself would have had in the 1806 session, even if Canning and his followers had remained loyal.

Portland's government was thus fairly secure. However, with by-elections, the loss of Canning and Castlereagh from the government in 1809, and its own weak Commons debating talent, the Perceval ministry, operating in the latter years of this Parliament, was in danger in the 1810 session, until victories both political and military strengthened it.

The first half of 1807 was highly significant, not only in producing the election victory that set up 23 years of Tory rule, but also in revolving around the two issues where Liverpool's record is most troubling to modern susceptibilities: Catholic Emancipation and the slave trade/slavery.

19. Ibid., cols 526-27 (23 April 1807).
20. Namier and Brooke, *The History of Parliament: Parliaments – 1807* say the new Parliament had 384 Ministerial and 218 opposition. Sidmouth's followers presumably voted with the government on the Address, increasing its majority.
21. *Annual Register, or A View of the History, Politics and Literature for the Year 1807* (London: W. Otridge & Son, 1809) p. 235.

As the 1807 election showed, the cause of Catholic Emancipation was a massive political loser in early nineteenth-century Britain. Not only did Portland win a huge electoral victory by opposing it but, when it was pushed through in 1829, followed by an election within a year caused by the death of George IV, it destroyed the Tory majority of the previous half-century and let in the Whigs with their gerrymandering 'Parliamentary Reform'.

As Liverpool said in 1805, it made no sense to attempt Catholic Emancipation in the middle of a war. It also made no sense to attempt it during the major post-war depression of 1816-20. Liverpool himself was to wonder whether its time had come in 1825 but passing it that year would probably have let the Whigs in at the 1826 election. The best opportunity to pass it was probably around 1823, when the economy had recovered and there were still three to four years to go until the next election. Still, Liverpool was correct when he said that the Protestant settlement was an integral part of the constitution, and it is hard to fault a statesman for pursuing a policy favoured by the great majority of his electorate.

Liverpool believed that slavery and the slave trade were immoral but, as he pointed out, feared that unilateral abolition of the slave trade would merely push it into the hands of other less scrupulous countries. After the Abolition of the Slave Trade Act of 1807, Liverpool was in the forefront of pursuing the cause for abolition amongst other countries at the Congress of Vienna and elsewhere and for the 1808 establishment of the naval 'West Africa Squadron' to police the West African coast.

Slavery itself was a more difficult matter because of the need to compensate the slave-owners. (Abolishing slavery without compensation, as the United States did after a civil war costing 500,000 lives, thereby depriving the South of its capital and devastating its economy, was not deemed an acceptable alternative.) Even with the cheeseparing Whigs in power in 1833 and slave-owners undercompensated, the £20 million cost, 40 per cent of annual government expenditure, was a heavy burden on the exchequer. (Inadequate compensation impoverished the islands of the West Indies for decades.) Thus, the abolition of slavery would have been financially impossible during the war or in the high-debt, impoverished post-war years, and only became practical politics around the mid-1820s (the Anti-Slavery Society was founded in 1823).

The new ministry was not entirely harmonious, partly because of Portland's feeble leadership. When it met at Perceval's for dinner on 25 June to discuss the King's speech, Canning absented himself, presumably miffed at not having been made Leader of the House of Commons, even though he was Foreign Secretary and had only previously been a junior minister.

Back at the Home Office, Liverpool became again embroiled in the debate about Britain's military preparedness against an enemy who was the more formidable for lacking any opposition on the Continent. By the Militia Transfer

Act, Liverpool increased by 25,000 the militia element of the defence forces established by Windham's 1806 Act and restored the allowances to volunteer forces which that Act had abolished.

The two major foreign policy events of 1807 were the attack on Copenhagen and the establishment of the Orders in Council preventing neutrals from trading with France and its allies and conquered satraps in Europe.

The attack on Copenhagen was typical Canning: a brilliant military coup that violated conventional norms and the ill-defined laws of neutrality, brought Denmark into the war alongside France, albeit without its fleet, and burned the first modern translation of Beowulf.[22] After the treaties of Tilsit, signed on 7 July, Danish neutrality was vulnerable to an attack from France and its new ally Russia, closing the British navy off from the Baltic, with its vital supply of wood. Liverpool, who knew from his days as Foreign Secretary the capabilities of Britain's intelligence network, was to claim in the Lords in January 1808 (after the fact)[23] that the Cabinet had information that the Tilsit agreements contained clauses allowing France to use the navies of Denmark and Portugal against Britain. (John VI took the Portuguese fleet to Brazil with a Royal Navy escort in November 1807, leaving Lisbon just ahead of a French invading army.)

Moving quickly, during the second half of July the Cabinet decided to send a fleet of 50 ships under Admiral James Gambier[24] to the Kattegat and an army of 25,000 troops to the area under General Lord Cathcart[25] with Major-General Sir Arthur Wellesley, recommended by Liverpool, as second-in-command. This expedition left on 27 July, less than three weeks after the Tilsit treaties were signed.

Having reached Copenhagen, the expedition demanded the surrender of the Danish fleet, after which Denmark declared war on Britain. Wellesley overcame the local Danish troops on August 29 and the British fleet bombarded Copenhagen from September 2-5, at which point the Danes surrendered, giving up their fleet. The expedition returned to Britain and the Danish fleet was duly forfeited to the Crown, while Denmark remained at war with Britain until 1814.

---

22. The unfortunate translator, Grimur Jonsson Thorkelin (1752-1829), lost 20 years' work but finally published a translation in 1815.
23. Note that Wikipedia's claim that Liverpool made this disclosure in January 1807, before the event, is incorrect; the treaties were not signed until July.
24. James Gambier (1756-1833). Baron Gambier from 1807. Captain, Royal Navy, 1778, Rear-Admiral, 1795, Vice-Admiral, 1799, Admiral, 1805, Admiral of the Fleet, 1830. Lord Commissioner of the Admiralty, 1795-1801, 1804-6, 1807.
25. William Schaw Cathcart (1755-1843). 10th Lord Cathcart from 1776. Viscount Cathcart from 1807. Earl Cathcart from 1814. Major-General, British army, 1795, Lieutenant-General, 1801, General, 1812, Commander-in-Chief, Ireland, 1803-6, Commander-in-Chief, Scotland, 1806-12. PC, 1798. Ambassador to St Petersburg, 1812-20.

After Trafalgar, Napoleon decided that the only way to defeat Britain was by destroying her trade. Accordingly, the Berlin Decrees of November 1806, tightened by the Milan Decree the following year, forbade French allied or neutral ships from trading with Britain. In retaliation, in January 1807 the Grenville government issued limited restrictions on neutral shipping, preventing it from trading between French and Spanish ports. Then, in November 1807, the Cabinet issued the more effective Orders in Council, forbidding French trade with Britain, its allies or neutrals and instructed the Royal Navy to blockade French ports. Liverpool, for the last months of 1807 acting as understudy Secretary of State for War and the Colonies while Castlereagh was ill, played a major role in this decision. He favoured including all countries allied to France, not just France and the countries it directly occupied,[26] which addition turned out to be highly effective.

In practice, there were two major differences between the two blockade systems. First, Britain had far more intercontinental trade than France, and gained even more trade by escorting the Portuguese royal family to Brazil. (John VI repaid British help by abandoning traditional Portuguese mercantilism. Shortly after his arrival in Brazil, he issued a 'Decree Opening the Ports to Friendly Nations', thus opening a major new market for British merchants.) Second, after Trafalgar Britain had full (though not quite undisputed) command of the seas, while France had little effective naval power with which to enforce its decrees. Hence British trade thrived despite the French blockade, with heavy naval activity throughout the world stimulating it further, while French trade stagnated.

There was one major third-party loser by the Orders in Council: the United States, then under the relatively pro-French presidency of Thomas Jefferson.[27] At a crucial juncture in July 1807, the situation was inflamed by the action between the USS *Chesapeake* and the smaller British frigate, *Leopard*, in which the *Leopard* attacked and boarded the *Chesapeake* off the coast of Norfolk, VA, killing three Americans, wounding eighteen and impressing four former British sailors into the Royal Navy.

Jefferson's response was the Embargo Act, forcing American merchants to shut down all trade with belligerent nations of either side. This did huge economic damage to New England merchants (almost all Jefferson's political opponents) but had little effect on the belligerents themselves. The Embargo

26. Sir Spencer Walpole, *The Life of the Rt Hon. Spencer Perceval* (London: Hurst and Blackett, 1874) Vol. 1, p. 269, quotes Liverpool's response to Perceval's memo on the subject.

27. Thomas Jefferson (1743-1826). Secretary of State, 1790-93. Vice-President, 1797-1801. President, 1801-9. Principal author of the 1776 Declaration of Independence, an extended whine about George III, in which he replaced John Locke's well-chosen trio of 'Life, Liberty and Property' with French rubbish about the pursuit of happiness.

Act was revoked at the end of Jefferson's term in 1809 but the British Orders in Council were held in place for five years. Being more effective than either the Berlin Decrees or the Embargo Act, they were to poison relations between Britain and the United States.

Liverpool's departmental duties in the remainder of 1807 were mostly routine. He was not a legal reformer as Home Secretary, believing that, although the law was severe in theory, its administration was relatively mild in practice. As he was to say in a Lords debate in 1810: 'Whatever might be said of the theory of our law, no one could doubt but that in practice it was the mildest on earth; and however sanguinary the statute book might appear, it must be confessed the administration in any country was never so much tempered with mercy.'[28] His view was overstated but represents a useful corrective to the modern, popularly held belief that the penal laws at this time were uniquely bloody. While an annual average of 580 death sentences were ordered in England and Wales between 1770 and 1830, only a fifth of those were carried out.

Most notably, Liverpool was able to prevent a further breach in the Royal Family by persuading the King to receive Princess Caroline. [29] The Whig-led 'Delicate Investigation' of the previous year had cleared her name (sort of) but, despite this, Grenville's Cabinet had been unable to persuade the King to receive her. After considerable unpleasant negotiation, managed by Liverpool, she was granted apartments at Kensington Palace and some access to her eleven-year-old daughter, Charlotte, and there the matter rested for the next few years. The King was also grateful to Liverpool in May the following year when he secured a pension for the King's sister Augusta, the widowed Duchess of Brunswick.[30]

It was not only the British Royal Family who caused problems for Liverpool; in November 1807, the future King Louis XVIII[31] arrived in Britain, travelling under the name of the Comte de Lille. After discussion with the King, Liverpool agreed that the rules of hospitality meant that Britain must fund Louis' entourage but that he should not be allowed to settle too close to London. When the Royal offer of the Palace of Holyroodhouse in Edinburgh was turned down, Louis was eventually housed in one of the Marquess of Buckingham's[32] spare properties at Hartwell near Aylesbury. Presumably some

28. Hansard, *Parliamentary Debates from the Year 1803 to the Present Time*, Vol. 17, col. 198 (30 May 1810).
29. Princess Caroline of Brunswick-Wolfenbuttel (1768-1821). Married George, Prince of Wales, 1795, separated 1797. By courtesy, Queen Caroline, 1820-21.
30. Princess Augusta Frederica (1737-1813), m. 1764 Charles William Ferdinand (1735-1806), Duke of Brunswick-Wolfenbüttel from 1780.
31. Louis Stanislas Xavier (1755-1824). King Louis XVIII of France *de jure* from 1795, *de facto* from 1814. Younger brother of Louis XVI, elder brother of Charles X.
32. George Nugent Temple-Grenville (1753-1813). From 1779 3rd Earl Temple and from 1784 1st Marquess of Buckingham. Son of Charles Jenkinson's old boss,

financial arrangement was made: the Marquess, having been Pitt's patron in 1783, was loosely allied with the opposition, led by his brother; while rich, he was already heavily in debt and Grenvilles rarely did anything for nothing.

Liverpool saw early on the troubles that were likely to arise from the *Chesapeake*/*Leopard* affair and the mutual trade restrictions, writing late in the year:

> The civilians are of opinion that Admiral Berkeley was not justified in his orders, which authorized the searching of a man-of-war for deserters. . . . An American war, in addition to all our other difficulties, would certainly be an evil at the present moment; but experience has proved that we shall not avoid it by unbecoming concessions, and the losses, if it shall occur, will fall more heavily upon the Americans than upon the people of this country.[33]

While these matters of foreign policy did not fall within Liverpool's official responsibility, he had been a leading member of the Cabinet that decided on the Denmark expedition and the Orders in Council and was compelled as Leader of the House of Lords to defend them when Parliament reassembled in January 1808. To Grenville's demand that he produce the information justifying the Copenhagen expedition, he responded, 'If government were to communicate private information there would be an end of all confidence, and at this time, when Europe is under the control of France, the lives of individuals, friendly to this country, would inevitably fall sacrifice.' Liverpool further claimed that French plans were known most quickly among the disaffected in Ireland.[34]

Liverpool later gave a more detailed defence of the Copenhagen expedition, basing it on the right to self-defence and pointing out that France could easily invade Denmark from Holstein with sufficient forces to overcome the weak Danish Army: 'Nothing prevents France from acquiring universal dominion but the naval power of Great Britain.'[35]

Liverpool's main defence of the Orders in Council came the following week:

> I compare the measure with that of the late administration, and contend that while by the Order of January 7 [1807] the ordinary law of nations was just as much violated as by the Orders of November 11 the latter secured to the country benefits which the former was not

George Grenville, nephew of the 2nd Earl Temple and elder brother of William Wyndham Grenville. Lord Lieutenant of Ireland, 1782-83 and 1787-89.

33. Quoted in Yonge, *The Life and Administration of Robert Banks Jenkinson*, Vol. 1, p. 242.
34. Hansard, *Parliamentary Debates from the Year 1803 to the Present Time*, Vol. 10, cols 28-31 (21 January 1808).
35. Ibid., cols 368-75 (8 February 1808).

> calculated to obtain. It is intolerable that England has enjoyed little advantage from her maritime superiority; and that France, who dare not show a flag on the ocean, has carried on such a trade by neutral bottoms, that the people of that country consume colonial produce at a much less rate than the English.[36]

The subject came up again several times, and Liverpool, after reiterating his desire to have good relations with the United States, was able to tell the House of Lords 'there is good reason to believe, as indeed I wish . . . that America must shortly have a proper sense of its own interest',[37] – US elections loomed and the end of Thomas Jefferson's anti-British Presidency was on the horizon. In any case, it did not appear that the Orders in Council were greatly affecting British trade – a drop in exports in the fourth quarter of 1807 included only one month of the new regulations and was more likely due to the Berlin Decrees of the previous year.

The most difficult task for a Home Secretary was maintaining order in Ireland, where a substantial portion of the Catholic population 'thinks of nothing but Bonaparte's successes on the Continent, and relies with certainty on his invading their country and separating it from England; the poor saying that they cannot lose, and they believe they should gain by the change'.[38] During the summer of 1807 a nationalist group the 'Liberty Rangers' was formed, promising 'to effect all that the Croppies failed to achieve in the year 1798'.

Liverpool therefore determined to station more troops in Ireland, to fortify Cork and Dublin and to make Cork a large military depot. He was greatly helped by Castlereagh and Sir Arthur Wellesley both being Irishmen. Liverpool pointed out to Wellesley that the Cork depot would be useful in resupplying any military expeditions in that direction – as indeed it was to be for Wellesley/Wellington's forces in the Iberian peninsula.

Liverpool's work in the House of Lords focussed primarily on the government's foreign policy, both successful and unsuccessful. On 14 March he welcomed closer relations with Sweden, whose Finnish province had been invaded by Denmark and Russia. However, his enthusiasm for the 'proofs of unshaken firmness and fidelity which his Swedish majesty has displayed to his engagements with this country'[39] rings less encouraging, when we realise

36. Ibid., cols 483-85 (15 February 1808). The quotation here is obscure; I think it should be 'at *not* much less rate than the English'.
37. Ibid., cols 1282-83 (29 March). Export reference, ibid., Vol. 11, col. 709 (30 May 1808).
38. Letter from an Irish official to Liverpool, quoted in Yonge, *The Life and Administration of Robert Banks Jenkinson,* Vol. 1, p. 260.
39. Hansard, *Parliamentary Debates from the Year 1803 to the Present Time,* Vol. 10, cols 1076-77 (14 March 1808).

that Sweden was about to lose almost all of Finland and the eastern third of Sweden, with King Gustav IV Adolf being forced to abdicate his throne. Perversely, the long-term improvement in Anglo-Swedish relations would have to await the advent of Jean Bernadotte[40] to Swedish rule in 1810.

On a happier note, the previous month Liverpool had introduced the Brazil Trade Bill over considerable opposition querulousness about the Brazilian slave trade, declaring that 'there is no principle on which these commercial arrangements could have been refused'.[41] In truth, the removal of the Portuguese royal family to Brazil and its subsequent opening up was one of the more painless and commercially lucrative (to both sides) operations of the entire war.

Throughout his period as Leader of the House of Lords, Liverpool was responsible for submitting reports to the King about the previous night's debates. He was also responsible for ensuring that the various Royal relations, hangers-on and office-holders fulfilled their duty of supporting the government in divisions that were often tight. Late in the 1808 session, Grenville's motion to admit Catholics to the directorship of the Bank of Ireland did unexpectedly well and resulted in an exchange of views with the King, in which Liverpool said: 'If persons connected with the Government will leave London before the close of the Session and will not themselves feel any anxiety about what is going forward in Parliament, it is very difficult with every exertion on the part of Your Majesty's servants to secure a proper attendance.'[42]

On 2 May, the Madrid populace rebelled against the occupation of the city by French troops, which had been in place since the deposition of Charles IV,[43] who had been forced to abdicate in favour of his son Ferdinand VII.[44] The following day, the French troops carried out a mass execution and from then on Spain was in rebellion, made more general on 6 May when Ferdinand VII was seized on a visit to Bayonne and also forced to abdicate, to be replaced by Joseph Bonaparte, crowned as Joseph I. Liverpool referred to the Spanish uprising in a June Lords debate, when he said, 'the people of that country have manifested a spirit and determination to resist the attempts of the invaders, which would have done honour to the most glorious periods of their history, and which perhaps were not to be expected under the pressure of such formidable difficulties'.[45]

---

40. Jean Bernadotte (1763-1844). Prince of Pontecorvo, 1806-10. Crown Prince of Sweden, 1810-18. King Charles XIV John of Sweden from 1818. Son of a lawyer, served as a non-commissioned officer in French army, 1780-90, promoted rapidly after the Revolution to Major-General in 1794. Marshal of the Empire, 1804. Commanded corps at Ulm, Austerlitz and Wagram. Elected heir-presumptive to King Charles XIII of Sweden by the Riksdag, 21 August 1810.
41. Ibid., cols 734-35 (25 February 1808).
42. Aspinall, The Later Correspondence of George III, Vol. 5, p. 88.
43. Charles IV (1748-1819). King of Spain, 1788-1808.
44. Ferdinand VII (1784-1833). King of Spain, 1808, 1813-33.
45. Hansard, *Parliamentary Debates from the Year 1803 to the Present Time*, Vol. 11, cols

The provincial assembly of Asturias, in northern Spain, arrived in London on 8 June to request help, which was promised by Canning in a Commons speech. The help was quicker to arrive than might have been expected, since Castlereagh had already appointed Sir Arthur Wellesley as commander of 9,000 men assembled at Cork, with the intention of mounting an expedition to South America. This expedition was increased to 15,000 men and redirected to Portugal, where Wellesley landed on 30 July.

We now come to the central conundrum of Castlereagh's tenure as Secretary for War and the Colonies, one of two massive blunders committed by this otherwise capable minister (the other being the Walcheren expedition of the following year). Wellesley won a decisive victory over 14,000 French troops under Major-General Jean-Andoche Junot[46] at the Battle of Vimeiro on 21 August. Immediately thereafter he was superseded by not one but two dozy senior officers, Sir Hew Dalrymple[47] and Sir Harry Burrard,[48] who proceeded to negotiate the unnecessarily feeble Convention of Cintra, forcing Wellesley to sign. By this Convention, Junot and his troops were to be returned to France on British ships with all their equipment and their loot from Portugal. Even the Russian fleet which had surrendered at Lisbon was allowed to return to Russia. The appointment of both Dalrymple and Burrard over Wellesley's head was clearly an appalling decision; it's worth asking the eternal question: whatever were they thinking?

The traditional story is that Wellesley was too junior for such a major command and so was superseded by George III, the Duke of York and the War Office. However, Wellesley was already a lieutenant-general (promoted in April 1808), he had been successful at Copenhagen the previous year, he had won major victories in India, he had served as Chief Secretary for Ireland in the government in power and his brother, Richard, was a marquess with major political influence in the House of Commons. Dalrymple and Burrard were fifteen to 20 years older than Wellesley and a few years senior as lieutenant-generals, but neither had Wellesley's experience of successful command, although Burrard had commanded a division at Copenhagen. Although both were doubtless well connected at the War Office, neither had Wellesley's connections in the wider world.

According to Sir John Moore, the reality seems to be that:

1108-9 (30 June 1808).

46. Jean-Andoche Junot (1771-1813). Commander of the French forces in Portugal, 1807. Duke of Abrantes, 1807. Supposed to have committed suicide in 1813 after further failures but there's some evidence he faked his death and escaped to New Orleans.
47. Sir Hew Whitefoord Dalrymple (1750-1830). Knighted 1779. 1st Baronet from 1815. Lieutenant-General, 1801, General, 1812. Governor of Gibraltar, 1806-8. Commander of the Portuguese expedition, 1808.
48. Sir Harry Burrard (1755-1813). Baronet from 1807. Lieutenant-General, 1805. Commanded 1st Division in Copenhagen expedition, 1807.

> Ministers did everything in their power to give the command to Wellesley, but he was so young a Lieutenant General that the Duke of York had objected to it, and, afraid of disgusting the Army by such an appointment, they had given it up. Disappointed in their favourite object, they were determined it should not be given to me and to prevent the possibility of its falling to me Sir Harry Burrard was named as second.[49]

Moore had been a Pittite MP in 1784-90 but was from a middle-class background so objected to the well-connected Wellesley; he was also paranoid and prone to fits of depression, according to Liverpool.[50]

That explains it, though not entirely. Dalrymple was Governor of Gibraltar and a Royal favourite; he was the obvious man to command an expedition so close to his area of responsibility. Burrard is less explicable; he was junior to Moore, so could not have blocked him even if Ministers had wanted to. Part of the problem was the expansion of the expedition after it had been committed to; with the reinforcements brought by Burrard, it amounted to 30,000 men, thought to require a more senior general than Wellesley.

Nevertheless, Castlereagh and the Cabinet should have stuck to their guns. Wellesley could have dealt with one dozy senior officer but two was too many. Moore's verdict on Dalrymple in his *Diary* was unequivocal: 'Sir Hew Dalrymple was confused and incapable beyond any man I ever saw head an army. The whole of his conduct then and since has proved him to be a very foolish man.'[51]

Dalrymple, Burrard and Wellesley were recalled to England in late September, to face a Court of Inquiry in November and December, and Moore was sent out with another 12,000 men (over Canning's strong objection – he despised Moore's habitual pessimism). Seeing that his troops outnumbered the French, Moore advanced into Spain but was soon faced by Napoleon himself and an army of 200,000, who forced Moore back through a harsh winter march to Corunna. Moore fought a successful defensive battle at Corunna on 16 January 1809, allowing the British troops to re-embark, but was killed in the fighting. His death inspired a cult following, eulogised in a poem by Charles Wolfe which was a standard part of the schoolboy repertoire until my youth 50 years ago:

> Not a drum was heard, not a funeral note,
> As his corse to the rampart we hurried;
> Not a soldier discharged his farewell shot
> O'er the grave where our hero we buried.[52]

49. *Diary of Sir John Moore*, Vol. 2, pp. 239-40, quoted in Aspinall, *The Later Correspondence of George III*, Vol. 5, p. 109.
50. 1815 Letter to his cousin, Col. George Jenkinson, quoted in Yonge, *The Life and Administration of Robert Banks Jenkinson*, Vol. 2, p. 168.
51. *Diary of Sir John Moore*, Vol. 2, pp. 239-40, quoted in Aspinall, *The Later Correspondence of George III*, Vol. 5, p. 109.
52. Charles Wolfe (1791-1823), *The Burial of Sir John Moore after Corunna* (1817).

In the meantime, following Wellesley's success at Vimeiro and Moore's initial advance into Spain, a French courier was sent to Britain with a Franco-Russian peace offer that still gave Napoleon a free hand in Spain. Liverpool intersected the courier at Walmer Castle and, after briefing the King, produced a Royal declaration that: 'Neither the honour of His Majesty, nor the generosity of the British nation, would admit to His Majesty's consenting to commence a negotiation, by the abandonment of a brave and loyal people, who are contending for the preservation of all that is dear to man.'[53]

The end of 1808 was a quiet and sad period for Liverpool. His father died on 17 December, after which Liverpool and his family travelled down to Hawkesbury to bury him in the family vault on 30 December. Castlereagh took over Liverpool's Home Office duties in his absence. Liverpool received a nice letter from George III, referring to Jenkinson's 'integrity and fidelity in the able discharge of his duty'[54] over a period of 48 years.

Whitehall Yard, 1811, St Paul's in distance.
Fife House is half-hidden, to the left of St Paul's.

Following his father's death, and his inheritance of most of his father's fortune, Liverpool leased a splendid and convenient Whitehall residence, Fife House, which became vacant after the death of the second Earl of Fife. Liverpool and, after his death, his brother, Charles, were to occupy the house until Charles' death in 1851. (The house was demolished in 1869.) Fife House

53. Quoted in Anon., *Memoirs of the Public Life and Administration of the Rt Hon. The Earl of Liverpool*, pp. 330-31.
54. Aspinall, *The Later Correspondence of George III*, Vol. 5, p. 160.

had been built or rebuilt in 1756-7 for the Earl; it occupied part of the ground of the old Whitehall Palace, destroyed by fire in 1698. It was thus extremely convenient for Liverpool's administrative duties, only a few hundred yards from Parliament and even closer to the Foreign Office, the War Office and Downing Street. On taking over the lease from Fife's executors in 1809, Liverpool again employed John Soane to make extensive renovations and alterations.

The new session began in January 1809 with Liverpool defending the Spanish/Portuguese campaign and the Convention of Cintra in the House of Lords. Grenville opened by claiming that there was 'nothing which could justify our sending into the interior of Spain thirty or forty thousand British men to meet an army of 500,000. I can only compare such a measure to the far famed march on Paris, to which it is fully equal in wildness and absurdity.'[55] Given that Liverpool's position of Home Secretary had nothing to do with the Spain/Portugal campaign, it is striking that Grenville mocked Liverpool's youthful phrase of fifteen years previously. It is another indication that Liverpool, as well as being Leader of the Lords, was seen as the *primum mobile* behind Portland's government, and the Perceval ministry that followed it.

Liverpool replied by giving a robust defence of Spain's position:

> It is difficult to conceive any situation which would better warrant hopes of ultimate success, than that of Spain at this day. The people are unanimous in their resistance to the invader. . . . The territory of Spain is as large as France within its ancient limits, and the country possesses many local advantages which are extremely favourable to its defence.[56]

The Spain/Portugal debate in the Lords was resumed in April, on a motion proposed by Grey condemning the 'want of information and foresight in every part of the conduct of his Majesty's Ministers'. Liverpool began by suggesting that Grenville's criticism that ministers should have waited to offer assistance to Spain was ridiculous – to refuse help while resistance was in its infancy and only offer it when it was in full flower was the reverse of good policy. They could not, however, have sent a full-scale force to Spain initially, because they held no Spanish port through which they could have supplied it. Wellesley had been despatched with discretion as to whether he landed on the Spanish coast or at the Tagus, which was the best approach to getting the expedition under way quickly.

Liverpool went through the fate of the Portuguese expedition, the advance into Spain and the retreat to Corunna point by point, arguing that, while mistakes had been made, such as the fiasco of replacing Wellesley by Dalrymple and Burrard, in general, the decisions taken had accurately reflected the strategic situation at the time. He ended by summarising the progress made:

55. Hansard, *Parliamentary Debates from the Year 1803 to the Present Time*, Vol. 12, cols 11-21 (19 January 1809).
56. Ibid., cols 21-25 (19 January 1809).

> By it we have gained the possession of the Russian fleet, while our own has been relieved from the tediousness and difficulty of a blockade; we have materially assisted the cause which we undertook to support; and I maintain, whatever may be the final result of the contest we are engaged in, France has not yet succeeded in subduing Spain.[57]

Grey's motion of censure lost by 145 votes to 92.

In February, Liverpool had defended the Orders in Council:

> I consider the evil of the Orders in Council, as they affected America, only as incidental consequences of the just retaliation, which as a neutral nation she could have no right to impute to Great Britain as an act of hostility, or of unjustifiable violence upon her neutrality. . . . America has showed no disposition to act properly towards us, but has held out every temptation to France.

Later he identified the cause of the problem: 'If the same disposition to friendship prevailed in America now as when Washington and Adams were in office, the same difficulties would not be felt.'[58]

Fortunately, some relief was shortly to arrive with the installation on 4 March of the moderate James Madison as President.[59] However, Liverpool was forced, later in the session, to apologise to the House for a mix-up caused by Canning and the Whig diplomat David Erskine (appointed to the post by Fox before his death), who had offered Washington the unconditional withdrawal of the Orders in Council, directly contrary to his instructions, thus worsening relations with the new administration when he was disavowed.[60]

In May, Liverpool, playing a role in foreign and military policy as Leader of the Lords, asked the House for a loan of £600,000 to support the Prince Regent of Portugal in his exile in Brazil, indicating that the government intended to make the Spanish/Portuguese campaign a long one. Later that month, he asked for a vote of credit of £3 million, to subsidise Austria in the Fifth Coalition being assembled against France.

On a motion to extend the war taxes in June, Liverpool admitted that fighting a war on two fronts, in the Iberian peninsula and (initially via subsidies) in

57. Ibid., Vol. 14, cols 150-64 (21 April 1809).
58. Ibid., Vol. 12, cols 800-2, 803 (17 February 1809).
59. James Madison (1751-1836). Confederation Congress delegate, 1781-83. Congressman from Virginia, 1789-97. Secretary of State, 1801-9. President, 1809-17. Active member of Constitutional Convention, 1787. Drafted Bill of Rights, 1791. Author with Alexander Hamilton of the majority of the Federalist Papers.
60. Hansard, *Parliamentary Debates from the Year 1803 to the Present Time*, Vol. 14, cols 693-94 (25 May 1809). David Erskine (1776-1855). 2nd Baron Erskine from 1823. MP for Portsmouth, 1806. Minister to the United States, 1807-9. Minister to Württemburg, 1824-28. Minister to Bavaria, 1828-43.

Austria, had increased expenditure beyond what had been thought necessary. He then touched on the central strategic question of the war, on which, later that year after he had become Secretary of State for War and the Colonies, his decision was to determine his ultimately successful war-winning strategy:

> With respect to the actual amount of expenditure, it might be a question of policy as to whether we should carry on the war on a certain definite scale, with a view to its long continuance, or whether we should carry it on for a short time on a more enlarged scale, with a view to more immediate advantages.[61]

The session's final major debate was on Curwen's Reform Bill, proposed by the moderate Whig, John Curwen, after the Duke of York scandal, to reduce corruption in parliamentary elections. Liverpool strongly supported the bill and introduced it in the House of Lords. He began by making clear that Curwen's Bill:

> does not in the least partake of the nature of what has been denominated Parliamentary Reform. . . . Sorry should I be to see the representation of our country so changed, that the whole of our elections should be similar to those of Middlesex and Westminster. Look, my Lords, to those elections, and you will perceive the evil of such a representation! Every noble lord who now hears me has had an opportunity there of observing how perjury, subornation of perjury, and all the vices which are consequent thereon, abound on these occasions and tend to degrade and disgrace the community.

He explained that Curwen's Bill related to the abuse of purchase of parliamentary seats:

> Supposing it be doubtful, whether the buying and selling of parliamentary seats is or is not an offence punishable by common law, yet my Lords, I cannot hesitate a moment to assert that, according to all analogy of law, and according to the true principles of the constitution, it is an offence which ought to be punished.[62]

The Cabinet sent Wellesley back to Portugal in April 1809, this time without any interfering senior officers. However, Castlereagh regarded the peninsula as a sideshow to the main campaign against Napoleon by Austria, which had begun with an Austrian invasion of Bavaria. The Austrians favoured a British

61. Hansard, *Parliamentary Debates from the Year 1803 to the Present Time*, Vol. 14, cols 910-12 (7 June 1809).
62. Ibid., cols 1032-35 (15 June 1809).

attack on north Germany, to encourage the Prussians to join the Fifth Coalition against France, but Castlereagh and the Cabinet decided instead in June to send a substantial force to the Low Countries, specifically to the island of Walcheren. Liverpool facilitated this by allowing for the release of some troops from Ireland to assist Wellesley, since the Austrian victory at Essling in May appeared to mean that Napoleon's efforts would be directed eastwards for the rest of the year. At the same time, he undertook to the Lord Lieutenant, the Duke of Richmond,[63] that the force in Ireland would never be allowed to decline below 120,000 men.

Meanwhile Canning, after two years at the Foreign Office, was again indulging his passion for intrigue, this time using the ailing Portland as leverage to manoeuvre himself into the top job once Portland retired. He began in April by approaching Portland to demand a reorganisation of the Cabinet with Castlereagh replaced by Marquess Wellesley. (Canning, an old foe of Moore, blamed Castlereagh for the failure of Moore's Spanish expedition and for the Convention of Cintra.) Already, at the end of April, he was intriguing with the Speaker Charles Abbot[64] to recruit him to his cause.[65]

Portland consulted some of his senior colleagues and the King, but not Liverpool or Castlereagh himself, then sat on the request for several months. The Cabinet clearly needed to be reconstructed but Portland was by this time not up to the task. The only change he made was to admit Granville Leveson-Gower, Canning's Whiggish acolyte, to the Cabinet as Secretary at War in July. At this time, Portland extracted from the King a promise that the change could be made if necessary, while still omitting to discuss the matter with Castlereagh (against which secrecy Canning remonstrated by letter, realising correctly that the blame for the intrigue would inevitably fall on him).

Liverpool found out about Canning's intrigue in July and penned a lengthy letter to the King. He admitted that Canning was at that time a more essential colleague than Castlereagh but took strong exception to the plan to remove Castlereagh from his office just as the Walcheren expedition was sailing. He continued:

> Lord Liverpool is most fully aware that the resignation of Mr. Canning, followed at this time by the events which would necessarily follow it, would lead in a very short space of time if not immediately

63. Charles Lennox (1764-1819). 4th Duke of Lennox from 1805. 4th Duke of Richmond from 1806. Founder of Marylebone Cricket Club, 1787. MP for Sussex, 1790-1806. Lord Lieutenant of Ireland, 1807-13. Governor General of British North America, 1818-19. His wife was hostess to the Brussels ball before the Battle of Quatre Bras, 1815.
64. Charles Abbot (1757-1829) 1st Baron Colchester from 1817; MP for Helston, Heytesbury, Woodstock and Oxford University, 1795-1817; Chief Secretary for Ireland, 1801-02; Speaker of the House of Commons, 1802-17.
65. Charles Abbot (ed.), *The Diaries and Correspondence of Charles Abbot, Lord Colchester* (London: J. Murray, 1861) Vol. 2, pp. 180-81.

> to the dissolution of the present Administration, and with a view to preventing a catastrophe which might be so repugnant to your Majesty's feelings, and so prejudicial, as Lord Liverpool conscientiously believes, at this moment to the publick service, Lord Liverpool most humbly requests that your Majesty would accept of his office of Secretary of State for the Home Department for the purposes of obviating in the least unsatisfactory manner the difficulties which at this time exist in your Majesty's Government.
>
> This office might be offer'd to Lord Castlereagh together with a Peerage and the conduct of the business of government in the House of Lords, with the understanding likewise that the correspondence relative to the expedition which is about to sail, and which has been arranged under his auspices, might still be left in his hands. . . . Lord Liverpool believes that such an arrangement, but such an arrangement alone would prevent at this time the dissolution of your Majesty's Administration.

Liverpool then went on to say that he did not want any other office but would nevertheless continue 'to exert himself so vigorously in [the government's] defence and justification in the House of Lords as if he held the most important and responsible situation.'[66]

Two things are notable from this letter. First, it is yet another example of Liverpool being prepared to sacrifice his position in the interests of the government, in a way that was not common then and has since disappeared altogether. In this context, it shows a marked contrast to Canning's more 'modern' approach to politics.

Second, it shows Liverpool's old-fashioned 'Church and King' Toryism, inherited from his father. In his eyes the administration was genuinely His Majesty's, and the King's well-being was a major consideration in the possible government restructuring. Liverpool had accepted the Home Office in 1807, even though its duties were then of only moderate importance, because it involved the most Royal contact and he was the minister with whom the King was most personally comfortable. He was now prepared to sacrifice his career, at least temporarily, if it led to the continuation of an administration the King valued.

It was an attitude that was to die with George III's descent into his final age-related madness the following year; neither Liverpool nor anyone else would have such a close and trusting relationship with the vain, foolish and duplicitous Prince Regent. Later ministers had close relationships with their monarch – one thinks of Disraeli's with Queen Victoria – but there was never any question of Disraeli sacrificing his career for his Queen's comfort and convenience.

---

66. Aspinall, *The Later Correspondence of George III*, Vol. 5, pp. 310-12.

The King sent no response to Liverpool's letter – what response could he have sent, without losing his most trusted minister? In consequence, since all were agreed that Castlereagh should not be removed until the Walcheren expedition had borne fruit, nothing was done. The Walcheren expedition finally set out on 30 July, even though the Austrians were now beyond help, having lost the Battle of Wagram on 5-6 July – news of the Austro-French armistice had already reached London before the expedition left.

Portland had a mild stroke on 11 August, after which negotiations began on forming a new government, during which Canning insisted to Perceval that the Prime Minister should be in the Commons, ruling out a leader in the Lords such as Liverpool. Perceval discussed the matter with Liverpool, who agreed with him that as Leader of the House of Commons he could not be expected to serve under Canning. Canning and Perceval discussed Perceval's becoming leader without Canning, with Canning pointing out that Perceval would have double strength as First Lord and Chancellor, and Perceval responding elegantly: 'It may be very true that any man who holds both these offices is of twice the weight in importance and public opinion; but Canning single is of more Parliamentary strength than Perceval doubled.'[67]

Then, on 10 September, Canning decided that the Walcheren expedition, which had seized the island of Walcheren but failed to take Antwerp, had effectively ended and demanded fulfilment of Portland's promise. Liverpool, seeing that Portland's health was no longer adequate to deal with this crisis, persuaded him to resign, and the government fell.

Perceval, Liverpool and Eldon consulted and, after obtaining the King's reluctant agreement, agreed that Perceval and Liverpool should approach Grey and Grenville to see whether a coalition could be formed. The remainder of the Cabinet, with the exception of Granville Leveson-Gower, agreed to stand together and to support the King.

At this point Castlereagh discovered what had been going on behind his back and, reasonably by the standards of 1809, challenged Canning to a duel. Being Anglo-Irish (who were renowned for their duelling propensity) and having fought a duel in his youth, Castlereagh knew he had an advantage against the sedentary blowhard Canning. They met on Putney Heath at 6 a.m. on 21 September. Shots were exchanged, Canning still refused to apologise, and second shots were fired. Canning's shot was deflected by a button on Castlereagh's coat while Castlereagh's shot inflicted a flesh wound on Canning's thigh. Castlereagh returned home after the duel and Liverpool called on him later that day, indicating where his sympathies lay.

Although this duel excluded both ministers from the next government (duelling was illegal), Castlereagh was back in office as Foreign Secretary just over two years later, whereas Canning's exile was of longer duration (mostly

67. Abbot, *The Diaries and Correspondence of Charles Abbot*, Vol. 2, p. 203.

through his own fault). It must be said, however, that the experience was salutary in terms of Canning's behaviour. From now on, while he was still an intriguer, his behaviour towards his Cabinet colleagues was less impossibly devious and inconsiderate than it had been on several occasions before 1809.

With Canning was now out of the picture, Liverpool could have taken the premiership himself, but the new government, without either Castlereagh or Canning, was bound to be weak in Commons debating talent. (Even if Grenville and Grey had joined, they were both in the Lords, and their young heir-apparent, Henry Petty, was about to succeed as third Marquess of Lansdowne, as his brother was terminally ill.) Thus, Liverpool deferred again to Perceval and might never have become Prime Minister, had Perceval lived.

Grey (based in Northumberland) refused to come to London to discuss any possible arrangement and Grenville came to London determined to reject any arrangement. Thus, Perceval was compelled to form an administration with little experienced talent. Marquess Wellesley, now attached to the government (thereby keeping Canning to some extent in line), was made Foreign Secretary. That filled Canning's place but still left a gap for a third Secretary of State. An attempt to recruit Robert Dundas[68] as Secretary of State for War and the Colonies was vetoed by his father, Melville, who wanted a Cabinet position himself, presumably as a sign his name had been cleared after the impeachment.

In the event, the gap was filled by Harrowby's brother, Richard Ryder,[69] a close friend of Perceval but not otherwise especially qualified for high office, although he was a useful Commons support to Perceval. Since Ryder, like his brother, was said to suffer from poor health, it was thought impossible to put him into the stressful War and the Colonies post. Thus, Liverpool was transferred to War and the Colonies, by far the busiest post in government during a major war – 'of a much more anxious nature'[70] than the Home Office, as Liverpool wrote to the King – while Ryder was given the relatively light duties of the Home Office. Ryder like his brother lived decades longer but his delicacy was used to explain the transfer to George III, who had daily contact with the Home Secretary and was close to Liverpool.

Elsewhere in the reshuffle, Granville Leveson-Gower by mutual agreement left the position of Secretary at War, which was filled by the young Lord Palmerston,[71] the first of a new generation of Tory ministers. Palmerston was one

68. Robert Dundas (1771-1851). 2nd Viscount Melville from 1811. MP for Hastings, Rye and Midlothian, 1794-1811. President of the Board of Control, 1807-09, 1809-12. Chief Secretary for Ireland, 1809. First Lord of the Admiralty, 1812-27, 1828-30.
69. Richard Ryder (1766-1832). MP for Tiverton, 1795-1830. Home Secretary, 1809-12.
70. Aspinall, The Later Correspondence of George III, Vol. 5, pp. 428-29.
71. Henry John Temple (1784-1865). 3rd Viscount Palmerston (Irish) from 1802. MP for Newport, Cambridge University, Bletchingley, Hampshire South and Tiverton, 1807-65. Secretary at War, 1809-28. Turned Whig, 1830. Foreign Secretary, 1830-41, 1846-52. Home Secretary, 1852-55. Prime Minister, 1855-58, 1859-65. Lord Warden of the Cinque Ports, 1861-65.

of no fewer than five up-and-comers to be offered the Exchequer (presumably because of his studies in political economy at Edinburgh University under Dugald Stewart)[72] but modestly demurred as did the other four, so in the end Perceval kept the Exchequer himself. The second significant such addition for the future, Robert Peel, was to succeed Liverpool's brother a year later as one of the Under-Secretaries for War.

Liverpool in his last days as Home Secretary oversaw the modest arrangements for George III's Jubilee, held on 25 October 1809, at the beginning of the King's fiftieth year on the throne. The King and other members of the Royal Family attended a private service in Windsor, followed by a grand fête and firework display at Frogmore. On the same day, the Lord Mayor and Corporation rode in procession to a service of thanksgiving at St Paul's Cathedral, followed by a dinner at the Mansion House. It was the first such Royal Jubilee celebration, setting a pattern for the subsequent such celebrations of Victoria, George V and Elizabeth II.

The Secretaryship of State for War and the Colonies was the first office in which Liverpool really distinguished himself. As Foreign Secretary, he had at first been overmatched, though he grew into the job, but his introversion was always a problem given the Foreign Secretary's busy schedule of interactions with foreign Ambassadors – even George III remarked on their hostility to him.[73] However, his experience was to enable him to provide helpful advice to Castlereagh in the vital period of 1812-15. As Home Secretary, he was neither an imaginative reformer like Peel, nor did he have the opportunity to prove his mettle against major outbreaks of sedition, as did Dundas (1791-94), Portland (1794-1801) and Sidmouth (1812-22).

Liverpool's principal interest throughout his career, inherited from his father, was economic policy, in which he was to excel throughout his tenure as Prime Minister. As War Secretary, he inherited some knowledge of logistics from his father's period as Secretary at War in 1778-82 and was to prove himself highly capable both as administrator and as military/economic strategist.

The office Liverpool was to occupy had been created only in 1794 (with the Colonies added in 1801) to give Dundas one of three secretaryships of state after he made room at the Home Office for Portland. It covered military strategy and most logistical matters and was distinctly senior to the non-Cabinet Secretary at War, which office was, as Liverpool described, 'the finance minister of the

72. Dugald Stewart (1753-1828). Professor of Moral Philosophy, University of Edinburgh, 1785-1810. Gave the first undergraduate course in political economy, attended by Lord Palmerston, 1800-1.

73. Hay, *Lord Liverpool*, p. 81, quoting George Rose, *The Diaries and Correspondence of the Rt Hon. George Rose* (London: R. Bentley, 1860), Vol. 2, p. 157, from a diary entry of 30 September 1804, relating a meeting with George III at Weymouth. The contempt for Liverpool expressed by George III in that entry is incompatible with multiple other sources confirming that the King liked and esteemed him. The entry thus reflects either Rose's own disdain for Liverpool or the Royal malady in action.

Army'.[74] Armaments were covered by the Master-General of the Ordinance, although Chatham (forced to resign in May 1810) and Mulgrave were less senior figures than the third Duke of Richmond had been in 1784-95.[75]

Finally, the Commander-in-Chief remained responsible for the army as a whole, including promotions. This office was filled by Sir David Dundas,[76] respected but without much political clout, in 1809-11, followed by the return of the Duke of York in May 1811. York had plenty of political clout, but as heir-apparent to the Regency and later the throne for all but ten months in 1817 (between Princess Charlotte's majority and her death), he had responsibilities far beyond the army. Liverpool, as the keystone member of the Cabinet with a close Royal relationship and Leader of the House of Lords, was thus in overall control of the war from October 1809.

Liverpool's first decision was what to do with the island of Walcheren and the British expedition to it. At a Cabinet on 27 October, the majority opinion was that retaining Walcheren as a naval station made no sense if Austria and France concluded a peace treaty (as indeed they had on 14 October, although this was not yet known in London). Liverpool therefore requested a formal report from the Admiralty on the subject, as well as a report from civil engineers on the requirements for destroying Walcheren's fortifications. He also recommended the sick to be removed immediately from Walcheren island, and a force of 4,000 to 5,000 men to be moved to the Kent coast to reinforce Walcheren if necessary.[77] Eventually, all fortifications on the island were destroyed, and by Christmas the entire force had returned home.

The other more important strategic decision awaiting Liverpool related to the Peninsula. Sir Arthur Wellesley, leading an Anglo-Spanish army, had won a substantial tactical victory over the French under Marshal Soult[78] at the Battle of Talavera, on 27-28 July, after which he was created Viscount Wellington. However, he was then forced by Soult to retreat into Portugal, leaving Spanish forces to face a series of defeats by the French (Arzobispo, Almonacid, Ocaña, Alba de Tormes) in late 1809, followed by a French advance to besiege the

74. Quoted in the entry on Palmerston in Fisher, *The History of Parliament.*
75. Charles Lennox, 3rd Duke of Richmond (1735-1806). Master General of the Ordnance, 1782-83, 1784-95. Uncle of the 4th Duke.
76. David Dundas (1735-1820). Colonel, British Army, 1782, Major-General, 1790, Lieutenant General, 1797, General, 1802, Commander-in-Chief, 1809-11. PC, 1809. KB, 1803. GCB, 1815.
77. Letter to the King, 28 October 1809, Aspinall, *The Later Correspondence of George III*, p. 429.
78. Jean-de-Dieu Soult (1769-1851). Duke of Dalmatia from 1808. Brigadier, French Army, 1794, Major-General, 1799, Marshal, 1804. Austerlitz, 1805. Jena, 1806. Peninsula, 1808-12, 1813-14. Royalist Minister of War, 1814-15. Bonapartist Peer of France, 1815. Chief of Staff at Waterloo, 1815. Restored to Marshal of France, 1820. Peer, 1827. Marshal General of France, 1830. Minister of War, 1830-34, 1840-44. Prime Minister, 1832-34, 1839-40, 1840-47.

Spanish government in Cádiz. On 20 October, Wellington had ordered the construction of the defensive Lines of Torres Vedras north of Lisbon, but they would not be ready until the following year. Thus, when Liverpool took over, it was unclear whether Wellington could survive in the Peninsula against the much larger French armies, and what he could achieve.

The underlying problem was financial, as Liverpool understood well. Public spending had reached £65.5 million in 1801, the last full year of the French Revolutionary Wars, and revenues notably failed to keep up, being only £39.1 million, 14.8 per cent of GDP against spending's 24.8 per cent of GDP. (Viewed in that light, the Peace of Amiens looks a considerably better deal for Britain.) Spending rose further, to £71.4 million in 1805 (not surprisingly, with Trafalgar and the failed expedition to North Germany), then plateaued in the following two years before rising to £78 million in 1808 and £81.5 million in 1809, at 25.1 per cent of GDP a level that could be sustained but not increased.

Revenues had done rather better. Addington's 1803 income tax reform and Lord Henry Petty's 1806 income tax hike raised tax revenues to 20 per cent of GDP in 1806-07, and Perceval's combination of sound administration and tweaking the tax system raised them further, to 21.2 per cent of GDP by 1809. Again, this was a level that could be sustained but not increased except in the short term (many modern governments gouge double this percentage of GDP out of their taxpayers, but they don't have the great majority of the population living close to subsistence).

The deficit, at 3.8 per cent of GDP in 1809, had been kept much better under control than under Pitt – an average of 4.0 per cent of GDP in 1803-10 compared with an average 8.9 per cent of GDP in 1793-1801. (The suspension of gold convertibility in February 1797 is unsurprising when one considers that the deficit in the year to October 1797 was a horrifying 15.9 per cent of GDP.)[79] Pitt's claims to be a master government financier fell apart in the heat of war; it was his less famous and flamboyant successors, Addington, Petty, Perceval and later the Liverpool/Vansittart duo, who enabled the Napoleonic Wars to be financed without bankruptcy.

Government deficits at this period were financed by two means. One was short-term (normally one-year) Exchequer bills, bought by the public market or the Bank of England (which normally acted as backstop) and bearing interest at say three pence or 3½ pence per day per £100 (equivalent to 4.56 or 5.32 per cent per annum). Long-term financing consisted primarily of Consols, perpetual bonds mostly bearing a three per cent annual interest rate but

79. GDP: Website ukpublicspending.co.uk. Income and expenditure: B.R. Mitchell (ed.), *British Historical Statistics* (Cambridge: Cambridge University Press, 2011) p. 581 – Income, p. 587 – Expenditure. The year-end for years from 1801 onwards is 5 January. Thus, in order to get the figures for the (approximate) calendar years 1801, 1805 and 1809, it is necessary to use the 1802, 1806 and 1810 figures in the tables. The GDP figures may well be inaccurate but the relative movements are probably about right.

issued at a deep discount in wartime (when interest rates were high), normally through one large financing on Budget Day each year. Thus, a budget deficit of £10 million might require the government to issue £18 million nominal in three per cent Consols. The large annual bond issue was then expected to be used partly to refund outstanding Exchequer bills, with mid-year financing needs met by new issues of Exchequer bills.

It is thus unsurprising that Perceval could find no takers for the job of Chancellor of the Exchequer among the administration's up-and-comers. It would have required an even more self-confident and ambitious young man than Palmerston (or a foolish one) to take on the delicate balance of British public finance in late 1809, when spending, taxation, deficits and debt were all so close to unsustainable levels. Indeed, Huskisson as Secretary to the Treasury had prepared a report during the summer (he resigned with Canning in September) stating that expenses must be reduced or Britain would face national bankruptcy. Fortunately, an upturn in trade in 1809-10 provided extra revenues that allowed existing expense levels to be maintained.

Given these financial constraints, the central principle of Liverpool's military strategy was put most clearly in a letter to Wellington in September 1810 (though he had already made the point in his House of Lords speech in June 1809):

> The question, in short, must come to this. We must make an option between a steady and continued exertion on a moderate scale, and a great and extraordinary effort for a limited time, which neither our means, military or financial, will enable us to maintain permanently. If it could be hoped that the latter would bring the contest to a speedy and successful conclusion, it would certainly be the wisest course; but unfortunately, the experience of the last fifteen years is not encouraging in this respect.[80]

It was this central conclusion that made Liverpool a more successful strategist than Pitt; he realised that the economy of Britain and her empire was far solider than that of Napoleon's regime and that moderate pressure applied over several years was most likely to bring final success. When the crisis came, in 1813-14, Liverpool pushed the British economy and taxation base to its limits and achieved his objective, but it was the steady pressure over a prolonged period which led to the opportunity for final success. Pitt's coalitions, maintained for short periods and based on exceptional strains to the British economy and government finance all failed, as did the Fifth Coalition of 1809. It was Liverpool's strategy of moderate pressure, backed by a sounder and more productive system of government finance than Pitt had created, which was to win the day.

80. Liverpool to Wellington, 10 September 1810, quoted in Yonge, *The Life and Administration of Robert Banks Jenkinson*, Vol. 1, pp. 334-37.

This is not to say that, once the correct strategy had been identified, it was easy to execute. By 1809, after sixteen years of war, British finances were in an overstretched situation. Ratcheting up the pressure on Napoleon's Empire required a careful balancing of Britain's financial condition and the resources needed for success. Too little and Napoleon would score military successes or battles of attrition that would destroy Britain's effort. Too much and Britain would descend into bankruptcy. It says much for Liverpool's military relationship with Wellington and his understanding of the financial markets in which Britain raised money that, first alongside Perceval and then assisted by Vansittart, he navigated the path to British victory. That path was a narrow one; even in June 1813, when success was in sight, the government's short-term cash flow became very difficult for a month or so, until news of Wellington's victory at Vitoria provided relief to the markets for British debt.

Liverpool's central strategy applied as much militarily as economically. Napoleon's famous aphorism that 'an army marches on its stomach' did not lead him to any great innovations in keeping that army's stomach filled. Unlike British forces in the Iberian peninsula, Napoleon's armies were expected to provision themselves by purchase or seizure of both food and footwear from the territories through which they marched.

This was no problem in a one-season campaign with high mobility through fertile territories in Germany or Italy. It had already come horribly unstuck during Napoleon's campaign in Egypt and the Middle East in 1798-1801, where lack of success had forced Napoleon to abandon his army and then forced that army to surrender. It was to fail in textbook fashion during Masséna's campaign against the Lines of Torres Vedras in the winter of 1810-11, even though Wellington was to be surprised how well Masséna's army held out. Finally, it failed disastrously, essentially destroying Napoleon's Empire, during the Retreat from Moscow at the end of 1812.

Norman Gash, in his excellent 1984 biography of Liverpool, claims that: 'In the whole panorama of the Napoleonic Wars [the Peninsula campaign] was no more than large-scale diversionary activity – a running ulcer, in the classic phrase, but not a mortal wound.'[81] The Napoleonic Empire, based on the old-fashioned French economy and assembled at lightning speed, had military strength and numbers, but little economic structure supporting it. Accordingly, as Liverpool understood, it was highly vulnerable to steady military and economic pressure, such as Britain applied with the Orders in Council and the Peninsular campaign. Like the Third Reich 130 years later (whose Minister of War Production Albert Speer[82] understood the problem well), it could win extraordinary victories in a short campaign but would be overcome in the long run by attrition from a much stronger and better-organised economic power.

81. Gash, *Lord Liverpool*, p. 82.
82. Albert Speer (1905-81). Architect and, from February 1942, Minister of Armaments and War Production of the Third Reich.

The most important decision to be taken by Liverpool when he took over at the War Office was whether to maintain Wellington in the Peninsula and what priority to give his efforts. In a private letter of 20 October, Liverpool began by reassuring Wellington:

> I think I may be, perhaps, of more use to you in your command in Portugal than any other person who could be placed in the same situation. Let me know your wants and wishes, and I will do my best for you, though I cannot promise that I will always succeed.[83]

He then asked Wellington a series of questions on the prospects in the Peninsula:

> 1st. As there is every reason to believe peace has been concluded between France and Austria, and that the whole military efforts of France will probably in a short time be directed in consequence of this event against Spain, what is the chance of these efforts being successful: – I mean their leading, with partial exceptions, to the complete subjugation of the country?
>
> 2nd. Would the French be likely to make a serious attack upon Portugal before they had acquired a tolerably quiet possession of every part of Spain north of the Sierra Morena? Are they likely to be able to spare an army sufficient for this purpose, before the north and centre of Spain are subdued?
>
> 3rd. If a serious attack is made by the French on Portugal, what is at present the prospect of successful resistance?
>
> 4th. If resistance is not likely to prove ultimately successful, how far would the British army be endangered, and its embarkation be likely to be prevented, by delaying to withdraw it till the French had penetrated in force into Portugal?[84]

Liverpool continued: 'Though we should not be justified, from want of timely precaution, in sacrificing that army, which formed the greater part of our disposable force, yet it would neither be just nor politic to abandon Portugal before such a measure was absolutely necessary.'[85]

Wellington responded on 14 November that the French would have to provide a very large reinforcement indeed to subjugate Spain, that they were likely to attack Portugal before subduing Spain, that successful resistance

83. Quoted in Rory Muir, *Wellington: The Path to Victory, 1769-1814* (New Haven, CT: Yale University Press, 2013) p. 350.
84. Col. John Gurwood, *The Dispatches of Field Marshal the Duke of Wellington*, 12 vols (London: John Murray, 1836-39) Vol. 5, p. 280.
85. Quoted in Yonge, *The Life and Administration of Robert Banks Jenkinson*, Vol. 1, p. 302.

was likely and that Wellington was confident of successful re-embarkation of the army if necessary. He also asked for an additional subsidy of £130,000 per annum to raise the pay of Portuguese officers and requested an overall establishment of British forces of 30,000 effectives to be maintained in Portugal. Given the disruption caused by war, the Portuguese government was running a large budget deficit, and the British subsidy of £500,000 annually would not be enough to stabilise its finances.

Liverpool laid this letter before the Cabinet, together with a statement of the reinforcements needed, and before the end of the year was able to promise Wellington that the Peninsula would receive the government's priority attention, that his army would be maintained at a level of 30,000 men as he wished, through the addition of 5,000 reinforcements, and that the subsidies to Portugal would be increased from £600,000 to £980,000 annually. It was also agreed that the Peninsula would take priority; as Liverpool wrote to Wellington the following June: 'When I accepted the seals of the War Department I laid it down as a principle that, if the war was to be continued in Portugal and Spain, we ought not to suffer any part of our efforts to be directed to other objects.'[86]

By this time, Liverpool was already wondering how the Peninsula war could be expanded, writing to Wellington about the possibility of supporting the eastern Spanish provinces, where resistance to French occupation had been especially strong. He also warned Sir John Stuart[87] that any attempt to take over the Ionian islands using forces from Sicily must not be allowed to weaken the forces in the Peninsula. Nevertheless, the cost, over a prolonged period, would be stupendous: 'I do not believe as great a continued effort has ever been made by this country, combining the military and pecuniary aid together, as His Majesty is making for Portugal and Spain,'[88] wrote Liverpool to Wellington in December. Step by step, the two able strategists were to piece together a path to victory, to be achieved over the next five years.

At this most difficult moment for the government, as a result of Portland's death, the Chancellorship of Oxford University came up for election. The Oxford MAs who made up the electorate were predominantly Tory and strongly opposed to Catholic Emancipation, so Liverpool had an excellent *a priori* chance of election. However, as the Duke of Beaufort,[89] with extensive connections with the university, was known to be interested Liverpool withdrew, to avoid

86. Quoted in Yonge, *The Life and Administration of Robert Banks Jenkinson*, Vol. 1, p. 331.
87. John Stuart (1759-1815). KB 1806. GCB, 1815. Colonel, British Army, 1794, Major-General, 1802. Won Battle of Maida, 1806. Lieutenant General, 1807. Commander, Mediterranean, 1807-10.
88. Quoted in Yonge, *The Life and Administration of Robert Banks Jenkinson*, Vol. 1, p. 316.
89. Henry Charles Somerset (1766-1835). 6th Duke of Beaufort from 1803. MP for Monmouth, Bristol and Gloucestershire, 1788-1803. Lord Lieutenant of Brecknock, 1803-35, Monmouthshire, 1803-35, and Gloucestershire, 1810-35. KG, 1805.

splitting the Tory vote against the Whig and pro-Emancipation Grenville. In the event, the vote was split anyway, because Eldon entered at the last moment, and the result was an unexpected victory for Grenville.[90] Grenville was to serve until his death in 1834, to be succeeded by Wellington.

When the new session began, Liverpool was initially doubtful of survival, as he wrote to Wellington in December: 'It is impossible to form any calculation yet of our strength in Parliament. We have some awkward questions to manage at the outset (particularly that of Walcheren) which must put us under considerable difficulties. I trust however that by patience and temper we shall get through them.'[91]

In the event, the opposition overreached itself by condemning both Walcheren and the Peninsula and attempting to censure the ministry without any inquiry having been held. No doubt the apparently feeble state of the government encouraged the opposition to think that with one good shove they could remove it but, by overplaying their hand, they ended by cementing the administration in office.

Grenville had an additional motive: he believed that, by attacking the administration, in general, and Castlereagh's management of Walcheren, in particular, he could attract Canning to his side, in which case the administration would have quickly bitten the dust. In the event, Canning had learned his lesson from the troubles of past years and remained more or less favourable to the government, so much so that in the spring Perceval approached Canning, Castlereagh and Sidmouth to attempt to strengthen the government by including all three; the attempt fell apart on Sidmouth's refusal to work with Canning.

The sclerotic and now ancient St Vincent began intemperately in the debate on the Lord Commissioners' speech opening the session:

> I will maintain, my Lords, that we owe all our disasters and disgrace to the ignorance and incapacity of His Majesty's present administration. But what could the nation expect from men who came into office under the mask of vile hypocrisy, and have maintained their places by imposture and delusion.[92]

Grenville then moved an amendment condemning the ministry for subjecting the country to 'unexampled calamity and disgrace', an extreme move when the House had not yet been provided with the necessary documents to consider the question.

---

90. Subject of an excellent Gillray cartoon, *Introduction of the Pope to the Convocation at Oxford, by the Cardinal Broad-Bottom*, 1 December 1809. Copy in my possession.
91. Quoted in Yonge, *The Life and Administration of Robert Banks Jenkinson*, Vol. 1, p. 317.
92. Hansard, *Parliamentary Debates from the Year 1803 to the Present Time*, Vol. 15, col. 7 (23 January 1810).

The extremism of the attack made it easier for Liverpool, winding up for the government. He defended the Portuguese and Spanish campaigns as thoroughly beneficial to Britain and claimed that the Walcheren expedition had been undertaken partly to remove the fortifications at the mouth of the Scheldt, a purely British objective. He also claimed that, by retaining Walcheren until the winter rather than evacuating quickly, Britain had improved the peace terms for Austria – that claim, at least, looks like a stretch. In the event, Grenville's amendment was defeated by a majority of 144 to 92.

Three days later the opposition again overplayed its hand by attempting to block the customary vote of congratulation to Wellington for his victory at Talavera. Liverpool set out Wellington's tactical mastery at the battle and the valour shown by British troops in that important defensive victory. He ended by rejoicing that the 'nation of shopkeepers', as Napoleon had called Britain, had 'the good fortune to unite a military spirit with our commercial pursuits'.[93] After a further supporting speech by Wellesley, the motion was carried without a division, as was the vote of a pension to Wellington.

Grenville returned to the attack in February, in a debate on the alliance with Portugal: 'Would anyone say, that in the present situation of affairs in Portugal and Spain, there was the least ground of rational expectation of success?' Liverpool focussed on the attitude of the Spanish and Portuguese themselves, pointing out that the Spanish populace were the first in Europe to rise actively against French occupation, instead of remaining neutral:

> What was the feeling of the people of Spain, even in that awful moment of national convulsion and existing revolution? It was that of the most complete deference to the British minister and government; and so perfect was their confidence in both, that they placed their fleet under the command of a British admiral.[94]

Grenville's amendment was defeated, though by only a modest majority of 124 to 94. Liverpool could breathe a sigh of relief that the main thrust of opposition attack had been on the Peninsula campaign and not on the much more questionable Walcheren fiasco.

Late in the session, Grey proposed a general motion of censure compounding the administration's military strategy, its controls over foreign trade, its excessive issues of paper money, the lack of government economy and a breach of parliamentary privilege by the House of Commons in imprisoning Sir Francis Burdett in the Tower.[95] Liverpool began his response by citing the

93. Ibid., cols 131-36 (26 January 1810).

94. Ibid., cols 511-25 (Grenville), 525-29 (Liverpool) (22 February 1810).

95. Sir Francis Burdett (1770-1844). 5th Baronet from 1797. MP for Boroughbridge, Middlesex, Westminster and Wiltshire North, 1796-1804, 1805-44. Radical early in his career, Tory after 1832. He had condemned the House of Commons for

mob's intimidation of the National Assembly during the French Revolution, saying: 'With such a dreadful example before their eyes, I am astonished how any persons of consequence can be found in this country to urge the necessity of yielding to any expressions of popular sentiment, not conveyed through the legitimate medium.'

After a further defence of the Peninsular campaign and of the administration's decision to assist the Spanish uprising, he moved on to the overall state of the economy, which the ten per cent increase in tax revenue from 1807 to 1809 (on his figures – modern analysis suggests about eight per cent) showed was flourishing. He concluded that the French had altogether been driven out of the West Indies, which had never been achieved before.[96] Grey's motion was defeated by 134 votes to 72.

The other half of Liverpool's administrative responsibility, Britain's colonies, took up considerable time. The conjuncture of the two responsibilities under a single Secretary of State would have made synergistic sense in the eighteenth century, when wars were undertaken to obtain colonies (or in the American War, to keep them). It made less sense in the context of a major global conflict in which after 1803 colonies were of modest relevance. Indeed, the office's responsibilities were to be split in 1854, during the next significant conflict. Nevertheless, with senior ministers so lacking during the Perceval administration, the consolidation had the virtue of centralisation.

Of most immediate importance were developments in Canada. Pitt and Grenville's 1791 Act had divided the colony into Upper Canada, inhabited largely by Anglophone Protestants, and Lower Canada, inhabited largely by Francophone Catholics thought to be sympathetic to Napoleon. The Governor General, Sir James Craig,[97] wrote to Liverpool in the summer of 1810 suggesting changes in the 1791 Act which he thought might mollify the Francophones of Lower Canada.

Liverpool's response, after consulting the Attorney General[98] and the Master of the Rolls,[99] demonstrates his mastery of the problem:

---

imprisoning the radical orator John Gale Jones, was himself charged with contempt and committed to the Tower after barricading himself in his house for two days. He was released after the session ended.

96. Hansard, *Parliamentary Debates from the Year 1803 to the Present Time*, Vol. 17, cols 533-78 (Grey), 578-85 (Liverpool) (13 June 1810).

97. Sir James Craig (1748-1812). Fought in the Battle of Bunker Hill, 1775, and the defence of Quebec, 1775-76. Major-General, 1794. Governor of Cape Colony, 1795-97. Lieutenant General, India, 1801. Governor General of British North America, 1807-11.

98. Sir Vicary Gibbs (1751-1820). MP for Totnes, Great Bedwyn and Cambridge University, 1804-12. Solicitor General, 1805-6. Attorney General, 1807-12.

99. Sir William Grant (1752-1832). MP for Shaftesbury, Windsor and Banffshire, 1790-93, 1794-1812. Solicitor General, 1799-1801. Master of the Rolls, 1801-18.

> You may rely upon it, that if the subject of the constitution of Canada was brought under the discussion of the British Parliament, the cause of the Canadians would be supported by all the democrats and friends of reform in this country. It would most probably receive the support likewise, under present circumstances, of Lord Grenville, the original framer of the Act of 1791, and of his friends. The support of so powerful a combination, even if it was for the moment successfully resisted, could not fail to have the effect of encouraging the factious and disaffected in Canada. They would look to the chance of their friends coming into Government for a revision and alteration of the system which might at this time be adopted. In short, we would have the game of the American war played over again.
>
> The object of Opposition would be, in the first instance, to embarrass the Government, but by the measures they would adopt for that purpose they might separate the North American colonies from the mother country. . . . We are therefore of the opinion that the great object ought to be to keep the subject of Canada out of Parliament as long as possible, unless a connexion could be proved between the popular party in Canada and the Government of France.[100]

The attack by the United States only two years later cemented Canada's loyalty to Britain and made Liverpool's fears of its tendency to rebellion seem excessive. Still, Liverpool had drawn the proper lessons from his father's experiences forty years earlier. The poisonous feedback between irresponsible House of Commons radicals and potentially rebellious colonists would not repeat itself under Liverpool.

The 'War and the Colonies' synergy of Liverpool's responsibilities was significant during this period of the Napoleonic Wars, when the French and British embargoes restricted European trade. There were several remarkable successes in these years adding to Liverpool's colonial responsibilities. While most such expeditions were naval, thus, primarily the responsibility of the First Lord of the Admiralty, Lord Mulgrave or, from May 1810, Charles Philip Yorke,[101] the overall strategy was Liverpool's.

Britain had been steadily capturing French islands in the West Indies from 1804 and, in February 1810, finally eliminated France from the region by capturing Guadeloupe, the last French bastion. This gave Britain an integrated and lucrative West Indian empire for the next five years, until Britain handed back most of the captured West Indies possessions to France in 1815.

---

100. Quoted in Yonge, *The Life and Administration of Robert Banks Jenkinson*, Vol. 1, pp. 312-14.

101. Charles Philip Yorke (1764-1834). MP for Cambridgeshire, St Germans and Liskeard, 1790-1818. Home Secretary, 1803-4. First Lord of the Admiralty, 1810-12.

In the Indian Ocean, a British force under Commodore Josias Rowley,[102] 'the Sweeper of the Seas', captured Réunion (called Île Bonaparte by the French at that time, thus increasing the triumph) in July 1810 – it was the subject of Liverpool's last letter to the King before darkness fell on His Majesty.[103] Then, in December 1810, with reinforcements from Vice-Admiral Albemarle Bertie,[104] he captured Mauritius, thus eliminating the French from the Indian Ocean. Réunion was handed back at the peace treaty but Mauritius was kept, giving Britain control over the Indian Ocean and the passage to India.

Finally, in the East Indies, Britain captured the Dutch stronghold of Ambon (Amboyna) in February 1810, gaining control of the Molucca Islands. The same year, France formally annexed Holland, making Dutch possessions fair game for British attacks. Thus, in the following year Stamford Raffles,[105] of the East India Company's service, persuaded the Governor General, Lord Minto, to mount a naval expedition against Java, which was captured in August 1811, thereby ending the war in the East Indies. Liverpool gave full credit to Minto for the successes in Indonesia and promised him that the Prince Regent would grant him a step in the peerage as soon as the Regency restrictions were lifted.[106]

The additions to Britain's colonial possessions, extending over three continents, at a time when Napoleon was at the height of his powers in Continental Europe, vindicate further Liverpool's belief that Napoleon's empire had severe economic and strategic weaknesses, and that steady pressure would bring it down. By ending the French presence in the West Indies and the Dutch presence in the East Indies, Liverpool made Britain's economic war on France more effective, forcing France's allies and neutral states in Europe to buy West Indian sugar and East Indian spices from British possessions and through British channels.

In the summer of 1810, Liverpool was compelled to address colonial policy in another form, with the burgeoning of the independence movement in the Spanish colonies of Latin America. The council of Caracas, Venezuela forcibly

102. Josias Rowley (1765-1842). 1st Baronet from 1813. Captain, Royal Navy, 1795, Rear-Admiral, 1814, Commander-in-Chief, Ireland, 1818-21, Vice-Admiral, 1825, Admiral, 1837. Commander-in-Chief, Mediterranean, 1833-37. MP for Kinsale, 1821-26.

103. Letter to the King, 24 October 1810, cited in Aspinall, *The Later Correspondence of George III*, pp. 637-38.

104. Albemarle Bertie (1755-1824). 1st Baronet from 1812. Captain, 1782. Played inglorious role in Glorious First of June 1794. Rear-Admiral, 1804, Vice-Admiral, 1808, Admiral, 1814.

105. Thomas Stamford Raffles (1781-1826). Knighted, 1817. FRS. Lieutenant Governor of Java, 1811. Governor General of the Dutch East Indies, 1813-16. Founded Singapore, 1819.

106. Minto was created Earl of Minto in 1813.

deposed the Spanish Captain General Vicente Emparán[107] on 19 April 1810 and formed the Supreme Junta of Caracas, which appealed to Britain for help, through Brigadier General Lidyard, the Governor of Curaçao.

Liverpool responded on 29 June:

> In conformity to these sentiments, and the obligations of justice and good faith, his Majesty must discourage every step tending to separate the Spanish provinces in America from the mother country in Europe. If however, contrary to his Majesty's wishes and expectation, the Spanish state in Europe should be condemned to submit to the yoke of the common enemy, whether by real compulsion, or a convention that should leave only the shadow of independence, on the same principles his Majesty would think it his duty to afford every kind of assistance to the provinces of America that should render them independent of French Spain, . . . and preserve the remains of the monarchy to their lawful sovereign, if ever he should recover his liberty.[108]

Liverpool ended by suggesting that the Caracas Junta had been misled about the desperate state of affairs in Spain and would be happy to rejoin the Empire once the Spanish monarch was back in full control. The letter, which reflected Liverpool's own deep distrust of populist independence movements, was copied to the Council of Regency in Cádiz and published there. It removed for the remainder of the war and several years thereafter any ambiguity about British attitudes to Latin American independence.

The major question at the end of the 1810 session, to occupy Liverpool for the next decade, was monetary policy, notably the report of the Bullion Committee published on 8 June. The gold price, which had been set at £3/17/10½d for an ounce of 22-carat gold (£4.25 per ounce of pure gold) by Sir Isaac Newton[109] in 1717, had risen by about fifteen per cent after the suspension of convertibility in February 1797. The Bullion Committee had been set up in February 1810, following a series of letters in late 1809 in the Whig *Morning Chronicle* by David Ricardo[110] (not yet an MP), which were

107. Vicente Emparán (1747-1842). Captain General of Venezuela, 1809-10. I can alas find no biographical information on Brigadier General Lidyard, not even a mention in the 1811 Army List. Curaçao was captured by the naval Captain Charles Lydiard on 1 January 1807 but he was killed in a storm in December 1808.

108. *Annual Register for the Year 1810* (London: W. Otridge & Son, 1812) quoted pp. 230-31.

109. Isaac Newton (1642-1727) Physicist. Warden of the Royal Mint, 1696-1700; Master of the Mint, 1700-27

110. David Ricardo (1772-1823). MP for Portarlington, 1819-23. Stockbroker, allegedly making £1million from insider trading with knowledge of the Battle of Waterloo. (However, it's unlikely that he and Nathan Rothschild both made big money insider trading on the same event. Probably he simply took a large long position in Consols).

published as a pamphlet, *The High Price of Bullion, a Proof of the Depreciation of Bank Notes,* in January 1810. The committee was chaired by Francis Horner[111] and included among its members, Henry Thornton, William Huskisson and Alexander Baring.[112]

The Bullion Committee was to determine whether the problem was due to shortage of gold supply or excess printing of paper money by the Bank of England. In practice, it appears to have resulted from both causes. The committee was unaware (because it lacked knowledge of future trends) that its report came at the time of maximum gold supply strain on a world seeking to adopt and maintain a gold standard.

Annual global gold production in 1800 was only about 600,000 ounces of gold, of which 400,000 ounces came from Latin America, having risen only 0.5 per cent annually, roughly in line with world output, in the eighteenth century. Gold output did not rise significantly during the next fifteen years of global warfare, while demand for gold rose sharply, as a result of the increase in GDP and in population from early industrialisation and the needs of British troops in the peninsula and French troops throughout Europe. Only after 1823 did Russian production from Ekaterinburg produce a sharp upsurge in global gold production.

Gold production continued to increase markedly later in the nineteenth century, to 1.4 million ounces in 1846, even before the discoveries in California, then to a peak of fifteen million ounces in the late 1890s. Over the nineteenth century new gold supply thus rose at an annual rate of 3.3 per cent, well above the annual rise in real world GDP of around 1.8 per cent.[113]

The committee examined in detail the markets for both gold and silver, which was also about fifteen per cent above the Mint price, a product of silver shortages since the 1790s. At the same time, the value of the pound had declined on the Amsterdam, Hamburg and Paris exchanges, suggesting

---

One of history's foremost economists; his *On the Principles of Political Economy and Taxation* (1817) propounded the doctrine of 'comparative advantage'.

111. Francis Horner (1778-1817). Whig MP for St Ives, Wendover and St Mawes, 1806-12, 1813-17. Son of a Whig Edinburgh merchant, one of the founders of the *Edinburgh Review*. An able, if humourless, man, his early death removed a major link between the Grenville and Grey Whig factions.

112. Alexander Baring (1774-1848). 1st Baron Ashburton from 1835. MP for Taunton, Callington and Thetford, 1806-35. Moderate Whig, breaking from the Whigs over the Reform Bill after Grey had barred him as a *parvenu* from his 1830 government. Second son of Sir Francis Baring, the founder of Barings Bank. Partner in Baring Brothers and Co., 1807-30, where he became the world's leading banker ('the Fifth Great Power') by 1820, ahead of Nathan Rothschild. President of the Board of Trade, 1834-35. Negotiated Webster-Ashburton Treaty with the United States, 1842. Opposed repeal of the Corn Laws, 1846.

113. Gold supply: Website – Info.goldavenue.com. Accessed 2017. GDP: Wikipedia, 'Gross World Product'.

that the problem lay in the domestic currency rather than in the international bullion supply. (The committee was led astray here; the problem lay primarily in excess demand for bullion due to the war without supply rising to match it.) The committee also noticed the wartime inflation, which also suggested that the problem lay primarily in the domestic currency. (Here it was in accordance with modern thinking.)

The committee then examined the increase in paper money issued by the Bank of England and observed:

> It may indeed be doubted whether, since the new system of Bank of England payments has been fully established, Gold has in truth continued to be our measure of value; and whether we have any other standard of prices than that circulating medium . . . the variations of which in relative value may be as indefinite as the possible excess of that circulating medium.[114]

The committee concluded that issuing excess paper money beyond the value of gold held had the same effect on the price of gold as the currency debasement indulged in by Henry VIII. Since the suspension of cash payments in February 1797, the Bank of England had felt no need to restrict their issues of notes and so had issued too many, raising the amount outstanding from £11 million in 1796 to £21.2 million in May 1810 and causing the gold value of the currency to decline, even though efficiency improvements in banking had increased the velocity of money. When country bank notes were added in, 'the increase in the paper currency in the last year . . . would probably be little short of the amount which in any one year since the discovery of America has been added to the circulating coin of the whole of Europe'.[115]

Furthermore, the committee concluded that a change in the gold parity, while resorted to by governments in former times, would be a breach of faith and a dereliction of duty. The suspension of cash payments in gold by the Bank of England should be ended as quickly as possible without waiting for the end of the war. No more than two years should be allowed for the Bank of England to adjust, and the country banks' issue of notes should be ended within a short time thereafter, thereby returning the country to a gold standard at the pre-war parity. The alternative would be a potentially devastating loss of confidence in Britain's ability to meet its obligations.

Liverpool was well aware that, however sound the Bullion Committee's analysis and conclusions, resuming cash payments before the end of the

114. Report from the Select Committee Appointed to Inquire Into the Cause of the High Price of Gold Bullion, and to Take Into Consideration the State of the Circulating Medium, and of the Exchanges Between Great Britain and Foreign Parts (London: J. Johnson and J. Ridgway, 1810) p. 16.

115. Ibid., pp. 70-71.

war would be economically and militarily suicidal. The budgetary strain of maintaining a substantial force in Portugal and providing subsidies to the Portuguese government was simply too great, as was the need for specie to support Wellington. However, the committee's general conclusions were to govern his policy once the war had been won.

The shortage of specie was a continuing hindrance to Wellington's activities in Portugal. Wellington wrote to Liverpool several times upon the subject during 1810 and 1811, barely avoiding a local illiquidity crisis in March 1810 and sending in May a further demand for specie rather than bills (which could be turned into specie only at a ten per cent discount, even in Cádiz, where the Spanish treasure fleets arrived). Liverpool responded in July: 'We cannot expect to carry on a war on a large scale without some difficulties; those of a pecuniary nature are perhaps more trying than any others, but they are, at the same time, most common.'[116]

Wellington's liquidity and that of the Portuguese government was further weakened by the success of British traders in the newly opened markets of Brazil, which diverted traditional specie revenue from Portugal. The following March, Wellington was to estimate to Liverpool that obtaining specie for military expenses in Portugal had cost around £1 million, or a 20 per cent premium on the nominal sum needed.[117] In response, Liverpool attempted to persuade him that Exchequer bills could be used even in Portugal instead of gold and in practice much of Britain's expenditure in Portugal was covered by this means, though Wellington continued through the end of 1811 to demand additional shipments of bullion to Portugal.[118]

The administrative work of the War and the Colonies Department was much heavier than that of Liverpool's earlier positions. The job's intensity may be seen from the fact that a high proportion of the letters in Wellington's correspondence during this period are written to Liverpool, with lengthy letters, sometimes several of them, written weekly when communications were open. Many of these letters are among the most substantial in Wellington's correspondence, while the peninsula was only one of Liverpool's responsibilities.

---

116. Quoted in Yonge, *The Life and Administration of Robert Banks Jenkinson*, Vol. 1, p. 331.
117. Letter to Liverpool, 23 March 1811, in Gurwood, *The Dispatches of Field Marshall the Duke of Wellington*, Vol. 7, pp. 388-92.
118. Gash, op. cit. p86, quoting a monograph by G.D. Knight which he does not name in his bibliography (Lord Liverpool and the Peninsular War, 1809-12, PhD Thesis, University of Florida, 1976), believes £5 million of the £6 million spent in 1810 and £8.25 million of the £9 million spent in 1811 were raised by Exchequer bills. I have strong suspicion of double counting here; Exchequer bills could have been issued to cover purchases of bullion. Wellington's continued complaints of the lack of specie in Portugal (see Gurwood, op. cit., Vol 8 pp. 154-55 and 265-66) also suggests the Gash/Knight figures are in error.

At this early stage of the Peninsular War, the army's quality was not what Wellington might wish: 'I am still apprehensive of the consequences of trying them in any nice operation before the enemy, for they really forget every thing when plunder or wine is within their reach.'[119] Another problem was that Wellington could not promote officers without lengthy reference to the Commander-in-Chief's staff at Horse Guards in London, thus making it difficult to motivate his subordinates. (This problem was alleviated as Wellington's seniority and reputation grew; by 1813-15 the Horse Guards' staff were doing what they were told.)

One of Wellington's early letters to Liverpool contained a lengthy discussion of the methods by which he would carry out the agreed strategy of maintaining a British force in Portugal largely for the defensive purpose of preventing the French from controlling the peninsula securely, which Sir John Moore had claimed to be impossible over a long period.[120] However, there was also considerable discussion of what should happen if Wellington was forced to evacuate Portugal, in which he expressed a preference for going to Gibraltar rather than joining the mixed Spanish/British forces around Cádiz.[121]

Apart from providing specie for Wellington, and ensuring various supplies were shipped as requested, including such arcane items as 4,000 water decks for the cavalry,[122] and dealing with Wellington's complaints about sub-standard equipment quality, Liverpool was also engaged in the tricky coordination between Wellington's forces and those assisting the Spanish royalists holding Cádiz, not always to Wellington's satisfaction.

One perennial source of complaint was the appearance of military information or letters from Spanish informants in the press, most of which either favoured the Whig opposition or was part of the Radical network that had grown up during the disturbed 1790s. In general, Wellington and Liverpool shared a disdain and distrust of the newspapers of their time; as Wellington wrote to a Dr Frank in 1811: 'I hope that the opinions of the people of Great Britain are not affected by paragraphs in newspapers, and that those paragraphs do not convey the public opinion or sentiment on any subject.'[123]

Wellington blamed officers sympathetic to the Whigs writing indiscreetly to their contacts in Britain, who then passed the information to the opposition press. Eventually, Liverpool recommended to Wellington that he publish a General Order pointing out the dangers of publication of officers' letters, closing

119. Letter to Liverpool, 11 April 1810, in Gurwood, *The Dispatches of Field Marshal the Duke of Wellington*, Vol. 6, p. 31.
120. Letter to Liverpool, 2 April 1810, in ibid., pp. 5-9.
121. Letter to Liverpool, 30 May 1810, in ibid., pp. 157-8.
122. Letter to Liverpool, 19 April 1810, in ibid., p. 47. A water deck was a piece of canvas, 4 feet x 4 feet, used to cover the saddle when off the horse's back.
123. Letter to Dr Frank, 7 January 1811, in ibid., Vol. 7, p. 116.

the post altogether if necessary, at least for a short time. Wellington responded that the latter course was impossible: 'It could not be done if attempted, and the attempt would be considered an endeavour by an individual to deprive the British public of intelligence, of which the Government and Parliament do not choose to deprive them.'[124]

It is more likely that some opposition and Radical newspapers had correspondents on the ground in Portugal. In the days before a military press office, independent reporters on an allowance from a newspaper could gain information from junior officers and NCOs in Wellington's army, while avoiding coming to the attention of the high command. In two separate complaints to Liverpool, Wellington mentions details of gun emplacement positions and copies of letters written to the senior Spanish commander and published in *The Sun*, a radical newspaper. Both are more likely to have been sourced by journalists on the ground in Portugal rather than through military letters home.[125]

William Howard Russell achieved fame, fortune and journalistic legend by his reports to *The Times* from the Crimea. However, the press 45 years earlier seems to have employed similar on-the-spot correspondents, without Russell's social standing or his care about giving information useful to the enemy.[126] Like many Victorian legends, that of Russell may have been devised to cover up an earlier, more disreputable reality.

1810 was a year of defensive war in the peninsula. Early in the year, Liverpool sent General Thomas Graham[127] to command British forces defending Cádiz, the Spanish seat of government and thought to be crucial to the defence of Portugal. In June Marshal André Masséna[128] invaded Portugal with 65,000 men. There were only a few major events, such as the French capture of Ciudad Rodrigo, the unlucky explosion in August that destroyed Almeida and the defensive Anglo-Portuguese victory at Bussaco in September. Wellington worried about the effect of this on his reputation, writing to Liverpool in August:

124. Gurwood, *The Dispatches of Field Marshal the Duke of Wellington*, Vol. 7, pp. 368-69.
125. See example of one such complaint in the letter to Liverpool, 18 August 1810, in ibid., Vol. 6, p. 342..
126. For example, the lawyer Henry Crabb Robinson reported on a freelance basis for *The Times* in the German campaign of 1805 and the Spanish campaign of 1808.
127. Thomas Graham (1748-1843). 1st Baron Lynedoch from 1814. Whig MP for Perthshire, 1794-1807. A Scottish country gentleman, he joined the army aged 45 in 1793 after his wife died, raising a Perthshire regiment. Moore's *aide-de-camp* at Corunna. Major-General, 1809. Commanded a division in the Walcheren expedition. Lieutenant General, 1810. Cádiz, 1810-11. Won Battle of Barrosa, 1811. Wellington's second-in-command, 1811-14. General, 1821.
128. André Masséna (1758-1817). Duc de Rivoli from 1808. Prince of Essling, 1810. Marshal, 1804. Italy, 1796-97; Switzerland, 1799-1800; Poland, 1807; Austria, 1809; Portugal, 1810-11.

> Nothing can be more irksome to me than the operations which have been carried on for the past year; and it is very obvious that a continuation of the same cautious system will lose the little reputation which I had acquired, and the good opinion of the people of this country.[129]

In response, Liverpool wrote him a long soothing letter stating:

> I am at a loss to conceive upon what grounds you can have supposed that the King's ministers had no confidence in the measures adopted for the defence of Portugal. . . . I never knew a question on which there was less difference of opinion in Cabinet than upon the subject of Portugal . . . the contest never could have been maintained in Portugal during the winter and spring, if it had not been for the determination of Government to persevere in it, at all risks to themselves, against not only the declared opinions of their opponents, but the public remonstrances of many of their friends. . . . I can assure you that you are very much mistaken if you suppose that the defensive system of warfare, which you have felt it necessary and expedient to adopt during the present campaign, has lowered your reputation in this country.[130]

Liverpool then gave Wellington the good news that reinforcements were on the way, so that the total force in Portugal would be brought up to 40,000 effectives, though this addition should be temporary, while such large French forces were active in the country. Generals, as much as the rest of the army, need their morale kept up, and it is to the credit of Liverpool's calm sagacity that he undertook such efforts to achieve this.

Late in the year, Wellington retreated to the newly constructed Lines of Torres Vedras, which the British forces entered during October and, thereafter, Masséna suffered from supply shortages. The principal sufferers were the unfortunate Portuguese locals, who had their food supplies seized by the French army. Wellington was well aware of this and wrote to Liverpool:

> I would therefore beg leave to recommend the unfortunate portion of the inhabitants who have suffered from the enemy's invasion to your Lordship's protection; and I request you to consider of the mode of recommending them to the benevolent disposition of His Majesty's subjects, at the moment which I hope may not be far distant that the enemy may be under the necessity of evacuating the country.[131]

---

129. Letter to Liverpool, 19 August, 1810, in Gurwood, *The Dispatches of Field Marshal the Duke of Wellington*, Vol. 6, pp. 346-48.
130. Quoted in Yonge, *The Life and Administration of Robert Banks Jenkinson*, Vol. 1, pp. 334-37.
131. Letter to Liverpool, 27 October 1810, in Gurwood, *The Dispatches of Field Marshal*

In the event, Masséna remained in Portugal throughout the winter. Wellington, writing to Liverpool in November, described Masséna's Portuguese campaign as having been 'carried on and persevered in against every military principle'[132] and in December described it as 'astonishing that the enemy have been able to remain in Portugal so long; and it is an extraordinary instance of what a French army can do'.[133]

In the last months of 1810 George III began his final descent into old age and insanity, which saddened Liverpool on a personal level and also weakened his political position. The renewed attack of George III's malady was set off by the last illness and death of his favourite daughter, Princess Amelia.[134] The King's last letter was dictated on 26 October and the following day Liverpool wrote to Bathurst: [135] 'I am grieved to be under the necessity of informing you that the agitation arising out of the protracted illness of the poor Princess Amelia has had within these few days a serious effect on the mind of the King, and his situation is become truly alarming.'[136]

At first it seemed likely that the King would recover, as he had before. Since it was feared the appointment of the Prince of Wales as Regent would worsen the King's condition, Ministers felt it their duty to postpone the decision. Conversely, the opposition believed that this would deliver power into their hands, so they wanted to rush the process and make the Regency as unrestricted as possible.

In this belief the opposition leaders, Grey and Grenville were to be proved wrong by the Prince Regent's actions when he assumed power. They may also have underestimated the political changes that had taken place since the Regency Crisis of 1789. If they had formed a government in early 1811, they would have been forced to call an election as they had no majority in the 1807 Parliament. However, the national anti-Catholic feeling, so strong in 1807, would still have run against them in 1811. In addition, the Perceval ministry was beginning to become more popular, because of the progress made in the Peninsular War. With Royal and ministerial powers of patronage substantially reduced from their 1789 level, a Grey/Grenville ministry appointed by the Prince Regent might well have failed to gain a majority even after the election, as would Peel in 1835, forcing the Prince to reappoint Perceval and Liverpool.

the Duke of Wellington, Vol. 6, pp. 519-20.

132. Letter to Liverpool, 3 November 1810, in ibid., Vol. 6, pp. 552-56.
133. Letter to Liverpool, 21 December 1810, in ibid., Vol. 7, pp. 56-60.
134. Princess Amelia of the United Kingdom (1783-1810). Youngest child of George III and Queen Charlotte; a Royal favourite with poor health in her later years. May have had an illegitimate child with the Hon. Charles Fitzroy (1762-1831).
135. Henry Bathurst (1762-1834). 3rd Earl Bathurst from 1794. MP for Cirencester, 1783-94. Master of the Mint, 1804-06 and 1807-12. President of the Board of Trade, 1807-12. Foreign Secretary, 1809. Secretary of State for War and the Colonies, 1812-27. Lord President of the Council, 1828-30.
136. Letter to Bathurst, 27 October 1810, quoted in Aspinall, *The Later Correspondence of George III*, p. 639.

Parliament met on 1 November after the existing prorogation expired. With the King ill, no renewal prorogation was possible, so it was adjourned for the minimum possible period of two weeks. This adjournment was renewed on 15 November, at which time Eldon told the House of Lords the King appeared to be recovering and Grenville and Grey raised mild objections to the repeated adjournments.

However, by 29 November Liverpool's proposal of a third two-week adjournment, after a generally positive report from the King's doctors to the Privy Council, met with serious opposition. Spencer and Moira proposed to replace the adjournment with a summons to the King's physicians to testify before a committee of the House. Then Grenville rose, claiming authority as the only surviving member of the 1788 Cabinet. This was not true. He was Vice-President of the Board of Trade in 1788, subordinate to Jenkinson (also not then in the Cabinet), before succeeding as Speaker (ineligible to join the Cabinet) in January 1789 and Home Secretary with Cabinet membership in June 1789. Also, Chatham (First Lord of the Admiralty) and Buckingham (Lord Lieutenant of Ireland), both 1788 Cabinet members, were still alive and politically active in 1810.

Presumably nobody felt it worthwhile to correct the notoriously peppery Grenville, who then claimed that the government was automatically dissolved and that ministers should be impeached for high crimes and misdemeanours.[137] Even by Grenville standards, this was a notably unhelpful and intemperate contribution at this awkward moment; it may have prejudiced the Prince Regent against appointing him Prime Minister when the Regency was formed the following February. In any case, the adjournment passed by 88 votes to 56.

After the next adjournment, the Houses formed a joint committee to examine the King's doctors, of which Liverpool was naturally a member, then proposed Resolutions which would form the basis of a Regency Bill. Grenville and Holland objected, saying that power should be transferred directly to the Prince of Wales by means of an Address, as the Whig-controlled Irish Parliament had presented in 1788 (this would have given him unrestricted power immediately). However, after a considerable Commons debate, the House presented Resolutions to the Lords on 27 December requiring Parliament to devise a method whereby the Royal Assent could be given to legislation.

Liverpool, in proposing the Resolutions, made a detailed and heavily researched speech that was much admired. He set out as a principle that regencies could only be appointed by Parliament and that there was no presumptive right to a regency in the heir to the throne – thus, in 1751 Princess Augusta, not the Duke of Cumberland, had been appointed prospective Regent for the young George III in case George II should die before his coming of age.

137. Hansard, *Parliamentary Debates from the Year 1803 to the Present Time*, Vol. 18, cols 60-71 (Grenville) (29 November 1810).

Regencies were also almost always restricted, and the exceptions – the Duke of Gloucester for the young Edward V and the Duke of Somerset for the young Edward VI – were not happy precedents.

A Bill appointing the Prince of Wales Regent was thus preferable to an Address asking him to become Regent because, having the Great Seal affixed, it would be binding upon courts of law, who would have to recognise the Regent's authority. Even when the King was incapacitated, the affixing of the Great Seal gave legislation the force of law and only Parliament, not the law courts, could question whether it was properly applied. The Irish Address of 1788 was not fully valid because Buckingham, as Lord Lieutenant, had refused to transmit it to England. Legally, in 1811, unlike in 1688, the state was in full operation and so Parliament could make up the deficiency caused by the King's illness.

The validity of the proceedings had been vindicated by the actions of Parliament in 1789, which was opened under the Great Seal on 3 February, which opening was confirmed by a Commission signed by the King on 10 March, after his recovery. However, Acts of Parliament undertaken between those two dates had been taken as fully valid and property had been transferred according to them.[138]

Despite the opposition of no fewer than seven Royal dukes, the Resolutions were agreed to (a proposed amendment being defeated by 100 votes to 74). On 4 January, Resolutions were proposed to the House establishing a regency under which the Prince Regent would not be able to create peers or alienate Royal property for a year – the purpose of this being to prevent a mass creation of Whig peers by a Regent-appointed Grey/Grenville government while George III was temporarily incapacitated.

Liverpool proposed these Resolutions with an amendment that would have prevented the removal of members of the Royal Household, but the Lords rejected his amendment and passed the Resolutions as sent up by the Commons. Parliament was officially opened by Commission on 15 January, the Regency Bill was passed by both Houses on 5 February and the future George IV assumed the office of Prince Regent, with limitations, on 6 February. The King, who had made a partial recovery, accepted the Regency on the day it passed, partly because of his confidence in the ministers who had passed it.

The opposition leaders expected to be immediately summoned to power but were disappointed. The Prince Regent did not like Grey (he was later to impose a firm veto on Grey being included in any government) and resented the bullying of Grenville. His closest friends among the Whigs were Moira and Sheridan but Sheridan, against his own interests and producing a joint pompous squawk to the Prince Regent from Grey and Grenville, had advised the Prince Regent to maintain the Perceval government in office for now, since

138. Ibid., cols 388-402 (27 December 1810).

its retention would lessen any disturbance to the possibly recovering King. The Prince Regent had communicated this intention to Perceval by letter on 4 February, the day before the Regency Bill passed.

The Perceval government thus remained in office, though its survival would again come into question the following year, when the Regency restrictions expired. The King made a partial slow recovery until July 1811 when he suffered a sharp relapse, after which there was no expectation of him resuming direct rule.

Liverpool's political position was considerably weakened by the Regency. He never had more than a correct relationship with the Prince Regent, whereas both he and his father had been genuine and long-standing friends of George III, essential elements in any government that relied on Royal support. Royal favour had been a unique advantage, shared with few colleagues (maybe only Eldon in Liverpool's time) both to his father throughout his career and to Liverpool in reaching high office and outdistancing colleagues thereafter. However, just as Liverpool lost this advantage, he began to gain a sufficiently impressive track record as Secretary of State for War and the Colonies (a result of progress in the Peninsular War and the string of colonial acquisitions in 1810-11), such that other ministers could no longer reasonably object to him becoming Prime Minister when the opportunity arose.

Liverpool's speech on the Address on 12 February centred on defending the campaign in Spain and Portugal. He pointed out that opposition predictions of British expulsion from Portugal within a few months had not come to pass and that public opinion remained solidly behind the overall policy of helping Spain and Portugal resist the French invasion. He then regretted the effect of the Orders in Council on American commerce and reiterated his intention to be as conciliatory as possible to American interests.[139]

Before the next debate on Portugal, Graham made a sortie against Marshal Victor's[140] forces besieging Cádiz, which had been weakened by demands from Soult, who was besieging Badajoz. Graham's forces sailed to Algeciras, where they landed on 23 February, then met Victor's forces at Barrosa, where they defeated a force double their size in a tactically well fought battle. While this victory had little long-term effect, partly because Spanish forces failed to follow it up, it nevertheless strengthened both Spanish morale and the Anglo-Spanish alliance.

Meanwhile, Wellington was in the process of defeating Masséna. The British army improved in quality and health from its winter at Torres Vedras,[141] a

139. Ibid., cols 1163-67 (12 February 1811).

140. Claude Victor-Perrin (1764-1841). Duc de Belluno from 1808. Toulon, 1793, Marengo, 1800, Governor of Louisiana, 1802-03, Jena, 1806, Friedland, 1807, Marshal, 1807, Portugal 1808-11, Russia 1812. After being berated by Napoleon, switched allegiance to the Bourbons, 1814, accompanying Louis XVIII to Ghent, 1815. Minister of War, 1821-23.

141. 'We are becoming a better and more efficient army every day'; Wellington to Liverpool, 23 February 1811, in Gurwood, *The Dispatches of Field Marshal the Duke of Wellington*, Vol. 7, p. 290-91.

tribute to the efficient commissariat set up by Wellington and Liverpool over the previous year. The French army retired from the Lines of Torres Vedras on 5 March, and retreated into Spain, closely pursued and harried by Wellington's forces and losing many deserters and much equipment.[142] However, further progress in Portugal and around Cádiz was hampered after Badajoz, held by the Spanish, surrendered to Soult's forces. Nevertheless, by April Wellington had at least temporarily liberated Portugal from French occupation.

On 21 March, Wellesley introduced a motion in the Lords for a subsidy of £2 million to Portugal, necessary to equip that impoverished state's armed forces. Grenville repeated his belief that the effort in Spain and Portugal was futile and a waste of £2 million. Liverpool in response pointed out the valuable Portuguese contribution to the Battle of Bussaco and that, while former coalitions had collapsed in a matter of months, the Peninsular effort was now in its third year without France having fully established its authority in any province of Spain.

Graham's victory, Masséna's retreat and their effect on opinion improved the strength of the Perceval ministry. By proposing resolutions applauding Graham's success (he was a Whig), Liverpool and Perceval both disarmed Whig critics of the Peninsular campaign and demonstrated their ability to overcome party prejudice in appointing the best people for the job. Then Wellington's successful pursuit of Masséna reinforced the view that the ministry had a last found both a formula for military success and the generals to carry it out.

The following month, Liverpool proposed a Vote of Thanks to Wellington for his exertions in defeating Masséna's army. He gave a detailed account of the course of the campaign, based on a lengthy summary Memorandum sent to him by Wellington in February,[143] and the rationale for Wellington's defensive approach, paid tribute to his foresight and skill in constructing the Lines of Torres Vedras, and ended by declaiming: 'there has never been a plan of campaign, a series of operations more uniformly successful, or conducted with more manifest and decided skill and spirit'.[144] In response, Grey (though not Grenville) magnanimously admitted that his previous opinion of the likely failure of the Peninsular campaign had been wrong and added his congratulations to Liverpool's.

Earlier in April, Liverpool had tweaked, by means of the Militia Enlistment Bill, the bounty for militia joining the regular army, increasing it to fifteen guineas, in the hope of replacing an additional 10,000 of the roughly 25,000 annual wastage of the Army while on active service. This measure, together with the reports of Peninsular successes, proved effective, and the shortage of men that had afflicted the army since the 1790s abated for the remainder of

---

142. Wellington, in a letter of 9 April 1811 to Liverpool, estimated French losses in the 1810-11 Portuguese campaign as 45,000 men, in ibid., p. 448.
143. Wellington's 'Memorandum', dated 21 February 1811, quoted in ibid., pp. 291-313.
144. Hansard, *Parliamentary Debates from the Year 1803 to the Present Time*, Vol. 19, cols 762-66 (26 April 1811).

the war. The administrative details of war, as well as the finances necessary to sustain it, were essential props of Liverpool's strategy for prolonged pressure on Napoleon's empire.[145]

In February and March, Liverpool had reviewed with Wellington the progress of the Peninsular campaign and the next steps to be taken. Wellington had written that the Spanish Regency was likely to offer him command of Spanish forces and enquiring what position he should take.[146] In his response, Liverpool stated that the 1810 campaign had cost £6 million, compared to annual expenditures of less than £3 million in 1808 and 1809. For 1811, the expense would relate to an army in Portugal of 50,000 men. Thus:

> I am under the necessity of stating it to be the unanimous opinion of every member of the Government, and of every person acquainted with the finances and resources of the country, that it is absolutely impossible to continue our exertions upon the present scale in the Peninsula for any considerable length of time.

If the war could be finished quickly, the costs must be met, but otherwise the scale of operations must be reduced. Accordingly, Britain should not hold out to the Spanish government any prospect of Britain being able to help them materially or with a subsidy in addition to that paid to Portugal. Therefore, Wellington should avoid becoming commander-in-chief of the Spanish armies, except on a limited basis to command those contiguous to Portugal.[147] In the event, Wellington was not made commander of the Spanish armies until after Salamanca in the following year.

In reply, Wellington pointed out that the 1809-10 figures did not include the cost of transports and that the army would cost almost as much to maintain in Britain as in Portugal. He reviewed the strategic advantage of the Peninsular campaign and suggested that Britain should keep the maximum possible proportion of its forces in Portugal. He suggested one saving, by releasing the transports which had been kept in Portugal for an emergency evacuation; with the French in retreat they were no longer necessary. Finally, he suggested that withdrawal from Portugal would almost certainly result in France making another attempt to invade the British Isles, a much more dangerous proposition.[148]

145. See, for example, Wellington's letter to Liverpool of 5 January 1811, concerning officers' ability to transport Merino sheep to England and informing him: 'I can assure you that I have no Merino sheep, and do not intend to have any'; in Gurwood, *The Dispatches of Field Marshal the Duke of Wellington*, Vol. 7, pp. 109-11. Liverpool dealt ably with Merino sheep as well as grand strategy.
146. Letter to Liverpool, 2 February 1811, in ibid., p. 224.
147. Quoted in Yonge, *The Life and Administration of Robert Banks Jenkinson*, Vol. 1, pp. 364-67.
148. Gurwood, *The Dispatches of Field Marshal the Duke of Wellington*, Vol. 7, pp. 388-92.

Liverpool wrote back enquiring what Wellington thought necessary for British troops to maintain themselves in Portugal, what should be done in the peninsula going forward and whether maritime operations on the coast of Spain would help. Wellington responded that 30,000 effectives would be sufficient to maintain the British presence in Portugal and that, after the capture of Badajoz (which proved to be impossible in 1811), British forces should advance into Spain either south to relieve Cádiz or north to liberate northern Spain. Maritime operations on the Spanish coast would be a useless diversion of resources, since they would receive no effective Spanish support without massive subsidies.[149]

While the British forces were now in excellent shape, the Portuguese army, poorly supplied by the Portuguese government (despite British subsidies) and often unpaid, had only 20,000 effectives instead of the 50,000 that were being paid for.[150] As Wellington wrote to Liverpool: 'The unfortunate desire to obtain and retain a vulgar popularity, and to please and flatter the lower orders, which has characterized almost every man who has appeared in a conspicuous situation throughout the recent events in Spain and Portugal, prevented the adoption of any of these [remedial] measures until very lately.'[151]

Wellington's success against Masséna, the partially successful Battle of Fuentes de Oñoro, the successful Battle of Albuera and the recapture of Almeida (partly negated by the failure to recapture Badajoz in June after a two-month siege), together with Grey's generous support for the campaign, removed the need for economies in the Peninsular forces, and allowed a gradual build-up to continue.

Liverpool did not propose a Vote of Thanks for Fuentes de Oñoro, instead proposing one to Beresford,[152] the Spanish General Joaquin Blake[153] and the British, Portuguese and Spanish forces under them for the Battle of Albuera. Wellington agreed that the government was quite right in both judgements.[154] However, Liverpool did bring him one significant reinforcement in June, allowing Graham to leave Cádiz and join Wellington as second-in-command, in which position he remained until September 1813.

Liverpool's last major intervention of the 1811 parliamentary session was on the Bullion Committee report and the general subject of the appreciation in the gold price. The House of Commons had debated the Bill at length, and

149. Ibid., pp. 521-25.
150. Wellington to Liverpool, 1 May 1811, quoted in ibid., Vol. 7, pp. 516-17.
151. Wellington to Liverpool, 30 May 1811, quoted in ibid., Vol. 7, pp. 624-26.
152. William Carr Beresford (1768-1854). 1st Baron Beresford from 1814. Viscount Beresford from 1823. Marquess of Campo Maior (Portugal) from 1812. MP for County Waterford, 1811-14. Captured Buenos Aires, 1806. Commander-in-Chief of the Portuguese army, 1808-20. Master General of the Ordnance, 1828-30.
153. Joaquin Blake (1759-1827). Spanish General. Albuera, 1811. Surrendered Valencia to French forces, 1812.
154. Gurwood, *The Dispatches of Field Marshal the Duke of Wellington*, Vol. 8, p. 51.

on Liverpool's advice the government had rejected the Bullion Committee's recommendation for a fixed date for resumption of gold payments, while issuing additional Exchequer bills to allay shortages in the coin supply.

In the Lords, the Radical third Earl Stanhope[155] introduced a bill to make it illegal to pay more than 21 shillings for a gold guinea in order to prevent landlords and others from demanding additional amounts for payment in notes. Liverpool in reply suggested that demanding excessive amounts of notes in payment was an isolated occurrence, not yet a normal practice, so the bill should be deferred for three months. On the second reading the following Monday, he announced that a bullion dealer mostly opposed to the government had told him that guineas could not be obtained at any price. He then added a clause saying that bank notes should be legal tender at par in payments of rent as well as in debt payments, and another limiting the term of the bill to 25 March 1812.

On the third reading debate Liverpool pointed out that the Bank of England's issue of notes amounted to £23 million, compared to government revenues of £70-£80 million, hence there was no possibility of *assignat*-type depreciation of their value. After the passage of this bill, Stanhope introduced another bill to tighten the requirements for legal tender, exclaiming that, 'To believe gold necessary for a circulating medium was an idea fit only for Hottentots.'[156] Liverpool ended the debate by remarking:

> The value of the gold coin in this country was not to be estimated according to its weight in gold, but according to the value fixed on it by the reigning sovereign of the country. The value of bank notes, as for every purpose of internal negociation [*sic*], I contend, was by the general consent of the country declared not to be depreciated."

The remainder of 1811 was relatively quiet. The Perceval government had as a result of the successes in the Peninsular War gathered considerable strength; as Liverpool wrote to Wellington that spring, 'Perceval's character is completely established in the House of Commons; he has acquired an authority there beyond any minister within my recollection, except Mr. Pitt'.[157] In the same

155. Charles Stanhope (1753-1815). 3rd Earl Stanhope from 1786. MP for Wycombe, 1780-86. Accomplished scientist and less accomplished author (he wrote a riposte to Burke's *Reflections on the Revolution in France*). Supported Pitt in his early years but defected to Radicalism after 1786. Married Pitt's sister Hester in 1774 (d. 1780), then Grenville's cousin Louisa. Father of Lady Hester Stanhope (1776-1839) who became Pitt's hostess, then a noted traveller and archaeologist.

156. Hansard, *Parliamentary Debates from the Year 1803 to the Present Time*, Vol 20, col. 982 (Stanhope) (16 July 1811). Liverpool's speeches in this series of debates, cols 764, 828, 844, 878, 983, 1115 (sentences quoted, 22 July 1811.)

157. Quoted in Yonge, *The Life and Administration of Robert Banks Jenkinson*, Vol. 1, p. 372.

letter, he foresaw a resumption of war in northern Europe and wondered what advantage Britain could take of it; this was a key factor behind Wellington's more aggressive strategy in the early months of 1812.

Wellington, promoted to full General in July, spent the last months of 1811 preparing for his 1812 advances and accumulating men and supplies. A letter to Liverpool in late July reveals that he had already settled upon a siege of Ciudad Rodrigo, on the Spanish/Portuguese border, as a key initial objective of his next campaign. He began a somewhat ineffective blockade of the city in August, though it was several months before he acted further, partly because the British forces suffered badly from sickness in September-October 1811.

These months produced rumours of peace in France. As Wellington wrote to Liverpool, echoing Liverpool's predictions of two years earlier, the drain of resources required to supply large forces in Spain seriously tempted Napoleon to end the campaign. Conversely, while the Portuguese army showed admirable discipline, the Portuguese government was half-hearted in its prosecution of the war, and Wellington believed that even the possible return of the Prince Regent (John VI) from Brazil would probably not help matters. Late in the year and into January, the successful French siege of Valencia, held by 16,000 Spanish troops, demonstrated that Spanish forces remained unreliable.

The year 1811 saw a bad harvest in Britain, due to a blight on the corn crop in June. Liverpool informed Wellington in November[158] that he must get corn supplies from America and the Barbary states as far as possible, and that supplies of specie would be even more restricted than usual because of the need to buy corn for domestic use. A further result was a worsening in domestic unrest, leading to the Luddite riots of the following year.

Wellington set out his plans for 1812 to Liverpool in a December letter, in which he outlined a plan to besiege Ciudad Rodrigo, after which, whether or not successful, he would advance southwards to besiege Badajoz, thus securing the entire Portuguese/Spanish frontier by the end of March.[159] He also thanked Liverpool for his kindness to his young son[160] – by this time the two men had become genuinely close and would remain so until Liverpool died.

At the end of 1811 Napoleon reigned supreme in Europe, with Russia, Austria and Prussia apparently resigned to his rule. While France had effectively lost almost all her overseas possessions, there were few cracks in the edifice of her military and economic strength extending across most of Western Europe.

---

158. Liverpool's letter of 21 November 1811, quoted in Gurwood, *The Dispatches of Field Marshal the Duke of Wellington*, Vol. 8, p. 446.
159. Ibid., pp. 454-57.
160. Most likely Arthur Wellesley (1807-84). 2nd Duke of Wellington from 1852. MP for Aldeburgh, 1829-32, Norwich, 1837-52. Major-General, 1854. Master of the Horse, 1853-58. Possibly also Charles Wellesley (1808-58). MP for South Hampshire and Windsor, 1842-55. Perhaps both. Liverpool was known to be good with children.

Wellington had achieved considerable success in the Iberian peninsula, making it a running sore on Napoleon's backside, but it was no more than that and there was little sign that it could be so. The Orders in Council remained in full force, and opinion in the United States was being whipped up towards a break with Britain, but they were having a considerable effect in starving Napoleon of essential commerce, while British commerce was growing rapidly despite 1811's bad harvest.

Finally, Liverpool himself was well established in his office of Secretary of State for War and the Colonies and had some substantial achievements to his credit. However, Liverpool's career looked likely to flourish without him ever gaining the highest office.

IV.

Year of Destiny, 1812

The year 1812 was to prove very important. It was the year Liverpool moved from the position of senior cabinet minister into that of a prime minister destined through his success to serve a near-record term. It was the crucial year of the Napoleonic Wars, producing a decisive victory for Wellington at Salamanca and an even more decisive disaster for the Napoleonic Empire in the retreat from Russia. At home, the effects of the industrial revolution and of the government's response were to result in the most severe of the Luddite riots and the Frame-Breaking Act.

The year opened with the siege of Ciudad Rodrigo, which Wellington invested on 8 January and, thanks to the unpredictable weather, took on 19 January, with just under 1,000 casualties – completing the operation in half the time he had estimated.[1] Wellington then immediately prepared to besiege Badajoz, which he believed should be done during the winter and early spring, while his troops had supply advantages over the French. After several weeks assembling the necessary equipment and transport, he invested Badajoz on 16 March. By that time, Wellington had been promoted to an earldom.

Meanwhile, back in London, Parliament reassembled on 7 January. On the Royal Address, Grenville referred to the country as being on 'the brink of ruin' to which Liverpool ventured a mild protest. Later that week, Liverpool proposed a Vote of Thanks to Minto for the capture of Réunion, Mauritius and Java, observing that, with French privateering rife, 'It was thought necessary to make France feel that the ocean was the undisputed domain of Britain; and that ships, colonies and commerce, those favourite objects

1. These dates are confirmed in letters from Wellington to Liverpool, 9 January and 20 January, Gurwood, *The Dispatches of Field Marshal the Duke of Wellington*, Vol. 8, pp. 518-24 and 526-33. 'Half the time' – personal letter to Liverpool, 20 January, ibid., p. 534. Gurwood, then a lieutenant, himself commanded the 'Forlorn Hope'.

Arthur Wellesley, first Duke of Wellington in 1814, a mass of medals and victory.
Source: Wellcome Collection.

of the ruler of France, were at the mercy of this country.'[2] On this occasion, Minto being a Whig, even Grenville was benign and the motion passed *nem. con.*

Even though the Regency restrictions were to expire on 6 February, on 31 January Fitzwilliam[3] introduced a strong measure of Catholic Emancipation, a subject which the Prince Regent was known to oppose. Liverpool made a

2. Hansard, *Parliamentary Debates from the Year 1803 to the Present Time*, Vol. 2, cols 126-29 (10 January 1812).
3. William Wentworth-Fitzwilliam (1748-1833). 4th Earl Fitzwilliam from 1756. Whig grandee. Nephew and heir of the 2nd Marquess of Rockingham, who died in 1782. Lord President of the Council, 1794. Lord Lieutenant of Ireland, 1794-95, 1806. Minister without Portfolio, 1806-7. Lord Lieutenant of the West Riding of Yorkshire, 1798-1819.

modest speech in opposition, suggesting that the middle of a major war was not the best time to bring up the question and that arraigning the court system as an instrument of Protestant oppression, as Fitzwilliam had done, was not the best argument in its favour to moderate minds.[4] Fitzwilliam's motion was defeated by 162 votes to 79, with even the pro-Emancipation Wellesley voting against it on the grounds of bad timing.

The following week the House of Lords first debated an entirely new topic, the 'Nottingham riots'. The bad harvest of 1811 after several years of poor ones led to an increase in the price of corn, which in early 1812 reached 122 shillings, twelve per cent above the previous decade's 1809 peak and second only to the 1800 peak of 131 shillings. This brought enormous distress.[5] In November 1811, in an action attributed to Ned Ludd, who supposedly smashed two stocking frames in 1779, textile workers began holding drills around Nottingham and smashing textile machinery. Similar outbreaks, including a pitched battle with local soldiers, were reported in Lancashire and Yorkshire.

The outbreak of frame-breaking, while not unprecedented, was a response to the pains of early industrialisation. Despite a general increase in overall living standards (with occasional setbacks after bad harvests as in the 1790s, 1811 and later 1816), several large categories of workers were losing out badly. E.P. Thompson[6] identifies three such groups: the handloom weavers, replaced by power looms; the framework knitters, replaced by stocking-making machinery; and the 'croppers', who dressed cloth by cutting it with large shears, who were replaced by shearing frames. The croppers were concentrated in Yorkshire, the framework knitters in Nottinghamshire and Leicestershire and the handloom weavers were scattered throughout the textile industry in the Midlands and North.

Each of these groups contained hundreds of thousands of workers, in 1800 organised through the 'outwork' system whereby they worked at home, with materials provided by an employer. They were relatively well paid in the early years of the textile industry, as rising output increased demand but after 1800 their wages declined sharply and continued to decline to below subsistence levels.

The last immiserated handloom weavers were commemorated in Disraeli's 1845 novel *Sybil*, a Dickensian 'wallow-in-squalor' that tugged on the heartstrings and derived its information from an 1842 Royal Commission report.[7] By 1850, the handloom weavers had disappeared but the transition

4. Hansard, *Parliamentary Debates from the Year 1803 to the Present Time*, Vol. 21, cols 474-75 (31 January 1812).
5. Thomas Tooke, *A History of Prices and of the State of the Circulation from 1793 to 1837*, 6 vols (London: Longman, Orme, Brown, Green & Longmans, 1838-57) Vol I p. 475.
6. Thompson, *The Making of the English Working Class*. Handloom weavers pp 269-313, Croppers pp 522-30, Framework knitters pp 530-41.
7. Disraeli's true distaste, however, was reserved for the self-governing workmen of 'Wodgate' – Willenhall, Staffordshire – who existed in a state of drunken, dog-fighting squalor making locks over a four-day working week, and whose misery

period between around 1815 to 1850 was a hard one, and handloom weavers who did not find a new trade led miserable lives. For croppers and framework knitters, the end came earlier; they were in difficulties from the 1790s and had mostly disappeared by 1825.

For all three groups of 'outworkers', a move to the factories seemed unattractive despite the potential for higher wages, because of the long hours and harsh discipline; outwork provided a freedom that factory work lacked. With more freedom, outworkers were also able to organise politically, with both industrial demands for a ban on the new machines and a minimum wage and political demands for parliamentary reform (by which they meant manhood suffrage and annual parliaments, not the limited measures favoured by some Whigs).

Luddism was an almost entirely working-class movement, a novelty in England (the 1790s rioters, like the French Jacobins, had been led by middle-class Radicals). Luddism also involved violent action against local factory owners and magistrates, though not yet a national armed uprising. In 1811-12, there was little coordination between the various areas of unrest, the handloom weavers were as yet little involved and the agitation was primarily industrial, involving frame-breaking and an attempt to get restrictive legislation against new machinery and for a minimum wage.

In this first Lords debate Liverpool, in a brief response to Holland's question on the subject, recognised the novel nature of the disturbances: 'There might be riots more alarming in appearance, but arising from a sudden ebullience of resentment, and therefore easily quelled in a short time; but the system adopted in the county of Nottingham undoubtedly gave those disturbances a new character.'[8] Liverpool announced that 'two of the most intelligent magistrates' had been sent to Nottingham to deal with the disturbances and that the government would shortly introduce legislation on the subject. In response, Lauderdale claimed that the Nottingham riots 'might all be traced to the system and conduct of His Majesty's Ministers, in reducing the commerce of the country to a gambling speculation'.[9]

At the end of February, Liverpool proposed the Frame Work Bill (known after its passage as the Frame-Breaking Act), by which frame-breaking would be subject to the death penalty and those whose frames had been broken would be compelled to report the crime to local magistrates. The Act superseded a 1788 Act that had made destruction of stocking frames subject to seven-to-

---

resulted from a lack of local government and social structure, not abject poverty as with the weavers.

8. Hansard, *Parliamentary Debates from the Year 1803 to the Present Time*, Vol. 21, cols 602-3, col. 603 (Lauderdale) (4 February 1812).

9. James Maitland (1759-1839). 8th Earl of Lauderdale (Scottish) from 1789. 1st Baron Lauderdale (GB) from 1806. MP for Newport and Malmesbury, 1780-89. Radical and proto-Keynesian economic theorist.

fourteen years' transportation. It was designed to be temporary and to expire on 1 March 1814. By that time a further Act had been passed, once again reducing the maximum sentence to transportation, before the legislation was toughened again to restore the death penalty during the post-war disturbances of 1817. Around 60-70 Luddites were executed in 1812-14 but in no cases do the magistrates appear to have used this Act specifically.

In introducing the measure, Liverpool stressed that it was experimental, intended to be temporary and gave protection to manufacturing by stocking frames the same protection as was given to other kinds of machinery. In response, Lord Byron (in his maiden speech) claimed in an emotional address that the work done by the new frames was inferior in quality, 'not marketable at home and merely hurried over with a view to exportation'[10] so that men were put out of work to no purpose other than the enrichment of the masters. It was an argument that would become familiar over the next two centuries but was at that time novel.

In the Third Reading debate, Liverpool denied that the Orders in Council had caused exceptional distress:

> It happened that at a late period there was a sudden excitement of trade; that it was followed by a glut of the market; and that glut, by distress among the workmen. . . . But the present interposition of Parliament is called for, not by the distresses of the workmen, but from a conspiracy against the machinery, which has regularly exhibited itself at all times when machinery has been employed to the disuse of manual labour. We have found penal statutes necessary for the protection of every successive kind of machinery.

Liverpool then read a passage from Archdeacon Paley,[11] implying that the intensity of punishment was to be adapted, not to the enormity of the crime, but to the difficulty of preventing it in society: 'It is on this principle that a man is hung for stealing a sheep or a horse.'[12] The bill passed its second reading by 32 votes to 17, passed its third reading without a division and received the Royal Assent on 20 March.

Liverpool proposed a vote of thanks to Wellington for the capture of Ciudad Rodrigo on 10 February. In his speech he emphasised Wellington's skill in capturing it in only eleven days; the thanks were agreed to without dissent.

---

10. George Gordon Byron (1788-1824). 6th Baron Byron from 1798. Radical poet. Hansard, *Parliamentary Debates from the Year 1803 to the Present Time*, Vol. 21, cols 966-72 (27 February 1812).
11. William Paley (1743-1805). Christ's College, Cambridge, Senior Wrangler, 1763. Archdeacon of Carlisle, 1782. *The Principles of Moral and Political Philosophy* (1785).
12. Hansard, *Parliamentary Debates from the Year 1803 to the Present Time*, Vol. 21, cols 1082-83 (5 March 1812).

Ten days later, he proposed an Address to the Prince Regent, thanking him for bestowing an earldom on Wellington and adding a parliamentary pension of £2,000 a year to the honour. Again, the Address and the pension were agreed to without dissent, indicating that both Wellington and the Peninsular campaign had now risen above party strife, except for Grenville's occasional griping. Even a continued £2 million subsidy to Portugal was agreed to without dissent.

By this time, the first of 1812's upheavals in the government had occurred. The ending of the Regency restrictions produced no changes, with the Prince Regent alienated further from the Whigs by the previous week's Catholic Emancipation debate. At the same time, he wanted to bring a section of the Whigs into a coalition government, if this could be done without major alteration in policies that were proving successful; however, Grey and Grenville rejected his overtures for such an arrangement. The petulant Prince Regent did not like Perceval, writing to the Archbishop of York[13] that 'I have now only Lord Liverpool' to trust.[14]

Wellesley had already announced his intention of leaving the government and retiring to the back benches. Liverpool, in a tactful letter to his brother, mentioned that Wellesley was disgruntled at not having his opinion taken into account sufficiently:

> However, I do not believe that he has attended more than half the Cabinet meetings which have taken place since he has been in Government; and this circumstance, combined with others, unavoidably prevented him from having the same common feelings with his colleagues as exist among those who not only act but live together.[15]

Wellesley then unsuccessfully attempted to persuade the Prince Regent to replace Perceval by a ministry led by Wellesley and Canning, albeit including Liverpool in his current job, with a partial concession on Catholic Emancipation. He finally resigned on 19 February. Perceval was then able to add significantly to the government's abilities by appointing Castlereagh to the Foreign Office, where he was to remain until his suicide ten years later. Castlereagh would have preferred to return to the War Office, with Liverpool returning to the Foreign Office, but Perceval and Liverpool were united in vetoing that idea.

While Castlereagh's abilities added to the government's stature, Perceval was also able to add to its Commons strength by bringing back Sidmouth as Lord President of the Council, together with two of his adherents in minor positions,

---

13. Edward Venables Vernon Harcourt (1757-1847). Bishop of Carlisle, 1791. Archbishop of York, 1808-47.
14. Quoted in Gash, *Lord Liverpool*, p. 89.
15. Quoted in Yonge, *The Life and Administration of Robert Banks Jenkinson*, Vol. 1, pp. 377-78.

while retaining Camden in the Cabinet as Minister without Portfolio. With the war proving the government's capability, and reinforcements in both the effective and political spheres, Perceval's government was now a strong one indeed.

After Wellington invested Badajoz, he wrote to Liverpool to discuss strategic possibilities for the rest of Spain, suggesting that a primarily naval attack on Tarragona or Barcelona in north-east Spain by Bentinck[16] and Pellew[17] would prove the most useful in dividing French forces, although he thought in unlikely either would succeed because of the possibility of reinforcements from France.[18] However, the witless Bentinck[19] decided to invade Italy instead, much to Wellington's fury, since an attack on Spain's east coast would have been extremely useful around or after Wellington's victory at Salamanca.

Badajoz was captured by storm on 6 April, after a remarkably swift siege (Wellington was worried about Marmont[20] sending a relief expedition), albeit with the loss of almost 5,000 men killed and wounded. Wellington sent several letters to Liverpool after the victory, one of which (now lost) recommended the establishment of a corps of sappers and miners, as inadequacies in that area had greatly increased the casualties of the assault.

During the remainder of April, Wellington ensured that Ciudad Rodrigo and Badajoz were garrisoned by local troops and provisioned in case of any attack by the French; this task proved protracted. However, he was delighted to hear from Castlereagh that a subsidy of £1 million was to be given to Spain, since this would increase his control over Spanish troop operations.

On 12 May, Wellington wrote to Liverpool that the American government had imposed a three-month embargo on supplies of grain to his troops. Fortunately, having been warned by Liverpool the previous November that

---

16. Lord William Bentinck (1774-1839). Whig MP for Camelford, Nottinghamshire, King's Lynn and Glasgow, 1796-1803, 1812-14, 1816-28, 1836-39. Governor of Madras, 1803-7. Major-General, 1805. Lieutenant-General, 1811. Commanded British forces in Sicily 1811-14. Governor General of India, 1828-35.
17. Edward Pellew (1757-1833). Baronet, 1796. 1st Baron Exmouth from 1814. 1st Viscount Exmouth from 1816. GCB, 1832. MP for Barnstaple, 1802-4. Captain, 1782. Captained frigate *Nymphe* to defeat French frigate *Cléopâtre*, 1793. Captained HMS *Indefatigable* to capture French 74-gun *Droits de l'Homme*, January 1797. Rear-Admiral, 1804. Commander-in-Chief, East Indies, 1804-09. Vice-Admiral 1808. Commander-in-Chief, Mediterranean, 1811-14, 1815-16. Admiral, 1814. Victor at battle of Algiers, 1816.
18. Gurwood, *The Dispatches of Field Marshal the Duke of Wellington*, Vol. 9, pp. 7-9.
19. Castlereagh wrote to Liverpool (27 April 1814, quoted in 3rd Marquess of Londonderry [ed.], *Memoirs and Correspondence of Viscount Castlereagh, Second Marquess of Londonderry*, 12 vols [London: William Shoberl, 1851] Vol. 9, p. 410) of Bentinck's 'impracticability and Whiggism, which seems to follow him everywhere'.
20. Auguste de Marmont (1774-1852). Duke of Ragusa from 1808. Served in Toulon, Italy and Egypt with Napoleon. Marshal, 1809. Stayed loyal to Louis XVIII during the Hundred Days but, as Major-General of the Guard, surrendered to Orleanist revolutionaries, July 1830.

no grain shipments were to be expected from England because of the poor harvest, he had bought sufficient grain from America in advance to increase his stocks to 200 days' supply from the previous 3 months, and he expected to maintain them there until he heard news of the 1812 British harvest.

Wellington's last long letter to Liverpool as Secretary of State for War and the Colonies, dated 26 May, set out his plans for an invasion of the Castilian heartland, with a view to bringing Marmont to battle before the harvest in central Spain allowed Marmont's troops to re-provision themselves. Wellington's troops would have access to secret stores of grain.[21] He arrived at Salamanca in late June and spent the next month besieging the city's forts, which he captured on 27 June, and awaiting an attack by Marmont, which he believed more advantageous than attacking first.

On 3 June, Wellington informed Liverpool that Graham would shortly return to England because of his deteriorating eyesight and requested that no successor be sent out as second-in-command: 'There are but few officers who should be sent from England as second-in-command, who would not come here with opinions formed, probably on very bad grounds, and with very extravagant pretensions.'[22] It is notable that this request was made in a private letter to Liverpool and not to the Commander-in-Chief; it indicates the high confidence between the two men.

In April the House of Lords returned yet again to Catholic Emancipation on a motion by the Earl of Donoughmore.[23] Liverpool in response was more definitive than in the past. His central argument was that the Catholic Church subjected the state to a foreign power and that power was currently under the domination of Napoleon's France. Donoughmore's motion was rejected by a majority of 174 votes to 102 and a similar motion was rejected by the Commons by an even larger majority. This indication that majority opinion in the Lords, the Commons and the country remained opposed to Catholic Emancipation was to be important in the negotiations over the succession to Perceval the following month.

On 24 April, Liverpool laid a declaration of the Prince Regent before the House, which stated that France had repealed the Berlin and Milan Decrees with respect to the United States by an order of 28 April 1811 (in fact, backdated from August 1811). Accordingly, the government was reviewing the possibility of repealing the Orders in Council as they applied to the United States (although it did not appear that full repeal of the Berlin and

---

21. Gurwood, *The Dispatches of Field Marshal the Duke of Wellington*, Vol. 9, pp. 172-78.
22. Ibid., pp. 209-10.
23. Richard Hely Hely-Hutchinson (1756-1825). 2nd Baron Donoughmore (Ireland) from 1788. 1st Viscount Donoughmore, 1797. 1st Earl of Donoughmore, 1800. Irish representative peer from 1801. 1st Viscount Hutchinson (UK), 1821. MP (Ireland) for Dublin University, Sligo Borough, and Taghmon, 1776-88. Colonel, 1800. Major-General, 1805. Lieutenant-General, 1812

Milan Decrees, the contingency for automatic withdrawal of the Orders in Council, had in fact occurred). News of this formal notice of the likely repeal of the Orders in Council thus reached Washington, three weeks' sailing away in summer, well before the US declaration of war on 18 June, and probably before President Madison's 1 June Message to Congress.

On 27 April in the House of Lords, Liverpool proposed a Vote of Thanks for the capture of Badajoz, pointing out that the level of resistance made it an exceptionally worthy object for such a vote. Liverpool singled out 'the body of officers forming under Lord Wellington, which would constitute a shield of strength such as had, perhaps, never existed in any other country, or indeed in this, on any former occasion'.[24] The Vote of Thanks was carried unanimously after a favourable speech by Holland.

Liverpool returned to the American question on 5 May, when he denied that Captain John Henry,[25] an agent of Sir James Craig, Governor General of Canada, had attempted to persuade the New England states to secede from the United States. Relations at the time (the winter of 1808-9) had been poor, with the Embargo Act in force and Madison declaring that the US would be justified in invading Canada without a formal declaration of war. However, Henry's instructions had been simply to obtain information as to the temper in New England and he had been withdrawn when Craig learned that Madison had settled differences with the British ambassador.[26]

On Monday, 11 May, Perceval was assassinated in the House of Commons by John Bellingham,[27] a British national, who was imprisoned in Russia in 1804 and who held a long grudge against the British government for not upholding his compensation claim for his imprisonment. He went to Parliament with the express intention of shooting someone in power and Perceval was unhappily the first he came across. Eldon believed he was the intended victim, having walked past Bellingham in an ordinary greatcoat a few minutes earlier, but Bellingham failed to recognise him out of his official regalia.

In the House of Lords Liverpool, when he heard that Perceval had been shot, immediately proposed an Address to the Prince Regent deploring Perceval's death and calling for the apprehension of the murderer.

Bellingham was allegedly cheered by the crowd as he was taken to justice; this reaction, if it existed, was exaggerated by the Radical press (the government

24. Hansard, *Parliamentary Debates from the Year 1803 to the Present Time*, Vol. 22, cols 1042-48 (27 April 1812).
25. John Henry (1776-1853). Captain, US Army, 1798. Employed as spy by Sir James Craig, 1809. Sold probably fraudulent papers to President Madison through certainly fraudulent French agent for $50,000, February 1812.
26. Hansard, *Parliamentary Debates from the Year 1803 to the Present Time*, Vol. 23, cols 14-17 (5 May 1812).
27. John Bellingham (1769-1812). Imprisoned in Russia over a business dispute, 1804. Refused compensation by Britain, 1809-12, on grounds that diplomatic relations with Russia had been broken off in 1808. Blamed Perceval.

was after all to win a large general election majority later that year). However, the reaction to Perceval's death in Nottingham was indeed one of joy, and the militia had to be called out and the Riot Act read. Bellingham was tried on 15 May, found guilty and hanged on 18 May. Brougham[28] condemned the trial as 'the greatest disgrace to English justice' but it is difficult to see why; there were dozens of witnesses to Bellingham's action, and only by the wildest stretch of the imagination can Perceval be held responsible for his misfortune.

Liverpool eulogised Perceval in the House of Lords on 12 May, saying, 'few men ever existed, who were endowed with more virtues; and no man had fewer faults'.[29] Perceval's funeral was held on 16 May, with Liverpool, Eldon, Harrowby and Ryder as pallbearers. Even before then, Eldon had sent a memorandum to the Prince Regent expressing the willingness of the government to carry on under any of the present Cabinet, but that the chances of success were limited without at least attempting to bring Wellesley and Canning into the government.[30]

The Prince Regent therefore named Liverpool interim Prime Minister to take charge of negotiations, while Castlereagh offered his resignation to the Prince Regent, if it would help attract Canning. Liverpool, however, while accepting the possibility of moving Castlereagh from the Foreign Office, insisted in the negotiations with Canning and Wellesley on 17 May that Castlereagh should remain Leader of the House of Commons.

Canning and Wellesley responded that they could not serve in any administration opposed to Catholic Emancipation, that Whigs should be invited to join the government and that Wellesley thought inadequate resources were being devoted to the Peninsular campaign. Accordingly, the government decided to carry on without them. There appeared no reason why they should not succeed; the addition of Castlereagh and Sidmouth to the administration had strengthened a team that was already strong.

John Walter,[31] the proprietor of *The Times*, is said to have hesitated at supporting 'a body of men so critically situated and so doubtful of national support' but *The Times* was still an ordinary Whig/Radical paper, without

28. Henry Peter Brougham (1778-1868). 1st Lord Brougham and Vaux from 1830. Whig MP for Camelford, Winchelsea, Knaresborough and Yorkshire, 1810-12, 1815-30. Lord Chancellor, 1830-34. His *Historical Sketches of Statesmen who Flourished in the Time of George III* (1839) is scathing about Liverpool, especially about the gold standard decision.

29. Hansard, *Parliamentary Debates from the Year 1803 to the Present Time*, Vol. 23, cols 168-69 (12 May 1812).

30. Quoted in A. Aspinall (ed.), *The Letters of King George IV, 1812-30*, 3 vols (Cambridge: Cambridge University Press, 1938) Vol. 1, pp. 74-75.

31. John Walter (1776-1847). Son of John Walter (c. 1739-1812), the founder in 1785 of *The Times* (c. 1739-1812). Manager/Editor of *The Times* from 1803. Whig MP for Berkshire, 1832-37, for Nottingham, 1841, 1842-43. Gash, *Lord Liverpool*, p. 91, gives Walter's view but Walter was hardly impartial.

the towering influence it was later to gain. It did, however, play a role by publishing (possibly without permission) Wellesley's statement justifying his resignation, which accused both Perceval and the rest of his colleagues of downright incompetence and alleged that the Peninsular War had been fought on a 'narrow and imperfect scale'.[32]

Thus, when on 21 May Stuart Wortley,[33] a generally pro-government backbencher connected to Liverpool by marriage, proposed a Commons motion asking the Prince Regent to appoint a 'strong and efficient administration', the motion was carried by 174 votes to 170 with Wellesley's supporters and the unreliable Canning voting against the government.

Stuart Wortley's motivation in bringing down the embryonic Liverpool government is unclear. His father had been a Whig who crossed the aisle with Portland in 1794, and he had been a reliable supporter of the Portland and Perceval ministries and a friend of Perceval. However, his political views were modifying; he had recently announced his support for Catholic Emancipation. Later, he was to prove by no means reliable in support of Liverpool's government but was, nonetheless, rewarded with a peerage in 1826, after which he was included in Peel's Cabinets of 1834-5 and from 1841 until his death in 1845.

In the first days when the Liverpool administration was being formed there was dismay among some country gentlemen that Liverpool had been unable to attract Canning and Wellesley and this, together with his new-found sympathy for Catholic claims, may have motivated Stuart Wortley to propose his motion. It was so unpremeditated that he had not lined up a seconder but the Whig Lord Milton,[34] heir to Fitzwilliam, was happy to second a motion that promised to disrupt Liverpool's new government.

Stuart Wortley deplored the failure of the next three weeks' negotiations and on 11 June proposed a second motion regretting the failure of attempts to broaden the government and calling for further such attempts, which was rejected by 289 votes to 164. In the end he congratulated himself that Liverpool's government 'stood better than at its first formation in the eyes of the country'.[35] Liverpool, a forgiving man, appears to have preserved

---

32. A copy of Wellesley's statement is contained in Hansard, *Parliamentary Debates from the Year 1803 to the Present Time*, Vol. 23, cols 367-70.
33. James Archibald Stuart Wortley (1776-1845). 1st Baron Wharncliffe from 1826. MP for Bossiney and Yorkshire, 1802-26. Lord Privy Seal, 1834-35. Lord President of the Council, 1841-45. Married to a niece of Louisa, Lady Liverpool.
34. Charles Wentworth-Fitzwilliam (1786-1857). 3rd/5th Earl Fitzwilliam from 1833. MP for Malton, Yorkshire, Peterborough, Higham Ferrers, Northamptonshire and North Northamptonshire, 1807-33. His Yorkshire election in 1807 cost £100,000; it is believed to have been the only pre-reform election where expenditure exceeded the 1754 Oxfordshire contest (for further information, see Namier and Brooke, *The History of Parliament*).
35. Thorne, *The History of Parliament: the House of Commons 1790-1820*. "Stuart Wortley, James Archibald."

cordial relations within the family but notably failed to give Stuart Wortley preferment, which came only from Peel a generation later. It should be noted that the delay caused by Stuart Wortley's motion prevented the repeal of the Orders in Council until 24 June, i.e. after the US Congress had declared war, and thus significantly contributed to the outbreak of that unnecessary conflict.

The day after Stuart Wortley's motion, even though the vote was a narrow one in a fairly thin House, the Cabinet resigned, while pledging to carry on their departmental work until the Prince Regent had formed an administration. The Prince Regent began by approaching Wellesley but Wellesley had already wrecked his relationship with his former colleagues by his statement in *The Times*, which his former colleagues blamed for the Stuart Wortley motion, and by his publication the following day of Liverpool's letter to him on the Catholic question.

Thus, when on 23 May Canning, on Wellesley's behalf, asked Liverpool whether he would join them, Liverpool responded that both he and the entire outgoing Cabinet would not serve in any government of which Wellesley was a member.[36] Liverpool also wrote to Canning disclaiming any personal hostility to Wellesley but pointing out that the publication by Wellesley of an attack on Perceval and his Cabinet colleagues made it impossible to work with him.

The Prince Regent asked them to reconsider but, via a further Cabinet minute of 27 May (from which Castlereagh and Camden, his uncle, were absent 'out of delicacy'), they confirmed their refusal to unite with Wellesley and Canning. At the Prince Regent's request, Liverpool, Melville, Mulgrave, Sidmouth, Westmorland, Buckinghamshire, Eldon, Harrowby, Ryder and Vansittart reinforced the point in separate letters, pointing out that Catholic Emancipation and Castlereagh's position were further obstacles to any such combination.[37] The loyalty of the Cabinet to Liverpool is notable and in marked contrast to the squabbles that had taken place in the previous decade. Liverpool's position was thus strong.

Wellesley then opened negotiations with Grey and Grenville, asking whether they would serve in an administration pledged to Catholic Emancipation and vigorous prosecution of the war. This epitomised the problem facing the attempt to construct an administration without Liverpool and his team. On Catholic Emancipation, the Wellesley/Canning group and the Whigs were united but were faced with a public opinion massively opposed. On the war,

---

36. Most of the relevant correspondence is contained in Hansard, *Parliamentary Debates from the Year 1803 to the Present Time*, Vol. 23, Appendix, cols i-xliv.
37. Both the two Cabinet minutes and the nine supporting letters are contained in Aspinall, *The Letters of King George IV, 1812-30*, Vol. 1, pp. 83 and 90-98. Liverpool's letter is not there but it is contained in Yonge, *The Life and Administration of Robert Banks Jenkinson*, Vol. 1, p. 393.

Wellesley's claim that the Perceval administration had been feeble made little sense and was in complete opposition to the Whigs, who had mostly favoured pulling out of the peninsula altogether.

Moira, the Prince Regent's close friend, expressed enthusiasm for a joint administration, provided Grey and Grenville were included, as did Lansdowne, so Wellesley then formally invited Grey and Grenville to join him in an administration with himself at the head and with Whigs making up four or five of the twelve to thirteen members, plus Erskine[38] and Moira. On 3 June, having led Wellesley on, Grey and Grenville then refused to serve in a Cabinet in which Whig participation was limited in advance. Moira attempted to change their opinion, but to no avail.

That same afternoon Liverpool told the House of Lords that he was serving only until a new government could be formed. Wellesley growled darkly that 'dreadful personal animosities' on the part of Liverpool and his colleagues had prevented him from forming one, after which Stanhope nicely described Liverpool's position as 'not a minister, but a daisy, a flower, that appears in bloom in the morning, that dies at night and is no more thought of'.[39]

After Wellesley showed Grey and Grenville's memorandum to the Prince Regent, he withdrew Wellesley's commission and on 6 June, possibly at Arbuthnot's earlier suggestion,[40] instructed Moira to open discussions in an attempt to form an administration. Grey and Grenville then raised an additional objection, requiring the officials of the Royal Household to be changed by the new administration. Moira was not authorised to offer this, so negotiations again broke down.

Wellesley also refused to take second place in a Moira government,[41] so Moira was reduced to trying to form an administration with Canning, Melville (who had inherited his father's cadre of loyal Scottish Commons supporters) and some second-tier Tories, such as Huskisson and Arbuthnot. Liverpool undertook to support such a ministry but not to serve in it. The Prince Regent, realising that any such administration would not be remotely 'strong and efficient' then terminated Moira's commission and on 8 June authorised Liverpool to resume his efforts to form a government.

Liverpool's final accession to office was thus a matter of chance even after Perceval's assassination. Wellesley's foolish publication of correspondence and Grey and Grenville's extraordinary intransigence were the only obstacles to

38. Thomas Erskine (1750-1823). 1st Baron Erskine from 1806. Whig MP for Portsmouth, 1783-84, 1790-1806. Lord Chancellor, 1806-7.

39. Hansard, *Parliamentary Debates from the Year 1803 to the Present Time*, Vol. 23, cols 332-34 (3 June 1812).

40. Arbuthnot letter of 29 May to Colonel McMahon, the King's Secretary, in Aspinall, *The Letters of King George IV, 1812-30*, Vol. 1, p. 99. Arbuthnot's reasonable argument was that nobody hated Moira, unlike Wellesley, so a combination might be more feasible. Colonel Sir John McMahon (1754-1817). MP for Aldeburgh, 1802-12. Prince Regent's Private Secretary, 1811-17.

41. Wellesley papers, quoted in Aspinall, *The Letters of George IV, 1812-30*, Vol. 1, p. 104.

forming an administration without him, either mostly Tory or mostly Whig, based on support for Catholic Emancipation. Given the prima donna-ish natures of Grenville, Wellesley, Canning, and to a lesser extent Grey, and the major policy differences between them, such an administration would not have survived for long, especially as it would soon have had to fight an election with an electorate that remained staunchly anti-Catholic. However, the disruption caused by such a short-lived administration would have been highly damaging to the war effort and to Britain's overstretched finances.

Before forming a government, Liverpool had to face the House of Lords. He announced that the Prince Regent had commissioned him to form a government, whereupon the Duke of Norfolk enquired what the government were doing about the Orders in Council, saying that not a single day should be lost before repealing them and pacifying the United States. Liverpool responded that the US Congress had shown signs of becoming more hostile but that no definitively hostile acts had yet taken place.

Then, after Moira had paid a gentlemanly tribute to Liverpool's response to his attempts to form a government and Liverpool had moved that the House adjourn, Wellesley lowered the tone by accusing Liverpool and his colleagues of holding 'dreadful personal animosities' against him. Liverpool wisely let the well-liked Harrowby respond to this, by pointing out that, only a few days before Stuart Wortley's motion, Liverpool and his colleagues had been attempting to form a government with Wellesley. However, the publication of Wellesley's attack on both Perceval and his ministers, accusing the whole team of incompetence, had naturally changed the situation. Wellesley denied authorising the publication but reiterated that he did not consider Perceval 'a fit man to lead the councils of this great empire'.

Grey then intervened to claim that he and Grenville could not enter a government in which their principles would not be allowed their full expression, as had been the case in both the Wellesley and Moira negotiations, after which poor Moira expostulated reasonably that: 'I shall not be satisfied with being told that I conducted myself with frankness, but that I was only a dupe, and that I was not aware of the designs to which I was instrumental.' Grenville then claimed that he and Grey were constitutionally entitled to demand the replacement of the Royal Household, after which Eldon thankfully moved the adjournment for a second time.[42] It had been an unedifying discussion, from which only Harrowby and Moira emerged with credit.

Liverpool was well aware of the Prince Regent's high regard for Moira and of the need to see him well provided for. Accordingly, the following November the East India Company elected Moira as the next Governor General, with Liverpool's support, even though Moira was a Whig. The huge salary and perquisites attached to this post solved Moira's financial difficulties and it was

42. Hansard, *Parliamentary Debates from the Year 1803 to the Present Time*, Vol. 23, cols 356-81 (8 June 1812).

to prove an excellent appointment. Moira remained in office for a decade of high achievement, working well with Liverpool's government, and would be promoted Marquess of Hastings in 1816.

To form a stable administration, it was essential for Liverpool to establish a *modus vivendi* on the vexed subject of Catholic Emancipation, since his administration would contain both pro- and anti-Emancipationists. He did so by leaving it a completely open question, allowing ministers on both sides to speak for and against such a measure, without committing the government either way. This was a major breach of the already half-formed doctrine of collective Cabinet responsibility but it worked. Intended initially as a stopgap for a short-lived government, it remained a central principle of Liverpool's government and its successors for over sixteen years.

Liverpool had little difficulty remaking the Cabinet he had inherited from Perceval. The feeble Ryder was removed as Home Secretary and replaced by Sidmouth, an able administrator with major Commons support. Sidmouth's ally Vansittart had already been installed as Chancellor of the Exchequer in May, a post made vacant by Perceval's death. Another Sidmouth ally, Charles Bragge Bathurst[43] was installed in the lucrative office of Chancellor of the Duchy of Lancaster, also vacated by Perceval's death. Liverpool's old office as Secretary of State for War and the Colonies was filled by the Earl Bathurst, promoted from the Board of Trade. The reliable Harrowby was given Sidmouth's former office as Lord President of the Council. The Earl of Buckinghamshire, President of the Board of Control (responsible for India) was promoted to the Cabinet.

With Liverpool and six ministers remaining in place, Eldon as Lord Chancellor, Castlereagh at the Foreign Office, Westmorland as Lord Privy Seal, Melville as First Lord of the Admiralty, Mulgrave as Master General of the Ordnance and Camden as Minister without Portfolio, this made a Cabinet of thirteen, reduced to twelve after Camden retired later in the year with a marquessate.

Junior ministers with significance for the future included Palmerston, remaining as Secretary at War, and Peel, promoted in August from Under Secretary for War and the Colonies to the important job of Chief Secretary for Ireland, under the Duke of Richmond, who remained Lord Lieutenant (outside the Cabinet) until the following year. At that time Henry Goulburn,[44] previously Under Secretary at the Home Office was transferred to Peel's old

43. Charles Bragge Bathurst (1754-1831) MP for Monmouth, Bristol, Bodmin and Harwich, 1790-1823, Treasurer of the Navy, 1891-03, Secretary at War, 1803-04, Master of the Mint, 1806-07, Chancellor of the Duchy of Lancaster, 1812-23, President of the Board of Control, 1821-22. Married Charlotte Addington, Sidmouth's sister, 1781.

44. Henry Goulburn (1784-1856) MP for Horsham, St. Germans, West Looe, Armagh and Cambridge University, 1808-56. Under Secretary, Home Office, 1810-12, Under Secretary, War and the Colonies, 1812-21, Chief Secretary for Ireland, 1821-27, Chancellor of the Exchequer, 1828-30, Home Secretary, 1834-35, Chancellor of the Exchequer, 1841-46.

job. Frederick Robinson, a Lord of the Treasury from June, was promoted in September to Vice-President of the Board of Trade, where his skills were useful – he and Huskisson, who joined the government in 1814, provided Liverpool with invaluable support on financial and economic matters.

The only remaining question was the fate of Canning, Liverpool's oldest friend and less tainted with the 'dreadful personal animosities' that had caused the Cabinet to form a solid wall of resistance to Wellesley. Liverpool offered him Castlereagh's post at the Foreign Office, with Castlereagh moving to the Exchequer but remaining Leader of the House of Commons. However, Canning refused to allow Castlereagh to 'lead' him in the Commons, even though Canning would have the senior and more lucrative office. Liverpool and even Castlereagh himself pleaded with him repeatedly, but to no avail.

By his final refusal Canning was shut out from Cabinet office for four years and from senior Cabinet office for a decade – he was only eventually recalled because of Castlereagh's suicide. His faction in the House of Commons was also decimated at the 1812 election, reduced to no more than a dozen. From the viewpoint of posterity, we can breathe a sigh of relief that he rejected the Foreign Office at this time; his combination of insubordination, hatred of the Continental autocracies, scheming and quarrelsomeness would have been hopelessly counterproductive at the Congress of Vienna.[45]

Henry, 3rd Earl Bathurst as elder statesmen, 1834. A rock of support and reliability for Liverpool's Cabinet.

Liverpool wrote to Wellington on 10 June to tell him of the formation of the new government, apologising for the friction with Wellesley and encouraging him about Bathurst's capabilities and the government's commitment to the Peninsula. Thereafter most of Wellington's correspondence with the government was conducted through Bathurst and the few letters to Liverpool were primarily personal.

On 16 June Brougham proposed a Commons motion demanding immediate abolition of the Orders

45. More on Liverpool and his colleagues at the website www.lordliverpool.com/chronology

in Council banning trade with French-controlled territories. The motion failed, but Liverpool was well aware of the urgency and hence the Orders in Council were repealed completely on 24 June. It was too late; on 18 June the United States had declared war. Meanwhile, a tentative approach to France for peace in April was rejected because it demanded recognition of the 'actual dynasty of Spain', i.e. Napoleon's brother Joseph, whose unsteady grip on the country was weakening further.

On 17 June Vansittart presented the Budget for the fiscal year to 5 January 1813, which had been mostly prepared by Perceval before his death but which Vansittart had gone through with Liverpool in the preceding week after the government was formed. Total expenditure was projected at £58.2 million, up about seven per cent from the previous year's budget, with army expenditure rising slightly to £17.8 million, plus £5.2 million extraordinary expenditure relating to the Peninsular campaign, while navy expenditure had declined about three per cent to £19.7 million. A special expenditure of £90,000 for a Marylebone barracks had been eliminated by Liverpool for lack of proper time for consideration.

Vansittart had that morning raised a loan of £15.65 million from the City, £27.54 million principal amount of three per cent stock, on which he regretted that the interest rate payable had risen to 5.28 per cent (7.09 per cent including the sinking fund provision). Two days later, he and Liverpool met with the Bank of England and agreed that only one quarter of this money would be applied to replacing short-term Exchequer bills, even though the total thereof had risen sharply during the lengthy interregnum between administrations.[46] Liverpool well knew how crucial the government's liability management was for the war effort.

In terms of raising new taxes, Vansittart raised a laugh by claiming his first tax was one nobody would pay – he intended to abolish a bounty totalling £308,000 on the export of printed goods, which had become redundant: 'Wherever British manufactures are permitted to enter, their superiority is universally acknowledged.'[47] He doubled the tax on hides and shoes, which had not previously been raised since 1711. He would also double the tax on glass, little used by the poor. He would add ten per cent to the tobacco duty. He would charge the duty on auctioned property on inclusion of the property in a public auction whether or not it was actually sold. He added a penny to the tax on postage – he regretted this additional burden on business correspondence.

Perceval had proposed a tax on private brewing, calculated at five shillings per head of families where brewing was undertaken. However, Vansittart believed this tax fell too harshly on the poor, whose beer was inferior and should not be taxed so heavily, and so abandoned it. Instead, he increased the

46. Bank of England, Minutes of the Court of Directors, 25 June 1812.
47. Hansard, *Parliamentary Debates from the Year 1803 to the Present Time*, Vol. 23, cols 559-74 (17 June 1812).

'assessed taxes' on such items as carriages and manservants, horses and dogs, which acted as sumptuary imposts. The total raised by new taxes would thus be £1.9 million.

This first Liverpool/Vansittart budget, although carried over from Perceval, included several features that were to be a staple of fiscal management for the next decade. Taxes were increased, to finance more of the extraordinary war expenditure incurred, so that a higher percentage of expenditure was covered by tax than was generally the case in Pitt's wartime budgets. At the same time, the new taxes were spread around, with only a small part of them (the hides and shoes tax) falling primarily upon the poorer members of society. Notably, the new taxes would fall on consumption, not on income as under Lansdowne's 1806 doubling of income tax, nor on economically valuable production. It is not surprising that Vansittart became unpopular but his austere fiscal management was to pay immense dividends.

According to modern computations,[48] the deficit for the calendar year 1812 was £24.5 million, up from £16.4 million in the preceding year. The 1812 fiscal gap was thus 26 per cent of public spending (including interest), up from nineteen per cent of public spending in the previous year; for context, in the year to October 1797 the peak fiscal gap ratio was 63 per cent, in 1801, 40 per cent and 23 per cent in 1805, Pitt's final year.

On 29 June news of serious disturbances in several manufacturing districts was reported to Parliament by Sidmouth and Liverpool. The matter was referred to a select committee. Stanhope feared the suspension of habeas corpus, and described Liverpool as a 'minister who had no fixed principle at all, and was more versatile than a weather-cock, turning about with every change of wind'.[49] The opposition also claimed that the distress was due to the Orders in Council but Liverpool pointed out that Birmingham, badly affected by the Orders in Council, had suffered few disturbances whereas Huddersfield, with among the worst disturbances, had suffered little from the Orders in Council. The Select Committee reported within a couple of weeks, and by the end of July a Public Peace Act had been passed, operative only until March 1813, giving magistrates in affected districts the right to search houses and seize arms caches. The Act passed the Lords by seventeen votes to six at the end of the session.

In a separate discussion on the Framework Knitters Bill, attempting to set hours and wage rates in that sector, Liverpool expounded the virtues of *laissez-faire* and non-interference by government, saying:

---

48. Mitchell, *British Historical Statistics*, pp. 581 (Income), 587 (Expenditure), 577 (1797, Income), 580 (1797, Expenditure). The year-end for 1797 is 11 October, that for 1801, 1805 and 1812 is 5 January, so to get the figures for the (approximate) calendar years 1801, 1805 and 1812, you should use the 1802, 1806 and 1813 figures in the tables.

49. Hansard, *Parliamentary Debates from the Year 1803 to the Present Time*, Vol. 23, cols 796-800 (29 June 1812).

> Were we once to entangle ourselves in the principle which this bill sought to establish, I know not where we are to stop until the commerce and manufactures of the country are utterly ruined. It is to machinery that we owe our superiority in commerce and manufactures amongst the nations of the world.[50]

The bill was defeated, with the enthusiastic agreement of the Whig Holland.

On 1 July Wellesley brought up a motion for Catholic Emancipation, the third that session, in an effort to exploit the differences between members of Liverpool's Cabinet on the issue. The Cabinet was indeed split, with Harrowby and Melville supporting Wellesley's motion on the grounds that some modest progress towards Emancipation should be made, while Liverpool and Eldon opposed it on the grounds that tranquillity was essential at that difficult time. The division was extremely tight, with Eldon's motion for returning to the previous question passing by 126 votes to 125. It was the closest Catholic Emancipation had come to passing so far, but it put Liverpool on record firmly against it; useful with an election due soon.

Finally, Liverpool introduced a Toleration Bill which repealed the seventeenth-century Conventicle Act, the Five Mile Act and other legislation against dissenters, reducing the requirement for dissenting meetings to one of simple registration. He pointed out that 'an enlarged and liberal toleration was the best defence of the Established Church' and that the restrictions against dissenters were outdated. In this legislation, he was supported by most public opinion; the public attitude towards dissent was now far more tolerant than that towards Catholicism. The legislation also had the effect, which would become apparent in the autumn's elections, of drawing many Methodists away from the Whigs and towards Liverpool's government.

The disquiet caused by the American declaration of war was alleviated within a few weeks by news of Wellington's victory at Salamanca on 22 July. For the first time, British forces had obtained a decisive strategic victory over French forces in the Peninsula, even though the French enjoyed slightly superior numbers, with 13,000 French casualties against 5,000 Allied, allowing Wellington to occupy Madrid for three weeks.

Wellington was rewarded by the Prince Regent with a marquessate just six months after his earldom, with a proposed Parliamentary grant of £100,000. He still wrote to Liverpool occasionally, congratulating him for the 'favourable prospect which you have before you' [51] but suggesting his government still needed additional support, preferably Canning or his brother Wellesley-Pole.[52]

50. Ibid., Vol. 23, cols 1249-50 (25 July 1812).

51. Wellington to Liverpool, 7 September 1812, in Gurwood, *The Dispatches of Field Marshal the Duke of Wellington*, Vol. 9, p. 401.

52. William Wellesley-Pole (1763-1845) 1st Baron Maryborough from 1821, 3rd Earl of Mornington (Ireland) from 1842. MP (Ireland) for Trim, 1783-90 MP for East

Later in September, he wrote thanking Liverpool for his work in identifying a country seat for Wellington to buy: 'It rarely happens that a person in your situation has leisure to attend to his own private affairs, much less to those of any other individual.'[53]

Wellington's Salamanca success paid important electoral dividends for Liverpool; it also allowed the government to loosen the purse strings on Wellington's activities. The Budget's additional £2 million of new taxes to support him sailed through Parliament in the first flush of the victory.

In the autumn the Bank of England objected to a request from Bathurst and the Privy Council to supply £400,000 in bullion to Wellington's troops on the grounds of lack of bullion in its vaults, protesting in person to Liverpool.[54] However, the government repeated their order to the Bank to supply Wellington with £400,000, in four monthly instalments of £100,000 each. It then opened a new channel of bullion supply to Wellington through the Rothschild[55] banking dynasty, which had offices all over occupied Europe.

After unsuccessfully besieging Burgos, having had a narrow escape – 'the worst scrape I ever was in' – from the entire French force of 90,000 men, Wellington retreated into winter quarters in Portugal. However, it represented only a temporary check to Wellington's success. The failure of Napoleon's Russian campaign had left him in an excellent position to advance quickly in 1813.

The success of Stuart Wortley's motion in May had demonstrated to Liverpool that the government could not be sure of a majority in the Parliament elected in the different circumstances of 1807. While convention would indicate that an election should not be called before the spring of 1813, six years after the last poll, the precedents of 1784, 1806 and 1807 had demonstrated that a government could call an election earlier, provided the monarch agreed.

Two factors convinced Liverpool that an early poll might produce favourable results. First, the three attempts in the 1812 session by the Whigs, allied with Canning and Wellesley, to push through Catholic Emancipation had aroused considerable hostility in the country. Having seen the electoral results achieved by Portland in 1807, Liverpool could hope for something of a repeat

---

Looe, 1790-95, MP for Queen's County, 1801-21. Secretary to the Admiralty, 1807-09; Chief Secretary for Ireland, 1809-12; Master of the Mint, 1814-23; Master of the Buckhounds, 1823-30; Postmaster-General, 1834-35.

53. Wellington to Liverpool, 15 September 1812, in Gurwood, *The Dispatches of Field Marshal the Duke of Wellington*, Vol. 9, p. 427.
54. Bank of England, Minutes of the Court of Directors, 8 October 1812.
55. Nathan Mayer Rothschild (1777-1836). Freiherr von Rothschild (Austria) from 1818. He had begun in 1798 trading in textiles from Manchester, then from 1804 began to deal in bills and bonds in London, as well as foreign exchange. He became a bullion dealer in 1809. Entered the international loans business in 1818 with a £5 million loan to the Prussian government and solved the Bank of England's liquidity problems in December 1825. Co-founded Alliance Assurance Co. in 1824. Worth about £3 million at his death in 1836.

performance. In later years, the Whigs would have more sense than to push Catholic Emancipation just before an election; indeed, it was the Wellington government's final passage of that measure in 1829, followed by an unexpected election due to George IV's death, that brought to an end the Tory hegemony of this period. Nevertheless, Portland's triumph of 1807 had been the first time public opinion had played a decisive electoral part, and politicians were not yet accustomed to electoral management on this basis, rather than on the old basis of ministerial, Court and local influence.

The second factor influencing Liverpool was the victory at Salamanca. With this triumph, prospects for an election were too good to miss and accordingly Parliament was dissolved on 29 September.

The result was a triumph for Liverpool – like Portland's in 1807, but slightly larger. The favourable war situation pushed voters towards the government, although economic hardship, extensive in 1812 but easing late in the year after the good harvest, operated in the opposite direction. According to Thorne's calculations,[56] the government gained some 30 seats, bringing its total to 419 against the opposition's 239, a majority of 180 compared to a government majority of about 150 following Portland's victory. As important, Canning's pro-Emancipation supporters were reduced from about 30 to eleven members and those of Wellesley to twelve, greatly reducing their potential for disruption.

Canning, however, won a personal triumph in the trading port of Liverpool, being elected with 1,631 votes ahead of the Tory anti-Catholic (and pro-slavery) sitting member Isaac Gascoyne with 1,532 votes (both well ahead of the Whigs Henry Brougham and Thomas Creevey[57] with 1,131 and 1,068 votes, respectively).

This was the first of Liverpool's four electoral triumphs. Apart from providing him with a secure majority for the next six years, it also marked a setback for Catholic Emancipation. Grattan's[58] motion of 1813 received less support than Canning's Commons motion of the previous year, while in the House of Lords it never got as close as the one-vote margin by which Wellesley's motion was defeated. The issue was thus on the 'back burner' during this Parliament, a blessing considering the excessive economic hardships of the early post-war years.

Liverpool knew that electoral conditions had changed since the 1780s. In a letter to Eldon's brother, who was anxious to secure a seat, Liverpool pointed out that he had only one Treasury seat available, which had gone to

56. Thorne, *The History of Parliament. the House of Commons 1790-1820* Presumably the Portland and Perceval governments had lost some seats in by-elections.

57. Thomas Creevey (1768-1838). Whig MP for Thetford, Appleby and Downton, 1802-6, 1807-18, 1820-26, 1831-32. Secretary to Board of Control, 1806-7. Diarist.

58. Henry Grattan (1746-1820). MP (Ireland) for Charlemont, Dublin City and Wicklow, 1775-1801, MP for Malton and Dublin City, 1803-20. Notable orator. Pushed through Act making Irish parliament independent, 1783, and Irish Catholic Emancipation, 1793.

Vansittart, and two others whose patronage had been given to him. Since Curwen's Act of 1809, it was no longer possible for government funds to be used to buy support from borough proprietors. Instead, public opinion and the general good reputation of government must be used to win support in open boroughs.[59]

The remainder of 1812 saw a modest positive balance for British arms against the United States, even though Britain had only 6,000 regular troops in Canada and reinforcements were impossible until Napoleon's defeat in 1814. On the negative side, in August 1812 the 38-gun frigate HMS *Guerriere* was sunk by the 44-gun USS *Constitution* and later in the year two more frigates, HMS *Macedonian* and HMS *Java*, were captured (HMS *Java* off the cost of Brazil). These losses were to result in a debate on naval administration in the House of Lords the following May, in which Liverpool successfully defended government policy by pointing out that repeal of the Orders in Council had been expected to appease the Americans and that, while isolated frigates could be captured whatever the balance of forces, in general, British forces were stronger than American on all the west Atlantic stations. Further, no British merchantmen had been lost other than those which sailed without convoy.[60]

On the positive side, in August US General William Hull, after attempting to invade Canada, was forced to surrender Detroit to a smaller force of Canadian soldiers led by Major-General Isaac Brock and First Nations[61] forces led by Tecumseh. Brock then won a second victory when a US invading force led by Steven van Rensselaer was defeated by a British/First Nations force at the Battle of Queenston Heights.

Nevertheless, Britain's naval losses were sufficiently disquieting that Wellington, dependent on a sea-borne supply line, wrote to Vice-Admiral George Martin in December: 'Government appear to be at last making a serious effort to get the better of the American navy, which might as well have been made before.'[62]

Of far more importance than the skirmishes in North America was the Battle of Borodino on 7 September, a huge engagement involving 250,000 troops, with 70,000 casualties, and a tactical French victory in which the

59. Quoted in Yonge, *The Life and Administration of Robert Banks Jenkinson*, Vol. 1, p. 444.
60. Hansard, *Parliamentary Debates from the Year 1803 to the Present Time*, Vol. 26, cols 201-2 (14 May 1813).
61. I am happy to be as politically correct as I can but to call Tecumseh's forces Native Americans is inaccurate. The Canadian term 'First Nations' seems more appropriate, even though many of them inhabited what is now the United States. The old-fashioned 'Indians' while also appropriate runs the risk of confusion with the inhabitants of today's India, even though the context generally clarifies this.
62. Wellington to Vice-Admiral Martin (10 December 1812), in Gurwood, *The Dispatches of Field Marshal the Duke of Wellington*, Vol. 9, pp. 611-12. Sir George Martin (1764-1847). Commander-in-Chief, Lisbon, 1812-14. Captain, 1783. Rear-Admiral, 1805. Vice-Admiral, 1810. Admiral, 1821. Admiral of the Fleet, 1846.

Russians under General Mikhail Kutuzov[63] nevertheless acquitted themselves well. Liverpool, writing to Wellington when the news arrived, immediately recognised its significance: 'If Russian perseverance should continue for six weeks or two months longer, Bonaparte will be in a situation more critical than any in which he has ever yet been engaged.'[64] Even more significant, in Liverpool's view, Czar Alexander I had ordered the Russian fleet to sail to Britain for safe keeping.

In a second letter to Wellington, apart from commending the Russian abandonment of Moscow, Liverpool went in detail into the dangers surrounding Napoleon and the difficulties he was now facing. He also pointed out that, even if Napoleon somehow managed to extricate his forces, the whole of French resources must be employed in either extricating Napoleon from Russia or sustaining him there, so there would be no reinforcements for French forces in Spain. He requested Wellington's thoughts on the next year's campaigning and suggested that, if France could be driven out of the Peninsula, an attack on southern France would be preferable to any other operation.

Wellington in reply explained his strategic thinking. With a tired army and heavily outnumbered (he gave his reasons for thinking the French forces against him numbered 90,000 men), it was difficult for him to take the strategic initiative – also, his army needed a winter's rest to recover. However, he believed that, if the French entered Portugal they would be beaten, since Wellington holding the border forts could cut their supply lines, and that the large French army would be broken up over the winter, giving him excellent opportunities in the New Year.

During the winter Wellington, who had now been appointed Commander-in-Chief of Spanish forces, would go to Cádiz, the siege of which had been raised, and attempt to improve Spanish organisation and discipline. Wellington recounted the achievements of the year and apologised for the failure of the Burgos siege, which stemmed from his troops' inexperience and a failure by the commander of the initial assault. Still, the siege of Burgos had been entirely his idea and should certainly not be blamed on the government.

The guns were fired in Hyde Park to celebrate Napoleon's retreat from Smolensk, which marked the end of his hopes in Russia. He was to leave the army by sleigh on 5 December, after rumours reached him of an attempted coup in Paris; the army left Russian territory on 14 December.

The Prince Regent opened the new Parliament in person on 29 November. In the debate on his speech Wellesley began with a blistering attack on the

63. Mikhail Kutuzov (1745-1813). Count from 1811. Prince from 1812. Brigadier, Russian army, 1782. Major-General, 1784. Lieutenant-General, 1791. Governor General of Crimea, 1787-91. Austerlitz, 1805. Russo-Turkish War, 1806-12. Borodino, 1812.

64. Quoted in Yonge, *The Life and Administration of Robert Banks Jenkinson*, Vol. 1, pp. 438-39. Second letter to Wellington, pp. 440-42.

government for not properly funding Wellington's Peninsula campaign. Liverpool responded that the resources in the Peninsula were far greater than had been imagined in 1809 and that, while Napoleon's defeats in Russia opened a new opportunity, it was still necessary to tailor resources to a long campaign, because an overwhelming short-term effort opened up too great a risk of failure. Grenville, supporting Wellesley, then claimed that the retreat after Burgos proved that, even after three campaigns, the government was no closer to achieving its objectives in the Peninsula. However, the government's position was so strong that the opposition did not divide the House. The opposition's weakness was emphasised during a subsequent debate on the £100,000 grant to Wellington, which Holland supported and was agreed without dissent.

On 13 December the Prince Regent delivered another message to Parliament asking for a charitable grant of £200,000 to assist Russians hurt by Napoleon's invasion. Liverpool took the opportunity to extol the Russian people, who had emulated the Spanish in their resistance to French invasion, and to rejoice in the commercial benefits of Russian alliance: 'Was it nothing to have the market of 36 million people? . . . Every channel of commerce had received fresh life and vigour through the success of the Russians.'[65] Again, the Whigs failed to divide the House.

Liverpool summed up his view of the military situation in another letter to Wellington. He believed Napoleon's defeat in Russia meant he might withdraw troops from Spain, because he would need a large force to maintain order in Germany. While Napoleon did not abandon Spain until he was forced to, Liverpool was prescient in pinpointing the attitude of Austria as critical in the attempt to liberate Europe. Castlereagh's diplomacy through the first half of 1813 would be devoted to drawing the cautious Austrians into what became the Great Alliance.

For the first time it now appeared possible that Napoleon's hold over Europe might be loosened and a stable peace achieved. War with the United States added another difficulty; but events there had suggested that the danger to Canada was manageable and the resources required would be modest. After the distress and unrest early in the year, a good harvest and firm policy had quietened the manufacturing districts and economic prospects had brightened. Finally, Liverpool himself had won a notable election victory and consolidated himself in power; it was now likely that he would make a major mark on the future of Britain. For Liverpool and the world, 1812 was a truly memorable year.

65. Hansard, *Parliamentary Debates from the Year 1803 to the Present Time*, Vol. 24, cols 319-22 (13 December 1812).

V.
Years of Victory, 1813-15

In the next three years Liverpool attained his first truly historic achievement: presiding over victory in the Napoleonic Wars. That was the principal reason for his longevity as Prime Minister; it gave him stature and credibility during the difficult years that followed. These three years also provide much of the basis for granting Liverpool the epithet, 'Britain's Greatest Prime Minister'.

Wellington opened the year 1813 with an address to the Cortes of Cádiz (the Spanish parliament), thanking them for making him Commander-in-Chief of Spanish forces, followed by an Address to the Spanish army and meetings with the leading generals. He then sent an envoy to the court of Austria (still allied with France) to tell them of his progress in Spain and that he expected to tie up 200,000 French troops in 1813. The remainder of early 1813 was occupied in building up the British and Portuguese forces and reorganising the Spanish forces for the campaign that would begin in early May.

Wellington's real opinion of the Spanish government was contained in a letter to Bathurst of 27 January:

> It is impossible to describe the state of confusion in which affairs are at Cadiz. . . . I am astonished at the patience of my brother, and that he has been able to do anything with these people. . . . I have taken for the military, nine tenths of all the resources of the country.[1]

Diplomatically, 1813 was the critical year of the war. It began with Napoleon and the *Grande Armée* expelled from Russia but no alliance formed to oppose him. Indeed, if Napoleon assembled a new and powerful army, the formation of any such alliance seemed unlikely, since Marie Louise,[2] the daughter of

---

1. Letter to Bathurst, 27 January 1813, in Gurwood, *The Dispatches of Field Marshal the Duke of Wellington*, Vol. 10, pp. 51-55.
2. Marie Louise (1791-1847). Married Napoleon I, 1810. Empress of France, 1810-14. Duchess of Parma from 1814. Mother of Napoleon II, Prince Imperial (1811-32).

the Austrian Emperor Francis I,[3] was married to Napoleon, while Prussia was poorly led by Frederick William III[4] and had lost half her territory by the 1807 Treaties of Tilsit. Furthermore, the failure of five previous coalitions against Napoleon made both Austria and Prussia highly cautious about committing themselves.

One preliminary step had already been taken: on 30 December the Russian Major-General Johann von Diebitsch[5] had signed a preliminary agreement, the Convention of Tauroggen with the Prussian Lieutenant-General David von Yorck,[6] withdrawing Prussian forces from opposition to the Russian advance towards Prussia. Kutuzov's forces crossed the River Vistula in January 1813 and entered East Prussia. Kutuzov made every effort to treat the inhabitants well and was generally welcomed. By this time Metternich was wriggling vigorously out of the French alliance. As far back as 9 December he had offered Austria's services to Napoleon as mediator of a general peace, and on 30 January Schwarzenberg,[7] commanding the Austrian forces, signed an armistice of indefinite duration with the Russian forces.

As Henry Kissinger masterfully set out in *A World Restored*,[8] Metternich[9] did not want Austria to face Napoleon's wrath without Russia and Prussia fully committed by its side; that had brought disaster in 1805-6 and 1809. Accordingly, he moved tentatively until August, playing a complex game. That game ended with (probably his ultimate objective throughout) Austria locked into an alliance with Britain, Prussia and Russia to push France back out of Germany.

---

3. Francis I (1768-1835). Holy Roman Emperor Francis II, 1792-1806. Emperor of Austria Francis I from 1804 (referred to herein as Francis I, his title during the period we are concerned with). Capable, if somewhat paranoid, but from 1809 dominated by Metternich.
4. Frederick William III (1770-1840). King of Prussia from 1797. Ineffectual reactionary, father of Frederick William IV and Emperor William I.
5. Hans-Karl von Diebitsch (1785-1831). Graf from 1829. Field Marshal from 1829. Played role in crushing Decembrist revolt of 1825. Commanding General in Russo-Turkish War of 1828-29 and suppression of Polish insurrection, 1830-31.
6. Johann David Ludwig von Yorck (1759-1830). Graf Yorck von Wartenburg from 1814. Generalfeldmarschall from 1821. Prussian army, 1772-79, 1782-85, 1786-1821.
7. Karl Philipp, Prince of Schwarzenberg (1771-1820). Field Marshal, 1813. Commander of the forces of the Sixth Coalition, 1813-14.
8. Henry Kissinger (1923-) (US Secretary of State, 1973-77), *A World Restored: Metternich, Castlereagh and the Problems of Peace, 1812-22* (London: Weidenfeld & Nicolson, 1957). One of the few books on this period written by a genuine expert. Kissinger's only flaw is that, not being an expert on British history of the period, and having few reliable sources, he does not appreciate the extent to which Liverpool was involved in foreign policy and setting the overall direction for Castlereagh.
9. Klemens von Metternich (1773-1859). Prince from 1803. Duke of Naples from 1818. Austrian Foreign Minister, 1809-48. Chancellor, 1821-48.

Prussia initially repudiated Yorck's armistice but, after reassurances from Metternich that Austria would stand with her, on 28 February signed the Treaty of Kalisz, an alliance with Russia, thus beginning the process of forming the Sixth Coalition and opening the path to joining with Metternich's Austria. By the end of March Metternich had obtained from Alexander a guarantee of Austria's 1805 frontiers, which Prussia had not achieved.

However, Austria was still moving only to the position of a neutral intermediary rather than a participant in the war. It finally wriggled out of its French alliance on 1 May, while promising the Czar that Austria would eventually end up a full ally. Meanwhile, Russian forces, without opposition from Prussia and Austria, were steadily advancing and by early April had passed the Elbe in central Germany. Even the death of Kutuzov on 28 April did not slow their advance – he was succeeded by Peter Wittgenstein.[10]

For Liverpool and Castlereagh, the long-term implications of Metternich's scheming were as yet impenetrable. Indeed, in a letter to Cathcart, Castlereagh speculated that Metternich's machinations might be dictated by Napoleon, to obtain a separate peace with his Continental adversaries while he still controlled most of Europe. Castlereagh recommended, 'the general principle, of giving confidence to all powers which can be induced to take a part in reducing the power of France and restoring the independence of Germany'.[11] Accordingly, Liverpool and Castlereagh looked to form an alliance with the self-confident Sweden. In 1810 Jean Bernadotte, one of Napoleon's marshals, had been elected heir-presumptive to the throne of Sweden, becoming Regent (and a Lutheran) on his arrival in Stockholm; he would succeed to the throne in 1818.

While Bernadotte had brought Sweden into France's alliance system in 1810, its allegiance was purely nominal and the French invasion of Swedish Pomerania in January 1812 brought both Bernadotte and Swedish public opinion firmly to an anti-French position. The Treaty of Orebro of July 1812 ended the war between Sweden and Britain but it was only in March 1813 that Sweden entered a definitive alliance with Britain, after Britain had agreed to recognise its claims to Norway. Thus, by the end of April Sweden and Prussia were allied in principle with Britain and Russia in coalition against Napoleon, while Austria had become neutral.

In North America, the first months of 1813 saw mixed fortunes. On 18-22 January a mixed British/First Nations force under Colonel Henry Procter and Tecumseh defeated the US forces under Major-General William Henry

---

10. Ludwig Adolph Peter, Count Wittgenstein (1769-1843). Prince Wittgenstein from 1834. Colonel, 1798. Major-General, 1799. Austerlitz, 1805. Friedland, 1807. Commanded right wing of Russian army at Battle of Polotsk, 1812, saving St Petersburg. Commanded entire army after Kutuzov's death, suffering defeat at Lützen and Bautzen, then commanded corps under Schwarzenberg.
11. Londonderry, *Memoirs and Correspondence of Viscount Castlereagh*, Vol. 8, pp. 301-5.

Harrison[12] at the Battle of Frenchtown, Michigan, which was followed by a massacre of the US wounded by First Nations auxiliaries (around 500 men), their worst loss of the war. Then, on 22 February, the British Colonel 'Red George' Macdonell captured Ogdensburg, New York, cutting off a threat to British supply lines.

However, on 27 April a US force under Zebulon Pike captured York (present-day Toronto), the capital of Upper Canada, forcing the British forces to retreat to Kingston, Ontario. The following month, US forces also captured Fort George, the westernmost British fort on Lake Ontario, at the mouth of the Niagara River. These US victories were counterbalanced on 1 June, when HMS *Shannon* captured USS *Chesapeake* in a brief but intense frigate action off Boston harbour. Thus, by the middle of the year honours remained about even. In May Russia offered to mediate between Britain and the United States but Liverpool turned the offer down; as Wellington said: 'the object of this offer must be to create a division between us and the Russians'.[13]

In London, Parliament reassembled in mid-February with a debate on the American war. Liverpool pointed out that impressment could not be the true *casus belli* because America's ports were crying out against the war, while the war hawks came from interior states, for whom impressment of seamen could not possibly be an important issue. He then described the war as 'one of passion' on the US part and, reasoning from Britain's position as guardian of the Atlantic sea lanes, said: 'She ought to have looked to this country as the guardian power to which she was indebted, not only for her comforts, not only for her rank in the scale of civilisation, but for her very existence.'[14]

The following month, Wellesley returned to his complaint that the government had starved the Peninsular campaign and demanded a parliamentary committee to examine the matter. Bathurst took the main burden of response to this, but Liverpool followed up, describing Wellington's 1812 campaign as 'the most brilliant achieved by British arms during the last century'[15] and going through Wellington's plans in detail. Wellesley's motion was defeated by 115 votes to 39.

12. William Henry Harrison (1773-1841). Youngest son of a prominent Virginia planter who was a signatory to the Declaration of Independence. Secretary of the Northwest Territory, 1798-99. Congressmen from the Northwest Territory, 1799-1800. Governor of the Indiana Territory, 1801-12. Major-General, 1812-14. Congressman from Ohio's 1st District, 1816-19. Senator from Ohio, 1825-28. Minister to Gran Colombia, 1828-29. 9th President of the United States, 1841. He died 31 days into his term and would probably have been a pretty good President if he had lived longer.

13. Letter to Henry Wellesley, 23 May 1813, in Gurwood, *The Dispatches of Field Marshal the Duke of Wellington*, Vol. 10, p. 395.

14. Hansard, *Parliamentary Debates from the Year 1803 to the Present Time*, Vol. 24, cols 584-86 (18 February 1813).

15. Ibid., Vol. 25, cols 84-88 (12 March 1813).

In the Commons, the government's strength was demonstrated by the fate of another attempt by Princess Caroline to stir up trouble. Her access to her daughter Princess Charlotte, now sixteen years old and being educated at Windsor, was restricted by the Prince Regent. Caroline wrote to the Prince Regent via Liverpool, who responded that the Prince Regent would not receive her letter, at which point she published it in the Radical press. In response to this, the Prince Regent instructed a committee of the Privy Council to examine the case. The committee recommended that, even though the 'Delicate Investigation' of 1806 had not formally found Caroline guilty of adultery, the Prince Regent should be allowed to restrict her access to her daughter.

Thereupon on two occasions Andrew Cochrane-Johnstone,[16] an independent Radical member, brought the case up in the House of Commons. With the aid of a violent speech by Whitbread, Cochrane-Johnstone attempted to embarrass the government, or possibly get paid off by the Prince Regent. On these occasions however, Parliament favoured the Prince Regent and the administration, and the motions failed without a division.

Throughout his almost 26-year tenure of the Lord Chancellor's office, Eldon was bombarded with criticism about the backlog in the Court of Chancery,[17] over which he and the Master of the Rolls presided and which was frequently up to twelve years in arrears. (Its business had grown proportionately with the increase in both population and wealth since its formation in the Middle Ages.) In 1812-13, Eldon agreed to a reform under which a Vice-Chancellor would be appointed, who would preside over the Court of Chancery in the Lord Chancellor's absence. After considerable debate, the Bill accomplishing this received its Commons Third Reading and was signed into law in March 1813.

Eldon then met with criticism because the first Vice-Chancellor, the Attorney General Sir Thomas Plumer,[18] was thought to lack sufficient knowledge of equity law. It appears that Plumer, a *protégé* of Perceval, was anxious to leave the House of Commons for a top legal appointment and Liverpool was happy to oblige him. Despite Plumer's best efforts, the backlog of Chancery cases was only modestly reduced and the Court again became a subject of hostile Parliamentary inquiry in 1824.

Unlike the previous year, the 1813 Budget was presented in two parts, in March and June, with the spending estimates covered in the second part. Vansittart began by announcing that he had refinanced £12 million

16. Andrew Cochrane-Johnstone (1767-1833). MP for Stirling Burghs and Grampound 1791-97, 1807-8, 1812-14. Governor of Dominica, 1797-1803. Expelled from the House of Commons after fraud conviction and absconding, 1814.
17. The Court of Chancery dealt with matters of equity in civil lawsuits that were thought too arbitrarily dealt with under common law. It was folded into the High Court in 1873.
18. Sir Thomas Plumer (1753-1824). MP for Downton, 1807-13. Solicitor General, 1807-12. Attorney General, 1812-13. Vice-Chancellor, 1813-18. Master of the Rolls, 1818-24.

of Exchequer bills by five per cent navy annuities of 15.5 per cent greater principal amount, at an interest cost of 5.78 per cent, being a 0.5 per cent greater interest cost than the previous year's Budget funding, but 0.16 per cent lower cash flow cost including the sinking fund provision.

This funding was one of the few during the war made by a near-par five per cent bond rather than by three or four per cent Consols at a deep discount. However, Vansittart also gave buyers an option of investing an additional 50 per cent of their subscription in a five per cent medium-term note that would be convertible at the holder's option twelve months after the end of the war into either cash or into 150 per cent of three per cent stock, 120 per cent of four per cent stock or 100 per cent of five per cent navy bills. By this ingenious mechanism, allowing the holders of the notes to choose their coupon and issue price, he would save 0.65 per cent in interest costs on the amount raised. Alas, the new notes were undersubscribed, raising only £800,000. The 'urgent necessity' expressed by the Bank of England at a meeting with Liverpool and Vansittart for a further drawdown of Exchequer bills would thus have to be postponed.[19]

To raise enough money to cover sinking fund payments and a deficit due to the previous year's auction tax having been rejected, Vansittart claimed he needed £970,000 in new taxation. He raised £100,000 of this sum by an increase in tobacco duty and £870,000 by a 25 per cent increase in customs duties, which had not been increased since 1804 and would cause little hardship since trade with the Continent had only just restarted. In addition, he proposed an additional excise of thirteen pence a bottle (eighteen pence at the retail level) on French wines 'an article of mere luxury, entirely confined to the higher orders'.[20] This tax should yield more revenue as trading links with France recovered.

Vansittart also proposed further temporary war taxes, such as a doubling of all duties on items imported from France or countries dependent on it – these imports had been prohibited by the Orders in Council but import licences were expected to be resumed. Finally, he proposed an additional duty on imports of American raw cotton, so that colonial production from India could be stimulated, and any removal by the Americans of the current embargo would not result in losses to importers of colonial cotton. Alexander Baring and Sir Robert Peel (father of the future Prime Minister) objected strongly to this measure, both 'talking their own books'.[21]

19. Bank of England, Minutes of the Court of Directors, 8 April 1813.

20. Hansard, *Parliamentary Debates from the Year 1803 to the Present Time*, Vol. 25, cols 473-81 (31 March 1813). The duty is the equivalent of about £14 ($18) at the retail level today but it must be remembered there was no cheap French 'plonk' in Britain in 1813 because of transportation costs – the first such cheap wine was the 'Gladstone claret' of the 1860s after the 1860 Cobden free trade treaty.

21. A useful merchant banking term; it means advocating measures that would lead to your own financial gain, based on securities positions you already hold. Nathan Rothschild was prone to this, and in later years Liverpool was to show himself wise to it.

On 11 June Vansittart outlined the spending estimates. Naval expenditure was up £872,000 over the previous year, while army expenditure was up £1.17 million. However, extraordinary army expenses in the previous year had exceeded the amount budgeted by £4.66 million, so this year Vansittart proposed an extraordinary army budget of £9.5 million, of which £5 million had already been voted. Thus, total expenses for Great Britain and Ireland would be £72.1 million, up 24 per cent from the amount budgeted in the previous year. He had raised another £20.9 million cash that morning, increasing the debt principal by £35.7 million. The total debt created in the 1812-13 session was £54.8 million, at an average charge of 5.2 per cent per annum.[22]

According to modern estimates 1813 saw a seventeen per cent jump in spending to £111.1 million (including emergency increases during the year). Even though revenue rebounded from 1812's hardship year by 6.2 per cent, the fiscal gap increased to 33 per cent of public spending, the highest such gap since that of 1801 (40 per cent).[23] The huge increase in the war effort was thus causing the country's fiscal discipline to deteriorate.

This was demonstrated in a series of letters between Liverpool and the Bank of England in May and early June. The Bank of England were not happy about the government's earlier failure to pay down Exchequer bills, so when asked to buy another £2 million of bills, they made it clear that it must be the last such demand and that both it and substantial amounts of other Exchequer bills must be cleared by the next loan. Then, the following week, Vansittart requested that the Bank roll over £5 million of its May and June Exchequer bill maturities to 17 June, promising in return to reduce the Bank's Exchequer bill outstandings by an additional £2 million by October and to apply at least half the early instalments of the forthcoming loan to such reduction. Finally, on 10 June, Liverpool and Vansittart asked, first, that the July 1812 bills be held until the latter part of July 1813, rather than presented for payment immediately, and, second, that the Bank advance a further £2 million in Exchequer bills as the government did not have sufficient funds to make the July interest payment on Consols.[24]

This correspondence shows that in the early summer of 1813 the government's cash flow management was very difficult, requiring discipline and iron nerves from Liverpool and Vansittart, as well as high-level negotiating skills with the Bank of England. Overall, the government came closer to insolvency in May/June 1813 than at any time since 1797-98.

In March 1813 Vansittart also proposed a new plan of finance, revising the Sinking Fund Acts of 1786 and 1792. He pointed out that taxes had been

22. Hansard, *Parliamentary Debates from the Year 1803 to the Present Time*, Vol. 26, cols 574-80 (11 June 1813).

23. Mitchell, *British Historical Statistics*, pp. 581 (Income), 587 (Expenditure). The year-end is 5 January so, to get the figures for the (approximate) calendar year 1813, you have to use the 1814 figures in the tables.

24. Bank of England, Minutes of the Court of Directors, 20 May, 27 May and 10 June 1813.

increased to a level that almost matched the normal expenses of wartime, but that extraordinary expenses since 1808 had once again unbalanced the budget. However, raising an additional £14.5 million of additional expenditure through further taxation would place an excessive burden on the economy and might prove unnecessary if special wartime expenses could again be reduced. Vansittart therefore proposed that new debt incurred each year should not require sinking fund taxes for the first four years but should continue to bear them after the sinking fund's final redemption, then supposed to be in 1830.

This was the first of several alleviations of the sinking fund, to reduce the burden of taxes and the annual funding need, while reassuring the market that the sinking fund principle was being maintained. Liverpool, introducing the legislation in the House of Lords, said that the scheme's purpose was not to dilute the sinking fund but simply to smooth its operation, while maintaining the principle that every new debt was to be extinguished by the sinking fund within 45 years. The nation had raised £20 million in excess annual taxes over the last decade, reducing the potential debt by £200 million. On the present scale of expense, the war could be carried on for four years without raising any new taxes, or six years taking into account the natural buoyancy of tax revenues. Russia had repelled Napoleon and the Continental System was dead, so, if taxes remained constant, British merchants could be expected to expand into the space allowed. In short, 'no period could be more favourable than the present to resort to this measure'.[25]

A younger generation used to ever-increasing national debt often scoffs at the sinking fund principle. However, the funding of the 22-year French Revolutionary and Napoleonic Wars in the bond markets, the build-up without market panic (except to a limited extent in 1797) of debt which at its peak in 1819 totalled 260 per cent of GDP, and the fiscal discipline required to bring that debt down (such that, by Liverpool's departure in fiscal year 1827, it was below 200 per cent of GDP),[26] are achievements never subsequently matched in any country. The sinking fund, allowing the government to finance unprecedented budget deficits while keeping the market calm, was a vital part of this achievement.

The major issue during the remainder of the 1813 session was the East India Company's charter renewal, undertaken every twenty years and due in 1814. The Commons debate on the East India Company was distinguished by the appearance of Warren Hastings to give evidence, invited by Castlereagh as a partial recompense for the disgraceful impeachment trial of 1788-95. The House rewarded Hastings appropriately by giving him a standing ovation. Hastings took this opportunity to warn against allowing too many Britons to settle in India, especially the lower orders because they tended towards despotism over the Indians. The tolerance and respect for Indian customs, languages and religions

25. Hansard, *Parliamentary Debates from the Year 1803 to the Present Time*, Vol. 25, cols 765-68 (12 April 1813).
26. Debt to GDP ratios calculated from figures in UKpublicspending.co.uk.

and fear of British racism established by Hastings as East India Company policy in India were to be thrown overboard by the Whiggish Bentinck/Macaulay[27] and Dalhousie[28] regimes of 1828-35 and 1848-56.

Grenville began the debate on the East India Company in the Lords by saying the subject covered the well-being of 40 million subjects of the British crown; modern estimates put the population of areas ruled by Britain at around 60 million of a total Indian population of 200 million, itself a fifth of the world's total population of one billion. He then called for an end to the East India Company's monopoly of British trade with the Indies, which induced Indian trade to be carried out with foreign nations before Britain. Liverpool in response assured him that a bill would be presented later in the session and referred the matter to a Select Committee.

Later in the debate, Liverpool stated that 'the government of India, from the year 1784 up to the present, had been most advantageously carried on by the Company'. He was therefore not in favour of revoking the Company's governmental privileges. Conversely, with world trade so much greater, it was now impossible to prevent foreigners from trading with the East Indies, and so he was in favour of revoking the East India Company's nominal monopoly, which would allow British traders to participate in that lucrative trade.[29] However, Liverpool later confirmed the Company's monopoly on trade to China, particularly in tea, where the Chinese government's restrictions made it unattractive to open the trade to all comers. (Exporting opium from Bengal to China was, alas, the East India Company's solution to the payments imbalance caused by insatiable British demand for China tea.)

One last matter was resolved. The appointment of a bishop and archdeacons at Kolkata to serve the 150,000 British people in India and also the gradually increasing number of Indian converts. This was the first Anglican hierarchy in the colonies; it was to be followed in other colonies.

---

27. Thomas Babington Macaulay (1800-59). 1st Baron Macaulay from 1857. MP for Calne, Leeds and Edinburgh, 1830-34, 1839-47, 1850-56. Secretary to the Board of Control, 1832-33. Law Member of the Governor General's Council, 1834-38. Secretary at War, 1839-41. Paymaster-General, 1846-48. Wrote his *Minute on Indian Education* of February 1835, stating: 'A single shelf of a good European library is worth the whole native literature of India and Arabia.' Hastings, on the other hand, had remarked in 1784 that knowledge of and sympathy for the peoples of India could be obtained by study of their writings, which 'will survive when British domination in India shall have long ceased to exist, and when the sources which once yielded of wealth and power are lost to remembrance'.
28. James Brown Ramsay (1812-60). 10th Earl of Dalhousie from 1838. 1st Marquess of Dalhousie from 1849. MP for Huntingdonshire, 1837-38. President of the Board of Trade, 1845-46. Governor-General of India, 1848-56. Lord Warden of the Cinque Ports, 1853-60.
29. Hansard, *Parliamentary Debates from the Year 1803 to the Present Time*, Vol. 25, cols 752-54 (9 April 1813).

The Catholic Emancipation question came up again in the Commons, where Grattan carried by 40 votes a motion referring their claims to a Committee of the whole House. However, a bill removing the disability of Catholics to sit and vote in Parliament lost by four votes after opposition by the Speaker, prompted by Liverpool. On the other hand, Liverpool supported a minor bill removing the need for Catholics to forswear the doctrine of transubstantiation if promoted to a position with the army outside Ireland.

After several preliminary skirmishes, the Swedish treaty finally came up for discussion on 13 June. The Whigs' principal point of attack was the treaty's provision giving Norway to Sweden but Liverpool pointed out that Denmark, previously in control of Norway, had remained allied to France throughout. Since Sweden had been forced to give up Finland to Russia by the treaty of Tilsit, and had already agreed the Norway acquisition with Russia, there was little purpose in resisting it.

From the British viewpoint, since Norway was a major source of naval stores and had many deep harbours, it was in Britain's interest to keep it as independent as possible from France and that could not be achieved while Denmark controlled it, because of that country's German possessions, which were vulnerable to French attack. As for Guadeloupe, which the Treaty also gave to Sweden, since Britain had captured all the French West Indian islands during the war, it was a matter of indifference to give one of them to Sweden.[30]

To wind up the session, Liverpool proposed a £5 million vote of credit, to allow the government to take advantage of any contingencies during the parliamentary recess, such as the subsidies to Russia and Prussia which had been agreed (though that news had yet to reach London) and the likely subsidy to Austria if she joined the war on the Allied side. This was carried without a division although Holland claimed that peace negotiations with Napoleon should be opened. The government's parliamentary path on foreign affairs had now become easy.

At the end of the session, the proto-Keynesian[31] Lauderdale moved a motion deprecating the cost of issuing Exchequer bills and demanding either an immediate withdrawal of all paper currency or a paper currency issued by

30. Ibid., Vol. 26, cols 719-26 (13 June 1813).

31. John Maynard Keynes (1883-1946). 1st Baron Keynes, 1942. Economist. Wrote *The Economic Consequences of the Peace* (1919), *The End of Laissez-Faire* (1926), *A Treatise on Money* (1930), *The General Theory of Employment, Interest and Money* (1936). Headed British delegation to the Bretton Woods Conference, 1944, during which he surrendered just about every British interest that mattered. Some but not all of the Whigs and Radicals during the Liverpool years favoured unbalanced budgets and loose paper-money policies of the kind later associated with John Maynard Keynes. I have risked anachronism in these pages in describing such ideas as 'Keynesian', reflecting the fact that Keynes' ideas in many areas were not original, but reflected the wishes of big-spending, funny-money dirigiste statesmen. Keynes merely wrapped these primordial urges in a theoretical gloss and apparent economic rigour.

the government. Liverpool in response gave a clear exposition of his views on currency, pointing out that gold had risen in value partly because of the restricted supply from South America, reduced from £30-40 million per annum in peacetime to £7-8 million per annum in the past few years, and partly due to the vast war expenditures on both sides, which increased the demand for specie.

Liverpool continued:

> The noble earl, however, has urged the extraordinary proposition, that a paper currency should be issued by government. Upon this point, all experience is against the noble earl, as in every country where that has been tried, it has uniformly produced the most ruinous effects. The great mistake continually made on the continent was, that such a paper currency having produced those ruinous consequences in every country in which it had been tried, it is therefore expected that a paper currency must produce the same consequences here. The great security of our paper currency, and that which constitutes the important difference between it and the paper currency of other countries is, that it is issued by an individual banking company, or by individuals for the sake of their own interest. The Bank of England would no doubt be willing to accommodate the public service, but they could refuse to issue their notes, and whenever they acted on any ground other than their own interest, it would be the first step to their ruin.[32]

Liverpool then expressed a desire to return to a metallic standard and said it should be possible within a short period after a definitive treaty of peace, though possibly not within six months.

Ireland was relatively quiet during 1813; a better harvest in 1812 had quelled the discontents of the previous year. In June Liverpool sent Lord Whitworth, his stepbrother-in-law, and previously the ill-fated Ambassador to Paris, to Ireland as Lord Lieutenant, with a promotion to an English viscountcy and in 1815 an earldom. Despite the famine following the 1816 'Year Without a Summer', Whitworth was to remain in Ireland for four years of relative peace, a rare distinction, although he was assisted by the efficient Peel as Chief Secretary.

Once Napoleon had assembled a new army of some 300,000 men, the summer campaigning season in Germany began with a defeat for the forces of the embryonic Alliance, at Lützen on 2 May. This was followed by a further defeat at Bautzen. The combined forces in both battles totalled over 250,000 men.

---

32. Ibid., cols 1178-80 (9 July 1813).

However, with Blücher[33] leading stout Prussian resistance and Ney failing to cut off the Allies retreat after Bautzen, French casualties at the two battles totalled over 40,000 men, compared with about 30,000 in the combined Russian and Prussian forces. Consequently, when Metternich proposed an armistice and peace negotiations, Napoleon was amenable. Hostilities temporarily ceased on this front on 4 June, by the Armistice of Pleiswitz, after which all the belligerents except Britain met in Prague to discuss a possible peace deal.

British diplomacy made considerable further progress in June. By the Treaty of Reichenbach, signed with Prussia on 14 June, Britain agreed to supply Prussia with a subsidy of £666,667 in return for Prussia keeping 80,000 troops in the field against France. Then, by the second Treaty of Reichenbach signed with Russia, Britain agreed to provide Russia with a subsidy of £1,333,334 in return for Russia to maintaining 160,000 troops in the field. Finally, under the third Treaty of Reichenbach between Russia, Austria and Prussia, Austria agreed to declare war on Napoleon if he rejected the Allies' peace terms being hammered out in Prague. The Sixth Coalition was coming into shape; it needed only further machinations by Metternich to become fully operational.

In the Iberian peninsula, Wellington's army finally moved on 15 May. Once in motion it moved remarkably quickly and entered Salamanca only eleven days later. Around that time, the French abandoned Madrid and on 12 June the French abandoned Burgos, which Wellington's forces entered the following day.

On 21 June Wellington, with 57,000 British troops and 24,000 Spanish and Portuguese, attacked the 60,000 French troops led by Jourdan[34] that had made a stand at Vitoria, the last major Spanish city on the road to France, and gained a complete victory, capturing the entire French baggage train. 'I have reason to believe that they carried off with them one gun and one howitzer only',[35] wrote Wellington to Bathurst. Casualties were 5,158 Allied and 8,000 French. The battle led to the collapse of Joseph Bonaparte's rule in Spain and the retreat of French forces across the Pyrenees. However, as Wellington wrote in a letter to Bathurst a week later, Vitoria 'totally annihilated all order and discipline. The soldiers have got among them about a million sterling in money'.[36]

33. Gebhard Leberecht von Blücher (1742-1819). Prince of Wahlstatt from 1814. Swedish army, 1758-60. Captured by Prussians and joined the Prussian army. Resigned 1773 after being passed over for promotion to major, reinstated in 1787 after Frederick the Great's death. Major-General, 1794. Lieutenant General, 1801. Commanded cavalry at Jena-Aurstedt, 1806. General, 1809. Lützen, Bautzen, Leipzig, 1813. Field Marshal, 1813. Waterloo, 1815. State visit to England; while resting on Blackheath, he said of the view of London: 'What a city to sack!'

34. Jourdan, Jean-Baptiste (1762-1833). Major-General, 1793. Battle of Fleurus, 1794. Marshal, 1804. Comte, 1819.

35. Letter to Bathurst, 22 June 1813, in Gurwood, *The Dispatches of Field Marshal the Duke of Wellington*, Vol. 10, pp. 446-53.

36. Letter to Bathurst, 29 June 1813, in ibid., pp. 472-73. His famous remark, 'We

As for the Spanish Cortes at Cádiz:

> we and the Powers of Europe are interested in the success of the War in the Peninsula, but the creatures who govern at Cadiz appear to feel no such interest. All that they care about really is to hear the praise of their foolish constitution. . . . If this war against the Bishops is carried on, we and the French will change sides; they will have the clergy and lower orders in the favour in future. . . . I do not believe that Spain will be a useful ally if the Republican system is not put down.[37]

When the news of Vitoria reached London, the nation's cash flow did not immediately improve, but market sentiment did. When Liverpool and Vansittart wrote to the Bank of England in late July, telling the directors they had paid back £6,776,000 of Exchequer bills, using half the paid-in proceeds of the latest loan to do so, but that they wanted the Bank to underwrite another £5 million of Exchequer bills, there was not a squeak of protest, even when £2 million of the bills failed to sell and were sold to the Bank.[38] Further issues of £2 million of bills in September and early October were met without protest, perhaps because the Bank was also receiving deposits of bills on behalf of the Allied sovereigns.

Following his victory at Vitoria, Wellington continued his rapid advance, investing and blockading Pamplona, in the foothills of the Pyrenees, on 26 June and San Sebastián on 7 July. However, Sir John Murray[39] had failed to capture Tarragona, losing artillery and stores in the process, and, even though the French forces in Catalonia were now cut off, Marshal Suchet[40] continued to hold off the British until the end of the year, achieving a significant tactical victory over the hapless Lord William Bentinck at Ordal in September.

Meanwhile, Wellington was promoted by the Prince Regent, over the Duke of York's objection, to the rank of Field Marshal, far ahead of his nominal seniority among generals. Liverpool wrote to him, first, hailing the effect of the victory on the armistice negotiations in progress at Prague and hoping the Germans, Austrians and Russians got the news before signing any compact with Napoleon, who would doubtless receive it sooner. Liverpool then asked pertinent questions about how to preserve the independence of Spain once the French had been driven out, whether fortifications like the Lines of Torres Vedras could be drawn across the Pyrenees, whether a Spanish militia with

---

have in the army the scum of the earth as common soldiers', was in a private letter to Bathurst on 2 July.

37. Private letter to Bathurst, 29 June 1813, in ibid., pp. 473-75.
38. Bank of England, Minutes of the Court of Directors, 29 July and 12 August 1813.
39. Sir John Murray (1768-1827). Major-General, 1805. Tory MP for Wootton Bassett and Weymouth and Melcombe, 1807-18. Lieutenant-General, 1811. General, 1825.
40. Louis-Gabriel Suchet (1770-1826). Duc d'Albuféra from 1812. Colonel, 1797. Marshal, 1811.

British officers could hold northern Spain against French incursions, and whether a moderate British force of 25,000-30,000 men, combined with this militia and the Spanish army, could be sure of holding off a French invasion. Finally, Liverpool urged Wellington to persuade the Spanish government to return from Cádiz to Madrid, thereby reducing the influence of the liberals and building confidence in its long-term viability.[41]

In response, Wellington suggested that a Pyrenean defensive line was impracticable because of the border's length, said that Spain had an ample force of 160,000 soldiers but that feeding and provisioning them was impossible under the current Spanish government, which left them unpaid, and that British expenses would be greatly reduced by shortening supply lines once San Sebastián had been captured, with store depots now in south-west England rather than Lisbon.[42]

On 27 July Soult, with 40,000 men, attacked the Allied forces blockading Pamplona, also interrupting the siege of San Sebastián. After the four-day Battle of Sorauren, Soult was compelled to retreat, effectively ending the French occupation of Spain (except for Suchet's force in Catalonia). Although San Sebastián did not fall until 8 September and Pamplona, blockaded rather than besieged, held out until 31 October, Wellington's advance into France was now a foregone conclusion.

Meanwhile, Metternich's machinations were bearing fruit. He designed the conditions to be presented to Napoleon at the Congress of Prague, which convened in earnest on 29 July. Emboldened by Wellington's victory at Vitoria, the Allies proposed that Napoleon should give up Germany, Holland, Spain and Italy. Napoleon refused to give his negotiators full power and only began to take the Congress seriously in August.

Since Napoleon had shown no sign of accepting the Allied conditions, Metternich broke up the Congress at midnight on 10 August and, in accordance with the third Treaty of Reichenbach, declared war on France, with Schwarzenberg appointed nominal Commander-in-Chief of all the Allied forces. Napoleon agreed to some concessions on 11 August but it was too late. By the Treaty of Teplitz, signed by Austria, Prussia and Russia on 9 September, with the young Earl of Aberdeen[43] adding his signature for Britain on 3 October, all four powers agreed to collaborate until France had been defeated and sketched between them preliminary agreements.

---

41. Quoted in Yonge, *The Life and Administration of Robert Banks Jenkinson*, Vol. 1, pp. 471-73.
42. Letter to Liverpool, 25 July 1813, in Gurwood, *The Dispatches of Field Marshal the Duke of Wellington*, Vol. 10, pp. 567-70.
43. George Hamilton-Gordon (1784-1860). 4th Earl of Aberdeen from 1801. British Ambassador to Austria, 1813-14. Chancellor of the Duchy of Lancaster, 1828. Foreign Secretary, 1828-30, 1841-46. Secretary of State for War and the Colonies, 1834-35. Prime Minister, 1852-55.

Klemens von Metternich, in 1808, so only a Graf and Ambassador to Paris, not yet a Prinz. Friend of Castlereagh, Wellington and Britain.

Liverpool and Castlereagh had achieved their overarching objective. Apart from providing subsidies to all participants, they had barely needed to lift a finger. Metternich had done all the work for them – their principal difficulty had been working out what complex form of four-dimensional chess Metternich was playing. Two principal Austrian armies were added to the forces confronting Napoleon in Bohemia and Italy, totalling 300,000 men. The forces confronting Napoleon now totalled 800,000 in Germany, plus a strategic reserve of 350,000 plus 150,000 in Spain, against a total of around 900,000 French effectives, of which some 650,000 were in Germany.

Castlereagh recognised Metternich's contribution, both at the time and later – he wrote to Aberdeen, 'Metternich performed miracles, both in the negotiations and in his armaments.'[44] That memory was to underpin his foreign policy until his death in 1822. Canning was to have no such memory, and Liverpool should have reminded him repeatedly of Metternich's past services as the Quadruple/Holy Alliance disintegrated. Metternich himself fled from revolution in 1848 and came to England but, although some old friends, notably Wellington, helped him, he was pained to be shunned by the court of the ungrateful (or ignorant) Whiggish Queen Victoria.

44. Letter to Aberdeen, 13 November 1813, in Londonderry, *Memoirs and Correspondence of Viscount Castlereagh*, Vol. 9, pp. 73-76. 3

In North America, the second half of 1813 saw some major US victories but strategically marked the end of US hopes for massive territorial gains. Commodore Oliver Hazard Perry's victory on 10 September at the Battle of Lake Erie, in which six British ships were captured and after which control of the lake fell to the United States, was followed by the estimable Harrison crossing the lake into Canada, after which Detroit fell to the US. Then, on 5 October came the most important US victory of the war, the Battle of the Thames, at which, with 3,500 troops, Harrison defeated Colonel Procter, with about 800 British regulars, and Tecumseh, with some 1,000 men of the First Nations. Casualties were around 45 British killed and wounded and no fewer than 600 captured, while Tecumseh was killed, ending organised First Nations resistance in the region and re-establishing US control over the north-west frontier.

Nonetheless, British forces foiled the major US strategic effort of the year, an attack on Montreal, the St Lawrence Campaign, organised by Secretary of War John Armstrong[45] and led by the notorious Major-General James Wilkinson.[46] On 26 October a force of 1,600 primarily French-Canadian '*voltigeurs*' (or elite skirmishers) under Lieutenant-Colonel Charles de Salaberry[47] won an important defensive victory at the Battle of the Chateauguay, defeating 4,000 US regulars under Major-General Wade Hampton.[48]

Then, on 9 November at the Battle of Crysler's Farm (near Cornwall, Ontario) 900 British regulars and 270 Canadians and First Nations under Lieutenant-Colonel Joseph Morrison[49] defeated no fewer than 8,000 US

---

45. John Armstrong, Jr (1758-1843). US Senator from New York, 1800-4. US Minister to France, 1804-10. US Secretary of War, 1813-14. Was convinced in 1814 that the British would not attack Washington.
46. James Wilkinson (1757-1825). Brevetted Brigadier General in 1777 at age of 20, then became Clothier-General of the Continental Army. 1787 swore allegiance to King of Spain in 'Spanish Conspiracy', attempting to get Kentucky to unite with Spain. Senior Officer of the US Army, 1796-7, 1800-12. Participated in Burr's Conspiracy, 1804-5, then betrayed Burr to Jefferson, 1806. Governor of Missouri Territory, 1805-7. Major-General, 1813. US Envoy to Mexico, 1816-25.
47. Charles-Michel d'Irumberry de Salaberry (1778-1829). Born in Beauport, Quebec, from a long line of French officers, he continued the tradition under British rule, becoming Lieutenant-Colonel in the British Army and then equipping and training the French-Canadian force which won at Chateauguay. CB, 1817.
48. Wade Hampton (1752-1835). Lieutenant-Colonel of South Carolina Volunteers, 1777-81. Congressman (Democratic-Republican) 1795-97, 1803-5. US Army Colonel, 1808, Brigadier General, 1809. Wealthiest planter in South Carolina when he died, gave his name to Hampton County, SC. Grandfather of the Confederate Civil War General.
49. Joseph Wanton Morrison (1783-1826). Born in New York under British occupation, he became Lieutenant-Colonel of the 2nd battalion of the 89th foot, dispatched to Canada in 1812. Later became Lieutenant-Colonel of the 44th Foot, posted to India in 1821, where as a Brigadier General he captured the Burmese province of Arakan

Lieutenant-Colonel Joseph Wanton Morrison, the hero of Crysler's Farm, November 1813, strategically the most important battle of the War of 1812.

regulars (though only about 5,000 actually engaged) under Wilkinson himself, in a battle later described as 'the absolute nadir of the history of the US regular army'.[50] The US forces retreated into winter quarters and the attempt to capture Montreal was over.

Since the 1814 campaign would allow Britain to deploy its full resources in North America following Napoleon's downfall, Crysler's Farm ended the US threat to Canada and was the strategic turning point of the war, as important in its theatre as the Battle of Leipzig three weeks earlier and far more important than the later Battle of New Orleans. Alas, while the victors of New Orleans and the Battle of the Thames became Presidents of the United States, Morrison's career ended in a malarial Burmese swamp.

---

before succumbing to malaria.

50. Donald Graves, *Field of Glory: The Battle of Crysler's Farm, 1813* (Montreal, QC: Robin Brass Studio, 1999) p. xi. Foreword by Col. John R. Elting, US Army (retired).

In November Castlereagh drafted a note to the US government offering to open peace negotiations. This was accepted by the United States. Thereby began the lengthy peace process that eventually led to the Treaty of Ghent.

The late summer of 1813 was notable for two appointments made by Liverpool. In August he made William Howley[51] Bishop of London. Howley was an excellent scholar, formerly Oxford Professor of Divinity, and was also a staunch High Church Tory, later appointed by Wellington to the Archbishopric of Canterbury in 1828. As the last true Laudian Archbishop of Canterbury, he was to perpetuate Liverpool's influence in ecclesiastical matters well into the Victorian age, remaining Archbishop until 1848.

Liverpool's other appointment was Robert Southey[52] as Poet Laureate – the incumbent mediocrity Henry Pye, appointed by Pitt in 1790, had died in August. Liverpool first offered the position to Walter Scott, over mild objections from the Prince Regent, who preferred Southey. However, when Scott declined it, Liverpool, through the Marquess of Hertford as Lord Chamberlain, appointed Southey.[53] He proved an excellent choice both in the quality of his poetry and in his staunch Toryism. He lived to 1843 and was succeeded by Wordsworth (appointed by the 'Conservative' Peel), again bringing Tory elements of the Liverpool era into Whiggish Victorian Britain.

The last months of 1813 saw steady progress for Wellington in the Peninsular campaign and southern France. In a letter to Bathurst on 8 August, Wellington raised the question that would occupy Liverpool for the next eight months: whether the removal of Napoleon and the restoration of the House of Bourbon was an Allied objective, or whether the Allies would be satisfied with a negotiated peace with a chastened Napoleon reduced to governing France, possibly with some adjacent territories.

At this stage, Russia was in favour of keeping a chastened Napoleon rather than restoring the Bourbons. However, the Austrian Emperor Francis I deeply distrusted Napoleon, even though his sister was married to him. Metternich pretended to favour his retention, but in reality had been determined to rid Europe of him since 1809 or even earlier.[54]. Emperor Francis stated a few

51. William Howley (1766-1848). Oxford University Regius Professor of Divinity, 1809. Bishop of London, 1813-28. Archbishop of Canterbury, 1828-48, crowning William IV and Victoria.

52. Robert Southey (1774-1843). One of the Lake Poets, along with Wordsworth and Coleridge. Sympathetic to the French Revolution, he moved rightwards politically, contributing to *The Quarterly Review* from 1809. Made Poet Laureate by Liverpool in 1813.

53. https://pastnow.wordpress.com/2013/09/20/september-20-1813-how-southey-became-poet-laureate/ Letter from Southey to Charles Watkins Williams-Wynn, 20 September 1813.

54. Siemann, Wolfram, *Metternich – Strategist and Visionary* is very enlightening on Metternich's view of Napoleon, and of the future of Europe.

months later that peace would never be secure so long as he lived.[55] British public opinion, conversely, was already staunch in its wish to remove Napoleon and, on balance, to restore the Bourbons.

The question was prompted by the Duc de Berri,[56] the future Louis XVIII's nephew and younger son of Charles X,[57] who contacted Wellington to offer to join his army with 20,000 French royalists. Wellington was firm on the question, even this early: 'My opinion is, that the interests of the House of Bourbon and of all Europe are the same, *viz.* in some manner or other, to get the better of and get rid of Bonaparte.' As for Napoleon, 'If he can be confined to the limits of France by any means, his system must fall. He cannot bear the expense of his internal government and of his army, and the reduction of either would be fatal to him.'[58]

Wellington's next success was the final capture of San Sebastián on 8 September. A month later, he crossed the Bidasoa river and entered France. His next victory came at the Battle of Nivelle on 10 November, when he split Soult's forces (losing 2,500 men to Soult's 4,000) and drove him back from his fortified positions on the river. Soult retired to defensive positions on the river Nive, around Bayonne but, in a four-day battle between 9 and 13 December, he was again driven back, although the French continued to occupy Bayonne until February, as bad weather prevented much action. Losses were even, but two Nassau battalions and one from Frankfurt, totalling 2,000 men, deserted from Soult's army to Wellington and were sent to join Allied forces in Germany.

Wellington continued to have problems with the anti-clerical Spanish government at Cádiz, to the extent that he resigned from the command of the Spanish army. His resignation was accepted on 22 September but the Cortes never confirmed it. Wellington later asked Bathurst for the right to install a British garrison at San Sebastián, to guarantee a British retreat into Portugal, rather than having to rely on an increasingly hostile Spanish officialdom.[59]

The problem was solved in principle by the Treaty of Valençay of 11 December, by which Joseph Bonaparte abdicated and Ferdinand VII was restored to the Spanish throne. It took another three months before Ferdinand

55. Letter from Aberdeen to Castlereagh, 24 December 1813, in Londonderry, Memoirs and Correspondence of Viscount Castlereagh, Vol. 9, pp. 111-14.

56. Charles Ferdinand d'Artois, Duc de Berri (1778-1820). Second son of Charles X, the most glamorous of the French royal family after their restoration. Assassinated at the Paris Opera in 1820. However, his wife bore a posthumous son, Henri, Duc de Bordeaux, Comte de Chambord (1820-83), known as 'the miracle child' because he renewed the legitimist line after Berri's murder (later unhappily taught mathematics by Augustin-Louis Cauchy).

57. Charles Philippe (1757-1836). Comte d'Artois until 1824. The last legitimate King of France, Charles X, 1824-30. Hero of Rossini's 1825 opera, *Il viaggio a Reims*.

58. Letter to Bathurst, 8 August 1813, in Gurwood, *The Dispatches of Field Marshal the Duke of Wellington*, Vol. 10, pp. 613-15.

59. Letter to Bathurst, 27 November 1813, in ibid., Vol. 11, pp. 325-28.

could escape Napoleon's clutches but in March 1814 he re-entered Spain. The Cortes liberals had asked Ferdinand to guarantee the constitution of 1812 before he re-entered Spain but Ferdinand, buoyed by popular support, avoided giving such guarantees, repudiated the Constitution and had the liberal leaders arrested. Wellington was to write of this: 'The imprisonment of the liberals is thought by some, and I believe with justice, unnecessary, and it is certainly highly impolitic; but it is liked by the people at large.'[60]

In a November letter to Bathurst, Wellington reported the feelings of the French people towards Napoleon:

> They all agree in one opinion, *viz.* that the sentiment throughout France is the same as I have found it here, an earnest desire to get rid of him, from a conviction that as long as he governs they will have no peace. The language common to all is, that although the grievous hardships and oppression under which they suffer are intolerable, they dare not have the satisfaction even of complaining; that, on the contrary, they are obliged to pretend to rejoice, and that they are allowed only to lament in secret and in silence their hard fate.[61]

There was, however, no strong opinion in favour of the House of Bourbon, which had been in exile for 20 years and 'was equally, if not more unknown to France than the Princes of any other Royal house in Europe'. Local opinion was highly favourable to the British occupants but Britain was not taxing them so, as Castlereagh remarked to Bathurst: 'It is perhaps the only spot in Europe free to enjoy the whole of their income, paying to the state nothing. We must not therefore be too elated by our reception or infer from this they are prepared to risk all against their detested government.'[62]

After the Allied armistice with France had expired, Blücher recommenced hostilities on 14 August and the Allies won a couple of tactical victories against Napoleon's subordinates. On 26-27 August, however, Napoleon, with 135,000 troops, defeated near Dresden an Allied force of 215,000 troops commanded by Schwarzenberg (38,000 Allied soldiers were killed, wounded or captured against 10,000 French). However, on 29-30 August, Russian forces inflicted a decisive defeat on a French force at Kulm, inflicting 5,000 casualties and capturing some 10,000 troops.

60. Letter to Sir Charles Stuart, 25 May 1814, in ibid., Vol. 12, pp. 27-28. Charles Stuart (1779-1845). KB, 1812. GCB, 1815. PC, 1814. 1st Baron Stuart de Rothesay, 1828. Minister to Portugal and Brazil, 1810-14. Ambassador to the Netherlands, 1815. Ambassador to France, 1815-24, 1828-30. Envoy Extraordinary to Portugal and Brazil, 1825-6. Ambassador to Russia, 1841-44.
61. Letter to Bathurst, 21 November 1813, in Gurwood, *The Dispatches of Field Marshal the Duke of Wellington*, Vol. 11, pp. 303-7.
62. Letter to Bathurst, 1 January 1814, in Londonderry, *Memoirs and Correspondence of Viscount Castlereagh*, Vol. 9, p. 133. 4

After the Treaty of Teplitz was signed, Austria immediately opened negotiations with Bavaria and within a week an armistice had been agreed, with Bavaria joining the Allies on 8 October. This added another 50,000 men to Allied forces and subtracted them from the forces available to Napoleon. It also brought the other German princes closer to the Alliance. Württemberg joined in early October, while Saxony, which dallied with Napoleon until the Battle of Leipzig, was denied membership in the victorious grouping, and thus faced potential dismemberment at the Congress of Vienna.

Meanwhile Blücher was advancing steadily, removing Jérôme Bonaparte from his Westphalian capital, Cassel, although he suffered a setback on 3 October, losing 5,000 troops. Napoleon attempted to trap him, but failed, and therefore in the middle of the month concentrated his forces around Leipzig.

In a letter to Wellington on 20 October, Liverpool observed that, with Bavaria on the side of the Allies, victory was likely:

> the fate of [Napoleon's] army might be considered as certain if there was one head that directed the operations of all the allies, and that a head in which all had confidence. . . . With this advantage on his side, I think we need not now be apprehensive of the result; but the difference will, nevertheless be great between his retiring to the Rhine with his present forces nearly entire, or that force being completely defeated in its present position.[63]

Liverpool's letter showed his usual strategic acuity, but the Battle of Leipzig on 16-19 October had already given the Allies the decisive victory.

Leipzig was the largest battle of the Napoleonic Wars, with 605,000 troops initially engaged, 380,000 on the Allied side and 225,000 on the French side (around 50,000 Württemberg and Saxon troops defected from the French to the Allies during the battle). This was three times the forces engaged at the Battle of Waterloo (including the Prussians),[64] four times the forces engaged at Vitoria, four times the forces at Austerlitz and twice the forces at the two previous leaders, Borodino and Wagram. British forces were unrepresented, except for a company of the Rocket Brigade, armed with the inaccurate but effective Congreve rockets, serving with the Swedish forces under Bernadotte. However, all the Allied countries at the battle except Bavaria had benefited from massive British subsidies organised by Liverpool.

Liverpool's worry about the Allied forces' direction was well founded, with Czar Alexander I, 'Supreme Commander' of the Allied forces, and Schwarzenberg, 'Field Commander', disagreeing about the strategic direction

---

63. Quoted in Yonge, *The Life and Administration of Robert Banks Jenkinson*, Vol. 1, pp. 473-74.
64. Twice the forces involved in the entire Waterloo campaign, including Grouchy's corps and the Prussians who did not arrive at the Waterloo battlefield.

of the battle. However, even though there were more Russian troops than Austrian on the field of battle, once battle was joined Alexander deferred to Schwarzenberg's greater experience. Schwarzenberg was thought not to be a great general, being too cautious, but he had a secret weapon: his Chief of Staff was the future Field Marshal Radetzky,[65] already a former chief of the Austrian general staff and a true military genius.

The Allies had throughout 1813 been operating on the Trachenberg Plan, supposedly agreed at a meeting between Allied sovereigns at Trachenberg on 7 July but probably cooked up between Schwarzenberg, Radetzky and the mortally ill Prussian general Gerhard von Scharnhorst[66] at an earlier meeting on 31 May. Under this plan, Allied armies would avoid engaging with Napoleon until they could be gathered in overwhelming force and would concentrate on attrition against peripheral French forces. Thus, when Napoleon confronted the entire Allied army at Leipzig, the Allies had a massive numerical superiority.

The battle itself was a four-day affair. On 16 October Allied attacks were repelled by the French, then a French coordinated attack at 2 p.m. was repelled by Allied forces reinforced by 50,000 fresh troops under Blücher. They paused the following day while Allied reinforcements arrived, and Napoleon decided to attempt a decisive blow rather than retreating. On 18 October, sheer Allied numbers began to overwhelm French defences, while a shortage of ammunition also hampered French efforts. Finally, on 19 October, the French attempted to retreat through the city of Leipzig and a substantial part of their force was cut off when the only bridge over the Elster river was blown up.

Allied losses totalled around 58,000 dead, wounded or missing, while French losses were 38,000 dead and wounded, 20,000 captured and around 50,000 men who defected to the Allied side. Strategically, Leipzig was a major Allied victory, forcing Napoleon to retreat to France, denuding him of his German allies and removing French control of territories east of the Rhine.

About 20,000 of the retreating French were intercepted by 43,000 Austrian and Bavarian troops at Hanau on 30 October. Nevertheless, the French succeeded in capturing the town and opening lines of retreat. By 5 November the French had crossed the Rhine and were encamped near Mainz.

The 1813-14 Parliamentary session opened on 4 November. Liverpool had already expressed his intention to Wellington of securing as much money as possible and then adjourning until March. The Prince Regent opened Parliament in person, wearing his robes over a field marshal's uniform, with Liverpool carrying the Sword of State. He reported Wellington's arrival in France and the

65. Joseph Radetzky von Radetz (1767-1858). Colonel, Austrian army, 1799. Major-General, 1805. Lieutenant Field Marshal, 1809. Chief of the General Staff, 1809-12. Field Marshal, 1836. Battle of Novara, 1849. Viceroy of Lombardy-Venetia, 1848-57.

66. Gerhard von Scharnhorst (1755-1813). Military theorist. Born near Hanover, he transferred to the Prussian army as Colonel, 1801. Major-General, 1807. Reorganised Prussian army. Chief of Staff to Blücher, 1812-13. Died from wound received at Lützen.

battle of Leipzig and claimed that the US advance on Canada had been repulsed, although Crysler's Farm was still in the future. He also rejoiced in a bountiful 1813 harvest, which alleviated Liverpool's fiscal problem. Notably, he proposed a magnanimous peace: 'No disposition to require from France sacrifices of any description inconsistent with her honour or just pretensions as a nation will ever be on my part, or on the part of His Majesty's Allies, an obstacle to peace.'

The Lords debate on the Address was notable for both Wellesley and Grenville abandoning their criticism and Grenville expressing, 'my entire approbation of the tone and language of the speech delivered this day by His Royal Highness to Parliament' and calling for a balance of power in Europe. In reply Liverpool emphasised the importance of Britain appearing to be completely unified and pointed out that the war was now one of nationalism, which had made even Portuguese troops stand up to the mighty armies of France.

Liverpool also echoed Grenville's call for political justice and moderation:

> but it becomes us to be more moderate, as we are more vigorous. I agree in this with the noble baron [Grenville] who thought that some fixed and certain terms of peace should be abided by – terms consistent with justice to all parties – with justice not only to our friends but to our enemies. We should not ask from our enemies such terms, as in their situation we should not think it reasonable to concede. There is no principle on which to prosecute the war, but a desire to obtain a peace, by which a fair addition of strength should be made to those powers which have suffered in the contest.[67]

Together with the hint in the Prince Regent's Address (which then, as now, the government had drafted), this was the first statement of Britain's self-denying approach to the forthcoming peace negotiations. Their central principle, expressed most fully at the Congress of Vienna, was that Britain would give back the colonial possessions she had acquired during the war, to ensure that the balance of power in Europe was re-established and that countries which had been weakened by invasion and occupation should regain their historic weight in Europe. While Russia and Prussia were to attempt to use the peace to gain additional territory, Britain, and eventually Austria, were to maintain the view that a solid, lasting peace, accepted by France, was more important than territorial gains.

This central principle would be followed by Castlereagh in the prolonged negotiations and was in notable contrast to the vengeful and meddling spirit that was to actuate the Paris Peace Conference and the Treaty of Versailles. After twenty years of war, it was a notable political achievement to restrain the vindictiveness which most of the British people undoubtedly felt in

67. Hansard, *Parliamentary Debates from the Year 1803 to the Present Time*, Vol. 27, cols 1-6 (Prince Regent), cols 11-20 (Grenville), cols 20-22 (Liverpool) (4 November 1813).

the interests of making a peace that could last. It can be argued that the avoidance of vindictiveness went too far in the case of Napoleon, who, by being exiled only to Elba, was able to return and threaten the peace of Europe once more. However, the opposite error, of building resentments that would last a generation or more, was to be only too vividly demonstrated by Lloyd George,[68] Wilson[69] and Clemenceau[70] in 1919.

In the Commons, the enthusiasm was even more extraordinary, with the Radical Whitbread exclaiming, 'the existing administration are entitled, I think, to every praise and . . . I do not wish to see any one of [His Majesty's ministers] displaced, seeing what measures are in progress and relying upon the moderation of their views, in endeavouring to accomplish a general and lasting peace.'[71] Alas, Whitbread, an admirer of Napoleon, was speaking under the misapprehension that his idol would accept moderate peace terms; he would commit suicide in July 1815 after Napoleon's final defeat.

Nevertheless, the enthusiastic reception of both Lords and Commons to the Prince Regent's speech and Liverpool's outline of the approach to be taken in peace-making gave Liverpool's government a mandate for their negotiating process that was to prove invaluable in the months ahead.

On 15 November, Vansittart announced a new loan of £22 million, at a significantly reduced interest cost of 5.31 per cent (the money had been raised by issuing three per cent bonds, in an amount of £38.9 million). This clearly indicated the improvement in the market from the war's successes. Vansittart also confirmed that the revenues for the September quarter had been £1.9 million higher than anticipated, an indication of the improvement in the economy. By this new loan, the government's needs would be covered until the usual spring Budget. From this point, the Bank of England was meekly acquiescent to the government's cash flow demands and even supplied another £400,000 of bullion for Wellington's army in January.

On 20 December Liverpool adjourned Parliament until 1 March, since the government had raised the money it needed and other business had been passed remarkably quickly.

Meanwhile, on the Continent, on 14-15 November Amsterdam rebelled against French rule, to be followed by several other Dutch cities, proclaiming the House of Orange as the Netherlands' legitimate rulers. Russian light troops had already crossed the Dutch frontier and the French administration had left

68. David Lloyd George (1863-1945). 1st Earl Lloyd George of Dwyfor, 1945. MP for Caernarvon Boroughs, 1890-1945. President of the Board of Trade, 1905-08. Chancellor of the Exchequer, 1908-15. Minister of Munitions, 1915-16. Secretary of State for War, 1916. Prime Minister, 1916-22.

69. Thomas Woodrow Wilson (1856-1924). 28th President of the United States, 1912-20.

70. Georges Clemenceau (1841-1929). Prime Minister of France, 1906-9, 1917-20.

71. Hansard, *Parliamentary Debates from the Year 1803 to the Present Time*, Vol. 27, cols 38-41 (4 November 1813).

Amsterdam after the uprising, so the Russian advance was swift. A Prussian corps began advancing into the eastern Netherlands, the Prince of Orange[72] landed at Schieveling on 27 November and his father[73] was proclaimed Sovereign Prince of the United Netherlands in Amsterdam on 6 December. Clancarty arrived at The Hague and was proclaimed British Ambassador to the Netherlands and Sir Thomas Graham with 8,000 British troops landed in the south. The final recapture of what became the United Netherlands took several more months; Antwerp held out until May 1814.

A further difficulty arose when Sweden invaded Denmark in December. Military fortunes were mixed but in January 1814 the two countries signed the Treaty of Kiel by which Norway was to be transferred to Sweden. The Norwegians objected to this and rebelled. However, a Swedish army entered Norway in late July and an armistice was concluded in August. A definitive union by which Charles XIII was elected King of Norway was ratified by the Norwegian Parliament in November.

The Dutch rebellion, even the anticipation of it, left Castlereagh unwilling to sign any peace deal that did not return France within her ancient frontiers. Thus, when he learned of the Frankfurt proposals made by Austria, by which Napoleon would remain Emperor and France would retain Belgium, Savoy and the Rhineland, he opposed them. He realised, however, that he needed to be closer to the Allied leaders in person.

Even after the Allies had restated their alliance and the proposed peace terms under the Declaration of Frankfurt on 1 December, Castlereagh was concerned that they had given Napoleon too good a deal. Accordingly, he resolved to join the Allied delegations on the Continent and to help steer the alliance to final victory. He received full plenipotentiary powers from the Prince Regent and left England on 3 January 1814. As he lay becalmed at Harwich, he cautioned Liverpool against being too quick to throw in Britain's lot with the Bourbons: 'If Bonaparte will give you your own terms, you ought not to risk yourselves and the confederacy in the labyrinth of counter-revolution.'[74]

Napoleon, however, delayed accepting the Frankfurt proposals and by the end of December, Schwarzenberg, with 200,000 soldiers, had crossed the Rhine between Basel and Schaffhausen, while Blücher, with 50,000-75,000 men, was poised to cross the Rhine between Rastatt and Koblenz. The survival of Napoleon's regime was now in doubt.

---

72. William II of the Netherlands (1792-1849). Prince of Orange, 1813-40. King of the Netherlands, 1840-49. Colonel, British army, 1811. Major-General, 1813. General, 1814. Commanded Dutch forces at Quatre Bras and Waterloo.
73. William I of the Netherlands (1772-1843). Prince of Orange from 1806. Sovereign Prince, then King of the United Netherlands, 1813-30. King of the Netherlands, 1830-40, until he abdicated.
74. Letter to Liverpool, 31 December 1813, in Londonderry, *Memoirs and Correspondence of Viscount Castlereagh*, Vol. 9, pp. 123-25.

At the turn of the year, the Bourbon restoration question came up in London and, after a lengthy meeting with the Comte d'Artois (the future Charles X), Liverpool, who had been briefed by Castlereagh, wrote a memorandum on the meeting for consideration of the Cabinet.

Liverpool had told Artois of Schwarzenberg's advance into Switzerland, which confirmed that Austria was indeed determined to pursue the war fully. Artois stated his intention to sail for south-western France with his two sons, Angoulême[75] and Berri. Liverpool, in response, made it clear that Britain could not provide support for such an expedition, or even allow Wellington to receive Artois officially, without either prior agreement of the Allies or a rising in France to show the people's receptiveness to the Bourbon cause. However, Liverpool believed that the outstanding negotiations with Napoleon would not end in peace, because his character would preclude his accepting Allied terms. Thus, Liverpool urged delay, since a declaration in favour of the Bourbon cause by a town such as Bordeaux would greatly alter the question.[76]

Artois reserved the right to embark immediately for France, even though Liverpool confirmed that the Cabinet agreed with his judgement. In the event, however Artois, eager to preserve good relations with Britain, crossed to Holland in early February, then sailed for Bordeaux to join Angoulême only in late March.

However reluctant to restore the Bourbons Castlereagh and Liverpool were, Wellington, while accepting political direction, had always favoured this alternative, as did most of the British people, except for a few Radicals. As the winter wore on and peace with Napoleon remained elusive, the three men began to manoeuvre to secure a Bourbon restoration, overcoming the disinclination of Alexander I and to a lesser extent Francis I.

On the way to Basel, Castlereagh, on behalf of the Prince Regent, proposed to William I, recently elevated as Sovereign Prince of the Netherlands, that his son, the Prince of Orange, should marry Princess Charlotte. William I was delighted with the idea and arrangements were agreed by which the two Royal families would be kept separate in future generations. Princess Charlotte, however, would have other ideas.

Throughout January Allied armies advanced deeper into eastern France, as the forces opposed to them numbered only 70,000 compared with a combined Allied strength of 200,000. By this time, Alexander I was seeking a 'march on Paris' as advocated by Liverpool back in 1794, a fact not lost on Liverpool's colleagues, including the Prince Regent, who had joked with

75. Louis Antoine, Duc d'Angoulême (1775-1844). King Louis XIX for 20 minutes in 1830, between Charles X's abdication and his own. Led Vendée uprising in 1795 and French invasion of Spain in 1823. Wife, Marie-Thérèse of France (1778-1851), daughter of Louis XVI and Duchesse d'Angoulême, was an important Royalist personage in her own right.

76. The memorandum is given in Yonge, *The Life and Administration of Robert Banks Jenkinson*, Vol. 1, pp. 483-88.

Liverpool about it two years before. With Blücher reaching Joinville on the River Marne on 18 January, and Schwarzenberg occupying the southern plateau around Langres, complete military victory over Napoleon now seemed possible.

Napoleon, in addition to his military difficulties, was now facing considerable domestic unrest and consequently agreed to a peace conference at Châtillon. The Allies were, however, still divided on whether to make peace with Napoleon. Britain and Austria were now in favour of restoring the Bourbons, while Alexander had come up with the bizarre scheme of replacing Napoleon with Bernadotte, thought to be something of a Russian puppet. (Bernadotte as Prince Charles John of Sweden favoured making peace only with the Bourbons.)

Fortunately, Castlereagh, who arrived at Basel on 18 January, quickly allied with Metternich to steer Alexander away from such a bizarre notion and keep the Allies working together, on the basis that Napoleon and the Bourbons were the only acceptable rulers of France, but that some evidence of popular support in France would be required before the Allies could back the Bourbons. Indeed, he worried that the peace negotiations themselves could cause trouble; on 30 January he wrote to Liverpool: 'I am afraid pending negotiations are likely to give an advantage to Jacobinical and military intriguers over the more honest sentiment of the nation.'[77]

Before the Châtillon conference had opened, Blücher had inflicted two further defeats on Napoleon, at Brienne and La Rothière. As a result, when the Allied plenipotentiaries arrived at Châtillon, there was a general consensus that Napoleon should be offered terms that would be sure to keep France contained, including withdrawal close to its 1792 boundaries and a Netherlands state that extended to the Meuse. These terms were offered to the French delegate, Armand-Augustin-Louis, Marquis de Caulaincourt,[78] on 7 February, after which the conference was adjourned for Caulaincourt to show the terms to Napoleon – who threw a tantrum.

Liverpool's own views on the Châtillon negotiations were contained in a letter to Wellington. He remarked that the people of eastern France were showing no great love for the Bourbons, while the imprudence of Artois in relaying the contents of a private conversation with the Prince Regent to the press made it almost impossible to help them secretly. He hoped that a major

77. Letter to Liverpool, 30 January 1814, in Londonderry, *Memoirs and Correspondence of Viscount Castlereagh*, Vol. 9, pp. 212-14. 4

78. Armand-Augustin-Louis, hereditary Marquis de Caulaincourt (1773-1827). Imprisoned in 1793, he escaped, rejoined the Army and served under General Hoche. Delivered the Duc d'Enghien to his death, 1804. Duke of Vicenza, 1808. Ambassador to Russia, 1807-11. Russian campaign, 1812. Grand Marshal of the Palace (chief French negotiator), 1813-14. Minister of Foreign Affairs, 1815. Memoir of Russian campaign, *With Napoleon in Russia*, published in 1933, avidly read by soldiers of the Third Reich.

Allied victory in eastern France would shortly bring out pro-Royalist French sentiment, allowing the Allies to agree on a policy of deposing Napoleon. He encouraged Wellington to become more aggressive in capturing French territory, to improve further the prospects of obtaining and keeping a good peace.[79] He also wrote to Castlereagh saying: 'You can scarcely have an idea how insane people in this country are on the subject of any peace with Bonaparte.'[80]

Far from a major Allied victory being imminent, Napoleon then demonstrated that he could still sting. The successes of the Six Days' Campaign of 9-14 February resulted in four defeats for Blücher and over 30,000 casualties with Napoleon's own army of only 40,000 men. Schwarzenberg, leading a larger army, continued a steady advance towards Paris but, following a tactical defeat at Montereau, at which Napoleon himself set the French artillery, Schwarzenberg proposed an armistice, so that peace talks could continue without the fortunes of war affecting them. Local peasants in eastern France were shooting stragglers from the Austrian and Prussian armies, indicating that French opinion was at best mixed.[81]

In southern France, Wellington made slow progress in January and February, hampered by the weather. On 2 February Angoulême arrived in San Sebastián but Wellington told him he could not yet receive him in an official capacity. Throughout February Wellington kept Angoulême informed of British operations but warned him continually that the interests of the French royal family would be best served by not getting ahead of public opinion. Then, on 27 February, Wellington beat Soult's army decisively at Orthez, forcing it to retreat in disorder towards Bordeaux.

The conference at Châtillon resumed a day later and Allied unity, threatened by Napoleon during the armistice, was cemented by the Treaty of Chaumont, drafted by Castlereagh and signed on 10 March, by which the Allies agreed again to make no separate peace with Napoleon until their definitive war aims had been achieved. In a letter to London, Castlereagh calculated that, taking into account Britain's subsidies, its contribution to the alliance was equivalent to that of all the other powers put together.[82] Caulaincourt had been given a deadline of 10 March for French acceptance of the Allied terms; on that date he said that only France's 'natural' frontiers on the Rhine would suffice. After further desultory negotiations and the rejection of a French counterproposal, the conference finally broke up on 20 March.

---

79. The letter is given in Yonge, *The Life and Administration of Robert Banks Jenkinson*, Vol. 1, pp. 495-97.
80. Quoted in Gash, *Lord Liverpool*, p. 108.
81. Letter from Aberdeen to Castlereagh, 28 February 1814, quoted in Londonderry, *Memoirs and Correspondence of Viscount Castlereagh*, Vol. 9, pp. 297-99. Repeated to Liverpool in a letter the following day, p. 299.
82. Letter to Edward Hamilton at the Foreign Office, 10 March 1814, in ibid., pp. 335-36.

Wellington wrote to Liverpool on 4 March, pointing out that:

> in proportion as we advance, I find the sentiment in the country still more active against the Buonaparte dynasty, and in favour of the Bourbons, but I am quite certain there will be no declaration on the part of the people, if the allies do not in some manner declare themselves or, at all events, as long as they are negotiating with Buonaparte.[83]

Thus, the ending of the Châtillon negotiations gave Bourbon supporters around France a clear opportunity. Wellington had already sent Beresford northwards towards Bordeaux with 12,000 men, with orders to assist the town's authorities if they wanted to proclaim Louis XVIII, but not to force them to do so, and to warn them that the Allies were still in peace negotiations with Napoleon. Beresford arrived in Bordeaux on 12 March and was met by the mayor and his colleagues.

Even though news of the collapse of the Châtillon negotiations had not yet reached Bordeaux, the mayor and his colleagues read an address of welcome to Beresford, then stripped off their Bonapartist regalia, put on white cockades and scarves, and declared allegiance to the Bourbons, after which Angoulême arrived in the city to claim it. Regrettably, the mayor issued a proclamation to the citizens of Bordeaux claiming Allied support for the Bourbon cause and protection for those taking it up, which Wellington at that stage was forced to disavow.[84]

The essential precondition for Allied support of a Bourbon restoration had now been fulfilled. Liverpool changed official British policy in a letter to Wellington of 24 March, in which he declared his intention to avoid a treaty with Napoleon and encouraged Wellington to push the Bourbon rising forward as strongly as possible. He discussed the various possible reactions of the Allies to Wellington's news and suggested that the Austrians at least could be expected to be pro-Bourbon, though they would not push the matter forward, because of their fear of Napoleon's power.[85]

For some weeks the Bordeaux position was precarious, as there were not enough Allied troops nearby to prevent a Bonapartist attempt to retake the city; however, Wellington's forces came up and ended the danger. On 10 April, Wellington met Soult in a hard-fought battle at Toulouse, in which there were 4,600 British casualties, after which on 12 April he entered the city, which like Bordeaux proclaimed for Louis XVIII. News of Napoleon's

83. Letter to Liverpool, 4 March 1814, in Gurwood, *The Dispatches of Field Marshal the Duke of Wellington*, Vol. 11, pp. 546-47.
84. Beresford letter to Wellington, 12 March 1814, in Gurwood, *The Dispatches of Field Marshal the Duke of Wellington*, Vol. 11, pp. 577.
85. Letter quoted in Yonge, *The Life and Administration of Robert Banks Jenkinson*, Vol. 1, pp. 500-2.

capitulation reached the city the same evening. By that stage, as Wellington wrote to Angoulême on 13 April, '*Je porte la cocarde blanche à présent, comme tout le monde.*'[86] After a further bloody skirmish near Bayonne on 14 April, Soult agreed to an armistice. The Prince Regent rewarded Wellington with a dukedom.

In eastern France, Napoleon suffered tactical defeats at Laon and Arcis-sur-Aube. Then on 23 March, an Allied council of war decided to advance directly on Paris, which Napoleon had left open. On 31 March, the French commanders surrendered Paris to the Allies, with Alexander I, the King of Prussia and Schwarzenberg entering Paris to the cheers of crowds waving white cockades and shouting '*Vive le Roi*'.[87] After an address by Alexander I, the French Senate agreed to the Allies' terms and passed an Act deposing Napoleon. Napoleon abdicated in favour of his son but the Allies refused to accept this. On the same day Marshal Marmont transferred his allegiance to the new provisional government in Paris, ending all hope of effective resistance by Napoleon's forces.

Finally, on 6 April Napoleon abdicated unconditionally and on 11 April Napoleon and all the Allies except Britain signed the Treaty of Fontainebleau, by which Napoleon retained the title of Emperor but was exiled to Elba, over which he could rule, funded by an annuity payable by France. (This dangerous scheme was the work of Alexander I, in Castlereagh's absence at Dijon.) Castlereagh refused to sign the treaty, on the grounds that Britain had never recognised Napoleon as Emperor and that exiling him to Elba, so close to the French coast, was asking for trouble. A Convention on the Suspension of Hostilities was then signed on 23 April.

Immediately after the Treaty of Fontainebleau, Castlereagh wrote to Liverpool postponing his return to London until Louis XVIII had arrived in Paris and proposing Wellington as the first British Ambassador in Paris. Artois arrived in Paris on 12 April, followed by Louis XVIII on 3 May. (Liverpool had greeted Louis XVIII on his way through London and as Lord Warden of the Cinque Ports had accompanied him to Dover for his embarkation on the Prince Regent's yacht, *Royal Sovereign*.)

Meanwhile, Castlereagh, under Liverpool's detailed direction, was negotiating a peace treaty with France, which became the Treaty of Paris, signed on 30 May. In it, Britain gave up most of the French colonies it had captured, except Mauritius, which was of no value to France without Indian colonies, and Tobago, which had been surrendered to France only in 1783 and whose white population was almost all British. Britain even returned Guadeloupe to France, which it had promised to Sweden, paying Sweden an indemnity of £1 million in lieu. The most contentious proposal was a French promise to

86. Letter to Angoulême, 13 April 1814, in ibid., pp. 639-40.
87. Charles Stewart letter to Castlereagh, 1 April 1814, in Londonderry, *Memoirs and Correspondence of Viscount Castlereagh*, Vol. 9, pp. 418-21.

abolish the slave trade after five years, which Liverpool, knowing the state of British public opinion, made Castlereagh insist on, pointing out that France might as well abolish the trade immediately, since its West Indian colonies had already been ruled by Britain for several years without it.[88]

The Anglo-Dutch treaty was less contentious, although it was not signed until 13 August. It provided for: the return of all Britain's Dutch conquests to the Netherlands, except the Cape of Good Hope and the South American settlements; for William I of Orange to become king of an extended Netherlands to include Belgium and Luxembourg; and for a subsidy from Britain of up to £5 million over ten years. In this context, Liverpool saw trouble ahead, writing to Clancarty:

> A new connection cannot be governed with as tight a rein as an old one. Recollect how Ireland is governed now, and what lost America to the crown of Great Britain. . . . The habits and prejudices of the Brabantes [sic], though not friendly to the French, approach nevertheless nearer to them than they do to those of the Dutch.[89]

In the event, the connection between the Netherlands and Belgium only modestly outlasted Liverpool, until rebellion in 1830.

June 1814 saw the arrival in London of Czar Alexander I, King Frederick William III of Prussia, Marshal Blücher and Metternich. Emperor Francis I had been invited to come but declined, much to the regret of Liverpool, who recognised the key role Austria had played in the alliance. At a special ceremony at Carlton House, the King of Prussia, Liverpool and Castlereagh were invested as Knights of the Garter – the only major honour Liverpool was ever to receive for his services. Later, the Czar and the King of Prussia were entertained to dinner by the Liverpools at Coombe Wood, on their way to Oxford. A Thanksgiving Service at St Paul's followed in July. Overall, as Vansittart wrote to Castlereagh: 'the public and Parliament are highly elated, and I think still more satisfied than elated, and indeed, if they were not satisfied, they must be the most unreasonable people that the world has ever produced'.[90]

Parliament had reconvened on 21 March, in an atmosphere where party animosity was still muted. In the House of Commons, almost the first subject debated was an attempt by Andrew Cochrane-Johnstone to clear his name after the Great Stock Exchange Fraud of 1814.

This was an extraordinary scheme, concocted by Cochrane-Johnstone, his nephew Thomas, Lord Cochrane[91] (also an MP) and Lord Cochrane's financial

---

88. The letter is quoted in Yonge, *The Life and Administration of Robert Banks Jenkinson*, Vol. 1, pp. 512-13.
89. Ibid., pp. 514-15.
90. Vansittart letter to Castlereagh, 28 April 1814, in Londonderry, *Memoirs and Correspondence of Viscount Castlereagh*, Vol. 9, pp. 520-22.
91. Thomas, Lord Cochrane (1775-1860). Marquess of Maranhão (Brazil) from 1824.

Cartoon 'Things as they have been, things as they now are'. Lord Cochrane as naval hero and Stock Exchange swindler.

advisor Richard Gathorne Butt, to defraud government bond investors by spreading a false rumour on 21 February 1814, when the outcome of the Châtillon peace negotiations was still highly uncertain, that Napoleon had been killed and the Allies had obtained a complete victory. The Cochranes' associate Charles Random de Berenger arrived at the Ship Inn in Dover that morning, posing as Colonel de Bourg, *aide-de-camp* to Lord Cathcart, with a forged letter to the Port Admiral at Deal to be transmitted by telegraph to London. This was done and Lord Cochrane sold £139,000 Omnium that morning, while Cochrane-Johnstone sold £241,000 and Butt sold no less than £392,000. Assuming an average profit of around five percentage points on the fraud,[92] Lord Cochrane cleared £7,000, Cochrane-Johnstone £12,000 and Butt £19,600.

Based on the eighteenth-century belief that 'stock-jobbers' were all crooks, the Cochranes doubtless expected to get away with this – St Vincent had described them as 'not to be trusted out of sight – they are all mad, romantic, money-getting and not truth-telling' in 1806.[93] However, the Committee of the Stock Exchange launched an investigation, discovered that £1.1 million of

10th Earl of Dundonald from 1831. Radical MP for Honiton and Westminster, 1806-18. Royal Navy Captain, 1801. Struck off Navy List, 1814. Restored as Rear-Admiral by Whigs, 1832. Vice-Admiral, 1841. Commander-in-Chief, West Indies and North America, 1848-51. Admiral, 1851. Vice-Admiral in Chilean navy, 1818-22. Admiral in Brazilian navy, 1823-25.

92. Aspinall, *The Letters of King George IV, 1812-30*, Vol. 1, p. 407, note 1 (Earl of Yarmouth letter to the Prince Regent, 12 March 1814) gives the rise in Omnium that morning as 5½ percentage points, from 27½ to 33. ('Omnium' referred to the partly-paid bonds of the latest Consols issue, in this case the £38.9 million nominal arranged by Vansittart on 15 November 1813.)

93. Thorne, *The History of Parliament: the House of Commons 1790-1820 'Cochrane Johnstone, Andrew James'*

government bonds sold on 21 February had been purchased only the previous week, and referred the matter to the High Court, headed by the draconian Ellenborough. Given Ellenborough's proclivities, had the Cochranes not been MPs and Lord Cochrane the heir to an earldom, all three conspirators might well have been hanged. As it was, they were sentenced on 21 June to £1,000 fines, twelve months of prison time and an hour in the public pillory. Lord Cochrane was also stripped of his naval rank and expelled from the Order of the Bath.

Much of the latter part of the 1814 parliamentary session was devoted to expelling the Cochranes from the House of Commons, accomplished on 5 July, by 140 votes to 44 in the case of Lord Cochrane and *nem. con.* in the case of Cochrane-Johnstone. The Radical-loving electors of Westminster re-elected Lord Cochrane quickly but Cochrane-Johnstone fled first to France and then to his West Indies slave plantations.

The Radical press, much of the populace (Cochrane was a somewhat spurious naval hero), many Whigs and many modern historians, failing to understand the nature of the 'money trail' evidence, sympathised with Lord Cochrane. So much did they sympathise that the Whig government of 1832 disgracefully granted Cochrane a free pardon and restored his naval rank and seniority, by then Rear-Admiral of the Blue. (He was to serve as Commander-in-Chief of the North America Station in 1848-51 and ended as an Admiral of the Red.) By doing so, they showed themselves less conscious than Liverpool's government of the need for integrity in public markets in bonds and stocks, and the unacceptability of major fraudsters as public servants.

On 1 April Liverpool told the House that the Châtillon negotiations had irretrievably broken down but that discussion should be held off until after the Easter recess. On 19 April he announced that fresh negotiations (Fontainebleau) were under way, which rendered discussion of the previous (Châtillon) negotiations unnecessary. Grey, in response, reserved the right to call for papers later, then launched into an encomium on Alexander I for his forbearance in not sacking Paris. Finally, on 27 April Liverpool announced that the Convention on the Cessation of Hostilities had been signed.

Britain's potential return to the gold standard, scheduled for six months after the war's end, came up for the first time on 26 April, with a prolongation of the Gold Coins Bill, and Liverpool said that, while:

> without these deviations from the ancient principle, the great exertions which had been made for some time past, and especially the exertions of last year, could not have been made. I admit however, that now it would be proper, as soon as it could conveniently be done, to revert to the ancient system, or rather to the principles of the ancient system.[94]

94. Hansard, *Parliamentary Debates from the Year 1803 to the Present Time*, Vol. 27, cols 544-45 (26 April 1814).

The only item in the preliminary peace treaties which aroused controversy was the provision whereby Denmark ceded Norway to Sweden, with Britain assisting the handover by a naval blockade if necessary. After preliminary skirmishes, this came up for debate on a motion from Grey, who was concerned about the Norwegians' desire for independence.

Liverpool pointed out that, as of 1814 the King of Denmark was the only absolute monarch in Europe, having gained that position by grant from a Danish Constituent Commission in 1660. Hence, he had the right to cede Norway in return for regaining the provinces of Holstein and Glückstadt, which Swedish and Russian troops had occupied in early 1813. Norway, as a province, resisted the cession but it had been stirred up to do so in a 'gross usurpation' by Prince Christian Frederick of Denmark[95] and the Danes resident in Norway. Thus, with Norway having acted as an enemy of Britain for the past eight years, Britain was justified in blockading its ports to ensure that Sweden's treaty rights were observed.[96] Grey's motion was defeated by 115 votes to 34.

On 11 May Liverpool proposed a grant of £100,000, plus an annuity of £10,000, to Wellington and smaller annuities to Graham (now Lord Lynedoch), Hill and Beresford; these were all agreed to without dissent. Then on 6 June Liverpool presented the Definitive Treaty of Peace between the Prince Regent and Louis XVIII, agreeing in principle with Grey's complaint that it had postponed slave trade abolition for five years.

At various points in the session, the Royal Family soap opera came up. Princess Caroline was granted a larger allowance of £50,000 per annum and departed for the Continent in August. Before she left, she sent a letter to Liverpool warning that she would return and cause a scandal if the Prince Regent attempted to divorce her – Liverpool pointed out drily to Canning that since Parliament would not allow a divorce except on proof of adultery there was no reason for her alarm unless her conduct is less likely to be correct upon the Continent'.[97] Liverpool contented himself with ensuring instructions were sent to ambassadors to make sure Caroline's life on the Continent was agreeable enough for her not to want to return.

Princess Charlotte[98] reached eighteen in 1814 and, encouraged, according to Liverpool, by a new Russian friend,[99] then refused to marry the Prince of Orange

95. Prince Christian Frederick (1786-1848). Christian VIII of Denmark from 1839. Elected King Christian Frederick of Norway, 17 May 1814. Abdicated after defeat by the Swedes, 14 August 1814.

96. Hansard, *Parliamentary Debates from the Year 1803 to the Present Time*, Vol. 27, cols 797-802, 808 (10 May 1814).

97. Gash *Lord Liverpool,* p 110.

98. Princess Charlotte of Wales (1796-1817). Daughter of George, Prince Regent, and, hence, Heiress-Presumptive to the throne. Married Prince Leopold of Saxe-Coburg-Saalfeld, 2 May 1816. Died after childbirth, 7 November 1817.

99. Aspinall, *The Letters of King George IV, 1812-30*, Vol. 1, p. 414, note 4, quoting Liverpool letter to Castlereagh, 30 April 1814.

because she would be required to live in the Netherlands. The Prince Regent told the Duke of York and the Bishop of Salisbury to scold her, with additional help from Alexander I and the Duchess of Oldenburg (the Czar's sister) while they were in London. Charlotte fled from Carlton House to her mother's residence at Connaught House, from where Eldon and the Duke of York brought her back. The Duke of Sussex, her uncle Augustus, brought the subject up in the House of Lords, only for Liverpool to refuse to discuss the Royal Family's domestic arrangements, a refusal in which he was backed up by Eldon.

Vansittart introduced the 1814 Budget in two parts.[100] On 13 June he had taken on a new loan of £24 million, of which £18.5 million was for Britain and £5.5 million for Ireland. This was obtained on favourable terms; for each £100 subscribed, contractors had been given £30 in navy five-per-cent bonds, £80 in three-per-cent Reduced bonds and £20 in three-per-cent Consols, to give an all-in cost of 4.6 per cent on £31.2 million principal amount of new bonds. The market was so strong that, by holding the offering open for bids for an extra day, £1 million of bonds was saved to the public.

Vansittart reported that trade and revenues had been buoyant during the year. For the year ending April 1814, customs and excise revenues were each up by 4.9 per cent, stamp duty revenue was up by 5.9 per cent and income tax revenue by no less than 9.5 per cent. Overall, revenues were up by 6.9 per cent, from £58.9 million to £63 million, of which the war taxes, representing £23.8 million, were up by 10.6 per cent. Modern numbers[101] show the calendar year 1814's expenditure to be £112.9 million, the highest figure until 1899, although the increase of £1.8 million from 1813 was less than the £2.7 million increase in debt service. Revenue was, however, buoyant, increasing by 4.3 per cent from 1813, so the fiscal gap declined from 33 per cent of expenditure to 31 per cent.

Cash flow management was still difficult, leading to a warning from the Bank of England on 6 July to Liverpool and Vansittart that no further advances would be given (the June bond issue instalments were coming in slowly).[102] However, the sharp fall in yield on Vansittart's June bond issue, compared to that of the previous November, showed that Britain's credit rating was beginning a major long-term improvement, whatever the cash flow difficulties. The only interruptions to that trend were the Hundred Days in 1815 and the abolition of income tax in 1816.

The peace treaty was debated on a motion by Grenville deprecating the treaty's failure to secure immediate abolition of the slave trade. Liverpool pointed out that Britain had secured abolition of the trade by Sweden,

100. Hansard, *Parliamentary Debates from the Year 1803 to the Present Time*, Vol. 28, cols 63-68 and 623-24 (13 June and 6 July 1814).

101. Mitchell, *British Historical Statistics*, pp. 581 (Income), 587 (Expenditure). The year-end is 5 January so, to get the figures for the (approximate) calendar year 1814, you have to use the 1815 figures in the tables.

102. Bank of England, Minutes of the Court of Directors, 6 July 1814.

Denmark and the Netherlands), and that the Treaty of Paris provided for its abolition within five years. In general, however, 'mankind have long agreed, my lords, that however sacredly binding soever moral obligation ought to be considered by individuals, or by a nation, the imposition of it upon another nation is not a legitimate cause of war'.[103] Liverpool's Westphalian concept of the rights of nations to their own internal arrangements here opposes that of modern 'human rights' advocates.

The next day, Liverpool propounded that:

> no peace with France could be secure or lasting, which did not maintain the honour and independence of that country inviolate. In becoming the negotiator of a peace I always wish to consider myself as the arbiter of the different interests at stake, and as forming my decision on a fair and comprehensive view of the circumstances and claims of all the parties.

He then outlined the minor boundary changes in favour of France and defended returning France's colonies to her because, 'it was exactly in proportion as she was colonial and commercial that we had a power over her by attacking her colonies and weakening her commerce'.[104]

Towards the end of the parliamentary session, one of Liverpool's remaining problems was eased by the return of Canning to full government support. Since Canning wanted to accompany his invalid son to a warmer climate, Liverpool sent him as special envoy to Lisbon to welcome back the Portuguese royal family from Brazil. At the same time Canning's followers were rewarded: Leveson-Gower with a viscountcy, Boringdon[105] with an earldom (both granted by the Prince Regent the following year), Huskisson, the most useful of them, with immediate office as First Commissioner for Woods and Forests and Sturges Bourne[106] with a position on the Board of Control and a Privy Councillorship.

The first months of 1814 were quiet ones on the American front. In the south, Andrew Jackson[107] won several victories over the Creek First Nations, the

103. Hansard, *Parliamentary Debates from the Year 1803 to the Present Time*, Vol. 28, cols 337-47 (27 June 1814).

104. Ibid., cols 369-72 (28 June 1814).

105. John Parker (1772-1840). 2nd Baron Boringdon from 1788. 1st Earl of Morley from 1815. Married Westmorland's daughter Augusta in 1804, divorced 1809 when he married Frances Talbot. Supported Pitt to 1801, then Canning, but turned Whig and voted for the Reform Bill in 1832.

106. William Sturges Bourne (1769-1845). MP for Christchurch, Bandon, Ashburton and Milborne Port, 1802-12, 1815-18, 1826-31. Lord of the Treasury, 1807-9, Member of the Board of Control, 1814. PC, 1814. Home Secretary, 1827.

107. Andrew Jackson (1767-1845). US Representative from Tennessee, 1796-97. US Senator from Tennessee, 1797-98, 1823-25. Major-General of Tennessee militia,

most decisive being at Horseshoe Bend on 27 March. At sea, both sides scored minor successes. Then Napoleon's defeat in April transformed the strategic situation, with Britain able to devote her full strength to the American conflict. However, in July, with War Secretary Armstrong eager to move aggressively before British forces were reinforced from Europe, US forces won two tactical victories in Canada at Chippawa and Lundy's Lane.

At Bathurst's request, Wellington had given him his strategic thoughts on the American theatre in a letter of 22 February:

> Any offensive operation founded upon Canada must be preceded by the establishment of a naval superiority on the lakes. But even if we had that superiority, I should doubt our being able to do more than secure the points on those lakes at which the Americans could have access. In such countries as America, very extensive, thinly peopled, and producing but little food in proportion to their extent, military operations by large bodies are impracticable, unless the party carrying them on has the uninterrupted use of a navigable river. . . . As to landings on the coast, they are liable to the same objections, though to a greater degree, than an offensive operation founded on Canada. . . . I do not know where you could carry on such an operation which would be so injurious to the Americans as to force them to sue for peace.[108]

Liverpool took this advice, relayed through Bathurst. He had always believed the war against the United States to be unnecessary and to be terminated as soon as possible; he now took on board the view that it was also unwinnable. Accordingly, his strategic decisions for the remainder of the war were devoted to imposing 'punitive' damage on the United States, that would demonstrate British power and force it to be reasonable in peace negotiations. The attacks on Washington and Baltimore were designed to this end. So was that on New Orleans, believed by British strategic thinkers to be the only point in the United States that Britain could hold militarily and, through its command of the Mississippi trade, thereby inflict significant economic damage on the United States.

After the defeat of Napoleon Liverpool sent reinforcements to North America, 15,000 of them Peninsular veterans, mostly to reinforce Prevost in Canada, although a brigade of Peninsula veterans under Major-General Robert Ross was sent to Bermuda. Naval operations were also reinforced under a new commander, Admiral Alexander Cochrane[109] – Thomas Cochrane's uncle and

---

1802. Major-General, US Army, 1814. Battle of New Orleans, 1815. Military Governor of Florida, 1821. 7th President of the United States, 1829-37.

108. Letter to Bathurst, 22 February 1814, in Gurwood, *The Dispatches of Field Marshal the Duke of Wellington*, Vol. 11, pp. 525-26.

109. Alexander Inglis Cochrane (1758-1832). Tory MP for Stirling Burghs, 1800-6. KCB, 1806. Captain, 1782. Rear Admiral, 1804. Vice-Admiral, 1809. Admiral,

Lord Castlereagh in 1821. After Sir Thomas Lawrence.

a Pittite Tory, unlike his relatives. The enlarged naval squadron's first operation was to capture Eastport, Maine on 18 July. Within a few weeks, the whole of eastern Maine was British-occupied, although the British never moved on Portland and southern Maine because they had hopes of Massachusetts (which then governed Maine) seceding from the United States.

The following month, the British landed at Benedict, Maryland, then inflicted a decisive defeat on a larger US army at the Battle of Bladensburg on 24 August, after which Ross and his forces moved on Washington. They burned the Capitol and the White House in retaliation for the Americans' burning of York the previous year but spared private property. Eating President Madison's dinner was a brilliant, if modest, additional stroke of psychological warfare.

Following the burning of Washington, British forces turned their attention to Baltimore but were unsuccessful in their attack on Fort McHenry on 13 September. Meanwhile Prevost[110] with 14,000 men, attempting to invade the United States (though warned by Bathurst not to overextend himself) was defeated by an inferior force in a combined naval-military operation at the Battle of Plattsburgh. Peace negotiations had begun at Ghent in August and military operations were winding down.

From the late summer, the attention of Europe focused on the forthcoming Congress of Vienna. These negotiations were carried on primarily by Castlereagh, but he consulted in detail both Liverpool and Wellington (now Ambassador to Paris) on the line to be taken, and Liverpool in letters to Castlereagh set out the overall British position.

The three men were clear in their view that, as Wellington wrote to Castlereagh, 'the situation of affairs in the world will naturally constitute England and France as arbitrators at the Congress, if those powers understand each other, and such an understanding may preserve the general peace'.[111] Thus, Talleyrand's attempt at the Congress to play all the other powers off against each other was highly distressing to Castlereagh. Fortunately, he was eventually able to persuade that devious gentleman that straightforwardness was the best policy for the Bourbon master he was currently supposed to be serving.

In a letter to Wellington, Liverpool set out the conference's central objective: 'For all our interests, but especially for those of France, every effort must be made to avoid drawing the sword in Europe under any pretence for a few years to come.' Accordingly, Murat[112] was reluctantly to be left in control of

1819. Commander-in-Chief, Leeward Islands, 1805. Governor and Commander-in-Chief, Guadeloupe, 1810-14. Commander-in-Chief, North America, 1814-15. Commander-in-Chief, Plymouth, 1821-24.

110. George Prevost (1767-1816). 1st Baronet from 1805. Colonel, 1798. Major General, 1805. Lieutenant General, 1811. Governor of Nova Scotia, 1808-11. Governor General of the Canadas, 1812-15.

111. Wellington letter to Castlereagh, 14 August 1814, in Londonderry, *Memoirs and Correspondence of Viscount Castlereagh*, Vol. 10, pp. 93-94.

112. Joachim Murat (1767-1815). Collected the artillery for Napoleon's 'whiff of

Naples, in spite of his treachery (he had joined the anti-Napoleon alliance in January 1813). More important, Austria and Prussia were both to be enlarged somewhat to make their strengths viable offsets to the power of France: 'It is quite essential, however, to any balance of power, that these two monarchies should be made respectable.'[113]

On 25 September, when Castlereagh had arrived in Vienna, Liverpool wrote to coordinate their views:

> It might be quite true that, if the Emperor of Russia does not relax his present demands, the peace of Europe may not be of long continuance; but for however short a time that peace may last, I should consider it of great advantage. In the course of two or three years, it may reasonably be expected that the King's power in France will be consolidated, and that the revolutionary spirit, which still exists to such an alarming degree in that country, will in a great measure have evaporated; the people will have returned to peaceful habits, and the landed and monied interests will feel their fate connected with the restored Government. . . . A war now, therefore, may be a revolutionary war. A war some time hence, though an evil, need not be different in its character and its effects from any of those wars which occurred in the 17th and 18th centuries, before the commencement of the French Revolution.[114]

Liverpool moved on to discussing Poland, where British public opinion favoured Polish independence, reversing the partition of 1792. Thus, Russian pretensions to dominance of a petty Duchy of Warsaw, changing the provisional agreement made by the 1813 treaties, made the question a difficult one in England. At the Congress itself, the problem was compounded by the King of Prussia's determination, if Russia gained further territory in Poland, to annex the entire Kingdom of Saxony. In instructions to Castlereagh on 4 October, Liverpool wrote:

> However this question of Poland may now end, it cannot be settled either creditably or satisfactorily. The Emperor of Russia need never have stirred it, and in that case the Powers of Europe would have left the three states most interested to settle the question à *l'aimable* among

grapeshot', 1795. General, 1796. Married Caroline Bonaparte (Napoleon's sister), 1800. Marshal, 1804. Duke of Cleves, 1806-8. King of Naples, 1808-15. Joined Allies, January 1813, but then supported Napoleon during the 'Hundred Days' 1815 and was defeated by Austrian forces, May 1815, and executed on 13 October.

113. Letter to Wellington, 2 September 1813, quoted in Yonge, *The Life and Administration of Robert Banks Jenkinson*, Vol. 2, pp. 24-27. By 'respectable' I take Liverpool to mean having enough power to be militarily respected; both monarchies were clearly completely legitimate and respectable in the modern sense.

114. Letter to Castlereagh, 25 September 1814, quoted in ibid., Vol. 2, pp. 31-33.

> themselves; but as it has been once mooted, it becomes a matter of serious embarrassment, and it is very material that we should lose no character by the part we take in it. I am inclined to think that the less we have to do with it, except as far as regards giving an opinion, the better.[115]

In a memorandum accompanying the letter, Liverpool set out the various possibilities, beginning by saying that, since Britain had not objected to the 1792 partition of Poland, it could hardly do so now. It was clear, however, that simple absorption of the Duchy of Warsaw by Russia would be the least attractive possible outcome and Britain should not sign any treaty which contained such a provision. Castlereagh was thus given the job of wearing down the Czar's resistance.

On 28 October Liverpool wrote again to Castlereagh, enclosing a paper from Vansittart suggesting that British efforts should not be concentrated on Poland since it was secondary to British interests and a Russia-dominated Kingdom of Poland would be a source of disaffection rather than strength. Liverpool continued that, if Britain remained recalcitrant, Russia might side with the United States in that ongoing war, the finance for which would put a strain of an additional £10 million on a budget that was already £27-£28 million in deficit. He recognised that the Whigs would want to repeal the property (income) tax so, 'We must therefore expect to hear it said, that the property tax is continued for the purpose of securing a better frontier for Canada.'[116]

The Czar remained recalcitrant and, indeed, a Polish compromise was reached only the following March, after Napoleon's escape from Elba. However, on Saxony Castlereagh was more successful; with assistance from Talleyrand and firm backing from Liverpool, he was by late November able to persuade the conference to leave the King of Saxony in possession of most of his territory, with only a modest cession to Prussia east of the Elbe.

At the end of the year, Liverpool drafted another letter of instruction to Castlereagh, suggesting that peace was the overriding consideration and that 'there is no mode in which the arrangements in Poland, Germany and Italy can be settled consistently with the stipulations of the Treaty of Paris, which is not to be preferred, under present circumstances, to a renewal of hostilities between the continental Powers'.[117]

Furthermore, Liverpool suggested that, since Louis XVIII needed peace and was trustworthy, Castlereagh should ally with Talleyrand in persuading reasonable compromise solutions on the other three powers, possibly through

115. Letter to Castlereagh, 4 October, quoted in ibid., pp. 35-37, Memorandum, pp. 37-39.
116. Letter to Castlereagh, 28 October 1814, quoted in ibid., pp. 46-47, Vansittart memorandum, pp. 47-49.
117. Quoted in ibid., pp. 85-87.

Metternich, who had responded to the Czar's rages and insults by telling the Czar he was used to similar rages and insults from Napoleon. If it proved essential to allow Russia control of Poland, it should be granted only on condition that Poland became a separate country, ruled by the Czar but with a liberal constitution, as the Czar had several times promised – in that way, the power of Poland would not be easily combinable with that of Russia in Eastern Europe. Liverpool's suggestion was carried out via a secret treaty between Talleyrand, Metternich and Castlereagh. signed on 3 January 1815, by which the three powers agreed to 'repulse aggression' and protect 'the state of security and independence'.

The other issue that came up before the Congress of Vienna was the slave trade, on which Thomas Clarkson[118] lobbied Liverpool, Wellington and Castlereagh, producing a correspondence between Liverpool and Wellington on whether French abolition could be accelerated from its five-year deadline. Liverpool authorised Wellington to offer £2 million or the island of Trinidad to France in return for immediate abolition, with a preference for the money offer. When Talleyrand responded with his usual dissembling, Liverpool authorised Wellington to repeat the offer but nothing came of it. Meanwhile, he wrote to Castlereagh suggesting that the British offer to France be used as leverage with other powers to secure abolition.

However, Castlereagh's view, which he expressed to Liverpool, was:

> I am convinced we cannot afford to become purchasers on such extravagant terms of indulgences for Africa. If we do, we shall get nothing without paying for it ten prices; and what is worse, they will break faith with us, in order to have the same thing to dispose of a second time in some new form.[119]

Later, Liverpool agreed to abandon the prospect of immediate abolition but insisted that Spain, Portugal and other minor powers agreed in the final treaty to abolish the trade at the latest within five years, the same time as France. Thus, by 1821 the slave trade had legally been abolished by all the countries of Europe.

By November, Louis XVIII and Wellington were becoming seriously concerned about Wellington's safety in Paris and the possibility of a revolt against the Bourbon regime. Liverpool gave Wellington advice for the French royal family: 'The first measure of precaution to which I would call their

---

118. Thomas Clarkson (1760-1844). Founder of Committee on Abolition of Slave Trade, 1787, introducing William Wilberforce to the problem. Also helped to found worldwide Anti-Slavery Society, 1825.

119. Liverpool letters to Wellington, in Yonge, *The Life and Administration of Robert Banks Jenkinson*, Vol. 2, pp. 119-22 and 123-25. Castlereagh to Liverpool, in Londonderry, *Memoirs and Correspondence of Viscount Castlereagh*, Vol. 10, pp. 112-13.

attention is never to allow a reunion of the whole royal family in Paris at the same time.'[120] In another letter he suggested that Wellington consider taking charge of the forces in America; as he wrote to Castlereagh, 'he would restore confidence in the army, place the military operations on a proper footing, and give us the best chance of peace'.[121]

Wellington acknowledged the danger, saying that, 'I do not see what means the King has of resisting the brisk attack of a few hundred officers, determined to risk every thing', even though 'the population of the country, and even of Paris, is favourable to the Bourbons' with only unemployed officers, especially former prisoners of war who had been imprisoned in Britain, being 'discontented and dangerous'. 'The only remedy is the revival of Buonaparte's system of war and plunder,' he continued.

Wellington discussed what he might achieve in North America, although he cautioned Liverpool against sending him there, because, if something happened in Europe, he warned presciently, 'there is nobody but myself in which yourselves, or your country or your Allies would feel any confidence'. He then continued:

> I confess that I think you have no right, from the state of the war, to demand any concession of territory from America. . . . If you had territory, as you hope you soon will have New Orleans, I should prefer to insist on the cession of that province as a separate article than upon the *uti possedetis* [keep what you hold] as a principle of negotiation.[122]

Liverpool preferred Wellington to leave Paris because of the danger of assassination but, after agreeing to do so, Wellington sent a further letter of protest. Liverpool then agreed that he should remain there until a satisfactory pretext for his removal could be found. However, on 17 December Castlereagh informed Wellington that he would have to be in London before the end of the parliamentary adjournment and that he wished Wellington to move to Vienna to represent Britain at the Congress, to which Wellington agreed.

The other peace negotiation in full swing by the autumn of 1814 was that at Ghent between Britain and the United States. On 31 August Liverpool drafted instructions to the British commissioners, Goulburn, Gambier and Adams, urging them to demand sovereignty over the whole surface of the Great Lakes, to prevent future attacks on Canada, and to demand a buffer state to provide security for the First Nations that had been British allies. Ongoing management was left to Bathurst, Acting Foreign Secretary in Castlereagh's absence.

---

120. Quoted in Yonge, *The Life and Administration of Robert Banks Jenkinson*, Vol. 2, pp. 55-56.
121. Quoted in ibid., pp. 58-59.
122. Wellington letter to Liverpool, 9 November 1814, quoted in Londonderry, *Memoirs and Correspondence of Viscount Castlereagh*, Vol. 10, pp. 186-89.

The American commissioners, John Quincy Adams,[123] Henry Clay,[124] James A. Bayard, Sr,[125] Jonathan Russell[126] and Albert Gallatin,[127] had arrived at Ghent in early July. They were a more distinguished group than the British commissioners but they were considerably further from home and therefore out of communication with it. Initially, as they wrote to the Senate: 'We need hardly say that the demands of Great Britain shall receive from us an unanimous and decided negative.'[128]

Even after news of Bladensburg and the Washington fiasco had slapped the US delegation down a bit, negotiations moved slowly; as late as 2 November Liverpool wrote that he saw little prospect of the Ghent negotiations ending in peace.[129] However, a counter-proposal then arrived from the Americans, which, given the state of British finances and public opinion, and Wellington's pessimism about the possibility of acquiring additional territory, Liverpool felt it politic to accept. Consequently, the Treaty of Ghent was concluded on 24 December.

Wellington had stated that New Orleans was the only important point which Britain could take and hold. However, in a letter to Canning, Liverpool described it as 'one of the most unhealthy in any part of America'. It was thus unfortunate that an expedition under Sir Edward Pakenham[130] landed nine miles south of New Orleans on 23 December. After beating off an initial attack by Andrew Jackson, the British force remained inert, allowing Jackson time to fortify the American position.

123. John Quincy Adams (1767-1848). Son of 2nd US President John Adams. US Minister to the Netherlands, 1794-97, to Prussia, 1797-1801, to Russia, 1809-14, to United Kingdom, 1815-17. US Senator from Massachusetts, 1803-8. Secretary of State, 1817-25. 6th President of the United States, 1825-29. US Representative from Massachusetts, 1831-48.
124. Henry Clay (1777-1852). US Representative from Kentucky, 1811-14, 1815-21, 1823-25. Speaker of the House of Representatives, 1811-14, 1815-20, 1823-25. US Senator from Kentucky, 1806-7, 1810-11, 1831-42, 1849-52. Secretary of State, 1825-29. Whig nominee for President of the United States, 1832, 1844.
125. James A. Bayard, Sr (1767-1815). Federalist US Representative from Delaware, 1797-1803. US Senator from Delaware, 1804-13.
126. Jonathan Russell (1771-1832). US Ambassador to Sweden, 1814-18. US Representative from Massachusetts,1821-23.
127. Albert Gallatin (1761-1849). US Senator from Pennsylvania, 1793-94. Democratic-Republican US Representative from Pennsylvania, 1795-1801. Secretary of the Treasury, 1801-14. US Minister to France, 1816-23, to United Kingdom, 1826-27.
128. Quoted in Yonge, *The Life and Administration of Robert Banks Jenkinson*, Vol. 2, p. 63, note 1.
129. Quoted in ibid., pp. 49-51.
130. Edward Pakenham (1778-1815). Son of 2nd Baron Longford. Member of Irish Parliament for Longford Borough, 1799-1800. GCB, 1815. Major-General, Peninsular War, 1814, succeeded Robert Ross as commanding general of British forces in North America. Sister Kitty married Sir Arthur Wellesley, later Duke of Wellington, 1806.

Pakenham attacked the US position twice, the second time on 8 January. He failed to capture it, despite having a force of 14,000 compared to only 4,700 Americans, and suffered heavy and rapid casualties, about 2,600 including Pakenham himself, before the British forces withdrew. Pakenham, doubtless misled by easy British successes such as Crysler's Farm and Bladensburg, had grossly underestimated the quality of the US troops and Jackson's generalship. In a frontal assault on a fortified position, manned by skilled Americans armed with 'Kentucky rifles' rather than muskets, Pakenham suffered an early foretaste of the horrors of the American Civil War and World War I. Nevertheless, peace was ratified by the US Congress in February 1815.

Parliament met on 8 November 1814, as Castlereagh had urged Liverpool to pull its opening forward to avoid substantive discussion on the American peace negotiations. It was soon apparent that the party truce had ended and party rancour was back in full swing. In response to a self-congratulatory Address by the Prince Regent, Grenville launched into a denunciation (albeit less intemperate than two years earlier) of the government's policies on several fronts, especially that expenditure was being kept at wartime levels. Liverpool defended the government point by point; this was all he could do as the negotiations at Vienna and Ghent were both at a critical stage.

Post-debate Liverpool expressed his pessimism to Castlereagh and Wellington on the government's chances of survival. The following week, Liverpool was on the defensive again, this time on the government's policy of keeping a force of 40,000 men in the Netherlands after the Treaty of Paris with France had been concluded. He pointed out that, until the Congress of Vienna ended, it was necessary for Britain to keep a substantial force in being. In the event, this force was to form the nucleus of Wellington's army at Waterloo.

On 21 November Lansdowne brought up the Ghent negotiations, for which the US government had published the American negotiating position. Liverpool replied that he never knew of any such proceeding before on the part of any civilised government; he would not however stoop to the US level in discussing in detail negotiations that were still under way. He also refuted an American allegation that Britain had induced slaves to desert from US forces, afterwards selling them in the West Indies. This brief impromptu debate justified the parliamentary timetable suggested by Castlereagh; by the time the Ghent negotiations reached a critical point in early December, Parliament had been adjourned until February.

Liverpool's final speech came in the adjournment debate on 1 December. Grenville had reverted to his intemperate worst on the motion, accusing Liverpool of 'subsidizing a few of the powers of Europe to destroy every vestige of freedom there', describing Liverpool's policy as attempting to reconquer the United States, with the proposed First Nations buffer state being 'a mere refuge of outlaws and robbers' and describing Britain's finances as 'a subject which it was impossible to touch on without shuddering'. Liverpool countered that foreign policy and finances should be discussed only when the country's external future was settled and described the army on the Continent as 'employed for objects that are essentially British, for objects that have been considered British by every statesman that had ever looked to them, and for objects that are ultimately connected with the best interests of this country'.[131]

With two wars to win (or, in the case of the War of 1812, draw) and two peace treaties to negotiate, 1814 had been a tough year for Liverpool. It is thus not surprising that he retired to Bath for three weeks in January 1815, while Parliament was not in session and the only remaining peace negotiation was in Castlereagh's capable hands. Having concluded the agreement with Talleyrand and Metternich to resist claims on Saxony, Castlereagh wrote to Liverpool explaining the need for him to remain at Vienna until negotiations were completed and to Wellington suggesting he delay his arrival at Vienna accordingly.

Liverpool wrote to Castlereagh from Bath, stressing the need for his return to London in early February for the Parliamentary debate about the continuation of income tax and the subsequent debate on the Corn Laws. He described the first-line Parliamentary support as inadequate and the second line – Manners-Sutton,[132] Robinson and Peel – as capable but limited to their departmental brief, with Robinson being 'very idle, scarcely opening his mouth'.[133] Having received Castlereagh's report on the question of Saxony, Liverpool said: 'I feel, I confess, little kindness for the King of Saxony personally, and therefore a provision for him is not my object; but I do not wish to see the system of totally annihilating ancient States extend beyond what is absolutely necessary.' Again, he re-emphasised the need for Castlereagh's presence, saying, 'You can have no idea how much ground the Government lost in the House of Commons, in the short session before Christmas. . . . We do not feel that the American peace has in any degree relieved our embarrassments.'

On 30 January, Castlereagh wrote to Bathurst excusing a further delay in his return: 'You might as well have expected me to run away from Leipzig (if I had been there) to fight Creevey and Whitbread, as to withdraw from hence until the existing contest is brought to a point.' He added, 'I beg you will not give any money at present to any of the Continental Powers. The poorer they are kept, the better, to prevent them from quarrelling.'[134]

131. Hansard, *Parliamentary Debates from the Year 1803 to the Present Time*, Vol. 29, cols 623-29 (Grenville), 629-31 (Liverpool) (1 December 1814).

132. Charles Manners-Sutton (1780-1845). 1st Viscount Canterbury from 1835. Son of Charles Manners-Sutton (1755-1828), Archbishop of Canterbury, 1805-28. Tory MP for Scarborough and Cambridge University, 1806-35. Judge Advocate General, 1809-17. Speaker of the House of Commons, 1817-35.

133. Liverpool letters to Castlereagh, 12 and 16 January 1815, quoted in Londonderry, *Memoirs and Correspondence of Viscount Castlereagh*, Vol. 10, pp. 239-40 and 240-42.

134. Castlereagh letter to Bathurst, 30 January 1815, in ibid., pp. 247-48.

Finally, on 6 February, Castlereagh wrote to Liverpool declaring that he had solved the Saxony question, was happy to leave the rest to Wellington, who had arrived in Vienna, and would leave for London on 13 February, with a day in Paris on the way to keep Louis XVIII in line. In the event, he was not back in the Commons until 6 March.

Parliament reassembled on 9 February in a truculent mood, as the opposition and many independent members believed the government wanted to maintain wartime taxation in a year of peace. Vansittart immediately attempted to defuse the situation by announcing that he would propose a new taxation package which would not include income tax. In this he had been directed by Liverpool. In a letter to Canning, Liverpool had explained that they would be able to keep income tax for one more year at most; farmers were suffering badly because of the decline in corn prices and so would have difficulty paying their 1815-16 assessment. Thus, it made sense to abolish it immediately, which should make it fairly easy to impose the necessary £5 million in substitute taxes.[135]

In a Lords debate about disbanding the militia, Liverpool explained that expenditure was still a major problem; the peace treaty with America was still not ratified and Britain had several obligations to keep troops on the Continent. Liverpool refused to discuss arrangements regarding the transfer of the port of Genoa to Sardinia or the question of the military's peacetime establishment until matters at Vienna were settled and Britain's commitments were fully known.

On 20 February in the Commons, Vansittart reiterated the decision to end income tax, which would expire on 6 April, subject to no adverse events occurring. He pointed out, however, that the Parliaments of 1805 and 1806, which had promised to repeal income tax on the return of peace, could not bind their successors. Vansittart defended the tax, calculating that over the period of its imposition it had saved the country borrowing of an additional £180 million. He considered it a 'great and powerful resource, which, in times of public emergency, might and ought to be resorted to', although in a year such as 1814-15, in which commodity prices had fallen precipitously, it might bear excessively on the operations of farmers.[136]

Vansittart calculated the peacetime expenditure of 1815 as £19.5 million, which with winding-up expenses would not be reached until 1819.[137] To meet this, Vansittart calculated £6.5 million from existing peacetime taxes and £6 million by war taxes other than income tax, while he planned to raise £5 million through new taxes. These would include the extension of window tax

---

135. Letter quoted in Yonge, *The Life and Adminstration of Robert Banks Jenkinson*, Vol. 2, pp.134-36.
136. Hansard, *Parliamentary Debates from the Year 1803 to the Present Time*, Vol. 29, cols 853-871 (20 February 1815).
137. Mitchell, *British Historical Statistics*, p. 587. The year-end is 5 January.

to hothouses and commercial premises, a 30 per cent increase in property tax assessments and their extension to commercial premises, and an 80 per cent increase in the tax on servants, carriages and horses, with a 50 per cent surcharge for bachelors. Then, £800,000 would be raised by increases in wine and tobacco duties (both of which commodities would be cheapened by the return of peace) and another £300,000 by raising the tax on licensed import/export houses. Postal charges on newspapers and foreign post and increases in stamp duties would bring the total tax increase to £4.4 million, with elimination of bounties and drawbacks raising the balance up to £5 million.

Vansittart had raised the bulk of the extra revenue from taxes on luxuries, since income tax abolition would mostly benefit the rich. He made a point of not increasing the tax on beer, the working man's drink as beer prices were already too high because of the high price of hops. In response, Whitbread reserved his views on Vansittart's taxation proposals but pledged that the brewers would indeed institute an immediate reduction in the beer price as hop prices had started to decline.

At the time, Vansittart's abolition of income tax appeared a necessary tactical retreat. As shown by his letters during the parliamentary recess, Liverpool was concerned about the opposition's ability to force abolition of the tax, especially with Castlereagh absent at Vienna. However, the decision was taken too early for fiscal prudence; the budget was still heavily in deficit and the debt burden was unprecedented. The decision to end income tax was also to cause the government difficulty in coming sessions. Abolition was reversed when Napoleon reappeared but, having abolished it once, the government was forced by the Whigs to do so again in 1816.

The British economy of the 1820s and especially the 1830s was held back by its narrow tax base and high tariffs. Governments in 1816-42 relied excessively on tariffs and on the fiddly and expensive-to-collect 'sumptuary' taxes on windows, servants etc., which replaced income tax ito balance the fiscal burden between classes.

Liverpool's next Lords interventions were brief statements on the forthcoming Corn Law; he reassured the House that the government's regulations on corn prices would be designed to press as little as possible on the living standards of the poor and stressed that street disturbances should not be allowed to affect their deliberations. On 6 March, a Corn Law riot in London had caused the magistrates to call out the militia, to which the Radical John Lambton[138] objected and Castlereagh replied that, 'the force was called out by the civil magistrates, and not with a view to menace the members of parliament'.[139]

138. John Lambton 'Radical Jack' (1792-1840). Radical MP for County Durham, 1812-28. 1st Baron Durham from 1828. 1st Earl of Durham from 1833. Lord Privy Seal, 1830-33. Ambassador to Russia, 1833-37. Governor General of Canada, 1838-39.

139. Hansard, *Parliamentary Debates from the Year 1803 to the Present Time*, Vol. 30, col. 28 (6 March 1815).

The riot was relatively serious; Castlereagh's windows were smashed, Robinson's house was attacked (he had introduced the bill), Eldon's front door was broken down and his hall furniture smashed, before the elderly Lord Chancellor led a corporal's guard of soldiers from the British Museum with bayonets fixed to expel the rioters, collaring one of them and exclaiming, 'If you don't mind what you are about, my man, you will be hanged.'[140]

The proposed Corn Law provided for a prohibition on imports when corn prices were below 80 shillings a quarter and free imports when prices were higher than that, while providing for free grain imports from Ireland.

On 15 March, Liverpool opened the Second Reading debate on the Bill. Unlike the Netherlands and Venice, which were primarily commercial republics that relied on imports, Britain was both a great agricultural and a great commercial country and, with a population (including Ireland) of 19.2 million in 1815,[141] could not follow the same policy without a serious strategic danger in wartime. Such a country must follow a balanced policy between commerce and agriculture, even though his own education had taught him to favour the commercial interest. Indeed, Liverpool maintained that the two interests were not in reality opposed, but identical.

Liverpool then punctured, thirty years in advance, the policy of unilateral free trade followed from 1846 to 1932:

> The general principle, supposing all nations, or at least the most considerable nations, to act on it, was that in these matters the Legislature must not interfere, but leave everything to find its own level. . . . It is unnecessary for me to tell your lordships, that the actual state of the world is very different from what it must be before any nation in particular could rely on this line of policy. . . . This at least I take to be clear, that no nation could so far act on it without exceptions. I admit that these exceptions ought to be as few as possible, that the legislative regulations ought to be as limited as the situation and circumstances of the nation will allow. But still, exceptions there must be.

He then focussed on balance: the woollen, cotton, pottery and other industries were all subjected to a high protective tariff, so that, if agriculture

140. Horace Twiss, *The Public and Private Life of Lord Chancellor Eldon* (London: John Murray, 1844) Vol. 2, pp. 262-63.

141. Mitchell, *British Historical Statistics*, p. 11. Liverpool would have had available an 1811 Census figure of 11,972,000 for England and Wales, and a generally accepted estimate of six million for Ireland. Ibid., p. 822, shows Mining, manufacturing and building as 21 per cent of GDP in 1811, Agriculture as 36 per cent and Trade and service sectors 43 per cent – so Liverpool was not conceptually wrong in dividing the economy roughly into 'agricultural and commercial'. Mining, manufacturing and building would peak at 40 per cent of GDP in 1901, of which mining and building were roughly nine per cent, their share in the more detailed GDP data available for 1925.

were not protected, it would relatively be discouraged. Even within agriculture, the import of foreign cattle was prohibited and it therefore made sense to protect the production of grain, the most basic of agricultural needs. Britain's manufacturing and commerce had trebled between the Restoration and 1750, and the country was a net exporter of grain, so the principle of Corn Laws, by which the country was encouraged to be self-sufficient in grain as far as possible, would not impoverish the poor.

Indeed, with production encouraged and price fluctuations dampened by protection, consumers should find the average price cheaper than in a full free-trade system. The bill would also lower prices by encouraging Irish production, as Ireland would be treated as a domestic supplier (as it had been since an Act of 1806). This would be additionally beneficial in developing the Irish economy, importing capital to take advantage of cheap Irish labour in grain production. At the import floor of 80 shillings a quarter, the quartern loaf should cost no more than one shilling, which he was confident consumers would see as a reasonable price.[142]

Even if agricultural protection raised the cost of manufacturing labour, this would not cause emigration or hinder manufacturing, since British wages were relatively high and manufacturers testifying to Parliament had confirmed that cheapness of capital, credit and fuel were far more important advantages to British manufacturing than cheap labour. In general, Liverpool believed that the balance of economic advantage for Britain lay with dearer corn and higher wages, rather than attempting to achieve rock-bottom labour costs. Finally, if the Bill was passed, it could later be adjusted quickly, while allowing full free trade might destroy British agriculture, which could not be recovered within fifty years.[143]

Liverpool's Corn Law policy made sense at the time and still makes sense in retrospect. The Bill passed the House of Lords by 144 votes to seventeen, while the main House of Commons vote was won by 245 to 77. Economic opinion favoured the Corn Law, including Ricardo, Huskisson and, most notably, Malthus, who had written two pamphlets supporting such a system in 1814. However, ever since the agitation for their repeal dating from the late 1830s, the Corn Laws have come in for abuse from Whig historians and, indeed, the distinguished *Economist* magazine would be founded in 1843 to oppose them.

There was no doubt that, as Liverpool freely admitted, the Corn Law would need to be modified as peacetime conditions returned and wartime inflation was wrung out. However, the agricultural distress of 1820-23, as wartime debts proved onerous and prices fell, indicated that protectionist measures had

142. The quarter was equivalent to eight bushels, and therefore contained 480 pounds of wheat. The quartern loaf was a standard size, containing 3.5 pounds of wheat and weighing approximately 4.33 pounds. Thus, a quarter of wheat would make 137.14 quartern loaves.

143. Hansard, *Parliamentary Debates from the Year 1803 to the Present Time*, Vol. 30, cols 175-86 (15 March 1815).

indeed been necessary over the post-war period, although a relaxation of the law was instituted in 1822 and a further relaxation was designed by Liverpool with Huskisson in 1826-27 as his last act in office. The principle outlined here, of balance in both taxation and tariffs between different sectors and interests was an important one, abandoned by the dogmatic Peel in his Corn Laws repeal of 1846. Liverpool also saw the fallacy of unilateral free trade, which damaged self-sufficiency and allowed foreign producers to dominate the market.

Finally, Liverpool was indeed correct in supposing that the Corn Laws would be helpful in Ireland. In 1847, the earliest figures we have, eighteen per cent of Irish arable land was given over to wheat production and another eight per cent to barley production – both more than the mere six per cent given over to potatoes in that famine year, although potato-growing land had rebounded to nineteen per cent of the total by the non-famine year of 1850. It was Peel's and the Whigs' unilateral free-trade policy, not Liverpool's Corn Laws, which destroyed Irish agriculture. Fifty years later, in 1897, arable land in production in Ireland had fallen by 37 per cent, only two per cent of which was devoted to wheat and seven per cent to barley, while the potato acreage had increased to 26 per cent of arable land. Irish wheat production in 1847 was 61,400 tons; it halved within two years and was only six per cent of that amount 50 years later. Without Liverpool's Corn Laws, the Irish potato famine would have been even more devastating.[144]

By the time the Corn Law debate began in the House of Lords, it was already known that Napoleon had escaped from Elba and landed in France. Liverpool and his colleagues knew that Napoleon was not secure in Elba, and for that reason they opposed the Treaty of Fontainebleau, but they probably did not anticipate that France would give him an excuse for escaping by not paying any instalments of the pension due under that treaty. In January 1815 Wellington warned Liverpool that the greatest danger was of him leaving for Italy and establishing a kingdom there with the help of Murat. On 26 February Napoleon left Elba for France, landing between Cannes and Antibes on 1 March. News of Napoleon's escape reached Wellington in Vienna on 7 March and news of his landing in France reached London three days later.

According to Clancarty, on the news of Napoleon's escape reaching Vienna, 'it was not difficult to perceive that fear was predominant in all the Imperial and Royal personages there assembled'.[145] However, the firm Wellington found a more helpful reaction: 'I found among all one prevailing sentiment, of a determination to unite their efforts to support the system established by the Peace of Paris.'[146]

144. Mitchell, *British Historical Statistics*, pp. 190 (Acreage), 198 (Production).
145. Clancarty letter to Castlereagh, 11 March 1815, in Londonderry, *Memoirs and Correspondence of Viscount Castlereagh*, Vol. 10, pp. 264-69.
146. Letter to Castlereagh, 12 March 1815, in Gurwood, *The Dispatches of Field Marshal*

This determination was codified by a formal, if preliminary, declaration signed on 13 March by Austria, Spain, France, Britain, Portugal, Prussia, Russia and Sweden, a copy of which was immediately sent to Louis XVIII and which included the determination that Napoleon should be considered an outlaw. This was Napoleon's great miscalculation: he assumed, largely correctly, that the French people would rally to him and desert the Bourbons, but he also assumed, from his study of the Vienna disputes, that the Powers would be disunited, with some of them inclined to support him after he had regained control of France.

By that evening, as set out to Castlereagh, Wellington and the three allied sovereigns had determined the form of resistance to Napoleon, should Louis XVIII fail to contain him. A purely Austrian corps of 150,000 men would be deployed in Italy, an Austrian and south German army of 200,000 men would be deployed on the upper Rhine, a third Prussian/British/Dutch force would be formed in Flanders, while a Russian force of 200,000 men would be held in reserve. Wellington would command the force in Flanders, while the other forces would be under the nominal command of a troika of the Emperor of Russia, the King of Prussia and Schwarzenberg.

By 18 March two organisational conferences between the Allies had been held and Wellington had agreed in principle to provide British subsidies to oil the wheels of Continental military deployment. In the end, as set out by Castlereagh in a letter to Nesselrode,[147] the subsidies totalled £8.5 million, being £5 million to the three Great Powers, £2.5 million to minor powers in lieu of the deficit below 150,000 soldiers supplied by Britain, and £1 million contingent subsidy if the reserve Russian army was required to make victory certain.[148] A final treaty forming the Seventh Coalition was signed on 25 March, after which Wellington left for Brussels, arriving there on 4 April.

Because of the rapid success of the Waterloo campaign, we think of its outcome as inevitable. Nevertheless, the battle itself was, as Wellington said: 'a damned near-run thing'. However, Wellington's rapid organisation of Allied resistance, keeping the Allies working together and creating one large force in Italy to deal with Murat, together with two further large armies that could take on Napoleon if the effort in Flanders failed, reduced Napoleon's ultimate chances of restoring his Empire to vanishing point. It was a very important achievement.

Liverpool coordinated closely with Wellington, sending two questionnaires to await his arrival in Brussels, and then sending Harrowby and Wellesley-Pole to Brussels to find out in detail Wellington's views on strategy, contingencies

---

the Duke of Wellington, Vol. 12, pp. 266-67 and 267-68.

147. Count Karl Nesselrode (1780-1862). Head of Russian delegation at Congress of Vienna, 1814-15. Foreign Minister, 1816-56.

148. Letter from Castlereagh to Nesselrode, 28 May 1815, in Londonderry, *Memoirs and Correspondence of Viscount Castlereagh*, Vol. 10, pp. 365-67.

and his needs. Both in this case and in the communication between the Allies, Liverpool and his colleagues made good use of earlier experience gained over twenty years of conflict.

Napoleon's return to France enjoyed startling success. His key success came on 14 March when Marshal Ney, who had said Napoleon should be captured and 'put in an iron cage', joined him with 6,000 men. Given that Ney had sworn oaths of fealty to Louis XVIII and was commanding the King's troops in southern France, this was a remarkable act of treachery; it is not surprising that the Royalists insisted on his execution after their eventual victory. Royalist resistance thereafter crumbled. After a well-received speech celebrating the constitution to the two Chambers[149] of the French parliament, Louis XVIII left Paris on 19 March, Napoleon entered Paris the following day and Louis XVIII retired to Ghent.

Meanwhile Murat, who had been growing increasingly discontented at the universal Allied distrust for him and tacit support for the legitimate king of Naples, Ferdinand IV,[150] declared war on Austria on 15 March and marched north. This opened the danger of a war on two fronts; as Wellington wrote: 'If we do not destroy Murat, and that immediately, he will save Buonaparte.'[151] However, Murat was checked at the Battle of Occhiabello on 8-9 April, then decisively defeated at the Battle of Tolentino on 2-3 May, after which he fled to Corsica. Ferdinand IV was restored the following day. Thus, the danger of a two-front war was averted before Napoleon put his armies in motion.

Liverpool's attitude during this exceptionally trying period is indicated in a letter to his cousin, Lieutenant-Colonel George Jenkinson, sent to help prop up the Bourbons, doubtless a depressing task in those weeks:

> In God's name, however keep up your spirits, or otherwise you can be of no use. . . . I never knew those feelings entertained by any one, that they did not, however unbeknown to himself, tinge the language of the person who imbibed them, and thereby produce incalculable mischief. Poor Sir John Moore was a melancholy example of what I am saying.[152]

Shortly after Napoleon's early success was known in Britain, the Bank Restriction Bill came up, suspending gold payments to 5 July 1816. Liverpool said that the current moment was wholly inappropriate for an attempt to

149. *La Chambre des députés* (the lower House) and *la Chambre des pairs* (the upper House).
150. Ferdinand IV of Naples (1751-1825). Third son of Charles III of Spain. King of Naples, 1759-99, 1799-1805, 1815-16. King Ferdinand I of the Two Sicilies, 1816-25.
151. Letter to Castlereagh, 5 April 1815, in Gurwood, The Dispatches of Field Marshal the Duke of Wellington, Vol. 12, pp. 287-88.
152. Quoted in Yonge, *The Life and Administration of Robert Banks Jenkinson*, Vol. 2, p. 168.

go back onto the gold standard but that the feasibility of doing so had been shown by a decline in the gold price from £5.50 in January 1814 to £4.50 in February 1815 (the gold standard price was £4.25), while huge specie outflows had continued at £23 million in 1813 and £30 million in 1814. However, regardless of the new crisis, outflows would continue as the forces in America could not return to Britain until the end of the summer.[153]

The Prince Regent presented a message to both Houses on 6 April, announcing the breach of the Treaties of Fontainebleau and Paris, calling for an augmentation of the forces and announcing the construction of a new coalition against French aggression. Liverpool confirmed that there was no secret clause in the Treaty of Paris binding the Allies to support Louis XVIII against internal subversion. On the following day, there was a full-scale debate, which Liverpool opened. He began by pointing out the liberality of the Treaty of Paris, allowing France her 1792 borders, already enlarged by revolutionary activity. The makers of that treaty had been aware of the likelihood of a punitive peace leading to further war and had concluded a treaty entirely honourable to France.

As to the Treaty of Fontainebleau, Castlereagh had acquiesced in it partly because of the cost of further war, but also because the Allies had already committed to it and could not back out with honour. Britain had not assented to those clauses in the treaty asserting that Napoleon was Emperor of France, because Britain had never recognised the title, nor to the monetary allowance, because Britain was not concerned in it. Since that allowance was stated only as an annual amount, it was technically not yet in default, since Napoleon left Elba after less than a year.

At this point, as Napoleon had shown himself untrustworthy and belligerent, there were two alternatives: to place ourselves in a state of armed defence or to declare war on France. Which alternative would be chosen was a matter for the Allies but Liverpool said that Britain would not push those Allies to a position more belligerent than they were prepared to occupy. Liverpool engaged in one slightly sharp sleight-of-hand here: he did not disclose the treaty signed on 25 March committing the Allies to war, as it was contingent on an event (Napoleon's ousting of Louis XVIII) that had not been known when the treaty was signed.

Grenville gave a generally supportive speech but Wellesley delivered a blistering attack on the Congress of Vienna, which 'established a system of absolute injustice and gross discordance' and suggested that Napoleon had justice on his side with regard to not only the allowance, but also the failure to install his wife Marie Louise as Duchess of Parma and Piacenza (the Congress of Vienna installed her, but with no hereditary rights for Napoleon's son). Finally, Grey deprecated the possibility of making war on France simply to remove Napoleon. Nevertheless, the Address was agreed without dissent.[154]

153. Hansard, *Parliamentary Debates from the Year 1803 to the Present Time*, Vol. 30, cols 306-9 (21 March 1815).

154. Ibid., cols 356-72 (7 April 1815).

The following week, Wellesley introduced a Motion of Censure and renewed his attack on the gross incompetence of the Treaty of Fontainebleau, to which Liverpool replied that no such attack had been made in the year since the Treaty was published, but only since Napoleon's escape. The Allies had taken the decision to deal with Napoleon while he was still a free man with most of the French marshals loyal and numerous forts in France and the Netherlands; Liverpool still believed that decision to have been correct. Given that decision, they could not imprison Napoleon and, if he was not imprisoned, he could intrigue and escape from wherever he was placed. The Treaty had not technically been breached and Liverpool knew that arrangements had been made to pay Napoleon's allowance punctually. Wellesley's motion lost by 53 votes to 21.[155]

The following day, Liverpool informed the House that an overture of peace had been received from Napoleon, which had been transmitted to Vienna. In fact, this was simply a bombastic declaration of a general desire for peace issued by Napoleon and sent to all the Allied powers; it was taken as seriously as it deserved to be. Nevertheless, Liverpool and Castlereagh had to be careful not to run ahead of parliamentary opinion in their preparations – they did not, for example, make Bourbon restoration an official war aim.

On 19 April the government proposed the revival of income tax for the year to April 1816, with the initial Commons speech being made by Castlereagh rather than Vansittart. There was considerable Whig heckling, both on the unfairness of income tax and on the desirability of entering into a measure of war finance when the nation was not at war. However, Vansittart pointed out that the House had already accepted an Address which called for military preparations to be made and those preparations needed to be paid for. A prolonged state of armed peace would be even more expensive than war, because it should not be paid for by borrowing. In return for the restitution of income tax, Vansittart was prepared to drop the additional taxes on windows and other assessed property taxes, since they would bear too heavily if combined with a reintroduced income tax.

The tax renewal was passed by 183 votes to 58. In the Lords debate on the subject three weeks later, Liverpool described income tax as 'the least unequal and the least oppressive way in which so great a sum could be collected; and perhaps there was no other way in which it could be raised with so little comparative pressure upon the poorer classes of the community'.[156]

Liverpool's failure to mention the 25 March treaty in the 7 April debate, and the treaty itself, were attacked by Wellesley on 27 April, in a speech in which he demanded that the Allies reject the objectionable parts of the Congress of Vienna's determination to present a united front against Napoleon. The elision was also to be criticised in a deeply hostile Commons motion by the last-ditch Napoleon fan Whitbread two days later. Nonetheless, the government prevailed in that debate by a majority of over 200.

155. Ibid., cols 557-65 (12 April 1815).

156. Ibid., Vol. 31, cols 234-35 (10 May 1815).

In the Lords, Liverpool pointed out that the new circumstance of Napoleon's resumption of power might have led the Allies to change their policy, so it was Liverpool's duty not to forestall them. Currently (as of 27 April) the country was still not formally committed to war but only to the Prince Regent's Address of 6 April. As for war aims:

> First, that we consider the present government of France as an evil that must be got rid of; secondly, that we deem it highly desirable to restore the legitimate monarchy of France, and will contribute our efforts to that restoration; and thirdly, that we do not, however, consider that restoration as a *sine qua non*, and disclaim any intention of imposing a government on the French people.[157]

Having reached Paris, Napoleon dissolved the existing Chambers and produced a new constitution, drafted by Benjamin Constant,[158] which included a House of Peers and freedom of the press; it was ratified by a plebiscite beginning on 26 April, with only 30 per cent voter participation, less than half the turnout in the 1802 plebiscites of the Consulate. Furthermore, armed resistance to Napoleon's rule continued. While attempts to resist him in the south by both the Duke and Duchess of Angoulême were quickly crushed by Grouchy,[159] a revolt in the Vendée, the most Royalist region of France, survived throughout his return. Elections were held for the lower Chamber, which sat from 3 June to 7 July and elected the monarchist (if independent-minded) Comte Lanjuinais[160] as President.

On 22 May, the Prince Regent sent a message called for all treaties to be presented to Parliament and for authorisation to take such steps as should be necessary to prevent the revival of Napoleonic rule. In his brief statement introducing the message, Liverpool said that it was brought down 'with a view to commencing hostilities against the system mentioned in the message, as soon as it should be found expedient to do so'.[161]

157. Ibid., Vol. 30, cols 882-86 (27 April 1815).
158. Benjamin Constant (1767-1830). Swiss French liberal writer on politics. Lover of Germaine de Stael (1766-1817). Anglophile proponent of constitutional monarchy; ideas used in Louis Philippe's 1831 constitution.
159. Emmanuel de Grouchy (1766-1847). 2nd Marquis de Grouchy from 1808. Major-General, 1793. Served in 1806 Prussian campaign, 1809 Austrian campaign and 1812 Russian campaign as Lieutenant General. Marshal of France, 1815. Chased north-eastwards after Prussians and missed Battle of Waterloo. In exile, United States, 1815-21. Restored to House of Peers and awarded French military distinction of Marshal by Louis Philippe.
160. Jean Denis, Comte Lanjuinais (1753-1827). Politician, lawyer and historian. Elected to Estates General in 1789 and National Convention in 1792, where he became a reactionary and fiercely opposed the Jacobins. Proponent of constitutional monarchy.
161. Hansard, *Parliamentary Debates from the Year 1803 to the Present Time*, Vol. 31, cols

The following day, Liverpool made a lengthy speech on the Address justifying a declaration of war. Regrettably, the character of Napoleon and his actions in violating fundamentally the Treaty of Fontainebleau (for which the central object, justifying the favourable treatment given to France, was his removal) suggested that long-term peace was impossible: 'From the whole of his acts, indeed, it was obvious that the desire for power, and a thirst for dominion, formed this person's predominant passion, to which passion every consideration of morality and good faith was unreluctantly sacrificed.' His return to France was not a call from the people, most of whom opposed him, but a call from the army, which saw new opportunities of glory and plunder. France's new constitution was wholly unable to restrain such a man.

It was thus fortunate that Napoleon had escaped while the Allies were still assembled at Vienna, because the coalition had been able to react with a speed and unity that might otherwise have been impossible. Since, at best, an expensive, and in the long term financially ruinous, armed peace was necessary, it made more sense to precipitate a crisis than to continue with an armed peace allowing Napoleon to strike whenever he had rebuilt his strength and the Allies might be disunited. Whatever our chances of success, we should never find a better or stronger confederation or a more favourable opportunity than the present. The contest was founded, 'on a sentiment of common sense, by which every man must have said to himself: "While this state of things remains, I cannot be safe."'[162]

After a speech by Grenville in support, and one by Grey in opposition that suggested the Bourbons were 'absolutely repulsive to all France' while Napoleon's wishes were pacific, but that the Allies' chances of defeating him in battle were slender, the Address was approved by a vote of 112 to 44.

Both Grey's estimate of Bourbon support and Liverpool's claim in his speech that 80 per cent of Frenchmen supported the Bourbons appear to have been wrong, in opposite directions. The 30 per cent referendum turnout on the 1815 constitution suggests that support for Napoleon was around that level, with support being greatest in Paris and among the army. However, a substantial proportion of the public supported either Louis Philippe, Duc d'Orléans[163] as Orleanist claimant to the throne (there had been considerable Orleanist scheming in 1814-15, although without much encouragement from Louis Philippe himself) or a return to a republican government led by Carnot[164]

286-87 (22 May 1815).

162. Ibid., cols 316-33 (23 May 1815).

163. Louis Philippe I (1773-1850). Son of 'Philippe Égalité' Orleanist (descended from Regent Philippe Duc d'Orléans [1674-1723] uncle of Louis XV), claimant guillotined 1793. Thereafter Orleanist claimant to throne, 1793-1830. King of France, 1830-48.

164. Lazare Nicolas, Count Carnot (1753-1823). Politician and mathematician. National Convention, 1792, voted for Louis XVI's execution. Directory, 1795-97. 'Organiser of Victory' in French Revolutionary War. Minister of War, 1800. Minister of Interior,

or some other 1790s leader. Thus, Bourbon support was probably a plurality of France's population but possibly not a majority overall, although it was undoubtedly a majority in the south and west. From these divisions stemmed the instability of French governments throughout the nineteenth century.

In late May and early June both Houses returned to the issue of Catholic Emancipation, with arguments much as in 1813. The occasion was notable, however, for the production of a letter by Monsignor Quarantotti,[165] the Secretary for the Propagation of the Faith, conceding that Catholic bishops and deans should be subject to approval by the King, and that the hierarchy would not attempt to subvert the Protestant nature of the state, other than by ordinary conversion. This might have allayed many of the fears of the anti-Emancipationists but its timing was unfortunate (although it had been written early the previous year) so Liverpool continued to oppose an inquiry into the Catholic question.[166]

A Royal veto on the appointment of bishops might have solved the constitutional problems of Catholic Emancipation (though not those of its unpopularity with the non-Irish electorate) but, in the event, it was never clearly offered. Quarantotti's letter had been written while Pope Pius VII was still a captive of the French; when he returned to Rome he sent a further letter referring the matter to the cardinals. The bigoted Roman Catholic 'bishop' John Milner[167] then organised opposition to a Royal veto, as did the Irish nationalist leader Daniel O'Connell, who referred to 'the odious, the stupid Quarantotti' so that the 'securities' that Liverpool believed essential accompaniments of any Catholic Emancipation were never formally available.[168]

Before condemning Liverpool unduly for failing to seize the opportunity Quarantotti had apparently (though illusorily) offered, we must remember that nearly 40 years later, after Emancipation had been granted, the arch-Whig, Lord John Russell[169] would attempt to resist the establishment of a Catholic hierarchy in Britain, terming it 'Papal aggression' and passing the Ecclesiastical Titles Bill of 1851.

1815. Exiled as regicide after 1815.

165. Giovanni Battista Quarantotti (1736-1820). Cardinal, 1816. Secretary of the Sacred Congregation for the Propagation of the Faith from some date after 1770, Pro-Prefect thereof, 1809-14. Prefect from May 1820.

166. Hansard, *Parliamentary Debates from the Year 1803 to the Present Time*, Vol. 31, cols 481-87 (Quarantotti letter), cols 680-83 (Liverpool speech) (8 June 1815).

167. John Milner (1752-1826). Vicar Apostolic of the Midland District, 1803-26.

168. This is discussed in detail in Antonia Fraser, *The King and the Catholics: The Fights for Rights 1829* (London: Weidenfeld & Nicolson, 2018). O'Connell quote, p. 94.

169. John Russell (1792-1878). 3rd son of 6th Duke of Bedford. Earl Russell from 1861. MP for Tavistock, Huntingdonshire, Bandon, Devonshire, Devonshire South, Stroud and City of London, 1812-17, 1818-61. Paymaster of the Forces, 1830-34. Home Secretary, 1835-39. Secretary of State for War and the Colonies, 1839-41. Leader of the House of Commons, 1835-41, 1846-55. Prime Minister, 1846-52, 1865-66. Foreign Secretary, 1852-53, 1859-65. Lord President of the Council, 1854-55. Colonial Secretary, 1855.

Nicholas Vansittart, Lord Bexley, Lawrence, 1824. The real victor of the Waterloo campaign – his £27 million bond issue was 40 times what Napoleon raised.

Liverpool's last Parliamentary intervention before military action reshaped the landscape came on 12 June, when he defended British assumption of Russia's debt to the Netherlands, resting his case on Russia's efforts and sufferings during the war. In reality, this had been a case of Castlereagh's excessive generosity to the Netherlands when its strength needed rebuilding in 1813-14, turning dubious Russian obligations of £4 million into cast-iron British ones.

Vansittart's Budget[170] in the new and difficult fiscal situation, was presented on 14 June. He itemised the expenditures necessary, including £18.6 million for the navy (including transports), £39.2 million for the army, £4.4 million for the ordnance and £9 million for foreign payments, coming in total to £81.4 million. If he thought that current levels of expenditure would continue for more than one year, he would meet more of them by new taxes but, as it was, he believed that, even if the war continued, expenditure on it would not continue at this extraordinary level.

Vansittart had already contracted a loan of £18.1 million, and that morning had contracted a new loan of £27 million, for each £100 of which buyers would be given £130 in three-per-cent Reduced stock, £10 in four-per-cent bonds and £44 in three-per-cent Consols, for an all-in cost of 5.71 per cent for the two loans incurred in 1815. That was just 0.31 per cent higher than had been incurred in 1813, since when £187 million in new funded debt had been issued – this was an extraordinary tribute to the improvement in public credit since the late 1790s. The healthy state of credit was further shown by the decline in the gold price since April, from £5.35 per ounce to £5.25. Unlike 1813-14, the government had not made special demands on the Bank of England, with only two requests for Exchequer bill finance, of £2 million each.

Looking forward, Vansittart suggested that, if the war continued on its current military pattern, there would be a saving on the navy, which had already been reduced from 140,000 men to 70,000. Conversely, if the Allies reached a truce with Napoleon so that naval activities increased, there would be a saving on the army. Either way, expenditure should decrease somewhat in future years.

Modern figures,[171] taking account of the rapid pacification after Waterloo, put calendar 1815 expenditure at £99.5 million, significantly down from 1814's £112.9 million, with debt interest up by £2.2 million to £32.2 million, army and ordnance expenditures down £10 million to £39.6 million and naval expenditures down £6 million to £16.8 million. Gross income was up 1.5 per cent to £79.1 million, so the year's deficit fell by more than 40 per cent, from £35 million to £20.4 million. Vansittart was thus perhaps overcautious in undertaking the normal sensible Treasury policy of contracting the whole year's debt at the time of the Budget, four days before the Battle of Waterloo.

Napoleon's *Champ de Mai* grand rally on 1 June accepted the constitution but turned into more of a military parade, after which he began to lead the bulk of the newly collected troops northwards. Since Prussian, Austrian and

170. Hansard, *Parliamentary Debates from the Year 1803 to the Present Time*, Vol. 31, cols 795-822 (14 June 1815).

171. Mitchell, *British Historical Statistics*, pp. 581 (Income), 587 (Expenditure). The year-end is 5 January so, to get the figures for the (approximate) calendar year 1815, you should use the 1816 figures in the tables.

Russian armies were also threatening France from the east, Napoleon was compelled to leave substantial forces to face them and suppress the rebellion in Vendée, so his *Armée du Nord* contained only 128,000 of France's 250,000 troops. Nevertheless, as Wellington's British forces were mostly inexperienced and the Anglo-Prussian armies in Belgium were widely dispersed, Napoleon believed success was more likely if he defeated the forces in Belgium first, rather than wait for a general Allied assault on France by a total of up to 850,000 men, which had been scheduled for 1 July.

Napoleon's plans were overoptimistic in two respects. First, lacking access to the London money market, he had raised a total of 17.5 million francs[172] during his return to power – about £700,000 at the prevailing exchange rate, a mere 2.6 per cent of the gigantic £27 million loan Vansittart raised on 14 June. By this stage, even though France's population was 30 million compared to Britain's nineteen million, Britain's ability to command resources for war was disproportionately greater.

Second, Napoleon claimed in his memoirs that: 'I had relied mainly . . . on the idea that a victory over the English army in Belgium would have been sufficient to produce a change of administration in England, and have afforded me a chance of concluding an immediate general peace.'[173] In this belief Napoleon had failed to keep up with the increase in British political stability since 1810. With Sidmouth, Canning and their followers safely part of Liverpool's government, the Prince Regent onside and the large majority Liverpool had gained in 1812, the government was secure against a British defeat in Belgium, at least in the short-term. The main danger from such a defeat was a remotely possible collapse in the London money market, bankrupting large holders of Vansittart's new loan.

Wellington spent late April, May and early June at Brussels collecting forces, coordinating supplies and training those that required it – many of the British forces were from Ireland and had not seen action. As Wellington wrote to Charles Stewart in a moment of irritation: 'I have got an infamous army, very weak and ill equipped, and a very inexperienced Staff. In my opinion they are doing nothing in England.'[174]

While the Allied plan was to advance into France from 1 July, Wellington always thought it more likely that Napoleon would attack first, though in early May he thought Napoleon would strike first at Prussian forces on the Rhine and that any Allied advance should also begin there. There was a mutiny among the Saxon troops (whose attachment to Napoleon was greater than that to Prussia, with which they were serving) so Wellington recommended they be sent to carry out garrison duties where they could do no harm.

172. Andrew Roberts, *Napoleon: A Life* (London: Allen Lane, 2014) p. 745.

173. Quoted in ibid., p. 751.

174. Letter to Charles, Lord Stewart, 8 May 1815, in Gurwood, *The Dispatches of Field Marshal the Duke of Wellington*, Vol 12, p. 358.

Later in May Wellington wrote to Metternich that the only hope of a peaceful France lay with the legitimate Bourbons. Rule by Orléans, Napoleon's infant son or the Jacobins would undoubtedly lead to permanent armament and a French attack on Austria or one of the other Allies.[175] In a later letter to Orléans himself, Wellington suggested it was his duty to support the King when the Allies re-entered France, as the King had been ousted by a military revolt and not by a general rebellion.[176]

Liverpool also favoured restoration of the Bourbons but, in a letter to Canning, saw the difficulties of maintaining them as rulers of France against Orleanist and republican opposition:

> The latter will be a work of much difficulty. The King is certainly personally popular; Monsieur [the future Charles X] and the Duc de Berri hated, the Duchesse d'Angoulême respected and pitied, but not loved, the Duc d'Angoulême rather liked. You will be surprised that our old friend Monsieur is perhaps the most unpopular of the set. This arises from the influence the emigrants have over him, and from him being regarded as the essence of emigration. There appears to me to be a great resemblance between his character and that of many of the princes of the Stuart family. He is a perfect chevalier but has no quality which belongs to a king or prince in difficult times. The greatest danger to the old line of Bourbons is from the Duke of Orleans.[177]

At least in foreseeing France's history over the next fifteen years, this was perspicacious.

Napoleon arrived at his army on 14 June and advanced into Belgium the following day. On the evening of 15 June, his army arrived near a crucial crossroads, Quatre Bras, where the British fought a key defensive battle the following day, while the Prussians suffered a defeat at Ligny, to the east. On 17 June both British and Prussians retreated northwards along parallel roads, the Prussians to Wavre, chased by Grouchy's corps, and the British to Waterloo, on the road to Brussels.

Finally, on 18 June the crucial engagement of the war was fought at Waterloo and narrowly won by Wellington's forces after the vanguard of the Prussian forces arrived from the east as evening approached. Total British casualties over the three days were 2,400 killed, 9,500 wounded and 1,900 missing, a moderate number for such a struggle.

The tactical details of the Waterloo campaign are fascinating but part of Wellington's story, not Liverpool's. In any case, the battle was not quite as

175. Letter to Metternich, 20 May 1815, in ibid., pp. 409-11.
176. Letter to Orléans, 6 June 1815, in ibid., pp. 448-49.
177. Letter to Canning, 13 June 1815, quoted in Yonge, *The Life and Administration of Robert Banks Jenkinson*, Vol. 2, pp. 178-80.

important as it was subsequently painted. In terms of the forces involved, it was only half the size of Leipzig two years earlier, even if you count all the Prussian forces and Grouchy's corps. Waterloo was also less decisive than Leipzig, which was the battle that really doomed Napoleon. Even if Napoleon had won Waterloo, he was unlikely to achieve long-term success, since 800,000 Allied troops were approaching France under generals who, if not quite of Wellington's calibre, were certainly competent – and in the case of Schwarzenberg's chief of staff, Radetzky, more than that.

Liverpool himself thought Waterloo remarkable indeed, writing to Canning in the late summer of 1815: 'I know of no instance in the history of the world, at least in modern times, of one battle producing such decisive effects.'[178] However, Napoleon's return had been doomed, and Wellington or some other Allied general's victory assured, in those crucial few weeks after Napoleon's return when Wellington in Vienna locked the Allies into an agreement and a military strategy that left Napoleon with no pathway to success.

The news of Waterloo came to London in the form of Wellington's dispatch to Bathurst written the following morning, in which he said: 'It gives me the greatest satisfaction to assure your Lordship that the Army never, upon any occasion, conducted itself better. . . . I send with this dispatch three eagles, taken by the troops in this action, which Major Percy[179] will have the honour of laying at the feet of His Royal Highness.'[180]

Late in the night of 21 June, Major Percy, with eagles and tricolours sticking out of his post-chaise, after asking directions at the Colonial Office and picking up Arbuthnot there, arrived at Harrowby's house in Grosvenor Square, at which most of the Cabinet including Bathurst and Liverpool had been dining. The ministers read the dispatch, questioning Percy to learn the extent of the victory, after which Arbuthnot, responsible for the government's public relations, was sent out to give the news to the crowd outside and then contacted the printers of the following day's *London Gazette*. Percy, with most of the Cabinet following, then continued to 16 St James's Square, where the Prince Regent was dining, to deliver his trophies to the Prince Regent. On this occasion, Liverpool himself triumphantly read the dispatch aloud to the Prince Regent and the assembled company.[181]

The first three years of Liverpool's prime ministership had held enormous achievement, with two wars successfully concluded and the finances kept on an even keel. He had succeeded where Pitt, Addington, Fox, Grenville, Portland

---

178. Quoted in ibid., p. 219.
179. Colonel the Hon. Henry Percy (1786-1825). Grandson of the Duke of Northumberland. *Aide-de-camp* to Moore at Corunna and Wellington at Waterloo.
180. Dispatch to Bathurst, 19 June 1815, in Gurwood, *The Dispatches of Field Marshal the Duke of Wellington*, Vol. 12, pp. 479-84.
181. An account of Percy's journey is given in Brian Cathcart, *The News from Waterloo: The Race to Tell Britain of Wellington's Victory* (London: Faber & Faber, 2015).

and Perceval had fallen short. His efforts had been rendered both more effective and more enjoyable through his close and friendly working partnerships with Wellington and Castlereagh, both now generally acknowledged as Britain's greatest practitioners in their respective spheres. Let us, therefore, leave him for a moment, aged just 45 in the early hours of 22 June 1815, toasting the prospects for a victorious peace.

VI.

Penury and Progress, 1815-19

As Liverpool enjoyed a well-deserved triumph, he may even in his euphoria have suspected that the early years of peace would prove more difficult for him and for Britain than the war years. The most important obstacle he faced was Britain's immense public indebtedness, which was far higher than ever previously. Indeed, it would be higher in terms of GDP (a concept then unknown) than at any time in the future except immediately after World War II. The famine caused by 1816's 'Year Without a Summer' was also especially ill-timed, while the 1819 Peterloo Massacre was a failure by local magistrates that caused widespread unrest elsewhere and had serious long-term repercussions on the Liverpool government's reputation.

Liverpool's successful weathering of these uniquely troublesome years, building a foundation for future success, was the greatest achievement of his premiership, even greater than winning the war. It assured Britain a future of peace and increasing prosperity, without the upheavals of revolution seen throughout the rest of Europe in 1830 and 1848, for the remainder of the nineteenth century. The achievements of the Victorians, indeed their entire world, was built upon the work done by Liverpool and his colleagues.

Wellington entered France three days after Waterloo and Louis XVIII re-entered France on 23 June. Napoleon arrived in Paris on 21 June and resigned the next day, nominally in favour of his young son but leaving the country to a commission of the two Chambers, led by Joseph Fouché,[1] who attempted to form an armistice with Wellington and asked for a safe conduct for Napoleon to the United States. Wellington rebuffed them.

Both British and Prussian forces advanced on Paris steadily. On 30 June some of Blücher's troops crossed the Seine, surrounding Paris, and defeated the defenders of Paris on 3 July at the Battle of Issy. Paris surrendered on 4 July, the Allied armies entered Paris on 7 July and Louis XVIII re-entered his

1. Joseph Fouché (1759-1820). National Convention, 1792-95. Minister of Police, 1799-1810, March-June, 1815, July-Sept, 1815.

capital the following day. Napoleon retreated westwards, still hoping to escape to America, but faced a British naval blockade, so on 15 July he surrendered to Captain Frederick Maitland[2] of HMS *Bellerophon*.

Only a day after the news arrived in London, the House of Lords gave a vote of thanks, proposed by Bathurst, for Wellington, Blücher and the Allied armies. Following the Vote, Liverpool proposed an additional grant of £200,000 for Wellington, referring to Wellington's 'extreme disinterestedness' by which he had never drawn all the allowances to which he was entitled. Once again, the grant was passed unanimously.[3]

At the end of June, Liverpool supported a Foreign Slave Trade Bill, proposed by Lansdowne, that made it an offence to finance the slave trade in foreign countries, although he described it as having been 'drawn up in a slovenly manner'. The Bill was, however, lost in a thin House. The following week, he proposed that a bill to abolish the pillory should be referred to a panel of judges, although he agreed the punishment was obsolete except perhaps in the case of fraud. Stanhope raised a laugh, presumably joined by Liverpool, when he suggested that it was an unequal punishment, because if he and Liverpool were both committed to the pillory for some offence, he would escape scot-free while the Prime Minister would be pelted mercilessly because of the Corn Laws.

An Apothecaries Act was passed requiring licences for medical practitioners, the first step on this road to modernity. After a final speech supporting the unification of excise methods between Britain and Ireland, Liverpool's parliamentary duties ended with adjournment on 12 July.

The terms of the new peace were settled in letters between Liverpool and Castlereagh, who went to Paris to meet the armies and the Allied sovereigns. Since Paris was much closer to London than Vienna, Liverpool was more involved in the detail of negotiations after Waterloo than in the previous year, issuing detailed instructions even on minor points to Castlereagh (and to Wellington as commander of the Allied forces) after consultation with the Cabinet.

The generous peace of 1814 would no longer do – France must lose something by rebellion, since there had been only minimal resistance to Napoleon's return. (Wellington however disagreed here, writing to Castlereagh: 'It would be ridiculous to suppose that the Allies would have been in possession of Paris in a fortnight after one battle fought if the French people in general had not been favourably disposed.')[4]

2. Frederick Lewis Maitland (1777-1839). KCB, 1830. Captain, 1801. Rear-Admiral, 1830. *Protégé* of St Vincent. Blockaded Rochefort to capture Napoleon, July 1815. Commander-in-Chief, East Indies, 1837-39.

3. Hansard, *Parliamentary Debates from the Year 1803 to the Present Time*, Vol. 31, cols 977-79 (23 June 1815).

4. Letter to Castlereagh, 11 August 1815, in Gurwood, *The Dispatches of Field Marshal*

Liverpool also realised that Louis XVIII would hardly be safe on his throne, with the French army opposed to him and Orleanist and Republican opposition movements. Hence Liverpool proposed that France be left with her 1790 frontiers rather than the broader ones of 1792, that an Allied army occupy France for some period, at France's expense and that some of France's border fortresses be occupied by the Allies. Conversely, Napoleon's one positive step during the Hundred Days, of abolishing the slave trade, should be adhered to.[5]

In a subsequent series of letters, he turned to the fate of Napoleon, and to the art treasures looted by the French in 20 years of war, which Liverpool was determined to return to the Allies and associated Italian states from which they had been looted. This was done over the next three months, with all losses being replaced, even to entities such as the Papacy that had not joined the Sixth and Seventh Coalitions, and Wellington making a show of force so that Louis XVIII did not appear to be relinquishing them voluntarily.

Liverpool also expanded on the border fortress proposal, suggesting that they be held for five years or Napoleon's lifetime, and restored only to Louis XVIII or his successors by rightful inheritance, which would bolster the Bourbon regime. Liverpool also expressed concern about the slow pace of French army disbandment, and undertook to send some Peninsular regiments, now returned from North America, to join Wellington and prevent temptation arising among the French soldiery.

As for Napoleon, he was to be put in British custody, without Allied co-custodians, and Liverpool, after consulting with Sir John Barrow,[6] proposed St Helena as the best destination. Eldon expressed doubts as to the legality of this, so Liverpool obtained an Act of Parliament early in the next session[7] which retroactively removed all doubt.

The coming financial difficulties cast their first shadow in Liverpool's letter to Castlereagh of 11 August, which began, 'I am obliged to call your serious attention to the state of our foreign expenditure.' It continued: 'We must not, however, conceal from ourselves that the country cannot go on for any length of time at its present scale of expense.' He foresaw the difficulties of the following year in prolonging income tax but pointed out that, without it, it would be impossible to keep up the necessary peace establishment. France, which had repudiated its debts, would be well able to pay the costs of its occupation, so Liverpool stressed the necessity for its doing so and for the

---

the Duke of Wellington, Vol. 12, pp. 596-600.

5. The letters are set out in Yonge, *The Life and Administration of Robert Banks Jenkinson*, Vol. 2, pp. 184-91 *et seq.*
6. Sir John Barrow (1764-1848). Second Secretary to the Admiralty, 1805-6, 1807-45 (appointed by the 1st Viscount Melville). Sponsor of numerous expeditions of Arctic discovery. Author of numerous books and *Quarterly Review* articles. Commemorated in the Barrow Strait.
7. The Custody of Napoleon Bonaparte Act, 1816.

termination of the various subsidies to the Allies, particularly those subsidiary Allies such as Spain and Denmark whose forces had not taken the field before the entry into Paris and 'where we have no chance of receiving money's worth for our money'.[8]

Vansittart also gave a pessimistic report to Castlereagh of Britain's financial difficulties, pointing out the decline in government bond prices. He suggested that this was due both to the large bond issues of the previous spring, which now hung over the market, and to the declining price of corn, which was causing distress among the landed interest and making the country banks cautious. These had already reduced their outstanding advances by a third and were thus causing taxpayers difficulties in paying income tax. On the other hand, overseas trade had rebounded, with the re-opening of the American market, so customs revenues were buoyant.[9]

The convocation of the new French Chambers on 21 September delayed a final treaty with France, which was also slowed by the subsidies to Austria and Prussia, due to be paid until April 1816, which would cease on signature of a definitive peace treaty. Even so, the progress being made led to the departure of the Allied sovereigns from Paris at the end of September. The new Chambers were, like Britain's Cavalier Parliament of 1661, initially ultra-Royalist, and forced the dismissal of Talleyrand and Fouché.

Thus, the treaty finally signed on November 20, inevitably unpopular in France, was blamed on the ultra-Royalists, rather than on Talleyrand and Fouché. As Liverpool wrote to Cooke:[10] "It is most extraordinary that the French princes, after living so many years in this country, should remain as ignorant of all the principles and practices of a popular or mixed government as if they had known no other atmosphere but that of Versailles under its former sovereigns."[11] However the new prime minister, the Duc de Richelieu,[12] proved both moderate and competent, though having spent the previous two decades in Russia he took time to settle into the job.

While Royalist elements in the populace entered into a "White Terror" of revenge that winter, killing around 300 Bonapartist officials by mob lynching, only two of Napoleon's generals were eventually executed, in both cases for deserting to him while commanding Royalist troops. One, the Comte de la

8. Londonderry, *Memoirs and Correspondence of Viscount Castlereagh*, Vol. 10, pp. 476-79.
9. Vansittart letter to Castlereagh, 4 September 1815, in ibid., Vol. 11, pp. 1-7.
10. George Cooke (1768-1837). Major-General, 1815. KCB, 1815. On Wellington's staff at Waterloo.
11. Quoted in Yonge, *The Life and Administration of Robert Banks Jenkinson*, Vol. 2, p. 224.
12. Armand-Emmanuel du Plessis (1766-1822). 5th Duc de Richelieu from 1791. Mayor of Odessa, 1803-14. Governor General of Yekaterinoslav, Kherson and Taurida, 1805-14. Prime Minister of France, 1815-18, 1820-21.

Bédoyère,[13] executed by firing squad, caused little stir. The other, the execution of Marshal Ney, on 7 December after a trial by the new, Royalist Chamber of Peers, was a major source of long-term anti-Royalist feeling.

Ney's wife had appealed to Liverpool and Wellington, who both expressed considerable sympathy. She also tried lobbying Lord Holland. However, it is not clear why Ney's case was more deserving than Bédoyère's, although, conversely, Soult and others of Napoleon's 1815 associates were lucky to escape a similar fate. Indeed, in September Liverpool expressed the opinion to Castlereagh that the proper procedure would have been to set up a military tribunal immediately the King re-entered Paris, to try and to execute the six to seven 'most flagrant offenders' among those corps commanders who had deserted the Royal armies for Napoleon before the king left Paris.[14]

Before the three Allied monarchs left Paris, they committed themselves to a further treaty much mocked by Whig historians: the Holy Alliance. This was the brainchild of Alexander I and took the form of a brief document initially signed by himself, the King of Prussia and the Emperor of Austria.

The agreement of 26 September declared that, since Divine Providence had given the three sovereigns victory, they would henceforth act on the principles of justice, charity and peace, which were as applicable to princes as they were in private life. According to the words of the sacred scriptures, they would enter a true and indissoluble brotherhood and, looking on their subjects as the father of a family, would act in fraternity to protect religion, peace and justice. They would also regard themselves as members of one Christian nation and would recommend to all their subjects to work every day in the principles of Jesus Christ. Furthermore, all other powers which wished to acknowledge these sacred principles and recognise that the happiness of humanity depended on these truths exerting all their influence on human destiny, were invited to join this Holy Alliance. The three sovereigns then asked the Prince Regent to sign the agreement.

Metternich himself expressed scepticism about this agreement to Castlereagh, probably because he knew the Enlightenment rationalist Castlereagh would disapprove. Castlereagh described it to Liverpool as 'sublime mysticism and nonsense', claiming that Wellington and he had difficulty keeping a straight face when Alexander I presented the agreement to them. He then suggested that Alexander I's mind was 'not entirely sound' and that he had been unduly influenced by a religious mystic called Barbara von Krüdener,[15] with whom

---

13. Charles, Comte de la Bédoyère (1786-1815). Colonel commanding regiment at Grenoble which went over to Napoleon on 8 March. Brigadier and aide to Napoleon in the Waterloo campaign, probably responsible for d'Erlon's 20,000 troops shuffling aimlessly between Quatre Bras and Ligny on 16 June.
14. Liverpool letter to Castlereagh, 15 September 1815, in Londonderry, *Memoirs and Correspondence of Viscount Castlereagh*, Vol. 11, pp. 16-18.
15. Barbara von Krüdener (1764-1824). Married 1782(?) Baron Burckhard Alexius

he had recently become infatuated. Castlereagh suggested that the Prince Regent sign the agreement in a personal capacity, without formally involving his ministers.

Liverpool, in response, was also sceptical of the initiative: 'I forbear discussing the question how far it might not have been advisable, on every account, to prevent such a proceeding altogether.' A personal agreement by the Prince Regent without the intervention of his ministers was contrary to the spirit of the British Constitution. He agreed with Castlereagh that the agreement itself would never be acceptable to the Whigs and got around the problem by drafting a letter for the Prince Regent to sign (which he did as Prince of Hanover), by which he agreed with the principles of the Holy Alliance, without committing to it as an Act of State.[16] The Holy Alliance is thus associated with – but distinct from – the later Quadruple Alliance, signed on 20 November 1815 by Austria, Prussia, Russia and the United Kingdom (the Quintuple Alliance after France's admission in 1818).

Liverpool, Castlereagh and Wellington, in their sceptical reception of the sovereigns' Holy Alliance initiative, were children of their rationalist educations. As the parliamentary debates were to show in the following year, the Whigs (and Whig-inclined historians thereafter) were even more hostile to the initiative, which to them combined monarchical absolutism and religiosity in a highly obnoxious manner.

Having been brought up as late eighteenth Century rationalists, British statesmen of Liverpool's generation were unsympathetic to the language in which the Holy Alliance was couched, albeit not to the principle of the Alliance itself. However, Alexander I, Francis I and Frederick William III occupied a world still much more centred on religion, closer to that of the English seventeenth century. So also did the great majority of their subjects, beyond a thin layer of the Enlightenment-educated, as also did most of the Prince Regent's subjects. The great Earl of Clarendon, founder of post-Restoration Toryism, would have found the wording of the Holy Alliance much more understandable than did Liverpool's generation of Tory statesmen.

The drafters of the Holy Alliance were trying to construct a bulwark against war and revolution that would have genuine emotional and spiritual resonance with future statesmen and with most of their subjects. By making the Alliance 'Holy' of whatever denomination (all four members had different dominant

Constantin von Krüdener (1748-1802). Religious awakening, 1801, becoming a preacher and founder of anti-Radical religious order, she influenced Alexander I deeply after they met in early 1815. Established Swiss colony in Crimea, 1821. She was thirteen years older than the Czar, over 50 at this time, so the relationship may well have been platonic.

16. The correspondence and text of the Holy Alliance agreement and the Prince Regent's letter are given in Yonge, *The Life and Administration of Robert Banks Jenkinson*, Vol. 2, pp. 226-34. Castlereagh letter to Liverpool, 28 September 1815; Liverpool reply dated 3 October 1815.

Christian denominations in their countries) they were attempting to prevent short-term considerations from leading its members to abandon it or to oppose its decisions. They were also trying to give it weight through the support of the religiously-inclined mass of their populace, thereby limiting the cynical manoeuvrings of their politicians, the revolutionary fervour of their Jacobin middle classes, and the belligerency of their military lobbies.

In the short term, the Holy Alliance achieved its objectives, to which Liverpool and his colleagues also subscribed. In the period 1815-22 Europe settled down after two decades of war and began to enjoy economic recovery, with even France generally accepting the restored Bourbon regime. The Alliance only fell apart when Castlereagh, who generally supported it if not its formulation, was succeeded by Canning, who had a Whiggish contempt for the Alliance itself, disliked the leading continental statesmen and saw no advantage for Britain in working with the continental powers.

Canning's hostility to the Holy Alliance, and the long-term failure to embed it in the European power structure, prevented it from achieving its maximum potential. It might have prevented future medium-sized wars, such as the Crimean War of 1854-56 and the Franco-Prussian War of 1870-71. It could even have proved valuable in deflecting the European powers from the ultimate tragedy of World War I. As such, the Holy Alliance deserves a great deal more respect from historians.

Liverpool retired to Walmer Castle for a well-earned rest in late September and remained there for most of the autumn, though the signing of the French treaty kept him in London for two weeks in November, the longest period he and Louisa ever spent apart.

In 1816 Liverpool entered a period when economic difficulties combined with widespread unrest and an increasingly hostile press to make his job exceptionally difficult. Fortunately, in terms of health, experience and temperament, Liverpool was at his peak. Economic stresses, together with those caused by the war, had produced similar unrest in the 1790s, however, the press was much more organised and powerful now. Moreover, the middle class was not as united in their support for law and order as they had been in the 1790s. Their growing agitation for parliamentary reform of combined with working class protest and Radical agitation to produce a revolutionary cocktail which to Liverpool and his Cabinet seemed to resemble that of early 1790s France.

Liverpool summed up the difficulties with the press in a letter to Castlereagh:

> You know full well that there are papers, which are vulgarly called Government papers, in consequence of the support which they give to the Government rather than the Opposition of the day: there are no papers over which we have any authority, or even any influence on which we can depend. . . . [N]o paper that has any character and consequently an established sale, will accept any money from government. . . . They

> make their way like sycophants with the public, by finding out the prejudices and prepossessions of the moment, and then flattering them; and the number of *soi-disant* Government or Opposition papers abound just as the Government is generally popular or unpopular.[17]

During the war, at least since 1803, much of the press had generally supported the war effort and most governments. Now the perennial call for government economy, exacerbated by the continuance of wartime-level taxation and, after 1819, a new agitation for parliamentary reform, pushed the press towards the opposition Whigs. Ironically, the Whigs' one great success during these years, forcing the abolition of income tax, both raised the burden of taxation on the working class and made the government's stabilisation of the country's finances more difficult.

At the beginning of 1816 the principal economic problem was low corn prices. They had fallen sharply with the end of the war and in January 1816 touched a low of 53 shillings, less than two thirds of the Corn Laws' benchmark price of 80 shillings. With the currency still depreciated from its gold value, this represented a nadir in real terms for several decades. Farmers both large and small, who had borrowed heavily to extend their cultivable acreage during the war, were suddenly plunged into financial difficulty. This gave extra strength to the agitation to end income tax. Ministers realised that many farmers, who should be assessed for large amounts of tax based on past years' incomes, would be unable to pay them from their depleted cash flow.

Before Parliament convened, Liverpool undertook a diplomatic initiative that could have had long-term importance, sending an embassy to China, the first since Lord Macartney's[18] mission in 1793, at the request of the East India Company, yet again in financial difficulties. China had become an important source of revenue for the Company through the opium trade and the temporary damming of that trade by Chinese officials in Canton had messed up the Company's finances. However, the long-term outflow of silver for opium was increasingly causing economic decline in China.

The embassy, led by Lord Amherst[19] left Britain on 8 February and arrived at Canton on 8 July. However, despite two months of trying, he was unable to

---

17. Liverpool letter to Castlereagh, 15 September 1815, in Londonderry, *Memoirs and Correspondence of Viscount Castlereagh*, Vol. 11, pp. 16-18.
18. George Macartney (1737-1806). 1st Baron Macartney (Ireland) from 1776. 1st Earl Macartney (Ireland) from 1792. 1st Baron Macartney (GB) from 1795. MP for Cockermouth, Ayr Burghs and Bere Alston, 1768-69, 1774-76, 1780-81. Ambassador to Russia, 1764-66, 1767-68, to China, 1792-94. Chief Secretary for Ireland, 1769-72. Governor of Grenada, 1776-79. Governor of Madras (Chennai), 1781-85. Governor of Cape Colony, 1797-98.
19. William Amherst (1773-1857). 2nd Baron Amherst from 1797. 1st Earl Amherst from 1826. Ambassador Extraordinary to China, 1816-17. Governor General of India, 1823-28.

gain an audience with the Jiaqing Emperor.[20] Macartney had obtained from the Qianlong Emperor,[21] his father, the unique privilege of an audience without performing the kowtow, thought objectionable by British envoys because it was held by the Chinese to signify the emperor's universal domination. However, the Jiaqing Emperor was neither as able nor as self-confident as the great Qianlong and Amherst was advised by the East India Company's Sir George Staunton[22] to remain a stickler for Macartney's position on the kowtow, even though his personal opinion leaned towards flexibility.[23]

Hence an opportunity was missed to open a fruitful dialogue between the Chinese and British governments. In such a dialogue trading privileges could have been exchanged for know-how. Moreover, the economically and socially damaging opium trade could have been controlled before it led to war two decades later and the subsequent Chinese accusation of Western exploitation through 'unequal treaties' that have been so resented by modern Chinese leaders.

In 1793 China's need for interaction had not been so great – as Qianlong said in his letter to George III, 'Our Celestial Empire possesses all things in prolific abundance and lacks no product within its own borders.' Furthermore, British attention would be consumed by two decades of war. By the time of the next great Chinese reforming leader, the Dowager Empress Cixi,[24] it was

---

20. Jiaqing, Emperor of China (1760-1820). 7th Emperor of the Qing dynasty from 1796, on behalf of his father until 1799. Fifteenth son of the Qianlong Emperor, chosen as successor in 1773. Faced two large-scale rebellions and economic decline. Opposed both Christianity and Western contact.
21. Qianlong, Emperor of China (1711-99). 6th Emperor of the Qing Dynasty from 1735, abdicated 1796 but retained ultimate power until his death in 1799. Son of the Yongzheng Emperor (ruled 1722-35) and favourite grandson of the Kangxi Emperor (ruled 1661-1722). Even though he was 82 at the time of Macartney's embassy he is believed by modern scholars to have had a shrewd understanding, better than his letter to George III indicated, of the strengths of Western technology. His valediction to George III, 'Tremblingly obey and show no negligence', may have been a deliberate attempt to discourage further contact in view of his own impending mortality.
22. Sir George Staunton (1781-1859). 2nd Baronet from 1801. MP for Mitchell, Heytesbury, South Hampshire and Portsmouth, 1818-26, 1830-52, initially as a Tory, becoming Whig after 1832, in both cases hoping for a good job. Accompanied father on Macartney's embassy in 1793, acting as interpreter on occasion. Second commissioner on Amherst's embassy in 1816. Joined East India Company in 1798. FRS, 1803. Involved in founding Royal Asiatic Society, 1823.
23. Sir Henry Ellis, *Journal of the Proceedings of the Late Embassy to China* (London: John Murray, 1817).
24. Empress Dowager Cixi (1835-1908). Married the Xianfeng Emperor, 1851. Regent from his death in 1861 on behalf of her son the Tongzhi Emperor (1861-75), her nephew the Guangxu Emperor (1875-1908) and for one day her great-nephew, the Xuantong Emperor Puyi (1906-67, reigned 1908-12). Jung Chang's *Empress Dowager Cixi: The Concubine Who Launched Modern China* (New York, NY: Alfred A. Knopf, 2013) is an excellent history of Cixi's incomplete but substantial modernisation of China.

too late. Western patterns of oppression and contempt, symbolised by the 1860 burning of the Summer Palace, had become too established and China's economic and relative political decline had gone too far to be easily reversed. The Jiaqing Emperor's refusal to meet Amherst caused the Imperial House to miss the opportunity to change Anglo-Chinese history for the better.

Back in Britain, the new parliamentary session opened on 1 February, with an Address that concentrated largely on the blessings of peace being restored. Lansdowne opened the Whig attack by demanding pledges on government economy and requests for information on the peace treaties. Liverpool replied with a pledge of economy and a promise that the peace treaties would be revealed the following day.

A week later, Lansdowne returned to the attack, demanding details of the peace establishments for the years 1786 through to 1792, to compare them with the post-war profligacy. The Whigs' economic approach during these years looks odd to a modern eye, or even to an eye accustomed to mid-nineteenth-century Whiggery. The party was old-fashioned in its keen focus on government economy. This derived from the seventeenth-century view that the Royal establishment and the government in general were irretrievably addicted to corrupt uses of state funds and extravagance.

The Whigs focussed little on 'relief' of poverty and economic hardship, considerably less than had the Foxite Whigs in the 1790s. Conversely, they achieved a major parliamentary success by forcing the government to abandon income tax, whose burden fell most heavily on the rich and the landed aristocracy. In these years, the Whigs were becoming the party of middle-class-focussed parliamentary reform and gaining grudging Radical support thereby; they were a long way from becoming the party of social reform.

On 14 February Grenville launched an attack on the peace establishment, claiming that, if £1.8 million for the army and £2 million for the navy was considered enough by Pitt in 1792, then £14 million for the army and an equivalent sum for the navy was excessive. Liverpool responded that the establishment was founded on public necessity and, if not, he was prepared to be censured by the House. However, the half pay of the army alone was more than the peacetime establishment of 1792. He had also known Pitt well before 1792 and Pitt would have agreed that the peacetime establishment of 1792 had been proved deficient by the defeats suffered in the first two years of the war, prolonged for almost a quarter of a century by those defeats.

With 30,000 men in France and 20,000 in the West Indies, the army now numbered 95,000 men, compared with 46,000 in 1792. Colonial forces, which now numbered 19,400, had been increased, partly to serve in colonies which in 1792 did not belong to Britain and partly to undertake new responsibilities, such as control of the slave trade and the 1,200 men stationed on St Helena to guard Napoleon. In a long period of peace, their numbers could be diminished. In Ireland, forces had been increased from 12,000 to

25,000 but, given the level of unrest, that did not seem excessive. In Britain, the force had increased from 16,000 to 25,000 but population had increased, as had government installations such as dockyards. The 1792 establishment had been set after a decade of peace; it was not to be expected that so small an establishment could be maintained in peace's first year.[25]

On 19 February Liverpool introduced the peace treaties to the House of Lords. He began by some justified self-congratulation in having defeated Napoleon within three weeks of the resolution declaring war:

> I think I may safely say, that there is no instance in the history of this or any other country, where, considering the magnitude of the operations and the object, the success was so rapid, and so complete and decisive in its nature. . . . But have I not also a right to say, that the government in such a trying moment had not been wanting in its duty when, under the circumstances which then existed, it had collected and brought to bear upon the enemy, within so short a time, a body of troops capable of performing such great and important services?

Liverpool then made an important point about Napoleon's support: 'If that power had been rooted in the affections of the people of France, as has been some times and in some quarters asserted, is it to be believed that it would have been so speedily destroyed?'[26]

The peace of 1814 had been designed on a principle of liberality and, while that liberality had been mistaken in some respects, it meant that Louis XVIII's mild government and the liberal peace conditions could not be blamed for Napoleon's return, which Liverpool regarded as primarily an army revolt. Initially, the Allies had simply called on the French people to resist Napoleon, regarding Louis XVIII as sovereign *de facto*. However, Allied policy changed once Louis XVIII left France and at the time of Waterloo Louis XVIII was not a party to the inter-Allied agreement, which did not require his return to power.

In May 1815 the Allies thus faced three possibilities: they might have to treat with a rebel French government, in which case they should insist on all possible securities; Louis XVIII might have been restored by French efforts alone, in which case the treaty of 1814 should be strictly adhered to; or Louis XVIII might have been restored only with Allied military help, in which case some additional security and indemnity should be required.

The treaty with France was thus based on three principles: the military occupation of part of France by the Allies; pecuniary compensation from the French government; and a territorial arrangement. The military occupation

25. Hansard, *Parliamentary Debates from the Year 1803 to the Present Time*, Vol. 32, cols 515-22 (14 February 1816).
26. Ibid., cols 634-53 (19 February 1816).

would be ended only after five years and payment of compensation, decided at 700 million francs (£28 million), would be a precondition of that termination.

Liverpool continued to believe that three quarters of the French people supported Louis XVIII, as evidence for which he pointed out that the Assembly elected under Napoleon's auspices had not reliably supported him, whereas that elected after Louis XVIII's Restoration had been strongly Royalist. Nevertheless, a substantial anti-Royalist party remained and military occupation would be necessary until full stability had been restored. The interference with French internal affairs was temporary and justified to preserve the quiet of Europe.

Finally, Liverpool commented on the economic situation: 'It must be the natural consequence of peace, that the numbers who subsisted upon a war expenditure should experience distress until capital took another direction, and the industrious habits which belong to a state of peace resume their activity and influence.'[27]

Despite a vigorous opposing speech by Grenville, Liverpool's arguments prevailed; the government majority was a comfortable 64.

Also in February, Liverpool offered Canning the Presidency of the Board of Control vacated by the death of Lord Buckinghamshire.[28] His letter was apologetic in offering such a junior office and gave a forecast of the government's prospects on income tax debate that would prove too sanguine. However, Canning responded accepting Liverpool's offer, writing that the Board of Control was perfectly satisfactory, indeed preferable to the Admiralty which had been discussed a few years earlier. While his return took a few months, it would strengthen the government's Commons position.

The principal cries of the 1816 session were for retrenchment and for relief from taxes. The Prince Regent's expenditure on the Brighton Pavilion were so unpopular that, after a formal request from Liverpool, Castlereagh and Vansittart,[29] he suspended construction for a time. Overall, Castlereagh was to describe the session in a May letter to Wellington as 'one of the most disagreeable sessions I ever remember; a sour, discontented temper among our friends, considerable distress throughout the country, and endless debates upon economy'.[30]

Income tax came up for debate on 7 March, when Lansdowne presented numerous petitions against it to the Lords. In response, Liverpool vigorously

27. Ibid.

28. Buckinghamshire died after a fall from his horse but Liverpool's letter referred to a previous 'precariousness of health'. Quoted in Yonge, *The Life and Administration of Robert Banks Jenkinson*, Vol. 2, pp. 253-55. Canning's reply, pp. 255-56.

29. Letter from Liverpool, Castlereagh and Vansittart to the Prince Regent, 15 March 1816, in Aspinall, *The Letters of King George IV, 1812-30*, Vol. 2, pp. 158-60.

30. Letter from Castlereagh to Wellington, 13 May 1816, in 2nd Duke of Wellington (ed.), *The Supplementary Despatches, Correspondence, and Memoranda of Field Marshal the Duke of Wellington*, Vol. 11, p. 401.

denied that ministers were committed, either directly or indirectly through previous governments, to its abolition immediately after the end of the war. Indeed, the 1806 government, in which Lansdowne himself as Chancellor of the Exchequer had increased income tax to ten per cent, had left open the possibility of continuing it into peacetime.[31]

To a different Lansdowne motion on military establishments, Grenville, with his usual intemperance, added his remarks. Liverpool replied that Grenville was accusing the government 'of having endeavoured to change the whole policy of the state, and to covert it from a government of law and liberty into a military government', and pointed out that, in practice, the country had possessed a peacetime standing army for over a century: 'The necessity of any military force must rest on one of three principles: 1^{stly}, the security of His Majesty's dominions, 2^{ndly}, the case which might be supposed to exist of affording aid to the civil authorities; 3^{rdly}, the preservation of the balance of power in Europe.' The 30,000 men needed in France were there to affect the balance of power in Europe; the rest of the army must be justified by one of the other two principles.

Liverpool continued that, at the end of each preceding war in which new colonies had been acquired, additional troops had been needed to guard them. While the country was in a state of peace, he had seen too much of life to believe that peace perfectly secure, being less than a year old. In Ireland, the government was as popular as any British government had ever been, yet only increased education and wealth among the Irish population could render that island completely secure from revolt. Finally, the force of 28,000 at home included some 7,000 that were needed for rotation for regiments on overseas service, so the net force of 21,000 was only 3,000 greater than the 18,000 normal before the wars, a smaller proportionate increase than the increase in population.[32]

The government won the division by 139 votes to 69.

Liverpool's defence of income tax proved nugatory, as the tax was defeated in the House of Commons by 238 votes to 201. Then a Motion of Censure was defeated by a majority of only 29, on an evening that Liverpool described to the Prince Regent's secretary as 'most unpleasant . . . if it had not been for Brougham's speech, which was little short of treason, and created a universal disgust among all parties, we should probably have been left in a minority'.[33]

In a Lords speech, Liverpool deprecated the loss of income tax, saying that:

> no one could feel more strongly than I do, the inexpediency of loans in time of peace, and my object has been to avoid them. It has been my

31. Hansard, *Parliamentary Debates from the Year 1803 to the Present Time*, Vol. 33, cols 8-11 (7 March 1816).
32. Ibid., cols 359-73 (15 March 1816).
33. Letter to Sir B. Bloomfield, Secretary to the Prince Regent, quoted in Yonge, *The Life and Administration of Robert Banks Jenkinson*, Vol. 2, pp. 270-71.

> judgement, and my opinion has not changed, that the continuation of the [income] tax at the amount which has been proposed, would have formed, not only the best plan of finance, but also the most effective relief to the distresses of the country.

However, the government was still considering whether to relieve the malt tax, which fell primarily on the poor, because, if an approach to the money market was necessary anyway, it did not much matter whether that approach was for £6 or £8 million.[34]

The Whig success in abolishing income tax and thereby unbalancing the budget proved economically damaging. The blow which abolition gave to the government's credit caused the post-war rise in Consols' prices to reverse, not to resume for more than a year. Thus, it was only from the late spring of 1817 that the buoyancy in Consols prices, increasing the wealth of their holders, began to improve the overall economic picture in a way that became so important in the 1820s. The total rise in Consols prices from 1815 to 1824 was some 70 per cent of GDP. Since Consols formed the principal savings vehicle for the monied classes both landed and industrial, Consols windfalls, increasing the wealth of their holders, paid for much of the 1820s' industrial expansion and its accompanying capital intensification.[35]

Liverpool foresaw this effect during the post-war economic downturn. In his 13 February letter to Canning he had written:

> I am satisfied likewise that those who raise this clamour have a narrow view of their own interest, as the restoration of public credit, *the run of the funds*, and the consequent fall of the interest on money will afford more relief to the existing distress of the country than any other measure of relief that could be adopted.[36]

The gloom of the country's difficulties was lifted in May by the marriage of Princess Charlotte to Prince Leopold of Saxe-Coburg-Saalfeld.[37] Liverpool did not attend, on the advice of his doctor. He had proposed to the Prince Regent

34. Hansard, *Parliamentary Debates from the Year 1803 to the Present Time*, Vol. 33, cols 518-19 (22 March 1816).
35. See Hutchinson and Dowd, 'The Apotheosis of the Rentier', for a full discussion of the wealth effects of this price rise.
36. Quoted in Yonge, *The Life and Administration of Robert Banks Jenkinson*, Vol. 2, pp. 253-55. The italics are mine and I take 'the run of the funds' to be a direct reference to the price rise to be expected as public credit recovered.
37. Leopold of Saxe-Coburg-Saalfeld (1790-1865). Married Princess Charlotte of Wales, 1816, and widowed 1817. Refused Greek throne, then became King of Belgium, 1831-65. Married Louise-Marie of Orléans, daughter of King Louis Philippe, 1832. Uncle of Albert of Saxe-Coburg and Gotha, Prince Consort to Queen Victoria.

that the Royal couple should have an allowance of £60,000 per annum, to avoid the risk of their running into debt,[38] but the parsimonious Parliament voted only £50,000. Liverpool had said of Leopold, when announcing the Royal couple's engagement, that 'all the courts of Europe agreed in bearing testimony to the propriety of his conduct and the goodness of his character'.[39] In the event, Leopold was to be an admirable and loving husband to Princess Charlotte during their lamentably short marriage and later became a capable King of Belgium and a wise uncle to Queen Victoria.

Later, in May, Liverpool proposed a Bank Restriction Act, under which restrictions on payments in gold should be prolonged for a further two years, until 1818. The Act of 1797 had provided for the resumption of gold payments six months after the end of the war but, given the war's length and cost, this was too short a time for the country's gold reserves to replenish themselves. The Bullion Committee of 1810 had declared that the depreciation in sterling had been caused by the overissuing of bank notes, while Liverpool believed it was caused by the outflow of specie to Spain and Portugal after 1808; the improvement in sterling's value after that outflow ceased suggested that his belief had been correct. Liverpool was confident that it would be imprudent to resume gold payments before 1818 and Parliament would have the right to consider the situation further then; if it did nothing, gold payments would automatically be resumed.[40]

Vansittart's 1816 Budget was a makeshift affair, as he admitted, because the House had rejected the prolongation of income tax. He began by announcing that the Bank of England had agreed to lend £3 million to the government at three per cent interest in return for being allowed to increase its capital by the same amount. Earlier in the year, Liverpool and he had also negotiated a sale of a novel instrument: two-year Exchequer bills bearing interest at four pence per day per cent (6.08 per cent). Even at the higher interest rate, the flexibility given by two-year funding was attractive, especially as it allowed refunding by Consols in two years' time, after the market had recovered further and their price had risen. On ordinary Exchequer bills, the interest rate had fallen by March to 3¼ pence per day per cent (4.94 per cent) – it was to fall to three pence per day per cent (4.56 per cent) in December.[41]

Army costs had declined to £9.6 million and navy costs to £10.1 million, so the government's total costs were £25 million (this calculation left out the costs of troops in France, which were to be paid for by France). With the £3 million

---

38. Letter from Liverpool to the Prince Regent, 3 March 1816, in Aspinall, *The Letters of King George IV, 1812-30*, Vol. 2, pp. 150-51.
39. Hansard, *Parliamentary Debates from the Year 1803 to the Present Time*, Vol. 33, cols 957-58 (5 April 1816).
40. Ibid., Vol. 34, cols 572-74, 578-79 (17 May 1816).
41. Bank of England, Minutes of the Court of Directors, 8 February, 21 March and 19 December 1816..

from the Bank, an additional £5.6 million unspent from the previous year and £2.5 million in re-issued Exchequer bills, the total borrowing would be £11.1 million, including provision for the sinking fund.[42]

By modern calculations, total expenditure for the year to 5 January 1817 was £71.3 million, of which £32.9 million was debt charges, against revenues of £69.2 million (which included £11.8 million from income tax, paid in arrears).[43] Thus, the budget was already close to balancing, despite huge debt interest costs, only a year after the long war had ended. However, the ending of income tax would make the budget calculation considerably more difficult in 1817.

On 28 May Liverpool brought forward a Message from the Prince Regent for a new issuance of silver coinage, a topic central to his father's career which had brought Liverpool his first ministerial office as Master of the Mint. Charles Jenkinson had undertaken a famous copper recoinage in 1797, which, together with a supplementary 1806 issue, had provided a copper coinage that was still adequate. He had also managed a gold recoinage in 1773-4. However, few silver coins had been minted since Queen Anne's reign and the last full silver recoinage had been undertaken by William III's ministers and overseen by Sir Isaac Newton in 1696.

Liverpool outlined the government's coinage proposals, beginning with a tribute to his father. He explained that the country's wealth made gold the natural standard: 'The progress of this country in agriculture, commerce, manufactures and riches has made gold, in fact, the measure of value in this country in a way more powerful than any declaration.' The Coinage Act of 1816 thus put Britain formally on the gold standard at a rate of 44½ guineas per troy pound (£3 17s. 10½d. per ounce) of 22-carat gold, once cash payments were resumed – the parity lasted until the gold standard was finally abandoned in 1931.

Liverpool then explained that a silver coinage was necessary for smaller denominations and that the price of silver governing its manufacture value should be high enough to ensure that silver coins were not melted down, but not so high as to cause the export of gold. With silver trading at 5s. 1½d. per ounce he believed that a mint price of 5s. 9d. per ounce, rather than the old Mint price of 5s. 2d., would allow sufficient room for market fluctuations. (The final Coinage Act set the price of silver at 5s. 6d. per ounce – 66 shillings per troy pound, up from 62 shillings.)

Liverpool then turned to the mechanics of recoinage. There were in circulation around £3.7 million Bank of England tokens (issued in 1811 and 1812 in three-shilling and 1s 6d denominations), the silver in which was priced at 6s. 8d. or 6s.

42. Hansard, Parliamentary Debates from the Year 1803 to the Present Time, Vol. 34, cols 822-38 (27 May 1816).

43. Mitchell, *British Historical Statistics*, pp. 581 (Income), 587 (Expenditure). The year-end is 5 January so, to get the figures for the (approximate) calendar year 1816, you should use the 1817 figures in the tables.

9d. per ounce. These should be called in immediately the new coins were ready, because 'base and good coin could not circulate together'. (They were exchanged for current coin from August 1817.) He proposed an immediate new coinage of £2.5 million, which with the new machinery could be produced in about six months – in King William's time it had taken four years.

While other countries on a recoinage took in old coin only by weight, as had Britain in the 1696 recoinage, Liverpool recommended that coins should be taken in at face value, an important concession since the century-old Mint coinage was found to have been worn by 26 per cent from its original weight. Only counterfeits would be taken in by weight and fineness as 'it would be impolitic and unjust to burthen the country with an expenditure, to repay losses that were the consequence of the knavery or simplicity of individuals'. Finally, Liverpool believed that a silver recoinage was a necessary step in returning to cash payments of gold, which he sincerely hoped to accomplish in two years. He estimated the cost of the silver recoinage at £500,000.[44]

After a short further discussion, the Address was passed with no dissension. The Coinage Act that resulted brought Britain's first gold sovereigns since 1604, replacing the previous guineas. A successful exchange was carried out in February 1817, led by Wellesley-Pole as Master of the Mint, and new issues of crowns, half crowns and shillings were made legal tender for payments up to £2.

Around 120 million of the new silver coins, with a value of £7 million,[45] were minted over the next four years (compared with the 1696 recoinage with a value of £5.1 million), before a new design was introduced for George IV in 1820. The £4 million of net liquidity injected into the economy through this silver recoinage usefully offset the deflationary return to the gold standard.

The following year, the gold sovereign was introduced with Benedetto Pistrucci's[46] 'St George and the Dragon' on the reverse, a design and a size that, with a hiatus between 1825 and 1871, has been used to this day. In 1817-20 George III sovereigns to the value of £7.7 million were minted and in 1821-26 no less than £33 million of George IV sovereigns, reflecting the full return to gold and the expansion in commerce.[47]

The British economy was already in difficulties in the winter of 1815-16, with a sharp downturn in exports, a decline in iron prices and a surge in bankruptcies to 1811 levels in 1816.[48] During the summer of 1816, the

44. Hansard, *Parliamentary Debates from the Year 1803 to the Present Time*, Vol. 34, cols 912-17 (30 May 1816).
45. Kevin Clancy, 'The recoinage and exchange of 1816-17', PhD thesis, University of Leeds (1999), Tables 11.12 and 17.
46. Benedetto Pistrucci (1783-1855). Chief Medalist at the Royal Mint, 1817-49, though his involvement with the coinage lasted only until 1825, when St George was replaced.
47. Mintages from: http://www.cruzis-coins.com/sovs/Sovmintage.html. Accessed 13 July 2020.
48. *The London Gazette*, 2,145 bankruptcies in 1816, compared to a peak of 2,112 in

economy's struggles and the government's problems were worsened by the 'Year Without a Summer'. The eruption of Indonesia's Mount Tambora in April 1815 was an event of 'Volcanic Explosivity Index' 7, one of only five in the Holocene (last 10,000 years) and not exceeded for 25,000 years. This combined with the Dalton sunspot minimum, in which sunspot activity in 1816 was the lowest ever recorded, to produce a temperature drop of one degree Celsius in the northern hemisphere summer, with unusually high cloud cover and rain.

In North America and Western Europe this produced exceptionally poor harvests, described as 'the last great subsistence crisis in the Western world'.[49] Within Britain, the effect was worst in Ireland, producing a crop failure and an outbreak of typhus that caused an estimated 100,000 deaths. The price of corn rose to 103 shillings per quarter by December 1816 and 117 shillings by June 1817 but, although the Corn Laws provided for opening the ports when the price reached 80 shillings, imports were limited because the harvest in Germany and other producer countries was equally bad.[50]

Liverpool was acutely aware of Ireland's problems. These were highlighted in a letter from Peel, which suggested that emigration from the overpopulated areas in the south might solve Ireland's problems but that, unfortunately, emigration levels (running to around 700 families per week) were higher in the north, where overpopulation was less of a problem. In October, Peel wrote again to Liverpool, warning of the growing famine and that fuel, normally not a problem in southern Ireland, was also in shortage because of the heavy rains, which prevented the peat turves from drying.

In England, the distress was less extreme but nevertheless severe. The estimated wheat yield fell from 37 bushels per acre in 1815 to 25.3 in 1816, 32 per cent below the preceding year, before recovering to 33.4 in 1817, according to reports made by Liverpool agents. The year 1816 represented both the largest decline in yield and the lowest yield of any year between 1815 and 1859, for which these statistics exist. The other year of dearth, 1819, saw a yield of 27.7 bushels per acre, a decline of 15 per cent from 1818.[51]

The first significant unrest of 1816 occurred in May, before the bad weather had any effect but after the disbandment of the wartime army and navy had increased the number of unemployed. Even at this stage, while grain prices at around 73 shillings per quarter were still lower than the average of previous

---

1811 and 1,759 in 1815. Quoted in Arthur Gayer, W.W. Rostow and Anna Jacobson Schwartz, *The Growth and Fluctuation of the British Economy, 1790-1850* (Oxford: Clarendon Press, 1953) Vol. 1, p. 147.

49. John D. Post *"The last great subsistence crisis in the Western World"* Baltimore: Johns Hopkins University Press, 1977.

50. Tooke, *A History of Prices*, Vol. 2, pp. 14-18.

51. Mitchell, *British Historical Statistics*, Table Agriculture 3, p. 195. This is the only crop yield table covering the years concerned.

years, they had risen sharply since January. Thus, the riots at Littleport and Ely on 22-24 May were triggered partly by the squeeze on real agricultural wages brought by rising prices and partly by general post-war distress.

The trouble started in Littleport, where a group of labourers fuelled by alcohol trashed the homes of several local worthies. The Littleport rioters then marched on Ely, where many of them occupied the town. A squadron of dragoons, sent from Bury St Edmunds, dispersed the rioters and arrested their ringleaders on the following day. Five of the rioters were hanged, ten imprisoned for twelve months and another nine sentenced to transportation to New South Wales.

For ministers and the British public, the summer of 1816 was brightened by one last Naval triumph. The Barbary pirates had bedevilled Mediterranean commerce for the previous two centuries. In August 1815 Castlereagh wrote to Bathurst pointing out that every other power including the Americans would expect Britain to eliminate the Barbary corsair menace; he sought only to delay matters until the Ionian Islands were safely in British hands, which took place that November.[52] The Americans under Commodore Stephen Decatur meanwhile sent a squadron which successfully negotiated an end to attacks on Americans but that did not solve the general problem.

Early in 1816 Admiral Lord Exmouth, commander in the Mediterranean, led a diplomatic mission to Tunis, Tripoli and Algiers in an attempt to get the pirates shut down. Tunis and Tripoli agreed, but the Dey of Algiers was recalcitrant and, after signing a treaty with Britain, massacred 200 Corsican, Sicilian and Sardinian fishermen who were under British protection. Exmouth returned to Algiers with five ships of the line and 22 other ships, including bomb ketches, and on 27 August bombarded the batteries, navy and dockyards of Algiers for nine hours, sustaining 800 casualties and firing 50,000 round shot and 960 mortar shells. The following day, he demanded the surrender of Algiers and the Dey accepted, not realising that the British fleet was almost completely out of ammunition. A definitive treaty was signed on 24 September, 4,000 slaves were freed and Barbary piracy was greatly diminished though not entirely eliminated. It was the last great victory of the Nelson/Hornblower navy.[53]

The autumn of 1816 was an anxious time for Liverpool; during it Louisa suffered the first of her recurring bouts of illness which were to end in her death in 1821. The political and economic prospects were also poor. In an October 1816 letter to Castlereagh, Liverpool commented that, while the excise and assessed tax returns showed that trade was not badly affected, the quarterly funding deficit was still substantial so the 1817 financial debates were likely to be stormy. However, the underlying economic advance continued; in October 1816 the Leeds to Liverpool Canal was completed, a project which had been in germination for half a century.

52. Londonderry, *Memoirs and Correspondence of Viscount Castlereagh*, Vol. 10, p. 483.
53. I agree with Wellington that the 1827 Battle of Navarino was an 'untoward event' rather than a victory.

Diplomatically, the second half of 1816 saw an attempt by Spain to annex Portugal as recompense for the South American colonies they were in the process of losing. The Portuguese John VI succeeded his mother in 1816 but remained in Brazil until 1821; his Spanish wife Queen Carlota Joaquina[54] meanwhile was attempting to acquire dominion over parts of Spanish South America, in particular Uruguay, which was to be annexed by Brazil in 1821 as Cisplatina and held until 1828. Castlereagh, with Liverpool's agreement, was firm that this would be a violation of the Treaty of Vienna and that both Spain's ambitions in Portugal and Queen Carlota Joaquina's in Latin America would be opposed by Britain. Wellington, when consulted, suggested that Britain should intervene against Portugal, if at all, to forestall its Latin American ambitions.

Liverpool, reasonably given recent history, took most interest in events in France and sent Canning to Paris in November to report on the French elections. Louis XVIII had called these on the advice of Wellington and Richelieu in order to reduce the power of the Ultra-Royalists, whose dominance at the 1815 elections had produced a '*Chambre Introuvable*' of furious reaction. The previous winter's White Terror had seriously increased popular discontent, as had the harvest failure of the 'Year Without a Summer'.

In the event, the Doctrinaires, supporting a liberal monarchy, handily defeated the Ultras. (They were to dominate French governments until the election of 1824, shortly before Charles X's accession, at which the Ultras regained control.) This period of moderate French governments facilitated the attainment of Liverpool's objective of stabilising France, restoring her as a positive factor in European diplomacy and reducing and later eliminating the occupying forces. However, French insolvency and popular distress made achieving those objectives a delicate matter in the short term.

France's solvency was greatly improved by loans led by Barings, beginning in early 1817. The first payment of France's indemnity to the Allies had been met by Napoleon's gold but France's budgetary position was inadequate for further payments. Alexander Baring obtained confirmation from the British government that international lending was acceptable at a meeting with Liverpool, Castlereagh and Vansittart in January 1817.[55]

Then Barings led several international issues of French five-per-cent *rentes* (government bonds), the first in February, with five-per-cent *rentes* issued at 55 per cent at a franc yield of 9.1 per cent. Further issues followed in April and July, with French banking houses' participation increasing from a quarter to a half and the price for the July issue rising to 61.5 per cent, after Wellington

---

54. Carlota-Joaquina of Spain (1775-1830). Eldest daughter of Charles IV of Spain. Married the future John VI of Portugal in 1785. Staged a coup with her son Miguel against her husband in 1824.

55. Castlereagh letter to Wellington, 17 January 1817, in Wellington, *Supplementary Despatches*, Vol. 11, pp. 600-1.

Henry Addington as Prime Minister in 1803,
not yet the immensely successful Home Secretary Viscount Sidmouth.

had vetoed a further loan at 55 per cent.[56] Liverpool confirmed in the House of Lords in February that the British government had not guaranteed or officially authorised the French loan and that only a small part of the money would be raised in London.[57] Later in the spring, Alexander Baring wrote to him:

56. Figures from Yousseff Cassis and Philip L. Cottrell, *Private Banking in Europe: Rise, Retreat and Resurgence* (Oxford: Oxford University Press, 2015) pp. 114-16. Veto from Wellington, *Supplementary Despatches*, Vol. 11, p. 619, letter to Castlereagh, 3 February 1817.

57. Hansard, *Parliamentary Debates from the Year 1803 to the Present Time*, Vol. 35, cols 226-29 (6 February 1817).

> in general, public credit throughout the country is decidedly improved and improving, and though a plant that requires to be treated tenderly, is likely, I believe, to be found adequate to a reasonable settlement of the heavy claims which it was required to support, a burthen which a year ago I was looking at almost with despair.[58]

Economic distress and the high price of corn for urban consumers turned into direct opposition to the government with the Spa Fields meetings late in 1816. At the first, on 15 November, attended by about 10,000 people, a petition demanding universal male suffrage, annual general elections and relief from distress was drafted for 'Orator' Hunt[59] and Sir Francis Burdett to present to the Prince Regent – Burdett, always a strongly constitutional Radical, pulled out. These demands bore little relation to official Whig policy, which was not even committed to moderate Parliamentary Reform.

The Prince Regent refused to receive the petition and so a further, more dangerous meeting with twice the attendance was held on 2 December. On this occasion, revolutionary Spenceans,[60] under the leadership of Arthur Thistlewood[61] and James Watson,[62] attempted to lead the crowd to take control of the Tower of London and the Bank of England, pillaging gun shops on the way. Troops at the Royal Exchange dispersed the crowd and arrested the ringleaders. The failure of this conspiracy is a remarkable tribute to the efficient system of informers built up by Sidmouth and to the well-judged deployment of troops which prevented the rioters achieving more than they did.

Watson was tried and acquitted after the court, led by defence counsel Charles Wetherell[63] (later Attorney General) and John Singleton Copley[64]

---

58. Quoted in Yonge, *The Life and Administration of Robert Banks Jenkinson*, Vol. 2, p. 311. Clearly from spring 1817 but no date is given.
59. Henry 'Orator' Hunt (1773-1835). MP for Preston (1830-32). Radical agitator, favouring working classes and opposing both Whigs and Tories. Imprisoned for two years after Peterloo Massacre.
60. Followers of the late Thomas Spence (1750-1814). An English Radical who believed in common ownership of land through local parishes. His Society of Spencean Philanthropists was an ultra-Radical group committed to overthrowing the government; while extreme, it was small, probably with fewer than 50 members.
61. Arthur Thistlewood (1774-1820). Radical activist. Organiser of the Spa Fields riots (1816) and the Cato Street conspiracy (1820) for which he was executed. Challenged Sidmouth to a duel in 1817 and was imprisoned.
62. James Watson (1766-1838). Surgeon or apothecary whose main occupation was as an agitator, together with his son (who was involved in the Cato Street conspiracy). Died in New York.
63. Charles Wetherell (1770-1846). MP for Rye, Shaftesbury, Oxford, Hastings, Plympton Erle and Boroughbridge, 1812-18, 1820-32. Solicitor General, 1824-26, Attorney General, 1826-27, 1828-29. Die-hard opponent of both Catholic Emancipation and parliamentary reform.
64. John Singleton Copley, Jr. (1772-1863). Son of the painter. 1st Baron Lyndhurst

(later Lord Chancellor) threw doubt on the government witnesses. The case against Thistlewood was then dropped; he was to be executed in 1820 after masterminding the Cato Street conspiracy.

With the general distress and poor harvest, unrest continued at a high level. In rural areas, rick burnings were common and there was a further outbreak of Luddite machine breaking in several counties (as it turned out, the last major such outbreak). Then on 25 January 1817, on the way to open Parliament, the Prince Regent was shot at with an air rifle and his carriage was pelted with stones. It was thus unsurprising that the government decided to introduce new law-and-order measures, appointing a Special Committee in the House of Lords to decide what was needed. The leading Whigs including Grey responded favourably. In Parliament on 4 February Liverpool commented: 'Designing men, I know, will be at all moments disposed to do mischief and create confusion, if they can . . . it must always be in time of difficulty, either internal or external, that such attempts can be successfully resorted to by the designing.'[65]

While the Select Committee considered suitable action, there was considerable concern in Radical circles that the government would introduce repressive measures as severe as those of 1795 – the Secretary of the London Union Society petitioned the House of Lords against such a move. Liverpool used the petition to show that there was a nationwide chain of these societies, ostensibly agitating for parliamentary reform and annual parliaments, but shading into organisations that attempted to overthrow the government by force.[66]

The first recommendation of the Select Committee was the suspension of *habeas corpus* and on 24 February Liverpool spoke in favour of the bill which would enact this:

> On the present occasion, you have the fullest proof (if you believe the report) of a treasonable conspiracy in the metropolis, to overturn, by a general insurrection, the laws, the government and the constitution of the kingdom. It is also a matter of great notoriety, that the same system is spread over a great part of the country. There is a double engine at work; the operation of the one is evidently aiming at what everyone must agree would overthrow the constitution; the operation of the other (I allude to the Spenceans) is calculated to produce a complete convulsion in the elements which compose the system of

---

from 1827. MP for Yarmouth, Ashburton and Cambridge University, 1818-27. Solicitor General, 1819-24. Attorney General, 1824-26. Master of the Rolls, 1826-27. Lord Chancellor, 1827-30, 1834-35, 1841-46.

65. Hansard, *Parliamentary Debates from the Year 1803 to the Present Time*, Vol. 35, cols 196-98 (4 February 1817).
66. Ibid., cols 539-42 (24 February 1817).

> social life. . . . Never was there a more determined and avowed design to sap all the foundations of morals and religion, and more assiduity in the prosecution of that design.[67]

The second reading of the bill passed the Lords by 130 votes to 35, with Grenville, but not Wellesley, joining the government, while the first reading passed the Commons by an equally emphatic majority of 273 to 98. The suspension was extended in June but allowed to lapse the following year.

In retrospect, the fear of Liverpool and the government about nationwide unrest appears justified but a little overblown. The ideological hostility to the British constitutional system appears to have been less widespread than in 1794-95. Nevertheless, the economic distress was nearly as bad as in 1795 and an ill-organised, if narrowly based, conspiracy to overthrow the government undoubtedly existed, according to modern evidence. Also, many of the opposition Whigs supported the repressive moves, whereas they were to be much more united in opposition to the Six Acts of 1819. Finally, it was certainly possible that another bad harvest could have made the situation spiral into something really serious.

Further control measures introduced that spring included a Treason Act, which extended the treason provisions to attempts against the Prince Regent's life, and the Army and Navy Seduction Act, which extended an expired Act against attempts to suborn the armed forces. The most severe new measure was a Seditious Meetings Act, modelled on that of 1795, which made it illegal to hold meetings of 50 or more without giving seven days' notice and requiring meeting halls to be licensed. The draconian nature of the Act was significantly tempered by a sunset clause allowing most of its provisions to expire on 24 July 1818. Again, this Act split the Whigs, the Third Reading passing the House of Lords by 111 votes to 23.

In May, Liverpool, attempting still to do something for popular distress, moved for a Select Committee to examine the Poor Law, setting up a committee of the House of Commons on the same subject. He said:

> It is now generally admitted, that our system of Poor Laws is an evil; but then it is an evil which has existed for 200 years, and is so intermixed with the prejudices and habits of the people, that remedies which might at an earlier period have been applied cannot now be adopted.[68]

Legislation was to follow in each of the two subsequent years, partly to address the huge increase in the system's costs during the economic disruptions of 1816-20.

67. Ibid., cols 568-73 (24 February 1817).
68. Ibid., Vol. 36, cols 297-99 (9 May 1817).

A month later, Liverpool moved the third reading of the Poor Employment Act, which provided for loans to local authorities to facilitate infrastructure improvements which would employ the poor:

> I admit that the general principle is against measures of this nature, because it is much better, with regard to the greater part of public works, to leave them to those who undertake them as a commercial speculation, and with a view to profit, than to interpose the assistance of government. . . . With regard to public works, I conceive that an advance of money for the purpose of commencing or carrying on works of public utility, would be, under the pressure of present circumstances, most beneficial in its consequences, by giving employment to a number of persons, for whose labour there is at this time no demand. . . . On the continent, with respect to the distress arising from the scarcity of food, the people are much worse off than in this country and I have myself received accounts from Germany and France, respecting this subject, which are quite appalling. It of course follows, that provisions being raised on the continent to four times their former price, the incomes of a great number of persons are wholly employed in procuring subsistence, and they have no surplus whatever to lay out in items of manufacture. This necessarily increases the pressure on the manufacturing interest here and precludes a demand for labour.[69]

It will be seen from this speech that Liverpool fully understood the theory of 'stimulus' more than a century before Keynes, that he was prepared to apply it in extreme circumstances, understood what had made circumstances extreme in 1817 and yet was rightly determined that the 'stimulus' should be temporary. Further attempts to improve the lot of the poor this year were a Truck Act, forbidding payment in goods and a Passenger Transport Act, regulating transatlantic steerage travel by the impoverished of southern Ireland.

Liverpool's government provided another benefit to the working classes, of enormous importance in the long run, with the Savings Bank Act of 1817, which established what were to be known until their amalgamation and effective abolition in the 1980s as the Trustee Savings Banks. The Act provided for savings banks administered by unpaid trustees, which would be forced by law to invest their money only in government securities or deposits at the Bank of England. This was an important principle: it made the savings risk-free and meant that small savers did not have to risk their money in the hundreds of private banks lending to business and against real estate, which as the 1825

69. Ibid., cols 928-30 (10 June 1817).

crash was to show, were by no means secure. The first such savings bank had been set up by the Rev. Henry Duncan[70] at Ruthwell in Dumfriesshire in 1810 and Duncan had publicised the scheme widely.

The 1817 Act was introduced by George Rose,[71] the aged Treasurer of the Navy who had managed the 1784 election for Pitt. Rose wrote a pamphlet on savings banks in 1816 and introduced the bill in 1817. Its official sanction was shown by the readiness with which it became law, and a necessary amending Act was introduced by Vansittart in the following year after Rose's death.

In introducing the bill, Rose said that it was 'not very likely, that application would be made to parliament by persons in that condition of life, the improvement of which was contemplated by this measure. Both the principle and the detail of such an institution are beyond the common ideas of persons engaged in daily and manual labour.'[72] After considerable debate, it was agreed that a savings bank holding of up to £30 should not make the holder ineligible for poor relief – an important incentive toward saving. There was an attempt to divert savings bank investment into mortgages 'to the relief of the agricultural interest' but it was beaten back.

The Savings Bank Act was one of the Liverpool government's most important pieces of legislation. By 1825, only eight years after the Act, savings bank deposits had grown to £13.3 million,[73] 27 per cent of the share capital of the Stock Exchange in that year, and more than the total of outstanding country bank notes, default on which caused such hardship. Trustee savings banks were to be an important feature of the British financial landscape for the next century, their growth only restricted by Gladstone's 1861 creation of an unnecessary public-sector competitor in the Post Office Savings Bank (whose deposits overtook the savings banks' in 1885).

The central principle, that savings banks could only buy government bonds, gave working-class savers complete security for their holdings in them. In the early years, as Britain resumed full convertibility of payments in 1821, it also allowed the savings banks to grow their capital, since the Consols in which they invested increased sharply in value.[74] It separated the

70. Henry Duncan (1774-1846). Ordained 1798. Minister at Ruthwell, 1799. Discovered Ruthwell Cross, 1818. Presented paper on fossil footmarks to the Royal Society of Edinburgh, 1828. Moderator of the General Assembly of the Church of Scotland, 1839. Helped found Free Church of Scotland, 1843.

71. George Rose (1744-1818). MP for Launceston, Lymington and Christchurch, 1784-1818. Senior Secretary to the Treasury, 1783-1801. Vice-President of the Board of Trade 1804-6, 1807-12. Paymaster of the Forces, 1804-6. Treasurer of the Navy, 1807-1818.

72. Hansard, *Parliamentary Debates from the Year 1803 to the Present Time*, Vol. 35, cols 348-49 (13 February 1817).

73. Mitchell, *British Historical Statistics*, Table XII-8, p. 671.

74. It must be granted that another 1797 (when Consols dipped below 50) would have caused a problem, and the system got into deep trouble with the irresponsible

capital accumulation and protection function of financial institutions from their lending function, to the great benefit of the saving public and of the entire financial system.

The year 1817 also saw another attack by the Whigs on pensions and sinecures, which resulted in a series of government bills abolishing offices and providing for compensation to their holders. In his speech proposing the measures, Liverpool said: 'The principle on which I recommend these measures to your lordships' attention is this – that whatever regulation of this kind might be adopted, there is a necessity of reserving to the Crown the means of rewarding public services.' Thus, if sinecure offices were abolished, pensions must be provided, or only the rich would be able to engage in political careers, the expenses of which generally exceeded any income from offices.[75]

Vansittart's 1817 Budget announced a reduction in expenditure from £24.9 million to £18 million, with army expenditure down from £10.8 million to £9 million and navy expenditure down from £10 million to £6 million. In addition, there was a £4.1 million charge for interest on unfunded debt and uncollectible Irish receivables (the Irish and British Exchequers had been integrated on 5 January). With receipts of £9.5 million, Vansittart would therefore borrow £12.6 million in Exchequer bills, expecting to re-finance in future years when Consol yields had further declined. This was not a concern; even though revenues had declined by £5-£6 million in the past year Consols had risen from 62 per cent to above 74 per cent, indicating that Britain's credit had substantially improved.

In the short-term markets, Vansittart had been able in February to sell Exchequer bills to the Bank, secured on malt, sugar, tobacco and snuff duties, at three per cent per annum 'being the usual rate in time of peace' as Vansittart had informed the Bank in his application – but nevertheless fully 1.56 per cent lower than the rate only two months before, albeit for secured paper.[76] The following week, he told the Bank his entire financing for the year would be sold at only 2½ pence per day per cent (3.80 per cent per annum).[77] In practice, the portion of it directly secured on tax revenues was raised at two pence per day per cent, or 3.04 per cent per annum. By the end of the year, even unsecured Exchequer bills sold in the market at two pence per day per cent, although the Bank was still unwilling to buy them at that rate.[78]

Vansittart discoursed on the new investments in both land and commerce that were being made from Consols profits. In addition, the Bank of England

---

inflationary Keynesianism after World War II.

75. Hansard, *Parliamentary Debates from the Year 1803 to the Present Time*, Vol. 36, cols 1254-58 (30 June 1817).

76. Bank of England, Minutes of the Court of Directors, 13 February 1817. (Vansittart letter, 11 February 1817).

77. Bank of England, Minutes of the Court of Directors, 20 February 1817 (Vansittart letter, 19 February 1817)..

78. Bank of England, Minutes of the Court of Directors, 27 November and 4 December 1817.

had moved towards resuming cash payments, sending notice to the Speaker of the House of Commons that it would repay £1 and £2 notes (but not larger denominations) in cash from 2 May 1817[79] and redeeming bills issued before January 1817 as they came due. Vansittart estimated total borrowing of around £14 million and debt redemption of £16.5 million, making a net debt reduction of £2.5 million.[80]

On modern figures, gross income was £57.6 million in 1817, while gross expenditure was £58.7 million, including £31.3 million in debt charges, down from 1816's record level of £32.9 million.[81] Thus, with income tax revenues collapsing, the budget remained in small deficit. Nevertheless, given the £9.5 million decline in income tax revenues and a £3.7 million shortfall in excise revenues caused by the depression, to near budget balance only two years after the war was a remarkable achievement.

While economic conditions began to ameliorate, the spring of 1817 saw further outbreaks of working-class violence. On 8 March 5,000 spinners and weavers, 'Blanketeers', met at St Peter's Fields, Manchester to march to London protesting against the downturn in the Lancashire cotton trade; they were dispersed by magistrates and 27 were arrested. There was considerable coordination between Radical cells during the spring, aided by a government agent employed by Sidmouth, William Oliver.[82] On 8 June several hundred men were dispersed by the authorities on the moors before they could descend on Huddersfield.

More seriously, the following day around 300 men armed with pikes and other weapons assembled at Pentrich and then marched on the Butterley iron works on the way to Nottingham, intending to kill the senior managers, seize weaponry and destroy the equipment. However, at Butterley the manager accompanied by a few constables faced them down and they were then rounded up by a squad of the 15th Light Dragoons. Around 85 of the rebels were arrested but only the three leaders were hanged for, by the time of the trials, economic conditions had improved and the government took the view that relative leniency would be the best way to quieten unrest.

The use of Oliver as a spy (and to some extent *provocateur* – he spread rumours of a mass uprising that encouraged the Pentrich rioters) was later used as a grievance by Radicals. However, while such informers had not been traditionally used except in wartime, the radicalisation of parts of

79. Bank of England, Minutes of the Court of Directors, 17 April 1817.
80. Hansard, *Parliamentary Debates from the Year 1803 to the Present Time*, Vol. 36, cols 1098-1109 (20 June 1817).
81. Mitchell, *British Historical Statistics*, pp. 581 (Income), 587 (Expenditure). The year-end is 5 January so, to get the figures for the (approximate) calendar year 1817, you should use the 1818 figures in the tables.
82. William J. Oliver (1774-1827). Home Office and police informer, 1817. Described by E.P. Thompson as the 'working class Judas'.

the working classes after 1793 and the Spa Fields riot justified Sidmouth in using untraditional methods. Even E.P. Thompson, highly sympathetic to Radicalism, admitted the existence of a conspiracy of extremists, a small minority of the Radical movement, to stage a national uprising, which inspired both the Spa Fields riot and the Pentrich affair.[83] Oliver himself, who had offered his services to the Home Office in March, was identified in the *Leeds Mercury* and emigrated to Cape Colony with government assistance in 1819.

The risings of early 1817, and the reaction against the government's use of Oliver, were regarded by E.P. Thompson as key elements in raising working people's class consciousness, transforming unrest from the random riots of the eighteenth century to the political movements of Peterloo, the 1831-32 Reform agitation and the Chartists. The Radical agenda of 1817 was still an extension of the Whig one; parliamentary reform (but generally to include full manhood suffrage), annual parliaments and the abolition of all 'places'. Some, but not all, Radicals wanted to abolish the monarchy but there was not yet much call for economic redistribution; that came only after Robert Owen's proselytising in the early 1820s, though even then many working-class Radicals remained devoted to individualism rather than to his communitarian ideal.

Liverpool was well aware of this burgeoning class consciousness and fought it with every means at his disposal. Quieting it was a central objective, in his view, of the Established Church and its Methodist offshoot. When Thompson described Methodism as 'interposing between the people and their revolutionary heritage a callow emotionalism which served as auxiliary to the Established Church',[84] he identified the core value of both the Anglican and Methodist churches to Liverpool in upholding the established order and subduing unrest.

Across the world 1817 was a notable year in India, under the active Viceroyalty of the Marquess of Hastings (the former Moira, elevated to Marquess in 1816). In 1814-16 Britain had fought a successful war against Nepal, acquiring part of western Nepal at the March 1816 peace treaty, which opened the trade route to the valuable cashmere goat herds of Tibet. The treaty also began the recruitment of Gurkha battalions into the British army.

In 1817 the Third Mahratta War took place, the final conflict against the Mahratta rulers of central India. Having received authorisation and funding from London, Hastings led British troops in person in an invasion of Mahratta territory with no fewer than 110,000 men, the great majority of them Indian. After a series of victories in 1817 and early 1818, in January 1818 Hastings signed the Treaty of Mundosir, giving Britain control of Indore and Rajput states in central India, and further treaties ending the Mahratta threat. By mid-

83. Thompson, *The Making of the English Working Class*, pp. 484-93, discusses this in detail.

84. Ibid., p. 54.

February, Hastings was able to write to the Prince Regent 'that our business is essentially finished, that our projected alliances are all settled and that all the European troops are preparing to return to their cantonments'.[85] As an expansionist of British rule in India, Hastings deserves to rank with Clive, Warren Hastings and Wellesley.

October 1817 saw one minor change in the government when Lord Whitworth was succeeded as Lord Lieutenant of Ireland by Charles, Earl Talbot.[86] Talbot was an agricultural expert (a Fellow of the Royal Society) and was given the freedom of Drogheda for his services to Irish agriculture. Regrettably, his staunch opposition to Catholic Emancipation raised Irish opposition to him from 1820, and he would be succeeded in December 1821 by the pro-Emancipation Wellesley.

In November 1817 national life was plunged into gloom with the death in childbirth of Princess Charlotte of Wales. Her labour had lasted 50 hours; the physicians took no steps to accelerate it with forceps and, indeed, her obstetrician Sir Richard Croft[87] committed suicide the following February. Princess Charlotte's penchant for the Whigs was perhaps a natural reaction to her father's Toryism, a similar reaction to that of all her Hanoverian ancestors. However, although she was much admired by the public, she appears from her own correspondence[88] to have been a somewhat unhappy young woman, who may well not have been successful if called to the Throne.

The national mourning for Princess Charlotte was deeply held by many, made more so by the knowledge that George III's sons were now all over 40, there were no surviving grandchildren and the Duke of Gloucester,[89] George III's nephew, was also childless. As Liverpool wrote to Peel:

> If it had pleased God to have spared either the mother or the child, we should have had something on which to fix our hopes and expectations; but as it is we are thrown quite out to sea, and there is no expedient to which we can look with real satisfaction.[90]

85. Letter from Hastings to the Prince Regent, 11 February 1818, in Aspinall, *The Letters of King George IV, 1812-30*, Vol. 2, pp. 246-47.
86. Charles Chetwynd Chetwynd-Talbot (1777-1849). 2nd Earl Talbot from 1793. Lord Lieutenant of Staffordshire, 1812-49. FRS, 1813. Lord Lieutenant of Ireland, 1817-21. KG, 1844.
87. Sir Richard Croft (1762-1818). 6th Baronet, 1816.
88. See, for example, her last letter to her mother, Princess Caroline, dated 10 October 1817, in Aspinall, *The Letters of King George IV, 1812-30*, Vol. 2, pp. 203-5.
89. Prince William Frederick (1776-1834). Duke of Gloucester from 1805. Son of Prince William Henry, George III's younger brother. MA, Trinity College, Cambridge, 1790. Chancellor of Cambridge University, 1811-34. Married Princess Mary (1776-1857), fourth daughter of George III.
90. Letter to Peel, 10 November 1817, quoted in Yonge, *The Life and Administration of Robert Banks Jenkinson*, Vol. 2, pp. 321-22.

Liverpool wrote urgently to Prince Leopold's equerry asking the Prince to inform Princess Caroline of her daughter's death[91] but in the event she heard the news from a courier.

The death of Princess Charlotte caused on outbreak of matrimony on the part of the Prince Regent's bachelor brothers. On 7 May 1818 the youngest, Adolphus, Duke of Cambridge, married Princess Augusta of Hesse-Cassel; their son George, Duke of Cambridge,[92] was born in March 1819. On 20 May Edward, Duke of Kent,[93] married Victoria of Saxe-Coburg, the sister of Prince Leopold; their daughter, the future Queen Victoria, was born in May 1819. The eldest unmarried brother, William, Duke of Clarence,[94] married Princess Adelaide of Saxe-Coburg on 11 July; they were not blessed with offspring. As a final insurance, Ernest, Duke of Cumberland, and his wife, who had been married in 1815, had a son, the future George V of Hanover,[95] in May 1819. Thus, within two years of Princess Charlotte's death, fears about the Royal succession were allayed.

In France 1817 had been a fruitful year; a key concern for Liverpool while a British and Allied Army of Occupation remained there. In January Wellington had recommended that, because of France's financial difficulties, the Army of Occupation should be reduced from 150,000 men to 120,000 on 1 April, even though French public opinion was unexpectedly hostile to it.[96] Later in the year, after Barings carried out three financings for the French government, the country's illiquidity was alleviated. With authorisation from Liverpool, Barings opened negotiations with France for a financing, to be carried out in 1818, which would allow France to repay the indemnity due to the Allies before the end of that year; these negotiations were still in progress at the year-end. At least, in correspondence with London, Wellington was now convinced that the occupation should end in December 1818.

The second half of 1817 saw an improvement in the British economy, with both imports and exports increasing sharply, iron exports rising by 31 per cent and cotton imports by 33 per cent, for example. The harvest was much

91. The letter is in ibid., pp. 323-24.

92. George, Duke of Cambridge (1819-1904). Major-General, 1845. Lieutenant General, 1854, serving in the Crimea. General, 1856. Field Marshal, 1862. Commander-in-Chief of the British Army, 1856-95.

93. Edward, Duke of Kent and Strathearn (1767-1820). Fourth son and fifth child of George III. Major-General, 1793. General, 1799. Commander of forces in North America, 1799-1800. Governor of Gibraltar, 1802-3. Field Marshal, 1805.

94. William, Duke of Clarence (1765-1837), later King William IV, 1830-37. Third son of George III. Rear-Admiral, 1789. Admiral, 1798. Admiral of the Fleet, 1811. Lord High Admiral, 1827-28.

95. George V of Hanover (1819-78). Blind from 1833. Crown Prince of Hanover, 1837-51. King of Hanover, 1851-66, when the country was annexed by Prussia.

96. Memorandum to Sir Charles Stuart, 9 January 1817, in Wellington, *Supplementary Despatches*, Vol. 11, pp. 589-94.

better than in 1816 and, with good growing weather appearing from June, corn prices fell rapidly, from 113 shillings per quarter in June to 77 shillings in September, although damp weather late in the harvest caused a rebound to 85 shillings in December.[97] The improvement in the economy caused a fall-off in unrest and the second half of 1817 was relatively tranquil.

Intellectually, the main event of the year was the publication of *On the Principles of Political Economy and Taxation* by David Ricardo. His ideas, particularly the doctrine of comparative advantage, were generally increasingly influential. Even though Ricardo was politically a Radical, Liverpool took his ideas seriously and in later years showed both in his speeches and his economic policies a strong commitment to free trade.

This commitment was evidenced by a modest ministerial reshuffle in the New Year, in which Liverpool strengthened his Cabinet, removing the absent Clancarty (permanently resident in the Netherlands) from the Board of Trade and promoting the young, clever and economically liberal Robinson, giving him a place in the Cabinet. From this point on the government began to pursue a barrier-removing trade and economic policy, with Liverpool leading a trio of junior ministers, Robinson, Huskisson, who was to succeed Robinson at the Board of Trade in 1823, and Thomas Wallace, Vice-President at the Board of Trade in Robinson's place.

The improvement in economic conditions and the resulting decline in unrest led Liverpool to end the suspension of *habeas corpus* early in 1818. It also led to the beginning of a rapprochement with Grenville and his supporters. Grenville, now 58, was beginning to withdraw from active politics and had become increasingly irritated by the Whigs' feeble attitude to unrest and their growing interest in Parliamentary Reform. He had been a member of the Select Committee set up the previous year to consider internal unrest and, after two letters from Liverpool, he agreed to continue serving in the new year. During the session, he supported Ministers on every issue except the resumption of cash payments and it became clear, in a year when a general election might well occur, that the Liverpool government had an important potential source of additional parliamentary support.

Parliament convened on 27 January 1818. In the debate on the Prince Regent's Address, Holland and Lansdowne both called for habeas corpus to be restored, while the new fourth Earl Stanhope[98] accused the French government of being hugely unpopular, maintained in office only by British bayonets, and suggested that France should be partitioned, as recommended by Julius Caesar.[99] Liverpool in response deprecated the slurs which 'his noble friend' had placed on the

97. Tooke, *A History of Prices*, Vol. 2, pp. 20-21.
98. Philip Henry Stanhope (1786-1855). 4th Earl Stanhope from 1816. Whig MP for Wendover, Hull and Midhurst, 1806-16. FRS, 1807. Moderate, albeit eccentric, son of a Radical father.
99. Caesar, *De Bello Gallico*: '*Omnia Gallia in tres partes divisa est.*'

French monarchy's popularity. Sidmouth, as Home Secretary, then announced that he was proposing a bill to end the suspension of *habeas corpus*. This was universally approved but, on several occasions during the session, the Whigs were to bring up cases of people who had been detained under the suspension in order to ensure ministers were not exonerated for their actions during the crisis.

The following week the question of the restriction of payments by the Bank of England came up in both the Commons and the Lords – the current restriction was due to end on 7 July. Liverpool assured the House that the Bank was ready to resume full payments and that there was no reason in terms of government finances why it should not do so. The only question was whether the restriction should be prolonged for another year while France raised the money necessary to pay the Allied indemnity.

In a letter to Wellington Liverpool expanded:

> With respect to the continuance of the Bank restriction, I entertain a very different opinion from that avowed by Mr. [Alexander] Baring. I know enough of the circumstances of the Bank to be perfectly convinced that they might resume their cash payments with safety, and without any material diminution of their issues and paper, if the financial difficulties of France, arising out of the claims of the Allies, were not a serious obstacle in their way. I give this, not as my own opinion and that of Mr Vansittart, but as the clear opinion of the present governor of the Bank, who is one of the most intelligent men in these matters I have ever known.[100]

Liverpool also criticised Barings' policy of distributing the new French loans as widely as possible among the different provinces of France, however politically desirable, for:

> the persons who would be concerned in the loan would never be able to manage it with the same prudence and advantage to themselves, and consequently to the public, as the great capitalists of Europe who contracted for the loan of last year, and a large part of it would probably very soon fall upon the general market.

Liverpool wanted to get the entire French financing operation done in 1818, with troops removed, quieting markets for resumption of cash payments to occur in 1819. In March he confirmed this view to Wellington, who consequently felt able to take a strong line with Richelieu and other French

100. Letter to Wellington, 10 February 1818, quoted in Yonge, *The Life and Administration of Robert Banks Jenkinson*, Vol. 2, pp. 332-35. The Governor was Jeremiah Harman (1763-1844). Director of the Bank of England, 1794-1827. Governor, 1816-18. Senior partner in the family bank, Harman & Co.

ministers, and with the other Allies regarding their claims against France. By the end of May the French government had agreed an acceptable settlement of the Allied claims against France, and Barings were ready to carry out the necessary financing.

In his letters to Wellington, Liverpool deprecated Richelieu's taking offence at his referring to Stanhope as 'my noble friend' when Stanhope had advocated dismembering France. He also commented on an attempted assassination of Wellington: 'I am aware that all public men are more or less exposed to this species of danger . . . but I am persuaded that there are facilities for executing so abominable a purpose, with a chance of escape, in a town like Paris which do not exist elsewhere.'[101] Wellington himself, in a letter to Clancarty, said the assassins acted, 'not, I presume, because they did not like my manners, or my face, or the colour of my coat, but because I was the main General of the Allies, and the main support of the system of tranquillity and order, which it is wished to establish in the world'.[102]

On 25 February the Duke of Montrose,[103] on behalf of the Select Committee, proposed a Bill of Indemnity for the actions of the authorities against unrest the previous year. Liverpool defended the Bill in the second reading debate two days later, stating that it was not a necessary corollary of the suspension of *habeas corpus*, but an opportunity to assure ministers that their powers had not been abused. He reminded the House of the disturbed state of London between November 1816 and January 1817:

> It is to be seen from the evidence, that many active and able persons, not, indeed, possessing property or respectability, in this town, were concerned in those machinations; but the internal state of the town was obvious to every one. . . . Is it nothing that the peace of the country has been secured, that apprehensions generally entertained have been allayed, that confidence has been every where restored?

The bills passed 'had the effect of abashing their boldest advocates, of taking the conspirators by surprise, of defeating their schemes both here and in the districts, of forcing them to distrust their cause and, what was often of greater importance, to distrust each other'.[104]

---

101. Liverpool note to Wellington, 15 February 1818, quoted in Yonge, *The Life and Administration of Robert Banks Jenkinson*, Vol. 2, pp. 335-36. Liverpool was right in that Wellington's attempted assassin was never captured; it was, of course, less than six years since the assassination of Spencer Perceval.
102. Wellington letter to Clancarty, 24 March 1818, in Londonderry, *Memoirs and Correspondence of Viscount Castlereagh*, Vol. 11, pp. 418-20.
103. James Graham (1755-1836). 3rd Duke of Montrose from 1790. MP for Richmond and Great Bedwyn, 1780-90. Master of the Horse, 1790-95, 1807-21. President of the Board of Trade, 1804-6. Lord Chamberlain, 1821-27, 1828-30.
104. Hansard, *Parliamentary Debates from the Year 1803 to the Present Time*, Vol. 37, cols

Liverpool then explained that the conspiracy of 1816-17 was more general than the Luddite unrest of 1812 and more directly aimed at overthrowing the constitution. A coordinated conspiracy aiming at insurrection had been under way in several different places:

> I well knew that the danger was materially increased by the peculiar circumstances of that period, and it was this consideration which rendered it an act of mercy to protect unhappy individuals from that delusion, which their private distress rendered more than ordinarily powerful. . . . As to the argument derived from the circumstance of no persons of consequence being concerned, I think we have lived in times when the impracticability of revolutionizing a state without the agency of men of rank, will no longer be advanced.

The Indemnity Bill passed the House of Lords by 100 votes to 33.

Considerable time was taken up by the settlements to the Royal Dukes as they hastily married to safeguard the succession. Liverpool had expressed his enthusiasm about these prospects to the Prince Regent and the government's intention to provide suitable allowances to the Royal newlyweds. The first two through the starting gate were the Duke of Clarence and the Duke of Cambridge, in April. Then, in May, the Duke of Kent (the eventual winner of the Royal sweepstakes, as father of Queen Victoria) was the subject of a similar message.

Liverpool, in his House of Lords speech, proposed that Clarence, as the senior, be given an allowance raised to £40,000 annually, while the other three Dukes (including Cumberland, who had been treated stingily on his marriage in 1815) were given £30,000 annually. Within two years the Prince Regent's debts would be fully paid, freeing up money for these allowances.[105] In the event, Commons cheeseparing prevailed and each Royal Duke was granted an allowance of £24,000 on his marriage, although Clarence successfully held out for more. Later in the session, Liverpool moved an amendment to the Regency Act, transferring responsibility for care of the incurably mad, but surviving, George III from the ailing Queen directly to the council appointed to care for him.

Liverpool's next major intervention was on his family's favourite topic of currency, in response to a motion by Lauderdale (who favoured paper money or a silver standard) to set up a committee to examine it. Liverpool began by stating that 'the best system of currency for any country, and particularly for a country such as this, is a paper circulation, measured by the precious metals as its standard, and supported in value by being convertible into cash at the pleasure of the holder.'

634-43 (27 February 1818).

105. Ibid., Vol. 38, cols 52-59 (15 April 1818).

After explaining his views on resumption of gold payments and discussing the international market for gold and silver bullion, Liverpool then explained why he felt any paper currency issue should have statutory limits:

> Unless some limit is adopted, property will become insecure, and the circulation will be subjected to repeated shocks, that might cause great public calamity and individual suffering. The evil of insecurity could not be a solitary evil. The repeated failures of country banks would give a shock to public credit, and the character of all paper currency would be affected by that of the most insecure.

Presciently, Liverpool thus anticipated both the crash of December 1825 and our present difficulties with unlimited expansion of credit.

Liverpool then commended the provision by which country banks would have to stop issuing small notes two years after return to the gold standard; in the event this was not carried out, resulting in the 1825 crash. Even in 1818 Liverpool was doubtful of the country banks' stability:

> Of the 700 country banks that existed in 1814, 200 have now been swept away and have disappeared, to the ruin of individuals and whole districts, and to the general injury of the agricultural and commercial interests. I have always been of the opinion that, although many of the difficulties out of which we are now emerging are to be traced to that convulsion which was caused by the rapid transition from war to peace, they are greatly aggravated by the failure of country banks.

He ended by reiterating that the delay in resuming cash payments was due to the difficulties surrounding the French settlement; the Bank of England was perfectly able to resume cash payments immediately.[106]

Vansittart's 1818 Budget speech showed considerably more optimism than in previous years. Army expenditure was down from £9.4 million to £9 million, navy expenditure from £7.6 million to £6.5 million and total expenditure was down from £22.3 million to £21 million, although this did not include the proposed £1 million church building fund (see below). He did not have a surplus from 1817 to offset this but he did expect a surplus in the year in progress. To fund this expenditure, and to remove £27 million of Exchequer bills from circulation, he intended to issue £34.9 million of 3½ per cent debt, irredeemable for ten years, which would provide an additional possible refunding mechanism for the outstanding four per cent and five per cent debt, without reducing the interest rate to three per cent.

---

106. Ibid., cols. 190-99 (20 April 1818).

Vansittart pointed out that the new 3½ per cent debt would be attractive because it would be difficult to convert into three per cent debt. Such a conversion would require the 3½ per cent debt to be standing well above par, equivalent to a price on three per cent Consols of 90 or more (par on 3½ per cent debt being equivalent to 85.7 per cent on three per cent debt). Such a price had been achieved only once in the past 40 years and was only to be achieved briefly in 1824 within the next 20 years.[107]

On modern figures, the economic recovery of 1817-18 caused the government's gross income to rise by three per cent to £59.5 million in 1818, while its gross expenditure fell by two per cent to £57.5 million (mostly on the army and ordnance), producing a modest surplus for the first time since the year to October 1792, as Vansittart predicted.[108]

Liverpool was to return to finance in May, moving the Bank Restriction Continuance Bill, extending Bank of England payment restrictions to July 1819. He reiterated his conviction that the Bank of England was ready to resume cash payments immediately, but the decision to wind up France's obligations to the Allies in three years, rather than five, required that country to raise £30 million quickly, inevitably disturbing money markets. Resumption of cash payments was a difficult undertaking, which should ideally be entered into when the exchanges were favourable; it would be foolish to attempt it when the exchanges were artificially disturbed.

Grenville and Lansdowne opposed the Bill, wishing to end payment restrictions immediately; Lauderdale also opposed it, not wishing to end them at all. Nevertheless, with the additional support of Bathurst and Harrowby, the Bill passed through Committee by 22 votes to nine. At the end of the debate Liverpool reiterated his support for the eventual ending of the restrictions, even though much of the country, as debtors, supported them, for 'the tendency of an inconvertible paper money is to create fictitious wealth, bubbles, which by their bursting, produce inconvenience'.[109]

In early May, Liverpool spoke briefly in favour of the second reading of the Cotton Factories Bill, eventually passed the following year after the intervening general election. This legislation forbade the employment of children younger than nine in cotton factories and limited their working day to twelve hours until the age of sixteen. It represented government's first effective step in regulating child labour and its first ameliorative response to the industrial revolution.

---

107. Sidney Homer and Richard Sylla, *A History of Interest Rates* (Upper Saddle River, NJ: Prentice-Hall, 2005) pp. 157-58 and 192.
108. Mitchell, *British Historical Statistics*, pp. 581 (Income), 587 (Expenditure). The year-end is 5 January so, to get the figures for the (approximate) calendar year 1818, you should use the 1819 figures in the tables.
109. Hansard, *Parliamentary Debates from the Year 1803 to the Present Time*, Vol. 38, cols 920-25, 948-50 (26 May 1818).

Sir Robert Peel, 1st Baronet. Father of the prime minister. Leading industrialist and author of the first child labour legislation.

Sir Robert Peel,[110] the richest mill-owner in Britain, a 'Church and King' Tory MP since 1790 and father of the Chief Secretary for Ireland, had sponsored a previous Act regulating apprenticeships in 1802. In conjunction with the socially reforming mill-owner (and future utopian socialist) Robert Owen,[111] he introduced the first version of this Bill in 1815 and re-introduced it annually until it finally passed into law. The divisions on the Bill matched those in political life generally; the Tories generally supported it, while the Whigs, especially those of Benthamite predilections, were opposed. Liverpool met Owen several times and was highly sympathetic to his benevolent capitalism at New Lanark though opposed to his overall Radicalism, while Sidmouth had Owen's essays circulated by the government to obtain comments from others.

Liverpool's speech introducing the second reading was brief. 'I highly approve of the Bill and consider it so much a principle of the common law of the land that children should not be overworked, that I desire some words to be introduced into the bill to declare this fact,' he began:

> I agree with the noble Earl [Lauderdale] that free labour ought not to be interfered with, however unwholesome or deleterious might be the nature of the manufacture; but to have free labour, there must be free

110. Sir Robert Peel (1750-1830). 1st Baronet from 1800. Tory MP for Tamworth, 1790-1820. Son of Robert 'Parsley' Peel (1723-95), himself a substantial cotton mill owner. Cotton mill industrialist, 1786-1817, when he sold out. Left £1.5 million in 1830, the largest industrial fortune to that date.

111. Robert Owen (1771-1858). Successful Manchester cotton mill owner. In 1800 bought control of larger mill at New Lanark, Scotland, which he ran on benevolent principles with an eight-hour working day and model housing. Formulated factory legislation with Peel, 1815. Embraced utopian socialism in 1817 and submitted a further report to Parliament on the Poor Law. Emigrated to United States, 1825, and founded a socialist community at New Harmony, IN, which failed. Sold New Lanark, 1828, and became a propagandist for the cooperative movement.

> agents, and I contend that the children to whom this bill applies are not free agents, . . . nor is there any doubt that such excessive labour is highly injurious to them.[112]

In a debate the following day, he reinforced this view: 'Is it possible to say that children compelled to labour more than fifteen hours a day are not overworked? What evidence could negative that proposition? If all the medical staff of Manchester were brought before the bar to prove it, I would not believe them.'[113]

Liverpool's next speech was in favour of an Aliens Act, which allowed the government to deport foreigners:

> If alien laws are in operation among foreign powers, and under them they choose to send all aliens out of their territories, are we to receive all the desperate and profligate characters of Europe, without the power of getting rid of them? . . . Is it to be contended that, because industrious individuals were sheltered from persecution, that therefore all the thieves, villains and murderers in Europe were to be received and sheltered without the slightest distinction?[114]

It was later found that, under an Act of 1695, aliens were able to gain Scottish citizenship (and thus after 1707 British citizenship) by investing in the Bank of Scotland. Later in the session, therefore, Liverpool was compelled to propose an additional Bill to repeal that anomaly.

On 15 May Liverpool moved the second reading of legislation close to his heart, the New Churches Bill, which provided a grant of £1 million for building new churches. The principle of the Bill had already been agreed so he was keen to move it forward: 'In moving the second reading of this bill I feel I am proposing the most important measure ever submitted to your Lordships' consideration. . . . It will, in its results, have the most beneficial effects on the religion, morality and general instruction of the country.'

Liverpool then went on to discuss the need for churches, concluding that, when infants, the old, the sick and dissenters were excluded, their capacity should total one in three to one in four of the population. The country's population had increased vastly in the past 20 years, especially in manufacturing towns, where churches were scarcest:

> With all the advantages the country has derived from the extraordinary extension of its manufactures, it is impossible for your Lordships to conceal from yourselves this fact: that great masses of human beings

112. Hansard, *Parliamentary Debates from the Year 1803 to the Present Time*, Vol. 38, cols 548-49 (7 May 1818).
113. Ibid., col. 582 (8 May 1818).
114. Ibid., cols 657-60 (14 May 1818).

> cannot be brought together in the manner in which they are situated in these towns, without being exposed to vicious habits, and to corrupting influences, dangerous to the public security as well as to private morality.

The example of Liverpool's namesake borough, a village at the beginning of George III's reign with a population now of 100,000, which had built six churches by subscription during the period and now had fourteen, showed what could be done. The new Bill would enable the construction of about 100 churches without voluntary subscriptions; Liverpool estimated that with such subscriptions the total built would be 150-200. (Yonge, writing 50 years later, claimed thousands of new churches had been built pursuant to the Act.[115])

While dissenters could build as many churches as they liked, new Anglican churches had to deal with the property rights of existing livings and were subject to the discipline of the Church. It was the duty of the Lords to balance these disadvantages. Furthermore, while he strongly favoured education for the poor, 'it is our duty to take care that those who receive the benefits of education should not be obliged to resort to dissenting places of worship by finding the doors of the church shut against them'.[116]

Later, Holland claimed that a previous such measure in Queen Anne's time to build 50 new London churches had resulted in only twelve churches being built, with excessive expenses on decoration (six being among the glories of Nicholas Hawksmoor[117]). Liverpool in response called for the new churches to avoid 'heavy expense for mere splendour' but to have 'the decent decoration which would mark the character of the Established church'.[118]

Keynes would have approved of the public-sector construction programme and would have assigned it an appropriate 'multiplier'. Liverpool would have argued that the economic multiplier from the improved happiness and behaviour of those served by the new churches was far above Keynes' figure.

In May 1818 Sir John Leach,[119] the new Vice-Chancellor, submitted his final report on the activities of Princess Caroline, in which he proposed that a Commission be sent to enquire more systematically in Italy and the other

115. Yonge, *The Life and Administration of Robert Banks Jenkinson*, Vol. 2, p. 367.
116. Hansard, *Parliamentary Debates from the Year 1803 to the Present Time*, Vol. 38, cols 709-14 (15 May 1818).
117. Nicholas Hawksmoor (1661-1736). Master of English baroque, designed six of the twelve churches built under the Act for the Building of Fifty New Churches in the Cities of London and Westminster or the Suburbs Thereof of 1711.
118. Hansard, *Parliamentary Debates from the Year 1803 to the Present Time*, Vol. 38, col. 832 (20 May 1818).
119. Sir John Leach (1760-1834). MP for Seaford, 1806-16. Vice-Chancellor of England, 1818-27. Master of the Rolls, 1827-34.

countries where she travelled. The result was a formal Milan Commission, of two barristers and a major, authorised by Leach,[120] which over the next year examined evidence as to the Princess' activities.

On 10 June Parliament was dissolved for a general election, which took place between 17 June and 18 July. The new Parliament would sit in January 1819. Since the previous election had been held in September 1812, the government could theoretically have carried on until the following year. However, Liverpool saw that the revival in the economy and the quiescence of popular unrest brought a good opportunity to renew his government's mandate. He may also have suspected that the resumption of gold payments could cause an economic downturn.

The result of the general election was a slightly reduced majority for the government, with the opposition gaining perhaps ten seats, albeit with a high turnover of members. There was a certain amount of grumbling about Liverpool's passivity – Sir Walter Scott said: 'How we want Billie Pitt now to get up and give the tone to our feelings and opinions.' However, as a member of the Lords, Liverpool could not constitutionally replicate Pitt's electioneering. Huskisson reported to Liverpool from Sussex that the voters in the county 'are no longer what they were ten years ago in their attachment to the old Tory interests and principles which are prevalent in the Nobility and Gentry'.[121]

This falling away of Tory enthusiasm may also have occurred among backbench MPs, explaining why the normal ministerial majority of around 100 was below that of about 180 after the 1812 election. However, Tierney's no confidence motion in May 1819 was beaten by 179 votes, suggesting that in practice the ministerial majority was only modestly reduced from the previous Parliament.

The autumn of 1818 was generally prosperous. The harvest was better than expected after a hot summer with four months' drought and substantial corn imports reduced the price marginally to 79 shillings per quarter at the end of the year. Meanwhile, trade was buoyant, as evidenced by a fourteen per cent increase in the government's excise revenues.

Peel resigned in August 1818 as Chief Secretary for Ireland, returning to England as a noted political talent and firm opponent of Catholic Emancipation. Although friends such as Croker were already canvassing support for him as a future prime minister,[122] he was tired of office and so served on the backbenches until 1822. He was succeeded by Charles Grant,[123] a *protégé* of Canning and

120. Letter from Leach to the Milan Commissioners, 8 August 1818, in Aspinall, *The Letters of King George IV, 1812-30*, Vol. 2, p. 252.
121. Both quotations from Gash, *Lord Liverpool*, p. 135.
122. Croker letter to Peel, 13 July 1818, quoted in Croker, *The Correspondence and Diaries of John Wilson Croker*, Vol. 1, pp. 114-15. Peel stated his weariness of office in an undated letter to Croker, ibid., p. 116.
123. Charles Grant (1778-1866). 1st Baron Glenelg from 1835. Tory MP for Inverness

a Catholic Emancipation sympathiser, after Goulburn and Huskisson had turned the job down. Grant was not a success; although intellectually able, he was a poor administrator and his liberal sympathies made him clash with Talbot, the Lord Lieutenant.

In the late summer, Queen Charlotte was taken ill, and correspondence between Liverpool and Castlereagh explored the possibility that Parliament would have to be recalled early to replace her guardianship of the aged King. However, she lingered on until November, and the Duke of York replaced her officially as the King's guardian in January 1819.

The autumn of 1818 contained two diplomatic successes. The Convention Respecting Fisheries, Boundary and the Restoration of Slaves was signed with the United States. It had been negotiated in London by Robinson and Goulburn for Britain; it was ratified in January 1819. The treaty granted the United States fishing rights in Newfoundland and Labrador and drew the boundary between the United States and the British North American dominions right across the Continent at the 49th parallel (except a small American enclave in Minnesota north of the parallel).

In October, the Congress of Aix-la-Chapelle (Aachen) met, with Alexander I, Francis I, Frederick William III, Castlereagh, Wellington, Richelieu, Metternich and other Allied ministers, to finalise arrangements for ending the Allied occupation of France. Both Liverpool and Castlereagh were keen to keep the Congress focussed on this limited objective, and not allow it to expand to a lengthy disputation, re-opening questions settled in 1815. The main questions were whether France should be admitted to the Quadruple Alliance and whether the Congress System should be formalised by regular meetings between the Allies.

On the meetings question, Castlereagh wrote to Liverpool saying: 'I am quite convinced that past habits, common glory, and these occasional meetings, displays and repledges, are among the best securities Europe now has for a durable peace.'[124] In another letter he said the Congress System:

> really appears to me to be a new discovery in the European Government, at once extinguishing the cobwebs with which diplomacy obscures the horizon, bringing the whole bearing of the system into its true light, and giving to the counsels of the great Powers the efficiency and almost the simplicity of a single State.[125]

Burghs and Inverness-shire, 1811-35, becoming Whig after 1830. Chief Secretary for Ireland, 1818-21. Vice-President of the Board of Trade, 1823-27. President of the Board of Trade, 1827-28. President of the Board of Control, 1830-34. Secretary of State for War and the Colonies, 1835-39.

124. Castlereagh letter to Liverpool, 4 October 1818, quoted in Londonderry, *Memoirs and Correspondence of Viscount Castlereagh*, Vol. 12, pp. 47-49.

125. Castlereagh letter to Liverpool, 20 October 1818, quoted in ibid., pp. 53-55.

Liverpool responded on behalf of the Cabinet, deprecating a formal pledge of repeated meetings:

> We are persuaded that the notion of such meetings would create a great degree of jealousy among the other powers of Europe, which no declaration that could be issued would adequately remove. The prominent necessity for them will cease to exist whenever the French government, left to itself, shall have proved that it can maintain tranquillity at home, and the relations of peace with other countries.

Furthermore, on the question of whether France should join the Quadruple Alliance: 'We continue of opinion that the greatest inconvenience would arise from inviting France to be an acceding party to the quadruple alliance of November 1815, and that there would be still greater objections, if possible, to the conclusion of a new and more extended treaty.'[126]

A letter from Bathurst to Castlereagh demonstrates that the Cabinet's view on the meetings question had been heavily influenced by Canning:

> He [Canning] thinks that system of periodical meetings of the four great Powers, with a view to the general concerns of Europe, new, and of very questionable policy; that it will necessarily involve us deeply in all the politics of the Continent, whereas our true policy has always been not to interfere except in great emergencies, and then with a commanding force. . . . He thinks that the meetings may become a scene of cabal and intrigue; and that the people of this country may be taught to look with great jealousy for their liberties, if our Court is engaged in meetings with great despotic monarchs, deliberating upon what degree of revolutionary spirit may endanger the public security, and therefore require the interference of the Alliance. . . . I do not subscribe to Canning's opinions, nor did any of the Cabinet who attended.[127]

In the event, while the Quadruple Alliance was confirmed without France, France joined the Alliance via a declaration of intimate union 'strengthened by the ties of Christian brotherhood'. No formal schedule was set up, but further meetings occurred in 1820, 1821 and 1822, although Britain was fully represented only at the 1822 meeting. Nevertheless, the momentum behind the 'system of tranquillity and order' as Wellington had called it diminished and, when the hostile Canning replaced Castlereagh in 1822, the Congress System fell apart.

---

126. Quoted in Yonge, *The Life and Administration of Robert Banks Jenkinson*, Vol. 2, pp. 344-45.
127. Bathurst letter to Castlereagh, 20 October 1818, quoted in Londonderry, *Memoirs and Correspondence of Viscount Castlereagh*, Vol. 12, pp. 55-58.

From the distance of two centuries, Castlereagh's and Wellington's support for the Congress System makes more sense than Canning's hostility to it. Liverpool was alas more influenced by Canning than by his wiser colleagues, being worried about the new Parliament 'which has not been tried, of a doubtful character, and certainly not accustomed to look at foreign questions as Parliaments were some years ago, when under the pressure or immediate recollection of some great foreign danger'.[128]

Following the Congress of Aix-la-Chapelle, the Allies withdrew their troops from France and, at a ceremony on 30 November, Wellington handed control over the Allied-held fortresses to Angoulême. Once Allied troops were removed, Allied influence over the French government diminished. Thus, in December, Richelieu's government fell, to be replaced by one controlled by the more liberal Comte Decazes[129] of the moderate Doctrinaire party. (Richelieu had been an *émigré* until 1815 and he lacked a domestic power base.) This caused rumblings from the absolutist powers, especially Metternich.

The removal of Allied troops from France freed Wellington for other responsibilities and Liverpool was delighted to receive him into the Cabinet – Mulgrave, Master General of the Ordnance, made way for Wellington but remained as Minister without Portfolio until 1820. In a letter to Liverpool after being offered the Ordnance, Wellington stated his wish to transfer his favour to whichever government held power:

> I don't doubt that the party of which the present Government are the head will give me credit for being sincerely attached to them and to their interests; but I hope that in case any circumstance should occur to remove them from power, they will allow me to consider myself at liberty to take any line I may at the time think proper. . . . [A] factious opposition to the Government is highly injurious to the interests of the country.

Naturally, Liverpool gracefully acceded to that request.

With Canning and Wellington added to the government, both owing considerable personal allegiance to Liverpool, and Grenville now generally friendly, the government's strength and Liverpool's own position were at the highest point they were to reach during his long administration. The following year of 1819 was to test that strength severely.

By far the most important event of January 1819 was the founding of Singapore by Sir Stamford Raffles. With Hastings' agreement, Raffles had looked for a port to act as *entrepôt* for the trade passing through the Malacca Strait and had determined on Singapore as unlikely to alienate the Dutch, who

128. Liverpool letter to Castlereagh, 23 October 1818, quoted in ibid., pp. 61-62.

129. Élie-Louis Decazes (1780-1860). Comte, 1816. Duc Decazes, 1820. Minister of Police, 1815-18. Minister of Interior, 1818-20. Ambassador to Britain, 1820-21.

attempted to control the trade from their capital of Batavia (modern Jakarta). Raffles therefore established a treaty with the elder brother of the Sultan of Johor under which Britain would back the elder brother's claim to Johor in return for the right to establish a trading port on Singapore island, for annual payments totalling 8,000 Spanish dollars (£2,000).

By 1825 the population of Singapore was 10,000 and the trade volume was over £6 million. After a period away Raffles returned to Singapore in 1822 and in late 1822/early 1823 drew up with Lieutenant Philip Jackson the Raffles Town Plan organising the city into functional and ethnic subdivisions. The Sultan of Johor was bought out in 1823.

The foundation of Singapore would be confirmed by the Anglo-Dutch Treaty of 1824, which established a British sphere of influence north of the Straits of Malacca and a Dutch sphere of influence on the south side. The Malay settlements were shortly afterwards consolidated as the Straits Settlements of Singapore, Malacca and Penang.

The Prince Regent's Address opening Parliament contained a hostage to fortune: 'The Prince Regent has the greatest pleasure in informing you, that the trade, commerce and manufactures of the country are in most flourishing condition.' Remarkably, this sentiment was echoed by Lansdowne, opening the debate for the opposition, who went to the unusual length of supporting the Address, since he agreed about the country's economic prosperity and was happy about both the British/US Convention Regarding Fisheries etc. and the withdrawal of Allied troops from France.

In response Liverpool began by praising 'the liberal view which the noble marquess has, in a manner so creditable to himself, taken of the speech and the address'. He then went on to praise the withdrawal from France, and to say: 'there never was a period in the history of the world when so general an anxiety prevailed to preserve the peace . . . and when the necessity of repose and the spirit of conciliation were more thoroughly acknowledged or acted upon over the European community.' On economic matters, he pointed out that taxes totalling £17.5 million had been remitted since the end of the war.

As for the return to gold, Liverpool was as keen as anyone but the French borrowings had destabilised the markets, so, 'I have no hesitation in saying that, considering the present state of the exchanges, and the progress of the pecuniary operations alluded to in the last session, I think it impossible that cash-payments could with safety be restored on 5th of July next.'[130]

Sometime in January the Committee of Treasury of the Bank of England had a preliminary meeting with the government to discuss the possible resumption of cash payments and expressed serious reservations about doing so in the near term.[131] On 2 February Liverpool proposed a Secret Committee

130. Hansard, *Parliamentary Debates from the Year 1803 to the Present Time*, Vol. 39, cols 28-33 (21 January 1819).

131. Bank of England, Minutes of the Court of Directors, 26 January 1819. The reference

of Inquiry on payments resumption, which should both consider evidence and draw what conclusions it should see fit. Accordingly, a Committee headed by Harrowby was appointed by the Lords; a parallel Committee headed by Peel[132] had already been appointed by the Commons.

Huskisson set out his views on resumption of cash payments in a memorandum to Liverpool. He set out four criteria for resumption to take place: (i) the foreign exchanges must be restored to par by reducing the supply of country banknotes; (ii) the Bank of England should supply extra bullion to the market; (iii) the debt from the government to the Bank should be diminished to £15 million; and (iv) the unfunded Exchequer bills debt should be diminished to £15-20 million.

Either a gold or a silver standard could be adopted, and Huskisson recommended the government taking a seigniorage on the gold to make its effective par value £4 per ounce rather than £3/17/10½. Either standard would be preferable to a continued reliance on paper money or a devaluation, which 'are founded on a delusion and being the first, would only pave the way for successive acts of fraud and bankruptcy'. Finally, Huskisson recommended that the austere policies necessary to resume cash payments should be undertaken within 1819.[133]

On 11 March the Bank of England prepared a Resolution that strongly opposed a resumption of cash payments. It began by expressing severe doubts whether the public would tolerate the severe contraction in the money supply which resumption would cause. To reduce this deflation, the Bank suggested that it needed to accumulate in gold the full amount of the 1797 money supply, of about £30 million, which neither South America nor the Continent could supply. With the 1818 French loans and the boom in imports in 1817-18, the balance of payments had swung heavily against the country and seemed unlikely to reverse. If the Bank reduced its outstanding banknotes, this would increase the demand for gold and thereby its price, while the government issuing debt to fund its Exchequer bills would give the Bank liquidity, but it would only incur losses if it bought gold at the fixed official price.

---

to the meeting is short and gives no details and the Resolution that follows merely commends the Committee of Treasury without saying what they had told 'the government' or vice versa. Since Huskisson produced his paper shortly afterwards, it may have been he who met the Bank's Committee of Treasury; since the Bank's Governor and Deputy Governor were not present, Liverpool and Vansittart may not have been present either.

132. Peel played a significant role in this debate, and it helped his career, but the resulting legislation was in no sense 'Peel's Act' as was claimed by his supporters a generation later and subsequently. Liverpool, as First Lord of the Treasury and the government's principal economic thinker, was always in control, with Huskisson as the ideas man in this case.

133. Yonge, *The Life and Administration of Robert Banks Jenkinson*, Vol. 2, pp. 382-84.

Two weeks later, the Bank issued a slightly revised Resolution, that declared flatly that it knew no reason why the Bank reducing note issuance would make the exchanges turn favourable. (Interestingly, there is a pencil note by this paragraph, saying 'Rescinded 6 Dec., 1827' – presumably by that time the Bank had come to recognise that this effect indeed existed). It ended by saying that resumption depended on circumstances they could not foresee and that no legislation could improve the position, though a reduction in government's debt to the Bank of £10 million was certainly essential. The Bank ended by offering to exchange its notes for bullion at the market price, but not at the official parity of £3/17/10½ per ounce.[134]

An introductory debate on the gold standard took place in both Houses on 5 April, after preliminary reports from both the Lords and Commons Select Committees had been received. Those reports confirmed that definitive reports on a full resumption of gold payments would be forthcoming shortly. They also advised that the Bank of England should stop its practice, followed since 1817, of converting £1 and £2 banknotes dated before January 1817 into gold sovereigns, since this had resulted in a drain of specie from the country to France. This resulted in Harrowby in the Lords and Peel in the Commons bringing in a Bill to prevent the Bank of England from exchanging further old notes for sovereigns. Liverpool in a brief speech emphasised that there was no question of the Bank of England being unable to pay its obligations, but the partial payment of notes in specie needed to be stopped for full payment to be resumed in an orderly manner.[135]

Definitive reports on cash payments resumption from the Commons and Lords Select Committees were presented on 6 and 7 May. By this time, the economy had definitely turned down and deflation had set in. There was justification for nervousness; Nathan Rothschild had told the Commons that resumption of gold payments would cause 'a great deal of mischief' given that money would be 'so very scarce, that every article in the country would fall to such an enormous extent, that many persons will be ruined'.[136] Fortunately, Liverpool was a canny enough operator to recognise when a none-too-scrupulous banker was 'talking his book' – the exchange business while sterling floated was highly profitable to the house of Rothschild.

The Commons report showed that, while in 1817 the Bank of England had enjoyed gold and cash reserves larger than at any previous time in its history, redemption of old notes had since drained bullion worth £6.76 million from it, of which around £5 million had been carried to France, according to Alexander Baring. The Commons Committee had accordingly recommended

134. Bank of England, Minutes of the Court of Directors, 26 March 1819.

135. Hansard, *Parliamentary Debates from the Year 1803 to the Present Time*, Vol. 39, cols 1396-97 (5 April 1819).

136. Rothschild quoted in David Kynaston, *Till Time's Last Sand: A History of the Bank of England, 1694-2013* (London: Bloomsbury, 2017) p. 113.

that small note redemption should cease temporarily, since only by a sharp contraction in its notes issue could the Bank reduce the bullion price to a level at which arbitrage was unprofitable.

Bank advances to the government totalled £19.4 million in Exchequer bills, down from a maximum of £34.9 million in August 1814. Conversely, the public balances held by the Bank had declined from around £11 million in 1807 to £7 million. For the Bank to resume cash payments fully, around £10 million of the Bank's outstanding Exchequer bills would have to be funded through longer-term government debt, or the Bank would have to reduce its loans to private traders, which would cause economic damage.

An immediate resumption of cash payments would require the Bank to eliminate suddenly most of its outstanding £25 million in notes, which would be highly deflationary and damaging to trade. Alexander Baring estimated that accumulating the necessary bullion worth £20 million in the country would take an additional four to five years. Accordingly, the Committee recommended that the Bank should be forced to deliver not less than 60 ounces of gold (worth some £234 at the official price) against their notes at £4/1/- in February 1820, and the same amount at par in May 1821, with full cash payments being resumed in May 1823. Finally, the Committee proposed the repeal of the laws preventing the melting down of currency, since they were ineffectual, with almost the entire 1817 issue of gold sovereigns having disappeared.

The Lords Committee report largely reflected that of the Commons Committee. The rapid expansion of the money supply in 1817 had caused over-trading, which had subsequently led to distress. The total note circulation from the Bank of England and country banks had between 1810 and 1818 varied between £42-£48 million, which demonstrated a massive increase in monetary velocity since the 1790s. The Committee thus recommended that the Bank should be compelled to pay its notes in bullion at gradually declining premiums over the period 1819-21, with full resumption of cash payments in coin in May 1823 or later, on Parliament giving one year's notice.[137]

On 18 May the Bank's Court of Directors met to consider the Reports of the Lords and Commons, saying it 'cannot but contemplate with the greatest anxiety' the proposed plan for resumption. Once again, it suggested that the Bank's obligation to supply bullion should be at the market price, not at £3/17/10½ per ounce.[138]

Then, two days later, the Bank relented somewhat and proposed to pay notes in bullion at £4/1/- per ounce from 1 February 1820 and at £3/19/6 per ounce from 1 October 1820. However, they still professed a 'repugnance,

137. The House of Commons Committee report is contained in Hansard, *Parliamentary Debates from the Year 1803 to the Present Time*, Vol. 40, cols 152-78; the House of Lords Committee Report is contained in ibid., cols 199-224.

138. Bank of England, Minutes of the Court of Directors, 18 May 1819.

however involuntary' to a system in which they would have little control over note issuance, since it would be set by market demands and the gold parity. They also warned of the adverse effect of 'pecuniary pressures' on the economy in general from the four-year transition to gold. They ended by suggesting that the Bank should exchange notes for bullion at the market price, that the government ought to repay a large part of its Exchequer bills and then see what effect these measures had on the markets. Anything beyond this was for Parliament and ministers to decide but the Bank would acquiesce under protest.[139]

After a petition had been presented by Lauderdale from 500 merchants of the City of London protesting against a resumption of cash payments, the debate proper began on 21 May with Liverpool producing the Bank's most recent letter. Harrowby then proposed six resolutions: first, to continue the payment restrictions for a limited time; second, to permit the Bank to exchange its notes for bullion at £4/1/- for some period before full resumption; third, to provide for a subsequent period, during which the Bank would exchange its notes for bullion at £3/17/10½; fourth, to provide for an intermediate period, with exchange for gold at an intermediate price and no ability to reverse the price decline; fifth, for the Bank to resume cash payments after being given notice by Parliament after bullion was exchangeable at the mint price; and, sixth, for repeal of all laws prohibiting the melting down or export of gold.

Lauderdale proposed an alternative set of resolutions providing for a bimetallic system with no fixed parity, while Grey proposed a further delay to allow more consideration of the topic.

After deprecating further delay, Liverpool proceeded to give his views on the question of resumption of the gold standard. There were three questions to be considered: whether to return to a fixed standard of value, whether to return to the pre-1797 standard; and how it was to be done. On the first issue, while there was no doubt that the bank restriction had enabled Britain to survive the war, it could not be a permanent part of the country's economic system, even in future wars, which were unlikely to be so total as that against Napoleon. As for the question of whether there should be a fixed standard:

> No body of men, I believe, was ever entrusted with so much power as the Bank of England, or has less abused the power entrusted to them: but will parliament consent to commit to their hands what they would certainly refuse to the sovereign on the throne, controlled by parliament itself – the power of making money, without any other check or influence to direct them, but their own notions of profit and interest?

139. Bank of England, Minutes of the Court of Directors, 20 May 1819.

It would make more sense for the government to issue bank notes directly but no country in the world had ever successfully established a currency without a fixed standard of value.[140]

As for returning to the former standard,

> Policy, good faith and common honesty call on the state to return to this ancient standard, if possible. . . . The engagement was to pay to a certain standard; and those who engaged to do so were bound by that engagement, if they meant to act honestly. . . . I am prepared to show that it is not only practicable, but that no permanent inconvenience can arise from the adoption of the principle I recommend.

Gold had returned from a price 30 per cent above the standard between 1813 and 1816, its price was now only three per cent above the standard. If the Bank had to contract the existing money supply, there might be some inconvenience, but far less than had been incurred in bringing the gold price down 30 per cent.

The Parliamentary committees had adopted a plan of returning to the gold standard as gradually as possible, thus minimising any inconvenience. It thus made no sense for Lauderdale to denounce their plan as a 'forced, precipitous and highly injurious contraction of the circulating medium' when the contraction was not to begin until next February and at a price three per cent above the current gold price. As for the question of whether the Bank could bring gold to par simply by contracting its note issue:

> I never could entertain a doubt, that if the circulating medium were gold, a reduction of the amount from £50 to £30 millions must increase its value, on the principle that the value of all property increases in proportion to the diminution of its amount: the same must also take place with reference to a circulating medium of paper.

As for the Committees' plan, its advantage was:

> that the Bank might open with a much smaller amount of treasure than if they were obliged to commence their operations by the resumption of cash payments. The next and the most striking advantage of the proposed measure is, that the Bank will begin to put it in operation upon a perfectly fair principle. Without recognizing any permanent depreciation of the standard, the report recommends to arrest the evil where it is.

---

140. It is not clear how aware British historians of Liverpool's time were of the Chinese Song dynasty's paper money system (1120s-1274), although it was mostly regional in its application.

Liverpool agreed that some reduction in the Bank's advances to government was necessary; these were currently below £20 million, and he believed that a reduction of £6 million rather than £10 million should give the Bank enough liquidity to undertake a gradual return to cash payments.

There was much difference of opinion on the money supply needed for Britain's commercial transactions: 'It will be found to be the opinion of some of the witnesses examined by the committee, that the commercial world will always be against the resumption of cash payments, as it would diminish the facility with which they at present obtain accommodation.' Indeed, Alexander Baring had said so; 'than whose statements and sentiments on the whole of this important subject I have never heard anything more intelligent and comprehensive'.

The present system 'must frequently give ease and facility to commercial transactions, and enable individuals engaged in those transactions to surmount obstacles, which in the ordinary state of the circulation, would be impossible'. However, 'the consequence of it is too often an encouragement to speculation, to unsound dealings, to the accumulation of fictitious capital; from all of which, in the course of a given number of years, a greater quantity of evil would probably accrue than of real advantage'.

Turning to the circulating medium itself, it was no greater than in 1792, despite the tripling or quadrupling of British trade, which caused many to argue that a return to gold might be unduly restrictive. However, the fallacy of this came from not recognising the difference between a gold and a paper circulation. Before the war, the circulation consisted of gold to the value of £30 million and paper to the value of £20 million; now it consisted of paper to the value of £50 million. Before the close of the American war there were few country banks, so people kept their wealth in small hordes of specie but, by the extension of the banking system, this habit was almost done away with: 'There is now scarcely such a thing as dead capital, except the small proportion which is kept in the respective banks.' Besides this, the system of bank clearing enabled merchants' payments of £1,457 million annually to be cleared by exchanging only £220,000 per day, or £68 million a year.

Liverpool then presented statistics on the circulation of Bank of England notes, showing that the £1,000 notes were in circulation for only thirteen days on average compared with 22 days in 1792. Thus, the increased efficiency of payments systems, and of paper over gold, would enable an unchanged circulation to satisfy a greatly increased volume of trade:

> In the county of Lancashire, where enterprise of every kind is carried to a greater extent than in any other district in the island, the greatest part of the circulating medium is carried on by bills of exchange; and when a respectable and intelligent individual, connected with that county, was asked whether any inconvenience resulted from that system, he replied 'None whatever.'

Liverpool ended by discussing the Mint regulations; he pointed out that, as silver was not legal tender above 40 shillings, and consisted of only around £5 million in total value, fluctuations in price between gold and silver were most unlikely to have a significant effect on the overall circulating medium. He ended by advocating that the House follow the recommendations of the Committee:

> My own persuasion is . . . that most, if not all the inconveniences that might be incurred from the experiment, have been incurred already, and that if parliament will steadily adhere to the course recommended, it will see the ancient standard of the country restored without material distress to any class of his majesty's subjects.[141]

After Lauderdale recommended his resolutions, Lansdowne supported the government's approach and, at the end of the debate, Lauderdale's resolutions were rejected and Harrowby's were agreed to without a division.

Liverpool's determination to push through resumption of the gold standard, against strong opposition from both the City and the Bank of England, was an act of great political courage. His judgement that gold payments could be resumed at the old rate 'without material distress' seems overstated, however. The deflation necessary to accomplish this caused a 28 per cent further decline in prices between 1818 and 1821 and another sharp recession.[142] However, the economic downturn, while severe (and including cases of actual starvation in areas around Glasgow and Paisley, where an influx of Irish workers had combined with mass layoffs by local manufacturers), was concentrated in the manufacturing districts of northern England and west-central Scotland. This concentration showed that the recession's cause was indeed monetary stringency (causing manufacturing credit to seize up) rather than a general downturn.

The 1819 recession, while unexpected, was not as deep as that of 1816-17, was highly localised and short. It had not begun at the time of the opening of Parliament in late January and it was already beginning to lift by the time of the autumn parliamentary session of November-December. Distress in the cotton manufacturing districts was indeed severe, with exports of manufactured cotton declining 22 per cent from 1818, almost to the 1816 trough, though still well above the 1811 level.[143] Bankruptcies surged moderately, but only

141. Hansard, *Parliamentary Debates from the Year 1803 to the Present Time*, Vol. 40, cols 610-28 (21 May 1819).

142. Rousseaux Overall Price Index, 1818=160, 1821=116; see Mitchell, *British Historical Statistics*, p. 722.

143. Official value of cotton manufactured goods exports: 1811 – £11.5 million, 1816 – £16.2 million, 1818 – £21.3 million, 1819 – £16.7 million. Figures from Gayer, Rostow and Schwartz, *The Growth and Fluctuation of the British Economy, 1790-*

to the 1817 level, far below those of 1811 and 1816. Brick production, too, reached a high in the year, far above the 1816 level, indicating that true distress was localised.[144] Corn prices remained stable at around 72-75 shillings.[145]

With no government providing Keynesian remedies and prolonging the suffering, and with a sound monetary system, even deep recessions were blessedly brief. Certainly, Liverpool's underlying judgement, that returning to gold was worth undertaking even at the cost of short-term disruption, was amply justified by the century of prosperity and economic growth that followed, with London becoming the unquestioned global financial centre, reaping untold rewards thereby.

Earlier, in May 1819, the House had debated the executions of Alexander Arbuthnot and Robert Armbrister by Andrew Jackson during the 1818 US invasion of Spanish Florida. Liverpool described Jackson as 'savage, cunning and cruel, in the greatest degree' in a private letter to Castlereagh[146] – which seems close to the judgement of history. However, in the House of Lords, he described Jackson's acts as 'not of a kind to justify a demand for reparation from this country'. He made the point that demands for reparation, once made, had to be followed up, and that Arbuthnot and Armbrister, in providing armed support to the Seminole Indians, had withdrawn themselves from British protection, even though Jackson's action in overruling the less severe verdict of a court was 'impossible to speak of without horror'.[147] At the end of the session, a Foreign Enlistment Act was passed, prohibiting British subjects from participating in wars against countries such as the United States and Spain with which Britain was at peace.

Since the Parliament was new, the subject of Catholic Emancipation came up again, with a joint Protestant/Catholic agitation in the country and a new bill introduced by Henry Grattan. Liverpool again made a major speech opposing Emancipation and, after Wellington had also spoken against it, Grattan's motion lost by 106 votes to 147 in the Lords; however, it lost by only two votes in the Commons. Later in the session, Liverpool spoke briefly in opposition to a related motion, an attempt by Grey to repeal the Test Acts requiring anyone accepting public office to swear the Oath of Supremacy and requiring him to subscribe to a declaration against Transubstantiation.

1850, Vol. 1, pp. 123 and 154.

144. Bankruptcies quoted in *The London Gazette*, 1,582 in 1819 as against 1,012 in 1818, 1,578 in 1817 and 2,145 in 1816. Brick production 1,101.6 million in 1819 as against 952.1 million in 1818 and 673 million in 1816. Figures from Gayer, Rostow and Schwartz, *The Growth and Fluctuation of the British Economy, 1790-1850*, Vol. 1, p. 147.
145. Tooke, *A History of Prices*, Vol. 2, p. 80.
146. Liverpool letter to Castlereagh, 18 September 1818, quoted in Londonderry, *Memoirs and Correspondence of Viscount Castlereagh*, Vol. 12, pp. 38-39.
147. Hansard, *Parliamentary Debates from the Year 1803 to the Present Time*, Vol. 40, cols 300-2 (11 May 1819).

Vansittart's 1819 Budget was necessarily restrictive, since it had been agreed that the government would repay £10 million of the Bank of England's Exchequer bills over the next two years, to assist the Bank in resuming cash payments. The House of Commons had already voted an additional £3.5 million in temporary excise duties. With the Exchequer bills repayment and the sinking fund requirement, the government thus needed to raise two loans of £12 million each, the first of which had been raised on the morning of the budget, while the other would be taken from the sinking fund in monthly instalments, thus reducing the net sinking fund to around £3.7 million and the amount of short-term debt outstanding from £49.5 million to £39 million. The Bank of England had been asked to fund the later instalments of a larger market loan but had refused.[148]

New taxes would include additional excises on foreign wool, domestic and foreign tobacco, coffee and tea, a reimposition of the malt duty – he hoped this would be offset by a reduction in malt prices – and an increase in the duty on domestically distilled spirits. Vansittart ended by hoping that 1820, with the second redemption of Bank Exchequer bills to finance, would be the last year in which the government went to the money market in time of peace: 'There is no reason to apprehend, that after that period, it will be necessary to trouble parliament or the country with a subject so painful as loans and new taxes.'[149]

On modern figures, gross income for 1819 was down by £1.4 million, as customs duties suffered from the recession. Expenditure was flat, as a savings in domestic expenditure had been offset by an increase in expenditure on the army, no longer benefiting from French subsidies. Thus, the surplus of the previous year had shrunk to a minuscule £0.6 million.[150]

Liverpool addressed the country's finances in the Lords on 21 June. He pointed out that Parliament, by abolishing income tax, had removed annual revenue of £18 million against the government's wishes, which might have allowed the gold standard to be restored more quickly and easily. In a departure from the policy pursued since Pitt established the sinking fund in 1786, Liverpool said he believed there was no effectual sinking fund; the only effective sinking fund was a surplus of revenue over expenditure. However, the nominal sinking fund allowed the markets and the public to trust the government's good faith, even though it borrowed against the fund. Other countries had sinking funds, for example, France had a sinking fund of one per cent of its debt. With continued economic

148. Bank of England, Minutes of the Court of Directors, 3 June 1819.

149. Hansard, *Parliamentary Debates from the Year 1803 to the Present Time*, Vol. 40, cols 1000-12 (9 June 1819).

150. Mitchell, *British Historical Statistics*, pp. 581 (Income), 587 (Expenditure). The year-end is 5 January so, to get the figures for the (approximate) calendar year 1819, you should use the 1820 figures in the tables.

growth, the government would soon have a clear surplus of revenue over expenditure of £8 million, or one per cent of the outstanding debt, which ought to be sufficient.[151]

The 1819 Commons session was notable for proposals that proved to have later importance. Sir James Mackintosh's[152] motion to reduce the number of crimes for which capital punishment was due passed by a majority of ten votes, foreshadowing Peel's liberalisation of the 1820s. Then a proposal for a committee to examine the possible reform of the Scottish burghs was carried by a majority of five votes, although Sir Francis Burdett's proposal for general parliamentary reform was rejected by 153 votes to 58. A committee was also formed to examine the question of whether steam engines could be compelled to consume their own smoke – one of the earliest attempts at environmental legislation.

On 18 May the Whigs, flushed by their earlier successes, proposed a motion of no confidence, which was defeated by 357 votes to 178, greatly reinforcing the government's position. Nevertheless, Liverpool had warned the Prince Regent that the government intended to make Vansittart's restrictive budget a matter of confidence and there was a possibility of their losing office thereby. This resulted in an anxious correspondence in which the Prince Regent suggested eliminating the malt tax and Liverpool replied that, given the necessary budget stringency to repay Exchequer bills to the Bank of England, the only alternative to the malt tax would be reviving income tax, which would produce even more opposition.[153]

In the Lords, the mediaeval provision of trial by battle, invoked in a celebrated case only the previous year, was repealed, together with the provision for acquittals in criminal cases to be challenged by private appeals. Even Eldon, proposing the repeal condemned the provision as 'containing so many absurdities, and principles so different from those most revered in the general system of our law'.[154]

In July the Milan Commission on Princess Caroline's activities reported its findings, providing the Prince Regent with the evidence of her adultery he felt necessary to obtain a divorce. Before the Milan Report arrived, the Cabinet addressed a Minute to the Prince Regent, stating that, even if Princess Caroline's adultery was proved, any attempt to obtain a divorce would involve 'serious hazard to the interests and peace of this kingdom'. To this, the Prince

151. Hansard, *Parliamentary Debates from the Year 1803 to the Present Time*, Vol. 40, cols 1229-31 (21 June 1819.
152. Sir James Mackintosh (1765-1832). Whig MP for Nairnshire and Knaresborough, 1813-32. Commissioner of the Board of Control, 1830-32.
153. Letter from Liverpool to the Prince Regent, 9 May 1819, Prince Regent responses, 10 and 11 May, Liverpool response, 11 May, in Aspinall, *The Letters of King George IV, 1812-30*, Vol. 2, pp. 289-92.
154. Hansard, *Parliamentary Debates from the Year 1803 to the Present Time*, Vol. 40, cols 1203-7 (18 June 1819).

Regent pointed out that any attempt to deprive Princess Caroline of her rights would equally require legislative approval and choosing separation rather than divorce would 'require the sacrifice of important public interests'.

In response, the Cabinet drafted a second Minute agreeing that adultery could probably be proved in court but that the witnesses were foreigners, 'many of whom appear of a low station in life' so that a proceeding in an ecclesiastical court was impracticable. The Cabinet believed that a proceeding in Parliament would require a greater standard of proof than would be required in a normal court and the poor quality of the witnesses would mitigate against its success. Finally, a prosecution for high treason might be possible, if the Law Officers thought such a charge could be proved.[155] By mutual agreement, the question was referred to the Law Officers, to report the following January.

Much more serious for the Liverpool government's long-term reputation, was an outbreak of unrest, fuelled by the temporary return of deep recession. There was a change from the disturbances of 1816-17, however. The millenarian, violent and poorly coordinated unrest of the Luddites, the Spa Fields rioters and the Pentrich rising had given way to a more broadly organised movement of mass meetings, less prone to random violence.

To some extent these represented a revival of the mass meetings of the 1790s, influenced by the writings of Thomas Paine, but they were largely driven by working-class mass organisers rather than by middle-class leaders. The mass meetings proposed a broad-ranging Radical 'reform', generally involving manhood suffrage and annual Parliaments, thereby distinguishing itself from the nascent 'Reform' movement within the Whigs, which sought only an 1832-style middle-class franchise.

The first manifestation of this was the election by a large meeting of Birmingham Radicals of Sir Charles Wolseley[156] as 'Legislatorial Attorney' to present the borough's grievances to the House of Commons. (Birmingham was among the most egregious examples of non-representation in the unreformed Parliament.) Wolseley had already chaired a giant Radical meeting at Stockport in June and debated whether to accept the Birmingham Radicals' honour at his nearby family estate Wolseley Hall, which had been granted to the family by the Saxon King Edgar for ridding the area of wolves.

Liverpool and Sidmouth were concerned at these signs of widespread and coordinated unrest and by reports of 'drilling' in Manchester, although according to E.P. Thompson the workers' leaders by their drilling were trying to keep any crowds orderly rather than stir armed uprising. Nevertheless, the

155. Minutes and letter quoted in Yonge, *The Life and Administration of Robert Banks Jenkinson*, Vol. 3, pp. 17-22. I take the second Minute to be wrongly dated 1820 instead of 1819; it refers to the 'Princess of Wales'.

156. Charles Wolseley (1769-1846). 7th Baronet from 1817. Like Liverpool, he had been present at the 1789 storming of the Bastille and implied in an 1819 speech that he had assisted it. Imprisoned for sedition, 1819-21.

Manchester magistrates had written to Sidmouth warning that they thought a 'general rising' was imminent. Thus when, on 16 August, 'Orator' Hunt arranged a meeting to press for 'reform', they called out both the local yeomanry (semi-trained militia) and the regular forces of the 15th Hussars.

The meeting according to modern estimates attracted around 60,000 participants, the largest held to that date, three times the Spa Fields crowd of 1816 and more than half the current population of Manchester. The great majority of this huge crowd were unarmed and well dressed, according to Hunt's instructions. When Hunt arrived, William Hulton,[157] chief magistrate, issued a warrant for his arrest and for that of three other organisers. Hulton ordered the regulars and Yeomanry stationed nearby to assist in the arrests. Sixty mounted yeomanry then advanced on the podium to clear a path for the magistrates to arrest Hunt. In the crush, both their inexperienced horses and the yeomanry panicked, laying about them with their sabres. Hulton perceived this as an attack on the yeomanry and ordered the Hussars, when they arrived, to disperse the meeting, which they did in a much more disciplined and careful way. The result was about 15 killed and 600 injured, and a disaster for both public order and the Liverpool government's subsequent reputation.

The 'Manchester Massacre', soon termed 'Peterloo', caused a nationwide uproar. The Aldermen and Common Council of the City of London addressed a petition to the Prince Regent sympathising with the Manchester crowd and condemning the government. In Yorkshire Fitzwilliam, Lord Lieutenant of the West Riding, called a public meeting to condemn the government's conduct in dealing with these assemblies – upon which Liverpool fired him. Indeed, unlike in 1816-17, most of the Whigs broke with the government to sympathise with the protesting populace, thus reverting to the Foxite approach of the 1790s.

In a September letter to Canning, Liverpool rejoiced that distress was this time localised to Lancashire, Cheshire, the West Riding, Glasgow and Paisley. There had been no disturbances in London because the reformers had no distress to work on. Crime in London and many other districts was also diminishing. Furthermore, unlike in 1816, the 1819 harvest was productive; indeed, there was a shortage of hands to get it in.

Nevertheless:

> nothing can be worse or more alarming than the state of those parts of the country which I first excepted. You will naturally ask whether the proceedings of the magistrates at Manchester on 16th were really

157. William Hulton (1787-1864) of Hulton Park. Studied at Brasenose College, Oxford. High Sheriff of Lancashire, 1810-11. Chairman of Lancashire and Cheshire Magistrates, 1819. Turned down a safe parliamentary seat in 1820. The Hulton family had owned the Hulton Park land since the twelfth century; they later discovered coal on the land and in 1910 their mine workforce suffered the third worst mining disaster in British history. Accident-prone.

> justifiable. To this answer, in the first instance, that all the papers on which they proceeded were laid before the Chancellor and the Attorney and Solicitor General, and that they were fully satisfied that the meeting was of a character and disposition, and assembled under such circumstances, as justified the magistrates in dispersing it by force. You will have seen in the public papers that the grand jury of Lancashire have in a degree sanctioned their opinion by throwing out the bills against the Yeomanry, and by finding the bill against Hunt and his accomplices.

However:

> when I say that the proceedings of the magistrates at Manchester on 16th ult. were justifiable, you will understand me as not by any means deciding that the course which they pursued on that occasion was in all its parts prudent. . . . Whatever judgement might be formed in this respect, being satisfied they were substantially right, there remained no alternative but to support them.

Liverpool then went on to consider the possibility of recalling Parliament and said that events in the next few weeks could make recalling it imperative, although he had no means of ascertaining whether Parliament would support the government in taking strong measures.[158]

Three weeks later, he informed Canning that the decision had been taken to recall Parliament on 23 November. Disturbances had continued throughout the worst affected parts of the country, with attempts at armed insurrection in Huddersfield, Burnley and Paisley; they were to continue with gradually declining frequency and seriousness until the Glasgow 'Radical War' of April 1820. The government took the possibility of a major coordinated rising very seriously. Wellington wrote to Major-General Byng,[159] the General Officer commanding the Northern District: 'The accounts which I saw yesterday of the proceedings of the Radicals in different parts of England tend to prove that we are not far removed from a general and simultaneous rising in different parts

158. Letter to Canning, 23 September 1819, in Yonge, *The Life and Administration of Robert Banks Jenkinson*, Vol. 2, pp. 407-12. In a letter to Wellington ten days earlier Liverpool had singled out Lancashire and its immediate neighbourhood as 'very alarming' and described the situation almost everywhere else as satisfactory. Letter to Wellington, 12 September 1819, quoted in 2nd Duke of Wellington (ed.), *Despatches, Correspondence and Memoranda of Field Marshal Arthur, Duke of Wellington* (in continuation of the former series) (London: John Murray, 1867) Vol. 1, p. 76.

159. Field Marshal John Byng (1772-1860). 1st Earl of Strafford from 1847. Whig MP for Poole, 1831-35. Colonel, 1810. Walcheren, 1809. Peninsula, 1811-14. Major-General, 1813. Waterloo, 1815. General Officer Commanding, Northern District, 1816-28. Commander-in-Chief, Ireland, 1828-31. Governor of Londonderry, 1832-60.

and at different places.' He then advised Byng on the garrisoning of his troops and of the need to prevent the mob overcoming any detachments of troops: 'As long as no misfortune happens to them the mischief will be confined to plunder and a little *murder* [author's italics] and will not be irretrievable.'[160]

Hulton as Manchester's chief magistrate messed up, there can be little question. While the crowd's military-style discipline appeared to Hulton more sinister than it probably was, attempting to arrest Hunt in front of 60,000 clamouring supporters was foolhardy and using the untrained yeomanry to enforce the law was asking for trouble. Thus, the casualties at Manchester in 1819 had the same immediate cause as those of an earlier event in Liverpool's career, the Tranent riot of 1797. Using regular soldiers as a police force in a riot situation could work, because of their high level of discipline; using militia, as at Tranent in 1797 and Manchester in 1819, was always likely to lead to trouble because of their lack of experience and training.

When it occurred, the local officials responsible, whether Liverpool as (non-present) militia colonel in 1797 or the Manchester magistrates in 1819, must be given the benefit of the doubt by government or social control could break down entirely. A letter from Sidmouth, with the backing of the Cabinet, conveying to the Manchester magistrates the thanks of the Prince Regent for their action in the 'preservation of the public peace' was thought necessary to ensure that other local authorities acted firmly.[161]

Over the autumn, various people suggested plans for dealing with the situation to Liverpool, most of which he had no difficulty in rejecting – the Duke of York's proposal to increase the army, for example. He was also firm in response to someone who suggested cultivating all the waste land in the country to employ the unemployed: 'I am fully satisfied that the principal cause of that [agricultural] distress was the quantity of land that was brought under the plough in the last years of the war, in consequence of the very high prices of corn.'[162]

Perhaps the silliest proposal came from Nathan Rothschild, who in October 1819, after the legislation to return to the gold standard had been passed, wanted to abandon it and continue the bank restrictions. Liverpool was suitably scathing on the subject in a letter to Vansittart:

> I am satisfied that no measure could be more fatal, and that the very notion of its being a matter for consideration would do harm. In the first place, there is not the smallest real pretext for it, supposing the exchanges to remain unfavourable for a short time, the Bank was only obliged to pay at £4/1/-, and this must be to them a sufficient security;

160. Letter to Byng, 21 October 1819, quoted in Wellington, *Despatches, Correspondence*, Vol. 1, pp. 80-82.
161. Referred to in Liverpool's 23 September, 1819 letter to Canning referenced above.
162. Letter to unnamed correspondent, 18 December 1819, quoted in Yonge, *The Life and Administration of Robert Banks Jenkinson*, Vol. 2, pp. 415-16.

> and as to their not having considerably augmented their treasure, I think it a fortunate circumstance in every respect. As to the continuing the restriction from the dread of diminishing their circulation too much, this would be a ground of a perpetual restriction, and is the idea of all others that it was most necessary to combat last year.

Liverpool stressed the need to pay the Bank before Parliament met the full £5 million due that year in Exchequer bills redemption.

A letter from Vansittart to the Bank asking for further Exchequer bills financing had just been refused, as £4 million of the previous July financing was still outstanding. The Bank had pointed out that substantial and growing sums were borrowed each quarter to meet the deficiencies on the Consolidated Fund. They requested early repayments of outstanding amounts and the £5 million promised to increase their stock of bullion to meet the expected demand with the first stage of payments resumption.[163]

In response, Liverpool and Vansittart wrote to the Bank, pointing out that £1 million had already been repaid and a second £1 million would be paid in silver bullion within a month. Of the remaining £3 million, £2.5 million would be repaid from loan proceeds arriving before 5 April 1820 and the remaining £500,000 would be paid by 5 April either in cash or silver bullion. The Bank accepted this proposal with only small modifications.[164]

Shortly before Parliament met, Liverpool's position was greatly strengthened by a letter and accompanying memorandum from Grenville. Grenville had left the Whigs the previous year but he still had considerable influence on moderate opinion and his support meant that Liverpool could meet Parliament with confidence.

Grenville took an extreme view of the disturbances:

> The object of effecting a revolution in this country by inflaming the worst passions of the lowest orders of society has been unremittedly pursued for many years past. . . . It seems no exaggeration to say, that if the promoters of general confusion can make as much new way in the next three or four years as they have done in the last, we must consider insurrection and civil blood as inevitable, though even then we may hope that their issue would not be doubtful.

Grenville regretted that the organisers of the Manchester meeting had not been charged with treason and proposed a set of Draconian measures restricting civil liberties that he believed Liverpool should introduce.[165]

163. Letter to Vansittart, 31 October 1819, quoted in ibid., pp. 416-17. Bank of England, Minutes of the Court of Directors, 7 and 21 October 1819.
164. Bank of England, Minutes of the Court of Directors, 18 November 1819.
165. Letter and Memorandum from Grenville, 12 November 1819, quoted in Yonge, *The*

In response, Liverpool agreed that the current situation was unprecedented:

> Though it cannot be denied that the great increase of our manufacturing population, the dependence of a great part of that population on foreign demand, and the refinements in machinery (which enable manufacturers to perform that work in weeks which formerly occupied months, and which lead consequently to extravagant wages at one time, and to low and inadequate ones at another) have recently subjected, and must in the nature of things subject this country to evils with which in the same degree we were formerly unacquainted; yet all these circumstances would not have accounted for the present state of the public mind in certain parts of the country, if the events of the French Revolution had not directed the attention of the lower orders of the community, and those immediately above them, to political considerations; had not shaken all respect for established authority and ancient institutions; and had not familiarized mankind with a system of organization which has been justly represented to be as ingenious and appropriate to its purpose as any invention in mechanics.

Liverpool then outlined what were to become the Six Acts, generally more moderate than the measures Grenville proposed, the most novel of which restricted attendance at large meetings to the parish in which they were held. Without preventing citizens' rights of assembly, these measures:

> get rid of the great evil of itinerant orators, and of all artificial measures of excitement. Novelty and curiosity are great aggravations of the evils of popular meetings. It is difficult to know who attends them, but parochial meetings would generally be flat, and in most cases the gentlemen who live in the parish would have influence enough to check those with whom they are so intimately connected, and whose actions in this respect could not be concealed from them.[166]

The short parliamentary session was a busy one. The Prince Regent's Address focussed on unrest, claiming that:

> a spirit is now fully manifested, utterly hostile to the constitution of this kingdom, and aiming not only at the change of those political institutions which have hitherto constituted the pride and security of this country, but at the subversion of the rights of property and of all order in society.[167]

Life and Administration of Robert Banks Jenkinson, Vol. 2, pp. 418-30.

166. Letter to Grenville, 14 November 1819, quoted in ibid., pp. 430-34.

167. Hansard, *Parliamentary Debates from the Year 1803 to the Present Time*, Vol. 41, cols

The potential for trouble was indicated by the normally moderate Lansdowne who supported Grey in proposing an inquiry into the causes of the Manchester disturbances. He condemned Sidmouth's letter commending the Manchester magistrates, condemned the removal of Fitzwilliam and continued: 'I believe a much greater danger threatens the nation from another source – I mean from the prevalence of an opinion among the public, that the institutions of the country are not so favourable to the lower as to the higher classes.'[168] It was a view that was to reverberate not only among the Whigs, but also among Liverpool and his colleagues, who after 1820 were to engage in numerous steps of social and constitutional reform.

Liverpool's speech on the Address began by pointing out that a parliamentary inquiry would mean the suspension of all the law courts' proceedings on the Manchester affair, which was impracticable. As to Sidmouth's letter of thanks, that was a decision of Liverpool and the whole government, on whom any blame should be distributed. The magistrates had been thanked because they had done their duty. The grand jury had brought bills of indictment against three of the ringleaders and had refused to bring them against the yeomanry. Hence, the government would not be doing its duty if it did not bring in legislation which supported the magistrates of Lancashire and elsewhere in doing their duty.[169] Grey's amendment was defeated by 159 votes to 34.

On 29 November, Liverpool spoke in favour of the first reading of four of the control measures introduced by the government: the Misdemeanours Bill to speed up court proceedings for misdemeanours; the Blasphemous and Seditious Libels Bill, which increased the sureties demanded from printers of seditious material and the penalties for a second offence of publishing it; the Seizure of Arms Bill, which allowed arms caches to be seized by magistrates; and the Training Prevention Bill (later the Unlawful Drilling Act), which made it illegal to carry out military training except by municipal bodies. He maintained that these bills were a system of protection, not coercion; if they prevented those acts which endangered the existence of our rights, they were the best safeguards of those rights. Only the Seizure of Arms Bill represented a temporary suspension of traditional rights.[170]

The following day, Liverpool gave a major speech in response to a Lansdowne motion demanding a Select Committee to inquire into manufacturing distress and the execution of the mass meeting laws. Liverpool began by pointing out that Lansdowne had not suggested that the distress was the fault of parliamentary action but was instead the inevitable aftermath of the long war. He could demonstrate this by showing that the United States, much more separated from Europe, was also in late 1819 in economic distress as great as Britain's (the Panic of 1819):

1-3 (23 November 1819).

168. Ibid., Lansdowne speech, cols 41-44 (23 November 1819).

169. Ibid., cols 44-48 (23 November 1819).

170. Ibid., cols 353-55 (29 November 1819).

> If your Lordships consider the situation of America, you will find there those principles of reform which have spread throughout this country. The Americans have no King, no nobles, no Established Church, no tithes. They have too – what is called equal representation – and we are told that they have no taxes; yet that country is more distressed than this, in which all those establishments exist. . . . For fifteen or twenty years that country remained neutral, carried on an extensive commerce, and made great progress in prosperity; and when the circumstances which had given rise to its prosperity changed, it is impossible that a country so situated should not go backwards.

Liverpool then went on to explain that the increase of the population in the preceding 60 years had led to a multiplicity of machinery, which in turn had made employment levels more unstable. Government was not responsible for this and attempts by government to improve the situation would in nine out of ten cases make it worse. As for the distress, Whigs who suggested it was unimportant because no people of consequence were involved had forgotten the damage done in former days by Wat Tyler and Jack Straw:

> I will not say, because I do not believe, that the great body of the French people were at first involved in the revolution which formerly ravaged that country. . . . The noble Lord, to prove that the meeting was peaceable, stated that it was attended by women and children. I never saw a mob in my life without women and children. I witnessed some of the most active scenes in the French Revolution: I was present at the capture of the Bastille; and I can assure the noble lord that I saw many women busily employed on that occasion.

Liverpool then entered into a detailed defence of the Manchester magistrates' action and paid a tribute to the Lord Lieutenant, the Whig 12th Earl of Derby. Finally, he concluded that, 'The fear of the mob always leads to arbitrary government; and the best friends of liberty are those who put down popular commotion, and secure the inhabitants of a country in the peaceable enjoyment of their rights.'[171] Lansdowne's motion lost by 178 votes to 47.

Liverpool later spoke in favour of the Second Reading of Eldon's Misdemeanours Bill to speed trials in seditious libel cases:

> I would be the last man to propose or recommend any additional restrictions on the liberty of the press, for I regard it as one of the best securities of public freedom. But that it stands in need of some regulation would, I think, be denied by no man who has attended to

---

171. Ibid., cols 494-506 (30 November 1819).

> that mass of licentiousness, of wickedness, indecency and profaneness, by which it has recently been contaminated. When doctrines contrary to every principle of religion and morals are openly promulgated, the law ought to be made effectual for its own purposes.[172]

On the Blasphemous Libels Bill, Liverpool responded to a speech by Grey, defending the blasphemy and sedition of the Radical press, by claiming that there was no subject on which Grey's views were further from the mass of public opinion: 'I am ready to admit that the British are a religious people, but the question is, how long the lower orders would continue so, if these publications are allowed to go on?' He believed that a tyranny in Britain would only be possible if religious belief disappeared and pointed out that the French Revolution had been more bloody and unpleasant than the English Civil War because it had been led by the wholly irreligious.[173] Liverpool later confirmed that writings against himself and his colleagues, or against the administration, would be mere personal libels; to become seditious libel, the writing must tend to undermine the foundations of the constitution.[174]

Finally, Liverpool spoke in favour of the Seditious Meetings Prevention Bill. He began by discussing the economic distress, proclaiming it to be the lingering after-effect of war and of the 1819 Panic in the United States which had disrupted the cotton manufacturing districts. There were calls for government to alleviate the distress with cash payments, but, 'If there is anything that could ruin this country, it is that government should take upon itself the support of the poor.' The system in place was local, with local funds being used to alleviate local distress, so 'supplies are collected with greater security and lenity, and applied with greater discrimination and effect, than it would be possible to do, if government managed the whole arrangement'. Meanwhile, the Seditious Meetings Prevention Bill, which would, after a Commons amendment, have a time limit of five years, would simply stop those multi-parish mass meetings that were an attempt to intimidate the public and were highly disruptive for business. The Bill would extend to Ireland, even though that country was currently peaceable, to prevent her from being visited by itinerant orators.[175]

Having passed the Six Acts, which included the Newspaper Stamp Duties Act, which imposed a fourpenny stamp on newspapers and opinion sheets selling for less than sixpence, Parliament adjourned until February. Overall, the legislation, modified somewhat by the Whigs, was a comprehensive and moderate response to the 1819 disturbances and some parts of the Six Acts became permanent law – the Unlawful Drilling Act remained in force until 2008.

172. Ibid., cols 684-687 (3 December 1819).
173. Ibid., cols 738-44 (6 December 1819).
174. Ibid., col 971 (9 December 1819).
175. Ibid., cols 1282-91, 1313-14 (17 December 1819).

The passage of six such substantial pieces of legislation in such a short session was a remarkable tribute to Liverpool and Castlereagh's skills in parliamentary management. Moreover, the legislation was effective in quieting disturbances – as early as 11 December, Wellington was advising Sidmouth on how in practice he and Byng should enforce the new Unlawful Drilling Act.[176]

Fortunately, the economy was already turning upwards and the end of 1819 thus marks a convenient demarcation between the heroic and turbulent first half of Liverpool's premiership and the reforming, more prosperous and more tranquil second half.

George Canning – long-term friend, occasional rival and eventual successor.

---

176. Wellington letter to Sidmouth, 11 December 1819, quoted in Wellington, *Despatches, Correspondence*, Vol. 1, pp. 89-90.

VII.

Challenges, Recovery and Transition, 1820-23

Norman Gash's magisterial 1984 biography of Liverpool says, '1820 was to prove the most difficult and dangerous year of Liverpool's whole career'.[1] I would disagree. The Queen Caroline scandal that erupted that summer threatened George IV but not Liverpool directly, although a disgruntled king might have tried to dismiss him. That became impossible once George IV discovered that Liverpool's Cabinet supported Liverpoolwhile most Whigs supported the Queen.

The economy, while still weak, was showing signs of recovery and national unrest to die down – Queen Caroline was a useful icon and figurehead for unrest but an impossible leader of it. The government was still unpopular but in the spring election the voting population rallied round it after the previous year's troubles. Only if the Cato Street Conspirators had achieved their wildest dreams would Liverpool have been seriously endangered either politically or physically.

The Law Officers reported in January 1820 on the findings of the Milan Commission on Princess Caroline's activities. They reported that a charge of high treason could not be sustained for the Prince Regent's wife or even a queen having sex with a foreigner, that an action in the ecclesiastical courts was inappropriate and that a divorce could only be obtained by Act of Parliament.

Also, in January came a disgruntled ultimatum from Canning, for whom four years in obscurity at the Board of Control had led to boredom. Liverpool offered him the Home Office, where Sidmouth's lengthy and successful tenure was nearing its end, but this was deemed insufficient. Canning, about to turn 50, wanted the leadership of the House of Commons or ideally the premiership itself. For Liverpool, attempting to satisfy Canning's frustrated ambitions became a recurrent theme until the tragedy of Castlereagh's death offered an apparent solution.

The Bank of England wrote to Liverpool saying they could no longer fund the quarterly deficits on the consolidated fund. The outstanding amount of Exchequer bills had grown despite the government's promise to repay bills to the value of £10 million over two years. The 1819 recession had caused tax

1. Gash, *Lord Liverpool*, p. 147.

payments to lag and the bond markets had not allowed a new funding of the size needed.[2] Liverpool and Vansittart responded on 15 February, after the King's death, requesting a postponement of the last £1 million of the first £5 million repayment until a new Parliament had met. This repayment was made in April, and an agreement was reached in May for repayment of the remaining £5 million by July 1821.[3]

On 30 January, Edward Bransfield,[4] who had risen from ordinary seaman to the rank of Master, became the first Westerner to sight and name Antarctica, having the previous day landed and named King George Island. Cook had circumnavigated Antarctica in 1773 but had never seen it; this was the first recorded discovery of the last continent.

In late January, two royal deaths occurred. On 23 January the Duke of Kent, father of the future Queen Victoria, died of pneumonia. Six days later, the old King George III finally breathed his last, raising George IV to the throne and bringing the question of Queen Caroline firmly to the forefront of politics. George IV was, however, confined to his bed with pleurisy; at one point it was feared he too would perish.[5]

Ceremonially, much of February was taken up with George III's funeral, which took place on 16 February at St George's Chapel, Windsor. George IV was too ill to attend, so the Duke of York presided as Chief Mourner and Liverpool travelled to Windsor with the entire Cabinet to attend.

The day after the King's funeral, news arrived of the assassination of the Duc de Berri, younger son of the future Charles X and ultimate heir-presumptive to the French monarchy. The verdict of Mrs Arbuthnot, who started her diary with the new reign, was typical of legitimists everywhere: 'If there was justice upon earth, that country and its accursed inhabitants would surely be swallowed up by an earthquake.'[6] From this point it was clear that the restored French monarchy was living on borrowed time. Nevertheless, in the short term Richelieu returned to power, which improved both the French government's quality and Anglo-French relations. (Alas, Richelieu would be ousted in December 1821 and die the following May.)

The new reign's first problem was whether to include Queen Caroline in the liturgy. The Cabinet recommended that the liturgy could be amended

2. Bank of England, Minutes of the Court of Directors, 6 January 1820.
3. Bank of England, Minutes of the Court of Directors, 17 February 1820.
4. Edward Bransfield (1785-1852). Royal Navy, 1803-1820. Master, HMS *Williams*, 1819-20.
5. Castlereagh wrote to his brother, 'The King's illness has had a most providential termination, entirely due to Sir M. Tierney's intrepid conduct in bleeding his Majesty almost to death.' Castlereagh letter to Stewart, 13 February 1820, quoted in Londonderry, *Memoirs and Correspondence of Viscount Castlereagh*, Vol. 12, pp. 210-14. We may mourn the loss of the early nineteenth century's constitutional arrangements but surely not its medicine!
6. Bamford and Wellington, *The Journal of Mrs. Arbuthnot, 1820-1832*, Vol. 1, p. 5.

to exclude her[7] although Canning said he would not have agreed to this if any penal action had been proposed.[8] After a display of fury by George IV, threatening to retire to Hanover, where a divorce could be obtained easily, he backed down. However, Queen Caroline was sufficiently annoyed by the exclusion of her name from the liturgy, and by the refusal of the authorities in Rome, where she was living, to recognise her new rank and status, that she began to move inexorably towards England.

The parliamentary session was short, since George IV's accession required a general election to be held. Before the dissolution, the Cabinet was threatened with assassination by the Cato Street conspiracy. This was not an isolated act of terrorism but an attempt by Arthur Thistlewood and a group of the most extreme backers of the 1816 Spa Fields riots to obtain power by force. It was a serious endeavour planned months in advance; according to Henry Hobhouse's diary,[9] the plotters had originally intended to strike at Westmorland's house in December. However, as Hobhouse outlines, 'Lord Sidmouth was well informed of all that was intended.' Thus, the conspirators' plan to murder the Cabinet on 22 February at the pre-session dinner at Harrowby's house in Grosvenor Square was known to the authorities well in advance.

Wellington wanted the Cabinet to go ahead as planned, meeting the conspirators armed to the teeth, but cooler counsels prevailed and the conspirators were arrested at their headquarters in Cato Street, although Thistlewood escaped and was hunted down. Harrowby and his family dined with Liverpool at Fife House until the conspirators were rounded up.

The Cato Street conspiracy, coming just before the election, was a stroke of luck for the Liverpool government. Without it, the government's reputation would have been overshadowed by Peterloo, and its Six Acts might have appeared an overreaction to unrest. The economy was in poor shape and unemployment in the industrial districts of the north and Scotland remained high. Thus, in normal circumstances, the government could have expected to lose seats to the Whigs and other opposition forces. However, after Cato Street, the ministry's precautions seemed sensible, and the obvious threat made it natural for moderate opinion to rally round a government led by the solid, capable Liverpool. On 27 February the Cabinet attended a service at the Chapel Royal, St James's Palace, to give thanks for their preservation, both physical and electoral.

7. The liturgy had previously excluded George I's wife, Sophia Dorothea of Celle (1666-1726), whom he imprisoned in the Castle of Ahlden from 1694 until her death 32 years later.
8. Yonge, *The Life and Administration of Robert Banks Jenkinson*, Vol. 3, pp. 25-33.
9. Henry Hobhouse (1776-1854). Permanent Under Secretary, Home Office, 1817-27. PC, 1828. Keeper of State Papers, 1826-54. Ecclesiastical Commissioner, 1830-54. A. Aspinall (ed.), *The Diary of Henry Hobhouse* (London: Home & van Thal, 1947) p. 12. Hobhouse (whose diary runs from 1820 to 1827) is less fun than Mrs Arbuthnot but especially knowledgeable on Home Office matters.

The general election was held between 6 March and 14 April. The Catholic Emancipation question was quiescent, with economic distress, high taxes, unrest and the ministerial reaction to it the main issues. The results saw only 87 new Members overall, with the government gaining a few seats, although short of its 1812 position. Liverpool wrote to Canning on 23 March:

> the public feeling has certainly been much more strongly with us than at the last general election. . . . The [Six Acts] are decidedly popular and scarcely any of the opposition have brought them forward as a ground of attack, while they have been most serviceable to many of our friends. The Whig party has shown itself very contemptible, and it appears clearer every day that there are but two national parties in the country: the church and king party, and the radicals. The latter however are become truly formidable.[10]

During the election campaign, the last major outburst of unrest occurred, in the Radical War or Scottish Insurrection. On 1 April a committee in Glasgow called for a national strike, which occurred in much of central Scotland. Two attempts were made to storm the Carron ironworks, successfully repelled by the Hussars. Then a convoy of prisoners was attacked, again being repelled by the reinforced military. The total casualty list of the week-long disturbances was around nine dead. Sidmouth's Home Office agents had infiltrated the committee, arrested several ringleaders and arranged to reinforce the military presence before the riots began. Three ringleaders of the unrest were executed and another fifteen sentenced to transportation.

April saw Liverpool's most determined attempt to head off the Queen Caroline problem. Alarmed by the news that she was coming towards England, the Cabinet drafted a proposal to be presented to her, by which she would receive £50,000 per annum for life and would be paid the honours due to her as Queen, provided she remained out of the country. This memorandum was presented to Brougham, who was acting as her lawyer, but Brougham did not present it to her as he had undertaken. When he finally met the Queen at St Omer, he discovered that she had fallen under the influence of a Radical city alderman Matthew Wood[11] and was determined to come to Britain to assert her rights. On 5 June she arrived, to be met with rapturous acclaim by the London mob.

---

10. Liverpool to Canning, 25 March 1820, quoted in Fisher, *The History of Parliament, 1820-32, -- Survey V -General Elections -- 1820*
11. Matthew Wood (1768-1843). 1st Baronet from 1837. Radical MP for the City of London, 1817-43. Lord Mayor of London, 1815-17. Inherited share of a fortune of £1 million from Gloucester banker Jemmy Wood (no relation) in 1836, through what was called 'conspiracy and fraud' at the Arches Court in 1839, in a verdict reversed on appeal by Lyndhurst as Lord Chancellor in 1841.

The King's Speech on 27 April pledged to accept a civil list equal to the Prince Regent's 1816 civil list, thus saving some money after George III's death. (Liverpool and the Cabinet had vetoed an increase.) It congratulated the previous parliament on its 'wisdom and firmness' in passing the Six Acts and ended with a wish that social peace should be quickly restored. In his speech on the Address, Liverpool hinted that he might partly agree with Lansdowne on the possibility of moving towards free trade and then expressed his satisfaction that the 'middle orders' had evinced respect for the laws in being willing as jurors to convict rioters.

The lapse of time since the war was producing movement on foreign affairs. On 5 May 1820, Castlereagh produced a State Paper, already agreed with the Cabinet, discussing what the government should do with respect to Spain. There King Ferdinand VII had been forced by an army revolt to restore the liberal 1812 constitution, generally against the wishes of most of his subjects. It was likely that France, at least, and the reactionary Powers might wish to intervene to support Ferdinand and might call on the Quintuple/Holy Alliance to act.

Castlereagh summed up the problem:

> There can be no doubt of the general danger which menaces more or less the stability of all existing Governments, from the Principles which are afloat . . . but the notion of revising, limiting or regulating the course of such experiments, either by Foreign Council or by Foreign Force, would be as dangerous to avow as it would be impossible to execute.

Accordingly, British policy should be to resist a further Congress, which might lead to intervention in Spain, and instead maintain friendly relations with the other Alliance powers from a distance.[12]

On 16 May a petition from Birmingham was presented to the House, complaining of the depressed state of trade, and Lansdowne moved for an inquiry into the complaint. Liverpool accepted the inquiry but objected to a subsequent claim that the government ought to do something about the depression:

> This I will say, that in political economy far more danger is to be apprehended from doing too much than from not interfering at all. A reference to the Statute Book will show that attempts to cure supposed evils have been the cause of great mischief. . . . Inconsiderate propositions, in such cases, from individuals are dangerous, but if brought forward by the executive government, they become ten times more dangerous.[13]

12. State Paper, 5 May 1820, printed in A. Aspinall and E.A. Smith (eds), *English Historical Documents: Vol. XI: 1783-1832* (London: Routledge, 2nd ed. 1996) pp. 1088-96.

13. T.C. Hansard, *The Parliamentary Debates, New Series, Commencing with the Accession*

The House then discussed a motion from Stanhope for providing employment for the poor via public works programmes, for example, cultivating waste lands and restricting the use of labour-saving machinery. To this Liverpool responded that:

> with the exception of the benevolent intentions entertained by my noble friend of benefiting the poor in the first place, and the country in the second, there is not a single position in his speech to which I am not prepared to give my most direct and unqualified disapprobation; for the propositions which my noble friend has maintained go to subvert the whole political economy of the country, and to make an entire change in the whole of its commercial relations.

McConnel and Co mills, Manchester. The Industrial Revolution in full swing; this mill had 5 thousand employees and was powered by Boulton & Watt engines.

Liverpool continued by deprecating the attempt to separate the manufacturing interest from the agricultural; the economy needed both, and they were interconnected:

> Manufactures have made great and rapid strides during the times in which it has been our fate to live and have raised the country to a degree of power and glory which it could never have obtained without them. In what manner have they made that progress? By restrictions upon agriculture? Most assuredly not; for when had they ever been supported in defiance of it? Agriculture, on the contrary, has been

of George IV, Vol. 1, cols 394-95 (16 May 1820).

> benefited by the increased circulation of manufactures, for is there any man who made a fortune by them who does not invest such of his capital as he can withdraw from his business in landed property; or if he does not so invest it himself, who is not desirous that it should be so invested, for greater security, by the heirs who succeed to it?

As for protection, manufactures had been protected, but so had agriculture by the Corn Laws. Investing additional capital in waste lands was counterproductive, since the current agricultural depression was the result of overproduction from cultivating waste lands during the war:

> I myself think, that if were to proceed to cultivate more waste lands, we would double, treble, quadruple, nay quintuple the present agricultural distress. . . . Several of the noble Lords whom I am now addressing are themselves agriculturalists, and well aware how small are the profits at present derived from agricultural pursuits: I myself, who sometimes engage in them, partly for health, and partly for amusement, know them to be so from my own experience. . . . Indeed, I would ask you, whether it is consistent with the dignity of government, to descend to speculations in land?

As for restricting machinery:

> I will take the opportunity of telling you that, next to the spirit of her people, England is indebted for her commercial power and greatness to the inventions which this people have made in machinery. It has given, as it were, legs to the lame and sight to the blind: it has inspired the dull with enterprise, and to the enterprising has given additional energy; it has placed the country, despite all its disadvantages, on a level with the most favoured nations, and has enabled its merchants, who pay a heavy price for labour, to compete with other nations, who pay but a trifle for it.

Liverpool then instanced Watt,[14] Boulton[15] and Arkwright[16] as:

> men who were as useful to their country, in their generation, as any of the legislators of old were in theirs. . . . Let him visit our manufacturing towns, for instance, Birmingham; and he will see the

14. James Watt (1736-1819). Invented the steam engine with separate condenser, as well as the concept of horsepower.
15. Matthew Boulton (1728-1809). Ironmaster and partner, with James Watt (1736-1819), in the development of steam-powered manufacturing.
16. Sir Richard Arkwright (1732-92). Invented the spinning frame. Known as the 'father of the modern factory system'. Knighted, 1786. High Sheriff of Derbyshire, 1787.

> greatest inventions matured, and brought to perfection, by those whom he might consider as the meanest and most abject of mankind, but who are, notwithstanding, daily rising from the humble situation in which Providence has originally placed them, to wealth and honour, and eminence in the state.[17]

Some days later a Lords debate initiated the move towards free trade that would prove the principal British economic policy of the next 40 years and culminate in the 1860 Cobden-Chevalier Treaty. The debate was precipitated by a merchants' petition to the House of Commons, calling for free trade, drawn up by economist Thomas Tooke[18] and presented by Alexander Baring on 8 May. Before then, the petition had been presented to Liverpool, Vansittart, Robinson and Herries at Fife House, by Tooke and a deputation of merchants led by Samuel Thornton,[19] a director of the Bank of England, and brother of the noted monetarist Henry Thornton, by then deceased.

As Tooke wrote:

> Lord Liverpool read the Petition aloud, sentence by sentence, very distinctly, and then addressed himself to the deputation in these words: 'Gentlemen – there is not a principle, not a sentiment, in the Paper that I have now read, in which I do not entirely and most cordially concur, and if I had to legislate for this country *de novo*, or for a country like the United States of America, having little or no public debt, these are the principles on which I should act. But in this country, which is burthened with so heavy a Debt; in which so many vested interests have grown up and are so connected and complicated with the existing commercial system, the case is very different; and the question of any change in that system ought not to be approached but with the utmost caution. I cannot, therefore on the part of Government, hold out the prospect of any great or immediate alteration.'

The merchants' deputation then asked for a select committee of the House of Commons to consider their petition and after a few days' reflection Liverpool sent a message agreeing to this. Tooke, a generation later, gave full credit to Liverpool and his government for the move towards free trade, contradicting the popular belief that Peel's 1841-46 government was responsible.

---

17. Hansard, *The Parliamentary Debates, New Series*, Vol. 1, cols 417-22 (16 May 1820).
18. Thomas Tooke (1774-1858). Economist and businessman. Governor of the Royal Exchange Corporation, 1840-52. Author of *A History of Prices and of the State of the Circulation During the Years 1793-1856*, 6 vols (London: Longman, Orme, Brown, Green & Longmans, 1838-1857).
19. Samuel Thornton (1754-1838). MP for Kingston upon Hull and Surrey, 1784-1812. Governor of the Bank of England, 1799-1801.

In the Lords' debate on 20 May Lansdowne, the most economics-minded of the Whigs, who had been shown the merchants' petition, proposed that the Lords establish a committee to examine the means of extending and securing the country's foreign trade. He began by theorising, contradicting Say's[20] Law, that the current distress was due to a surplus of labour, which had been overemployed during the war. He proposed a removal of import prohibitions (of which there were few) and a relaxation of the Navigation Acts, so that European produce could be brought to Britain by third-country ships. Duties on Scandinavian timber should be removed, since the war that had occasioned them was over. Duties on French wines and silks should be reduced, despite the hardship to Portuguese vintners and the Spitalfields silk weavers.

Lansdowne expounded on the benefits of freeing trade in general, pointing out that the opening of the India trade to free competition in 1813 had employed 4,720 seamen in the trade, whereas the East India Company had only employed 2,550. Moreover, the Americans had been gaining market share in the Canton tea trade from the East India Company monopoly of that trade. Finally, British trade with the United States had increased annually since American independence from £3 million to £30 million; Britain should therefore open trade with the rebelling Spanish colonies in South America to gain a huge trade.

In reply, Liverpool set out the country's economic situation and his thoughts on trade policy. He first praised Lansdowne's speech, emphasising the importance of internal and external trade and agreeing that agricultural, commercial and manufacturing interests could never be separated when considering the health of the whole economy. He proposed that the committee, if established, should quickly decide what it would not do, to minimise economic uncertainty and agitation.

Liverpool examined the consumption of tea, coffee, malt and spirits, on which duty was charged, and showed there was a slight increase in 1819-20 over the average of the previous three years. Whatever local distress there may be, this proved that the general welfare had not declined. However, exports had declined from an average £46 million in 1816-18 to £38 million in 1819, still higher than the best years of the war and 50 per cent more than in 1792. On close examination, half the fall-off was due to a decline in exports to the United States and the remainder mostly to slackening in the previously overexpanded trade to the East Indies.

Liverpool agreed with Lansdowne on the advantages in principle of free trade:

---

20. Jean-Baptiste Say (1767-1832). French economist, author of *Traité d'économie politique* (1803). Author of Say's Law. Published *De l'Angleterre et des Anglais* (1815). Co-founder of École spéciale de commerce et d'industrie, 1819, the world's first business school.

> I can entertain no doubt of what would have been the great advantages to the civilized world, if the system of unrestricted trade had been acted upon by every nation, from the earliest period of its commercial intercourse with its neighbours. If to those advantages there could have been any exceptions, I am persuaded that they would have been but few. . . . But my lords, we are now in a situation in which . . . it is impossible for us, or for any country in the world, but the United States of America, to act unreservedly on that principle. The commercial relations of the European world have been long established and cannot suddenly be departed from.

He pointed out that universal free trade would wreck British agriculture, which had grown up under a different system: 'To do so would be to unhinge the whole property of the country.' As for the Corn Laws, the average price of corn in 1815-20 was 78s 5d a quarter, which suggested that the Corn Laws' protective limit of 80 shillings a quarter had been well chosen and was working properly. He recommended that no change in them should be made. Similarly, no change should be made in the currency question that had been decided the previous year.

Liverpool then turned to the general subject of protection, pointing out that both agriculture and industry had enjoyed considerable tariff and other protection. Sometimes this had become unnecessary: 'The cotton manufacture, for instance, in which we have acquired so great a superiority over other nations, need not fear any thing from an abolition of all protection.' Woollen manufacture was similarly strong but, on the other hand, silk manufacture was so artificial in Britain that any removal of protection might kill it altogether, extinguishing the livelihood of 50,000 employees. Similarly, Irish linens, Ireland's principal manufacture, would be greatly damaged by full free trade. However fine the principle, Liverpool would not institute it where 'a great, immediate and positive evil may be incurred'. As for prohibitions, Liverpool agreed they should go but the protective duty that replaced them would normally be so high as to prevent significant trade.

Liverpool welcomed the idea of examining opportunities for freeing trade. The warehousing system, for example, had been set up by Pitt and should be extended, while all transit duties should be abolished. He agreed with Lansdowne that the timber and wine duties should be examined but cautioned that trade with France had in 1787-92, when freed, been only equivalent to that with Spain or Portugal, far below what would have been expected given France's size.

As for the East Indies trade, machinery had made British muslins half the price of Indian muslins in India but the market had been glutted in 1818, leading to a decline in 1819. China on the other hand was a largely closed market and its opening was a matter for the Chinese government. However,

Liverpool did propose to introduce legislation whereby trade from India would be opened to every country in the world, without the goods having to pass through Britain or Malta, as previously.

Liverpool ended by concurring with Lansdowne's motion, with the caveat that he believed the benefits likely to be less than Lansdowne expected. He added:

> there is nothing which alarms me so much, as a meddling disposition on the art of the legislature with reference to these subjects, upon insufficient grounds; a continual tampering with great questions, a change of regulation, session after session, to comply with temporary emergency, partial interests or unreasonable clamour. . . . Under such a course of policy, neither the merchants of this country, nor those of foreign nations, will be able to confide in us; and our distresses, instead of being relieved, will be multiplied ten-fold.[21]

Following Liverpool's speech, a Select Committee of the House of Commons was appointed, chaired by Wallace. In its report, Wallace outlined the existing state of distress and recommended for its relief the greatest practicable measure of free trade, including the relaxation of the navigation laws, the extension of the warehousing system and the simplification of the laws relating to commerce.

Liverpool's speech turned British economic policy decisively towards the removal of trade restrictions. It demonstrates that the 'liberal Toryism' of the 1820s was, except in foreign policy, entirely independent of Canning's advent.

Liverpool was truly regarded as the indispensable man of the Cabinet, as Wellesley-Pole said to Robert Plumer Ward:[22]

> Lord Liverpool could not exist out of office, and never would resign, but even if he were willing, and were to state to his colleagues that he thought the King might be more inclined to them without him, they would not permit it, and would all think it right to follow him.[23]

Regrettably, the second half of 1820 would be devoted to the question of Queen Caroline, which weakened Liverpool's position with the King, his Cabinet and the public. His resilience was not helped by Louisa suffering another prolonged and serious bout of illness during the summer, which was to lead to her death the following year.

21. Hansard, *The Parliamentary Debates, New Series*, Vol. 1, cols 546-65 (Lansdowne), cols 565-94 (Liverpool) (26 May 1820).
22. Robert Plumer Ward (1765-1846). MP for Cockermouth and Haslemere, 1802-6, 1807-23. Clerk of the Ordnance, 1811-23. Barrister, novelist and diarist.
23. Quoted in Gash, *Lord Liverpool*, p. 192.

On 6 June Liverpool presented a message from the King announcing Caroline's arrival in England (the day before) and presenting each House with a green bag of papers, purporting to contain his evidence of Caroline's adultery, for Parliament's consideration. That arrival, and the riots in her support, caused Royal consternation and the postponement of the Coronation, which had been due on 1 August. Liverpool then proposed a secret committee of fifteen lords to examine the evidence against the Queen and devise the appropriate measure. After Lansdowne had objected to the secret committee, because the House could not take judicial notice of the matter, Liverpool expanded on this, saying, if the Queen had committed high treason, only a court could determine it, but the best legal opinion held that adultery abroad was not high treason. Since no crime was likely to be proved, the matter was a civil one, and Parliament would be acting legislatively not judicially. The secret committee could then determine whether a Bill of Pains and Penalties was appropriate.

The following day, Liverpool proposed to proceed to a ballot, and a Whig motion for further delay was defeated by 108 votes to 29. The secret committee's first meeting was postponed several times for negotiations to see whether the Queen might leave the country.

Vansittart presented his Budget on 19 June. He began (extraordinarily to modern eyes) by apologising for presenting financial matters when the House's attention was directed elsewhere. Army expenditure was budgeted at £9.4 million, up from £8.7 million, due to the augmentation of the forces to deal with the unrest of 1819. Naval expenditure was also up, to £6.6 million, with 2,000 extra marines raised for garrison duties. Total non-debt expenditure at £19.3 million was thus up by £0.8 million from 1819 but the interest on Exchequer bills had been reduced by £0.5 million, offsetting this.

In addition, a further £9 million of Exchequer bills would be converted into funded debt, of which £5 million derived from the 1819 agreement with the Bank of England. Total unfunded debt would thus be reduced from £39.5 million to £30.5 million. To fund the deficit, he proposed to take a £12 million loan from the sinking fund and sell £5 million of debt to the public. The net surplus in 1819 was £1 million below expectations because of the depression; in 1820 Vansittart budgeted for a surplus of £3.5 million which he expected to increase to £5 million in a less depressed year.[24]

On modern figures, gross income increased by £1.8 million in 1820 while expenditure also increased by £0.9 million, mostly from additional debt charges, for a net surplus of £1.5 million, compared to £0.6 million the previous year.[25]

---

24. Hansard, *The Parliamentary Debates, New Series*, Vol. 1, cols 1161-68 (19 June 1820).
25. Mitchell, *British Historical Statistics*, pp. 581 (Income), 587 (Expenditure). The year-end is 5 January so, to get the figures for the (approximate) calendar year 1820, you should use the 1821 figures in the tables.

The 'Queen's Matter' then swung into full gear. On 22 June Wilberforce,[26] regarded as the voice of morality, proposed motions in the Commons imploring the Queen to accept the terms offered her. These were passed by 391 to 124 but the Queen refused to compromise.

The Queen's arrival and agitation had again raised unrest in the country, especially against George IV. There was unrest among the Household Guards, which naturally provoked concern, so Wellington wrote a memorandum to Liverpool on it. He suggested that the chain of command be simplified so that the Guards received orders from fewer sources, and that a London police force be established so that the government would not have to rely on the Guards to keep order there.[27] For the Queen's trial Liverpool made London's parishes recruit additional special constables, while the Home Counties reserved their yeomanry to march to London if needed.[28]

On 4 July the secret committee reported to the Lords, recommending a legislative proceeding, so Liverpool announced his intention to bring in a Bill of Pains and Penalties. He believed it had been the duty of ministers to prevent a public investigation but the Queen's arrival in England had left no middle course remaining, making an investigation inevitable.[29] The following day Liverpool introduced the Bill, explaining that impeachment was not available since no crime under English law had been committed. Although it was not a bill of divorce, its effect would be the same; it would deprive the Queen of her honours and privileges and dissolve her marriage to the King.

On 6 July, the Queen's petition was officially received and defended by Brougham. Liverpool proposed setting the second reading of the Bill for 17 August, that being the earliest date on which four of the twelve Law Lords would be present, and proposed that all voting should be in person and not by proxy, to ensure that peers had heard the relevant evidence.

In the interim, the Capital Punishment Act of 1820, the first attempt to reduce the number of offences requiring the death penalty, came before the House of Lords. Eldon objected, first to the removal of the offences under the 1723 Black Act, which specified over two hundred capital crimes, then to the removal of the death penalty for cutting down trees, killing cattle and cutting through the banks of rivers, on the ground that severe offences of these kinds, cutting down an entire forest, say, should deserve the death penalty.

Liverpool then raised another objection:

---

26. William Wilberforce, 1759-1833. MP, 1780-1825. Leader in the movement to abolish the slave trade, 1807, and slavery, 1833. Close friend of Pitt.
27. Wellington Memorandum to Liverpool, June 1820, quoted in Wellington, *Despatches, Correspondence*, Vol. 1, pp. 127-29.
28. Liverpool letter to Wellington, 31 July, quoted in ibid., p. 141.
29. Hansard, *The Parliamentary Debates, New Series*, Vol. 2, cols 165, 173-74 (4 July 1820).

> Several years ago, when transportation meant either to be transported to the worst and most noxious climate in the world, that of Africa, or to the British colonies in North America, where the parties transported became indentured servants, and were in fact treated worse than the negro slaves, this punishment served to excite some degree of terror. Now, however, the system was entirely changed, and the colonial office was besieged with applications without end (many more than could be complied with) from persons wishing to have liberty to settle in the delightful country and under the fine climate of New South Wales. . . . My opinion is, the inquiry has begun at the wrong end, and that we should first direct our attention to the discovery of some secondary punishment, the terror of which might serve in a number of cases as a substitute for the terror of death.[30]

The bill was passed with Eldon's amendments.

House of Lords during the trial of Queen Caroline, 1820, Sir George Hayter.

After a three-week adjournment, Liverpool moved to bring in the Bill of Pains and Penalties, with all peers compelled to attend on penalty of a £500 fine and imprisonment in the Tower.[31] There then followed three weeks of testimony from witnesses, at which Liverpool was present throughout, while confining himself to responses on points of order or decorum.

On 7 September Liverpool intervened to tell the House that the King no longer wished the Bill of Pains and Penalties to operate automatically as a

30. Ibid., Vol. 2, cols 526-27 (18 July 1820).
31. For the non-attendance penalty, Bamford and Wellington, *The Journal of Mrs. Arbuthnot, 1820-1832*, Vol. 1, p. 28.

divorce. If the House from religious or other scruples objected to the divorce provision, he would be happy to withdraw it. Liverpool had presented his view (and the Cabinet's) that the divorce clause must be abandoned because it could not pass the Lords, let alone the Commons, in a letter to the King; the King eventually agreed, but bore an increased grudge against Liverpool.[32]

The House then adjourned until 3 October to allow Brougham to prepare the defence case, which lasted another nineteen sittings. Three further days were devoted to the defence summing up and two more days by the Crown's lawyers in reply. Liverpool again intervened on procedural matters, somewhat more frequently than while the prosecution's case was being presented.

After the defence and the summings up, the House reconvened to consider the second reading and Liverpool made another major address. He reviewed the mass of sordid evidence for and against the Queen's adultery, with considerable fairmindedness, but came down firmly on the side of her repeated adultery with the servant Bartolomeo Pergami:[33] 'On this view of the subject, my Lords, I am perfectly ready to decide as if I were in a jury-box, and to declare that if ever there was case of adulterous intercourse clearly and fully established by circumstantial evidence, it is the case before your Lordships.'

Liverpool then went on to discuss the expediency of the measure. As a Bill of Pains and Penalties, it followed the course of a normal divorce bill, with no additional punishment for the adultery. Rejecting it would be a triumph of guilt. Liverpool claimed, finally, to be attempting 'to do justice, in the most important cause, between the Crown, the Queen and the Country'.[34] The second reading of the Bill was carried by 123 votes by 95, after an opposition vote to retain the divorce clause (thereby weakening the Bill's chances of passage) was carried by a majority of 64.

On 10 November the third reading of the Bill was passed by only 108 votes to 99, with several peers objecting to the clause granting the King a divorce. After the vote, Liverpool, realising that a Bill that had barely passed the Lords had no chance in the Commons, moved that the Bill be reconsidered on this day six months, thus effectively killing it.

The House was then adjourned until January. London, Dublin, Edinburgh and many other towns were illuminated at the news of the Bill's withdrawal. After proceedings ended, Liverpool arranged for the Queen to receive an unconditional £50,000 per annum but refused her request for a Royal Palace and did not include her name in the liturgy. Fortunately, the Queen's service

32. The letter is given in Aspinall, *The Letters of King George IV, 1812-30*, Vol. 2, pp. 361-63 (Liverpool's letter), 363-64 and 366 (the King's responses).
33. Bartolomeo Pergami or Bergami (1783-1842). Servant hired by Queen Caroline in 1814, who became her major-domo and, probably, lover.
34. Hansard, *The Parliamentary Debates, New Series*, Vol. 3, cols 1574-1619 (3 and 4 November 1820).

of thanksgiving at St Paul's and her attempts to subvert the government fell flat once her allowance was settled and popular infatuation with her died down thereafter.

The King was furious at the Bill's abandonment and informed Liverpool that he would 'take measures for the formation of a new Administration'.[35] He offered the aged and intemperate Grenville the premiership, but in vain.[36] While there were ministers who were more sympathetic to the King than Liverpool, they had no hope of forming a government, while a Whig administration, the available alternative, would be even more unsympathetic. Wellington, another potential supporter, wrote to the King a strong memorandum advising him to retain the incumbent ministry.[37] Liverpool was thus in little danger of imminent dismissal.

The stress on Liverpool of the Queen's trial, allied to Louisa's illness, was immense. As he wrote to Canning in September: 'In the whole course of my life I do not recollect to have undergone such fatigue as during the three weeks of the proceedings in the House of Lords.'[38] Mrs Arbuthnot described the proceedings as 'all far too disgusting to be more than just mentioned here'[39] and one tends to agree.

The entire saga was a huge waste of Parliament's and Liverpool's time; it also prejudiced the King against him for over a year. Wellington described Liverpool as being 'fretful and ill-tempered', while at a critical cabinet meeting Arbuthnot described him as 'in a phrenzy, and his rage got so high that for a time it stopped all deliberation'.[40] Liverpool also wrote to Arbuthnot:

> I feel I have few, very few publick friends in the world. I wish only to be thoroughly and honourably released. I will not abandon others but I am by no means sure that they will not abandon me and leave me to be the sole victim of the present clamour.[41]

This intemperateness, irritability and pessimism had not previously been a problem for Liverpool but similar complaints were repeated fairly often in the years ahead. They are a clear sign of the toll that the five hugely unpleasant months of the Queen's trial had taken.

From this point, there was a reduction in Liverpool's participation in House of Lords debates. He had taken an active role in the debates surrounding the

35. Aspinall, *The Letters of King George IV, 1812-30*, Vol. 2, p. 380.
36. Gash, *Lord Liverpool*, p. 166.
37. Wellington Memorandum to the King, dated December 1820, quoted in Wellington, *Despatches, Correspondence*, Vol. 1, pp. 150-63.
38. Liverpool letter to Canning, 12 September 1820, quoted in Yonge, *The Life and Administration of Robert Banks Jenkinson*, Vol. 3, pp. 106-8.
39. Bamford and Wellington, *The Journal of Mrs. Arbuthnot, 1820-1832*, Vol. 1, p. 33.
40. Ibid., pp. 45-46, 20 October 1820, and p. 52, 10 November 1820.
41. Quoted in Gash, *Lord Liverpool*, p. 166.

Queen's trial and had been among the most frequent speakers in the House throughout his premiership, but from 1821 onwards his interventions were less. There were still set-piece speeches, but they were fewer, and the day-to-day interventions to speed debate or make a Government point were less frequent.

In the middle of the Queen's trial, Liverpool had been asked about foreign policy; specifically, Britain's reaction to the July revolution in Naples (where the military had overthrown King Ferdinand I's government and installed the Spanish 1812 constitution)[42] and to the other Quintuple Alliance powers' apparent intention to suppress it by force. He responded that the revolution in Naples differed considerably from that in Spain: 'This difference consists of the state of the Sicilian dominions, for it is notorious, that there subsists a difference between the two members of that monarchy, and it does not appear that Sicily has yet acquiesced in the system of government established at Naples.' However, it was no part of the government's policy to interfere with the internal affairs of other states, and the government was not a party to any engagements for that purpose.[43]

The Congress of Troppau met on 20 October, without Castlereagh, with his half-brother Lord Stewart[44] as an observer. Given the Congress's wish to focus on Naples and Britain's resolution to have nothing to do with military intervention there, this was perhaps inevitable. France, in a liberal phase under Richelieu, was also without a plenipotentiary, but as well as the three eastern powers' foreign ministers, Alexander I and Francis I were present in person and Frederick William III was represented by his heir the future Frederick William IV.

In a series of conferences from which Stewart was excluded, Metternich steered the other delegates to the Troppau Protocol. This declared that no new principle was intended beyond those agreed in 1814-15, but – centrally – proclaimed that:

---

42. As Sir William A'Court, the Ambassador, wrote: 'A kingdom in the highest degree flourishing and happy, under the mildest of Governments, and by no means oppressed by the weight of taxation, crumbles before a handful of insurgents that half a battalion of good soldiers would have crushed in an instant.' A'Court to Castlereagh, 6 July 1820, in Londonderry, *Memoirs and Correspondence of Viscount Castlereagh*, Vol. 12, p. 279.
43. Hansard, *The Parliamentary Debates, New Series*, Vol. 3, cols 256-57 (5 October 1820). The two disputing members of the Neapolitan royal family were: Ferdinand IV (1751-1825), King of Naples, 1759-1799, 1799-1806, 1815-16, King of Sicily, 1759-1816, King Ferdinand I of the Two Sicilies, 1816-25; and his son, Francis I (1777-1830), King of the Two Sicilies, 1825-30.
44. Charles William Stewart (name changed to Vane from 1819) (1778-1854). 1st Baron Stewart (UK) from 1814. 3rd Marquess of Londonderry (Ireland) from 1822. 1st Earl Vane (UK) from 1823. MP (Ireland) for Thomastown and Londonderry, 1796-1801. MP for Londonderry, 1801-14. Army, 1791-1812. Adjutant-General in Peninsula, 1809-12. Under-Secretary for War and the Colonies, 1807-9. Minister to Prussia, 1813-14. Ambassador to Austria, 1814-23. Lord Lieutenant of Durham, 1842-54. KG, 1853.

> States, which have undergone a change of government due to revolution, the result of which threaten other states, *ipso facto* cease to be members of the European Alliance, and remain excluded from it until their situation gives guarantees for legal order and stability. If, owing to such alterations, immediate danger threatens other states the powers bind themselves, by peaceful means, or if need be, by arms, to bring back the guilty state into the bosom of the Great Alliance.

In its limitation of intervention, the Troppau Protocol expressed an important principle of foreign policy, highly relevant today. It stated that intervention was to be undertaken, not to overthrow governments of which the Great Alliance disapproved, but only to restore or maintain governments satisfactory to it. Considered as a limitation of intervention, the Troppau Protocol made sense; considered as an encouragement of it, the Protocol was more problematic from a British viewpoint. Castlereagh summed up the problem in a letter to his brother:

> It is singular . . . that it should have occurred to the three Courts to reform an Alliance, which has been found to adapt itself with great facility to all the exigences of affairs, upon the exploded doctrines of divine right and passive obedience. They might have foreseen that the House of Hanover could not well maintain the principles upon which the House of Stuart forfeited the throne. . . . We cannot adhere to their principles, and if they will be theorists, we must act in separation.[45]

The final upheaval of 1820 was the resignation of Canning, accomplished by a letter to the King stating that he differed with the government on the Queen Caroline issue, believing the Queen's name should be included in the liturgy. Mrs Arbuthnot, who hated Canning, rejoiced at this news, but it worried Liverpool, who believed him an asset to the government and a major danger if outside it.

Liverpool offered the Board of Control to Peel, who did not wish to re-join the government in its apparent weakness, so he gave the office to Bragge Bathurst as an interim measure. A certain amount of persuasion was needed; as Liverpool wrote to him: 'In the state to which the whole business now stands, it cannot be surprising that persons not connected with the Government should be unwilling to take responsible offices.'[46]

By the end of the year conversations with the country gentlemen, for example, a letter from Stuart Wortley,[47] convinced Liverpool that the clouds

45. Castlereagh letter to Sir Charles Stewart, 16 December 1820, quoted in Kissinger, *A World Restored*, p. 266.
46. Quoted in Aspinall, *The Letters of King George IV, 1812-30*, Vol. 2, p. 401, note 1.
47. Quoted in Yonge, *The Life and Administration of Robert Banks Jenkinson*, Vol. 3, pp. 114-19.

were lifting and that the government could go on. Liverpool's own equanimity had returned: Mrs Arbuthnot writes of him beating everybody in a house-party game of charades, though he did not participate in Blind Man's Buff.

Economically, in 1820 recovery took hold. The harvest was bountiful, perhaps a third above normal, which caused the price of corn to decline to 54 shillings by May 1821 and corn stocks to be held back, affecting prices and sales in the following two years.[48] Cotton exports rebounded to their 1818 level, while iron and steel exports recovered about half their 1819 declines. Meanwhile, prices continued to fall, which considerably improved workers' real wages. That, and the incipient recovery in employment, explain the decline in unrest.

The King, needing all the support he could get, opened Parliament in person in 1821. He began by thanking Parliament for the Civil List – there had been some criticism that the adjournment had come without any such acknowledgement. He then drew attention to the peaceful state of the world (with the partial exception of Italy) and congratulated himself on the improvement in trade and the revenue in the second half of 1820.

In reply, Liverpool contrasted the improved state of manufacturing with the worsened position in agriculture. There had been no corn imports in the past two years, so declining agricultural prices resulted from increasing domestic production. However, legislation was not required. Liverpool reiterated the government's desire for peace and its extreme reluctance to interfere in the internal arrangements of other states. In a revolutionary situation 'to interfere would be exercising a judgement without the means of forming a correct one'. Finally, the budget position had improved further: 'I feel pleasure in stating, that in the fifth year of peace we can go on without additional funding – a degree of good fortune which does not happen to other countries, which are frequently applied to as subjects of disadvantageous comparison.'[49] The Address was agreed to without dissent.

Before Liverpool spoke in the Lords on foreign policy, the Congress of Laibach (modern Ljubljana) had made the position even more complicated. Castlereagh had approved the presence at Laibach of Ferdinand I of Naples, but not the interventionist Troppau Protocol, which was supposed to govern the Laibach proceedings; hence he did not attend but sent Stewart as an observer. In his instructions to Stewart, he made a good point:

> I still think Metternich has weakened his position by making it a European instead of an Austrian question. . . . He would have carried public opinion (especially in this country) much more with him, had

48. Tooke, *A History of Prices*, Vol. 2, pp. 81-83. Export figures taken from Gayer, Rostow and Schwartz, *The Growth and Fluctuation of the British Economy, 1790-1850*, Vol. 1, pp. 140-70.

49. Hansard, *The Parliamentary Debates, New Series*, Vol. 4, cols 12-17 (23 January 1821).

> he stood simply on the offensive character of a Carbonari government to every Italian state, than embarking himself on the boundless ocean on which he has preferred to sail. . . . But our friend Metternich, with all his merit, prefers a complicated negotiation to a bold and rapid stroke.[50]

Castlereagh set out the official British position in a circular to British ministers abroad. He criticised the principles of the Troppau Protocol:

> Their adoption would inevitably sanction, and in the hands of less beneficent Monarchs might lead to, a much more frequent and extensive interference in the internal affairs of States, than [the British government is] persuaded is intended by the August Parties from which they proceed, or can be reconcilable either with the general interest, or with the efficient authority and dignity of Independent Sovereigns.[51]

At Laibach, Metternich's desire to get Europe behind a general principle of intervention severely damaged the Alliance. During the Congress, which lasted until 12 May, Austria occupied Naples and suppressed a Piedmontese revolt, both with the consent of the Congress. At the end of the conference, the three eastern powers reissued the Troppau Protocol. Meanwhile, Alexander I received news of Alexander Ypsilantis'[52] invasion of modern Romania, beginning the Greek War of Independence. Based on the Troppau principles, Alexander repudiated the Greek revolt, in which he was backed later in the year by Castlereagh (by then Marquess of Londonderry), who described it in a letter to the Czar as 'forming a branch of that organized spirit of insurrection which is systematically propagating itself through Europe, and which explodes wherever the hand of the governing power, from whatever cause, is enfeebled'.[53]

Liverpool's first foreign policy speech came in February. He referred to Castlereagh's circular, and said it merely reiterated the view that the government had held since the 1815 peace conferences. He then defended the principle that intervention was possible only in special cases:

---

50. Castlereagh to Stewart, 5 January 1821, *Memoirs and Correspondence of Viscount Castlereagh*, Vol. 12, pp. 340-41.
51. Foreign Office, British and Foreign State Papers, 1820-21, Compiled by the Librarian and Keeper of the Papers, (London: HMSO, 1830) pp. 1160-62.
52. Alexander Ypsilantis (1792-1828). Son and grandson of senior Ottoman officials. Colonel in the Russian service, 1812-13, then, 1817, Major-General in the Hussar Division. Elected Head of *Filiki Eteria*, 1820, Greek secret society fomenting independence. Invaded Romania and Wallachia, 1821; after defeat, blamed his men for failure. Imprisoned in Austria, 1823-27, then released at the request of Czar Nicholas I. Died in Vienna, 1828; body now in Athens.
53. Letter to Czar Alexander I, 16 July 1821, in Londonderry, *Memoirs and Correspondence of Viscount Castlereagh*, Vol. 12, pp. 403-8.

> A state cannot say 'We will attack another state, because the conduct of the people forms a bad example.' The right of interference must rest upon a more clear, decisive and intelligible object; because, if a dread of example could give to one country the right to interfere with another, a vicious and depraved state might assume the right of attacking a virtuous community, whose good example was disapproved of by the former.[54]

Liverpool then discussed the specific case of Naples, pointing out that the Whigs never appeared to allow rights to legitimate governments but only to liberal usurpers. King Ferdinand I of the Two Sicilies had reigned for more than 60 years and throughout that time had been a friend to Britain; he also had an estimable personal character. The Spanish rebellion had been a purely national movement, but in Naples the country had split, with Sicily wishing to maintain its ancient constitution.

Ten days later Liverpool returned to the subject, denouncing the Troppau Protocol:

> Never did Russia, Austria and Prussia do a more ill-advised act, than when they put forth that declaration. Till then it might be doubted whether there were two extreme principles in action. But that declaration set forth one extreme principle, the disposition to crush all revolutions, without reference to time, to circumstances, to causes, or to the situations of the nations in which they arose. The other extreme principle, which I am sorry to see manifested in the noble lords opposite is to uphold all revolutions, not looking to their causes or justifications. Revolutions seem to them to be certain good – the name cheers up their hearts.[55]

Britain's policy was neutrality. The Whigs wanted Britain to intervene in the conflicts of Europe, but Britain had not intervened in the partitions of Poland and the Whigs had not urged the country to do so. The country must not put itself in the position of offering up a vain remonstrance, without either becoming a laughing-stock or having to suffer the consequence of its rejection.

The Queen remained an issue, although an early Commons debate on the subject gave the government a majority of 101. Liverpool moved in the Lords for an annuity of £50,000 to be paid to her unconditionally, saying that, since such an annuity had been proposed in her marriage contract to be paid on King's demise, she had at least an equitable claim to it during his lifetime.

54. Hansard, *The Parliamentary Debates, New Series*, Vol. 4, cols 760-71 (19 February 1821).

55. Ibid., cols 1063-65 (2 March 1821).

In March the Queen initiated a correspondence with Liverpool and the King, making three demands. First, she asked to be included in a Royal drawing room reception. Next, she reiterated her demand to be included in the liturgy. Finally, she demanded to be invited to the King's coronation, scheduled for July. To all these requests, Liverpool returned a polite refusal, which he maintained throughout the unpleasant further correspondence. Fortunately, the government's popularity was now improving with the economy, while the Queen's was declining.

George IV was furious with Liverpool for not making the problem go away, abusing him to Wellesley-Pole for three hours in late February.[56] Indeed, for a week, Liverpool was thought about to resign; only the support of his colleagues, notably, Castlereagh, prevented him from doing so. Conversely, for most of the spring the King was determined to turn out Liverpool and the Cabinet but could not detach part of the Cabinet from Liverpool or find an alternative government with support in the Commons.

A Catholic Emancipation Bill with securities on the appointment of bishops introduced by the Irish MP William Plunket[57] passed its Commons third reading by a majority of nineteen on 2 April, reflecting the greater support for Catholic Emancipation in the new Parliament. At this point, Liverpool suggested to Sidmouth accepting the bill and trying to make amendments to it.[58] Liverpool's attitude was that Catholic Emancipation's passage was probably inevitable, although he retained his religious objections to it. By a 'back-channel' letter from Arbuthnot to the King's private secretary, Liverpool had warned the King that Catholic Emancipation was probably inevitable, so the King should not commit himself against it. However, across the country Catholic Emancipation remained highly unpopular in England and Wales; non-elite opinion was far less tolerant than elite opinion.

Liverpool spoke against the Bill at second reading. He objected to the principle of the Bill and hence would vote for it not to go into committee. He did not regard the penal laws against Catholics as part of the anti-Catholic code of the years after 1695, which was 'one of the most nefarious, oppressive and abominable systems that ever disgraced any country' because he regarded the right to political power as separate from the rights to liberty and property. Liverpool believed that the alliance between Church and State established in 1688 was the foundation of the constitution; if you believed that, the bill was

56. Bamford and Wellington, *The Journal of Mrs. Arbuthnot, 1820-1832*, Vol. 1, p. 75, 24 February 1821.

57. William Conyngham Plunket (1764-1854). 1st Baron Plunket from 1827. MP (Ireland) for Charlemont, 1798-1801. MP for Midhurst and Dublin University, 1807, 1812-27. Solicitor General for Ireland, 1803-5. Attorney General for Ireland, 1805-7, 1822-27. Chief Justice of the Irish Common Pleas, 1827-30. Lord Chancellor of Ireland, 1830-34, 1835-41.

58. Gash, *Lord Liverpool*, p. 202.

unacceptable. The establishment had not been settled properly at the time of the Reformation, and it had consequently been overturned twice in fifty years by Puritans and Catholics. Indeed, with the Emancipation Bill, if the heir to the throne were Catholic, he would have an irresistible argument to succeed. He believed granting Catholic Emancipation would do little good for Irish Catholics outside the elite and could irretrievably damage Irish Protestants; thus he would vote against the Bill.[59] The second reading of the Bill lost by 159 votes to 120.

The other major 1821 debate was on the disenfranchisement of the Cornish borough of Grampound for its corruption at the 1818 election. Lord John Russell[60] introduced a Bill in the Commons which transferred Grampound's franchise to the rapidly growing borough of Leeds. The case was notable in being the first constituency completely disenfranchised for delinquency since Maidstone in 1554,[61] as well as the first change to Parliamentary representation in England and Wales since the enfranchisement of Newark in 1673. Previous boroughs where corruption was proved[62] had been enlarged geographically, 'thrown into the hundred' to add uncorrupt electors to the corrupt ones, but that was impracticable in Grampound, because of Cornwall's low population and high density of Parliamentary representation.

Liverpool prepared a memorandum for the Cabinet setting out his view of this question. He began by assuming that Grampound would be disenfranchised, and the representation not 'thrown into the hundred'. However:

> I should then say, that the giving the right of election to the populous manufacturing towns was the worst remedy which could be applied. In the first place, it would be the greatest evil conferred on those towns; it would subject the population to a perpetual factious canvass, which would divert, more or less, the people from their industrious habits, and keep alive a permanent spirit of turbulence and disaffection among them. Against such a measure all the most respectable inhabitants of those towns would, I am convinced, protest.

59. Hansard, *The Parliamentary Debates, New Series*, Vol. 5, cols 339-46 (17 April 1821).
60. John Russell (1792-1878). 1st Earl Russell from 1861. MP for Tavistock, Huntingdonshire, Bandon, Devonshire, Devonshire South, Stroud and City of London, 1813-17, 1818-61. Paymaster of the Forces, 1830-34. Home Secretary, 1835-39. Secretary of State for War and the Colonies, 1839-41. Leader of the House of Commons, 1834, 1835-41, 1852-55. Prime Minister, 1846-52, 1865-66. Foreign Secretary, 1852-53. Lord President of the Council, 1854-55. Secretary of State for the Colonies, 1855. Foreign Secretary, 1859-65.
61. Maidstone appears to have been disenfranchised, not for corruption, but for participation in Wyatt's rebellion.
62. New Shoreham in 1770, Cricklade in 1782 and Aylesbury in 1804 had been enlarged by 'throwing representation into the hundred', as would be East Retford in 1828. The first such disenfranchisement attempt for corruption had been made on Stockbridge in 1693 but it failed, as did a similar attempt in 1793.

Liverpool then pointed out that, when Pitt had moved towards Parliamentary Reform in the 1780s, Manchester and Birmingham could never be induced to petition for it, and the Birmingham leaders to whom he had spoken, while favouring Parliamentary Reform, were opposed to Birmingham returning MPs.

He continued:

> In the next place, I think the proposed transfer [of representation to Leeds] would be the most injurious to the Constitution that could be devised. I do not wish to see more boroughs such as Westminster, Southwark, Nottingham, etc. I believe them to be more corrupt than any other places when seriously contested; and I believe the description of persons who find their way into Parliament through these places are generally those who, from the peculiarity of their station, are the least likely to be steadily attached to the good order of society.

He then explained that throwing the borough into the hundred had the virtue of changing the borough rather than the overall system of representation. However, he would prefer adding to the representation of the larger counties:

> County elections are the least corrupt of any in the kingdom. The representatives of them, if not generally the ablest members of the House, are certainly those who have the greatest stake in the country and may be trusted for the most part in periods of difficulty or danger.
>
> If you destroy something corrupt, the natural course seems to be to substitute something sound and safe in the place of it, and not to prefer adding to those which, taken by themselves, I must consider the great evils of our present system; though I am aware that, to the limited extent in which they now exist, some advantages may be derived from them as part of a mixed and comprehensive representation.

Liverpool ended by suggesting that he would favour a programme of borough reform which eliminated corruption but made no changes in the current proportions of the system, merely substituting pure and well constituted boroughs for corrupt ones.[63]

In the House of Lords, Liverpool spoke at both the first and second readings, as well as making a successful intervention at the Committee stage. On the first reading he reminded the House that he had voted against Parliamentary Reform in 1793 but had supported the disenfranchisement of the (Whig-controlled) borough of Stockbridge,[64] though not that of Barnstaple, where corruption

63. The Memorandum is given in Yonge, *The Life and Administration of Robert Banks Jenkinson*, Vol. 3, pp. 137-39.

64. In 1793 (Stockbridge) and 1819 (Barnstaple). Neither borough was disenfranchised.

had not been adequately proved. The franchise was a great advantage to those who possessed it, but it was a public trust, not a property right. He outlined the reasons why Grampound could not simply be extended but explained that transferring the representation to Leeds would require a voting qualification to be determined – anything close to household suffrage would make it both corrupt and damaging to the constitution. He therefore preferred adding two representatives to the large county of Yorkshire.

At the second reading, Liverpool expanded on the constitution's advantage of every class of electors being represented, which would be damaged by throwing Grampound into the hundred, because of Cornwall's overrepresentation: 'I support the present bill, not because I am a parliamentary reformer, but because I am an enemy to all plans of general reform. I would make no alteration on theoretical principles, but I will never refuse to pay due attention to any abuse which may arise.'

At the Committee stage, Liverpool proposed two amendments, one removing the proposed representation transfer to Leeds and a second transferring representation to Yorkshire. His first amendment won by 60 votes to 34 and his second by 60 votes to 26.[65] The Bill passed both houses, leaving Grampound's 1820 MPs (both Tories) in place for the 1820 Parliament but transferring its representation to Yorkshire for the 1826 election.

By this time, the Bank of England had resumed gold payments without restrictions, accepting the acceleration by a Resolution following a request from Liverpool and Vansittart, with the gold standard coming into force on 1 May 1821. During 1820 the Bank had made large purchases of bullion, helped by favourable exchange rates, and by February 1821 its gold holdings had reached £11.9 million, more than ever before. By the end of the year, the Bank was offering to ship gold to any town in the country, free of charge, in amounts of £3,000 or more – this ensured gold circulated throughout the country and reduced the demand for possibly spurious local bank notes.[66] The classical gold standard then lasted 93 years until 1914, although only after 1870 did other major economies adopt it.

Vansittart's 1821 Budget began by noting that expenditure on the army and navy had declined by £1.6 million, with total expenditure down by £1.8 million. Conversely, income in the first five months of 1821 was running about £240,000 ahead of 1820, and there was also a surplus of £500,000 from the indemnity payments from France, more than budgeted. After the normal sinking fund payments and a loan from the sinking fund, he budgeted a surplus of £3.6 million, well on the way to the £5 million annual surplus he had announced as a target.

---

65. Hansard, *The Parliamentary Debates, New Series*, Vol. 5, cols 629-32 (10 May 1821), cols 696-97 (14 May 1821) and cols 853-58 (21 May 1821).
66. Bank of England, Minutes of the Court of Directors, 20 December 1821 and 31 January 1822.

Vansittart ended by congratulating the House on the success of the great efforts made to resume bullion payments. He then outlined how the first post-war rise in Consols had pushed the economy from the depression of 1816-17 to the ebullience of 1818, and forecast that the recent rise, which was likely to be more sustained, would have a corresponding benefit on economic activity. Finally, he hailed the increased saving among the lower classes, which itself would contribute hugely to greater economic stability as well as to their comfort.[67]

On modern figures, gross public income rose by £1.7 million to £61.6 million in 1821, with most of the increase coming in customs duties. On the other hand, expenditure remained flat at £58.4 million. This left a surplus of £3.2 million, double the previous year and the first of five such substantial surpluses that began to reduce the huge outstanding debt.[68] From this point, fiscal policy became much easier, allowing for modest tax reductions that reinforced the economic recovery. Vansittart, however, who had done all the 'heavy lifting' of raising taxes and cheese-paring spending would enjoy the benefit of this for only one more year as Chancellor.

During the parliamentary session, the opposition had called for further economies of £4 million in public expenditure, which Liverpool felt to be impractical. In July, however, he sent the King a memorandum setting out his plan for economies of £1.59 million, by reducing both the army and navy by 12,000 to 13,000 men and making equivalent economies in ancillary services. Even at this time of high tension between King and minister, the King acquiesced in this plan but made clear his disappointment and expressed his hope (to which Liverpool agreed) that no further such economies would be necessary.[69]

During the spring Liverpool began the delicate task of restructuring his administration. He knew Sidmouth wanted to retire from the Home Office; the session had shown the Commons frontbench woefully short of front-line debating talent; he wanted to promote Peel; he thought a deal was possible with the Grenville faction; and, now that the agitation over Queen Caroline had died down, he wanted to do something for Canning. He would spend the next eighteen months satisfying this complex set of requirements.

After nine years in office, a modern prime minister would have demanded everybody's resignation and reconstituted his ministry wholesale along the lines he preferred, but Liverpool's position was one of '*primus inter pares*' so that option was not available. Nevertheless, he would have done better to have

67. Hansard, *The Parliamentary Debates, New Series*, Vol. 5, cols 1073-87 (1 June 1821).
68. Mitchell, *British Historical Statistics*, pp. 581 (Income) and 587 (Expenditure). The year-end is January 5 so, to get the figures for the (approximate) calendar year 1821, you should use the 1822 figures in the tables.
69. Aspinall, *The Letters of King George IV, 1812-30*, Vol. 2, pp. 449-51 and 452 (Liverpool's letters) and 451 (the King's response.)

brought in more new blood, for example, promoting Palmerston who had languished outside the Cabinet as Secretary at War since 1809. With more new blood in 1821-23, the core of the ministry might have continued more effectively after Liverpool's retirement and Canning's death.

Liverpool toyed with the idea of moving Vansittart to the Board of Control and giving Peel the Exchequer, but this was met with resistance from Castlereagh, who was suspicious of the bumptious and self-promoting Peel. According to Mrs Arbuthnot, Castlereagh felt that Peel 'had never done any thing to entitle him to so high a place as the one proposed'. Interestingly, Liverpool also discussed retiring in favour of Castlereagh, with Canning going to the Foreign Office. Liverpool and Castlereagh both agreed, however, that 'it would not be fair to the country' to offer Wellington a top non-military post.[70]

Liverpool's next shot was a letter to the King setting out an initial reshuffle plan. This had already been stymied by Peel's refusal to accept the Board of Control, which Liverpool thereafter proposed to offer to Grenville's relation, Charles Williams-Wynn, moving Melville to the Home Office and Canning to the Admiralty.

The King, however, objected to any changes in the existing government and further negotiations were then postponed because of the death of Louisa on 12 June. Louisa had been ailing since the previous year but her sudden decline in 1821 and death shocked Liverpool and he retreated from society for several months. She had provided Liverpool with emotional support, a considerable amount of advice and clerical help (copying many of his letters, for example) for 26 years.

Liverpool wrote to Arbuthnot on 13 June saying that the King's objection to Canning was 'personal pique and resentment' and that, by sending him to the Admiralty, Liverpool had chosen one of the offices with the least necessity for personal communication with the monarch. He also accused the King of wanting to keep the government weak so that he could change it easily.[71] Liverpool's colleagues met and agreed to persuade him to carry on and to support him over Canning; Sidmouth delivered this comforting message on 18 June.

Liverpool then left for Gloucestershire for Louisa's funeral, beginning the journey in a *cortège* of over 70 carriages belonging to sympathetic notables, including the Dukes of York and Clarence. The internment took place at Hawkesbury parish church; reportedly Liverpool was 'in an agony of tears as to be quite insensible to every thing that passed about him'[72] and had great difficulty lifting Louisa's emaciated body into the coffin.

---

70. Bamford and Wellington, *The Journal of Mrs. Arbuthnot, 1820-32*, Vol. 1, pp. 82-83, 17 March 1821.
71. Liverpool letter to Arbuthnot, 13 June 1820, quoted in Yonge, *The Life and Administration of Robert Banks Jenkinson*, Vol. 3, pp. 146-47.
72. Colonel George Jenkinson to Mrs Arbuthnot, 24 June 1821, in Bamford and Wellington, *The Journal of Mrs. Arbuthnot, 1820-32*, Vol. 1, p. 103.

Liverpool's love for Louisa was memorialised in a bust by Sir Francis Chantry,[73] which would be completed in 1825 and remain at Coombe Wood until Liverpool's death (after which it was placed in All Saints, Kingston-on-Thames). It is a fine marble bust of a young girl with a wistful expression, almost certainly taken from Romney's 1792 portrait of Louisa. The inscription reads:

> Louisa Theodosia
> Countess of Liverpool,
> Born February 1767
> Died June 1821
> She visited the fatherless
> and widows in their affliction
> and kept herself
> unspotted from the world.[74]

On his return, Liverpool expressed to Bathurst the constitutional difficulty in the King's veto of Canning: 'It is not Mr. Canning out of office, but Mr. Canning out of office, by the personal exclusion of the King, agreed to by his government, which is the question.'[75] To the King Liverpool reaffirmed the principle but agreed to postpone changes until the autumn, as the King had confirmed that he put no permanent bar on Canning.

In early July the news arrived in London of Napoleon's death in St Helena, relieving British taxpayers of a substantial cost, but also making the French government over-confident. Wellington joked: 'Now I think I may say I am the most successful General alive.'[76]

At the coronation of George IV on 19 July he was adorned with a new crown made specially for him, set with 12,314 diamonds and said to make him look like 'a gorgeous bird from the East';[77] it cost over £24,000 just to hire the stones. The coronation itself cost £243,000, twenty times the cost of George III's coronation, and involved all the guests dressing in specially-designed "Tudor" costumes. It was very splendid but Mrs. Arbuthnot noted that the King surrounded himself primarily by members

73. Francis Leggatt Chantrey (1781-1841). RA, 1818. Knighted 1835. Leading Regency sculptor. Left Chantrey Bequest, which was the main source of funding for acquisitions at Tate Britain until 1925.
74. The wording is an adaptation of the Epistle of James, 1:27, 'Pure religion and undefiled before God and the Father is this, To visit the fatherless and widows in their affliction, and to keep himself unspotted from the world.'
75. Quoted in Gash, *Lord Liverpool*, p. 178.
76. Bamford and Wellington, *The Journal of Mrs. Arbuthnot, 1820-32*, Vol. 1, p. 105, 4 July 1821.
77. Tessa Rose, *The Coronation Ceremony of the Kings and Queens of England and the Crown Jewels*, 1992, p. 85.

of the opposition. Liverpool, still in mourning for Louisa, did not attend. The Queen, however, did try to attend but was turned away at the doors of Westminster Abbey.

The occasion was marred for Liverpool by the King's attempt to make Lord Conyngham (his mistress's Whig husband) Master of the Horse; the post was eventually given to the reliably Tory Duke of Dorset.[78] A week later the King was pointedly rude to Liverpool at a dinner hosted by Wellington; so far had relations deteriorated.[79]

The unhappy Queen Caroline fell ill after the coronation and died on 7 August. Liverpool immediately resolved to pay her honours as if there had never been a question about her virtue. She had expressed a wish to be buried at her birthplace in Brunswick, so Liverpool, who had initially intended to organise a funeral at Westminster Abbey, arranged for the body to be transported to Germany.

Both Liverpool and the King wanted the Queen's body to leave London by water but the Admiralty raised objections, so it was decided to transport the body around the north of London, avoiding the central district, before embarking at Harwich. On the day of the funeral the official route was blocked by barricades and large crowds, and Sir Robert Baker,[80] the magistrate in charge of the funeral, gave in to the crowd and directed the procession through the City. It was another cheap Radical victory and added to the King's displeasure with Liverpool. Liverpool ensured that Baker was dismissed from his post and, on the advice of Wellington, the Radical General, Sir Robert Wilson,[81] who had attempted to disrupt the troops keeping order, was dismissed from the army.

When the Queen died, the King was on the way to Ireland on a goodwill visit, decided on, in consultation with Londonderry, earlier in the year. He was the first British monarch to visit Ireland since Richard II's ill-fated trip of 1399. There the King, Londonderry and even Sidmouth, who accompanied them, found themselves surprisingly popular. The economic upturn had now made the government popular, as it had been in 1813-14.

Liverpool returned to the task of restructuring the Cabinet in the autumn, conducting negotiations largely through Londonderry while he retired to Bath for several weeks. There was one new factor: Canning, who had for some time

---

78. Charles Sackville-Germain (1767-1843). 5th Duke of Dorset from 1815. KG, 1826. Master of the Horse, 1821-27, 1835.

79. Aspinall, *The Diary of Henry Hobhouse*, p. 69, 1 August 1821.

80. Robert Baker (1762-1840). Knighted 1820. Hatton Garden Magistrate, 1798. Sent by Liverpool to investigate Luddite disturbances, 1812. Chief Magistrate of Bow Street, 1820-21.

81. Robert Wilson (1777-1849). Knighted 1809. Radical MP for Southwark, 1818-31. Peninsula campaign, 1808-9. Colonel,1809. Seconded to Russia, 1812. Major-General, 1813. Dismissed from Army, 1821; fought in Spain against French forces, 1823. Reinstated, 1830, as Lieutenant General. General, 1841. Governor of Gibraltar, 1842-49.

been considering the financial and other attractions of succeeding Hastings as Governor General of India, learned that Hastings' retirement was likely. Having spent four years at the Board of Control, Canning was already familiar with India's problems and the East India Company were prepared to appoint him. Thus a few years of building the Canning family's modest fortunes in a very lucrative office (and receiving a peerage for doing so) were highly appealing.

The prospect of sending Canning six months' voyage away greatly improved the disposition of the King, also mellowed by a successful visit to Hanover, where he had met Metternich, who told him the current administration, especially Wellington and Londonderry, was much admired by the Continental powers, and that Francis I would downgrade his ambassador in London if it was dismissed.[82] In September, the King had kept Liverpool waiting for 24 hours for an appointment on his return from Ireland. In November, cheered by the news that Liverpool would consent to Conyngham becoming Lord Steward of the Household, the King received Liverpool cordially and made no difficulties about ministerial changes to cement Liverpool's government in office.

The main potential accession of strength was the jointure with the Grenville faction. Grenville had retired from active politics and thus would not have to serve in a Cabinet with Liverpool. However, his nephew Buckingham felt himself entirely suitable for Cabinet office, or, alternatively, the Lord Lieutenancy of Ireland, which his abler father had occupied in 1783 and again in 1787-89. Buckingham, who had strong elements of Whiggery and had served in the Talents ministry of 1806-7, at this stage opened negotiations with Lansdowne to see what could be done through the Whigs. However, he discovered that, even with Royal and Grenville help, the Liverpool ministry had become immovable.

Now that relations with the King were restored, Liverpool had a solution: to grant Buckingham the dukedom which his family had coveted for half a century. This was done the following February, cementing the Grenville connection to the government. Alas, the Dukedom of Buckingham and Chandos (Buckingham's wife was daughter of the third and last Duke of Chandos) was to last only 67 years, during which the second Duke suffered the largest bankruptcy of the nineteenth century in 1847. Williams-Wynn, nephew of Grenville and cousin of Buckingham, was made President of the Board of Control in January 1822 as the sole Grenville representative in the Cabinet.

Once the Grenville negotiations were settled, the other restructuring elements fell into place. Sidmouth retired from the Home Office but remained in the Cabinet as the King wished. He was replaced by Peel, a great accession of administrative and Commons debating strength, though not so great as Peel's admirers have subsequently claimed. Wellesley, who still had a dozen Commons followers and thus also added strength, became Lord Lieutenant

82. Aspinall, *The Diary of Henry Hobhouse*, p. 77, 13 November 1821. In the event, Prince Paul Esterhazy (1786-1866) was to serve as Ambassador until 1842.

of Ireland, to restore his shattered financial position, but without a position in Cabinet. Since Wellesley favoured Catholic Emancipation but was an idle administrator, Goulburn, who opposed it and was administratively capable, became Chief Secretary for Ireland. Plunket, author of the 1821 Catholic Emancipation Bill, and another Grenville connection who had served in the Talents ministry, became Attorney General for Ireland. Two Canning connections retired from junior office and on 27 March Canning was formally appointed Governor General of India, apparently ending his British political career, even if several months would elapse before he left for India.

For most of the first ten years of Liverpool's government, the Cabinet had been noted for its harmony, as both Londonderry and Wellington stressed in letters written in December 1821[83] – it was in notable contrast to their earlier experience in the Portland ministry of 1807-9, for example. Over the years, the personal relationships between the senior ministers became very strong, as did his colleagues' respect for Liverpool, evidenced on several occasions when the King or the opposition sought to replace him.

After this Cabinet reshuffle, more particularly, from the entry of Canning the following autumn, matters deteriorated; there were frequent rows between 1823 and 1827 and the Cabinet spilt completely when Liverpool retired in 1827. Part of this was doubtless due to Liverpool's own increased irritability, which worsened over the years. Even so, two centuries of further experience have shown that the harmony of 1812-21 was unusual, not the subsequent discord. In a supremely difficult period that harmony showed the remarkable quality of Liverpool at his best, as well as that of his ministerial team.

In December 1821, the French Ultra-Royalists, allied to the future Charles X, whose power was increasing as Louis XVIII's health declined, showed their overconfidence following Napoleon's death by ousting Richelieu – even though his Doctrinaire party was the largest in the Chamber of Deputies. Richelieu was replaced by the Ultra-Royalist, Joseph de Villèle,[84] who remained in office until 1828. While Villèle was both a moderate and pro-British, his colleagues followed policies that effectively attempted to reinstate the *Ancien Régime*. Wellington, in a letter to Londonderry foresaw the problems ahead: 'I cannot conceive a more unfortunate event than the formation of this royalist administration. In order to acquire a little popularity and a national character, they must meddle in foreign politics, and this against the system of the Quintuple Alliance.'[85] Even if Londonderry had lived, the Alliance system would have run into further trouble.

83. Gash, *Lord Liverpool*, p. 190.

84. Joseph de Villèle (1773-1854). Comte de Villèle from 1822. Mayor of Toulouse, 1814-15. Member of the Chamber of Deputies, 1815-28. Minister of Finance and Prime Minister of France, 1821-28.

85. Letter to Londonderry, 17 December 1821, quoted in Wellington, *Despatches, Correspondence*, Vol. 1, pp. 208-9.

The year 1821 saw the recovery in the industrial economy continuing to improve, with Hoffman's production index increasing by five per cent to above the 1818 level, and real wages (helped by continued deflation) and consumption the highest since the war. However, agriculture was in severe distress. In both Ireland and England, heavy rain made the 1821 wheat harvest inferior, yet its quantity was large, so wheat prices fell to a new low of 42 shillings by summer 1822.[86] In Ireland, the 1821 potato crop failed, but Ireland's dependence on potatoes had been alleviated by Liverpool's 1815 Corn Laws, so that, whereas in 1817 the balance of trade in corn was unfavourable to Ireland, by 1820-21 one million quarters was exported from Ireland to England. With wheat prices so low, English landowners with substantial debt and Irish landowners who had recently converted to corn were in severe difficulty. Moreover, most of the poorer Irish were still growing potatoes, so that crop's failure caused an outbreak of unrest.

At the beginning of 1822, the government decided on a novel attempt to influence public opinion, by producing an extended pamphlet: *The State of the Nation, at the commencement of the year 1822*. Individual statesmen had written pamphlets advocating or denouncing government policies – Liverpool and his father had both produced economic overviews, in 1796 and 1798 respectively – but this was the first attempt by the whole government to influence public opinion. As such, despite its 200-page length and untranslated Latin and even Greek, it was relatively successful, going through eleven editions.

The motivation behind it was not mere electioneering – the next election was four years away – but that:

> The ministers of a free and high-minded country cannot be without a feeling of the value of public character. They know that in public station, still more than in private life, a good name is connected with the due and effective performance of duties; that character is influence, and that influence is power; that power from influence will extend its operation, where power from law and positive authority cannot reach; and that the good will of the people towards government, has in all ages proved the readiest means of an effective administration.[87]

The introduction then explains that, if ministers were respected, a 'spirit of concurrent feeling between people and government' would be generated, making penal statutes to control disorders superfluous. Later the pamphlet

86. Tooke, *A History of Prices*, Vol. 2, pp. 83-84.

87. Robert Stewart, Viscount Castlereagh, and John Singleton Copley, Baron Lyndhurst, *The State of the Nation, at the commencement of 1822: considered under the four Departments of Finance, Foreign Relations, Home Department, Colonies and Board of Trade, etc. etc. etc.* (London: John Hatchard & Son, 1822) pp. 1-2.

returns to this subject, declaring: 'If it be the character of a light and inconsistent mind to be diverted from the performance of a grave and invidious duty by a mistaken popular clamour, it is no less a measure of prudence not to undervalue the aid of public opinion.'[88]

The pamphlet discusses government policy across four government departments. On finance, it defines the primary duty of the post-war government to be reducing government expenditure and the associated taxation, with an ancillary duty to create a taxation system that could finance expenditure stably and was not unduly burdensome. The pamphlet then identifies the ministry's financial policies, demonstrating that it had indeed achieved the defined objectives. It sets out a detailed account of economic developments since 1815, rejoicing in the growth of manufactures, especially cotton, 'now the leading manufacture of the kingdom and destined doubtless to become the clothing of the world'.[89]

On foreign policy the pamphlet sets out the principles of the 1815 peace settlement, before expanding on the nature of Britain's relationships. It explains the alliance system, and that:

> the leading principle and object of these treaties . . . are the maintenance of the general peace of Europe by the personal amity of the sovereigns, and by a system of mediation, which should on the one side recognize the perfect independence of the several states in their internal concerns; and, upon the other, should hold forth their common interest, and therein their common obligation, to consult the general policy of Europe in all questions affecting the safety of the whole.[90]

Thus, the core of the Alliance system is reaffirmed. The pamphlet also explains Britain's policy towards the rebelling Spanish in Latin America: although it would clearly be advantageous for Britain to have them as independent countries with full trade relations, our obligations to Spain prevented our helping them, and Britain had passed the Foreign Enlistment Act to deter British subjects from doing so.

On home affairs, the pamphlet reminds readers of the level of unrest in 1816-20 and congratulates the government on the greater tranquillity that followed: 'If the vessel of the state be now in port, surely some credit is due to those by whose labour she was worked through such a tempest.'[91] The pamphlet also makes the point that government policy during the disturbances was to rely on the menace of law, rather than its execution, since juries could not be relied upon to convict.

88. Ibid., p. 190.
89. Ibid., p. 56.
90. Ibid., pp. 87-88.
91. Ibid., p. 133.

Within the home affairs section, the pamphlet discusses the unrest in Ireland. It criticises the serious effect of landlord absenteeism, whereby a few hundred landlords resident abroad, and spending rent proceeds abroad, represented such a large portion of Ireland's potential consumption. The government is also aware that the surplus population drove the poor into subsistence potato farming on inadequate plots of land. While the population of Ireland was half that of England, the yield of excise taxes was only one fifteenth and other measures of manufactured products consumption put it at only a tenth. The pamphlet expresses considerable sympathy for the Irish poor, much of whose distress was due to 'the erroneous system of former times'. Overall, 'it is impossible but that her misguided peasantry must shortly return to the protection of a paternal government'.[92]

The colonial section gives the first place to Canada, because of its importance in consuming British manufactures and then to Jamaica, because the excise duties on sugar exceeded £5 million, more than the gross receipts for Ireland, while excise on all West Indian products, including rum and tobacco was £8.2 million. Third was the Cape of Good Hope 'a vineyard to the world'.

On trade, the pamphlet extols the policy of reducing tariff barriers and other protections, especially the Navigation Acts, under the Board of Trade's 'most intelligent President and Vice-President' (Robinson and Wallace). The pamphlet gives statistics on the growth of Britain's economy, extolling the country's relations with foreign powers and asserting that 'the general aspect of Great Britain, so far as regards the public tranquillity, is every thing which the most ardent lover of his country could desire'.

The pamphlet ends: 'Is it unreasonable to expect a confident assurance, that the future annalist, if not the passing generation, will recognize the public obligation to the ministers of George the Fourth?'[93] Alas, no such recognition has come from a dozy Whiggish posterity.

The first months of 1822 saw further Irish unrest, as the first potato harvest failure since 1807 brought severe distress. The arrival of the popular Wellesley made no difference to the impoverished Irish potato growers, who were subject to rent and tithe collection by middlemen rather than by often absentee landlords. Additional unrest arose from a millenarian movement among Irish Catholics following the writings of a bishop Charles Walmesley,[94] writing as Signor Pastorini, who had forecast the downfall of Protestantism between 1821 and 1825.

Liverpool's response came on several policy fronts. The government provided immediate food relief and a private subscription raised £250,000 for

---

92. Ibid., p. 196.
93. Ibid., p. 202.
94. Charles Walmesley (1722-1797) FRS. Educated at Douai and the Sorbonne, Vicar Apostolic of the Western District of England, 1770. *General History of the Christian Church* by Signor Pastorini (1771). Consecrated John Carroll, first US Catholic bishop, 1790.

Irish famine relief. In addition, the government granted bounties to fisheries on the Irish west coast and to help the spread of Irish linen manufacture from the north to the south.

The King's Speech opening Parliament in 1822 led with the disturbances in Ireland, rejoiced at the flourishing state of manufactures and the national finances, and indicated that the depressed state of agriculture might lead to legislation in that area. Lansdowne in response complained that government economies had been made too slowly, deprecated a scheme which he claimed Liverpool had been hatching, to borrow £5 million in Exchequer bills and lend it to agriculturalists, and then ended by hoping the Greeks would achieve independence.

Liverpool and Vansittart indeed wrote to the Bank of England on 2 February, asking whether an issue of Exchequer bills to the value of £3-£4 million might be possible to relieve agricultural distress, to which the Bank agreed.[95] Liverpool also met the Bank of England and leading bankers to see whether such a sum, lent to country bankers, might relieve agricultural distress, but was told it was useless, since the farmers' problem was not just illiquidity but lack of security against new borrowings.[96]

In the debate on the Address, Liverpool admitted the Bank of England discussions but said that, even though short-term loans had been used in the past to relieve commercial illiquidity, the nature of the problem in agriculture was different, and so short-term loans would not solve it. Since there had been no agricultural imports to Britain for some years, he believed the agricultural distress was due to the rapid increase in Irish production since the Corn Laws came into effect, leading to 1½ million quarters of corn sales from Ireland to Britain in the last nine months. As for government economy, while further economies were impending, they certainly would not significantly alleviate the plight of the agricultural sector. Liverpool then announced that, after consulting with Wellesley, he intended to introduce measures to arm the executive government in Ireland with additional powers, which would be limited in duration to the 1822 session of parliament, so that the House could examine their effects and decide whether to extend them. He pointed out that the King had been well received in Ireland and that Irish discontent did not relate to the King or the government but to deeper structural problems.[97]

The following Saturday, Liverpool introduced the Irish Insurrection Bill and the Irish Habeas Corpus Suspension Bill. While the Insurrection Bill gave government powers that had never been necessary in England (for example, the ability to impose a curfew) the current insurrections were directed, not against the government, but against property itself:

95. Bank of England, Minutes of the Court of Directors, 4 February 1822.
96. Gash, *Lord Liverpool*, p. 184.
97. Hansard, *The Parliamentary Debates, New Series*, Vol. 6, cols 15-19 (5 February 1822).

> This then, differs from ordinary insurrections, in which, although property might suffer, it is only incidentally attacked; its destruction not being the direct object of the discontented. On the contrary, in the present, the attack is directed immediately against the property and the lives of persons who are in a higher station than the assailants.

Liverpool explained further that the unrest was so widespread that more troops would be ineffective. Instead greater police powers were required. As for measures of conciliation, the problem related to the entire state of Irish society, so Catholic Emancipation would have little effect. Finally, Liverpool reiterated that this was not a local insurrection, it was set in motion by promoters who were not in the field but 'behind the curtain'.[98]

Liverpool's repressive measures succeeded in the short term; the unrest gradually declined and a better potato harvest removed the immediate cause of mass discontent, although the Irish Insurrection Act was renewed in July. However, Ireland's long-term problems of overpopulation and an unstable and unfair land distribution remained unsolved. Liverpool alleviated these problems via the Corn Laws and various measures supporting Irish industries, but they were to prove largely insoluble under direct British rule.

Politically, the more important issue was the agricultural distress in the remainder of Britain. Mrs Arbuthnot had discussed this with Westmorland, a large landowner:

> I insisted that the cry of agricultural distress was grossly exaggerated, that the pressure felt by that class now was *nothing* compared to that suffered by the manufacturing districts in 1819, when 10,000 able and willing workmen were starving in one town (Glasgow) for want of work, and every other manufacturing town suffering in a like degree; that the farmers had got into luxurious habits which they did not choose to give up and therefore joined in the cry of 'No Taxes;' that those persons who had borrowed money at 5 per cent interest during the war to buy land would suffer as any body did who borrowed money to buy any thing; but that the great landed proprietors would weather the storm and be just as well off as ever; that there would certainly be a transfer of property, but that the country generally would be as rich as ever and that there could not be a greater proof of it than the enormous increase of the Revenue in every branch. He said I talked nonsense and was very childish (which, by the way, is no argument) and that the transfer of property I talked of so quietly would be a greater revolution than even a bankruptcy of the funds.[99]

98. Ibid., cols 185-88, 217-20 (9 February 1822).

99. Bamford and Wellington, *The Journal of Mrs. Arbuthnot, 1820-32*, Vol. 1, p. 139, 2 February 1822.

Westmorland and his fellow landowners formed by far the largest interest in the unreformed House of Commons; their distress thus gave Liverpool trouble throughout the 1822 parliamentary session. Only a good quality harvest in 1822 somewhat alleviated the agricultural difficulties, which remained an important issue for the rest of Liverpool's tenure.

Liverpool responded to a petition from Kentish farmers calling for tax reductions to alleviate distress in agriculture. He began by surveying the British economy, noting the new Census figures for 1821 which showed a decennial population increase of 17.3 per cent in Britain, the buoyancy of revenue, which in 1821 had increased by over £1 million from the same taxes, with little difficulty in collection, and the increase of £1.2 million in deposits at the savings banks. Exports had increased by £2-3 million, leading to greater profits and higher wages in manufacturing everywhere except the iron trades.

Liverpool then turned to agriculture, where farmers had complained of excessive British taxation. He showed that depressed prices and overproduction were having the same effect on the Continent as in Britain. For example, agricultural distress was as great in Switzerland as elsewhere, even though Switzerland had low taxes and no standing army. Moreover, agriculture had been prosperous in the latter stages of the war, yet taxation had since then been reduced by 25 per cent (principally the abolition of income tax) which was fully as much as the appreciation of the currency through the return to gold.

Comparing 1822's position with the position before 1792, even though taxation had tripled, the country's exports had quadrupled. Even the consumption of tea, the excise on which had increased from 13 per cent to 100 per cent, had increased from 16.6 million pounds to 22.7 million, the same proportion as the population increase during the period. Similarly, the consumption of candles had risen from 49.9 million pounds to 83.6 million, far more than the rise in population, as had soap, leather and bricks; only salt had not.

The farmer's main need is a market: 'Ask the farmer in his sober reason, when he is divested of the delusions drilled into him by the sophistry practised at public meetings, what it is that he really wants, and he will tell you: "A market."' One problem was that the war's unnatural market had gone; government's annual demand for meat and other provisions had declined from £2 million to £200,000 when peace returned. Another was that the Corn Laws had brought a major increase of Irish corn production adding to the surplus.

Given the need for debt service, without which holders of government bonds would be hugely impoverished, £5 million was the maximum tax relief which could be provided, by abolishing the sinking fund, less than one fiftieth of the national income of £250-280 million.[100] The gain from this would be

100. Modern estimates put 1821 GDP at £322 million; if national income were 85.6 per cent of GDP, as in the United States' 2018 economy, that would put national income at £275.6 million. Liverpool did not have modern economic statistics or statistical concepts – GDP was invented in the 1930s – but he nevertheless had a solid, well-

modest, whereas the loss, affecting public credit and pushing up interest rates, would badly affect owners of mortgaged estates. In any case, eliminating the sinking fund would be immoral and dangerous, since Britain already had the highest public debt in the world.

While low food prices were hard for farmers, they were beneficial for the much greater number of consumers, who formed most of the population: 'In this metropolis, in which your Lordships are sitting, never were the lower orders of the people in better condition than they are at the moment.' Over time the markets would equilibrate, and government must hold the balance between the great interests of the country.

Public expenditure had been brought down to £1.2 million below the minimum estimated by a parliamentary committee in 1817, and the sinking fund had also reduced debt service payments. There would be further relief as the £5 million annually spent on army and navy half-pay began to reduce. The government now intended to refinance the higher-interest portions of public debt, enabling further tax reductions. In addition, the government proposed to borrow £4 million from the Bank of England in Exchequer bills and distribute it to parishes, allowing for poor relief or public works, alleviating costs on farmers – this resembled the scheme for relief in industrial districts in 1816-17. As for the Corn Laws, they should be re-examined to see whether a sliding scale might work better than the sharp cut-off at 80 shillings but any changes would be modest and would not affect much the current position of farmers.[101]

In the event, the Importation Act of 1822 added an additional refinement to the 1815 Corn Law, to be triggered only when corn prices had risen above 80 shillings per quarter, in prohibiting corn imports after the price had fallen below 80 shillings until it again reached 70 shillings – the ports were no longer to be opened on a small dip. The Act also added a modest sliding scale duty, of twelve shillings while the corn price was between 70 shillings and 80 shillings, declining to one shilling when the price rose to 85 shillings.

On 12 March Liverpool returned to public finance, introducing the Navy Five Per Cents Bill, which redeemed £135 million of five per cent bonds, the original tranche of which dated back to the American War. Liverpool went through the question of whether £25 million of three per cent bonds had been redeemed, the condition in the original 1781 legislation for redeeming the five per cent bonds, and concluded that they had, via the sinking fund, even though new three per cent Consols had been issued to replace them. The market's agreement with this was shown by the five per cent bonds never having traded above 108 per cent of par, even when they should arithmetically have traded at 120. Holders would be offered new government bonds at a lower rate or be redeemed at par. The redemption would save the government £1.3 million annually.[102]

grounded idea of the economic realities of his day.

101. Ibid., Vol. 6, cols 682-717 (26 February 1822).

102. Ibid., cols 1038-43 (12 March 1822).

Further pressure from the opposition and the agricultural lobby on public expenditure manifested itself in a motion proposed by the Whig economic specialist, Lord King.[103] Liverpool announced that in addition to a reduction in those public salaries which had been increased since the suspension of 1797, civil servants as a whole would take a further reduction of ten per cent – which further reduction the King had also agreed to for his own household – making an annual saving of £373,000 in a full year. This would also apply to ambassadors, of which there were eighteen.[104] After these announcements, Lord King's motion was lost without a division.

Late in the session, the government took a step towards increasing rural credit, by passing legislation allowing country bankers to continue issuing £1 and £2 notes; this would cause trouble in 1825. Liverpool also proposed a deal with the Bank of England whereby, in return for extending their Charter from 1833 to 1843, the restriction of six partners on country banks more than 65 miles from London would be removed, so that banks of all sizes could be formed, albeit without the privilege of issuing notes until 1844. This change could have alleviated the 1825-26 financial crisis and was the centrepiece of the reform that followed it. The Bank of England accepted this proposal but, after taking soundings in the House of Commons, it appeared that, given the agricultural distress and the strength of the country bankers' lobby, the deal agreed with the Bank could not pass the House. Banking reform would be taken up again successfully in 1826.[105]

Liverpool moved the second reading of the Navigation and Commerce Act, a major step towards the repeal of the Cromwellian and later Navigation Acts. He described the new bill as repealing 300 of the old statutes relating to commerce and discussed how, because of the laws' complexity, 'people get a livelihood – certainly a fair and honest one, but one far from advantageous to the commerce of the country – by informing merchants what they could or could not do, according to law'. The new law recognised the independence of South America and put its trade on the same basis as that of the United States and European nations. It also freed up exports, so all forms of payment by foreigners could be used.[106]

This legislation led to further relaxations of trade restrictions in following years, piloted by Huskisson as trade secretary, so that by the end of Liverpool's term few of the Navigation Acts' restrictions on British trade remained. The

103. Peter King (1776-1833). 7th Baron King from 1793. Whig political economist. Notable for refusing to accept paper money at par from his tenants in 1811.

104. Hansard, *The Parliamentary Debates, New Series*, Vol. 6, cols 1291-98 (26 March 1822).

105. Bank of England, Minutes of the Court of Directors, 25 and 27 April 1822. Liverpool letter to the Bank, 25 June 1822 in the 27 June Minutes.

106. Hansard, *The Parliamentary Debates, New Series*, Vol. 7, cols 1119-22 (17 June 1822).

Navigation Acts were abolished altogether in 1849 and during the remainder of Liverpool's term, Britain moved substantially towards free trade, in terms of regulation as well as tariffs.

Liverpool proposed a further tax-relieving measure, the Dead Weight Annuity Act, which commuted the half-pay of army and navy officers, running at £5 million per annum, into an annuity of £2.8 million per annum payable for 45 years. By this means, he secured the needs of the remaining unemployed officers, while relieving the immediate budget of £2.2 million per annum. In his speech, he explained that the objective of this was not primarily to reduce taxes but to remove the artificial financial strains caused by the war. The Act, with a minor amendment, was eventually passed the following year.[107]

Liverpool returned to the subject of Ireland on a petition introduced by the Duke of Devonshire[108] for commuting Irish tithes. Liverpool recognised that the collection of tithes in Ireland was severe and produced great injustices and was thus open to some change so long as the Anglican Church of Ireland was provided for. He did not believe tithes were a major issue in the discontents of 1821-22 and maintained that commuting Irish tithes had no bearing on whether English tithes should be commuted.[109]

There were repeated debates in the Lords about the Irish distress. Liverpool reassured the House that the government had sent food to Ireland, although careless interference from government could cause famine rather than alleviate it – the free market fed London, so should generally be left to itself. He later supported a further £50,000 subsidy to provide Irish employment.[110]

Finally, on 14 June 1822, Liverpool responded at length to a Lansdowne motion on the Irish troubles. He said that the problems in Ireland did not relate to its government but to the relationship between the propertyless and the propertied. In most countries, throughout human history, that relationship had been one of slavery, either partial, as in serfdom and villeinage, or total. Nine tenths of Ireland's problems related to this relationship, evidenced by the joyful reception of the King the previous year almost immediately succeeded by riots against the propertied. Ireland had suffered badly from the end of the war because southern Ireland had provided both food and its surplus population for the armies. Yet taxation was not excessive because Ireland represented a third of Britain's population but provided only a tenth of Britain's revenue.

While Ireland's legal administration had recently been reformed to make it more equitable between Catholics and Protestants, absentee landlordism was

---

107. Ibid., cols 1319-22 (25 June 1822).
108. William Cavendish (1790-1858). 6th Duke of Devonshire from 1811. Lord Lieutenant of Derbyshire, 1811-58. Lord Chamberlain of the Household, 1827-28, 1830-34.
109. Hansard, *The Parliamentary Debates, New Series*, Vol. 6, cols 1168-69 (15 March 1822).
110. Ibid., Vol. 7, cols 141, 671-72 and 727 (29 April, 17 and 23 May 1822).

a major problem, as much for moral as for economic reasons. As for tithes, they represented a right of property, just as solid as any other, and at least the clergy, unlike most large landlords, were resident in Ireland. He would prefer that tithes bear directly on tenants because indirect payment through landlords increased them and brought harsh administration. There was also the problem that, whereas a tithe income of £400 a year in England would be collected from 30 or 40 individuals, a similar income in Ireland would be collected from 1,400 or 1,500 people, mostly of the lowest class. It made more sense for clergymen to lease their tithe rights to landlords, who could then collect them directly. Thus, concluded Liverpool, every effort was being made to address Ireland's problems.[111] Lansdowne's motion was defeated by 108 votes to 60.

Liverpool's next major speech was on a mischievous measure proposed by Canning in the Commons to allow Catholic Emancipation but only for English Catholic peers. Canning's hope here was to split the anti-Emancipation forces, making them concede the principle by this bill, which would emancipate only 20 people. Liverpool objected to this bill because, unlike Plunket's bill of the previous year, it left the subject open to continual further agitation. Moreover, the House of Lords was most closely attached to the established religion and so it made no sense to admit Catholics into it before admitting them to the Commons. The current bill had none of the safeguards of Plunket's bill, increasing its danger to the Church and, while giving away the principle, it did nothing for Ireland. Moreover, it was thoroughly invidious in discriminating against Catholic commoners.[112] The Bill lost by 171 votes to 129, in a remarkably large turnout.

One marker for the future was Russell's motion for Parliamentary Reform. This avoided Radical pleas for annual Parliaments or manhood suffrage but followed the lines of the Reform Bill of ten years later, disfranchising pocket boroughs and expanding the representation in counties. His argument expounded on the massive economic and demographic changes of the past 30 years which in Mrs Arbuthnot's view formed a better argument for keeping the current system than for changing it. Russell's motion failed by a majority of 112 but received a surprisingly large total of 174 votes. For Mrs Arbuthnot: 'The truth is, the Opposition feel that under the present system they have no chance of getting in, and they would alter the Constitution in any way which would enable them to turn their adversaries out.'[113]

Vansittart's Budget was presented on 1 July. The continuation of peace had necessitated some changes; for example, the costs of Chelsea Pensioners could no longer be borne by prize money. Vansittart announced a general revision of the sinking fund to be carried out from 1823. In the current year, the malt

111. Ibid., cols 1058-66 (14 June 1822).
112. Ibid., cols 1244-51 (21 June 1822).
113. Bamford and Wellington, *The Journal of Mrs. Arbuthnot, 1820-1832*, Vol. 1, p. 160 (26 April 1822).

duty had been repealed, costing £1.5 million, as had the salt duty – both those repeals would directly benefit agriculture and the poor through reduction in their tax burdens. Overall, there would be a clear surplus of £3.1 million, which together with £2.2 million from the half-pay and pension arrangement and a saving of £700,000 from refinancing the five per cents, would give a total surplus well above the sinking fund provision of £5 million. He also projected a surplus of around £6 million for 1823.[114]

On modern figures, gross public income declined by £1.7 million to £59.9 million, a slightly smaller decline than the foregone revenues from the malt and salt duties. Gross public expenditures, however, declined by £1.9 million to £56.5 million, giving a £3.4 million surplus, larger than in the previous year. The main reductions in expenditure were on the army and navy, totalling £2.8 million.[115]

The long parliamentary session closed on 6 August. Less than a week later, on 12 August, Londonderry committed suicide by cutting his throat with a pocket-knife. Londonderry may have been subject to blackmail over a homosexual assignation[116] but the true cause of his suicide seems to have been that the stress of ten years' overwork cracked a psychological makeup that had always been brittle. His friends had been aware of the problem; Wellington had warned Arbuthnot of illness three days earlier, while a letter from his doctor to Wellington had talked of 'a preternatural fullness of the vessels of the head' and indicated that his nerves were unstrung.[117]

Londonderry's funeral at Westminster Abbey, after he had been pronounced of unsound mind (and therefore not by Church doctrine a suicide), was attended by an immense crowd of well-wishers, and Cobbett[118] failed to get more than a small group of Radicals to cheer as his body was carried into the Abbey. Liverpool was immediately faced with the problem of replacing him, possibly with two people since Londonderry had combined the jobs of Foreign Secretary and Leader of the House of Commons. It is worth looking at Liverpool's decision, because his eventual choice, Canning filling both roles, for which he overruled the King and much of his Cabinet, was not inevitable.

---

114. Hansard, *The Parliamentary Debates, New Series*, Vol. 7, cols 1413-23 (1 July 1822).
115. Mitchell, *British Historical Statistics*, pp. 581 (Income), 587 (Expenditure). The year-end is January 5 so, to get the figures for the (approximate) calendar year 1822, you should use the 1823 figures in the tables.
116. The possibility of Londonderry's homosexuality has been latched on to by fashionable modern historians; at the time the idea was promoted by his doctor to deflect responsibility from himself. It seems unlikely; certainly, Wellington and Mrs Arbuthnot believed it to be false. See, Bamford and Wellington, *The Journal of Mrs. Arbuthnot, 1820-1832*, Vol. 1, p. 253, 13 August 1822.
117. Letter from Bankhead to Wellington, 9 August 1822, in Wellington, *Despatches, Correspondence*, Vol. 1, p. 252; Letter from Wellington to Arbuthnot, pp. 258-60.
118. William Cobbett (1763-1835). Radical MP for Oldham, 1832-35. Tory, then Radical journalist. Founder of *Cobbett's Weekly Political Register*.

When Liverpool became Prime Minister, Commons management was difficult. The Whigs had had second-rate leadership since Grey and Lansdowne had succeeded to their titles and moved to the Lords – the next Whig Commons leader, Grey's uncle by marriage, George Ponsonby,[119] was a lightweight who died in 1817. However, the Grenville group was allied with the Whigs and contained considerable voting strength, while Canning and Wellesley, allied outside Liverpool's government, presented a formidable combination of Commons support and debating talent.

In the following decade, as Castlereagh/Londonderry led the Commons capably, the job had got easier. Canning joined the government, as recently had Wellesley. Grenville retired, and his supporters also joined the government. Even though the Whigs had gained numerical strength, there were now no significant independent sources of opposition.

For the Whigs, Tierney succeeded Ponsonby but proved an indifferent leader and retired in 1821. The Whigs had lacked Commons debating talent since Lansdowne left in 1809, and their Radical supporters like Whitbread or Burdett had died or moved towards the Tories. However, with the younger generation that was changing. William Lamb (the future Melbourne)[120] at 43 was diffident and centrist, but Althorp,[121] Russell and the young Stanley[122] were forming the nucleus of a powerful opposition.

If Canning had already left for India, Liverpool would have had little difficulty in filling Londonderry's shoes. The obvious choice for Foreign Secretary was Wellington, with deep international knowledge, experience and prestige. Liverpool and Londonderry had agreed that Wellington should be kept away from the sharp end of politics but the role of Foreign Secretary was the least political of the top offices and could easily be managed from the Lords.

Without Canning, Liverpool also had two obvious choices for Leader of the House of Commons, younger men who could rejuvenate the government. One was Peel, who would succeed in 1828, with whom Liverpool worked

---

119. George Ponsonby (1755-1817). MP (Ireland) for Wicklow, Inistioge and Galway, 1778-1801. MP for Wicklow, Tavistock and Peterborough, 1801-17. Lord Chancellor of Ireland, 1806-7. Whig leader in the House of Commons, 1808-17.

120. William Lamb (1779-1848). 2nd Viscount (Ireland) and Baron Melbourne from 1828. MP for Leominster, Portarlington, Peterborough, Hertfordshire, Newport (Isle of Wight) and Bletchingley, 1806-28. Chief Secretary for Ireland, 1827-28. Home Secretary, 1830-34. Prime Minister, 1834, 1835-41.

121. John Spencer (1782-1845). Viscount Althorp from 1783. 3rd Earl Spencer from 1834. MP for Northamptonshire and South Northamptonshire, 1806-34. Chancellor of the Exchequer and Leader of the House of Commons, 1830-34.

122. Edward Smith-Stanley (1799-1869). Lord Stanley from 1834. House of Lords from 1844. 14th Earl of Derby from 1851. MP for Stockbridge, Preston, Windsor and North Lancashire, 1822-44. Whig until 1834, Tory from 1841. Chief Secretary for Ireland, 1830-33. Secretary of State for War and the Colonies, 1833-34, 1841-45. Leader of the Conservative Party, 1846-68. Prime Minister 1852, 1858-59, 1866-68.

well but whose chilly temperament was unsuited to the job. The other was Palmerston, older than Peel, a minister for thirteen years, and a supporter of Catholic Emancipation, which would be useful if it became politically necessary to pass it, since no reversal of principle would be involved; it would also keep the Grenvilleites on board. By 1826, Palmerston and Liverpool were temperamental as well as political opponents, with Palmerston soured by waiting too long and Liverpool querulous with illness – but a newly promoted Palmerston in 1822 could have instilled fresh vigour into the government.

For Liverpool to make either Peel or Palmerston Commons leader would have been a step into the future. He could still have promoted Robinson and Huskisson, and brought Palmerston into the Cabinet if he chose Peel, and would thereafter have had a united Commons team equal to any difficulties. Canning, 52, factious and out of top office since 1809, was a recommitment to the older generation and a reversion to the past.

Liverpool's decision here is unquestionably one of history's turning points. Nevertheless, one can understand emotionally his enthusiasm for Canning. He had just lost the rock of his administration; the natural reaction was to reach out to his other longest-standing associate. Also, as a friend, he knew the burning force of Canning's ambition and realised he could now fulfil part of it. The Liverpool/Canning friendship seems one-sided to dispassionate observers but was nonetheless important to Liverpool.

Liverpool also had an important short-term decision to make: who to send to the Congress of Verona. Canning was unsuitable since he disagreed with the Alliance system. Wellington, respected by all the Congress participants, was the obvious choice.

Liverpool's negotiations with the King were hampered by the King having departed for Scotland, accompanied by Peel. His visit there was remarkably successful, inaugurating the Royal love affair with Scotland. Liverpool sent the King word of Londonderry's death, together with a proposal that any subsequent rearrangements should await the King's return. The King wrote in reply to Liverpool, emphasising that the arrangements regarding India should not be disturbed.

Over the next few weeks, Liverpool canvassed his colleagues, seeking their approval to give Canning the dual jobs of Foreign Secretary and Leader of the House of Commons. He met with a unanimous wish for Canning to depart to India, except for Wellington, who expressed a gentlemanly acceptance of Canning's claims.[123] His colleagues' opposition to his apotheosis is a remarkable tribute to Canning's ability to make enemies.

Liverpool's loyalty and determination as well as his colleagues' respect for him were demonstrated when he approached his Cabinet singly and obtained

123. Yonge, *The Life and Administration of Robert Banks Jenkinson*, Vol. 3, p. 198. Yonge is strongly pro-Canning and goes so far as to claim (p. 193) that there were no differences on foreign policy between Canning and Castlereagh, which is clearly wrong.-

their grudging acquiescence in Canning's promotion. Thus, when the King returned from Scotland, Liverpool was able to present Canning's appointment as the unanimous wish of the Cabinet, to which the King also grudgingly acquiesced, after a session with Wellington.

After securing Canning's services, Liverpool got married again on 24 September – the marriage had been planned for August but was postponed by Londonderry's suicide. He had been 'talked of' in relation to Bathurst's elder daughter Louisa Georgina, an 'old maid' at 30 and quite suitable by contemporary standards for the 52-year-old Liverpool.[124] However, in the event, he chose Mary Chester, a friend and companion of his first wife Louisa, then aged 44 so closer to his own age. Mary was the daughter of Charles Chester, himself the younger son of a baronet, so from Liverpool's ancestral gentry background rather than the inner-circle aristocracy of his first wife and his adult companions.

Liverpool then needed to fill the Indian Governor Generalship opened by Canning's promotion. The lucrative job inevitably proved attractive to people who lacked the capacity to fill it; the Grenvilleites Williams-Wynn (who was making heavy weather of the Board of Control) and Buckingham pushed hard to obtain it. There was also Lord William Bentinck, Wellington's bugbear during the Peninsular War, already dismissed for incompetence from the Governorship of Madras, and anxious to bring the benefits of Whig cultural insensitivity and racism to India's top job. Bentinck would be appointed to the job by his brother-in-law Canning in 1827, after which, together with his sidekick Macaulay, he reversed Warren Hastings' policy of leaving Indian administration as unchanged as possible. Instead, they imposed English language requirements on Indian administrators that placed the country in the hands of the British-educated Socialist left – a policy that took 70 years of independence to reverse.

Liverpool's favourite for the job was Charles Manners-Sutton,[125] the Speaker, but that would involve giving Williams-Wynn the Speakership which he coveted and including Buckingham in the Cabinet as the Grenvilleite representative. The King vetoed this, whereupon Liverpool settled unenthusiastically on the East India Company directors' preferred alternative, Lord Amherst. In the event, Amherst's inability to impose himself on a situation, demonstrated in

124. Louisa Georgina Bathurst (1792-1874). She appears never to have married; there is an 1858 reference to her in a letter of Emily Eden, see Violet Dickinson (ed.), *Miss Eden's Letters* (London: Macmillan, 1919): 'She always was in extremes. In her political days she did not think it possible that a Whig soul could be saved and may think so still.' She sounds ideal; would have added some backbone to Liverpool's last years!

125. Charles Manners-Sutton (1780-1845). 1st Viscount Canterbury from 1835. Son of Charles Manners-Sutton, Archbishop of Canterbury, 1805-28. MP for Scarborough and Cambridge University, 1806-35. Speaker of the House of Commons, 1817-35.

his failure to obtain an audience with the Jiaqing Emperor in 1816, made him an ineffective Governor General, leading to the bloody and expensive First Burmese War. It was not one of Liverpool's happier appointments.

Once Canning had his feet under the Cabinet table, he demanded favours for his followers, tilting the Cabinet balance further in his favour. Fortunately, the deterioration of Bragge Bathurst's health and his wish to retire opened up the job of Chancellor of the Duchy of Lancaster, to which Liverpool was able to move Vansittart in January 1823, consoling him with the English barony of Bexley. Canning's follower Robinson was then promoted from the Board of Trade to replace Vansittart at the Exchequer. Robinson, clever but lazy and ineffectual, proved popular and a good speaker while the economy remained favourable but failed in the crisis of 1825-26.

Liverpool also promoted Huskisson, another Canning acolyte, though a more diligent one, and a valuable assistant to Liverpool himself, to the President of the Board of Trade. Initially, the King vetoed his admission into Cabinet, an omission that rankled with Huskisson, even though Liverpool promised him Cabinet admission within a year. Huskisson's office of Commissioner of Woods and Forests was given to Arbuthnot, who wanted a less demanding job, while Arbuthnot's office as Secretary to the Treasury was given to J.C. Herries,[126] a future Chancellor of the Exchequer.

Huskisson's promotion over his head rankled the Vice-President of the Board of Trade, Wallace, whose work on trade had been invaluable; however, in August 1823, Lord Maryborough, Wellington's brother Wellesley-Pole, was pensioned off as Master of the Buckhounds, freeing up the Mastership of the Mint for Wallace and giving Huskisson Maryborough's Cabinet place. Notably not promoted was Palmerston, who was offered an English peerage if he would relinquish his office of Secretary at War to Huskisson but refused it.

Liverpool's prolonged reorganisation of his government has been hailed by Whiggish historians but overall it was not particularly successful. Canning was not an improvement on Castlereagh. Peel was cleverer than Sidmouth but less likely to control unrest in difficult times, as Sidmouth had done in 1816-20. Robinson was popular and a better speaker than Vansittart but without the diligence, the financial ability or, when the going got rough, the courage. Only Huskisson, while unpopular and a difficult personality, was an improvement on his predecessor. Most important, the close and amicable relations within the Cabinet, so notable in 1812-21, were lost with the prickly Peel and the mercurial Canning replacing the equable Sidmouth and Castlereagh. This made Liverpool's life more difficult.

126. John Charles Herries (1778-1855). MP for Harwich and Stamford, 1823-53. Secretary to the Treasury, 1823-27. Chancellor of the Exchequer, 1827-28. Master of the Mint, 1828-30. President of the Board of Trade, 1830. Secretary at War, 1834-35. Joint Conservative Leader in the House of Commons, 1849-51. President of the Board of Control, 1852.

In mid-September Wellington set out for Verona via Paris and Vienna. He was armed with a memorandum from Londonderry, presented to him by Bathurst, on the line he should take there.[127] Britain's two main objectives would be to prevent Russia from invading Turkey to secure Greek independence and to prevent France from invading Spain to abolish the 1812 constitution and restore Ferdinand VII to his full powers.

Wellington first tried to square the British and French positions, meeting Villèle in Paris. He discovered that France already had 100,000 men in the field in southern France. Villèle said he did not want a Franco-Spanish war but he thought the Spanish liberals would murder the king, at which point a war would become inevitable. (Invasion was popular among Ultra-Royalists, because they thought France would win and thus strengthen the French monarchy.) Villèle said he would ask the Congress for a declaration of support of the French position in Spain, and asked Wellington for a declaration of British neutrality if France invaded Spain. Wellington responded that Britain could not commit itself in a hypothetical case. Villèle also made it clear that France would do nothing effective against the slave trade, despite treaties it had signed, because French public opinion thought abolition a British plot.[128]

Having seen Wellington's report, Liverpool wrote to Canning that:

> The conduct and character of the King [of Spain] makes even the personal question the weakest I ever recollect in the case of revolution. . . . I am not at all prepared to say that if a change of dynasty should be the result it would or ought to be a ground for hostile interference, in any way, from other powers.

Canning sent Wellington a note reinforcing the instruction not to agree to any joint Allied declaration on Spain. He also informed Wellington of the rebels' capture of Quito and reaffirmed the British determination not to issue any joint defence of Spain's position in South America. In a separate letter Canning instructed Wellington to take a strong line against a recent Russian ukase claiming the west coast of the North American continent down to latitude 51 degrees, on the twin grounds that the Hudson's Bay Company was already occupying part of that territory and that a treaty had been signed with the United States agreeing to joint dominion over it.[129]

Wellington met Alexander I in Vienna, who informed him that Russia regarded Spain as the epicentre of revolution and wanted to invade it with a Russian army. However, since France refused to allow passage to a foreign army,

127. Londonderry memorandom, 14 September 1822, quoted in Wellington, *Despatches, Correspondence*, Vol. 1, pp. 284-88.

128. Wellington letter to Canning, 21 September 1822, quoted in ibid., pp. 288-94.

129. Liverpool letter to Canning, 27 September 1822, and Canning letters to Wellington, 27 September 1822, quoted in ibid., pp. 300-7, 311-18.

the two countries were at an impasse. At the Verona conference, Alexander I proposed to march a Russian army of 150,000 men into Piedmont, to hold itself ready in case the French army mutinied while in Spain, or the French Jacobins took advantage of the army's absence to rebel; this proposal was received with horror by all concerned.

The Verona conference formally began on 20 October. Wellington presented a memorandum stating that Britain would shortly have to recognise Spain's former colonies in Latin America, if only to suppress the pirates that were making use of their ports. However, the main result of the conference was that Austria, Russia, Prussia and France united to break off diplomatic relations with Spain, agreed to back any French invasion and sent a joint letter in terms bound to be unacceptable to the radical Spanish government.

Britain, with its doctrine of non-intervention, despite Wellington's influence and charm, found itself isolated. The Anglo-Austrian entente, with both Castlereagh and Wellington enjoying a warm relationship with Metternich, was spoiled by Wellington's need to press Austria for repayment of loans contracted in the 1790s. Fortunately a loan settlement was eventually reached by direct negotiation between Wellington and Francis I, to the relief of ministers facing parliamentary hostility.

The Congress of Verona failed on the main question of Spain but did produce a solution over navigation in the Black Sea, which Liverpool said: 'had more real difficulties attending it than any which has occurred'.[130] Verona was, alas, the last such meeting; the personal relationships built up between Alexander I, Castlereagh and Metternich were thrown away in the subsequent generation, even though Wellington was to subject himself to a St Petersburg winter in 1826, attempting to create a dialogue with the next Czar Nicholas I.

From our twenty-first-century perspective of constant 'summits' we forget that one of the major problems of pre-1914 diplomacy was that the participants, despite vastly better transportation and communications than in the 1820s, mostly did not know each other personally.[131] There was no pre-1914 equivalent to the friendship between Metternich, Castlereagh and Wellington, the benefit of which even during Metternich's lengthy tenure of office (until 1848) was thrown away by the doctrinaire 'liberalism' of Canning and Palmerston. That friendship was generated by the Congresses after the Napoleonic Wars, the abandonment of which, however modest their results, produced huge long-term damage to European civilisation.

Economically in 1822, the British economy broke decisively above its 1818 peak. Brick production, a proxy for capital investment, rose 15 per cent above the previous year, to just below the 1819 record. Hoffman's production index

130. Letter to Canning, 21 October 1822, quoted in Yonge, *The Life and Administration of Robert Banks Jenkinson*, Vol. 3, pp. 246-47.

131. See Christopher Clark, *The Sleepwalkers: How Europe Went to War in 1914* (London: Harper, 2013), for a discussion of the miscommunication in July 1914.

increased another five per cent, to a level ten per cent above the 1818 peak, while cotton exports' official value rose to 19 per cent above the 1818 peak. A continued decline in prices, especially of food, caused a substantial increase in real wages in both London and the cotton districts; this, combined with fuller employment, explains the year's labour peace. Only agriculture remained depressed, with an excellent 1822 harvest counterbalanced by a further fall in wheat prices, to a new low of 38 shillings per quarter. Financially, the great South American bond boom began, with issues for Chile, Colombia, Peru and the fictitious Central American country of Poyais,[132] as well as issues for Prussia and Russia.[133]

January 1823 was dominated by foreign affairs. While Villèle was determined, if possible, to avoid French involvement in a Spanish war, several of his colleagues, notably the new foreign minister Chateaubriand[134] and the bulk of the Ultra-Royalists, including the future Charles X, believed that such a war would be successful, binding the army, whose loyalties were uncertain and whose generals were mostly ex-Bonapartists, to the restored monarchy. Thus, France signed a secret treaty with the eastern Allies, who promised their support if France invaded Spain to restore Ferdinand VII's absolutist powers. Then, on 28 January, Louis XVIII announced that a hundred thousand Frenchmen were ready to march, invoking the name of St Louis, to safeguard the throne of Spain for a descendant of Henri IV. At that point, a French invasion of Spain became inevitable.

The King's Address on 4 February, began by stating that Britain had 'declined to be party to any proceedings at Verona, which could be deemed an interference in the internal concerns of Spain, on the part of Foreign Powers' and that he sought to avert war between France and Spain. The speech then continued to congratulate the country on the 'increasing activity which pervades the manufacturing districts, and the flourishing condition of our commerce in most of its principal branches' which he believed would soon alleviate the distress in agriculture.[135]

---

132. The Poyais bond issue was organised by the soldier and Latin American adventurer, Gregor McGregor (1786-1845). 'Poyais' referred to a stretch of the Nicaraguan Mosquito coast, mostly unfit for cultivation. The scheme, which involved a land swindle as well as a bond issue, was publicised in a 355-page guidebook detailing Poyais' supposed delights and a prospectus detailing the wide boulevards and domed cathedral of its supposed capital St Joseph.
133. Tooke, *A History of Prices*, Vol. 2, pp. 84-86. Export figures taken from Gayer, Rostow and Schwartz, *The Growth and Fluctuation of the British Economy, 1790-1850*, Vol 1, pp. 171-210.
134. François-René de Chateaubriand (1768-1848). Vicomte from 1815(?). Writer and diplomat. Ambassador to Sweden, 1814-15, to Prussia, 1821-22, to Great Britain, 1822. Foreign Secretary, 1822-24. Ambassador to the Holy See, 1828-29. Refused to recognise legitimacy of Orleanist regime after 1830.
135. Hansard, *The Parliamentary Debates, New Series*, Vol. 8, cols 1-3 (4 February 1823).

Stanhope moved an amendment asking for remedies to the continuing agricultural distress and suggesting that the country should have adopted a silver rather than a gold standard in 1819. In response, Liverpool asserted that changing the monetary standard would do more harm than good, then moved on to a Lansdowne speech criticising the government's foreign policy.

Contrary to Gash's claim,[136] Liverpool did not praise the Spanish constitution of 1812, which had caused so much difficulty to Wellington's operations in 1812-14. He merely said that in its adoption there had been 'a less taint of blood, of crime, and of violence, than was afforded by almost every other example of a similar revolution that had occurred in modern history'. On the constitution itself, Liverpool said that 'correction, not abrogation, was advised', implying that Ferdinand VII's abrogation of the constitution in 1814 was ill-judged and adding: 'Had the sovereign then corrected it, the country would have thanked him for its modification.' At this point, Britain was trying to preserve peace between France and Spain, by remaining neutral and offering its services as mediator. Stanhope's amendment was defeated by 62 votes to three.

Three weeks later Liverpool confirmed that Britain had no obligations to either side in a potential Franco-Spanish conflict, but that the government's main hope was that peace between the two countries could be preserved.[137] During this period the Cabinet split on foreign policy that was to bedevil the remainder of Liverpool's term in office first opened. Wellington and the King, working with the Russian and Austrian ambassadors, Lieven[138] and Esterházy,[139] attempted to preserve friendly relations with the Alliance powers.[140] On the other side, Canning in his hostile letters to Chateaubriand, and even to the future Charles X, made it clear that he favoured the Spanish liberals, was hostile to France and regarded friendly relations with the autocratic states of Europe as of little value.[141]

Liverpool had set out his thoughts on economic policy in a letter to Vansittart (soon to be replaced by Robinsons) in early January 1823. Including the repayment of the Austrian loan (which did not arrive until later in the

---

136. Gash, *Lord Liverpool*, p. 223.
137. Hansard, *The Parliamentary Debates, New Series*, Vol. 8, cols 237-38 (24 February 1823).
138. Christoph Heinrich von Lieven (1774-1839) Count Lieven. Married 1800 Dorothea von Lieven, *née* Benckendorff (1785-1857). Prince and Princess Lieven from 1826. Lieven was Ambassador to the Court of St James, 1812-34. Dorothea was a Patroness of Almack's and mistress of Metternich and possibly Palmerston.
139. Paul III Anton, Prince Esterházy (1786-1866). Ambassador to Britain, 1815-42. Minister besides the King, 1848.
140. Much deplored by Brock, *Lord Liverpool and Liberal Toryism, 1820-27*, pp. 240-41.
141. Even more deplored by Mrs Arbuthnot; see Bamford and Wellington, *The Journal of Mrs. Arbuthnot, 1820-1832*, Vol. 1, pp. 208-9, 29 January 1823 and through February and March.

year), Liverpool thought he would have a surplus of more than £10 million to dispose of. Accordingly, as well as fixing the annual sinking fund at £5 million and making a bonfire of the 'assessed taxes' (sumptuary taxes which fell most heavily on the distressed and illiquid agricultural sector) he proposed reducing the malt tax by another £1 million.[142] In a letter to Grenville, Liverpool described the reduction in the assessed taxes as 'far beyond the expectation of the country at large' and within half a million of the 1792 figure.

Early in the session, Robinson, the new Chancellor of the Exchequer set out to the Commons his view of financial prospects, which contemplated a surplus of £7.1 million before any reduction in taxes. His style differed from the prosaic Vansittart's – Robinson broke into verse, then purple prose: 'We have seen the opening of a brilliant dawn, and we may anticipate without hesitation the steady and glowing splendour of a meridian sky.'[143]

Robinson proposed to halve the hated window tax and abolish a series of small sumptuary taxes on servants, gardeners and carriages that had mostly arisen during the war. These tax reliefs benefited the agricultural sector and small traders but did little for the working class. The purple prose was well received after the dullness of Vansittart, with rousing cheers at the end, and the tax reductions made Robinson popular both in the Commons and the City.

In the Lords, Liverpool spoke on the National Debt Reduction Bill, which codified the new and lower sinking fund of £5 million per annum. He regarded the sinking fund as an invaluable aid to Britain's efforts in any war, because it gave debt buyers confidence that the debts would be repaid. In peacetime, a real sinking fund must be established:

> It is scarcely possible for any statesmen or legislator to go on during peace, without paying off a part of the debt incurred during war. . . . If, during a period of peace, no part of the debt incurred during war is paid off, not only must we commence war under great disadvantages, but ultimately certain ruin must ensue.[144]

Even after the declaration of 28 January, the French moved slowly to invade Spain. Four of the five corps of the French army were headed by former Napoleonic generals and their loyalty to the regime was not assured. This problem was solved by appointing Angoulême as Commander-in-Chief, despite his lack of military experience, and appointing staunchly Royalist deputies to the corps commanders. Eventually, on 6 April, the doubters were

142. Yonge, *The Life and Administration of Robert Banks Jenkinson*, Vol. 3, pp. 247-48 (7 January to Vansittart) and 251-53 (to Grenville, wrongly dated 23 July; from Yonge's references to it the date should be January or early February, probably 23 January).

143. Hansard, *The Parliamentary Debates, New Series*, Vol. 8, cols 194-213 (24 February 1823).

144. Ibid., cols 635-38 (21 March 1823).

justified when a force of 500 leftist French and Piedmontese men attacked the French forces and were repulsed, after which the 'Hundred Thousand Sons of St Louis' advanced into Spain. They were opposed by Spanish pro-radical forces of no great quality, allied to irregulars commanded by the British renegade general Sir Robert Wilson. The French advance was steady, notably assisted by the support of most of the Spanish populace, who favoured the absolutist French invasion of 1823 as fervently as they had opposed the revolutionary French invasion of 1808.

Eventually, on 30 September, Cádiz surrendered, the Cortes abolished itself and restored Ferdinand VII to freedom under French tutelage in an armistice promising continuing constitutional rule. The following day, the freed Ferdinand abrogated the constitution and resumed rule as an autocrat, executing many of his enemies and remaining in power until his death in 1833. Despite Ferdinand's manifold failings, this was the result desired by an undoubted majority of the Spanish population, though not by the urban middle-class intellectuals who made most noise.

Angoulême, disgusted by Ferdinand's treachery, returned to France, leaving 45,000 French troops in Spain, where most of them were to remain until 1828. His father Charles X, also disgusted by Ferdinand's treachery, refused the honours Ferdinand attempted to bestow on him. However, from a French viewpoint, Chateaubriand put it best in his memoirs: 'Striding across the Spains, succeeding where Bonaparte had failed, triumphing on the same soil where a great man's arms had suffered setbacks, doing in six months what he had failed to do in seven years, was a true miracle.'[145]

Liverpool set out the government's policy on the Franco-Spanish war on 14 April. He began by reviewing events in Spain since 1812, when the constitution had been established while the Cortes was confined to the Isle of León and 'had been established on many principles extremely erroneous, and not only erroneous in themselves, but wholly inapplicable to the state and feelings of the country'. When Ferdinand had returned, Sir Henry Wellesley had advised him to alter the constitution but instead, while promising a Cortes and a representative constitution, he had provided neither and had misgoverned the country abominably. It was thus no surprise when a revolution took place, restoring the 1812 constitution.

In Liverpool's view, while foreign powers could be alarmed at the means by which the 1812 constitution had been restored, its restoration should not have given them cause for alarm, let alone intervention, because that constitution had been in force from 1812-14, when all those countries were allied to Spain. Accordingly, Britain's policy of non-interference was repeatedly stated to the Allies. Liverpool then outlined the progress of the Verona negotiations.

---

145. François-René de Chateaubriand, *Mémoires d'outre-tombe* (Paris: Garnier, 1848-50).

After Verona, Britain continued to attempt to mediate between France and Spain, but Louis XVIII's address to the French Chambers convinced both Spain and Britain that a French invasion of Spain was likely. Louis's statement that 'all authority and liberty must necessarily emanate from the Crown' gave especial offence in Britain.

As to future policy, Britain must remain neutral: 'To embark in this war for Spain but not in Spain, to submit to most of the inconveniences of war, while we confine ourselves to a few maritime operations, which could afford the Spaniards no effective assistance, would be childish, and would render us deservedly the ridicule of Europe.' Furthermore, the situation in Spain was not as in 1808, when all Spain supported resistance; Spain was now engaged in a civil war, 'in which the intelligence may be on one side, but in which it is evident that all the old stubborn prejudices are on the other. The fanaticism of liberty may be with the government, but the fanaticism of religion is with those who oppose that government.'

Finally, support for the war in France was lukewarm but, if Britain entered on Spain's side, within three weeks every Frenchman would be energised in the war with Britain. As for the current war, 'I firmly believe the undertaking of France to be absolutely impracticable, unless she is assisted by the greater portion of the Spanish people.'[146]

Ten days later, on a motion by Ellenborough[147] suggesting Britain should have defended Spain against France, Liverpool ran over the same arguments, then stated the general principle that in a conflict between monarchy and democracy, Britain, with a constitution that was a 'compromise between the principle of democracy and that of monarchy', should pursue a middle course: 'We ought not to act as the abettors of despotism on the one hand, nor the supporters of wild and impracticable theories on the other.'[148]

Liverpool responded in May to a Grey speech complaining of the Government's reluctance to intervene. After pouring scorn on Grey for his opposition to the Peninsular War, Liverpool turned to the general European situation, saying the government's objective was to prevent war breaking out in Europe, because nobody knew where it could lead. Grey claimed that the Allies wished to destroy the liberty of every country in Europe, but Liverpool:

> cannot believe that the noble earl really entertains such a chimerical idea. . . . I cannot conceal from myself, that in the present state of the world, if there is danger on one side from arbitrary doctrines, there is

146. Hansard, *The Parliamentary Debates, New Series*, Vol. 8, cols 839-68 (14 April 1823).
147. Edward Law (1790-1871). 2nd Baron Ellenborough from 1818. 1st Earl of Ellenborough from 1844. MP for Mitchell, 1813-18. Lord Privy Seal, 1828-29. President of the Board of Control, 1828-30, 1834-35, 1841, 1858. Governor General of India, 1842-44. First Lord of the Admiralty, 1846.
148. Hansard, *The Parliamentary Debates, New Series*, Vol. 8, cols 1240-48 (24 April 1823).

> danger from new opinions and revolutionary doctrines on the other. The policy of this country should lead her to maintain that situation, moral and political, which will enable her to restrain the excesses of either.[149]

Throughout Liverpool's term in office, there was considerable public dissatisfaction with the House of Lords' juridical processes, which under Eldon were superbly performed but had developed huge arrears in several areas of business. Late in the 1823 session, Liverpool made a major speech explaining that the Lords' appeal function had become intolerably backlogged, even though the Lords sat three days a week to hear appeals. The main problem was Scotland, which submitted 40 appeals to the Lords annually, compared with eight to nine from Ireland and five from England.

Liverpool therefore proposed a bill by which appeals were heard five days a week, presided over by a Deputy Speaker, until the arrears were worked through. He also proposed the appointment of a Royal Commission to come up with a better system for Scottish appeals that did not rely on an ultimate court of appeal full of people unfamiliar with Scots law. After the Royal Commission had reported, the Scottish judicature was reformed by a bill passed the following year. The debate was notable for a magnificent diatribe from Eldon, in which he denounced Scotch lawyers for obfuscating all legal points with unnecessary paperwork, while claiming his own full conversance with Scots law, having been involved with it for forty years.[150]

The Catholic Emancipation question took a new form in 1823, with a bill to allow English Catholics the vote (Irish Catholics had been enfranchised by an Act of the Irish Parliament in 1793). Liverpool agreed to the proposed change: 'The Catholics of this country are a highly respectable body and have freely admitted their uniform loyalty.' Alas, the bill failed at second reading in the Lords by 80 votes to 73.[151]

Robinson's Budget followed generally the financial statement he had made earlier in the year. In the event, the surplus on the consolidated fund totalled £8.76 million, instead of the £7.2 million that had been expected. He ended his presentation by forecasting further tax reductions in future years.[152] On modern figures, the tax reductions of 1822-23, offset by economic growth, reduced 1823 public income by £1.4 million, with a sharper drop in excise and assessed taxes being offset by an increase in customs duties. Gross public expenditure also dropped by £2.2 million, mostly through a fall in debt service payments, so that the net surplus increased by £0.8 million to £4.2 million. Despite a debt-to-GDP ratio well above 200 per cent, the public finances were now healthy.[153]

149. Ibid., Vol. 9, cols 191-200 (12 May 1823).
150. Ibid., cols 1246-51, 1321-32 and 1355-56 (26 and 30 June and 1 July 1823).
151. Ibid., cols 1487-88 (9 July 1823).
152. Ibid., cols 1412-20 (2 July 1823).
153. Mitchell, *British Historical Statistics*, pp. 581 (Income), 587 (Expenditure). The year-

The 1823 session was also notable for the passage of the 1823 Masters and Servants Act, which codified the punishments for employees breaching their employment contracts, allowing for imprisonment with hard labour for up to three months for such breaches. Passage of the law indicated that the economy had tightened sufficiently by 1823 for contract breaches to have become a significant problem; it marked the first of three modifications to labour law in successive years, as the Liverpool government sought to catch up with industrialisation. The 1823 law was heavily used; one study has shown an annual average of more than 10,000 prosecutions under it between 1858 and 1875.[154]

Peel's major penal reforms began in 1823 without significant oratorical support from Liverpool. For the first time, under the Judgement of Death Act, judges were allowed to vary death sentences on the more than 200 capital crimes, other than treason or murder, by commuting them to imprisonment; this was thought more likely to bring jury convictions for moderate offences. By the Gaols Act, jailers were paid directly by the state and prisoners were segregated by sex; the Act was largely ineffective until inspectors were appointed in 1835. Most significant, almost all of the provisions of the 1723 Black Act was repealed, slashing the number of generally working-class felonies carrying the death penalty.

In general, the 1823 session was easier than previous sessions. The Whigs were demoralised by repeated failures and the accession of centre groups to the government in 1820-22. Canning's House of Commons presence was less and less in evidence; Sir William Fremantle, a Buckingham acolyte favourable to Canning, remarked at the end of the session that Canning had 'done nothing, had allowed Peel to take command, and the government would have done as well without him as a leader as with him'.[155]

In 1823-24, with government finances now satisfactory, Liverpool organised three items of public investment with a benign effect until our own day. First, George III had assembled a scholarly library of over 65,000 volumes, a highly important Enlightenment book collection. Early in 1823, George IV announced he was giving it to the nation. Liverpool arranged a £50,000 government grant for expansion of the British Museum to include a King's Library gallery, over 300 feet long, that became one of the central adornments of the Museum for 170 years after it opened in 1827.[156]

end is 5 January so, to get the figures for the (approximate) calendar year 1823, you should use the 1824 figures in the tables.

154. See, for example, S. Naidu and M. Yuchtman, 'How Green Was My Valley? Coercive Contract Enforcement in 19th Century Industrial Britain', Tech. rep., Harvard University, 2009.

155. Quoted Gash, *Lord Liverpool*, p. 221. Sir William Henry Fremantle (1766-1850). MP for Enniskillen, Harwich, Saltash, Tain Burghs and Buckingham, 1806-27. PC, 1822. Treasurer of the Royal Household, 1826-37.

156. Despite objections from the Museum's Trustees, the collection was moved in 1998 to

Also in 1823, one of the world's great art collections came on the market, that of the Lloyds underwriter, John Julius Angerstein, who had died in January.[157] Liverpool was helped here by the final repayment of Austria's old war debt, so he authorised the government to purchase the collection for £57,000. The collection, together with a further collection given by Sir George Beaumont, became the centrepiece of the National Gallery, opened in 1824, initially in Angerstein's old town house in Pall Mall.

Liverpool's third public investment was perhaps of even more long-term importance. It originated from a pamphlet by Charles Babbage explaining the workings of his proposed Difference Engine, the principal practical use of which was to eliminate the errors in hand-made nautical and gunnery tables. This pamphlet was discussed at a Treasury meeting presided over by Liverpool, after which a grant of £1,500 was given to Babbage to develop the large-scale Difference Engine. The initial grant came with promises of more if needed.

The Difference Engine proved more difficult than expected to construct, although Babbage's inheritance of £100,000 in 1827 made it easier to continue work. Wellington, a good friend to science, awarded Babbage a further grant of £3,000 in 1828. However, in the event no Difference Engine was constructed until another engineer, using Babbage's plans, made one for the International Exhibition of 1862.

Meanwhile, it was only after a total of £17,000 had been granted to Babbage, and the Difference Engine had been abandoned by Babbage in favour of a programmable Analytical Engine, that government funding was cut off by Peel in 1842. Peel had been a Babbage-sceptic even when the project was first proposed; as he wrote to Croker, 'I should like a little previous consideration before I move in a thin house of country gentlemen, a large vote for the construction of a wooden man to calculate tables from the formula x^2+x+41.'[158]

Babbage's failure can partly be attributed to the temperamental failings that often go with genius. The full-sized Difference Engine operated at the limits of early nineteenth-century metallurgical technology, requiring tolerances right at the edge of those available. Further, it is not clear, given the cost of each Difference Engine what success could have led to – without electronics, the engines were useful but technologically marginal. Still, the Liverpool government's modest 1823 grant marks an investment in the distant future that shows it very different from its traditional Whiggish and Disraelian portrayal.

---

a six-storey tower at the British Library.

157. John Julius Angerstein (1732-1823). Born in St Petersburg, possibly the illegitimate son of the Empress Anna. Lloyds underwriter and slave trader. Chairman of Lloyds, 1790-96.

158. Peel letter to Croker, 8 March 1823, quoted in Croker, *The Correspondence and Diaries of John Wilson Croker*, Vol. 1, pp. 262-63. Jennings describes the Difference Engine as 'a mechanical device of which a good deal was heard some years ago, but which never answered to the expectations that were formed of it'.

Liverpool was well aware of the technological and economic changes that were transforming Britain. In 1823, for example, he travelled to Walmer in a steamboat for the first time. He saw the economic and social benefits too; in a letter to Canning that autumn he remarked that 'it might fairly be said, that Great Britain was never in such a state of welfare and content, as at present'.[159]

During 1823. Liverpool refused to make the King's physician and confidant, Sir William Knighton, a Privy Counsellor on the proper constitutional ground that this would take authority away from ministers.[160] Knighton's influence was hereafter used against Liverpool, which over the next few years strengthened Canning's position. However, at this stage, Canning's strong influence was much resented by the King, who wrote to Liverpool in November: 'The misfortune of this Government is that it is a Government of departments, but Lord Liverpool must endeavour to correct this defect by suppressing the passion which seems to exist for speech making out of time and out of proper place.'[161]

Canning's gradual alienation of Wellington and other colleagues was to cause trouble in the years ahead. His foreign policy also alienated the former Allies, as his disdain for them became more apparent and the popularity in Spain of the French invaders made Whiggish and Canningite supporters of the bourgeois radical constitutionalists seem increasingly foolish. Their position was further weakened by John VI of Portugal's suspension of the country's constitution, thus defeating the army which had attempted to impose it and removing for the moment the danger of a French invasion. Already by June, the hitherto friendly Metternich was referring to 'the ill-will of the English minister'.[162]

After France's success in Spain, British fears naturally turned to possible French designs on the former Spanish colonies in Latin America. Canning was especially fearful of a Spanish 'indemnity' to France that allowed France to take over Latin American countries. Nevertheless, he devised a stratagem that effectively neutralised France's power in the region. Good relations with the United States had been a fixed policy of Liverpool's government since the war ended so, in August 1823, Canning opened discussions with the US Monroe[163]

159. Letter to Canning, quoted in Yonge, *The Life and Administration of Robert Banks Jenkinson*, Vol. 3, p. 259.
160. William Knighton (1776-1836). Baronet from 1813. Private Secretary to King George IV, 1822-30.
161. George IV to Liverpool, 6 November 1823, in Aspinall, *The Letters of King George IV, 1812-30*, Vol. 3, pp. 38-39.
162. Bamford and Wellington, *The Journal of Mrs. Arbuthnot, 1820-1832*, Vol. 1, p. 238, 4 June 1823.
163. James Monroe (1758-1831). Delegate to the Confederation Congress, 1783-88. US Senator, 1790-94. Minister to France, 1794-96. Governor of Virginia, 1799-1802 and 1811. Minister to UK, 1803-7. Secretary of State, 1811-17. President of the United States, 1817-25.

administration and Secretary of State John Quincy Adams, suggesting a joint declaration disapproving of third-party intervention in the conflicts between Spain and her colonies.

Adams, however, believed that an independent declaration by the United States would avoid accusations of following a pro-British policy (a big problem for a New Englander aiming to run for President in 1824). Hence in a message to Congress President Monroe propounded what became the Monroe Doctrine, committing the United States to international isolationism and calling for an end to any further colonisation by European powers. With the US Navy still inadequate to police this declaration, the country relied on Britain for its enforcement but it nevertheless achieved Canning's short-term objective, of discouraging any French attempts to seize Spanish colonies.[164]

1823 was a year of rapid progress economically and even agriculture began to recover from its deep depression. Wheat prices rebounded by more than a third during the year, as the harvest proved to be a moderate one and stocks were run down. There was not yet any great increase in the volume of £1 and £2 country banknotes issued under the 1822 Act, which later became one of the causes of the 1825 bubble; stamped issues increased only from £4.3 million to £4.5 million.[165]

Brick production rose no less than 22 per cent above the 1822 level and was now well above the previous 1819 peak. Exports of manufactured cotton and woollen goods remained flat, albeit at a high level. Overall, Hoffman's production index rose another five per cent, and was now 15 per cent above its 1818 peak. The foreign bond boom slackened somewhat, and focussed on Europe rather than Latin America, with £5.5 million of bonds raised for Austria, Portugal and Spain. Finally, of most importance for the future, the Act for constructing the first true railway, the Stockton and Darlington, with capital investment of £450,000 was passed. Like many other advances that we associate with the Victorians, the Railway Age thus had its genesis under Liverpool.[166]

---

164. Daniel Walker Howe, *What Hath God Wrought: The Transformation of America, 1815-1848* (Oxford: Oxford University Press, 2007) pp. 111-15, summarises the Monroe Doctrine's evolution from a US viewpoint.
165. Tooke, *A History of Prices*, Vol. 2, pp. 122-30.
166. Figures taken from Gayer, Rostow and Schwartz, *The Growth and Fluctuation of the British Economy, 1790-1850*, Vol. 1, pp. 171-210.

VIII.

Bubble, Reform, Death and Oblivion, 1824-28

In 1824, Liverpool's health began to deteriorate seriously. His pulse rate, normally around 75, dropped to an alarming 50, first one and then the other leg became painful and swollen and he complained of feeling weak, depressed and listless.[1] He went to Bath before the beginning of Parliament's Easter recess and his doctor informed the King that he did not think Liverpool would be able to carry on much longer. In the event, Bath seemed to agree with him, his pulse rate improved and he was back in London by 1 May. However, in June Colchester wrote of him: 'Lord Liverpool, who for some months has always favoured and laid up one leg, now coils both legs upon the bench where he sits and is evidently in worse health.'[2]

Knighton, the King's doctor and private secretary reported to the King that Liverpool's heart was defective, his blood vessels obstructed and his head affected in a manner reminiscent of the deaths of his father and grandfather. How Knighton knew the medical diagnosis for the obscure Colonel Charles Jenkinson, who had been dead for 74 years, is unclear;[3] as for Liverpool's father, he had lived in good health until almost 80. In any case, Liverpool's retirement for health reasons was a matter of constant gossip from 1824 forward, although the Cabinet was known to be so split that only Liverpool could hold it together.

The King's Address opening the session was positively exuberant on the state of the economy and its effects on public order: 'At no former period has there prevailed throughout all classes of the community in this island, a more cheerful spirit of order, or a more just sense of the advantages which, under the

1. Gash, *Lord Liverpool*, pp. 226-27.
2. Abbot, *The Diaries and Correspondence of Charles Abbot, Lord Colchester*, Vol. 3, p. 330.
3. William Watts, less obscure, died at only 42; maybe this is what Knighton meant.

Robert Banks Jenkinson, 2nd Earl of Liverpool in 1826. holding the deeds of the National Gallery. Sir Thomas Lawrence.

blessing of Providence, they enjoy.' The Address also raised a new question: the abolition of slavery, following a major slave revolt in Demerara[4] (now part of Guyana) the previous summer.

Liverpool's own speech began with rejoicing at the country's prosperity and pointing out that its former distresses had now been removed by natural causes 'and, I rejoice to say, without any tampering interference of Parliament'. He added that the difficulties had been caused by the transition from the artificial prosperity of the war years, with huge government spending, to the natural prosperity of peace. The return to gold had also caused difficulties but the country was now returned to a natural prosperity based on a solid monetary standard.

Liverpool then turned to foreign relations, where he deprecated the French attack on Spain because France 'could make out no specific case which gave her any title to interfere with the internal regulations of Spain'. He had advised the Spanish constitutionalists to compromise and his advice had been proved correct by events:

> Is it not evident, not only that the great majority, but a majority so great as to leave the minority an object of surprise with us, hailed the French as friends who came to overthrow the constitution? . . . Notwithstanding their jealousy to foreigners, and their dislike of Frenchmen, they hailed the French army as deliverers, and thus showed that they hated the constitution more than either.

Liverpool then praised the Duc d'Angoulême:

> However much I at first deprecated the invasion of Spain, I cannot withhold my praise from that illustrious prince, who instead of encouraging Ultraism among the Spaniards, did everything to check it, and who gave fair promise, in that mission, of what may be expected when he should ascend the throne of his fathers.[5] . . . The Ultraism complained of is the sentiment of the Spaniards, not of the invaders, and I have no more idea of sending British bayonets to make people free against their will, than to enslave them against their will.

Liverpool then turned to Latin America, where he announced that the government would like Spain to recognise its colonies' independence, but that

4. Centred on a plantation owned by Sir John Gladstone, the future prime minister's father. After the riots and the resolutions promising compensation to slave-owners on abolition, Gladstone bought major new plantations; in the event, although the largest recipient of compensation, he lost about half his investment.

5. Alas, Angoulême was to occupy the French throne as Louis XIX for only twenty minutes in July 1830, one of the great missed opportunities in French history.

its policy was unfettered from any obligations, whatever line Spain took. On slavery, he hoped that both Houses would do what was right, while treating the subject with care and temperance.

As in the previous year, Robinson presented the financial situation of the country early. Customs revenue had increased by almost ten per cent and, while excise duties had lagged, overall revenue had been well above Robinson's 1823 estimate. In addition, there had been an unexpected windfall from repayment of the 1790s Austrian loan. He also announced that £500,000 of the next instalment of the Austrian loan repayment would be devoted to an extension of the 1818 church building programme, and a further £300,000 to the rebuilding and extension of Windsor Castle. The church building grant met with noisier Whig opposition than in 1818 but nevertheless passed, much to Liverpool's satisfaction.

Robinson then turned to another refunding, by which £50 million of the four per cent stock should be refunded into 3½ per cent stock, which would itself not be refundable for five years, thus further reducing the national debt's interest after Vansittart's refunding of the five per cent debt in 1822-23. Robinson then conducted a novel thought experiment for that period, looking forward three years to 1827 and projecting small surpluses for those years, after sinking fund payments. From these he proposed to make tax reductions on rum and sea coals (those shipped to London or elsewhere) instead of reducing the national debt further. He also proposed to reduce duties on wool and silk, soaring into rhetorical heights: 'It is time to cut the cords which tie down commerce to the earth, that she may spring aloft, unconfined and unrestricted, and shower her blessings over every part of the world.' He ended with an encomium on the unreformed Parliament, which had brought these blessings to the country, and was met with resounding cheers.[6]

While Robinson was much better than Vansittart at bringing the House of Commons to its feet cheering, his economics were suspect. By employing for the first time a practice subsequently overindulged in, of forecasting revenues three years ahead in a roaring bull market, and then cutting taxes to meet them, he ran into fiscal trouble two years later. The exceptional economic effervescence of 1824 was partly caused by a wealth effect from the post-war rise in Consols prices. Thus, Robinson's premature tax cuts in 1824 and 1825 left the national debt uncomfortably large during the 1830s and early 1840s, when the abolition of slavery imposed an additional £20 million compensation cost and capital investment for the railways was exceptionally heavy.

Liverpool continued to fight a rearguard battle for the relationships of Castlereagh's Alliance system. He took the opportunity of the Austrian loan bill, regularising its repayment of 1790s debt, to praise the Austrian government. On Francis I, 'no sovereign ever sat on a throne who possessed nicer or more

6. Hansard, *The Parliamentary Debates, New Series*, Vol. 10, cols 304-37 (23 February 1824).

honourable feelings'. Liverpool also paid tribute to Metternich's conviction that some repayment on the loan should be made.[7] Alas, the strictures by Canning on the Austrian government prevented Liverpool's friendly words from pacifying Metternich.[8]

The session's major foreign policy debate was on a Lansdowne motion proposing the recognition without delay of the former Spanish colonies' independence. In reply, Liverpool began by agreeing with Lansdowne that commerce should be as unshackled as possible but pointed out that there was already considerable commerce with Latin America through Britain's West Indian colonies. From 1808, Britain had attempted to press on the various Spanish governments the desirability of dealing with their colonies more liberally. Then, between 1815 and 1822 Britain had attempted to mediate between Spain and her rebellious colonies but that mediation was never accepted.

In 1822, the government had brought the Spanish colonies into the Navigation Acts system, allowing them free trade with Britain in British ships but still not formally recognising their independence. The government had informed the Spanish government that it intended to send consuls to its ex-colonies but had not done so owing to the Franco-Spanish crisis. Then, after French success in Spain, a further step had been taken, opposing European intervention in those colonies:

> I know it has been said, that the intentions of the powers of Europe respecting the South American states, have been changed, in consequence of the speech of the President of the United States of America. What effect that speech might have had, it is not for me to say, but whatever its effect might have been, I feel it but justice to the King's ministers to declare, that weeks before that speech reached Europe, it was distinctly communicated by them to the government of France that, without interfering with the rights of Spain, Great Britain could not see with indifference any foreign power interfere in the struggle between that country and the South American states.

Liverpool then turned to the question of diplomatic recognition and pointed out that in a time of peace only Spain could recognise its colonies' independence. Liverpool felt that, contrary to the line France had taken when Britain's American colonies rebelled, Britain had no right to recognise the independence of Spanish colonies while a war between them and Spain continued actively: 'God forbid that, under any circumstances, Great Britain should feel disposed to follow such an example!'

7. Ibid., cols 877-80 (11 March 1824).
8. Metternich letter to Wellington, 15 April 1824, quoted in Wellington, *Despatches, Correspondence*, Vol. 2, pp. 249-50.

Liverpool contended that Britain's prohibition of foreign interference in Latin America was in practice worth a thousand ambassadors and that Latin America already had all the advantages of formal recognition. The government must be sure that the new Latin American governments were stable and capable of upholding international relations. It had therefore sent consuls to them with instructions to report back on their progress. Further, it was simple courtesy to give Spain the first opportunity to recognize the independence of its own colonies. Finally, if the states of Europe intended to convene a Congress to consider this question, Britain could not be a party to it. He ended by proposing an amendment to Lansdowne's motion commending the government's 'firmness, moderation and prudence'. Lansdowne's motion was defeated by 95 votes to 34 and Liverpool's amendment was agreed to without a division.[9]

The 1824 Parliament took a further step towards controlling the slave trade and towards the abolition of slavery altogether. Liverpool, supporting the legislation, said the immediate object was to improve the condition of the slaves, by regulation and by moral and religious instruction. On abolition:

> I have only to observe that the great feature of the present plan . . . is the introduction of some principle to enable every man to obtain his own manumission, and not only his own manumission, but that of his wife and children. If it shall hereafter be found that this plan cannot be carried into effect, or that its operation is not sufficiently prompt to prove beneficial, it will then be a question for consideration, whether parliament might not afford further facilities.[10]

Liverpool's thinking on slavery and the slave trade had evolved. During the 1806-7 debates, he had not been an unthinking supporter of the slave trade. His Evangelical Christianity made him sympathetic to the Clapham Sect and reformers such as Wilberforce. Thus by 1824, when anti-slavery agitation began in earnest, he was already sympathetic to its objective, although cautious about the means and costs of reaching that objective.

Liverpool returned to the subject of Ireland on several occasions, making a major speech on 8 April, on the Earl of Darnley's[11] motion calling for a select committee. Liverpool, speaking immediately after Darnley, began by apologising for speaking early, saying that in his present state of health, he might be exhausted before the appropriate hour should arrive. He opposed Darnley's select committee because he felt it would raise hopes in Ireland that could not be realised.

---

9. Hansard, *The Parliamentary Debates, New Series*, Vol. 10, cols 992-1003 (15 March 1824).
10. Ibid., cols 1215-16 (18 March 1824).
11. John Bligh (1767-1831). 4th Earl of Darnley (Ireland) from 1791, based in Kent. Notable cricketer.

While he had not visited Ireland and was therefore free of local prejudice (!), he had met many large bodies of Irish people and felt that:

> a more honest, a more industrious, set of people, or a people more alive to feelings of gratitude for favours conferred (whatever might be said of them in their own country) does not exist. . . . Whether we look to the services of the people of that country in our armies or our navies or in any other department in which their services are required, a more useful set of people do not exist in the world.

The Lords should also take account of regional differences; Ulster was as prosperous as any other part of Britain and so should be excluded from any remarks about the difficulties of the remainder of Ireland. Past English policy towards Ireland could sometimes be described as 'tyranny and oppression' and more often as narrow and selfish. However, he believed Ireland's main problem derived from having received English laws and English institutions at an unfit moment.

Conversely, at no period had so many acts been passed for the benefit of Ireland as during the reign of George III, and indeed he believed that no country had done more for any part of its empire than Britain had done for Ireland during the last few years. England was the highest taxed country of Europe, yet she had taken on the debt of Ireland, and Ireland was now the lowest taxed country of Europe except perhaps Switzerland, paying only one fifth as much as England. England had also forwarded Irish education, formerly in Protestant schools, but since 1817 in un-denominational schools, the number of which had increased from 30 in 1817 to 1,122 in 1823, teaching the Douai version of Scriptures to Catholic children.

Liverpool then observed that Irish poverty was largely due to the country having no poor laws, so that the impoverished Irish in times of famine fared worse than slaves, who were looked after by their masters. Landlord absenteeism also removed the normal protection which a landlord gave to his tenants and produced the oppressive evils of middlemen who detracted from the profits of both landlords and tenants.

Finally, Catholic Emancipation was a question to be argued in its own right but he did not see how it would make much difference to Ireland, as Ireland's property almost entirely rested with the Protestants, who would therefore continue to have most of the political power.[12] Darnley's motion lost by 57 votes to seventeen in the House of Lords. Nevertheless, the Commons appointed a Select Committee on Ireland.

While Liverpool was in Bath and Parliament in recess, a major row with the King blew up over Canning's attendance at the City of London's Easter

12. Hansard, *The Parliamentary Debates, New Series*, Vol. 11, cols 261-69 (8 April 1824).

Monday dinner hosted by the Lord Mayor, Robert Waithman.[13] As Sheriff of London in 1820, Waithman had been prominent in his support of Queen Caroline, and the King wanted the government to have nothing to do with him.

No minister had attended the Lord Mayor's Banquet the previous November, but Liverpool believed that boycotting Waithman completely gave the opposition an undue advantage and so had expected to attend the Easter Monday dinner. In the event, Canning and Williams-Wynn did so. The King was furious and there was an angry exchange of correspondence. Liverpool pointed out that attendance at such banquets followed a precedent set in Pitt's time and Canning made the point that the Government was fairly popular, so undue subversion was not expected and did not occur, except for a small pro-Greek demonstration which Waithman suppressed.

Robinson's 1824 Budget followed closely his earlier financial statement. It reversed the five per cent and ten per cent cuts in civil service salaries ordered two years earlier and restored the ten per cent cut in the Royal allowance. He ran through the cuts in duties he had already announced, which gave a small surplus after sinking fund payments, and announced that the refinancing of the four per cent Consols had been agreed to by £68 million of the £75 million outstanding. On modern figures, revenue in 1824 increased by £1.2 million, from the greater yield of excise duties. Expenditure increased by the same amount, with proportionate increases in civil, army and navy expenditures, presumably reflecting the restoration of the 1822 salary cuts. Thus, the surplus was again £4.2 million.[14]

The summer of 1824 saw the exceptionally favourable money market conditions confirmed by July's rate on the quarterly Exchequer bill funding being reduced to 1½ pence per day (2.28 per cent) a new low for several decades. The Bank of England also passed without demur Liverpool and Robinson's request to backstop the £50 million conversion of four per cent Consols with an issue of Exchequer bills to the value of £7 million to be repaid from the sinking fund, also at the 1½ pence per day rate but with a potentially longer maturity.[15]

Following his return from Bath, Liverpool spoke at length in favour of the Aliens Bill, which gave the Crown the statutory right to expel aliens from the country. He argued that revolutionary doctrines were still common and, while foreign revolutionaries should have the right of refuge in Britain, they should

13. Robert Waithman (1764-1833). MP for City of London, 1818-20, 1826-33. Sheriff of the City of London, 1820. Lord Mayor, 1823-24. Radical and prosperous self-made draper.

14. Mitchell, *British Historical Statistics*, pp. 581 (Income), 587 (Expenditure). The year-end is 5 January so, to get the figures for the (approximate) calendar year 1824, you should use the 1825 figures in the tables.

15. Bank of England, Minutes of the Court of Directors, 1 July 1824.

not be able to foment revolution from its shelter – British neutrality in foreign disputes required no less. The bill would not apply to any individual who had lived in Britain for seven years.[16] The bill's second reading was passed by 80 votes to 35.

Liverpool also proposed a bill righting some ancient injustices, reversing the attainders on the Scottish earldoms of Mar, Kenmure and Perth and the baronies of Strathallan and Nairn, all of whom had been attainted following the 1715 rebellion. He also proposed to reverse the attainder he called the 'greatest blot on our history' that of Baron Stafford, the aged Catholic executed at the behest of a Whig parliamentary mob in 1680.[17]

Liverpool spoke in favour of two limited measures of Catholic Emancipation, proposed by Lansdowne, which would give English Catholics the right to vote, open magistracies and local offices to them and restore the office of Earl Marshal, one of whose duties is to preside at coronations, to the Catholic Duke of Norfolk. Liverpool believed it was necessary to have a Protestant Parliament, a Protestant Privy Council and Protestant judges but the present bills related only to inferior offices. That Catholics in Ireland could vote for their own parliament was a powerful argument to extend the franchise to Catholics in England. He believed concession here would be the best way of preserving a Protestant constitution. Despite Liverpool's support, opposition from Eldon, Westmorland and others condemned Lansdowne's bills to defeat by 38 votes and 34 votes. However, a separate Bill restoring the Duke of Norfolk's privileges was passed.[18]

A late session bill on marine insurance, breaking the duopoly that had existed since 1720 and allowing new companies to be formed, drew notice from both Liverpool and Eldon that in the following session they would look again at the subject of establishing companies by Act of Parliament, and of ensuring that their proprietors remained responsible for their actions. The Bubble Act 1720, which banned the formation of new public companies unless approved by Royal Charter, was now causing real distortions to the economy and the government had become aware that something new was needed.[19] Equally, prevailing market speculation was already causing disquiet such that the House of Lords adopted a standing order which required that, before the second reading of a bill allowing a company to be formed, a committee must report whether its capital had been three quarters paid up.

In June Liverpool laid out the government's policy on recognising the South American republics. There were no engagements with countries other than Spain that would prevent such recognition, Spain itself had been given ample

16. Hansard, *The Parliamentary Debates, New Series*, Vol. 11, cols 628-33 (11 May 1824).
17. Ibid., cols 815-16 (24 May 1824).
18. Ibid., cols 840-42 (24 May 182.
19. Ibid., cols 1457 and 1472 (18 and 21 June 1824); The bill was sponsored by Rothschild interests, and resulted in the foundation of Alliance Assurance.

time to recognise its former colonies' independence, but had not done so, and the only remaining hurdle was official information from the government's commissioners, on whether the governments of those countries were sufficiently permanent as to make recognition desirable. That information had not yet been received but the government would act when it came in.[20]

These years were notable for new 'reforming' legislation. Generally, Liverpool played little part in the debates surrounding this legislation, though he made suggestions to the responsible minister on its content. The most significant legislation economically was a trio of bills relating to workers' rights. One repealed the 1799/1800 Combination Acts and all earlier anti-combination legislation, thus allowing completely free collective bargaining and the legal formation of trade unions; another abolished the punitive 1719 legislation forbidding 'artificers' from emigrating; and a third set up arbitration provisions for disputes between masters and workmen.

This package of legislation was sponsored by the Radical Whig Joseph Hume,[21] and partly drafted by the ultra-Radical agitator Francis Place.[22] However, it was supported by Huskisson, who had decided that the Combination Acts alienated the working classes and made it too difficult for them to defend their interests in wage negotiations. Thus, the Bill passed the Commons with little debate. When the legislation came to the Lords, it passed without debate. However, after a surge in industrial action convinced Ministers they had gone too far in liberalisation, the subject was re-considered the following year and the result was the 1825 Combinations of Workmen Act prohibiting trade unions from attempting to collectively bargain for better terms and conditions at work and suppressing the right to strike.

The Vagrancy Act 1824, introduced by Peel, is still largely in force. It was directed against the rising number of beggars in urban areas and made begging on the street an offence, punishable by up to one month's imprisonment. Not all the 'liberalizing reforms' sponsored by Peel and Canning were entirely liberalising, to modern sensibilities.[23]

---

20. Hansard, *The Parliamentary Debates, New Series*, Vol. 11, cols 1480-82 (24 June 1824).
21. Joseph Hume (1777-1855). MP for Weymouth and Melcombe, Aberdeen Burghs, Middlesex, Kilkenny City and Montrose Burghs, 1812, 1818-41, 1842-55.
22. Francis Place (1771-1854). Radical tailor. London Corresponding Society, 1794-7. Supported Chartism and Corn Laws repeal in old age but held back from the Radical agitation of 1816-19.
23. Civil liberties were a concern during the debate. As the Whig MP, John Smith (1767-1842) (MP for Wendover, Nottingham, Midhurst, Chichester and Buckinghamshire, 1802-34) said: 'Of the magistracy of the country generally, I think very highly, but unquestionably, in some of the small corporate towns, there are individuals in the commission of the peace, who are in the very lowest sphere of life, and it really is too much that the character of an English subject, under such peculiar circumstances, should be at the mercy of the immediate decision of one such person.'

The Weights and Measures Act, on the other hand, was a codifying piece of legislation on which all can agree, then and now. It repealed all previous legislation and introduced the Imperial system as a standardised system of weights and measures. It was introduced by Sir George Clerk,[24] a Lord of the Admiralty, with the encouragement of Melville and Barrow, and was the first full codification of British weights and measures, only effectively repealed by EU-mandated legislation in 1985.

During the spring, news reached London of the most difficult British military conflict of Liverpool's later years: the first Anglo-Burmese War. The Third Burmese Empire under the Konbaung dynasty had established itself over the previous century, and through expansion into Manipur and Assam had acquired a lengthy border with British India. Having been uniformly successful in battle, the Burmese believed they could drive Britain out of East Bengal and accordingly occupied Shalpuri island, claimed by the East India Company, in September 1823. The recently arrived Amherst was unwilling to lose face and hence declared war on the Burmese Empire.

From either a British or a Burmese viewpoint, the war was a near-disaster. British forces were highly successful, with the unsung hero of the War of 1812, General Joseph Morrison, capturing the coastal, low-lying province of Arakan, before falling victim to fever along with most of his troops. Meanwhile over two years, the main British force under General Archibald Campbell, after meeting with early defeats, captured both Rangoon and the ancient capital of Ava, forcing the Burmese into the Treaty of Yandabo, signed in February 1826, which included a £1 million indemnity and the cession to Britain of Arakan and several coastal or border provinces.

The war overall cost £13 million, however, nearly two years' full peacetime army estimates and causing the near bankruptcy of the East India Company. The unhealthy coastal Burmese climate also killed 15,000 British soldiers. Only Amherst's friendship with Canning prevented him being recalled in disgrace. As for the Burmese Empire, the indemnity impoverished it for decades and it then fell victim to British expansionism in two subsequent wars in 1852-53 and 1885.

The Anglo-Burmese War included one technological high note, when the East India Company's single paddle-steamer gunboat, the 60-horsepower *Diana*, built in Kidderpore, Kolkata in 1823 and commanded by Frederick Marryat,[25] the future inventor of the naval war epic, became the first steam

---

24. George Clerk (1787-1867). 6th Baronet from 1793. FRS, 1819. MP for Edinburghshire, Stamford and Dover, 1811-32, 1835-37, 1838-52. Lord of the Admiralty, 1819-27, 1828-30. Financial Secretary to the Treasury, 1841-45. Master of the Mint, 1845-46. PC, 1845. Uncle of James Clerk Maxwell.

25. Frederick Marryat (1792-1848). Navy from 1806. Commander, 1815. Captain, 1824. Left Navy, 1830. FRS. Author of *Mr. Midshipman Easy* (1836) and *The Children of the New Forest* (1847), *inter alia.*

vessel deployed in war. It achieved great success against the Burmese war praus, whose elite oarsmen fell exhausted and vulnerable after a few hours being chased up the fast-flowing Irrawaddy River by the *Diana*'s inexorable paddle wheels. Indeed, the *Diana* was so successful that the Burmese government insisted on acquiring it as part of the peace settlement.

The summer and autumn of 1824 were for Liverpool a relaxed, contented period, during which his health improved, with stays at Walmer and a further holiday at Bognor. He engaged in an extended correspondence with Croker on the history of the previous century, describing Horace Walpole as 'as bad a man as ever lived; I cannot call him a violent party man, he had not virtue enough to be so; he was the most sensuous and selfish of mortals'. As for Burke:

> the works of Burke with his letters will contain the whole strength and secret of the Whig cause during the last reign. . . . I differ from him on many points, but I look to him as one of the great oracles of my country. I wish the Tory cause had found as good an expositor.[26]

A useful corrective for the modern theory holding Burke as the founder of Conservatism!

On 16 September, the long-ailing Louis XVIII finally died, to be succeeded by Charles X, well known to Liverpool from the 1813-14 negotiations. Since Charles X had hankerings to restore the pre-1789 *Ancien Régime*, there were two dangers: that the regime might reorient its foreign policy away from Britain and towards Russia; and that it might become so unpopular as to fall (as indeed happened in 1830).

When he heard of the French king's death, Liverpool wrote to Canning setting out British policy. He was eager to follow the most punctilious rules of protocol, to provide an additional buttress to the restored regime. In view of Charles X's connection with Britain, Liverpool asked the King to bestow the Garter on him. He wanted to send a special mission to France, but felt that Canning should not lead it, to avoid giving it a political character and alarming the other powers who feared Britain's growing support for the Latin American states. As for France's orientation:

> I believe her interest to be to incline to this country, and I believe further this to be Villèle's opinion, but he does not act upon it. He is afraid of the Allies. He is afraid of the ultra-Royalists, who revolt at our limitations as to the principle of legitimacy, and he is afraid perhaps still more of the public opinion in France, which at all times, but most especially since 1815, is hostile to England.[27]

---

26. Liverpool letter to Croker, 23 August 1824, quoted in Croker, *The Correspondence and Diaries of John Wilson Croker*, Vol. 1, pp. 270-71.
27. Liverpool letter to Canning, 21 September 1824, quoted in Yonge, *The Life and*

Britain's approach to the new French regime was muddled by the coincidence that Westmorland was in Paris 'seeking adventures among a class of persons far removed from all political intrigue'[28] at the time of Louis XVIII's death and took the opportunity of congratulating Charles X. Charles X in return assured him that all France's troubles dated from its decision to aid the American rebels, a clear implication against Britain's potential recognition of the ex-Spanish colonies. This infuriated Canning, who wanted Anglo-French relations to be safely in the hands of himself and his crony Lord Granville (the former Granville Leveson-Gower), the new ambassador. When Villèle told Granville France reserved the right to keep troops in Spain for ten years, if necessary, Canning proposed a belligerent response, which only a lengthy Cabinet discussion persuaded him to tone down.

Liverpool's foreign policy fears of Charles X's regime were mostly unfounded. France kept a modest force in Spain until 1828 but had little influence on Ferdinand VII's policies. The main French military engagement before 1830, the 1827 Battle of Navarino, was fought in alliance with both Russia and the Canning government, while the major 1830 victory in Algeria of Charles X's regime was not opposed by Britain. Charles X's regime, and especially Villèle until he was ousted in 1828, was generally a friend to traditional British Tories and befriended by them; Whigs and Canningites were ambivalent to it.

However, Charles X's domestic policy was counterproductive. He paid an indemnity of 988 million francs (about £39 million) to nobles who had lost land in the Revolution, a huge burden on the struggling French economy and a policy avoided by the English King Charles II in a similar situation. He also passed an Anti-Sacrilege Act, including the death penalty for major sacrileges, which merely encouraged the strong French anti-clericalism. Charles X's loss of control in 1830, despite his successful Algiers campaign, was due to the same cause as Louis XVI's in 1789: chaotic public finances combined with general unpopularity. Louis Philippe's government, which succeeded it, was little improvement in its financial management and suffered from much worse corruption; one can only mourn 1830's missed opportunity for rule by Angoulême.

Liverpool remained friendly towards Alexander I's Russia and believed her threat to India was contingent on war breaking out between Russia and Britain for other reasons. He also hoped to restrain the 'war party' in Russia, which wanted to intervene militarily to secure Greek independence. Canning's refusal to consider attending a Congress made it impossible to procure a united Allied front on the Greek question, which could have restrained both Russian and Turkish policy.[29] Thus, the Congress held in St Petersburg without British or

---

Administration of Robert Banks Jenkinson, Vol. 3, p. 294.

28. Bamford and Wellington, *The Journal of Mrs. Arbuthnot, 1820-1832*, Vol. 1, p. 352, 21 October 1824.

29. Yonge, *The Life and Administration of Robert Banks Jenkinson*, Vol. 3, p. 295-96.

Turkish participation from January 1825 proved abortive and broke up in May amidst much recrimination – which should not have happened, given the general agreement between the Congress powers on the Greek question.[30] St Petersburg was the last of the Congress System meetings; this mechanism for settling disputes between the Great Powers would be sorely missed.

The other major issue with Russia was the boundary between Russian and British spheres of influence in the north-west of the American continent (Russia still held Alaska). The United States had agreed with Russia by a treaty of April 1824 that Russian claims to territory would be abandoned south of 54 degrees 40 minutes North. Draft treaties were exchanged between Britain and Russia through the autumn of 1824, until the Treaty of St Petersburg, signed in February 1825, defined the same latitude as the boundary between Russian and British spheres of interest. It then only remained to define the boundary between British and American spheres; this was not finally settled until 1846, by a line continuing the 49th parallel to the Pacific.

Late in 1824, the recognition of the Latin American republics became an immediate issue. Liverpool's views were set down in a detailed memorandum to the Cabinet, attempting to achieve unanimous agreement. He began by pointing out that the Latin American rebellions had begun in opposition to Joseph Bonaparte and in support of the legitimate Spanish king; Britain had therefore supported them. After the war ended, Britain repeatedly attempted to mediate between Spain and her colonies, as it appeared that a concessionary policy by Madrid would keep them in the fold. Thus, their loss could be ascribed to the rigid and inflexible obstinacy of the Spanish government. Therefore, the key question was: 'Are there any circumstances extrinsic to this internal character which should longer delay the recognition of the independence of such of those states as have established their independence *de facto*, and have constituted governments capable of maintaining relations of peace and amity with other Powers?'

Since Spanish America and Brazil geographically constituted one fourth of the globe, it was impossible for them to remain in 'outlawry' for long. Moreover, since the United States had already recognised them, they could force Britain to do so through trade sanctions. As for the Alliance powers, they had no practical stake in the matter but only feared the loss of legitimacy by the colonies' independence.

It had always been British policy to prevent Spanish America from falling into the hands of the French. Having liberated Spain, Britain could reasonably feel that danger was ended but the French invasion of Spain renewed it, and Spain was likely to remain subjected to France, at least in foreign policy.

Finally, the United States was a more formidable naval rival than the Netherlands ever had been:

30. Turkey disagreed, of course, but Turkey was not by this time considered a Great Power and was not invited to the Congress.

> Let us remember, then, that peace, however desirable, and however cherished by us, cannot last for ever. Sooner or later we shall probably have to contend with the combined maritime power of France and the United States. The disposition of the new states is at present highly favourable to England. If we take advantage of that disposition, we may establish through our influence with them a fair counterpoise to that combined maritime power. Let us not, then, throw the present golden opportunity away, which, once lost, may never be recovered.[31]

Liverpool's implied assumption was that Charles X's benign regime would not survive forever and a radical France, if allied to the United States, would present a formidable opponent.

Wellington opposed granting recognition to Latin America, because he saw it as destroying the Great Alliance and believed the new states were worthless by comparison. Liverpool wrote to Wellington, stressing the argument most likely to appeal to him, the danger of losing Latin America to the United States. George IV also objected, calling the policy 'a restless desire of self-interest in direct opposition to those wise and comprehensive principles, by which the peace and general interest of Europe were bound together'.[32] Canning, conversely, gloried in throwing over the Great Alliance.

There was thus a considerable battle, both in Cabinet and with the King, to get the new policy agreed but, in the end, Liverpool won the grudging acceptance of Wellington and only Westmorland held out. It did, however, provoke an angry letter from the King enquiring whether Liverpool's government had altogether given itself up to liberalism.

In discussions about the next year's financial arrangements, Liverpool wrote to Canning giving his own economic thinking:

> If we could do what we ought to do (do not be alarmed, I am not going to propose it) we should make an augmentation in our direct taxes of at least two millions; and as a compensation, take off indirect taxes to the extent of four or five millions. By such an arrangement we should not materially reduce our revenue, and we should considerably increase the wealth and resources of the country, by the relief which might be afforded to commerce.[33]

---

31. Liverpool's memorandum is given in full in Yonge, *The Life and Administration of Robert Banks Jenkinson*, Vol. 3, pp. 297-304.
32. George IV to Liverpool, 27 January 1825, in Aspinall, *The Letters of King George IV, 1812-30*, Vol. 3, pp. 58-59.
33. Letter to Canning, 19 October 1824, quoted in Yonge, *The Life and Administration of Robert Banks Jenkinson*, Vol. 3, p. 311.

By this stage, Liverpool's views were foreshadowing Peel's economic policies of the 1840s, although he would have stopped short of Corn Laws repeal, let alone unilateral free trade.

Even Ireland was looking better. Wellesley wrote to Liverpool:

> The condition of Ireland is greatly improved within the last year. . . . Prices have improved, rents and even tithes are better paid, and in the districts which had been most disturbed the people are turning their attention to pursuits of industry and honest labour, instead of plotting or executing schemes of outrage and violence.[34]

Wellesley then went on to suggest that only Daniel O'Connell's Catholic Association and its Ulster counterpart, the Orange Association, remained a problem but that Wellesley believed them to be containable. However, the Catholic Association had during 1824 begun to recruit new members by charging a 'Catholic Rent' of one penny per month, collected through the local Catholic churches. This gave it great strength through a mass membership which no previous such grouping had possessed. O'Connell was to be a major thorn in the British government's side until his death in 1847. Together with the Great Famine of the 1840s, O'Connell's efforts made the failure of union inevitable.

The balance of forces in the Cabinet was further disturbed in December 1824 by the retirement of Sidmouth, which made the old-line Tories, Eldon, Wellington, Bathurst and Westmorland feel even more beleaguered and further strengthened the liberalising wing led by Canning and Peel. It was also a loss to Liverpool personally, depriving him of one of his closest associates and throwing him further into the arms of Canning.

The year 1824 was economically the best year of the 1820s, indeed the best year until the late 1840s. Wheat prices strengthened to over 60 shillings a quarter in the first two months of the year, then, after a decline later in the spring, strengthened with a moderate harvest to 63 shillings, strong demand boosting prices as much as a mild deficiency in supply. Brick production increased another 18 per cent above the 1823 level and was now a full third above its 1819 peak. Exports of cotton manufactures jumped fourteen per cent, to an official value of £30.2 million, 34 per cent above the previous cycle's peak of 1818. Hoffman's index of total production rose another seven per cent, 23 per cent above its 1818 peak.[35]

Issue volume on the London bond market reached its peak, with £12.7 million of new issues (in actual proceeds), the largest of £4.2 million being for Colombia. Share issuance also surged, with the total volume of new shares

34. Wellesley letter to Liverpool, 22 November 1824, quoted in ibid., pp. 312-13.
35. Figures taken from Gayer, Rostow and Schwartz, *The Growth and Fluctuation of the British Economy, 1790-1850*, Vol. 1, pp. 171-210.

issued in 1824 and 1825 being double the volume outstanding, although only a small portion of the total capital, £15.2 million, spread among 127 share issues, was paid in before 1827. Of this surge, 36 per cent of the capital paid in was for 44 mining companies, fourteen per cent was for 20 gas companies, fifteen per cent was for fourteen insurance companies (legislation in 1824 had broken the insurance duopoly) and 35 per cent was for 49 miscellaneous company issues.[36]

The economy's overall strength had been combined with a steady increase in bullion held at the Bank of England until January 1824, but then began to show signs of outrunning prudence, with the Bank's bullion stock declining from £13.8 million to £10.1 million, the lowest since 1820, while notes in circulation increased from £19.8 million to £21.8 million. A modest increase in interest rates was clearly called for but the Bank of England did not increase rates until the middle of 1825, by which stage its bullion stock had collapsed to £4.4 million. The country banks also expanded their note issue rapidly, the issue of stamped country banknotes rising almost 50 per cent from £4.5 million to £6.7 million between July 1823 and July 1824.

Wages in both London and the manufacturing districts continued to increase in money terms, although real wages declined from their 1822 peak, because of the recovery in wheat prices. With the economy strong and employment high, real wages slightly declining and the Combination Acts entirely repealed, including the unions' liability for damage, strikes were inevitable. Trade unions, now legal, were formed across the country and in September 1824 alone there were serious stoppages among dyers, cloth-lappers, journeymen shoemakers and colliers in and around Glasgow, with rioting, picketing and intimidation. The most prominent strike was in the cotton trade, where from August to January 1825, almost all cotton spinners and power-loom weavers went on strike. They formed associations and held public meetings; the Weavers' Association even sent weekly reports of their proceedings to the newspapers.

Even the Radical Hume was worried; he wrote to the Glasgow weavers: 'I still do expect that great benefit will be derived from the Repeal if the imprudent conduct of the operatives does not urge the masters to obtain a renewal of the power they formerly had to oppress.'[37] Strikes continued into the New Year, making new trade union legislation a priority for 1825.

The year 1825 began pleasantly for Liverpool, with a trip from his usual spa haunt of Bath to Bristol with Canning, in order for them both to receive the Freedom of the City and the Freedom of the Merchants Company. Liverpool

36. Henry English, *A Complete View of the Joint Stock Companies Formed during the Years 1824 and 1825* (London: Boosey, 1827).

37. The quotation, and much of the information in these two paragraphs is contained in Gayer, Rostow and Schwartz, *The Growth and Fluctuation of the British Economy, 1790-1850*, Vol. 1, p. 209.

reminded the City fathers that for him it was a renewal of an old family acquaintanceship, for his forefather, Anthony Jenkinson, had been a Bristol merchant, 250 years before. However, he preferred to receive this honorary freedom, for every public man must feel that 'the approbation of his fellow subjects was a just reward of public service'.[38] In the evening the guests were entertained to dinner at the Mansion House, at which 28 toasts were drunk at a cost of £665, after which Liverpool journeyed sleepily back to Bath.[39] Possibly as a further memento of this visit, the *Earl of Liverpool* of 389 tons, owned by Bristol merchants, was registered in Bristol in December 1825 and spent the next 30 years as a New York packet and then in the West Indian trade.[40]

Before the 1825 session began, a dispute erupted between the King and the Cabinet over the recognition of the new Latin American republics and the separation from the Great Alliance. In a letter to Liverpool, the King claimed that: 'The Jacobins of the world (now calling themselves the Liberals) saw the peace of Europe secured by this great measure and have therefore never ceased to revile the principle of the Quadruple Alliance'; and asked whether 'the principles established by my government in the years 1814, 1815 and 1818 are or are not to be abandoned'. In response, the Cabinet justified the recognition of Latin America and claimed that even in 1815 Britain had only acceded to the Great Alliance with reservations. They proclaimed the need to 'maintain the system of confidence and reciprocal communication' with the Allies and pointed out that Latin American recognition was in no way inconsistent with this. In response, the King said that 'confidence and reciprocal communication' with the Allies was 'all that the King could require'.[41]

The King's Address opening the session took off rhetorically into the stratosphere: 'There never was a period in the history of this country, when all the great interests of the nation were at the same time in so thriving a condition, or when a feeling of content and satisfaction was more widely diffused among the British people.' It rejoiced that prosperity was spreading to Ireland and asked the government to consider ways of suppressing the Catholic and Orange Associations. The Anglo-Burmese War and increased security requirements elsewhere would require some increase in defence spending, though increased prosperity should permit further tax cuts. It praised the continued peace, highlighted commercial treaties with Sweden and the United States, and

38. Quoted in Gash, *Lord Liverpool*, p. 228.
39. John Latimer, *The Annals of Bristol in the Nineteenth Century* (London: W. & F. Morgan, 1887) Vol. 1, p. 112.
40. Grahame Farr (ed.), *Records of Bristol Ships, 1800-1838 (Vessels over 150 Tons)* (Bristol: Bristol Record Society, 1950) pp. 100-1.
41. King's Letter to Liverpool, 17 January 1825, Cabinet Minute in response, and King's further letter to Liverpool, 30 January 1825, quoted in Wellington, *Despatches, Correspondence*, Vol. 2, pp. 401-4.

confirmed that commercial treaties would be organised with Latin America. Finally, it praised the commercial gains from removing trade restrictions and urged Parliament to remove further restrictions.

In his response, Liverpool began by praising Parliament for having held firm during the difficult post-war years, accomplishing the 'Herculean task' of returning to the gold standard, for which the country was now reaping its reward. The country could now continue cautiously removing trade restrictions, for 'the general principles of free trade, I have always laid down as the great foundation of national prosperity, and as those which should be resorted to as soon as the general condition of England will permit'.

Finally, Liverpool turned to Ireland, which he said must be dealt with independently from Catholic Emancipation, because the Catholic Association's activities, extracting the 'Catholic Rent' from the unfortunate Irish peasantry, were designed to evade the law and were contrary to the constitution. He concluded by announcing that he would shortly move to reconvene the committee inquiring into the state of Ireland, to bring the Catholic Association before the House.[42]

On 8 February, Liverpool discussed potential legislation regulating the Catholic Association, saying he looked on it as the greatest enemy of Ireland, since it checked its prosperity, discouraged capital and excited animosities which the government was trying to allay and remove. If Parliament did not put down all associations, it must permit them all, producing 'a state of rancorous religious and political animosity, totally incompatible with the well-being of any country in the world'. Two days later, Liverpool moved the appointment of a committee to examine the state of Ireland.[43]

Liverpool's big Ireland speech came on the second reading of the Unlawful Societies in Ireland Bill. He began by repeating that the Catholic Association would prevent any Irish tranquillity; the Association itself was designed to provoke a rebellion at the opportune time – he reminded the House that the 1798 Irish Rebellion had failed partly because it was set off prematurely. He then discussed the Catholic rent, which, collected from all Catholics through the Church, must essentially be a compulsory levy. The legislation was drafted to cover all unlawful associations, not just the Catholic Association, since he had no doubt an equivalent Protestant group would form. Ireland was recovering economically and, just as the clamour for revolutionary change in Britain had died down once prosperity returned, so he was confident the same would happen in Ireland. There was no reason why the legislation should not be effective, just as the 1796 legislation against seditious meetings and the 1819 Six Acts had been effective.[44] The second reading passed by 146 votes to 44.

42. Hansard, *The Parliamentary Debates, New Series*, Vol. 12, cols 23-28 (3 February 1825).

43. Ibid., cols 137-42, 160-62 (8 and 10 February 1825).

44. Ibid., cols 872-81 (3 March 1825).

In the event, the legislation was ineffective. O'Connell set up a new Catholic Association, to evade its provisions. Hagiographers compare O'Connell to Gandhi; there is no doubt that, once he had devised the mechanism of the Catholic Association, he became equally difficult to stop. Catholic Emancipation and Irish tithe 'reform' made no difference whatever. O'Connell's effect on the 1830s Whig governments was so malign that had they been less unimaginative they would have repealed the 1801 Act of Union, just to be rid of him. In no other problem area was Liverpool's fifteen years of rule so unproductive.

Robinson, presented a report on the 'Financial State of the Country' in February, with no summer Budget at all – from 1825 on, the formal Budget was normally presented in February/March rather than in June. He began with an encomium on the economic boom – no warnings about speculation for him! 'If upon a fair review of our situation there shall appear to be nothing hollow in its foundation, artificial in its superstructure or flimsy in its general result, we may safely venture to contemplate with instructive admiration the harmony of its proportions and the solidity of its basis,' he opined. He announced that the surplus for the preceding year had been £1.44 million instead of the estimated £420,000. He then eulogised the:

> principle of mutual convenience, which creates new wants, stimulates new desires, seeks for new enjoyments and, by the beneficence of Providence, contributes to the general happiness of mankind. . . . [W] hen we reflect upon the facility which is given to its operation by the recent discoveries of modern science, and by the magical energies of the steam-engine, who can doubt that its expansion is progressive and its effect permanent?

Robinson projected income of £56 million and expenditure of £56.4 million for 1825, after paying £5.5 million into the sinking fund. Expenditure included an increase in the army and £250,000 to the United States for slaves freed by British forces during the War of 1812. He projected revenues and expenditure for 1826 and 1827, producing a total surplus of £4 million in 1824-27, including the £1.44 million surplus of 1824. He then reiterated his 'duty to do good' with this surplus. He reduced the duty on imported iron and that on hemp, coffee and wine. He also halved the duty on domestic spirits, to reduce illicit distillation and smuggling. This last provision had unfortunate effects, since the duty on beer remained high; it led to a profusion of elaborate 'gin palaces' where solitary drinking of low-priced spirits was encouraged, with domestic spirits consumption doubling from 3.7 million gallons in 1825 to 7.4 million gallons in 1826.[45]

45. Jessica Warner, 'Gin in Regency England', *History Today*, Vol. 61, issue 3 (March 2011).

After eliminating several small direct taxes, Robinson reduced the house tax for smaller houses and eliminated the window tax on houses with fewer than seven windows. Thus, the total of tax reductions was £1.53 million; the total for the three years was £4 million.[46]

Robinson's budgetary arithmetic, again greeted by the House with loud cheers, rested on two fallacies: it assumed that revenue would continue at least flat, with no possibility of a recession; and it applied four years of projected surpluses (including one already past) to pay for 2½ years of tax reductions. In a recession, he would run into trouble, as did indeed happen in 1826 and 1827.

On modern figures, revenue in 1825 declined by £2 million to £57.7 million instead of increasing as Robinson had projected. Expenditure also declined by £1.4 million to £54.1 million, mostly because of a saving of £1 million in debt charges. Thus, the surplus was £3.6 million, down from £4.2 million in the previous year, but still a healthy level, albeit less than the assumed payment into the sinking fund.[47]

Liverpool's next major Lords intervention remains mildly famous today; it is quoted in every speculative bubble. By late March 1825, the stock market was a little off its peak and the Bank of England's gold holdings were sharply down from their already depressed level of December 1824. However, note issuance was still healthy, as were money market conditions, and the flood of new stock financings continued unabated. It was still several months until the money markets began to cause concern, and more than eight before the banking crash of early December.

Liverpool began by claiming that speculation was unavoidable and, if kept within limits, beneficial:

> In a moment like the present, in a time of profound peace, and when the interest of money is low, it is to be expected that speculation will exist in a very considerable degree. To this, I have no objection, but I wish that the public should be set to rights as to the situation in which they stand.

He then asked what the position of the public would be if there were a war or any 'embarrassing event' short of war. In the recent war, when commercial embarrassments occurred, bankers and merchants were helped through issues of Exchequer bills:

---

46. Hansard, *The Parliamentary Debates, New Series*, Vol. 12, cols 719-44 (28 February 1825).
47. Mitchell, *British Historical Statistics*, pp. 581 (Income), 587 (Expenditure). The year-end is 5 January so, to get the figures for the (approximate) calendar year 1825, you should use the 1826 figures in the tables.

> I wish it, however, to be clearly understood, that those persons who now engage in Joint-Stock Companies, or other enterprises, enter on these speculations at their peril and risk. I think it my duty to declare, that I never will advise the introduction of any bill for their relief; on the contrary, if such a measure is proposed, I will oppose it, and I hope that parliament will resist any measure of the kind. I think that this determination cannot be too well understood at the present moment, nor made too publicly known.

He felt especially compelled to make this declaration because he understood that people were speculating, not only in the metropolis, where people could judge for themselves, but outside it, where country bankers were encouraging country people to engage in speculations, 'the object of which they could not possibly know'.

He concluded:

> I would be one of the last men ever to interfere, by legislative provisions, with the property of individuals, or to endeavour, by any means, to prevent men from spending their own money as they pleased. But as the consequences of the present speculations might be so serious I think, filling the situation which I do, that I would not discharge my duty, if I did not give that warning, and say that I shall be found, in common with their lordships, determined not to give relief, or listen to any claims made on account of distress, arising from such sort of speculations. In stating my opinion, it is in reference to no particular measure, but to that general spirit of speculation, which is going beyond all bounds, and is likely to bring the greatest mischief on numerous individuals.[48]

We hear frequently during periods of financial crisis that it is impossible to spot a bubble while it is in progress; well, Liverpool did so, even though there had not been a full-scale financial bubble since 1720. His firm declaration against bailouts, to which he stuck when the crisis erupted, was courageous and economically sophisticated.

May brought yet another debate on Catholic Emancipation. This time, the bill proposed by the Radical Sir Francis Burdett passed the Commons by 248 to 227, a larger majority than Plunket's bill of 1821, and it was combined with two other Irish measures, one to pay Irish priests and the other to raise the Irish voting qualification to £10 (to counteract the effect of Emancipation). Meanwhile, in the House of Lords, the Duke of York had in a rare intervention denounced Catholic Emancipation with great vehemence, arousing anti-Catholic sentiment in the country.

---

48. Hansard, *The Parliamentary Debates, New Series*, Vol. 12, cols 1194-95 (25 March 1825).

Liverpool himself was in two minds whether to let Emancipation through, since even the anti-Catholic Mrs Arbuthnot admitted that this time of peace and prosperity, with Ireland relatively quiescent, was an ideal moment to settle the question. However, Liverpool had indicated to Wellington his intention to resign if it passed (as Peel did briefly, when the bill to pay Irish Catholic priests passed the Commons) – he did not want to 'cling to office after losing the public voice, gaining humiliation and mortification, like Sir Robert Walpole and others'.[49] Then, at a Cabinet meeting at Liverpool's home, the anti-Emancipationists agreed to stay in office to see the main bill's fate in the Lords.

Liverpool began by reminding the House that the government had already been compelled to suppress the Catholic Association, and had set up a Select Committee, which had not yet had time to report findings. Nevertheless, the Commons had brought up not one but three bills, expecting the Lords to vote on them without proper information as to how they would operate:

> The least objectionable part of the Bill, as I think, is the concessions it proposes to make to the Roman Catholics; for on that subject I am content to put one short question to the House: will they relieve the Catholic from the disabilities under which he labours, or will they not? – and if they reply in the affirmative, I will engage to draw up a bill for the purpose in half an hour.

Liverpool believed that Catholics were not constitutionally entitled to equal rights in a Protestant country. Protestant allegiance to the sovereign was complete, Catholic was qualified; and, since half a day's work did not command the same day's wage as a full day's work, so partial allegiance should not command the same civil rights and privileges as full allegiance. The Pope still had powers, for example, to recommend to Irish bishoprics and, just as popes had taken the Stuart pretenders' recommendations for Irish bishoprics until 1766, so he might now use this power to take recommendations from the King of France, the King of Spain or indeed of 'that bugbear of the noble lords opposite', the Holy Alliance. Moreover, the operation of confession, in which the priest had an absolute duty of confidentiality, gave them further unwarranted power over their parishioners.

There were other problems: education, in which parishioners were not allowed to learn the Bible except through priests, and marriage, where the priests did not recognise non-Catholic marriages. Moreover, the power of excommunication gave a fearful authority to political priests, which could be dangerous in elections.

There were practical evils to Emancipation; after it, Britain could not truly be said to be a Protestant state; indeed, the King would be highly discriminated

49. Conversation with Arbuthnot, quoted in Bamford and Wellington, *The Journal of Mrs. Arbuthnot, 1820-1832*, Vol. 1, p. 393, 6 May 1825.

against if he was the only person constitutionally forbidden to be Catholic. Then, while the Catholic Church disclaimed all wish of despoiling the Irish Established Church, in practice that must be its object, for it had a religious obligation to advance its own faith at the expense of all others:

> What, then is the good which can result from this bill? Will it tranquillize, or will it tend to tranquillize Ireland? I am sorry that so much delusion exists throughout the country upon a point so important. . . . It is a proposition of the clearest demonstration, that the disturbed state of Ireland for the last twenty years, had nothing whatever to do with the Catholic question.

The Insurrection Act had never been invoked in Ulster, where the two religions were close to equality, but it had been invoked in southern Ireland, where there were no religious dissensions: 'Absenteeism, combined with the great subdivision of property, has occasioned an increase of population to a most enormous extent; this has brought the country into a state of beggary, and hence have sprung all the disorders of the state.' Catholics in Ireland, who could vote since 1793, had far more rights than Protestants under any of the Catholic despotisms of Europe.

Finally, paying Catholic priests would establish the Roman Catholic hierarchy 'in all its pride and power'. While the Coronation Oath did not prevent establishing the rights of Catholics, it certainly prevented the King's government from funding the Catholic Church.

Emancipation would produce peace only for a short time and then redouble dissension. There was a movement to re-establish the Catholic religion throughout Britain: 'And if once established, should we not revert to a state of ignorance, with all its barbarous and direful consequences?' The country had enjoyed religious peace for the last 130 years, due to the existing constitutional arrangements; he therefore preferred them to the change in this bill, or to any other that had been suggested. Liverpool's peroration was met with loud cheers, unusual in the Lords, and the bill was defeated by 178 votes to 130.[50]

This was the last time Catholic Emancipation was to be debated in Liverpool's lifetime. Liverpool's opposition to it gave him a great advantage in the 1826 election, as it had in 1812 and to Portland in 1807.

After the Lords vote, Canning called a special Cabinet meeting, at which he threatened to resign if the government did not push through Catholic Emancipation. Liverpool was still in two minds whether to resign, as he felt Emancipation was inevitable eventually; he was stiffened by Bathurst and other opponents of Emancipation. The King had also sent Liverpool a

50. Hansard, *The Parliamentary Debates, New Series*, Vol. 13, cols 739-752 (17 May 1825).

congratulatory note, telling him his speech was 'most powerful' and ending 'God be thanked' on the size of the Lords majority, although Liverpool told the King that some part of the majority was 'hollow'.[51]

It soon became clear that the unexpectedly large Lords majority had indeed settled the matter for the moment and that public opinion was heavily on the side of Emancipation's opponents. Moreover, the ministry was popular because of the economic boom. Accordingly, Canning withdrew his threatened resignation and the ministry carried on.

As a year of great stock market speculation, it was appropriate that 1825 should produce the final repeal of the Bubble Act of 1720. The Act had been drafted at the height of the South Sea Company mania, essentially to prevent competitors to the South Sea. It had incorporated two insurance companies, which formed a duopoly of marine insurance until 1824 but prevented any other incorporations without a Royal Charter. It had not thereby totally prohibited company formation. It was possible to establish a company by Act of Parliament and Royal Charter and, in the bull years of the 1820s, some did so; for example, canal companies had been popular for decades. Nevertheless, by impeding manufacturing companies with limited liability, the Act had been a drag on the development of a healthy equity capital market and a modest drag on industrialisation itself.

Repeal of the Act was first proposed in the Commons on March 1825 by Peter Moore,[52] a Whig East India Company nabob with a habit of investing in bubble companies. (He would flee from his creditors to France in 1827 and die there, near bankrupt, in 1828.) He claimed that the Act made too many ordinary transactions illegal and was so self-contradictory as to be a dead letter. Copley, as Attorney General, opposed the motion, since a quick repeal would have major legal consequences, which had not been researched. The Whig copper merchant, Pascoe Grenfell[53] supported repeal, since recent speculative companies had involved princes of royal blood and the Archbishop of Canterbury.

On 2 June Copley introduced a government bill to repeal the Bubble Act, which the law courts had ruled to be unintelligible and, by imposing heavy penalties, oppressive. Copley said, others had suggested that new legislation should be introduced to replace it but, since no such Act had existed before 1720, and no prosecutions had been brought under it, he believed such legislation was unnecessary. He then veered off the expected track by announcing that, as shareholders' limited liability made Parliament and the

---

51. The King to Liverpool and Liverpool to the King, 18 May 1825, quoted in Wellington, *Despatches, Correspondence*, Vol. 2, p. 451.

52. Peter Moore (1753-1828). MP for Coventry, 1803-26. East India fortune, Radical Whig.

53. Pascoe Grenfell (1761-1838). MP for Great Marlow and Penryn, 1802-26. Cornish copper merchant, moderate Whig and financial pundit.

King reluctant to grant charters, he would propose that charters could include a provision making shareholders liable for a company's debts (fortunately, that provision was made voluntary). Huskisson agreed that repealing the Bubble Act was necessary and the bill was introduced, to be passed by the end of the session. Incorporation thus became somewhat easier but remained expensive; low-cost limited liability would have to wait for the Companies Act of 1862.

The most important legislation of 1825 was the Combinations of Workmen Act, which replaced the 1824 Act that had sparked off so much industrial action. This made any combinations illegal beyond those with the sole purpose of raising wages or depressing working hours. Within those narrow restrictions, trade unions remained legal, although they also remained liable for damages caused by industrial action and could not legally coerce workers by violence. This was probably the optimal structure of trade union legislation. Unions' liability for damage was removed by a combination of Gladstone's 1871 legislation and Disraeli's further liberalisation of 1875, which together wrecked British labour relations and took over 100 years to reverse.

Liverpool made a brief speech at the committee stage of the bill. He explained that the Bill was necessary because of the strikes resulting from the previous year's hastily drafted bill and said the new legislation 'not only prevents the combination of workmen against masters, and of masters against workmen, but prevents the combination of workmen against workmen. This is a protection which the honest and good workman has a right to expect.'[54]

At the end of the session, Liverpool examined the possibility of a snap election, to take advantage of popular enthusiasm at the defeat of Catholic Emancipation. Under the Septennial Act, Parliament could carry on until the spring of 1827, but that would involve an undesirable mid-session dissolution. Hence the practical choices for a dissolution were the summer or autumn of 1825 or 1826.

Wellington suggested a snap dissolution, accepting that Liverpool could not, as the head of a government neutral on the question, go to the country with a direct anti-Catholic Emancipation appeal. However, he pointed out that, if Catholic Emancipation were the leading question in the public mind in an election campaign, it would greatly strengthen the 'Protestant' forces in the Commons. Liverpool responded that it was too late for an early summer dissolution: 'It has been usual, either to dissolve Parliament in the month of June, before the hay and corn harvest, or after they are over, about the middle or end of September.' Since 'we are now in the middle of the hay harvest and the wheat is in blossom in all the southern counties', they must wait until September, although he would favour a decision to dissolve at the September Cabinet meeting.[55]

54. Hansard, *The Parliamentary Debates, New Series*, Vol. 13, cols 1478-79 (4 July 1825).

55. Wellington to Liverpool, 22 June, and Liverpool to Wellington, 23 June 1825, quoted in Wellington, *Despatches, Correspondence*, Vol. 2, pp. 463-65.

By September, Liverpool's view had slightly changed; in a letter to Wellington he expressed indifference between a dissolution and continuing into 1826, provided the Corn Laws and Catholic Emancipation could be kept out of debate during the 1826 session.[56] Although Wellington argued strongly for a dissolution, Canning undertook to use his best efforts to keep the Catholic question out of debate, while Liverpool and Huskisson agreed to defer the corn question until 1827. With several anti-Emancipation peers having advised Liverpool that an immediate dissolution would damage their electoral prospects, the dissolution was postponed until June 1826.

August 1825 saw one of Liverpool's few foreign trips, when he took his relatively new wife Mary to France, the Hague and Amsterdam. Given the difficulties of travel at that period, the trip indicates that he was still reasonably physically robust. However, he did worry about possible crises during recess and disapproved of foreign travel by ministers – as he wrote to Wellington the following year:

> I still think we ought not to separate indefinitely as we have done, that we ought to reassemble at fixed and not very distant periods, and, though a culprit in one instance myself, I can by no means approve of the new practice of ministers passing a part of their holidays upon the continent, though in some particular cases it may be attended with advantage.[57]

During the same summer, Liverpool had the pleasure of appointing his cousin John Jenkinson Bishop of St David's. This was not an especially lucrative see but in July 1827, after Liverpool's resignation, it was added to by Canning appointed Jenkinson Dean of Durham Cathedral which came with a munificent £9,000 per annum. Jenkinson held both posts until his death in 1840.

September and October were largely occupied with Buckingham's quest to become Governor General of India. The expense of the Anglo-Burmese War, together with a (possibly mishandled) sepoy mutiny, had made the East India Company's Court of Directors keen to recall Amherst, and Buckingham saw an opportunity to replace him and restore the shaky Grenville finances. Liverpool took advice from Wellington, who told him the Anglo-Burmese War was on its way to a successful conclusion, and that the Governor of Madras, Sir Thomas Munro,[58] who understood Indian warfare, would be a better successor to Amherst, if necessary. Both Liverpool and Wellington were

56. Liverpool letter to Wellington, 16 September 1825, quoted in ibid., p. 499.
57. Liverpool letter to Wellington, 15 October 1826, quoted in ibid., Vol. 3, p. 422.
58. Sir Thomas Munro (1761-1827). Cadet in Madras (Chennai), 1779, and then army career in India. Brigadier, 1817. KCB, 1819. Baronet, 1825. Governor of Madras, 1819-27.

agreed that the Court of Directors' favourite, the Whig Lord William Bentinck should be avoided at all costs. The final coup occurred when Wellington nobbled Buckingham's doctor, who informed the Duke that given his size and sedentary habits, he would not survive six months in India. Buckingham then agitated for the Lord Lieutenancy of Ireland but Wellesley, who had just remarried to an insufficiently wealthy American lady, showed no inclination to give it up.

The financial crisis of 1825, the first crisis of a cyclical industrial economy unrelated to war, had begun in the late spring. According to Mrs Arbuthnot, who disapproved of Huskisson's trade liberalisations, Rothschild had told Herries in April:

> that the consequence of admitting foreign goods (which had not been met by corresponding liberality on the other side of the water) was that all the gold was going out of the country. He had himself sent two millions within the last few weeks; the funds fell rapidly, and no advantage is gained by any human being.[59]

The Bank of England's bullion reserves declined from £10.1 million in January 1825 to £7.3 million in April to £4.4 million in July, a grossly inadequate monetary base for an 1825 GDP of around £386 million.

One underlying cause of the over-speculation was the proliferation of weak country banks. Banking law restricted banks to a maximum of six partners, making most of them hopelessly undercapitalised and reducing the barriers to entry in the business. Then 1822 legislation had allowed country banks to issue £1 and £2 notes for a further ten years, with no limitations on their gold reserves when doing so. Liverpool had already warned of the excessive number of country banks in 1817; by 1825, after a period of excessive speculative activity, especially in foreign bonds, the problem was out of hand and there were almost 800 banks. The issue of notes by these country banks, which had increased by 50 per cent to £6.7 million in the year to July 1824 had increased by a further 31 per cent to £8.8 million by July 1825, almost double the level of 1823.

The Bank of England's performance was thoroughly undistinguished throughout the crisis, and Liverpool seriously considered revoking its charter. Instead of raising interest rates as gold flooded out of its vaults in the first half of 1825 (when the Prime Minister had made an official speech condemning the bubble), it kept monetary policy exceptionally easy, buying government bonds to replace the gold it lost, without raising interest rates. It thereby allowed the bubble to inflate further. Had it tightened control then, the crash would have been precipitated, but would not have been so extensive.

---

59. Bamford and Wellington, *The Journal of Mrs. Arbuthnot, 1820-32*, Vol. 1, p. 391, 30 April 1825.

Even in late summer, when its gold reserves seemed likely to disappear altogether, the Bank did not significantly raise interest rates; only in December, when the crisis was in full swing, did its discount rate reach five per cent. In a 24 November letter to Bexley, Liverpool was fairly forgiving:

> I am persuaded that the Bank is now in a right course, and that their only fault was taking the alarm a little too late. I foresee considerable distress and commercial embarrassment, but that is the natural result of the over-speculation of the last two years, and any attempt to interfere by the authority of Government would only aggravate the evil instead of remedying it.[60]

The London merchant banks had taken advantage of easy monetary conditions to issue Latin American bonds, without the banks or anyone else knowing which Latin American countries were creditworthy, or even in existence. All the merchant banks were thus damaged by the tightening of credit in late 1825, with Barings coming off worst because of the foolish Mexican speculations of Alexander Baring's second son, Francis.[61]

The first signal that something was seriously wrong came in late October when the merchant Samuel Williams with large American business closed its doors. The money market was tight during November, alarmingly so in the last week, although the Bank of England continued draining gold from its domestic correspondents rather than seeking it abroad. Then, on Saturday, 3 December, the major private bank Pole, Thornton,[62] whose name partner, Sir Peter Pole,[63] was a Tory MP, with extensive country bank business, came close to closing its doors and was rescued only by an emergency loan from Smith's, the Nottingham bank that founded the Carrington family fortunes.

The following day the Bank of England, which had reversed its policy to one of easing at the beginning of December, agreed to provide £300,000 in loan capital to bail out Pole, Thornton. However, confidence in the bank was shaken and, after the failure of the Yorkshire bank, Wentworth & Co.,

60. Quoted in Yonge, *The Life and Administration of Robert Banks Jenkinson*, Vol. 3, p. 355.
61. Francis Baring (1800-68). 3rd Baron Ashburton from 1864. MP for Thetford, 1830-31, 1832-41, 1848-57. His cousin Francis Thornhill Baring (1796-1866), 1st Baron Northbrook from 1866, son of Alexander's elder brother Thomas, was Whig MP for Portsmouth, 1826-65. Secretary to the Treasury, 1834, 1835-39. Chancellor of the Exchequer, 1839-41. First Lord of the Admiralty, 1849-52.
62. Henry Thornton, the noted monetary economist, banker and philanthropist, died in 1815; the bank was then being run by his 25-year-old son, Henry Sykes Thornton (1800-1881).
63. Sir Peter Pole (1770-1850). 2nd Baronet from 1813. MP for Yarmouth, Isle of Wight, 1819-26. Pole, Thornton reportedly yielded an average £40,000 per annum in profits in 1818-24 but had to pay out £1,250,000 in a weekend in the crisis; see Fisher, *The History of Parliament.- Pole, Sir Peter*

the pressure on Pole, Thornton again became intolerable, forcing it to close its doors after business ended on 10 December. Because of Pole, Thornton's extensive network, this directly caused the failure of 38 country banks and by the end of the crisis 73 of the 770 country banks in England and Wales had failed, as well as three of the 36 banks in Scotland.[64] Over the next month, Pole, Thornton's business was acquired by its competitor Williams &Co.,[65] which was also forced to stop payment temporarily on 13 December but was reconstituted with different shareholders thereafter.

Also on 13 December, Liverpool and Robinson, 'in order to relieve present distress', ordered the Bank of England to purchase £500,000 in Exchequer bills on the government's behalf and agreed to cancel them immediately if necessary.[66] The climax of the crisis came three days later when the Bank of England came close to stopping gold payments. (According to Tooke, its gold reserves bottomed out at £1,027,000, slightly below the nadir of February 1797, in an economy more than 50 per cent larger.[67])

On 16 December, a five-hour Cabinet meeting was called to discuss what should be done. Herries reported that the Bank was down to £100,000 in gold coin and wanted to suspend payments, thereby taking Britain off the gold standard. Huskisson, strongly anti-Bank, suggested that, if the Bank stopped payment, its charter should be removed. However, Herries reminded Liverpool that the government owed the Bank £30 million against Bank of England note circulation of £18 million – thus, if the Bank's charter was withdrawn, the government would have difficulty paying the army and navy.[68]

Eventually, the Cabinet did nothing drastic, being reminded by Wellington of Cicero's dictum that 'while there's life, there's hope'. The Cabinet's one concrete decision, probably instigated by Liverpool, was to encourage the Bank temporarily to issue £1 and £2 notes, using its dormant powers under the 1822 legislation – the first such notes were issued the following day. In the event, £150,000 in sovereigns had arrived from the Continent that morning and Rothschild paid them immediately into the Bank.

Over the weekend, the Bank of England, which held daily Court of Directors meetings through the crisis, ran out of £5 and £20 notes, but received an additional supply from the printers. On 20 December, massive shipments of gold began to arrive from the Continent, the first of £200,000 in sovereigns, at the order of Rothschilds. Nathan Mayer Rothschild had done very well

64. L. Neal, "The Financial Crisis of 1825 and the Restructuring of the British Financial System", Federal Reserve Bank of St Louis *Review*, Vol. 80, no. 3 (May-June 1998).
65. Williams & Co. Founded 1771. Re-founded, 1825-26, as Williams, Deacon, Labouchere. Became Williams, Deacon, Thornton in 1828. With mergers, had over 100 branches by 1914; acquired by the Royal Bank of Scotland in 1930.
66. Bank of England, Minutes of the Court of Directors, 13 December 1825.
67. Tooke, *A History of Prices*, Vol. 2, pp. 185, note.
68. Bamford and Wellington, *The Journal of Mrs. Arbuthnot, 1820-1832*, Vol. 1, pp. 426-28, 17 December 1825.

from British needs during the war, and from the big Consols issue immediately before Waterloo. Although he had been distinctly unhelpful in 1819, on this occasion he saved the Bank of England and the British financial system. Within a few days £8 million in notes had been issued, while the Mint went into overdrive and coined £1 million in sovereigns from the modest bullion store available.[69] Rothschild did well in the end; a Bank resolution in February 1827 ordered that he should be paid £3/19/0 instead of the normal £3/17/10½ for all the gold he had brought to the Bank since the crisis, a handsome 1.46 per cent commission.[70]

Although the Bank's gold reserves did not bottom out until 24 December, the worst of the crisis was now over and the panic was subsiding, so Liverpool retreated to Coombe Wood. Nevertheless, the effect on trade and even the aristocracy had been severe – Mrs Arbuthnot told the story of how Sir Charles Knightley:

> a gentleman of large property near Daventry, came to London and was obliged to ride part of the way and to borrow a few sovereigns, which his little girl had hoarded, to pay for the journey, and told us that at this moment he had not the means of getting a shilling.[71]

In late December, news reached London of the death of Czar Alexander I. Canning agreed with Liverpool that a senior visit must be paid to St Petersburg to get to know the new Czar, Nicholas I,[72] and Wellington was chosen to go, to his considerable reluctance, given the difficulties in travelling to St Petersburg in midwinter..

Wellington was to be away from early February to late April, spending about a month in St Petersburg and establishing a modest rapport with Nicholas I, who expressed a desire to avoid entering a war on behalf of the Greek rebels. The rapport was to prove useful in negotiating the Protocol of St Petersburg, by which Britain and Russia were to mediate between Greece and Turkey. The following year, that was to lead to the Treaty of London, by which France, Britain and Russia offered to mediate between Greece and Turkey and Russia foreswore territorial aggrandisement against Turkey.

In 1825 the industrial economy was adversely affected by financial conditions, beginning to turn down from the late summer and entering 1826

69. Yonge, *The Life and Administration of Robert Banks Jenkinson*, Vol. 3, p. 356.
70. Bank of England, Minutes of the Court of Directors, 14 February 1827.
71. Bamford and Wellington, *The Journal of Mrs. Arbuthnot, 1820-1832*, Vol. 1, p. 428, 20 December 1825. Sir Charles Knightley, 2nd Baronet (1781-1864). Conservative MP for Northamptonshire South, 1835-52.
72. Nicholas I (1796-1855). Younger brother (by nineteen years) of Alexander I. Czar of All the Russias, 1825-55. Politically reactionary, militarist autocrat, pursued successful expansionist policy in Central Asia, then became involved in Crimean War.

The opening of the Stockton and Darlington Railway, 1888 picture, with horseman preceding and passngers on the coal.

on a weak note. Exports were almost flat but imports soared by 26 per cent to £54.8 million, more than 50 per cent higher than in 1822 and a major source of the gold drain. Wheat prices, which had risen to 67 shillings, fell but only to 64 shillings. Brick production was exceptionally strong, rising by 33 per cent to 1,949 million bricks, double the level of only four years before and a level not matched again until 1846. Exports of cotton manufactures declined, to an official value of £29.5 million but still 30 per cent above the previous cycle's peak of 1818. On the other hand, Hoffman's index of total production rose another seven per cent and was now 31 per cent above its 1818 peak. Real wages came under pressure, as tight supply conditions pushed up consumer prices.[73]

Most significant for the future, the Stockton and Darlington Railway, the world's first public railway to use steam locomotives, was opened on 27 September. The two-hour journey over 8½ miles of completed track between Shildon and Darlington was undertaken in a train pulled by George and Robert Stephenson's Locomotion No. 1, with one passenger carriage and 21 wagons, some carrying coal, and over 450 passengers, many sitting on the coal. At the triumphant end to the trip, six wagons of coal were distributed to the poor.

73. Figures taken from Gayer, Rostow and Schwartz, *The Growth and Fluctuation of the British Economy, 1790-1850*, Vol. 1, pp. 171-210.

The next question was how to avoid future financial crises, or at least ensure they did not endanger the gold standard or the economy. To help him think about the legislation needed, Liverpool received papers from Herries, Huskisson and Bexley.

In his memorandum, Bexley began by correctly identifying the crisis: 'The crisis which threatened us, and from which we have not yet completely escaped, seems to me more to resemble that of France in 1719, and of England in 1720, than anything which has happened more recently.' He then gave a succinct account of why such speculation occurred and said the modest additional money creation by country banks was only marginally to blame (the currency was almost entirely metallic in 1720, with few country banks). Limiting issues of small-denomination notes would push transactions onto a metallic basis, improving the problem, but creating banks with a lot of partners (beyond the existing statutory limitation of six) would not necessarily help because large groups of partners would have no central control, and rich men would not risk their entire fortunes on unlimited-liability ventures in which they had a small share. As for the Bank of England, establishing provincial branches would 'preserve its ascendancy'.[74]

Huskisson's paper was much more radical and demonstrated both his animus against the Bank of England and his susceptibility to French economic thought. He proposed that Britain should operate a bimetallic system, with the Mint issuing receipts for deposits of £50 equivalent or more of silver, their value calculated at a fixed exchange rate of 15.5 to one against gold, and those receipts circulating as currency in addition to gold coins. This would have two advantages: it would stimulate trade with Latin America, which was the world's major source of silver, and it would allow the Bank of England to keep only modest quantities of unprofitable gold bullion in its vaults. He cited the example of France, which had a huge money supply in both silver and gold and suggested that British practice should follow French more closely.[75]

Liverpool had decided on a plan, closer to that of Bexley than of Huskisson, when he wrote (nominally jointly with Robinson but sent from Fife House) to the Bank of England's Court of Directors on 13 January asking that the Bank permit the formation of banks with more than six partners, provided they were more than a certain distance from London, and that the Bank itself open branches throughout the country. The full text of his (in my view, impressive) letter is included at the Appendix.'

The Court of Directors initially rejected this proposal, so Liverpool and Robinson asked the Bank to suggest conditions on which the proposal might be acceptable. The Bank suggested that a safeguard such as the Bank of Ireland

74. Bexley's memorandum is given in full in Yonge, *The Life and Administration of Robert Banks Jenkinson*, Vol. 3, pp. 358-61.

75. Huskisson's memorandum is quoted in Wellington, *Despatches, Correspondence*, Vol. 3, pp. 98-104.

had been given, whereby other banks' paper could not be paid in London, would be sufficient. Liverpool and Robinson gratefully accepted this and promised to put such a clause in the legislation. They again urged the Bank to open branches, pushing on an open door as a Special Committee of the Bank had already recommended that it do so.[76] The process had nonetheless been stressful; Liverpool was said to have flown into rage at the (admittedly annoying) Westmorland at a Cabinet dinner, something he could usually avoid.[77]

The King's Address opening Parliament began by deploring the financial crash. It then said: 'His Majesty relies upon your wisdom to devise such measures as may protect both public and private interests against the like sudden and violent fluctuations, by placing on a more firm foundation the Currency and circulating Credit of the country.' The speech went on to celebrate British mediation between Portugal and Brazil by which Portugal had recognised Brazil's independence, a trade treaty with France and one with the new Colombia, and to offer reassurances that the Anglo-Burmese War was headed for success.

Liverpool's speech on the Address began by noting that the financial crisis was anticipated by the government – he referred to his March 1825 speech. He emphasised that one cause predominated, the spirit of 'mad speculation' which had prevailed throughout the country, exacerbated by excess note issuance by country banks, far out of proportion to the increase in Bank of England notes. He announced his intention to restrict the issue of small notes, giving credit to Bexley for the idea, and to eliminate the exclusive privilege of the Bank of England:

> The Bank of England's privilege operates in a most extraordinary, and I think a most unfortunate manner for the country. Any small tradesman, a cheesemonger, a butcher or a shoemaker, can open a country bank; but a set of persons with a fortune sufficient to carry on the concern with security are not permitted to do so.[78]

By the following week, the government had ceased stamping £1 and £2 country banknotes to prevent country banks from front-running their anticipated legislation. Liverpool explained to the House of Lords that even a summary bill would have given country banks near London an unfair advantage over more distant ones; hence the government had acted through an order to the Stamp Office.[79]

---

76. Bank of England, Report to the Court of Directors, 20 January 1826, Available through the Bank's website.
77. Bamford and Wellington, *The Journal of Mrs. Arbuthnot, 1820-1832*, Vol. 2, p. 6, 27 January 1826.
78. Hansard, *The Parliamentary Debates, New Series*, Vol. 14, cols 15-20 (2 February 1826).
79. Ibid., cols 140-42 (9 February 1826).

On 17 February, Liverpool moved the second reading of the Country Bankers Bill of 1826, which allowed joint-stock banks with limited liability and banking partnerships with more than six partners to be formed and to issue bank notes of £5 or more, provided they were more than 65 miles from London. Liverpool began his speech by recalling the previous year's speculations, and his warning against them, which had included a caution against the part played by country bankers:

> Your Lordships must say, when you recollect the numerous speculations of the last year, the mining speculations, the loans to foreign countries, the various extravagant projects which were on foot, that it was impossible but that, sooner or later, a powerful reaction must take place. . . . The spirit of adventure – the spirit of gambling and speculation – was pushed to an extent never exceeded at any period of the history of this country since the celebrated South-sea Bubble. . . . Your Lordships have heard a great deal of the danger of giving freedom to trade and much of the evils have been ascribed by some persons to those acts of parliament by which some branches of trade have been liberated; but the greatest speculation took place in those articles, the trade in which had always been free.

However, 'I do not think that all these speculations and gambling transactions could have been carried to the degree they were carried, if they had not been aided by the paper currency.' Paper currency expansion came from two sources: the Bank of England and country banks. The Bank's note issuance did not affect the exchanges, Liverpool's favourite indicator, until September 1824, and from March 1825 was already being brought back under control.[80] Conversely, country banknote issuance had doubled in two years. Thus, whatever reduction in the paper circulation was made by the Bank of England was more than made up for by the country banks. Speculation had been facilitated by the country banks' overissue and, when the speculations failed, the country banks were first to suffer:

> For where did the distress begin? The first failure which took place was that of a great house in the West of England. The second, that of a London banking house, connected with not less than forty of the country banks. The third great stoppage was that of a large banking establishment in Yorkshire.

80. According to Gayer, Rostow and Schwartz, *The Growth and Fluctuation of the British Economy, 1790-1850*, Vol. 1, p. 202, Bank of England notes outstanding increased only slightly from £19.4 million in January 1822 to £20.4 million in October 1824, rose to £21.8 million in January 1825, declined again to £20.7 million in April and £20.9 million in July, then fell more sharply to £18.8 million in October. Then the liquidity injections of December 1825 pushed them to £24.9 million in January 1826.

The government therefore had proposed two remedies, one for removing £1 and £2 notes from circulation and the other in the proposed Country Bankers Bill.

Withdrawing notes from circulation and replacing them with metal would considerably check the circulation that trade required and cause distress. However, the measure was necessary; otherwise, 'the country might be left in a state of perfect delusion' even while the Bank of England reduced its issues. Moreover, since commercial crises were inevitable, 'it is necessary to provide against the consequences of this description of circulation to the poorer classes', who could be left destitute by the failure of their local bank, since they had no other reserves. In the recent crisis, working men who had received their pay in worthless banknotes were seen hawking them around at five shillings in the pound to buy necessities.

There was wartime experience of the need for £1 and £2 notes; they had then amounted to around £7 million. Thus, adding £6-£7 million from the country banks gave a total of £13-£14 million of £1 and £2 notes needed. Between 1819 and 1826, the Mint had coined more than £25 million in sovereigns, of which around £7.2 million had been exported and declared to HM Customs. Adding in undeclared exports, there was £16 million in sovereigns available, which should be ample to cover the country's needs, especially as three years would be allowed for withdrawing small notes.

Liverpool continued: 'However, though I prefer a metallic to a paper currency in small transactions, still I admit that a system of banking, established on sound principles, is attended with convenience, and even benefit to a country.' The measure he was proposing was a half-measure because they had the chartered rights of the Bank of England to deal with, which ran until 1833. Liverpool denounced the existing system of small country banks as 'the worst, in every respect, that could possibly be conceived'. However, the Bank of England had agreed to allow the creation of joint-stock or large partnership banks, provided they were more than 65 miles from London; in return, he had encouraged the Bank of England to open branches, which he believed it had a right to do.

Liverpool then touched on the Corn Laws, where he appealed for moderation and a measure that would stabilise prices. Finally, he was determined against issuing additional Exchequer bills to bail out the banking system but agreed that the Bank could make up to £6 million of secured short-term loans, providing liquidity, while the Treasury would then redeem Bank Exchequer bills for cash.[81]

The Exchequer bills issue was highly contentious. Pitt had issued Exchequer bills by which merchants could borrow against their inventories at a time of commercial distress in 1793, and another issue had been authorized in 1811

81. Hansard, *The Parliamentary Debates, New Series*, Vol. 14, cols 450-66 (17 February 1826).

when the Milan Decrees and Orders in Council had dried up trade. The Commons and the City were strongly in favour of the government repeating this procedure. However, Liverpool believed that this expedient should not be used in peacetime and that using it would contravene his warning of the previous year. Indeed, he even authorised Canning to tell the Commons that forcing such an issue would bring his resignation.

In the event, Liverpool and Robinson entered into an agreement with the Bank of England on 28 February that the Bank would make loans up to the value of £3 million secured against goods, repayable in three months, while Liverpool would undertake that the government would redeem £6 million of the Bank's advances to it within six months through the sinking fund.[82]

Liverpool participated actively in the committee stage of the Country Bankers Bill. He intended to extend the bank chartering and note withdrawal measures to both Ireland and Scotland, taking account of special circumstances in those countries. Finally, Liverpool announced the insertion of a clause in the Bill allowing the Bank of England to establish full branches, since under existing legislation it might only be able to establish agencies, which could not act independently of the centre.[83] By 1 June, the Bank was appointing its first branch manager, in Gloucester.[84]

Later, Liverpool returned to the subject of liquidity provision, engaging in a fluent technical discussion with Lansdowne as to the Bank of England's lending against goods, pointing out that, with the goods deposited in a bonded warehouse and loans made against only part of their value for two to three months, the risk was not great:

> This course is obviously preferable to that to which I have always so seriously objected: namely, to the converting the government into a Bank, and inducing the merchants not to look to themselves, or to the banks of the country for assistance, which they would otherwise naturally do. . . . At present it is the Bank that ought to be looked to by the merchants, and not the government; since the distress had not been brought about by any political events whatever, or by any public calamity, [but] by over-trading and other causes, respecting the nature of which there is a pretty general agreement of opinion. . . . There is, then a material difference between advances on goods which must be paid within two or three months, and on Exchequer-bills, which might be out a year or even several years. The Exchequer-bills of 1793 were not paid off within the year, and there was afterwards another issue of Exchequer-bills, which had not been wound up for twenty-two years from the date of the issues.

82. Bank of England, Minutes of the Court of Directors, 28 February 1826.
83. Hansard, *The Parliamentary Debates, New Series*, Vol. 14, cols 558-65 (20 February 1826).
84. Bank of England, Minutes of the Court of Directors, 1 June 1826.

There followed a tirade from Lauderdale accusing Liverpool of doing as much to cause commercial distress by his warnings against speculation as Pitt had done by declaring war in 1793. Lansdowne and Liverpool then resumed their economically higher-level discussion: Liverpool proposed the clause allowing the Bank of England to open fully independent branches; Lansdowne requested that each branch should be made to pay its notes locally in gold; and Liverpool agreed, suggesting that each local branch Bank of England's notes should be locally designed and printed, to reduce forgery.[85] The Country Bankers Act passed into law in May 1826.

Liverpool returned to the Exchequer bills question when discussing the Bank Notes Bill, formally preventing the issue of £1 and £2 notes. He claimed that they had not refused to issue Exchequer bills merely because of his March 1825 speech:

> We are not so strongly attached to our own opinion as to persevere in any system which we discover to be an injurious one. However, of this I am satisfied, that His Majesty's Government never effected a greater good, than by resisting the applications which were made on that subject. If those applications had been now acceded to, upon any future occasion, when any distress arose, relief would be demanded as a matter of right.

The 1793 precedent was a bad one, because this time there was no war, crisis or bad harvest. Bank of England assistance was quite different; it was to known persons and offered on market principles against good security. In response to the peer who warned that abolishing notes would encourage highwaymen, Liverpool pointed out that, having been a victim of highway robbery when he was a schoolboy, he knew the risks but that highwaymen had become much less common since he had introduced better policing regulations while Home Secretary.[86] He made the point that full reform was not possible until the Bank of England's charter expired in 1833 and ended: 'I am satisfied, that if the withdrawal of the small notes, and the introduction of a metallic circulation, does not effectually cure the existing evils, they will, at all events, have a great effect in removing them.'[87]

Finally, Liverpool gave his views on the Scottish and Irish banking systems. He regarded Scottish banks as much sounder than English, since their number was restricted by law and they were all substantial. Hence, he was easily persuaded by the agitation led by Sir Walter Scott, with his *Letters of Malachi Malagrowther*,

85. Hansard, *The Parliamentary Debates, New Series*, Vol. 14, cols 866-77 (27 February 1826).
86. See above Chapter II.
87. Hansard, *The Parliamentary Debates, New Series*, Vol. 14, cols 1353-56 (14 March 1826).

against the abolition of Scottish pound notes, agreeing to set up a committee to examine the question, where the proposal died. In Ireland, a new banking system had recently been set up and would be given time to settle.[88]

As on economic questions throughout his career, Liverpool's leadership on bank reform was decisive, carefully thought out, economically sound and eloquently expressed. The move to joint-stock banking is with us today, as are the Bank of England branches (agencies since 1997), while the abolition of £1 and £2 notes survived for the remainder of the gold standard period. Liverpool's reform stabilised the British banking system and made bank failures almost unknown – the next big British bank failure was that of Overend, Gurney & Co. in 1866.

The reform was also carried out with remarkable speed – the climax of the crisis occurred on 18 December 1825, the solution to the reform of the long-term banking system was propounded 26 days later and the relevant legislation was passed by both houses and signed into law on 22 March and 26 May 1826, the latter just 159 days from the crisis. The money markets were unsettled through late February but, once the Bank of England made its modest liquidity injection in March, recovery was swift – although the manufacturing districts remained distressed for most of the year.

Liverpool's next significant intervention was on slavery, when Bathurst introduced a debate on Commons resolutions of 1823 for ameliorating the condition of the slave population. Liverpool began by declaring that slavery should be abolished 'as soon as was consistent with the respective interests of all who were concerned in that condition'. Immediate steps should be taken to improve the condition of slaves and qualify them for enfranchisement. Whipping and Sunday work must be abolished, slave trials must be made more just, and a proper system of valuation should be instituted. While the colonies had done nothing in response to the 1823 resolutions, he still favoured the colonial governments acting on these principles, to teach the slaves to look up to them for their eventual enfranchisement. Parliament should call on the colonial assemblies to do what was right but allow a reasonable time for the infirmities of human nature.[89]

In a subsequent debate, Liverpool remarked that he opposed slaves' emancipation without proper preparation:

> I have always felt that this is a measure, which ought to be approached with caution and deliberation. The great interests and property at stake demand this caution, and it is also to be considered, that the government and parliament have been parties to the evils of slavery, in consequence of the direct encouragement, which has, for a hundred and fifty years, been given to the state of things existing in the West Indies.

88. Ibid., cols 1392 and 1396-97 (17 March 1826).
89. Ibid., cols 1152-54 (7 March 1826).

However, the colonial assemblies' reaction had been disappointing: 'they have shown a disposition, not to amelioration, but to resistance. . . . If they persist in refusing to attend to the recommendation which they have been given, it will be the duty of parliament to interfere.' Any colony which ameliorated the conditions of its slaves could rely on the support of the mother country; he hoped they would act in a spirit of peace and conciliation, and not compel parliamentary action.[90]

Liverpool's attitude to slavery appears unacceptably gradualist to a modern sensibility. The political arguments against change were weaker than those against Catholic Emancipation – there was no majority in favour of slavery, just wealthy vested interests. The money to purchase manumission, even on a more generous scale than the £20 million which Whigs managed in 1833, was available from the early 1820s onwards, once the national finances had stabilised. Still, the political clamour for emancipation was not yet deafening, and for the Prime Minister to accept the moral case for abolition was a big step forward.

In his financial statement, Robinson again resorted to flowery rhetoric: 'The violence of the storm has passed away, the clouds which impended over us have begun to disperse; and by the very conflict of the elements, the atmosphere has, to a certain degree, been cleared and purified.' He then turned to reality, congratulating himself for underestimating revenue in three successive years and went through the tax remissions since 1816, totalling them to £27.5 million, while consumption had increased substantially, and public debt had been reduced by £18 million since 1823, with a £1 million reduction in the annual charge for it. Finally, he turned to the estimates for 1826, showing expenditures of £56.3 million, including £5.5 million for the sinking fund and revenue of £57 million. He then estimated the revenue loss from the recession and the previous year's tax changes at £1.3 million. The surplus was thus £700,000 and he proposed to reduce that by continuing a reduction in tobacco duty from four shillings to three shillings which had been introduced erroneously in the previous year. Finally, he announced the intention to reduce outstanding Exchequer bills by £6 million through application of the sinking fund, to relieve the Bank of England's balance sheet.

On modern figures, Robinson was too optimistic. Public revenue declined by a substantial 4.4 per cent in 1826 from 1825, to £55.2 million, with most of the reduction in excise duties. Conversely expenditure, with substantial jumps in army and navy expenditure, mostly as a result of the Anglo-Burmese War, rose by £2 million to £56.1 million. Thus, instead of the substantial surplus which Robinson had projected, the budget fell into a £0.9 million deficit, the first since 1817.[91]

90. Ibid., Vol. 15, cols 393-95 (19 April 1826).

91. Mitchell, *British Historical Statistics*, pp. 581 (Income), 587 (Expenditure). The year-end is 5 January so, to get the figures for the (approximate) calendar year 1826, you

The year 1826 also saw Peel's second major set of Home Office reforms; a codification of the entire criminal law. This was an immense task, recommended by a Select Committee as far back as 1796 and pending for a century before that. It came in two parts, a bill for the improvement of justice administration, which passed in the 1826 session and a bill to consolidate the laws affecting larceny and other property crime, which was passed in the 1827 interregnum between Liverpool's stroke and his replacement. The effect of both measures, together with the 1823 reforms, was to cut drastically the crimes for which the death penalty was imposed.

Penal reformers wanted to go further but Peel himself was deterred by a steady rise in crime, which had doubled from 47,522 criminal commitments in England and Wales in the seven years to 1816 to 93,718 in the seven years to 1825, most of the increase being in property crime.[92] From 200 years away, it seems likely the increase was largely due to the increasing prosperity of the middle and artisan classes, which brought correspondingly more opportunities for property crime. Peel's other conclusion, that a professional police force was needed, also made sense. (The Metropolitan Police was introduced in 1829 and absorbed Liverpool's Bow Street Horse Patrol in 1837.)

The second half of the session was quieter than the first half but Liverpool's illness was becoming more severe. Indeed, at Easter, Canning, who had now through favours to the King's mistress and cronies put himself on better terms with the King, paid a surprise visit to Bowood to see Lansdowne, probably contingency planning for a possible cross-party government on Liverpool's departure.[93] For Liverpool himself, the main subject of contention was the Corn Laws.

The extended Corn Laws debate began with Lansdowne urging a direct grant to the distressed inhabitants of the manufacturing districts. Liverpool replied that the Poor Laws and private charity were the best means of alleviating such distress. Direct grants from the government would be unprecedented outside Ireland (where a private subscription during the last period of distress had brought in £300,000). Later, Liverpool explained that he did not think the present a good time to debate the Corn Laws question, though he accepted that the Corn Laws needed revising to bring down the fulcrum price of 80 shillings per quarter, since taxes on farmers had been relieved so much. He did not, however, believe that fully free trade in corn was desirable.

Liverpool rejected the thesis that the country's distress was due to the Corn Laws; it was due to overtrading, as demonstrated by the demand for many goods being now as much below the norm as it had been above the norm in 1825. However, he announced that the corn then in bond should be released

should use the 1827 figures in the tables.

92. Gash, *Mr. Secretary Peel*, p. 341.

93. Bamford and Wellington, *The Journal of Mrs. Arbuthnot, 1820-1832*, Vol. 2, p. 21, 23 April 1826.

to reduce the current high price, which had risen to 60 shillings, and that Ministers would be given the discretion to import another 500,000 quarters if the price rose.[94] In the event, a dry August with rising prices brought this provision into effect even though the harvest was eventually a good one. On the other hand, employment in the manufacturing districts began to recover over the summer.

On 11 May, Liverpool gave a major speech on the Corn Laws. He began by agreeing that the Corn Bill of 1815, or even that of 1822, were not applicable to the present time – the question of corn duties was by its nature variable. Since £27 million in taxes had been remitted since 1815, all should agree that a price of 60 shillings gave an equivalent return to a price of 80 shillings in 1815. The banking bills being considered by the Commons bore no relation to the Corn Laws but should on balance boost them. However, circumstances had made temporary relief necessary, 'not the partial insurrections, and the destruction of power-looms, which are as foolish as they are unwarrantable, but the sufferings incurred in Lancashire, Warwickshire, Derbyshire, and other districts'.

Since England, Scotland, Wales and Ireland could barely feed themselves in good years, the existing Corn Laws caused difficulty when there was a bad harvest, of which Britain had seen eleven in the past 32 years. In 1816, for example, the outlook in early June was good, yet by the end of the month, indeed after one disastrous day, the harvest was ruined and corn prices shot up from 52 shillings to 110 shillings. Under the current system, if a similar event occurred on 14 May, they could not open the ports until 14 August, or 14 November if the averages happened to be against them: 'There is no evil which would bear any comparison with this; it operates as a most enormous tax on the community, and especially upon the lower orders of it.' The government needed the power to open the ports immediately in years of distress.

It was said that manufacturing workers were short of work, not bread, but several who a short time ago had wages of eighteen or 20 shillings a week were now reduced to work at seven, six or even five shillings a week. Government needed the power to open the ports to prevent real distress; not just his own government, but any government. When the Prussian government had approached the government in February asking for free entry of corn in return for free entry of British manufactures, the government had refused to relax the Corn Laws; this showed that they did not place free trade principles above them. Ministers now wanted to look at the corn question from all points of view and arrive at a flexible solution, which took all interests into account; the emergency provisions he had announced in March were not intended to affect the Corn Laws' principles.[95]

94. Hansard, *The Parliamentary Debates, New Series*, Vol. 15, cols 294-97, 751-52, 762-63 (18 April and 1 May 1826).
95. Ibid., cols 1088-95 (11 May 1826).

Parliament was dissolved on 31 May. In his dissolution speech the King thanked Parliament for its work on banking reform and congratulated it on the British victory in the Anglo-Burmese War, for which preliminaries of peace had been signed. It also commended the 'exemplary patience' of the manufacturing classes during the recession.

At the dissolution, nine English peerages were created, carefully balanced between supporters and opponents of Catholic Emancipation, with Liverpool, Canning, the King, Peel and Grenville all having a say in who was ennobled. Most important for Liverpool, his former brother-in-law (through Louisa), Frederick Hervey, who had worked for him at the Foreign Office in 1801-3, was promoted from Earl of Bristol to Marquess, taking in addition the subsidiary title of Earl Jermyn. Given that neither Liverpool nor his half-brother Charles had any sons, this was almost equivalent to a step in the peerage for Liverpool himself.

In the late summer, Liverpool quarrelled with Wellington about promoting Wellington's youngest brother Gerald Wellesley[96] to a bishopric. Gerald Wellesley had separated from his wife some years earlier and therefore in Liverpool's eyes was ineligible for a bishopric. Liverpool held firm, and Gerald Wellesley, who lived to 1848, never was made a bishop. Wellington was sufficiently annoyed that Arbuthnot warned Liverpool he was thinking of resigning from the Cabinet.[97]

The principal issue at the 1826 general election, held from 7 June to 12 July, was Catholic Emancipation. Wellington had given Liverpool advice on the matter:

> I conceive it to be the duty of the government generally, and of its members individually, whatever may be their opinions regarding the question of further concessions to the Roman Catholics, to shape their course in respect to the dissolution of Parliament and to the elections in such manner as to afford the best chance of assembling a Parliament which shall enable the government to keep the Catholic question in the state in which it is.

He then explained that, with a substantial pro-Emancipation Commons majority in 1825, that would be impossible without more anti-Emancipation MPs, so Liverpool should use his influence in that direction.[98]

Liverpool officially remained neutral but behind the scenes appears to have exercised some influence as suggested. This resulted in a quarrel with

96. Gerald Valerian Wellesley (1770-1848). Prebendary of Durham, Chaplain of the Royal Household.

97. The relevant correspondence is given in Yonge, *The Life and Administration of Robert Banks Jenkinson*, Vol. 3, pp. 383-95.

98. Wellington to Liverpool, 2 May 1826, quoted in Wellington, *Despatches, Correspondence*, Vol. 3, pp. 314-15.

Palmerston, who felt that as a long-serving minister he should have Liverpool's support at Cambridge University (a high-prestige seat that returned two MPs elected by its graduates) but instead found himself and his anti-Emancipation colleague William Bankes[99] opposed by two further anti-Emancipation Ministers, Copley and Goulburn. Even though all four candidates were nominally Tory, the largely clerical electorate was badly split, rejecting Goulburn and Bankes and electing Palmerston an ignominious second, with Whig backing, a long way behind the persuasive Copley. Alas, Palmerston's ill-feeling against Liverpool provided the initial nudge in a process that sent him into the arms of the Whigs.

The election was more widely contested than in 1820, with an increasing level of public electioneering reflecting the larger electorate enfranchised by prosperity. The economy, still fragile, especially in the manufacturing districts, worked somewhat against the government – although less so than in 1820. The Corn Laws were also important; Liverpool's temporary relaxation of them was unpopular in agricultural districts, as was Huskisson's relaxation of protection in general.

Overall, this was the best of Liverpool's four election victories. The Whigs were on the wrong side of both the economic issue (where they supported free trade) and Catholic Emancipation. In Ireland, O'Connell's Catholic Association, now re-formed, had considerable success supporting pro-Emancipation candidates, in a campaign marked by more violence than usual. In the remainder of the United Kingdom, however, Catholic Emancipation remained deeply unpopular. The overall result saw a net gain of about a dozen seats for the anti-Emancipation forces but a much larger gain of over 30 seats for the government, increasingly split though it was becoming, against the Whigs. From Liverpool's viewpoint, this was remarkably satisfactory.

Alas, as the election results rolled in, Liverpool's health again deteriorated and he was only intermittently active for the remaining six months of his political life. He was bled and leeched after a cold in early December and was again out of action for some weeks in January, missing the Duke of York's funeral. Psychologically, he was now finding the job difficult; Mrs Arbuthnot tells of him complaining that Canning was far more difficult to work with than Castlereagh. She also quotes Wellington, on the Cabinet dinner of 8 November: 'Formerly Cabinet dinners were rather jovial meetings, but that now, after the ministers had not met for six weeks, there was scarcely a word spoken, every body seemed afraid or averse from speaking.'[100] Liverpool spoke frequently of retiring, but wanted to put a new Corn Law in place and feared the confusion his retirement would bring.

99. William John Bankes (1786-1855). MP for Dorset, 1832-35. A distant cousin of Liverpool, travelled extensively to Egypt.

100. Bamford and Wellington, *The Journal of Mrs. Arbuthnot, 1820-1832*, Vol. 2, p. 55, 9 November 1826.

The closing months of Liverpool's administration were, like its opening years, dominated by the politics of the Iberian peninsula. Spain had been ruled by the autocratic Ferdinand VII, with a French army occupying the country, since 1823. Portugal went into crisis when the monarch John VI died in 1826, leaving his liberal elder son running Brazil, which had declared independence in 1822, as Emperor Pedro I.[101] To avoid reuniting the two countries under one ruler, Portugal was to be ruled by Pedro's infant daughter Maria II,[102] under the regency of her aunt, the Infanta Isabel Maria.[103] Unfortunately Pedro I (Pedro IV of Portugal) during his brief period of less than two months as King of Portugal imposed a new liberal constitution, with the encouragement of Canning and the active participation of Sir Charles Stuart, who carried the constitution from Brazil to Portugal and presented it to the Infanta. John VI's absolutist younger son, Dom Miguel[104] was cut out of the succession (though there was a proposal to marry him to the seven-year-old Queen Maria) and was left plotting rebellion with considerable popular support.

A substantial section of the Portuguese army backed Miguel, entered Spain and gained assistance from the Spanish government. Accordingly, the Infanta's government requested the return of Beresford, who had commanded the Portuguese army during the Peninsular War. Wellington doubted whether Beresford should be sent but then agreed with Liverpool in early October that, if Portugal was to be liberal and Spain reactionary, Portugal's only security would lie in the efficiency of its army, so Beresford had better go there.

Canning had just spent several weeks in France and was able to report that the French government was not hostile, although its Ambassador to Madrid was anti-British. Liverpool drafted a potential response to Spanish aggression, suggesting that Spanish merchant shipping could be seized, neutral powers reminded that Spain was not entitled to invade Portugal, an independent power, and, if necessary, the Spanish constitutionalists could be unleashed to make mischief. He reiterated his view that the regency with the constitution was the legitimate government of Portugal and that absolutists like Metternich would not wish to see Britain intervene on the liberal side. He ended, however on a note of doubt: 'Are we confident that the Portuguese nation will stand by their Constitution and the existing regency? If not, our situation may be very perplexing.'[105] Given that the constitution was less than six months old and partly of Canning's design,

101. Pedro I (1798-1834). Emperor of Brazil, 1822-31. King of Portugal, 1826.
102. Maria II (1819-53). Queen of Portugal, 1826-28, 1834-53.
103. Infanta Isabel Maria (1798-1876). Regent of Portugal, 1826-28.
104. Dom Miguel I (1802-66). King of Portugal (usurper), 1828-34.
105. Liverpool letter to Canning, 10 October 1826, quoted in Yonge, *The Life and Administration of Robert Banks Jenkinson*, Vol. 3, pp. 406-7.

this was a good question – Mrs Arbuthnot said: 'However fond we are of Constitutions, the Portuguese by no means like having one forced down their throats.'[106]

Over the next few weeks, the situation on the ground slowly deteriorated – even after Beresford arrived in Portugal – with the Portuguese rebels, allied to some Spanish forces, making incursions into Portugal. Thus, when the Portuguese ambassador officially asked for assistance at the beginning of December, the Cabinet resolved to send out 5,500 men under Sir William Clinton, a decision confirmed by Parliament on 12 December. Clinton's force was assembled with remarkable speed; it arrived at Lisbon on 25 December. While Beresford was annoyed in early January by receiving only the post of 'temporary' Commander-in-Chief of the Portuguese forces, which he resigned within a few days, by mid-January the Anglo-Portuguese combination had achieved its objective of suppressing the Portuguese rebels and chasing the Spanish invaders back into Spain. It was a satisfactory, if limited, success.

The intervention in Portugal was popular, at least among Canningites and Whigs, but it made no long-term difference. When British forces were removed in 1828, Miguel swept to power, and was ousted in 1834 only following an intervention by Pedro I, who abdicated his Brazilian throne and enjoyed considerable support from the Whig British government and Palmerston as Foreign Secretary. Portugal's nineteenth-century history was a dismal one; the major reason for this was the conflict between 'liberals' with little popular backing and traditionalists with massive aristocratic and rural support but despised by the urban intellectuals.

The summer of 1826 was exceptionally warm and dry, with fears of a serious drought in late August. Corn prices remained firm, even though traders recognised that the 500,000 quarters in bond would be released for sale domestically during 1827. However, the drought caused prices for oats, rye, peas, beans and other foods to rise significantly. Accordingly, by an Order in Council, those commodities were permitted entry in payment of a small duty. Parliament was recalled early, in November, to ratify this action, although rain in September had alleviated the problem naturally.

Otherwise, 1826 was a year of sharp economic downturn, followed by modest recovery late in the year. Imports declined to 1824's level, with wheat imports rising sharply from 391,000 quarters to 582,000. Exports were affected by the decline in trade with South America, falling back to the levels of the preceding decade. Brick production also fell back but remained nine per cent above the healthy 1823 level. Exports of cotton manufactures declined by 14 per cent, to below their 1822 level, reflecting the sharp credit crisis in the early part of the year. Kondratieff's index of textile production declined sharply, by 18 per cent, but Hoffman's index of total production declined by only nine per cent.

106. Bamford and Wellington, *The Journal of Mrs. Arbuthnot, 1820-1832*, Vol. 2, p. 54, 9 November 1826.

To anticipate, the recovery in late 1826 continued during 1827. Imports recovered to almost the 1825 level, while exports recovered to their 1823-24 levels or rather above them except those to Latin America. Brick production fell further, to around the 1822-23 level. Exports of cotton manufactures, on the other hand, rebounded sharply, to a level twelve per cent above the previous 1824 peak. Both the Kondratieff and Hoffman indexes rebounded sharply, by 36 per cent and 21 per cent, respectively, leaving them ten per cent and two per cent above their 1825 peaks.[107] Thus, the overall picture is of a sharp but short-lived recession in the manufacturing districts, with recovery beginning in late 1826 and continuing strongly through 1827. The financial crisis of 1825 had caused only a short downturn in the strong economic uptrend of Liverpool's latter years in office.

Before the next Parliamentary session, the Cabinet's attention was devoted to the Corn Law. As usual on economic matters, the discussion was led by Liverpool, based on a memorandum produced by Huskisson that outlined the defects in the existing law and proposed changes. Eventually, Liverpool decided on a sliding scale, whereby the duty would be 40 shillings per quarter when the domestic corn price was 50 shillings, dropping by two shillings per quarter for every shilling price rise, to zero when the domestic price hit 70 shillings.

With this scale, it was estimated that imports would normally begin when the domestic price rose to around 60 shillings, so deducting the 20 shillings duty, the net receipt to the foreign producer would be 40 shillings. Imports would become a flood at 65 shillings. In another reform, the price calculations would be based on weekly rather than quarterly averages, which were thought less easy to manipulate. Overall, the reform would have stabilised the market and given foreign corn producers clear signals on when the British market would be open; it was the best of the Corn Laws attempted between 1815 and 1846. Alas, the toxic politics of 1827-28 would prevent its enactment.

Liverpool made his new proposal at the tense Cabinet dinner on 8 November and, after a few further Cabinet meetings, it was adopted as government policy. To maximise its acceptability to Parliament, it was agreed that Canning, rather than the unpopular Huskisson or the feeble Robinson, would introduce the proposal in the Commons, while Liverpool would introduce it in the Lords.

One final intervention occurred before the session began: a lengthy letter from the ailing Duke of York to Liverpool. This reiterated his general support for Liverpool's government but emphasised his die-hard opposition to Catholic Emancipation. It also claimed that the proposed reform of the Corn Laws was almost unanimously opposed by the landed interest and

107. Figures taken from Gayer, Rostow and Schwartz, *The Growth and Fluctuation of the British Economy, 1790-1850*, Vol. 1, pp. 171-210 (1822-26), 211-41 (1827-32). The 1827 Hoffman index is for consumer goods; the overall Hoffman index is not given for that year.

risked destroying the landed order on which British society rested. Liverpool responded verbally to the Duke but reminded the King that his government rested on a principle of neutrality on Catholic Emancipation and that a purely 'Protestant' administration could not command a Commons majority. As for the Corn Laws, 'I am quite certain I could satisfy your Majesty that His Royal Highness is acting under a misapprehension upon the whole of that subject.'[108]

After the new Parliamentary session opened the King presented his Address in person. He began by noting the Order in Council admitting foreign food, then rejoiced in the Burmese peace. He sympathised again with the manufacturing districts, and warned that revenues were lower than expected, but rejoiced that the economic problem appeared to be alleviating.

Liverpool confined his remarks on the Address to defending the Order in Council, reminding the Lords that 'there was about one fortnight in the course of the summer, as alarming with respect to the produce of the earth, as any period that has ever been remembered'. Fortunately, the weather had improved in September. The proposed Corn Bill would be introduced in the New Year, when attendance would be better.

On 13 December, Parliament was adjourned. On the previous day, however, had occurred the great Portugal debate in both Houses, following the decision to send troops. In the Lords, as Liverpool was too ill to participate, Bathurst gave a workmanlike account of the complex Portuguese political situation together with British obligations under the Treaties of 1661 and 1703, renewed in 1810 and 1815. He was supported by Holland and Lansdowne, as well as Wellington, and the decision to send troops was agreed to without dissent.

In the Commons, after a sober speech announcing the decision, Canning in a second speech responding to doubters indulged in one of his most famous flights of oratory: 'Contemplating Spain, such as our ancestors had known her, I resolved that if France had Spain, it should not be Spain "with the Indies". I called the New World into existence, to redress the balance of the Old.' He was met with resounding cheers from the Whigs and silence from his own side.

While justifiable, if arrogant, in describing his sparking off the Monroe Doctrine to secure Latin American independence, Canning's words had a very different implication when applied to the 1826 Portuguese crisis. In that case, also, he had brought in a New World (Brazilian) Emperor to impose a constitution on an Old World country (Portugal) that did not want one. Dom Miguel has received a bad press from Whiggish British historians, but rule by him without a liberal constitution was almost certainly the desire of a substantial majority of Portuguese citizens, then and for decades afterwards. Canning and later Palmerston were instrumental in thwarting their wishes.

---

108. Yonge, *The Life and Administration of Robert Banks Jenkinson*, Vol. 3, pp. 432-37.

Immediately after Parliament adjourned on 13 December, Robinson expressed a desire to leave the Exchequer and retire to the House of Lords. He had recently lost a favourite child. He also feared facing the House of Commons after his revenue estimates for 1826 had proved optimistic by some £4 million, throwing his 1826 Budget into disarray and making it difficult to formulate an acceptable 1827 Budget. Liverpool, in reply, told Robinson of his own illness and impending retirement. He pointed out that the Government's life was 'hanging by a thread' because of the Catholic question so a change in the 'efficient' offices would terminate it prematurely. He also deprecated Robinson leaving: 'This is the first session you will have had of real financial difficulty, and I do not think it would be for your credit that you should appear to shrink from it.'[109]

In the event, the Whig John Maberly[110] first harassed Robinson about the financial position on 16 February. Robinson delayed making a formal response, refusing to answer further questions as late as 26 March. Then he was called up to the Lords as Viscount Goderich as part of Canning's Cabinet-forming exercise. The definitive budget was presented on 1 June by Canning. It was a disgraceful display of cowardice and goes far towards explaining Goderich's failure to control his own administration after Canning's death.

During the Parliamentary adjournment the Duke of York died. Liverpool immediately made sure his office of Commander-in-Chief went to Wellington, rather than being held by the King directly, as His Majesty half wished. Liverpool's letter informing Wellington of the King's wish to appoint him and encouraging him to hold the Mastership of the Ordnance in parallel was sent within 48 hours of the Duke's death. Wellington's response was nicely sardonic, reflecting the confidence between the two men: 'We both understand the same thing, viz., that I am to hold both offices and perform the duties of both but receive the salary of only one.'[111]

The Duke of York's funeral threatened the health of two Prime Ministers and a Lord Chancellor. St George's Chapel at Windsor Castle was excessively cold and the funeral lasted five hours, largely through incompetence in its management. It caused Wellington and Canning to catch bad colds, the latter retiring to Brighton, absent from Parliament for more than a month. It only did not finish off Eldon because that wily gentleman had the sense to stand on his ceremonial cocked hat, rather than on the flagged stone floor. However, Liverpool had retired to Bath to recuperate from his exertions before Parliament reconvened, apparently with some short-term success.

---

109. Liverpool letter to Robinson, 16 December 1826, quoted in Yonge, *The Life and Administration of Robert Banks Jenkinson*, Vol. 3, pp. 438-39.
110. John Maberly (c.1775-c.1840). MP for Rye and Abingdon, 1816-32. Army clothing contractor and banker. Tory until 1818, then Whig. Declared bankrupt, 1832, and fled to Brussels.
111. Wellington to Liverpool, 8 January 1827, quoted in Wellington, *Despatches, Correspondence*, Vol. 3, p. 534.

During the period following the funeral, Canning and Liverpool exchanged their penultimate letters, on the Portugal situation. Canning began by acknowledging that France had been helpful in quelling the Spanish assistance to the Portuguese rebels, so that part of the rationale for the presence of British troops in Portugal had disappeared. Equally, he remained convinced that Dom Miguel intended to restore autocracy, initially as regent, which would now be a massive blow to British prestige.

Liverpool advised temporisation but said, significantly, that:

> We must take into account that our army has certainly not been well received in Portugal, and that we are by no means popular there. The parties likewise into which the country is divided, are much more nicely balanced than we had reason to believe when we decided on the expedition.

For Liverpool at least, there was no ideological knee-jerk for liberalism leading him to overlook the preferences of the Portuguese people.[112]

Liverpool's and Canning's last correspondence came on the scheduling of the debates on the Corn Laws and Catholic Emancipation. They agreed in preferring to debate corn first but believed that a Catholic Emancipation debate could not be postponed beyond early March. They both wanted the new Corn Laws to pass as the Cabinet had agreed them three months earlier. While they were on opposite sides on Catholic Emancipation, they believed that, if it passed the Commons, it could be amended in the Lords to provide additional safeguards for the Church. If both men's health had held up, there was no reason they could not have cooperated amicably for the 1827 session.

When Parliament reconvened, Liverpool announced his intention to introduce his proposed Corn Law Bill on 19 February or, at latest, 26 February. Alas, his stroke on 17 February prevented this and Canning's illness prevented the Commons debate on the proposed bill from occurring until 1 March. Just before, on 12 February, Liverpool proposed a message of condolence to the King for the death of the Duke of York, in a graceful speech that paid respect to the Duke's capabilities as Commander-in-Chief for three decades. Finally, in a speech that was brief and observers found more halting than usual, on 16 February he proposed an additional grant of £12,000 per annum to the Duke of Clarence, now the undisputed heir to the throne.

On 17 February 1827, Liverpool's political life ended. Around 10.30 that morning, while he was having breakfast alone reading documents, he suffered a massive stroke; he was found shortly afterwards by his servants flat on the floor. At first it seemed he might recover and he was removed to Coombe Wood for greater quiet. Over the next few weeks he was able to say a few

112. Canning to Liverpool, 5 February 1827, quoted in Yonge, *The Life and Administration of Robert Banks Jenkinson*, Vol. 3, pp. 443-47. Liverpool to Canning, 6 February 1827, quoted in Wellington, *Despatches, Correspondence*, Vol. 3, pp. 583-84.

words from time to time. Indeed, he sent two letters to the King in mid-March, in which he suggested visiting Windsor on 26 March.[113] However, his abilities never returned sufficiently to conduct business and there were frequent relapses. From late March, therefore, the King and other ministers began working towards a new administration.

Nevertheless, Liverpool was able to signal acquiescence to Lady Liverpool on 9 April, when she brought him the news that the King was relieving him of his office. He suffered a second more severe stroke on 7 July, then lingered on until his death on 4 December 1828, in the presence of his wife and his half-brother Charles.

Liverpool's body left Coombe Wood on 15 December for the long journey to Hawkesbury. Outside Liverpool's family, official mourning for him was limited but the Duke of Wellington as Prime Minister did propose that he, Bathurst, Melville and Peel, Liverpool's remaining Cabinet colleagues in Wellington's government, should wear mourning dress for a period of three weeks.[114] The mourning coaches accompanying the initial procession were far fewer than for his wife's funeral in 1821; just his brother, the Marquess of Bristol, the Duke of Clarence, Sidmouth and his local MP Charles Pallmer.[115] On 18 December, he was interred in Hawkesbury parish church. The personal estate left by his will was proved at £120,000, plus 3,000 acres of land in Gloucestershire; less than the estate his father had left. Unlike his father, Liverpool's even more distinguished career had left him poorer rather than richer.

Initially, there were just a few tributes that did Liverpool justice. For example, Ellenborough, speaking in the Lords on 2 May, said: 'the loss of the earl of Liverpool, who possessed the respect and esteem of the country to a degree hardly ever before accorded to any private individual, was not to be supplied'.[116] However, such whole-hearted tributes were few. Even by the time of his death, Liverpool's political footprint was sharply diminished.

There remain three questions unanswered: what would have happened if Liverpool had not suffered a stroke, what did happen, and why the political and intellectual footprint of Liverpool and his ministry shrank so rapidly into insignificance.

First, what would have happened. The best evidence here is a conversation between Londonderry (the third Marquess, Castlereagh's brother) and the King on 13 April 1827. Londonderry visited the King to beg him not to make Canning Prime Minister and the King responded:

---

113. The King responded to them in a letter of 24 March 1827, in Aspinall, *The Letters of King George IV, 1812-30*, Vol. 3, p. 206.

114. Wellington to Peel, 6 December 1828, given in Wellington, *Despatches, Correspondence*, Vol. 5, p. 311.

115. Gash, *Lord Liverpool*, p. 250. Charles N. Pallmer (1772-1848). MP for Luggershall, 1815-17, Surrey, 1826-30. Son of West India planter, solicitor. Bankrupt, 1831.

116. Hansard, *The Parliamentary Debates, New Series*, Vol. 17, col. 495 (2 May 1827).

> So things proceeded until the calamity of Liverpool, and what I formerly would have thought a desirable event, has certainly turned out for me one of the most unfortunate. It is true however that Liverpool would not have stayed in beyond the present session, and he declared to me, if he did not carry the Corn Bill, he would not remain prime minister; but had he gone out, he would have arranged matters so as not to place me in the dilemma in which I now stand.[117]

Assuming Londonderry is a reliable witness in this note to his ally Wellington, that the King was not deluding himself, and that Liverpool had not deceived him, this is significant. Liverpool intended to retire at the end of the 1827 session. The King had expected to welcome this – as we have seen, he was not very fond of Liverpool. However, Liverpool had expected to arrange for a smooth transition, not the angst-filled drama of April 1827.

Since Liverpool had repeatedly stated that he did not think Wellington should occupy a purely political office,[118] he would have had three alternatives, on retirement in, say, July.

First, he might have proposed a transition to Canning but without the angst, enabling the seven anti-Emancipation ministers who resigned on Canning's appointment to keep their jobs. This is the least likely of the three. In July 1827 Canning was within a month of death; any delay and he would have been removed from the equation. Liverpool was fully aware of Canning's weak points, especially his egotism and quarrelsomeness. He would have objected to Canning's desired Canningite/Whig coalition and would have fought it, pressing for the retention of Canning's existing colleagues. Liverpool had rescued his career in 1822; now with the King's help he could have ended it kindly, sweetening the end with an earldom and a pension.

A second course of action would have been a generational shift to Peel. We know Wellington would have served under Peel; Mrs Arbuthnot was contemplating it on his behalf in December 1826. Peel's reputation was high following five successful years at the Home Office and his man-management defects were not yet apparent. Except on Catholic Emancipation, he was regarded as a liberal, so Robinson and Huskisson would have served under him, more easily than under Wellington, in a government with Catholic

117. Londonderry memorandum to Wellington, 13 April 1827, given in Wellington, Despatches, Correspondence, Vol. 3, pp. 631-35.

118. There was also the problem that Wellington had just accepted the office of Commander-in-Chief, which he and others felt more suited to his talents. Mrs. Arbuthnot, of course, wanted Wellington to succeed Liverpool, generating enough waves on the subject to be described by Treasury Secretary Lushington as 'a meddling junta of the aristocracy, instigated by a foolish female'; (Aspinall, *The Letters of King George IV, 1812-30*, p. 208). Had it not been for her Diary, that would have been the poor woman's only footprint in the sands of Time!

Emancipation an open question as under Liverpool. Retire Canning with all the honours and cash he could carry, bring Palmerston into the Cabinet and everybody would have been (relatively) happy. Liverpool liked and admired Peel and this solution would have given him the best chance of anointing a long-term successor.

The third course was the 'Duke of Portland' solution. In 1807 Portland had been chosen to lead nominally a government of younger men, none of whom wanted to serve under the others. In 1827 there were several 'Portlands' available. Goderich (formerly Robinson), apparently considered for such a role, would not have been one of them, as Liverpool knew of his cowardice. However, Bathurst, an opponent of Catholic Emancipation and Harrowby, a supporter of it, were both liked by their colleagues and eminent enough to fill the role. If Canning and his supporters had objected vehemently to Peel's succession, this might have been an acceptable compromise.

Alas, Liverpool was in no position to arrange his succession. The difficulty of the transition was shown by the universal desire to put it off in the hope that Liverpool would recover, with even informal attempts to find Liverpool's successor not beginning until the last week of March and Liverpool not formally relieved of his duty until 9 April. The length of this hiatus appears to have been unique in the prime ministerial period of British history.

During the lengthy period of indecision, the main business of the 1827 parliamentary session took place. The Corn Bill was introduced by Canning and passed the Commons, with the majority at second reading no less than 243 votes to 78, the Whigs mostly abstaining and the protectionists voting against. By that stage the new government was being formed, with much of Liverpool's former Cabinet in opposition. Thus, when the Corn Bill came up in the House of Lords, introduced by Goderich, the new Leader of the House, Wellington felt free to propose a wrecking amendment, which passed by 133 votes to 122, with most former ministers voting for Wellington's amendment.

A revised Importation of Corn Bill, with Wellington's thumb firmly on the scale of the drafting, was brought in the following year and passed. Its main difference from the 1826-27 version was that the sliding scale was both more protectionist and fell away much more abruptly around 70 shillings. This caused the corn market to function erratically, with neither British nor foreign corn growers able to plan properly. For example, in 1829, when corn prices averaged 66 shillings per quarter, no less than 2.2 million quarters was imported, more than in any previous year as the wholesalers held corn back until the price reached 70 shillings, then flooded the market. Wellington's 1828 meddling was thus responsible for much of the following decade's agricultural distress.[119]

On Catholic Emancipation, the big Commons debate went well for the anti-Emancipation forces, Burdett's motion failing by 276 votes to 272. This

119. Mitchell, *British Historical Statistics*, pp. 221 and 756.

demonstrated the net shift of about a dozen votes between the two sides in the 1826 election. It also meant that the issue would not have plagued Liverpool's government for the remainder of the session. Since he would presumably also have persuaded Wellington and his colleagues to support his Corn Bill, a healthy Liverpool would thus have steered the government ship safely into the July 1827 recess.

Canning's succession to power was highly contentious. Peel had already refused to serve under him, because of his pro-Emancipation views, but the remainder of Liverpool's Cabinet was in principle available. However, Canning had very likely already come to an agreement that Lansdowne and some moderate Whigs would join a Canning government, while Grey and Russell held aloof. From Canning's point of view, this appeared an ideal solution. Lansdowne, Tierney, Carlisle and William Lamb (the future Lord Melbourne) would bring major new talent to the administration and give it a colour distinctly different to Liverpool's. Adding Parliamentary Reform to Catholic Emancipation as topics that Ministers could disagree about would remove his ideological differences with those moderate Whig figures. The Canningite/Whig Coalition appears to have been Canning's first choice, not his fall-back position.

Accordingly, Canning was delicately offensive to Wellington in his overture to join his government, so Wellington, Peel, Bathurst, Eldon, Westmorland and Melville refused to join him. Wellington even resigned the non-political office of Commander-in-Chief. Of the anti-Emancipation Cabinet ministers, only two remained: Copley, promoted to Lord Chancellor as Lord Lyndhurst, and Bexley, who after tendering his resignation joined Canning's government as a favour to the King.

Canning's government lacked a Commons majority, as the 1826 Parliament was strongly Tory – the dismal fate of the Corn Bill in the Lords demonstrated the damage Tory backwoodsmen could do. Canning, unlike the feeble Goderich, would have met Parliament in 1828, relying on his charisma but would then have run into trouble.

When Canning died suddenly on 8 August, one feels the government could have done better than choose Goderich to lead it. Lansdowne, for one, was an outstandingly capable figure, an excellent fit to lead a Canningite/Whig coalition. However, Lansdowne doubtless saw that the only chance for a Commons majority was to attract Tory support, which he could not easily do.

Hence Goderich succeeded without much discussion and strengthened the Tory side of the government by adding Herries as Chancellor of the Exchequer. Wellington, having no great objection to Goderich, returned as Commander-in-Chief. It was not enough. Herries and Huskisson quarrelled – they were both capable but prickly – and that quarrel, combined with dread of the looming Parliamentary session, caused Goderich to resign in January 1828.

Wellington then resigned the office he really wanted, Commander-in-Chief (to which he was blocked from returning until 1842), and formed a government, gritting his teeth and taking back Huskisson, Palmerston and other Canningites. He rejected Eldon (much to the latter's fury), Westmorland and Bexley, the last of whom would have provided useful financial wisdom. Alas, Wellington's hamhandedness with finance and somewhat peremptory leadership style caused him to lose Huskisson in May 1828, followed by the resignation of the other Canningites. This loss was unnecessary and, given what the future was to bring, remarkably foolish.

Following the unexpected loss of an Irish by-election at County Clare to Daniel O'Connell, Wellington and Peel decided their policy of the past quarter of a century must be reversed and Catholic Emancipation granted. The Roman Catholic Relief Act was passed in April 1829, infuriating the right wing of the Tory party, who concocted the bizarre belief that Parliamentary Reform would stop any similar legislation in the future. Peel's betrayal of his anti-Emancipation followers was especially resented and his chilly personality and poor man-management skills made the problem worse.

Liverpool had left his successors an 1826 Parliament so solidly, splendidly Tory that, even with both wings of the party cut off, like Monty Python's Black Knight, the Wellington/Peel government had a majority. Nevertheless, the hatreds generated by Canning's ministry and Catholic Emancipation weakened the Tory position incomparably. Canningites who before 1827 had thought of themselves as Tories started looking to possible alliances with the Whigs. Palmerston was especially tempted by the chance of achieving top office in a Whig government short of ministerial experience. Meanwhile, ultra-Tories like the Duke of Richmond[120] were motivated by a simple thirst for revenge against Wellington and, particularly, Peel.

Thus, when George IV died in July 1830 and caused an untimely general election in which the government lost about another 20 seats, the Tories were no longer able to command a majority. Negotiations with Huskisson to return to the fold were ended by Stephenson's Rocket on 15 September. Without Palmerston and other Canningites and without the ultra-Tories, Wellington's government lost a vote of no confidence on 15 November by 233 votes to 204. The next two years saw the passage of a Reform Bill, which mostly through gerrymandering rather than expansion of the franchise locked the Tories out of government for nearly two generations. I discuss the Reform Act in Chapter IX, since it was central to the 'Whig view of history' that undervalued Liverpool.

The miserable history that followed Liverpool's retirement explains the decline in his reputation. Liverpool's party was already split between two mutually hostile wings before he retired and the party fell apart with his disappearance. No re-creation of Liverpool's government was possible, as Wellington proved in 1828.

---

120. Charles Gordon-Lennox (1791-1860). 5th Duke of Richmond from 1819. MP for Chichester, 1812-19. Postmaster General, 1830-34.

IX.

Conclusion

I have looked at Liverpool's life in detail and so will now draw conclusions. I will discuss the historical importance of re-evaluating Liverpool's career, at the lessons we can draw today from Liverpool's policies and, after summarizing Liverpool's achievements, briefly at a comparison between Liverpool and other claimants to the title of 'greatest prime minister'.

Why does a re-evaluation of Liverpool's career matter?

Ever since Liverpool's departure, we have been conditioned by the Whig view of history, which sought to portray nineteenth-century British history as a steady progress towards late Victorian affluence and power. I believe that this view is wrong and that the apogee of British power, economic dynamism and quality of government came during Liverpool's tenure. This section will examine why it is necessary to challenge this Whig view of the period.

The Whig view of history was established during the Whig supremacy of 1714-60 and gained important further influence during the long Whig hegemony after 1830. Thomas Babington Macaulay's history of the post-1688 period was vital in this effort but so was the mythologisation of the 1832 Reform Act. As a corollary to that mythologisation, Liverpool's fifteen-year ministry was written out of the record, portrayed as an unimportant period of black reaction before Reform was ushered in. In re-examining Liverpool, removing the Whig aspersions cast over his record, we should thus begin by examining the Reform Act itself, and determining what it really was and what it was not.

In the Whig myth, the Reform Act was the first great extension of the franchise, leading inexorably on to modern democracy, put into effect by Whigs who, while fearful of full democracy, were nevertheless united in seeking to broaden substantially the basis of parliamentary representation. This is not accurate.

Liverpool's opposition to parliamentary reform, first expressed in opposition to a Grey proposal of 1793, was not based on a simple aversion to change. In his view, the existing constitution, as modified in 1688, was uniquely conducive to good government because of its balanced nature. The King, the Lords and the Commons each had their separate powers and only after all three freely consented could major initiatives be undertaken. The Lords had its own role to play as representative of tradition, the Church and the large landed interests and, except on money bills, was coequal with the Commons.

The Commons franchise had grown up haphazardly since 1295 but now had the virtue of being usefully 'mixed', representing all segments of the people in a way that could not be reproduced by a simple Cartesian division into richer voters and poorer non-voters as imposed by the 1832 Reform Act. While the working classes, the most numerous, were represented in the system as they would not be except residually between 1832 and 1867, they did not dominate it as they would under pure democracy (anathema to both political parties at this time). From experience, county seats produced better members, more securely attached to the constitution, than populous boroughs with broad franchises. Thus, except in cases of extreme corruption, Liverpool wanted to change the existing system as little as possible, because it produced capable government and any meddling might well make things worse (as indeed it did, to any supporter of Liverpool's policies and beliefs).

According to Fisher's *History of Parliament*, [1] the electorate expanded by about 37 per cent between the 1820 and 1831 elections, through natural means. The 1832 Reform Act expanded it only by a further fifteen per cent. To produce the unique 'mixed' constitution, the pre-1832 electorate arose from a wide variety of franchises, only some of them restrictive. Potential voters included traditional '40-shilling freeholders' in the counties, while 'freemen' votes in many boroughs enfranchised most long-resident artisans, and other boroughs enfranchised 'scot-and-lot' voters (direct payers of 'rates', property taxes) or 'potwallopers' (occupiers of houses with their own fireplaces, boiling their own pots). There were no registration requirements; you could just turn up at the polls and vote.[2]

The 1832 Reform Act disenfranchised freeholders with value between 40 shillings and £10, as well as many others who voted through time-honoured local franchise schemes. While those already on electoral rolls were 'grandfathered', any such voter moving after 1832 or succeeding to his father's modest estate lost out – by 1867 there were few 'ancient rights' voters

1. 'Survey IX: The English Reform Legislation' in Fisher, *The History of Parliament*, gives a detailed account of the 1832 Reform Act, its redistribution and estimates for the extension of the franchise in 1820-31 and through the Act.
2. Philip Salmon and Kathryn Ris, 'Who Should Have the Vote? What Electoral Rights Did Britons Have in the Century Before 1918', *History Today*, Vol. 68, issue 8 (August 2018), gives valuable details of pre- and post-1832 voting rights.

remaining. While most 'freemen', 'scot-and-lot' and 'potwalloper' voters in borough constituencies would regain the vote by the Second Reform Act of 1867, in county constituencies '40-shilling freeholders' would not regain the vote until the Third Reform Act of 1884.

The 1832 Act also imposed a strict requirement for registration with a one-shilling fee, serious money for an artisan, and a one-year residence requirement, disenfranchising those who moved. The franchise, which had been somewhat balanced between the classes, became artificially limited to the middle classes and above by a sharp cut-off at the £10 level. Overall, the franchise was considerably more restricted after the Reform Act than before it. The modest increase in the electorate and numbers voting came from seat redistribution, disenfranchising small constituencies and enfranchising larger ones.

While doing nothing for the working class, indeed damaging its interests significantly by restricting the 40-shilling freeholders' voting, the Reform Act did a huge amount for the Whigs, gerrymandering the electoral system so that the Tories won only one majority between 1832 and the next Reform Act in 1867. This was achieved primarily by rigging the lists of boroughs disenfranchised and boroughs enfranchised with two new seats. For example, the 1830 election, finely balanced between the two parties, saw the thirteen Cornish seats that were to be disenfranchised in 1832 return nineteen Tory and seven Whig members. In 1837, also a finely balanced election, the 22 boroughs given two new seats under the 1832 Act, primarily Northern manufacturing towns and downmarket London boroughs, returned eight Tories/Conservatives, 26 Whigs/Liberals, and ten (Whig-voting) Radicals. From this portion of constituency revision alone, the Whigs achieved a net gain of 40 seats.

In total, 56 boroughs with 111 seats were disenfranchised in England and Wales, while another 30 boroughs lost one of their two seats, for a total of 141 seats disenfranchised. 22 boroughs were given two new seats and nineteen were given one new seat. An additional 62 new seats were given to counties, increasing their representation from 82 to 144 members.

It was the massive scale of the borough disenfranchisement that caused a huge shock to the House when the preliminary bill was first read in the House of Commons on 1 March 1831.[3] Previous discussions of parliamentary reform among serious statesmen had envisaged a more limited disfranchisement, of perhaps 20-25 of the most corrupt and electorally indefensible boroughs, with their seats redistributed primarily to the Northern industrial cities and to counties.

However, Grey had subcontracted the drafting of the bill to a group of four Whigs including the most Radical senior figures, Russell and Grey's son-in-law, Lord Durham.[4] Both Russell and Durham were well to the left of their

3. An excellent recent account of the reform crisis, albeit written by a strong supporter of the Whigs and the Reform Act is Antonia Fraser, *Perilous Question: Reform or Revolution? Britain on the Brink, 1832* (London: Weidenfeld & Nicolson, 2013).

4. The other two members were Althorp (Leader of the House of Commons) and John

party; Durham, who led the group, far outside its mainstream. Thus, the bill they produced, although restrictive in its enfranchisement provisions, was both radical and highly gerrymandering in its redistribution provisions, far more so than would have been envisaged by mainstream Whigs, such as Melbourne, Lansdowne and Palmerston, now Foreign Secretary.

Moreover, even though the new franchise would include only a small percentage of the population, the redistribution abandoned the age-old principle of representing distinct 'places' and went by population itself. Most disenfranchised constituencies, such as Wootton Basset and Ilchester, were distinct urban entities with distinct civic personalities; many new constituencies, such as Finsbury, Lambeth and Tower Hamlets, had no separate existence but were mere agglomerations of mostly impoverished (so non-voting) people in sections of London.

After the first version of the Reform Bill passed its second reading by only one vote, 302 to 301, on 22 March 1831, it then lost a key vote in committee. Since many of the ultra-Tories and some Canningites had been 'scared straight' by four months of incept Whig government and the radical Reform Bill, there was now a Tory majority in the Commons of at least 40[5] for a Wellington/Peel government. As the new Parliament had been in existence for well under a year, on past precedent King William IV should have refused the Whigs a dissolution and the Tories would have returned, possibly in a coalition, to calm popular unrest and pass compromise legislation. However, the King foolishly granted the Whigs the dissolution they craved and they used the popular unrest they had stirred up to engineer a large pro-Reform parliamentary majority.

The best opportunity had been lost for a compromise Reform measure, which might have taken a limited step in the redistribution of say 25-30 constituencies, widened the franchise modestly and rationalised it, while agreeing any gerrymandering between moderate figures on both sides of the House. Calming popular unrest, such a measure would have stabilised the political situation. As the crisis worsened and unrest intensified, William IV became increasingly hostile to the reform project, which involved him in promising a mass creation of peers. However, by the time he attempted to replace Grey with a Wellington ministry in May 1832, serious popular excitement and the large Whig majority in the Commons had made it impossible for Wellington to take office.

Two further factors made the 1832 Reform Act especially destructive to the existing constitutional settlement.

William Ponsonby (1781-1847). Viscount Ducannon (Ireland) from 1793. 1st Baron Ducannon from 1834. 4th Earl of Bessborough from 1844. MP for Knaresborough, Higham Ferrers, Malton, Bandon, Kilkenny County and Nottingham, 1805-6, 1810-34. Home Secretary, 1834. Lord Lieutenant of Ireland, 1846-47.

5. '1830-31 Parliament', in Fisher, *The History of Parliament*, estimates a Tory government majority of 42 after the 1830 election.

The first was popular agitation, which the Whigs encouraged (on false pretences – as E.P. Thompson has pointed out, the working-class supporters of parliamentary reform got nothing from the 1832 Act).[6] The trouble began with the 'Swing' riots in late 1830, which were violent, but caused largely by a poor harvest. Then mass popular agitation in favour of Reform began as the Whigs took office, with strong encouragement from the more radical Whig MPs. The demonstrations remained largely peaceful through the first half of 1831 but, after the House of Lords blocked the bill by a majority of 41 on 7 October, violent riots broke out in several cities, with those in Bristol lasting three days, destroying much of the central city, killing twelve rioters and injuring more than 100 others.

From then on, opponents of Reform were in physical danger, especially during the week in May 1832 while Wellington was attempting to form a government (the Duke was indomitable but Peel showed signs of squishiness). Even after the violence but, before the bill had passed the Lords, Grey welcomed Thomas Attwood,[7] leader of the (Radical but non-violent) Birmingham Political Union, to the Treasury on 19 May 1832 and thanked him: 'We owe our situation entirely to you.'[8]

Riots had been common enough in previous decades but the use of the mob to intimidate opposition was new and painfully reminiscent of events in Revolutionary France. Furthermore, since the working classes gained nothing from the Reform Act, and were hurt further by Whig legislation, such as the 1834 Poor Law, popular discontent remained high, far above the 1820s level, for the next fifteen years, until the late 1840s brought cheaper food and greater prosperity.

The second factor exacerbating the destructive effect of the crisis was the forced promise from the King to create enough extra peers to ensure passage of the Act, which, given the majority of 41 against it in the Lords, would have required 50-60 new peers in one creation. This was not entirely unprecedented; Queen Anne had created twelve new Tory peers on 1 January 1712 to ensure passage of the Treaty of Utrecht. The abuse to which this could lead had been recognised at that time. After the Hanoverian succession, the Whig government attempted to prevent it via the Peerage Bill of 1719 but that unduly restrictive measure was defeated by a rebellion of Whig backbenchers led by Walpole.

6. As the *Poor Man's Guardian* remarked after the Reform Act passed: 'Our English Whigs extended the franchise to the small middlemen in order the more effectively to keep down the working classes. Of all governments, a government of the middle classes is the most grinding and remorseless.' See Thompson, *The Making of the English Working Class*, p. 821.

7. Thomas Attwood (1783-1856). MP for Birmingham, 1832-40. Country banker, proto-Keynesian economist. Founded Birmingham Political Union to agitate for Reform, 1829.

8. Fraser, *The History of Parliament*, p. 247.

Nevertheless, the difference in scale was important and the final abstention by the Tory leaders in the Lords to avoid mass creations, which in the end allowed the Bill through, marked a serious diminution in the power of the House of Lords. The precedent of 1832 was then held to justify a still larger potential creation in 1911, the threat of which was used to pass the 1911 Parliament Act which brought to an end the legislative veto of the House of Lords.

In Liverpool's time, the House of Commons was already nominally supreme. However, Liverpool's own elevation to the Lords in 1803, for example, had been undertaken because the main Whig leaders were in the Lords and his debating talents were needed there. Throughout Liverpool's term in office, the Whig leaders in the Lords, Grenville, Grey and Lansdowne, were far weightier than the Commons Whig leadership and Lords debates were as important as those in the Commons, except on strictly budgetary matters. Thus, the US Ambassador Richard Rush, in his memoirs, expressed surprise at finding the Lords' debates in 1818-19 more impressive than those in the Commons.[9]

After 1832, even though some prime ministers such as Aberdeen, Rosebery and Salisbury were in the Lords, the House of Commons was a much more important centre for legislation and serious debate was concentrated there. In this area also, therefore, the Reform Act upset the balance of the constitution.

Rethinking the 1832 Reform Act brings into focus that period's politics. The 1830s and early 1840s were politically an unhappy time, with continual unrest, economic stress (partly but not entirely caused by the capital cost of the railway network) and ineffectual government. The 1850s and early 1860s, still with predominantly Whig governments, but free from the overhang of the Reform Act and with improved economic conditions, were much happier years.

The other major policy initiative misevaluated by Whig historians was Liverpool's 1815 change to the Corn Laws, reviled by posterity ever since their repeal in 1846. The Corn Laws had three purposes. First, they attempted to stabilise the market for grains so that British farmers could be sure of a reasonable price for their output. Second, they were intended to keep Britain as self-sufficient in food as possible, a reasonable ambition after two decades of war. Third, and less known, they were intended to make Ireland, with its low labour costs and potato monoculture, a supplier of grain for Britain as a whole. This last purpose was only partially achieved – 17 per cent of Ireland's land was under grain crops by 1847 – but even its partial success alleviated the 1840s potato famine.

The Corn Laws did not prevent grain price fluctuations but, contrary to myth, while sustaining prices when they were low, they did not increase them in times of scarcity. However, by the 1820s the return to gold had deflated prices in general, making 80 shillings per quarter too high an equilibrium. Thus, in late 1826 Liverpool and Huskisson prepared a revised Corn Law with

9. Richard Rush, *Memoranda of a Residence at the Court of London* (Philadelphia, PA: Key and Biddle, 1833).

a sliding scale duty centred on 60 shillings a quarter. That bill was defeated in the Lords in the chaos after Liverpool's retirement but a subsequent less well-designed bill, slightly more protectionist but still a liberalisation of the 1815 Act, was passed in the following year.

Peel liberalised the Corn Laws further in 1842, then repealed them altogether in 1846. This reduced food prices overall, producing an improvement in living standards for industrial workers. However, it also left agriculture hugely vulnerable to US competition, which became effective with the completion of the midwestern US railway system in the 1870s. The result was an agricultural depression that began in 1873 and lasted until World War II. Liverpool's belief that the Corn Laws were essential for British self-sufficiency in wartime was borne out in World Wars I and II, when Britain twice came close to starvation through assaults on her food imports.

Peel's repeal of the Corn Laws was combined with further moves towards unilateral free trade in the years between 1846 and 1860, which resulted in the hollowing out of British industrial capability over the next century. Conversely, repeal did not benefit Ireland; it did nothing to alleviate the immediate potato famine and caused the growing of corn in Ireland to become uneconomic, so within a decade the nascent Irish granary had disappeared.

The Corn Laws had only a modest effect on living standards. The decade 1812-22, in which they were introduced, was one of sharp price deflation in agriculture and elsewhere, during which wages declined less than prices in agriculture and remained approximately static in other sectors, thus producing a sharp rise in real wages (at the cost in 1822-23, when corn prices were exceptionally low, of large losses for farmers). The recovery in corn prices after 1822, and the more sluggish economy of the 1830s, then caused a modest rise in living standards in the late 1820s, flattening until the early 1840s. Corn Laws repeal caused a further decline in overall prices, which produced a rise in living standards except in agriculture itself, where wages fell. Overall, post-war deflation and the vigorous industrial prosperity of the 1820s did considerably more for working-class living standards than repeal of the Corn Laws, while the capital requirements of railroad building and inept Whig economic management in the 1830s caused a pause in the overall betterment of working-class conditions that otherwise persisted through the rest of the century.

In relative terms you can argue that the 1820s were Britain's period of greatest economic strength in relation to her main competitors. In 1820 Britain had a GDP of $36.2 billion 1990 international dollars, close to that of France (whose population was 50 per cent larger) and representing 15.2 per cent of the Greater European total, including Russia and the important European offshoot of the United States (then with a GDP only one third that of Britain).[10] Only two countries had larger GDPs, China, at

10. Figures in this section are from Angus Maddison, *The World Economy: Historical Statistics* (Paris: OECD, 2003).

$229.6 billion 1990 international dollars and India at $111.4 billion 1990 international dollars – and Britain by 1820 was fully in political control of India.

In 1870, just before the major downturn started in 1873, Britain's share of the Greater European whole had grown slightly, to 16.4 per cent, and it had now marginally the largest Western GDP at $100.2 billion 1990 international dollars, with the US just behind it and France and Germany each 30 per cent smaller. By this time, China's GDP had shrunk to $189.7 billion 1990 international dollars, while India's had grown modestly – staying flat per capita – to $134.9 billion. By 1913 Britain's share of the Greater European GDP was only 11.6 per cent and its GDP was behind that of the United States (more than double its size) and Germany (five per cent larger).

Britain was already the largest Western economy by 1820 and enlarged its position within the Western bloc modestly further in the next 50 years, as industrialisation and railways took hold. Then after 1870, Britain's relative position began to decline, largely owing to its unilateral free trade policy, and by 1913 its GDP was already exceeded by that of the United States and Germany, although on a per capita basis only the United States was about eight per cent richer by the latter date.

However, in the 1820s, in addition to its absolute position and relatively rapid growth trajectory, Britain had the inestimable advantage of a near monopoly of the new industrial technologies, which Liverpool himself recognised and rejoiced in. Even with its massive burden of war debt, Britain in that decade was able to seize markets from its competitors and increase its economic dominance.

In foreign policy also, the same general pattern applies. For more than a decade after 1815, Britain was the arbiter of Europe and, indeed, of the world. At no point during the Napoleonic Wars did Britain field the largest armies. However, its navy had been utterly supreme after 1805, its Allies' armies depended on British subsidies, and its own army was substantial and had the best general on the Allied side. Those advantages did not disappear quickly, although Britain's military adventures were confined to small-scale colonial wars. Thus, even though Britain pulled out of the Great Alliance after 1822, it remained the arbiter of Europe for several decades after that.

This position began to change only after the middle of the century. With regard to the Royal Navy, the move to steam and iron made Britain's position less obviously invincible. Militarily, Britain's performance in the 1854-56 Crimean War was distinctly questionable. Consequently, beginning with the Schleswig-Holstein crisis of 1863-64, Britain found itself no longer an automatically important factor in European quarrels. In the Franco-Prussian War of 1870-71, it was a mere spectator.

Then, after the 1890s, the United States emerged as a rival and at least economically superior power, a source of strength to Britain only when firmly allied to it. Salisbury maintained Britain's pivotal influence by avoiding Continental entanglements but, after he retired from the Foreign Office in 1900, Britain joined one of the two mutually hostile alliances in Europe. When the 1914 crisis came, Britain did not have a say in either side's decision to go to war.

We must thus reverse the standard optimistic Whig view of steady progress through the nineteenth century towards an apotheosis of power and prosperity in the 1890s. Strategically, and in terms of relative economic strength, Britain achieved both supreme military triumph and a position of unique economic superiority in the early part of the century. Strategically, after about 1850 it was living on past glories and became gradually less important in European and world affairs. Economically, it continued to build modestly until about 1870, although with increasing foreign competition; then after 1870 its relative though not absolute position began to decline.

Overall, the apogee of Britain's greatness came when Liverpool was prime minister. The changes in economic policy and constitutional structure following his departure were a substantial contributor to the ending of the centuries-long advance and the beginning of relative decline. Winning the Napoleonic Wars, navigating the most difficult years of the industrial revolution, returning Britain to the gold standard and stabilising and beginning to reduce the unprecedented mountain of public debt: these were all Liverpool's achievements. Through them, he made the business of statesmanship much easier for his successors throughout the nineteenth century.

What can we learn today from Liverpool's policies?

Liverpool's fiscal and economic policies were sophisticated and successful, not just for his time but by any standards; several aspects of them are applicable today. We can also learn from his foreign policy, which embodied some universally useful principles. Constitutionally, Liverpool's belief in a mixed constitution and a balance of interests would work better than today's unbalanced constitutional system.

Liverpool regarded the British constitution of his day as ideal because it was 'mixed' with elements of monarchy, oligarchy and democracy comingled and thus the various interests in British society each had an influence on decision making. A Liverpool today would want to return to such a system.

Since Liverpool believed the constitution was and should be mixed, he also believed that policy should be balanced between the various interests in society. Thus, the needs of the country for food security and of the agriculturalists for income stability produced the Corn Laws, even though Liverpool believed in free trade. Similarly, Liverpool believed in direct action to alleviate famine, as in 1800, even though this was not in accordance with abstract economic theory – he would have handled the 1845-49 Irish potato famine differently from Peel and Russell.

A modern Liverpool would regard it as critically urgent to reverse the 1911 emasculation and 1958 and 1998 distortion of the House of Lords. He would have two reasons for this. First, he would regard a genuinely powerful and independent second chamber as a vital part of a 'mixed' constitutional set-up. If legislation can be passed by a single chamber, all elected at the same time on the same franchise, extremism and tyranny can result and, at best, much legislation will be ill-considered and dictated by party prejudice.

Second, Liverpool would regard the current structure of the House of Lords as an abomination. He would recognise the Royal right to create peers and the unfortunate precedent created by Queen Anne in 1712, creating twelve peers to get the treaty of Utrecht through. However, he would regard the misuse and expansion of that precedent by Grey in 1832 and Asquith in 1911 as illegitimate and would want to prevent further such abuses He would also regard the 1958 invention of life peers as undesirable, since it allows for too many new peerages, mostly with connections to the current government. Finally, he would despise the 'Tony's cronies' House of Lords created in 1998 with a majority for foolish political correctness.

In his ideal world, Liverpool would revert to a House of Lords consisting only of the currently existing hereditary peers, plus a limited number of new creations if desired, to act as a generator of long-term policies. Overall, a second chamber consisting of hereditary legislators is an ideal check on the short-term-oriented House of Commons. If an elected element were thought necessary, a limited number of say 100 life peers popularly elected for ten-year terms, who would after that period keep the title but not the Lords seat, would be a plausible addition to a hereditary chamber.

Whatever its composition, the new second chamber would have the powers of the pre-1832 House of Lords: a full veto, the power (as now) to originate legislation, security against gerrymandering as happened in 1832 and 1911 and a subordinate but nonetheless important role in the government of the country. It would once again be overseen by the Lord Chancellor.

Beyond its purely constitutional application, the principle of balance between national interests in a modern setting would produce rational, well-considered policy, not governed by powerful lobbies or the opinion polls. As his administration demonstrated, Liverpool was fully aware of public opinion but believed good government based on sound principles to be more important than short-term popularity. However, sound government also requires awareness of the prejudices and wishes of the electorate, seeking to satisfy them wherever possible. A Liverpool government would have as its primary objective today the preservation and enhancement of the fabric of society, maintaining the balance between interests.

In the maintenance of social order, Liverpool's society was far less intrusive into privacy than our own – Sidmouth's agents were nowhere near as knowledgeable of private matters as modern electronic surveillance techniques. Liverpool also believed that moral guidancewas no concern of the state but valued the Church of England as a helpful moral stabiliser and preserver of social order. Here today a Liverpool would have no equivalent assistance – the Church of England is both feeble and compromised, and no replacement has arisen.

Economically, Liverpool's understanding was superior to that of most statesmen today. In general, the quality of economic thought among British policymakers of Liverpool's period was high. Adam Smith,[11] Thomas Malthus and David Ricardo gave them an excellent grounding in free market economics, and few statesmen opposed their doctrines. Liverpool read Smith as a teenager and was educated thoroughly by his father, a knowledgeable, albeit sceptical, disciple of Smith. Liverpool guided the country successfully through the most economically difficult years of war spending and post-war depression and returned Britain to the gold standard, before overseeing an unprecedented economic upturn. Then in 1825-26, he anticipated the Austrian economists by forecasting a crash resulting from overspeculation and reorganised the British banking system to guard against it happening again.

The first deviation from economic good sense among British policymakers was their move after 1846 to unilateral free trade. Free trade itself was pioneered by Liverpool, based on principles enunciated by Smith and Ricardo, but he never contemplated leaving British agriculture vulnerable to competition from the US Midwest, let alone subjecting British industry to depredation by protected foreign competitors. After 1846, Peel and blinkered Whig statesmen eliminated first the Corn Laws and then British tariffs, keeping free trade even as other countries turned protectionist after 1860. The result was a gradual erosion of Britain's competitive position, eventually worsened by two world wars, but avoidable had better economic policies been followed.

Beyond the writings of economic theorists, the overriding economic principle governing Liverpool's economic policy was property rights. These were far more sacrosanct than they are today, even though modern capitalist economies nominally respect them. Liverpool's era respected the idea of a 'freehold place', for example – a job to which you had a property right, which you could buy or sell on the market. Thus, when the Irish parliament was abolished in 1800, there was no question of doing so without proper compensation to those who controlled Irish boroughs. Similarly, when the abolition of slavery was first discussed in 1824, Liverpool made it clear that however immoral slavery was, there could be no question of abolishing it without compensation to the slaveholders.

Modern governments do not take property rights anything like seriously enough. Leftist sentimentality holds that they conflict with human rights and

11. Adam Smith (1723-90). Scottish economist. Professor of Moral Philosophy, University of Glasgow, 1753-63. Commissioner of Customs in Scotland, 1778-90. Rector of the University of Glasgow, 1787-89. *Theory of Moral Sentiments* (1759). *The Wealth of Nations* (1776).

should thus be held subordinate. However, without property rights, human rights are meaningless: if the government has the right to seize your property, it has rights over your entire existence. Moreover, to the extent that property rights are owned by the government rather than by individuals, they are subject to the 'tragedy of the commons', in which, because an item of property has no owners, it is not cared for and quickly becomes degraded. Modern governments interfere with regulations and price controls, seeking to force property to be used for the 'general good'. They also engage excessively in compulsory purchase of private property for public-sector schemes of one kind or another or even, as in the US Kelo vs City of New London (2005) Supreme Court case,[12] for more politically favoured private interests.

Since modern statesmen are not brought up to respect property rights in the way Liverpool did, the best way to ensure those rights is probably by a constitutional amendment, framing it as part of a second 'Bill of Rights' in the British system. Thomas Jefferson did great damage to the future of his country when he changed John Locke's 'Life, Liberty and Property' in the US Declaration of Independence to the intellectually sloppy, French-inspired 'Life, Liberty and the Pursuit of Happiness' – the latter provides far less protection to the individual than a straightforward guarantee of property rights. Any country that wishes to be considered a free society needs a solid protection for property rights in its constitution; the assets of the propertied are otherwise too great a temptation for unwashed leftists.

Turning now to Liverpool's economic policies, the most important, an objective throughout his administration, was to return Britain to the gold standard, with a banking system designed to operate effectively on such a standard. To achieve this, he had to overcome only modest political opposition – the two recent examples of fiat currencies, the American continentals and the Revolutionary French *assignats*, were not encouraging. On the other hand, the economic difficulties involved were considerable, with British public debt around 250 per cent of GDP and prices in 1815 around 56 per cent above 1792 levels.

Liverpool had two reasons for favouring a gold standard. First, as had been known throughout history, it provided price stability because of gold's durability and scarcity. Second, it prevented government from issuing money directly; Liverpool correctly regarded such direct issuance as vulnerable to government meddling and unlikely to command the international market respect which a major currency required.

Liverpool's 1819 gold standard lasted for the remainder of the nineteenth century, only upset by the arrival of European war in 1914. It was, however, increasingly difficult to maintain, because over the course of the nineteenth

12. A benchmark case in which the state's power of eminent domain was held to extend to the City of New London's seizure of Suzette Kelo's house for a private sector "comprehensive redevelopment plan" that was later abandoned.

century both economic growth and population growth accelerated, increasing the demand for money faster than new supplies could be obtained. That was why the gold discoveries of 1849 in California and the 1890s in the Yukon were so stimulative to global growth; both new finds ended periods of substantial deflation, thereby easing monetary conditions. By 1914, global population was increasing by close to one per cent per annum, while global economic growth per capita was running at about 1.3 per cent per annum; global gold supplies could not keep up with this and the gold standard was running into trouble.

By the 1920s, global population growth was even faster, at 1.1 per cent per annum, with only a slight dip for World War I and the Spanish influenza of 1918-19. Hence Britain's return to the gold standard in 1925, at the pre-1914 gold parity, was a high-risk proposition. Not only was a substantial one-off deflation required, as had been undertaken in 1819, but the gold standard would continue to be deflationary on a year-by-year basis. While policymaker fecklessness and indiscipline were substantial contributors to Britain's abandonment of the gold standard in 1931, they were not the only causes.

After World War II, global population growth had increased still further, to 1.8 per cent per annum in the 1950s and over two per cent in the 1970s, so a true gold standard was impossible. The Bretton Woods standard of 1944 was worse than pure floating exchange rates; it allowed governments to delude themselves and their citizens that an inflation-preventing gold standard was in effect, thus bringing global inflation and, in Britain, effective debt repudiation through inflationary erosion of principal and interest. Nevertheless, during the period 1950-2000, a global gold standard would have been impossibly deflationary. However, that is now changing.

The global population's rate of increase peaked in the early 1970s and is now declining, at around 1.09 per cent per annum in 2015-20, according to 2017 UN Population Survey estimates. It is expected to decline further to 0.63 per cent per annum in 2040-45 and 0.32 per cent per annum in 2065-70.[13] Once the global population's rate of increase drops below one per cent per annum (expected in the next quinquennium, 2020-25) a gold standard becomes feasible without excessive deflation. Moreover, maintaining a gold standard indefinitely becomes straightforward at the lower population growth projected a generation or two in the future.

Provided global population growth remains at one per cent per annum or below, there is now no reason not to return to a gold standard. Conversely, the reasons for moving in that direction are as valid as they were in Liverpool's time. When even central banks are aiming not at price stability but at creeping inflation of two per cent per annum, the gold standard's provision of price stability is enormously important for anyone whose assets are long term in nature.

13. United Nations Department of Economic and Social Affairs, Population Division, *World Population Prospects: The 2017 Revision* (New York, NY), custom data acquired by website.

Even more important, the gross irresponsibility of the world's central banks in the last decade (actually, since around 1995) demonstrates just how essential it is to wrest the process of money creation out of the hands of governments, who can always find paid-for economists to justify whatever inflationist, property-destroying nonsense they come up with. We have all endured a decade of productivity growth close to zero as a result of central bank meddling, subjecting us to Brezhnev-era, Soviet-style stagnation.[14] A gold standard would guard against any further such experiments.

Once a gold standard is in place, banking regulation becomes straightforward, as Liverpool demonstrated in 1826. The trick is to restrict the issue of notes by any other than the central bank, if there is one – either to zero, or to a low level. By doing this, excessive money supply expansion can be prevented and bubble/crash episodes like 1720, 1825 and 2008 can be eliminated. The 1819-25 banking system had too many small banks, each allowed to issue their own notes; after 1826 note issuance was restricted and the natural process of bank consolidation allowed to proceed. The 1844 Bank Charter Act, restricting even Bank of England note issuance to a low level, was too restrictive because it had to be suspended three times within the next 20 years; the 1825-44 system was a good balance.

In today's world, a system without a central bank is optimal, because the central bank will not be truly independent of the government or of academic fads encouraging it to expand credit. The ideal banking system contains commercial banks, large and small, with their leverage governed by painful experience and no bailouts or deposit insurance, along with brokerages and secondary lenders that depend on commercial banks for their liabilities. In addition, for retail savers who wish to avoid the banking casino, Trustee Savings Banks along the lines of Liverpool's 1817 Act, investing only in Treasury securities, are an excellent alternative. They provide the most important function of a bank, securing private savings, without venturing into the less important and more dangerous areas of loan provision and bond/stock market operations.

Liverpool's fiscal policies can be an important lesson to us today. He inherited a public debt that by the end of the war was 250 per cent of GDP, then in the first year of peace lost a major source of revenue in income tax. Yet, by cutting non-debt-service expenditure by 69 per cent in three years, he and Vansittart managed to balance the budget, and keep it balanced, making a start on repaying the huge debt and refinancing the most expensive portions of it.

The main fiscal skill that has been lost is cutting public expenditure, which appears to become more and more difficult with each year that goes by. It is also necessary for a leader to take Liverpool's attitude to the national

14. I have written on this at length but see, also, Ernest Liu, Atif Mian and Amir Sufi, 'Low Interest Rates, Market Power and Productivity Growth', University of Chicago Working Paper No. 2019-09, which demonstrates the mechanism by which artificially low interest rates suppress small companies and reduce productivity growth.

debt: determination to bring it down without indulging in expropriation of bondholders through inflation (as did British post-World War II governments)[15]. A gold standard will greatly help; it removes the temptation to cheat bondholders through monetary fiddling.

The past decade of profligacy has worsened the problem and made it likely that a Liverpool/Vansittart approach will be needed to prevent the first British debt default since 1672. A stringent attitude to public expenditure and readiness to forgo popularity will then prove vital – fiscal balance will only be attainable through cutting back 'sacred cows' such as the National Health Service, the education system and entitlement programmes generally. Only by 'zero-based budgeting', as Liverpool and Vansittart undertook in 1815-20, examining every item of government expenditure to determine whether it is truly necessary, will the appropriate level of public sector austerity be achieved.

Among politicians, Liverpool was the foremost expert of his time on international trade. He understood perfectly the benefits of free trade, but also the need to preserve British agriculture and the self-defeating nature of a unilateral free trade policy, removing tariffs when competitors left them in place or increased them. His Corn Laws gave Britain the chance to remain close to self-sufficiency in food and to develop Ireland as a grain-producing area.

Today therefore, Liverpool would protect rather than subsidise agriculture, thus eliminating the budgetary costs of agricultural subsidies. He would also attempt to reach supply agreements with politically reliable agri-surplus nations such as Canada, Australia and New Zealand.

With regard to tariffs in general, Liverpool would attempt to reach a global system of low tariffs, which would provide revenue for the Exchequer, thereby reducing the tax burden on the domestic economy, while taking advantage of substantial, but not of trivial, comparative advantages of foreign producers in some product and service sectors. He would bear in mind the importance of maintaining domestic living standards, which Say had identified as a problem in 1814-15, but would recognise that in today's much richer economy the few individual cases of hardship from rises in the cost of staples are better dealt with through the welfare system than by distorting the economy.

Liverpool's foreign policy principles would translate well. He would welcome the increased opportunities for meetings between world leaders, recognising that such contacts can prevent the dangerous build-up of hostility, such as occurred between 1904 and 1914. On the other hand, he would oppose the plethora of international organisations, from the United Nations downwards,

15. My Great-Aunt Nan, retiring in 1947 without a state pension, put her substantial savings into 3½ per cent War Loan, a perpetual bond like Consols. By the time she died in 1974, the nominal price of her bonds was below 30 per cent of par (because of high interest rates) while inflation had reduced the purchasing power of her semi-annual interest payments and her principal by 75 per cent. Truly a disgrace.

as he opposed a permanent secretariat for the Great Alliance in 1818. He believed that such organisations become self-perpetuating, with agendas that do not reflect the interests of their members.

One important principle where he would differ from modern statesmen is the rationale and direction of foreign intervention. Liverpool never subscribed to the Troppau Protocol of 1820, because he believed it unduly interventionist, but he wholeheartedly subscribed to its central principle: that any intervention that was undertaken must be made to prop up a failing government, not to overthrow it. Liverpool believed that overthrowing governments leads to anarchy and revolution, possibly in third countries. Since maintaining global stability and, if possible, peace was his overriding principle, it followed that even unsatisfactory regimes must be kept in power, lest what succeeded them prove worse.

Thus, in the last 40 years, according to the Troppau principles, the West should have intervened in Iran in 1978 to prop up the Shah. It did intervene in Kuwait in 1991 to remove Saddam Hussain's troops and it should have intervened in Egypt in 2011 to prop up Hosni Mubarak. It should not have intervened in Iraq in 2003, Libya in 2012 or Syria in 2013. The Middle East might have been much more stable and happier had such an approach been followed.

Liverpool would also be less inclined to intervene than modern statesmen in countries violating human rights. He believed more strongly than we do today in the 'Westphalian' concept that nations are entitled to their internal arrangements. Hence, he would be disinclined to propose military intervention or even sanctions in cases such as Iran and Venezuela where nations had offended the broad international consensus on such arrangements.

Finally, a modern Liverpool would have left the European Union, and would enter into trading arrangements with it on an arms-length basis, as with any other nation. He would regard the EU as a major potential danger to British liberties and security, and would seek to weaken it, at least preventing it from becoming a more coherent single entity. A united Europe was a bugbear of British foreign policy from Louis XIV's time, and Liverpool spent his early career in a successful attempt to defeat one such scheme. Thus, while Liverpool would attempt to maintain the closest possible relations with individual EU countries, his relationship with the EU as an entity would be minimally correct, and he would encourage individual countries to break away from it if they wished.

Liverpool as 'Britain's Greatest Prime Minister'

The following discussion of his achievements demonstrates that Liverpool was in the very top tier of British prime ministers. His achievements included the following:

(i) Organiser and strategist of Napoleonic wars victory

Prime ministers are not generally good at military strategy. Churchill[16] was not the military genius he thought himself, while Lloyd George was regarded by his generals as a major menace (not that they were much better). In his leading general Liverpool had a highly self-confident military genius. Thus, he was careful not to second-guess operational decisions and equally careful to take Wellington's advice when decisions arose about areas such as North America where Wellington was not directly involved.

However, at the highest strategic level, Liverpool made one call that proved crucial to the war's success: he outlined the rationale for application of steady and moderate force, by which Napoleon's unstable, gimcrack Empire could be brought down.

Previous leaders, during the First, Second, Third, Fourth and Fifth Coalitions, had attempted to bring overwhelming force against France and Napoleon through a coalition of allied powers, to defeat him in one campaign. This brought repeated failure, largely because in a single campaign Napoleon was a better general than anyone the allies could muster and the theoretically superior allied forces were weakened by lack of coordination between the different powers, enabling them to be attacked piecemeal.

Liverpool reasoned that Britain had a stronger and more advanced economy than France, her ability to raise money without causing a financial crisis was much greater and her ability to call on the resources of the world through maritime trade was infinitely greater (and was increased still further by naval and colonial victories during Liverpool's period at the War Office). The economy of Napoleon's Empire relied excessively on looting the non-French territories under his control, which could work for only a limited time before their economic collapse left him nothing further to loot. Hence moderate pressure, requiring Napoleon to expend military and other resources to combat it, would over time cause Napoleon's overextended Empire to collapse. Napoleon's invasion of Russia was an attempt to gain additional resources to overcome this weakness; when that failed, his resources were fatally weakened and an allied coalition, if assembled carefully and well managed, might finally succeed.

In 1813 Liverpool, with Castlereagh, assembled the coalition that could bring enough military superiority to bear on defeating Napoleon. The October 1813 Battle of Leipzig, without significant British forces, but with

16. Sir Winston Churchill (1874-1955). Knight of the Garter, 1953. MP for Oldham, Manchester NW, Dundee, Epping and Woodford, 1900-64. President of the Board of Trade, 1908-10. Home Secretary, 1910-11. First Lord of the Admiralty, 1911-15, 1939-40. Chancellor of the Duchy of Lancaster, 1915. Minister of Munitions, 1917-19. Secretary of State for War, 1919-21. Colonial Secretary, 1921-22. Chancellor of the Exchequer, 1924-29. Prime Minister, 1940-45, 1951-55.

almost all allied powers heavily subsidised by Britain's strong Treasury, was the triumph, even more than Waterloo, that changed the history of the nineteenth century.

Liverpool's strategy involved a level of economic thinking and management that was not present in Napoleon's Empire. It was also not matched by either of Britain's subsequent wartime leaders, Lloyd George or Churchill, although possibly some of her peacetime leaders, such as Palmerston or Thatcher,[17] could have matched it had they been faced with the situation (though Pitt, fine political economist though he was, failed to do so). It does not alone place Liverpool ahead of all his prime ministerial rivals, but it gives him a unique selling point that they lacked.

(ii) Managed peace settlement that lasted 99 years

The 1814-15 Congress of Vienna and its peace settlement have generally been given a good press by historians (especially in light of the lamentable failure of the 1919 Congress of Versailles, which forgot several lessons taught by Vienna). The territorial adjustments brought 99 years without a general European war, while the Quadruple/Holy Alliance set up some principles of foreign policy still applicable today.

Credit for the success of the Congress generally goes to Metternich and Castlereagh, but the overall British strategy for a peace without the usual spoils of victory was set out by Liverpool in his House of Lords speech of November 1813. British negotiating positions were agreed by Liverpool and Castlereagh before Castlereagh's departure for Vienna, and in several letters of guidance to Castlereagh during the negotiations. Liverpool was Castlereagh's boss throughout Castlereagh's tenure as Foreign Minister and played a more detailed part in determining diplomatic strategy and tactics than he did with Wellington in determining military strategy and tactics.

Liverpool also played a full part in the successful and rapid reintegration of France into the international concert of nations after 1815, facilitating the series of large financings in 1817-18 that enabled it to happen. However, at the time of the Congress of Aix-la-Chapelle in 1818, under the influence of Canning, Liverpool was less supportive of the emerging Congress System than Castlereagh, refusing to commit to a formal timetable of Congress meetings.

Liverpool was instrumental in the appointment of Canning as Foreign Secretary after Castlereagh's suicide in 1822. Once Canning was in place, Liverpool withdrew somewhat from foreign policy, allowing Canning to break Britain's relationships with the major European powers in favour of isolationism and a chimerical hope of huge commercial benefits from the

17. Margaret Thatcher (1925-2013), Baroness Thatcher from 1992. MP for Finchley, 1959-92. Secretary of State for Education and Science, 1970-74. Prime Minister, 1979-90.

newly independent states of South America. However, in foreign as in domestic policy, Liverpool should be judged primarily on the immense successes of his first decade in office rather than on the more equivocal record of his last five years, when in all areas save economics his control was lessened.

(iii) Directed British economy through industrial revolution

Liverpool was Prime Minister when the British economy was going through changes both unprecedented and unequalled in world history. Jean-Baptiste Say, travelling through Britain in the autumn of 1814, described his surprise at the plethora of steam engines being used in all kinds of applications, a liberation from the limitations of naturally occurring power sources that had been absent in his previous visit a generation before. In addition, the period 1815-20 saw massive economic disruption caused by the end of two decades of war, the largest natural failure of the European harvest in 1816 and a savage monetary deflation caused by the return to gold.

Liverpool received a superlative early economic education from his father Charles Jenkinson. He also received tutelage from his mentor William Pitt, whose Cabinet early in its existence received live tutorials from Adam Smith. Hence throughout his time in office he was well aware of the effect of economic factors.

Liverpool and his contemporaries lacked the Keynesian arrogance that leads modern statesmen to believe they can 'steer' the economy. They also lacked the massive public sector that makes their acts affect the economy throughout, although the Liverpool government's public spending peaked briefly at over 30 per cent of gross domestic product (GDP) in 1813-15. At that level, it was unprecedented in size and Say, writing in 1814-15, believed that the size of Britain's government, and the charges on the national debt would make British goods forever uncompetitive in European markets. While there was little Keynesian 'stimulus' from this spending (because the money was borrowed in an essentially closed system), there was a substantial technological knock-on effect.

Liverpool and Vansittart freed the British private sector to compete by cutting non-interest public spending by around fifteen per cent of GDP over the three years 1814-17. After an inevitable period of post-war retrenchment lasting two years, and exacerbated by 1816's 'Year Without a Summer' caused by the Mount Tambora volcano, the economy recovered rapidly in the second half of 1817 and 1818. There was then a second downturn, probably caused mainly by the sharp deflation surrounding the 1819-21 return to the gold standard, after which the economy took off, producing levels of real economic growth never before seen.

Some modest errors in monetary policy were partial causes of a banking crash at the end of 1825, so 1826 saw a further mild recession, but recovery was returning from the middle of that year and continued into 1827. Overall, the Liverpool years saw a substantial growth in the British economy and a significant improvement in real *per capita* incomes despite the period's rapid population growth, the fastest in British history. Liverpool's budgetary, monetary, regulatory and trade policy were all important factors in this success.

The structure of government financing provided an important additional boost to the 1820s economy. As yields on existing government debt rose during wartime, instead of issuing new debt bearing a higher interest coupon, the government issued three per cent bonds with a deep discount, often at little more than 50 per cent of par. When peace returned and the government ran a budget surplus, Britain's credit improved, providing investors with large capital gains, some 70 per cent of GDP overall. These profits provided the capital that financed Britain's industrial take-off, enabling the economy to become more capital-intensive without more than modest erosion of labour's share of GDP. The early industrial revolution years were tough for Britain's workers, but would have been much tougher without this additional fillip to the system.[18]

(iv) Managed social unrest of 1816-20

E.P. Thompson's *The Making of the English Working Class*, the classic study of its radicalisation during the industrial revolution, paid tribute to Liverpool and his contemporaries: 'One is impressed with the extraordinary skill with which Government, between 1792 and 1820, succeeded in forestalling serious revolutionary developments, and in maintaining a steady flow of reliable information as to insurrectionary conspiracies.'[19]

The early phase of industrialisation put unprecedented strains on the social fabric. For Britain to industrialise, resources had to be diverted from labour to capital, which exerted downward pressure on wage rates. Moreover, as Say discovered on his 1814 visit to England, at the end of the wars government debt and taxation placed an unprecedented burden on the economy. Several large groups of workers, such as hand-loom weavers, stocking-frame knitters and 'croppers', all 'outworkers' paid by the piece and largely independent of their employer, were sharply immiserated during this period by competition from factory-based machinery and were consequently radicalised.

The result was an outbreak of machine-breaking, 'Luddism', in 1811-12, after the bad harvest of 1811, and then two periods of national unrest, with plots to overthrow the government by force, in early 1817 and 1819, when economic conditions were especially harsh. Liverpool and Sidmouth

18. A paper on this topic, *'The Apotheosis of the Rentier'* by Martin Hutchinson and Kevin Dowd, was published in the Fall 2018 *Cato Journal.* Dowd (kevin.dowd@durham.ac.uk) is Professor of Finance and Economics at Durham University.
19. E.P. Thompson, *The Making of the English Working Class* (Vantage, 1966 edition) p. 493.

made active use of informers to detect widespread conspiracies, passed strong legislation, much of it temporary, to deter subversive activity, but enforced it mildly to avoid exacerbating discontent.

Two additional factors softened social discontent. First, Liverpool and Sidmouth were anti-Benthamite, and therefore accepted the inefficiencies of 'outdoor relief' and did not attempt to impose a system of 'workhouses' as the Whigs would later impose through the 1834 Poor Law. Second, Liverpool recognised that organised religion and the Church of England, in particular, were important factors in improving the behaviour and lessening the misery of the impoverished. The Church Buildings Acts of 1818 and 1824, measures close to his heart, thus subsidised the building of hundreds of churches in industrial areas, which became important influences for social peace.

There can be no question that one of Liverpool's key objectives was to avoid the creation of the anti-government, working-class consciousness that Thompson celebrates. It was a close-run thing, but he succeeded; after 1819 working-class radicalism first diverted to the defence of Queen Caroline and then died down through the prosperous 1820s. Only in 1831-32 did a true working-class consciousness arise, as the Whigs encouraged Radical agitation in favour of their gerrymandering Reform Bill which did nothing for the working classes.

(v) Brought down without default or inflation the highest debt ever

There have been three occasions on which a major nation's government debt has reached 250 per cent of GDP: two in Britain, after the Napoleonic Wars and after World War II, and one in Japan today. Of the three, only Britain in Liverpool's time brought the debt down without default, rescheduling or virulent inflation (though it is possible that Japan will achieve the same feat).

At first glance, the British governments of Clement Attlee[20] through to roughly Edward Heath[21] were even more successful, reducing public debt from 250 per cent of GDP to around 50 per cent of GDP in thirty years. However, they achieved this by keeping interest rates at artificially low levels and allowing inflation to run into the middle or high single digits for several decades, peaking at 24 per cent in 1975. Holding government bonds in 1947-75 was equivalent to hand-loom weaving in the early Industrial Revolution.

20. Clement Attlee (1883-1967). 1st Earl Attlee from 1955. MP for Limehouse and Walthamstow West, 1922-55. Chancellor of the Duchy of Lancaster, 1930-31. Lord Privy Seal, 1940-42. Secretary of State for Dominion Affairs, 1942-43. Lord President of the Council, 1943-45. Deputy Prime Minister, 1942-45. Prime Minister, 1945-51.
21. Edward Heath (1916-2005). Knight of the Garter from 1992. MP for Bexley, Sidcup and Old Bexley and Sidcup, 1950-2001. Chief Whip, 1955-59. Minister of Labour, 1959-60. Lord Privy Seal, 1960-63. President of the Board of Trade, 1963-64. Prime Minister, 1970-74.

This disgraceful performance decapitalised the British economy, destroyed middle-class savings and made Britain's economic performance far inferior to those of its competitors.

The Liverpool government's first step after hostilities ceased was to stabilise the debt position through budget stringency. This did not produce popularity, either short-term among the populace or long-term among Keynesian economists, but it was one of the Liverpool government's greatest achievements.

Liverpool's next step was to restore full confidence in Britain's credit by returning to the gold standard, which was achieved in 1819-21. Initially, this was massively deflationary and increased the burden of government debt in terms of GDP (the debt-to-GDP ratio probably peaked in 1819). It also produced a savage albeit brief second recessionary 'dip' in 1819, with a resurgence in industrial and political unrest.

However, from 1819 on Britain's credit was undoubted, as was the value of the currency and its purchasing power. Government debt was reduced without inflation from 260 per cent of GDP in 1819 to 192 per cent of GDP when Liverpool left office in 1827, on its way to below 100 per cent of GDP by the 1850s.

(vi) Designed two Corn Laws and began the move towards free trade

Schoolchildren brought up on traditional British history learned that the 1846 repeal of the Corn Laws led to free trade and general prosperity. In reality, besides destroying the British landed interest when American competition in cereals intensified from the 1870s, the move to unilateral free trade also in the long term destroyed Britain's industrial competitive advantage. It allowed other countries to develop behind tariff walls industries such as steel which Britain had pioneered, sell into free-trading British Empire markets and eliminate Britain's industrial lead.

The 1815 Corn Laws were a legislative compromise, designed to cushion the effect on landowners of the transition from war to peace, in which grain prices would decline and international competition intensify. Part of their rationale was strategic rather than economic; Liverpool's government wanted Britain, whose population was rising rapidly, to be as far as possible self-sufficient in foodstuffs in a war. The Corn Laws had an additional rationale in making it economically attractive to grow corn in Ireland, thus partially weaning the overpopulated Irish from dependence on the potato monoculture. The Irish corn production so developed would mitigate the awful tragedy of the 1840s Irish potato famine.

By the mid-1820s, the Corn Laws had become too restrictive. Corn prices had declined by two thirds, leading to a massive depression in the agricultural sector in 1822-23. Prices in general had declined by about 40 per cent with the return to gold, so the 80-shillings-per-quarter hard limit in the 1815 law was higher than grain prices were likely to reach in all but dearth years. Hence as his last act in politics, Liverpool together with Huskisson designed a new sliding scale Corn Law, that reduced protection as prices rose, with a fulcrum around 60 shillings per quarter, a little above the level at which prices had settled. Regrettably, Liverpool suffered a stroke before being able to introduce this and the eventual legislation of 1828, while based on the Liverpool/Huskisson draft, was both more protectionist and less market-friendly, being subject to manipulation by corn suppliers. However, any reasonably designed Corn Law would have prevented much agricultural distress had it still been in force after 1873.

The campaign for free trade, which dominated the political world until the Cobden-Chevalier Treaty of 1860, was begun by the 1820 House of Lords debate in which Lansdowne and Liverpool outlined the case for easing and removing trade restrictions, forming a consensus on setting up a committee to do so. Liverpool then presided over a repeated series of tariff cuts and trade liberating measures, designed in detail by Huskisson, Robinson and Thomas Wallace. This removal of restrictions was a significant contributor to the prosperity of the 1820s.

(vii) Took Britain back onto the gold standard against strong opposition

Britain's return to the gold standard, enacted in 1819 and completed in 1821, was a brave decision. It added about 40 per cent to the real value of Britain's heavy outstanding debt, burdening future generations. It damaged the fortunes of the politically powerful country gentry, who had borrowed excessively during the war based on high grain prices. It produced a short second recessionary 'dip' in the economy, leading to widespread unrest including the Peterloo Massacre.

Yet the decision was generally supported except by a few proto-Keynesians and Radicals like Henry Brougham; indeed, a substantial faction followed the 1810 Bullion Committee in thinking it overdue. It re-established British credit on rock-solid foundations and allowed interest rates to remain low and capital values correspondingly high for the remainder of the century.

While later legislative meddling deprived it of the automaticity of a truly free-market monetary system, the nineteenth-century gold standard was quite close to this ideal. It led to London dominating the world's financial system for the next century, with incomparable benefits to British trade and the economy in general. While the monetary system established by Liverpool was not perfect, we have yet to find a better one.

Liverpool performed a useful additional service for the British economy in stabilising the coinage, by his recoinage of 1816-17. During the eighteenth century, there had been no pound coin and the economy suffered periodic shortages of silver and copper currency, stifling trade and resulting in the production of numerous 'Bank Tokens', which were issued above their bullion value and therefore subject to default. Charles Jenkinson had alleviated this problem with his 1797 'Cartwheel' copper coinage, which gave faith to the working classes that sterling was not about to go the way of the *assignat*, and his 1805 *Treatise on the Coins of the Realm* became a standard work for the next century that set out the necessary solution.

By his recoinage, Liverpool implemented Jenkinson's solution. He issued the first gold sovereigns since James I's time and provided a silver and copper coinage that became standard until decimalisation in 1971. This considerably eased small-scale trade and contributed to the recovery in confidence that was cemented by the return to gold.

(viii) Ended with a vigorous period of social reform

By his restructuring of 1821-23, Liverpool changed the nature of his government. One such change was forced, by Castlereagh's suicide and Liverpool's determination to replace him with Canning. However, that change, Sidmouth's replacement by Peel and Vansittart's by Robinson all replaced highly effective and strong if unpopular ministers with successors who were considerably more Whig-historian-friendly.

Nevertheless, the last five years of Liverpool's government produced a high level of achievement on several fronts, which has been celebrated by posterity. Even William Gladstone is alleged to have said: 'England was never better governed than between 1822 and 1830.' Economically, the government lowered taxation, made substantial moves towards free trade and produced an economic upsurge that marked the take-off stage of the industrial revolution. In foreign policy, the government abandoned Castlereagh's system of European alliances for Canning's policy of isolation and global assertion, a policy that remained in force for the rest of the century. In domestic policy, Peel undertook a massive programme of legal and social reform that modernised British society and laid the foundation for the Victorian age.

(ix) Reformed the English banking system

The English banking system before 1825 was flawed, making it both unstable and incompatible with the gold standard monetary framework. Except for the Bank of England, no bank could have more than six partners, so there were by 1825 over 800 country banks and no large banks of undoubted stability.

Liverpool recognised that the most critical function of banks was to act as safe havens for money, especially for poorer citizens who had few alternatives. Hence, by the Savings Bank Act of 1817, he established Trustee Savings Banks, administered by trustees, which could invest only in government securities and deposits at the Bank of England, providing an absolute haven for savings, secure from the vagaries of the loan market. Trustee Savings Banks lasted until the 1980s; even by 1825, they had total deposits of £13.3 million, more than the stamped, country bank notes worth £8.8 million that caused such trouble.

With the conventional English banking system unsound, the 1825 crisis was inevitable and was predicted by Liverpool eight months before it broke (an analytical success not equalled by subsequent statesmen). The crisis was caused by speculation, much of it encouraged by over-issue of £1 and £2 notes by the country banks. Gold flowed out of the country, to return only when the Bank of England sharply increased interest rates. This led to a wave of bank failures.

In January 1826, Liverpool presented a paper to the Bank of England, outlining a banking reform that was essentially adopted in toto. This reform made the English banking system, based on the gold standard, secure for the rest of the century, with only one major bank failure, that of Overend, Gurney & Co. in 1866.

(x) Led an outstandingly able government including six prime ministers

Liverpool's government included Sidmouth, Canning, Robinson/Goderich, Wellington, Peel and Palmerston. In addition, he had negotiations with Grenville in 1818, he used Aberdeen as a diplomat and his principal lieutenant was Castlereagh, unquestionably of prime ministerial calibre. Eldon, Bathurst, Melville, Huskisson and Copley were all notably successful ministers in their respective departments.

* * *

Of Britain's 55 prime ministers since Sir Robert Walpole became *de facto* its first Prime Minister, there are about six who have a plausible claim to be considered the greatest. Apart from Liverpool himself, these are, in chronological order, William Pitt the younger, William Gladstone, Winston Churchill, Clement Attlee and Margaret Thatcher. Some others, such as the elder Pitt, Sir Robert Peel and David Lloyd George, had careers that when examined closely show serious character flaws rendering their legacy more ambiguous than appears at first sight.[22]

Pitt was regarded by Liverpool's contemporaries as the *beau idéal* of prime ministers. His fine reputation rests mostly on the first half of his first ministry, when he was a strong, reforming prime minister who sharply reduced corruption, increased efficiency and introduced Adam Smith's free market principles into economic management. Once war began, he never solved the strategic problems of how to win it, and his economic management largely

22. My thoughts on Britain's 54 prime ministers other than Liverpool, the contenders for the accolade of "Britain's Greatest Prime Minister" are at the website: www.lordliverpool.com/contenders

fell apart under the fiscal strain. The Act of Union with Ireland, regarded as a crowning achievement by the Victorians, looks highly equivocal today. Overall, while he gets major points for economic innovation, he was not as successful in war or even peace as Liverpool.

Gladstone's high reputation as Chancellor of the Exchequer is overblown; he had it very easy, with the hard work having been done by Liverpool and Vansittart. As Prime Minister, the highly successful first ministry, with several important and long-lasting reforms, and moderately successful second ministry must be balanced against foreign policy failures and what eventually became disaster in Ireland – he made the Irish question much more politically toxic than necessary. Overall, with a discount for governing in quiet times, he is not a serious contender for number one spot.

Churchill gets a large boost for inspiring war leadership, mostly concentrated in a period of about eighteen months in 1940-42. His support for scientific innovation gives him another boost. However, he was an indifferent military strategist (Gallipoli, Crete and the Dieppe raid), although he worked better with his generals than did Lloyd George. He was less than adequate economically, sending Maynard Keynes to betray British interests at Bretton Woods and blocking the 1952 'ROBOT' scheme for freeing the British economy from exchange controls. His peacetime administration achieved little. He thus does not deserve to rank number one, as most lists have him.

Attlee was an extremely effective deputy to Churchill during World War II, then after 1945 he capably implemented an agenda that changed Britain forever. His economic policies did not work but their defects could have been quickly corrected had the Conservatives who succeeded him been more competent. Bevan called him the 'Arch-Mediocrity'; this is by no means his only parallel to Liverpool. Overall, he should rank among the top few prime ministers.

Thatcher was untested in a major war but could have matched Churchill's determination and rhetoric; she might, however, have had difficulty leading an all-party War Cabinet. However, her contribution to Cold War victory and her economic achievements were beyond anything Churchill managed. Even with several mistakes, she should rank with Pitt, Liverpool and Churchill near the top of the list.

* * *

British history has been distorted for almost two centuries by the Whiggery of British historians. Liverpool's government has been relegated to a distant past, irrelevant to modern concerns and deemed to be of no great quality. That delusion has distorted our understanding and resulted in poor, national decision making in our own day. If this book enables a broad readership to realise the magnitude of this error, it will have achieved its objective. Britain's Greatest Prime Minister will then inspire the land and indeed the world of his distant successors.

Appendix

Liverpool's letter to the Bank of England, 13 January, 1826

Fife House, 13 January, 1826

The panic in the Money Market having subsided and the pecuniary transactions of the Country having reverted to their accustomed course, it becomes important to lose no time in considering whether any measures can be adopted to prevent the recurrence in future of such Evils as we have recently experienced.

However much the recent Distress may have been aggravated, in the judgement of some, by incidental circumstances and particular Measures, there can be no doubt that the Principal Source of it is to be found in the rash Spirit of Speculation, which has pervaded the country for some time supported, fostered and encouraged by the Country Banks.

The Remedy therefore for the Evil in future must be found in an improvement in the Circulation of Country Paper and the first measure which has suggested itself to most of those who have considered the subject is a recurrence to a Gold Circulation throughout the country, as well as in the Metropolis and its neighbours by a Repeal of the Act which permits Country Banks to issue One and Two Pound Notes until the Year 1833, and by the immediate enactment of a Prohibition of any such Issues at the expiration of two or three Years from the present period.

It appears to us to be quite clear that such a measure would be productive of much good, that it would operate as some Check upon the Spirit of Speculation and upon the Issues of Country Banks, and whilst on the one hand it would diminish the Pressure upon the Bank and the Metropolis incident to an unfavourable state of the Exchanges, by spreading it over a wider surface, on the other hand it would cause such pressure to be earlier felt and thereby insure an earlier and more general adoption of the precautionary Measures necessary for counteracting the Inconveniences incident to an Export of the precious Metals. But though a recurrence to a Gold Circulation in the Country for the reasons already stated, might be productive of some good, it would by no means go to the root of the evil.

We have abundant proof of the truth of this Position in the events which took place in the Spring of 1793, when a Convulsion occurred in the Money

Transactions and Circulation of the Country more intensive than that which we have recently experienced. At that period nearly a hundred Country Banks were obliged to stop payments and Parliament was induced to grant an Issue of Exchequer Bills to relieve the distress. Yet in the year 1793 there were no One or Two Pound Notes in circulation in England, either by Country Banks or by the Bank of England.

We have a further proof of the truth of what has been advanced in the response of Scotland, which has escaped all the Convulsions which have occurred in the Money Market of England for the last thirty five years though Scotland during the whole of that time has had a Circulation of One Pound Notes, and the pecuniary transactions of that part of the United Kingdom have been carried on exclusively by the means of such Notes.

This issue of smaller Notes though it be an aggravation cannot be the sole or even the main cause of the evil in England. The failures which have occurred in England, unaccompanied as they have been by the same occurrences in Scotland, tend to prove that there must have been an unsolid and delusive System of Banking in one part of Great Britain and a solid and substantial one in the other.

It would be entirely at variance with our deliberate opinion, not to do justice to the Bank of England, as the great centre of circulation and Commercial Credit.

We believe that much of the Prosperity of the Country in the last Century is to be ascribed to the general Wisdom, Justice and fairness of all its dealings and we further think that during a great part of that time, it may have been <u>in itself</u> and <u>by itself</u> fully equal to all the important Duties and Operations confided to it. But the progress of the country during the last thirty or forty years in every branch of Industry, in Agriculture, Manufactures, Commerce and Navigation has been so rapid and extensive as to make it no reflection on the Bank of England to say that <u>the Instrument</u> which <u>by itself</u> was fully adequate to former transactions is no longer sufficient without new Aids, to meet the demands of the present times.

We have to a considerable degree the Proof of this Position in the establishment of so many Country Banks.

Within the memory of many living and even of some of those now engaged in Public Affairs, there were no Country Banks except in a few of the great commercial Towns.

The Money Transactions of the Country were carried on by Supplies of Coin and Bank Notes from London.

The extent of the Business of the country and the improvement made from time to time in the mode of conducting our increased commercial transactions, founded in pecuniary Credit, rendered such a System no longer adequate and Country Banks must have arisen, as in fact they did arise, from the increased wealth and <u>new wants</u> of the country.

The matter of regret is not that Country Banks have been suffered to exist, but that they have been suffered to exist so long without control or limitation, or without the adoption of Provisions calculated to counteract the Evils resulting from their improvidence or Excess.

It would be vain to suppose that we could now by any act of the Legislature extinguish the existing Country Banks, even if it were desirable, but it may be within our power gradually at least to establish a sound System of Banking throughout the Country, and if such a System could be formed, there can be little doubt that it would ultimately extinguish and absorb all that is objectionable and dangerous in the present Banking Establishments.

There appear to be two modes of attaining this object:

First, that the Bank of England should establish branches of its own body throughout the country.

Secondly, that the Bank of England should give up its exclusive Privilege as to the number of Partners engaged in Banking except within a certain distance of the Metropolis.

It has always appeared to us that it would have been very desirable that the Bank should have tried the first of these Plans, that of establishing Branch Banks upon a limited scale.

But we are not insensible to the difficulties which would have attended such an experiment, and we are quite satisfied that it would be impossible for the Bank under present circumstances to carry into execution such a System to the extent necessary for providing for the wants of the Country.

There remains therefore only the other Plan, the surrender by the Bank of their exclusive Privilege as to the number of Partners beyond a certain distance from the Metropolis.

The effect of such a measure would be the gradual establishment of extensive and respectable Banks in different parts of the Country, some perhaps with Charters from the Crown under certain Qualifications and some without.

Here we have again the advantage of the experience of Scotland.

In England there are said to be between Eight and Nine hundred Country Banks and it is no exaggeration to suppose that a great proportion of them have not been conducted with a due attention to those precautions which are necessary for the safety of all Banking Establishments even where their Property is more ample. When such Banks Stop their creditors may ultimately be paid the whole of their demands, but the delay and Shock to credit may in the mean time involve them in the same difficulty and is always attended with the greatest injury and suffering in the districts where such Stoppages occur. If this be the case where the Solidity of the Bank is unquestionable, what must be, as too often happens, when they rest on no solid foundations.

In Scotland there are not more than Thirty Banks, and those Banks have stood firm amidst all the convulsions in the Money Market in England and amidst all the distresses to which the Manufacturing and Agricultural interest in Scotland as well as in England have occasionally been subject.

Banks of this description must necessarily be conducted upon the general, understood and approved Principles of Banking.

Individuals are from the nature of the Institutions precluded from speculating in the manner in which Persons engaged in Country and even in London Banks speculate in England.

If the concerns of the Country could be carried on without any other Bank than the Bank of England there might be some reason for not interfering with their exclusive Privileges, but the effect of the Law at present is to permit every description of Banking except that which is solid and secure.

Let the Bank of England reflect on the dangers to which it has recently been subject, and let its Directors and Proprietors then say, whether for their own interests such an Improvement as is suggested in the Banking System is not desirable and even necessary.

The Bank of England may perhaps prepare as they did on a former occasion the extension of the term of their Privileges as to the Metropolis and its Neighbourhood beyond the year 1833 as the price of their concession.

It would be very much to be regretted that they should require any such condition.

It is clear that in point of Security they would gain by the concession proposed to them, inasmuch as their own safety is now necessarily endangered by all such convulsions of the Country circulation as we have lately and formerly witnessed.

In periods of profit would they lose any thing by it for which they would be entitled to demand compensation?

It is notorious that at the present time their Notes circulate in no part of England beyond the Metropolis and its Neighbourhood except in Lancashire and perhaps for that District some special provision might be made.

But as it is the Interest, so it ever will be the endeavour of the Country Bankers to keep the Bank of England Notes out of circulation in those parts of the Kingdom where their own circulation prevails. In this they must always be successful while Public Credit continues in its ordinary state and the Exchanges not unfavourable to this Country. The consequences are that in such times the Bank of England becomes the sole depositary for Gold, and in times of an opposite tendency, the sole resort for obtaining it; that at one period their legitimate profit is curtailed by an accumulation of Treasure beyond what would be required by a due attention to their own and private safety as a Banking Establishment and at another period they are exposed to demands which endanger that safety, and baffle all the ordinary calculations of foresight and prudence.

If then the Bank of England has no Country circulation except in the County above named, the only question for them to consider is whether on the grounds of Profit as well as Security to themselves the existing Country circulation shall or shall not be improved.

With respect to the extension of the term of their privileges in the Metropolis and its Neighbourhood, it is obvious from what passed before that Parliament will never agree to it.

Such Privileges are out of fashion and what expectation can the Bank under present circumstances entertain that theirs will be renewed? But there is no reason why the Bank of England should look at this consequence with dismay. They will remain a Chartered Corporation for carrying on the Business of Banking. In that character they will we trust always continue to be the sole Bankers of the State and with these advantages so long as they conduct their affairs wisely and prudently they always must be the great centre of Banking and circulation.

Theirs is the only Establishment at which the Dividends due to the Public Creditor can be paid.

It is to be hoped therefore that the Bank will make no difficulty in giving up their exclusive Privileges in respect to the number of Partners as to any District (blank) Miles from the Metropolis.

Should the Bank be disposed to consent to a measure of this nature in time to enable the Government to announce such a concession at the opening of Parliament, it would afford great facilities to the arrangement which they may have to prepare for insuring the stability of Private Credit, on which the support of Public Credit and the maintenance of Public Prosperity is materially and closely involved.[1]

1. Bank of England, Minutes of the Court of Directors, 20 January 1826.

Bibliography

Primary Sources

Abbot, Charles (ed.), *The Diaries and Correspondence of Charles Abbot, Lord Colchester*, 3 vols. (London: John Murray, 1861)

Annual Register, or A View of the History, Politics and Literature for the Year 1807 (London: W. Otridge & Son, 1809)

Annual Register, or A View of the History, Politics and Literature for the Year 1810 (London: W. Otridge & Son, 1812)

Aspinall, A. (ed.), *The Letters of King George IV, 1812-30*, 3 vols (Cambridge: Cambridge University Press, 1938)

———, *The Correspondence of Charles Arbuthnot* (London: Royal Historical Society, 1941)

———, *The Diary of Henry Hobhouse* (London: Home & van Thal, 1947)

———, *The Later Correspondence of George III*, 5 vols (Cambridge: Cambridge University Press, 1962)

Aspinall, A., and E.A. Smith (eds), *English Historical Documents: Vol. XI: 1783-1832* (London: Routledge, 2nd edn 1996)

Bamford, F., and 7th Duke of Wellington (eds), *The Journal of Mrs. Arbuthnot, 1820-1832*, 2 vols (London: Macmillan, 1950)

Bank of England, Minutes of the Court of Directors. Available on the Bank's website: https://www.bankofengland.co.uk/sitemap/minutes.

Bickley, Francis (ed.), *The Diaries of Sylvester Douglas, Lord Glenbervie*, 2 vols (London: Constable, 1928)

Burke, Edmund, *Thoughts on the Cause of the Present Discontents* (London: J. Dodsley, 1770)

Castlereagh, Robert Stewart, Viscount, and John Singleton Copley, Baron Lyndhurst, *The State of the Nation, at the commencement of 1822: considered under the four Departments of Finance, Foreign Relations, Home Department, Colonies and Board of Trade, etc. etc. etc.* (London: John Hatchard & Son, 1822)

Croker, John W., *The Correspondence and Diaries of John Wilson Croker*, 3 vols (London: John Murray, 1884)

Debrett, John, John Stockdale and John Almon, *The Parliamentary Register; or, History of the Proceedings and Debates of the House of Lords and House of Commons*, 77 vols (1780-1803)

Eden, Robert, 3rd Baron Auckland (ed.), *The Journal and Correspondence of William, Lord Auckland* (London: R. Bentley, 1861-2)

Foreign Office, *British and Foreign State Papers, 1820-21*, Compiled by the Librarian and Keeper of the Papers (London: HMSO, 1830)

Fortescue, Sir John (ed.), The Correspondence of George III, 1760-83, 6 vols (London: Macmillan & Co. Ltd, 1927)
Gurwood, Col. John (ed.), *The Dispatches of Field Marshal the Duke of Wellington*, 12 vols (London: John Murray, 1836-39)
Hansard, T.C., *Parliamentary Debates from the Year 1803 to the Present Time, 1803-27*
———, *The Parliamentary Debates, New Series, Commencing with the Accession of George IV*
Horn, D.B., and Mary Ransome (eds), *English Historical Documents: Vol X: 1714-1783* (London: Eyre & Spottiswoode, 1969)
Jenkinson, Charles, *Dissertation on the Establishment of a Natural and Constitutional Force in England independent of a Standing Army* (1756)
———, *Discourse on the Conduct of Great Britain with Respect to Neutral Nations* (London: Hulton Bradley, 1758)
———, *A Collection of all the Treaties of Peace, Alliance and Commerce between Great Britain and Other Powers from the Treaty signed at Munster in 1648 to the Treaties signed at Paris in 1783* (London: J. Debrett, 1785)
———, *State of the Country in the Autumn of 1798* (London: J. Wright, 1798)
———, *A Treatise on the Coins of the Realm: In a Letter to the King* (London: Oxford University Press, 1805)
Jenkinson, Robert Banks, *Reflections on the Present State of the Resources of the Country* (London: John Stockdale, 1796)
Jucker, Ninetta S. (ed.), *The Jenkinson Papers, 1760-1766* (London: Macmillan, 1949)
Laprade, William T. (ed.), *Parliamentary Papers of John Robinson, 1774-1784* (London: Royal Historical Society, 1922)
Londonderry, 3rd Marquess of (ed.), *Memoirs and Correspondence of Viscount Castlereagh, Second Marquess of Londonderry*, 12 vols (London: William Shoberl, 1851)
Maurice, F. (ed.), *The Diary of Sir John Moore*, 2 vols (London: Edward Arnold, 1904)
Melville, Lewis (ed.), *The Wellesley Papers: The Life and Correspondence of Richard Colley Wellesley, 1760-1842* (London: Herbert Jenkins, 1914)
Mitchell, B.R., *British Historical Statistics* (Cambridge: Cambridge University Press, 2011)
The National Archives, *French Revolution – How did the British react to July 1789*, Source 4, Letter from a Mr Jenkinson in Paris, available at: https://www.nationalarchives.gov.uk/education/resources/french-revolution/. Accessed 29 June 2020.
Report from the Select Committee Appointed to Inquire into the Cause of the High Price of Gold Bullion, and to Take Indo Consideration the State of the Circulating Medium, and of the Exchanges Between Great Britain and Foreign Parts (London: J. Johnson and J. Ridgway, 1810)
Rose, George, *The Diaries and Correspondence of George Rose*, 2 vols (London: Richard Bentley, 1860)
Say, J.-B., *De l'Angleterre et des Anglais* (Paris: Chez Arthur Bertrand, 1815)
Smith, W.J. (ed.), *The Grenville papers: Being the Correspondence of Richard Grenville, Earl Temple, K.G., and the Rt Hon. George Grenville and their friends and contemporaries*, 4 vols (London: John Murray, 1852-53)
Styles, Dr John, *Memoirs of the Life of the Rt Hon. George Canning*, 2 vols (London: Thomas Tegg, 1828)
Tomlinson, John R. (ed.), *Additional Grenville Papers 1763-65* (Manchester: Manchester University Press, 1962)
Watts, William, *Memoirs of the Revolution in Bengal, Anno. Dom. 1757* (London: A. Millar, 1760)
Wellington, 2nd Duke of (ed.), *The Supplementary Despatches, Correspondence, and Memoranda of Field Marshal Arthur, Duke of Wellington*, 15 vols (London: John Murray, 1858)
———, *Despatches, Correspondence, and Memoranda of Field Marshal Arthur, Duke of Wellington* (in continuation of the former series), 8 vols (London: John Murray, 1867)

Biographical Works on Jenkinson and Liverpool

Anon., *Memoirs of the Public Life and Administration of the Rt Hon. The Earl of Liverpool* (London: Saunders & Otley, 1827)
Brock, W.R., *Lord Liverpool and Liberal Toryism, 1820-27* (London: Frank Cass & Co., 1941)
Buckland, C.E., *Dictionary of National Biography* (London: Swan Sonnenschein & Co., 1906), entry on 'Charles Jenkinson', in the micrographic edition (1975) p. 1074
Cookson, J.E., *Lord Liverpool's Administration, 1815-22* (Edinburgh: Archon Books, 1975)
Gash, Norman, *Lord Liverpool: The Life and Political Career of Robert Banks Jenkinson, Second Earl of Liverpool, 1770-1828* (London: Weidenfeld & Nicolson, 1984)
The Gentleman's Magazine, March 1829
Hay, William Anthony, *Lord Liverpool: A Political Life* (Martlesham, Suffolk: Boydell & Brewer, 2018)
Petrie, Sir Charles, *Lord Liverpool and His Times* (London: James Barrie, 1954)
Yonge, C.D., *The Life and Administration of Robert Banks Jenkinson, Second Earl of Liverpool*, 3 Vols (London: Macmillan, 1868)

Other Sources

Allen, Robert G., *The British Industrial Revolution in Global Perspective* (Cambridge: Cambridge University Press, 2009)
Anon., *The Oxfordshire Contest, or the whole controversy between the Old and New Interest* (London: J.B. Owen, 1753)
Ashton, T.S., *The Industrial Revolution 1760-1830* (Oxford: Oxford University Press, 1948)
Ashworth, William J., *The Industrial Revolution: The State, Knowledge and Global Trade* (London: Bloomsbury, 2017)
Bew, John, *Castlereagh: Enlightenment, War and Tyranny* (London: Quercus, 2011)
Blackwood's Magazine, 'An Echo from Old Bengal, Vol. 182 (1907)
Bolingbroke, Henry Viscount, *LETTERS, on the Spirit of PATRIOTISM: on the Idea of a PATRIOT KING: and On the STATE of PARTIES, At the Accession of King GEORGE the First* (London: A. Millar, 1749)
Bowler, R. Arthur, *Logistics and the Failure of the British Army in America, 1775-1783* (Princeton, NJ: Princeton University Press, 1975)
Brougham, Henry B., *Historical Sketches of Statesmen who Flourished in the Time of George III* (Philadelphia, PA: Lea & Blanchard, 1839)
Bryant, Sir Arthur, *The Age of Elegance, 1812-1822* (London: Collins, 1950)
Buckland, C.E., *Dictionary of Indian Biography* (London: Swan Sonnenschein & Co, 1906)
Bunker, Nick, *An Empire on the Edge: How Britain Came to Fight America* (New York, NY: Alfred A. Knopf, 2014)
Burke, Edmund, *Reflections on the Revolution in France* (London: James Dodsley, 1790)
Butterfield, Sir Herbert, *George III, Lord North and the People, 1779-80* (London: Bell, 1949)
———, *George III and the Historians* (London: Macmillan, 1957)
———, *The Whig Interpretation of History* (London: W.W. Norton, 1965) (1931)
Camden, William, *The History of the Most Renowned and Victorious Princess Elizabeth, Late Queen of England* (London: E. Flesher, 1675)
Campbell, Lord John, *The Lives of the Lord Chancellors and Keepers of the Great Seal of England*, 8 vols (London: John Murray, 1847)
Cannadine, David, *The Decline and Fall of the British Aristocracy* (New Haven, CT: Yale University Press, 1990)
Cannadine, David, *Victorious Century: The United Kingdom, 1800-1906* (London: Viking, 2017)
Cassis, Youssef, and Philip L. Cottrell, *Private Banking in Europe: Rise, Retreat and Resurgence* (Oxford: Oxford University Press, 2015)

Cathcart, Brian, *The News from Waterloo: The Race to Tell Britain of Wellington's Victory* (London: Faber & Faber, 2015)
Cecil, Lord Robert, 'Lord Castlereagh', *The Quarterly Review*, Vol. 111 (January 1862)
Chateaubriand, François-René de, *Mémoires d'outre-tombe* (Paris: Garnier, 1848-50)
Clancy, Kevin, 'The Recoinage and Exchange of 1816-17', PhD thesis, University of Leeds, 1999
Clark, Christopher, *The Sleepwalkers: How Europe Went to War in 1914* (London: Harper, 2013)
Clark, J.C.D., *English Society, 1660-1832: Religion, Ideology and Politics during the Ancien Régime* (Cambridge: Cambridge University Press, 2000)
Cole, G.D.H., *The Life of Robert Owen* (Edinburgh: Archon Books, 1966)
Colley, Linda, *In Defiance of Oligarchy: The Tory Party, 1714-60* (Cambridge: Cambridge University Press, 1982)
Curley, Thomas M., *Sir Robert Chambers: Law, Literature and Empire in the Age of Johnson* (Madison, WI: University of Wisconsin Press, 1998)
Defoe, Daniel, *A Tour Through the Whole Island of Great Britain*, 3 vols (London: G. Strahan, 1724-26)
Dickinson, Violet (ed.), *Miss Eden's Letters* (London: Macmillan, 1919)
Disraeli, Benjamin, *Coningsby, or the New Generation*, 3 vols. (London: Henry Colburn, 1844)
Ehrman, John, *The Younger Pitt: The Years of Acclaim* (London: Constable, 1969)
———, *The Younger Pitt: The Reluctant Transition* (London: Constable, 1985)
———, *The Younger Pitt: The Consuming Struggle* (London: Constable, 1996)
Ellis, Sir Henry, *Journal of the Proceedings of the Late Embassy to China* (London: John Murray, 1817)
Engels, Friedrich, *The Condition of the Working Class in England* (Leipzig: Otto Wigand, 1845)
English, Henry, *A Complete View of the Joint Stock Companies Formed During the Years 1824 and 1825* (London: Boosey, 1827)
Fairman, William, *The Stocks Examined and Compared; or, A Guide to Purchasers in the Public Funds* (London: Lane, Darling & Co., 1807)
Falkiner, C. Litton, *Studies in Irish History and Biography, Mainly of the Eighteenth Century* (London: Longmans, Green & Co., 1902)
Farr, Grahame (ed.), *Records of Bristol Ships, 1800-1838 (Vessels over 150 Tons)* (Bristol: Bristol Record Society, 1950)
Feiling, Sir Keith, *A History of the Tory Party, 1640-1714* (Oxford: Clarendon Press, 1924)
Feiling, Sir Keith, *The Second Tory Party, 1714-1832* (Oxford: Clarendon Press, 1938)
Fisher, D.R. (ed.), *The History of Parliament: The House of Commons, 1820-32* (Cambridge: Cambridge University Press, 2009)
Fletcher, C.R.L., *Historical Portraits, 1700-1850*, 2 vols (Oxford: Clarendon Press, 1919)
Floud, Roderick. 'The Changing Value of Money', *History Today*, Vol. 69, Issue 3 (March 2019)
Foljambe, C.G.S.,1st Earl of Liverpool (of the 1905 creation), and Compton Reade, *The House of Cornewall* (Hereford: Jakeman & Carver, 1908)
Foster, J., *Alumni Oxonienses, 1715-1886* (Oxford: Parker & Co., 1888)
Foster, Sir Augustus, 'Foster's Notes on the United States', *The Quarterly Review*, Vol. 68 (1841)
Fraser, Antonia, *Perilous Question: Reform or Revolution? Britain on the Brink, 1832* (London: Weidenfeld & Nicolson, 2013)
———, *The King and the Catholics: The Fight for Rights 1829* (London: Wiedenfeld & Nicolson, 2018)
Gash, Norman, *Politics in the Age of Peel* (New York, NY: W.W. Norton & Co., 1953)
———, *Mr. Secretary Peel: The Life of Sir Robert Peel to 1830* (Cambridge, MA: Harvard University Press, 1961)
Gash, Norman 'The Tortoise and the Hare: Liverpool and Canning', *History Today*, Vol. 32, Issue 3 (March 1982)

Gayer, A., W.W. Rostow and A.J. Schwartz, *The Growth and Fluctuation of the British Economy, 1790-1850* (Oxford: Clarendon Press, 1953)
Gleick, James, *The Information: A History, A Theory, A Flood* (London: Fourth Estate, 2012)
Goulstone, John, and Michael Swanton, 'Carry on Cricket – the Duke of Dorset's 1789 Tour', *History Today*, Vol. 39, Issue 8 (August 1989)
Graves, Donald, *Field of Glory: The Battle of Crysler's Farm, 1813* (Montreal, QC: Robin Brass Studio, 1999)
Grayling, A.C., *The Age of Genius: The Seventeenth Century and the Birth of the Modern Mind* (London: Bloomsbury, 2016)
HM Revenue and Customs, *A Tax to Beat Napoleon*, National Archives. Available at: https://webarchive.nationalarchives.gov.uk/20100512190349/http://www.hmrc.gov.uk/history/taxhis1.htm (accessed 23 July 2020)
Hague, William, *William Pitt the Younger: A Biography* (New York, NY: Alfred A. Knopf, 2005)
Hague, William, *William Wilberforce: The Life of the Great Anti-Slave Trade Campaigner* (London: HarperPress, 2008)
Hathaway, W.S. (ed.), *The Speeches of William Pitt in the House of Commons*, 3 vols (London: Longman, Hurst, Rees, Orme and Brown, 1817)
Hibbert, Christopher, *Wellington: A Personal History* (London: HarperCollins, 1997)
Hilton, Boyd, *Corn, Cash, Commerce: The Economic Policies of the Tory Governments, 1815-1830* (Oxford: Oxford University Press, 1977)
Hilton, Boyd, *A Mad, Bad and Dangerous People? England, 1783-1846* (Oxford: Oxford University Press, 2006)
Homer, Sidney, and Richard Sylla, *A History of Interest Rates* (Upper Saddle River, NJ: Prentice-Hall, 2005)
Howe, Daniel Walker, *What Hath God Wrought: The Transformation of America, 1815-1848* (Oxford: Oxford University Press, 2007)
Huntley, R.W., *Chavenage: A Tale on the Cotswolds* (London: James Burns, 1845)
Hutchinson, Martin, and Kevin Dowd, 'The Apotheosis of the Rentier: How Napoleonic War Finance Kick-Started the Industrial Revolution', *Cato Journal*, Fall 2018
Johnson, Allen S., *A Prologue to Revolution: The Political Career of George Grenville* (Lanham, MD: University Press of America, 1996)
Kissinger, Henry, *A World Restored: Metternich Castlereagh and the Problems of Peace, 1812-22* (London: Weidenfeld & Nicolson, 1957)
Knight, G.D., 'Lord Liverpool and the Peninsular War, 1809-12', PhD Thesis, University of Florida, 1976
Knight, Roger, *Britain Against Napoleon: The Organization of Victory, 1793-1815* (London: Penguin, 2014)
Kynaston, David, *Till Time's Last Sand: A History of the Bank of England, 1694-2013* (London: Bloomsbury, 2017)
Latimer, John, *The Annals of Bristol in the Nineteenth Century*, 2 vols (Bristol: W. & F. Morgan, 1887)
Little, Patrick, 'Lady Bankes Defends Corfe Castle', *History Today*, Vol. 65, Issue 2 (February 2015)
Maddison, Angus, *The World Economy: Historical Statistics* (Paris: OECD, 2003)
Malthus, Thomas, *An Essay on the Principle of Population* (London: J. Johnson, 1798)
Miller, James, *The Lamp of Lothian or the History of Haddington* (Edinburgh: James Allan, 1844)
Miller, John, of Lincoln's Inn (attrib.), 'Article IX – Internal Policy', *The Quarterly Review*, Vol. 42, no. 33 (January 1830)
Muir, Rory, *Wellington: The Path to Victory, 1769-1814* (New Haven, CT: Yale University Press, 2013)
———, *Wellington: Waterloo and the Fortunes of Peace, 1814-52* (New Haven, CT: Yale University Press, 2015)

Naidu, S. and M. Yuchtman, 'How Green Was My Valley? Coercive Contract Enforcement in 19th Century Industrial Britain', Tech. rep., Harvard University, 2009
Namier, Sir Lewis, *The Structure of Politics at the Accession of George III* (London: Macmillan, 1929)
Namier, Sir Lewis, and J. Brooke (eds), *The History of Parliament: The House of Commons, 1754-1790* (Martlesham, Suffolk: Boydell & Brewer, 1964)
Neal, Larry, *The Financial Crisis of 1825 and the Restructuring of the British Financial System*, Federal Reserve Bank of St Louis *Review*, Vol. 80, no. 3 (May-June, 1998)
Newton, John Frank, *Early Days of the Right Honorable George Canning: First Lord of the Treasury and Chancellor of the Exchequer* (London: T. Cadell, 1828)
O'Brien, Patrick K., 'The Political Economy of British Taxation, 1688-1815', *Economic History Review*, Vol. 41, Issue 1 (February 1988)
Osborne, Roger, *Iron Steam and Money: The Making of the Industrial Revolution* (London: Pimlico, 2014)
O'Shaugnessey, Andrew Jackson, *The Men Who Lost America: British Leadership, the American Revolution, and the Fate of the Empire* (New Haven, CT: Yale University Press, 2013)
Paley, William, *Principles of Moral and Political Philosophy* (London: R. Faulder, 1786)
Pellew, The Hon. George, *The Life and Correspondence of the Right Honourable Henry Addington, First Viscount Sidmouth*, 3 vols (London: John Murray, 1847)
Phipps, The Hon. Edmund, *Memoirs of the Political and Literary Life of Robert Plumer Ward*, 2 vols (London: John Murray, 1850)
Post, John D. *"The last great subsistence crisis in the Western World"* Baltimore: Johns Hopkins University Press, 1977.
Reeve, Henry (ed.), *The Greville Memoirs: A Journal of the Reigns of King George IV and King William IV*, 3 vols (London: Longmans, Green, 1875)
Ricardo, David, *On the Principles of Political Economy and Taxation* (London: John Murray, 1817)
Roberts, Andrew, *"Napoleon: A Life* (London: Allen Lane, 2014)
Robson, Eric, 'Lord North', *History Today*, Vol. 2, Issue 8 (August 1952)
Robson, R.J., *The Oxfordshire Election of 1754* (Oxford: Oxford University Press, 1949)
Rodger, N.A.M., *The Command of the Ocean: A Naval History of Britain, 1649-1815* (New York, NY: W.W. Norton & Co., 2004)
Rose, Tessa *The Coronation Ceremony of the Kings and Queens of England and the Crown Jewels*, HMSO 1992
Ross, Ian S., *The Life of Adam Smith* (Oxford: Oxford University Press, 1995)
Rubinstein, W.D., *Men of Property: The Very Wealthy in Britain since the Industrial Revolution* (London: Croom Helm, 1981)
Rush, Richard, *Memoranda of a Residence at the Court of London* (Philadelphia, PA: Key & Biddle, 1833)
Sack, James J., *The Grenvillites, 1801-29: Party Politics and Factionalism in the Age of Pitt and Liverpool* (Chicago, IL: University of Illinois Press, 1979)
———, *From Jacobite to Conservative: Reaction and Orthodoxy in Britain, c.1760-1832* (Cambridge: Cambridge University Press, 1993)
Salmon, Philip, and Kathryn Ris, 'Who should have the vote? What Electoral Rights Did Britons Have in the Century Before 1918?' *History Today*, Vol. 68, Issue 8 (August 2018)
Satia, Priya, *Empire of Guns: The Violent Making of the Industrial Revolution* (London: Penguin Press, 2018)
Selgin, George, *Good Money: Birmingham Button Makers, the Royal Mint, and the Beginnings of Modern Coinage, 1775-1821* (Oakland, CA: The Independent Institute, 2008)
Siemann, Wolfram, *"Metternich – Strategist and Visionary"* Belknap-Harvard University Press, 2019
Sinclair, Sir John, *The Correspondence of the Right Honourable Sir John Sinclair, Bart*, 2 vols (London: Henry Colburn and Richard Bentley, 1831)

Smart, William, *Economic Annals of the Nineteenth Century*, Vol. 1, 1801-1820, Vol. 2, 1821-1830 (London: Macmillan, 1915-17)

Smith, Adam, *An Inquiry into the Nature and Causes of the Wealth of Nations*, 3 vols (London: W. Strahan, 1776)

Smith, E.A., *Wellington and the Arbuthnots: A Triangular Friendship* (Stroud, Gloucestershire: Alan Sutton, 1994)

Stanhope, Philip Henry, 5th Earl, *Life of the Right Honourable William Pitt*, 4 vols (London: John Murray, 1861)

Thal, Herbert van, (ed.), *The Prime Ministers: Volume 1, Sir Robert Walpole to Sir Robert Peel* (London: Allen & Unwin, 1974) (see chapters by Asa Briggs on Peel and Norman Gash on Liverpool)

Thom, Colin, 'Fine Veneers, Army Boots and Tinfoil: New Light on Marc Brunel's Activities in Battersea', *Construction History*, Vol. 25 (2010)

Thompson, Edward P., *The Making of the English Working Class* (London: Victor Gollancz, 1963)

Thorne, R. (ed.), *The History of Parliament: The House of Commons 1790-1820* (Cambridge: Cambridge University Press, 1986)

Thornton, Henry, *An Enquiry into the Nature and Effects of the Paper Credit of Great Britain* (London: J. Hatchard, 1802)

The Times, '*The Times*'s Top 50 Prime Ministers', 5 May 2010

Tooke, Thomas, *A History of Prices and of the State of the Circulation During the Years 1793-1856*, 6 vols (London: Longman, Orme, Brown, Green & Longmans, 1838-57)

Trinder, Barrie, *Britain's Industrial Revolution: The Making of a Manufacturing People, 1700-1870* (Lancaster: Carnegie Publishing, 2013)

Twiss, Horace, *The Public and Private Life of Lord Chancellor Eldon*, 2 vols (London: John Murray, 1844)

Uglow, Jenny, *In These Times: Living in Britain through Napoleon's Wars, 1793-1815* (New York, NY: Farrer, Straus and Giroux, 2014)

Valentine, Alan, *Lord North*, 2 vols (Norman, OK: University of Oklahoma Press, 1968)

Vaughan, James, *The Politics of Empire at the Accession of George III* (New Haven, CT: Yale University Press, 2019)

Ventura, J., and H.J. Voth, 'Debt into Growth: How Sovereign Debt Accelerated the First Industrial Revolution', National Bureau of Economic Research Working Paper No. 21280 (2015)

Vibart, Col. Henry M., *Addiscombe, its Heroes and Men of Note* (London: Constable, 1894)

Walmesley, Charles, *General History of the Christian Church, by Signor Pastorini* (a pseudonym) (Dublin, 1771)

Walpole, Sir Spencer, *The Life of the Rt Hon. Spencer Perceval*, 2 vols (London: Hurst and Blackett, 1874)

Warner, Jessica, 'Gin in Regency England', *History Today*, Vol. 61, Issue 3 (March 2011)

Williamson, J.G., 'Why Was British Growth So Slow During the Industrial Revolution?' *Journal of Economic History*, Vol. 44, no. 3 (1984)

Wilmot, E.P.E., and E.C. Streatfield, *Charterhouse, Old and New* (London: John C. Nimmo, 1894)

Wraxall, Sir Nathanial, *Posthumous Memoirs of His Own Time* (Philadelphia, PA: Carey, Lea & Blanchard, 1836)

Index

SD - #0024 - 140725 - C0 - 234/156/24 - PB - 9780718895648 - Gloss Lamination